W9-BZV-453

METHODS THAT WORK

A SMORGASBORD OF IDEAS FOR LANGUAGE TEACHERS

John W. Oller, Jr., and
Patricia A. Richard-Amato
Editors

NEWBURY HOUSE PUBLISHERS
A division of HarperCollins*Publishers*

Library of Congress Cataloging in Publication Data
Main entry under title:

Methods that work.

Bibliography: p.
Includes index.
1. Languages, Modern--Study and teaching--Addresses,
essays, lectures. I. Oller, John W. II. Richard
-Amato, Patricia A.
PB35.M554 1983   418'.007   83-13495
ISBN 0-88377-330-9

Cover design by Rodelinde Albrecht

NEWBURY HOUSE PUBLISHERS
A division of HarperCollins*Publishers*

Language Science
Language Teaching
Language Learning

Copyright © 1983 by Newbury House Publishers, Inc. All rights reserved. No part of this book
may be reproduced or transmitted in any form or by any means, electronic or mechanical, including
photocopying, recording, or by any information storage and retrieval system, without permission in
writing from the Publisher.

First printing: December 1983

Printed in Singapore   10

Acknowledgments

In an undertaking of this type, the persons to be thanked are many. We can name only a few of those who have helped, encouraged, inspired, criticized, in some cases even followed, and above all tolerated us. First, of course, our families who have put up with our long hours at the typewriters, and in libraries, or on the telephone, and the students and colleagues who have generously set us free from many other tasks in order to concentrate for several months on this project.

We also express our appreciation to all of those language teachers who taught us or allowed us to observe their classes over the years. A number of the contributors to this book have been among those teachers. We also thank the students, who have sought to learn from us, some of whom are now language teachers or teacher trainers themselves.

We thank Newbury House Publishers for the encouragement to pursue this project and for the speed with which they have made it available to the public. And, most of all, we thank all of our contributors, the authors, publishers, and in the cases indicated, the editors as well who allowed us to use their work. We are grateful for permission to reprint the following items published and copyrighted by

Addison-Wesley:
Nina Wallerstein, 1983. *Language and Culture in Conflict: Problem Posing in the ESL Classroom*. Reading, Massachusetts: Addison-Wesley, Chapter 2, 11–25.

the American Council of Teachers of Foreign Languages in the *Foreign Language Annals:*
Otto W. Johnston, 1980. Implementing the intensive language model: an experiment in German at the University of Florida, *Foreign Language Annals* 13 (2):99–106;
Theodore B. Kalivoda, Genelle Morain, and Robert J. Elkins, 1971. The audio-motor unit: a listening comprehension strategy that works, *Foreign Language Annals* 4:392–400;
Stephen D. Krashen, in press. The din in the head, input, and the language acquisition device, *Foreign Language Annals*.

the University of Chicago Press in the *International Journal of American Linguistics:*
Leonard Newmark, 1966. How not to interfere with language learning, *International Journal of American Linguistics* 32. Also in Edward W. Najam and Carleton T. Hodge (eds.), 1966. *Language Learning; The Individual and the Process*. Bloomington, Indiana: Indiana University Press.

Counseling-Learning Publications, Box 383, E. Dubuque, Illinois 61025:
Charles A. Curran, *Counseling-Learning in Second Languages*, Box 383 E, Dubuque, Illinois: Counseling-Learning Publications, 1976, Chapters 2 and 3, 19–59.

Educational Solutions in New York:
Caleb Gattegno, 1972. *Teaching Foreign languages in Schools: The Silent Way*. New York: Educational Solutions, as excerpted.

ERIC and the National Council of Teachers:
Robert H. White and Raymond J. Rodriguez, Appendix C: The open language experience, and Appendix D: Sample plan for an open language experience—shopping at the supermarket, in *Mainstreaming the Non-English Student*, Chicago: ERIC and NCTE, 1982, 332–40.

the International Organization of Teachers of English to Speakers of Other Languages in the *TESOL Quarterly*:
Robert J. Di Pietro, 1981. Discourse and real-life roles in the ESL classroom, *TESOL Quarterly* 15 (1):27–33;
Robert J. Di Pietro, 1982. The open-ended scenario: a new approach to conversation, *TESOL Quarterly* 16 (1):15–20;
Kathleen Green, 1975. Values clarification theory in ESL and bilingual education, *TESOL Quarterly*, 9 (2):155–164;
Robin Scarcella, 1978. Socio-drama for social interaction, *TESOL Quarterly* 12 (1):41–46.

Language Learning:
Susan L. Stern, 1980. Drama in second language learning from a psycholinguistic perspective, *Language Learning*, 30 (1):77–100.

Newbury House:
Merrill Swain, 1978. Home-school language switching, in J. C. Richards (ed.), *Understanding Second and Foreign Language Learning*. Rowley, Massachusetts: Newbury House, 238–248;
Earl W. Stevick, 1980. *A Way and Ways*, Rowley, Massachusetts: Newbury House, Chapters 18 and 19, 229–259.

Oxford University Press in New York:
Carolyn Graham, 1978. *Jazz Chants*. New York: Oxford University Press, as excerpted;
Marina K. Burt and Heidi C. Dulay, 1981. Optimal language learning environments, in J. E. Alatis, H. Altman, and P. Alatis (eds.), *The Second Language Classroom*. New York: Oxford University Press, 177–192.

Oxford University Press (Oxford, England) and the British Council in the journal *English Language Teaching*:
Camy Condon, 1979. Treasure hunts for English practice, *English Language Teaching* 34 (1):53–55;
Hugh Leong, 1979. The debate: a means of eliciting semi-spontaneous communication in the TEFL classroom, *English Language Teaching* 34 (4):287–289.
Mario F. G. Rinvolucri, 1980. Action mazes, *English Language Teaching* 35 (1):35–37.

the Peace Corps:
John T. Rassias, 1970. *New Dimensions in Language Training: The Dartmouth College Experiment*. Peace Corps Faculty Paper No 6, (February):1–12.

The Smithsonian:
Richard Wolkomir, 1980. A manic professor tries to close up the language gap, *The Smithsonian* 11 (May):80–86.

SPEAQ (the Association for Teachers of English as a Second Language in the Province of Quebec; SPEAQ is the French acronym) in their *SPEAQ Journal*:
J. J. Asher, 1979. Motivating children and adults to acquire a second language, *SPEAQ Journal* 3:87–99.

the University of Wisconsin Press in the *Modern Language Journal*:
Shirley J. Adams, 1982. Scripts and the recognition of unfamiliar vocabulary: enhancing second language reading skills, *Modern Language Journal* 66:155–159.
J. J. Asher, Jo Anne Kusudo, and Rita de la Torre, 1974. Learning a second language through commands: the second field test, *Modern Language Journal* 58:24–32.

W. Jane Bancroft, 1978. The Lozanov method and its American adaptations, *Modern Language Journal* 62:167–175.

John Macnamara, 1973. Nurseries, streets and classrooms: some comparisons and deductions, *Modern Language Journal* 57 (5–6):250–254;

Sandra J. Savignon. 1981. Three Americans in Paris: a look at 'natural' second language acquisition, *Modern Language Journal* 65 (3):241–247;

Tracy D. Terrell, 1982. The natural approach to language teaching: an update, *Modern Language Journal* 66 (2):121–132;

Finally, we thank the staff of the Reference Department of the University of New Mexico Zimmerman Library, who helped us track down many a wayward date, page number, or what-have-you. Of course, we alone must take the responsibility for the final condition of the references, the present texts, and the material which we have contributed.

*to our parents and teachers, and,
especially, in memory of John W. Oller, Sr.
who inspired us both*

Preface

During our own initiation as language teachers (Oller, at first in Spanish and French, and later in ESL; Richard-Amato, in ESL), we heard plenty about "the subtle difficulties of language instruction," but we heard considerably less about success in surmounting those difficulties. Coursebooks and especially anthologies tended to deal primarily with problems. Theorists in particular were often failure-oriented. In recent years there have been exceptions, such as Stevick and Krashen and a few others, but by and large the theoretical picture has been one of gloom.

In some cases, recommendations from the experts seemed tantamount to defeat and capitulation. Perhaps this is why Krashen (1982) notes that many teachers "lost faith in theory." During the last couple of decades, foreign language teachers (as distinct from second language teachers), especially in the United States, were sometimes even encouraged to give up the goal of *ever* enabling students to communicate in the target language. As a result, some settled for teaching *about* the target language and culture. This was less true among second language teachers, but here too the emphasis was often on explaining failure rather than ensuring success.

Naturally, we wondered about the success side of the story. Having seen plenty of gray clouds of doubt, it occurred to us that somewhere above them the sun must be shining. There just had to be *some* success stories for language teachers to look to for inspiration.

Consequently, we began to track down and gather together papers about *Methods That Work*. It is true that our trade journals and newsletters sometimes carry sections about such methods, but we found no coursebook which presented the commonly rumored success stories in an accessible format. It seemed that such a book was needed. Two feelings encouraged our efforts: first, we'd have loved to have had such a book back when we set out to become language teachers, and second, from our more recent perspective, now as teacher-trainers, we have often wished for a book of success stories to replace, or at least supplement, the standard readers which, more often than not, are concerned more with the difficulties than with the solutions of our practical problems.

Starting out with a handful of sources in mind we soon found a substantial number of articles, chapters, and tidbits that we shaped into this "lumpy rag-bag of a book" (as David Eskey might be wont to describe it). No doubt we have excluded some good material, owing in one way or another to the limits of our resources—whether physical or mental. Nonetheless, the students and colleagues with whom we have shared our results have so far been remarkably pleased. We hope you will be too.

At long last, you hold the book in your hands. We expect it to be controversial, not because teachers aren't looking for success, but because anyone who claims to achieve it, even in small measure, will have to face down those naysayers who are still wagging their fingers and saying it can't be done. According to them we'd all be better off to give up our aspirations of getting our students to communicate in the target language because, they claim, "A language just can't be acquired in a classroom setting." For our own part, we agree with Stevick, Krashen, and others who have argued on the contrary that the classroom *can be* an *optimal* setting for language acquisition.

We will be pleased, then, if even a few of the methods that are capsulized in this book of readings should stand the test of time. We fully expect that any methods included here which are *merely* gimmicky, or cultish, or based on faulty reasoning will eventually be found out. In the meantime, we have done our best to select a smorgasbord of success stories which we hope will both inform and interest language teachers. We call it a "smorgasbord" because we do not expect everyone to sample every dish. Readers are invited to choose only what they like.

In a great measure any success that the book itself may achieve will be owed to the several contributors who have offered their ideas for our consumption, and in greater measure still, the credit for any ultimate effectiveness must eventually accrue to the teacher out there in the classroom, putting it all together.

As language teachers ourselves, all the papers included here have in one way or another served us as sources of ideas, new techniques, and sometimes even inspiration. With best hopes, therefore, we offer the entire collection to language teachers everywhere. We hope that you like it and that some of the ideas contained here will work for you.

John W. Oller Jr.
Patricia A. Richard-Amato

Albuquerque, New Mexico
April 1983

Contents

Introduction

The main criterion for inclusion of any given item in this volume was a high mark on our own subjective index of *applicability*. Our aim was to offer tried and proven methods, and for the most part, we limited attention to ones that have been tested in classrooms—often our own. However, a few observations of a distinctly theoretical bent are included on the basis of the old adage that "nothing is so practical as good theory." Another criterion for selection was whether a given approach seemed to require *attention to meaning*. If it didn't, generally, we excluded it. With the possible exception of Graham's "Jazz Chants" (Chapter 21 in Part VI, Fun and Games) the methods included all focus attention first and foremost on meaning. Even the "chants" may be "episodically organized," as may be seen from the argument presented in Chapter 1.

As might be expected, we did not agree completely on everything that we decided to include in this volume. In fact, we agreed to disagree on some issues. Although we did not include any methods which we did not feel had some claims to success, we did include some chapters concerning which one or both of us held some personal reservation(s)—sometimes about the methods themselves, sometimes about their philosophical basis. We realize that our readers, of course, in the final analysis, like each of us, have their own beliefs and will make their own choices. In fact it may seem quaint even to say this, but we language teachers are a surprisingly close professional family and sometimes we act like one. Perhaps it is for this reason that we feel free to share our differences along with our points of agreement.

In that spirit of freedom, we mention at the outset one point of difference that became clearer as we worked through the writing of our "Editors' Introductions" and "Discussion Questions." It nearly put us at loggerheads at the end of Part II and especially in Part III. Now, looking back, it seems useful to reflect a moment on that point. Some will consider this exercise unnecessary or even inappropriate, and those readers are asked to skip the next two paragraphs.

A general uneasiness finally became focused in a certain assumption that seemed to Oller to underlie philosophies expressed by Lozanov, Curran, Rath, and Freire. Richard-Amato, incidentally, is not convinced that the assumption even exists or is relevant. However, Oller sees it as a sometimes explicit but more often implicit idea that play acting, meditative reflection, mind-relaxing techniques, self-examination, and social activism can lead to "self-worth" or

xii   METHODS THAT WORK

personal "wholeness" (a close cognate of "holiness"). To Oller this seems to place the burden of what Curran explicitly calls "redemption" squarely on the shoulders of the language teacher, who also is in need (according to the biblical outlook) of the same work of grace. To suggest that personal "wholeness" can be achieved through language acquisition seems to Oller to assign to the language teacher a messianic role (a godlike status) and to invite the student to a kind of submission that is idolatrous. Oller holds, following the biblical gospel, that "redemption" (a term used by Curran and a concept implicit in the notion of attaining "self-worth") is God's grace—Christ on the cross dying for man's sin, being buried, and rising from the dead. Language teaching, though it is a high calling, in Oller's view, is something other than the "incarnation" of God (another theological metaphor used by Curran) and is something less than the "redemptive" work of Christ.

In spite of this difference, we do agree that there are potential benefits to be had from some of the therapeutic techniques recommended by Lozanov, from the cathartic play acting of Suggestopedia, and from the counseling-learning approach of Curran. Also, the techniques of "values clarification" and Freire's dialectic approach to social activism can lead to intense communicative interactions which are known to result in language acquisition. Hence, we agree fully in the idea that we can learn much from authors who have put some of these techniques into action in language classrooms. For Richard-Amato's interpretation of some of the useful ideas in these chapters in particular, see Chapter 32.

Apart from advising the reader of our basis for selecting materials included in this volume, it is also the purpose of this introduction to preview the major sections and to highlight some of the themes that, we believe, bind the work together into a coherent whole. As with all anthologies the problem of arranging the various contributions into sections was solved more or less arbitrarily. Other bases for categorization occurred to us, as we were working, but we settled on seven sections as a practical thematic arrangement.

Part I, Pragmatic Orientations, deals in some detail with the biases that we bring to the methods courses that we ourselves teach. As will be apparent to the discerning reader, these ideas are drawn from many sources and may even represent the edges if not the center of a new paradigm (in the sense of Kuhn 1962). For instance, along with some of our British and American colleagues, we appeal to the current interest in pragmatics as an alternative to surface orientations in language teaching. Paralleling in certain points the expositions of Wilkins and others on the design of a notional/functional course syllabus, a number of hypotheses are offered concerning optimum materials and conditions for language acquisition.

Another thread that binds several of the contributions together is the growing recognition of the importance of what has come in recent years to be called "text-linguistics." As language teachers we are convinced that the field of interest must be broadened from the sentence (as a separable unit) to the whole fabric of discourse. Along with a growing number of colleagues, we believe that whole episodes of communication comprise the minimal units to be used in the language classroom. Principles behind this conception are discussed in Chapter 1 and illustrated in Chapter 2 in terms of practical classroom applications. The importance of the environment of language acquisition is stressed by Burt and Dulay in Chapter 3, and certain misconceptions from structural linguistics are refuted by Newmark in Chapter 4.

Part II, Teacher/Individual Orientations, includes four approaches that have gained currency in recent years among rank and file teachers. Many teachers are already familiar with one or more of these methods. They come from James Asher (see especially Chapter 5 in Part II and Chapters 26 and 27), Caleb Gattegno (Chapter 6), John Rassias (see Wolkomir, Chapter 7), and Georgi Lozanov (see Bancroft, Chapter 8). Each method has its distinctive characteristics, but all of them seem to focus a good deal of attention on the teacher as a director of what happens in the classroom. In addition to this, each in its own way is also very much attuned to what goes on inside the student, and what the student as an individual brings to the classroom and takes away from it. Some teachers may say of one or all, "It just isn't me," or "That's not my style," but for others one or all of these methods will strike a chord. We believe that to the extent that any of these methods works it will be because they enable the student to spotlight his or her attention on meaning—that is, to concentrate on the pragmatic connection of utterances in the target language with meaningful states of affairs and episodes of experience.

Part III, Social/Therapeutic Orientations, shifts the focus from the teacher and student as individuals per se, and moves it into the realm of therapeutic or social interaction and the effects that such interaction may have on the learner within a community. In this section, we include a discussion of Lozanov's Suggestopedia from a rather different viewpoint than the one advocated by Bancroft in Chapter 8. In fact, according to Stevick's understanding (Chapter 9 in two parts) Lozanov's philosophy seems to go well with Curran's counseling-learning (as advocated by Curran himself in Chapter 10). Two other social/therapeutic approaches included in this section are "values clarification" and Freire's brand of social activism, interpreted respectively by Kathleen Green (Chapter 11) and Nina Wallerstein (Chapter 12). All these social/therapeutic approaches seem to share an emphasis on the role of the society/community in shaping the language abilities of the learner. Perhaps they attract attention partly because of their apparent escape from traditional orthodoxies. We believe that their emphasis on genuine acts of communication may offer the best explanation for their practical appeal as well as their apparent successes.

Part IV, Roles and Drama, continues themes initiated in Parts II and III. Especially apparent will be the thematic ties to the Rassias "madness," and in some ways the papers in this part also echo strains of the social and therapeutic philosophies. However, the emphasis in general seems to move back to language teaching proper. Stern (Chapter 13), Di Pietro (Chapter 14), Scarcella

(Chapter 15), and Rodriguez and White (Chapter 16) all advocate role playing and drama as methods for eliciting communicative acts and also for encouraging students to internalize the competence necessary for communication in the target language. Di Pietro's contributions, moreover, offer some important insights into the nature of strategies for interaction and how they differ across cultures and across settings within a given culture. Empirical evidence from Stern, and observations by Scarcella and by Rodriguez and White as well, sustain the impression that students and teachers alike find drama and role playing both invigorating and profitable. Moreover, Rodriguez and White show how it is possible to smooth out the transition from role-playing activities to genuine communication in the world at large.

Part V, Natural Orientations, seeks to explain language acquisition both inside and outside the classroom. Macnamara (Chapter 17), for instance, discusses the salient differences of "Nurseries, Streets and Classrooms" as environments for language acquisition. His reflections seem as apropos in 1983 as they were a decade ago when they first appeared in print. Terrell (Chapter 18) pursues the theme of "natural" language teaching, drawing heavily on Krashen's theorizing. Both of them make a convincing case for bringing some of the features of nurseries and streets *into* the classroom. This section concludes, then, with papers by Savignon (Chapter 19) and by Krashen (Chapter 20) reflecting on processes that the language acquirer seems to go through.

Part VI, Fun and Games, is admittedly lighthearted and brief, but it offers some practical activities that can be used to good advantage in the language classroom. The entries included are intended not only to break the lockstep routines which teachers tend to fall into, but they also provide some practical ways to enhance classroom interaction and peer teaching. They also contribute to that community spirit which is so crucial to successful teaching of any kind. Graham, a professional entertainer as well as an ESL teacher, offers "Jazz Chants" (Chapter 21); Condon, "Treasure Hunts" (Chapter 22); de Berkeley-Wykes, "Jigsaw Reading" (Chapter 23); Leong, "The Debate" (Chapter 24); and Rinvolucri, "Action Mazes" (Chapter 25). Practicing teachers will no doubt be able to enrich this and other sections out of their own experience.

Part VII, Program/Experiment Reports, contains seven chapters each reporting on an experimental study or program implementation, or in some cases both. Asher (Chapter 26) provides a rich supply of information on the command approach and how it has fared in a variety of applications. His chapter here also complements and ties in with Krashen (Chapter 20) and Terrell (Chapter 18) in Part V. Immediately following is a report on a modification of Asher's approach recommended by Kalivoda, Morain, and Elkins (Chapter 27). Their work shows how Asher's nontraditional method can be fitted into a more traditional classroom format. The next two chapters, by Otto Johnston (Chapter 28) and John Rassias (Chapter 29), respectively, report on applications of the Rassias "madness" at the University of Florida and Dartmouth. Then, focusing attention on the reading process, complementing the earlier paper by de Berkeley-Wykes, Shirley Adams (Chapter 30) describes an experimental study showing how scripts and expectancies can be as important to second language reading as to reading in the first language. Swain (Chapter 31) gives an indispensable look at the Canadian immersion programs, and finally, Richard-Amato (Chapter 32) concludes with a discussion of the development of an ESL center at Alameda High School in the Jefferson County School District in Colorado. Her contribution draws on many of the recommendations of previous selections.

Part I
Pragmatic Orientations

The four chapters in this section introduce the reader to an overall philosophy of language teaching which has a great deal in common with the methods and ideas expressed by many other authors throughout the book. In a way it *is* an eclectic philosophy, and even more obviously it may *appear to be* an emergent eclecticism. However, back in the late 1950s and early 1960s when it was beginning to take shape in a few isolated and largely independent language teaching centers, the pragmatic orientations of this section were regarded by mainstreamers as somewhat outlandish. To some of the still numerous survivors of that period, who were steeped in its structuralist philosophy, this section may yet seem a little flaky.

All this is to say that the pragmatic orientations summarized here constitute less an eclecticism than a revolutionary way of looking at language acquisition and language teaching. For at least two decades now this pragmatic approach has had to run against the current of popular opinion. Happily, it seems now that the tide may be turning and a new consensus may in fact be developing. Be that as it may, our purpose here is not to promote such a consensus for its own sake, or even less to applaud it, but to offer for consideration as clear a presentation as we can of pragmatic orientations for successful language teaching.

Chapter 1 opens with a survey of some ideas (working hunches) concerning the nature of language acquisition and how it may be promoted. Appeal is made to tried and proven principles of successful fiction writers. Chapter 2 offers an overview of a fully integrated pragmatic curriculum for the teaching of Spanish as a foreign language which exemplifies the principles of Chapter 1. Chapter 3 by Burt and Dulay casts some of the critical issues in terms of their own highly practical theoretical perspective, and finally, Chapter 4 by Leonard Newmark clinches the argument, as it were, by anticipating nearly the whole of it during the heyday of structural linguistics and the audiolingual habit-formation era clear back in 1966. It is our hope that our readers will feel something of the same

1

2

exhilaration that still courses through our own veins as we look back to the decade of the 1960s when many of the battles chronicled here were being fought out by a few champions like Leonard Newmark.

SUGGESTED ADDITIONAL READINGS

HEIDI DULAY, MARINA BURT, AND STEPHEN KRASHEN.
1982. *Language Two*. New York: Oxford.

This handsome book covers a great deal of the research on the acquisition and learning of second languages. It is quite readable in spite of the fact that it contains some highly technical information at points. It provides as well many practical hints about how to employ the findings from research to good advantage in the classroom.

STEPHEN KRASHEN.
1980a. The input hypothesis. In J. E. Alatis (ed.). *Current Issues in Bilingual Education*. Washington, D.C.: Georgetown University. Also in J. Oller (ed.). 1983. *Issues in Language Testing Research*. Rowley, Massachusetts: Newbury House.

This paper presents what Earl Stevick has characterized as one of the most provocative theories to date in nonprimary language acquisition theory. It is a very readable account of the major tenets of Krashen's approach. It also provides the best basis that we know of for the successful methods of language teaching discussed throughout this book.

STEPHEN KRASHEN.
1981. *Second Language Acquisition and Second Language Learning*. London: Pergamon.

This book won the Kenneth Mildenberger award for the best book on foreign language teaching published in 1981. It discusses the difference between "learning" and "acquisition" and provides a good deal of impressive evidence in favor of the input hypothesis and other ideas which it advances.

JOHN OLLER.
1979. *Language Tests at School: A Pragmatic Approach*. London: Longman.

Though the focus is on making, giving, and interpreting the results from pragmatic language tests, this book discusses in some depth the pragmatic basis dealt with in Part I of the present book. Also, it insists, and we agree in this, that language testing should be an integral part of a coherent philosophy of language teaching (and vice versa).

Chapter 1

Some Working Ideas for Language Teaching

John W. Oller, Jr.
University of New Mexico

EDITORS' INTRODUCTION

This chapter considers four working ideas. The first is Krashen's *input hypothesis*. It suggests that second language acquisition requires input just a little beyond the acquirer's present stage of development (also see Burt and Dulay, Chapter 3, on this point). As this input is comprehended, acquisition progresses. Krashen's hypothesis helps to clarify the question that a theory of second language acquisition must answer: *How does input become intake?* (Also see Krashen's contribution, Chapter 20, and Terrell's, Chapter 18.) To answer this question, the process of pragmatic mapping is invoked. It is defined as the inferential linking of utterances to contexts of experience. In relation to this process, three additional hypotheses are considered. *The textuality hypothesis* suggests that the events of experience have a textual character—that they are temporally organized and arranged in a sequence. *The expectancy hypothesis* calls attention to the cognitive momentum that accompanies the production or comprehension of discourse, and *the episode hypothesis* suggests that text (in the sense of *any* stretch of discourse) will be easier to produce, to understand, to recall, and in general to profit from if it is episodically organized. Better and worse example texts are considered. It is suggested that the written and oral texts used in language teaching should respect episodic organization. Following the lead of good story writers, six specific recommendations for language teaching are offered: (1) use motivated text with significant conflicts in the pursuit of meaningful goals; (2) seek out stageable action; (3) respect the logic of experience; (4) first establish the facts; (5) break the text down into manageable chunks; and (6) make multiple passes through the text, deepening comprehension on each pass. Applications are discussed in Chapter 2.

In the last two decades, more and more language teachers have committed themselves to the objective of bringing students to a point where they can effectively communicate in the target language. As the pressure to achieve this objective has grown, and as the difficulty of bringing students to nativelike communicative competence has become more and more apparent, some have reacted by doubting that this goal can be attained at all, at least in formal classroom settings. Among them are some foreign language teachers who have retreated to the less challenging goal of mere "exposure to the target culture" as a substitute objective.

Not all language teachers have capitulated, however. Many of us still believe that ability to communicate in the target language in a specified range of experiential contexts is a reachable goal. Clues about how to move toward the goal can be gained from the reservations that some have had for a very long time about the traditional approaches. For instance, it was not without humor that Jespersen criticized the French texts of his day:

The reader often gets the impression that Frenchmen must be strictly systematical beings who one day speak merely in futures, another day in *passé définis* and who say the most disconnected things only for the sake of being able to use all the persons in the tense which for the time being happens to be the subject for conversation while they carefully postpone the use of the subjunctive until next year (p. 17).

He went on to suggest that

we ought to learn a language through sensible communications; there must be (and this as far as possible from the very first day) a certain connection in the thoughts communicated in the new language ... One cannot say anything sensible with mere lists of words. Indeed not even disconnected sentences ought to be used (1904, p. 11).

More than half a century later, during the 1960s, Jespersen's thesis was finally carried into practice in a Spanish program published by Encyclopaedia Britannica Films. The author's preface states:

We believe that language on the useful, everyday level is situational and sequential and that the moment a student can react automatically ... to a given situation identified with his own experience, he "knows" the foreign language used in *that* situation. The proper procedure then is to immerse the student in the world in which this language is used, a world inhabited by people about whom he knows and cares. This sharing of everyday experiences with people of a foreign tongue creates the climate of sympathy necessary and establishes the *sine qua non* for the teaching of the language, the desire of the students to learn to communicate with the people of that language (Oller 1963, p. ix).

We examine this foreign language program in greater detail below in Chapter 2. However, it may be useful first to develop some ideas about communication and just how it works. In particular, it may be helpful to begin to understand the sort of organization that Jespersen found absent in his French texts. The missing ingredient may be termed *episodic organization*. It is that design aspect which causes us to regard texts (whether written, spoken, or merely contemplated) as meaningful. In particular, episodic organization is the connectedness of events, ideas, and intentions, as well as of the elements of discourse which are often linked to them. Some have argued that this "connectedness" is merely an illusion caused by a western European outlook. However, this objection may be answered effectively by pointing out, as Karl Lashley did back in the 1950s, that the connectedness of experience is as much a function of physical facts and of physiological mechanisms as it is of psychological tendencies.

With all of the foregoing in mind, four working hypotheses about second language acquisition are considered each in its turn. These hypotheses form the basis of a discursive investigation of episodic organization. Finally, some observations about texts to be used or generated in the course of language instruction are offered. These suggestions, then, are carried into practice in a variety of ways in subsequent chapters.

THE INPUT HYPOTHESIS

In 1980, Stephen Krashen stated explicitly an idea that many language teachers and even some theorists had been considering for a long time. He called it "the input hypothesis." Roughly put, it says that *the acquisition of a second language depends on access to and utilization of comprehensible input.* Krashen's hypothesis makes it clear that more than mere "access" is required. Or, as the author of the above cited Spanish program put it:

All teachers of foreign language know that simple "exposure" is not enough. . . . We all know that until a language becomes an integral part of the student's experience, until he can react to and activate automatically language which has been *made a part of his experience,* he cannot communicate effectively in the language (his italics; Oller 1963, p. ix).

Of course, this "hypothesis" is not really testable in the traditional sense of experimental science. It is rather a working theory—a sensible basis for practice, and no doubt many would also agree that it has some theoretical value as well. Another helpful feature of Krashen's formulation is the idea that to be maximally beneficial, the input should be just a little beyond the student's present stage of development.

In an interesting way, the input hypothesis helps us to formulate the theoretical problem of second language acquisition. The input hypothesis differentiates mere "input" from "intake." The latter is input that gets comprehended. This differentiation helps us to formulate a crucial question: *How does input become intake?* The question can be represented as shown in Figure 1. The problem is to explain how it is that the leap is made from the spoken or printed elements of the target language (*input*) to comprehension (*intake*).

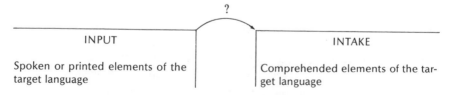

Figure 1   A schematic representation of the language acquisition process as expressed in the input hypothesis.

This question, how input becomes intake, can be construed as a special case of the general process of pragmatic mapping. The latter may be defined as the systematic linking of discourse structures to the events of ordinary experience (and vice versa). If we transform Figure 1 into Figure 2, the rough outlines of the

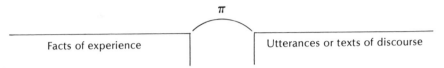

Figure 2   A schematic representation of the process of *pragmatic mapping*—the linking of elements of experience with the texts of language.

process of pragmatic mapping emerge. It is by this mapping process that the event sequences of experience are set in meaningful correspondence with discourse structures.

Input in a second language is merely one of the many types of event structures which constitute ordinary experience. Therefore, the left side of Figure 1 is expanded upon in Figure 2 so as to encompass the broad range of "facts of experience." On the right side of Figure 2 are represented the utterances (or written forms) of discourse, or texts. As with the input hypothesis, the problem is to determine how it is that the inferential leap is made from the facts of experience to the comprehension of discourse. In order to call attention to the inferential pragmatic linkage of the facts of experience with the strings of verbal elements in discourse, the bridge in Figure 2 is labeled with the Greek letter pi.

The process of pragmatic mapping may be construed at either a microcosmic or macrocosmic level. At the microcosmic level the problem is to explain the *comprehension* (or production) of any text or portion thereof (i.e., to explain the conversion of input to intake, or of experience to text, and vice versa). Also, as will be seen below, the term text will be interpreted broadly so as to include realized or inferred sequences of events often referred to as "the *contexts* of experience." At the macrocosmic level, the problem is to explain the development of language, and still more generally, the advance of knowledge and the maturation of the ability to make sense of experience.

Before going on to discuss the other working ideas closely related to Krashen's input hypothesis, it may be useful to say a bit more explicitly just what the process of pragmatic mapping is. The general problem is to link meaningful utterances (or their surrogates, e.g., printed forms) with the appropriate facts of experience. For instance, consider the foreign visitor at an American airport who read the sign "Bus Stop, No Standing" and sat down on the curb. He understood correctly that the "Bus Stop" was a place to catch a bus, but he wrongly interpreted "No Standing" to mean that pedestrians were not allowed to stand at the bus stop. The problem was one of pragmatic mapping—correctly linking the elements of the printed forms with the facts of his own experience. After he had been sitting on the curb for a while, it dawned on him that the sign had to apply to drivers passing by in their cars. It was the cars which were not supposed to "stand" at the bus stop because they would interfere with the loading and unloading of passengers.

Consider the process. It is necessary to associate the phrase "Bus Stop" with the passenger-carrying vehicles which pick up and let off people at the location where the sign appears. That is, the noun "bus" must be associated with a certain class of passenger-carrying vehicles, and "stop" with the location where the sign appears, a location where in fact a certain class of events can be expected to occur periodically; namely, one or more buses will stop to pick up and let off passengers. Similarly, "No Standing" must be understood to refer to a class of forbidden events. The trouble is to determine the subject of the verb "stand" in the underlying deep structure and to relate that subject to a probable referent or class of referents. In this case the intended class of referents consists of persons passing by in automobiles who might be tempted to stop in the way of the buses and to load or unload passengers at the bus stop.

Therefore, the process of pragmatic mapping is, among other things, a process of determining referential meaning or deixis. Of course, it is more than that because one must also infer antecedent propositional meanings (e.g., the fact that buses stop to pick up and let off passengers) and consequent propositional meanings (e.g., the fact that any car which stopped there would get in the way of the buses). Also there are whole complexes of relationships between such propositional values.

The foreigner's interpretation of the "Bus Stop, No Standing" sign illustrates the sense of "pragmatic mapping" as it relates to the immediate problem of comprehension at a particular point in time. It also suggests something of the process of language acquisition in the broader sense of the term.

But consider another example. Not long ago my wife and I had been out at the malls on a shopping trip to buy an overcoat for yours truly. Son Stephen, age three, was seated in the back. When there was a lull in the conversation, he said, "I want my [kʰoʔ]." As it so happened the evening was a particularly blustery one and he was already wearing his coat, a fact I pointed out. Exasperated, he repeated his request, saying, "No! I want my [kʰoʔ]." His mother understood on the second try and handed him the McDonald's root beer which was between the front seats just beyond his reach. It had been there all the time while we were in the stores at the mall, ever since our quick stop at McDonald's when the shopping trip began earlier that evening. Wanting to make a linguistic lesson out of the whole affair and seeing an opening, I pointed out, "Oh," addressing myself to Stephen, "You mean [kʰokʰhh]." I prominently aspirated the final "k." Stephen repeated, "Yeah, Daggy, [kʰokʰhh]!"

Up until that time he had called me "Daggy," presumably on analogy with "doggie," an early entry in his lexical repertoire. A few days later, Stephen overheard me telling the story to Jack Damico, one of my doctoral students. From the other room we heard him repeat the punch line with emphasis, "Yeah, [kʰokʰhh]!" which showed that the incident had stuck in his mind about as much as in mine. But there is more. After about another week had passed one morning

Stephen said, "I call you 'Daggy,' but that's not your real name, hunh."

I was curious what he thought my real name was, so I asked, "What *is* my real name, Son?"

"Your real name's 'Daddy.' "

Not only did he sort out the contrast between velar and alveolar consonants in final position, apparently due to the incident with the "coke," but he generalized the refined phonological contrast to other lexical items.

This is a brief glimpse of the pragmatic mapping process in macroperspective. Pragmatic mapping is in fact the process of linking every element of surface form with meaningful facts and states of affairs in experience. Also, as I understand it, this process is the central item on the agenda for linguistic theory in the coming years. Thus, the reader is cautioned that the exposition here is intended merely to give a more or less operational definition, not to provide a full-blown theory.

Nonetheless the characterization of the pragmatic mapping process has led me to formulate three additional hypotheses which help to address the question implicit in Krashen's input hypothesis—namely, how is it that input is sometimes converted to intake? My hypotheses have roughly the same character as the input hypothesis, and they serve chiefly to elaborate upon it. They too are really working hunches, but like the input hypothesis, they may at least subjectively be tested on the basis of readily available empirical evidence. Before going into any of them in detail, it may be useful here to preview all three. *The textuality hypothesis* suggests that the events of experience have a textual character—that they are temporally organized and arranged in sequence. *The expectancy hypothesis* calls attention to the cognitive momentum that rises and falls during the production or comprehension of discourse, and *the episode hypothesis* suggests that text (in the sense of *any* stretch of discourse) will be easier to produce, to understand, to recall, and in general to profit from if it is episodically organized.

THE TEXTUALITY HYPOTHESIS

Whereas the diagram of Figure 2 might suggest that the facts of experience are static and solid, the textuality hypothesis suggests that the elements of experience themselves are dynamically interrelated and must of necessity be represented in a temporalized logic (sequentialized) in order for us to make sense of them. Further, this hypothesis claims that the highly temporalized event-structures of experience are propositionally complex. Simply put, the textuality hypothesis says that *the event-structures of experience are textual in nature.*

This idea seems to underlie the following remarks by Karl Lashley from his well-known paper on "The Problem of Serial Order in Behavior":

The organization of language seems to me to be characteristic of almost all other cerebral activity. There is a series of hierarchies of organization; the order of vocal movements in pronouncing the word, the order of words in the sentence, the order of sentences in the paragraph, the rational order of paragraphs in a discourse. *Not only speech, but all skilled acts seem to involve the same problems of serial ordering, even down to the temporal coordinations of muscular contractions in such a movement as reaching and grasping* (italics mine; Lashley 1951, p. 187).

Of course, what Lashley is talking about has nothing to do with "western civilization." He is talking about *brain functions*—especially the analytic temporalizing functions that seem to be the specialty of the left hemisphere. These functions, probably, are relatively unaffected by differences in the details of culturally determined experience.[1] In other words, the textuality hypothesis argues that event-structures are propositional in nature quite independently of any cultural overlay that may, over the course of development, result in adjustments in their interpretation.

Lashley, however, was focusing his attention explicitly on motoric behavior. The textuality hypothesis is broader in scope. There is an important sense in which all event-structures are temporalized—even when viewed from the vantage point of an independent observer rather than a participant actor. For instance, consider the following example which was originally offered in a slightly different form by someone who was seeking to refute the textuality hypothesis. Suppose that we are observing a worker at an American Embassy somewhere in the Middle East. We note that the crowd outside the Embassy is growing increasingly unruly. Suddenly a brick comes crashing through a window above the worker. He sees it coming and ducks his head just in time. The brick falls harmlessly to the floor near where he is sitting.

To illustrate the textuality hypothesis, it will help if we take a closer look at the event sequence. The important thing to see is that the event sequence itself has a kind of grammatical (propositional) as well as a presuppositional and implicational structure to it.

Why did the brick come crashing through the window? For one thing, it had sufficient momentum to break the glass. But before that could happen, it had to acquire the momentum somehow. We infer that it was thrown by someone. Now notice the sequence of events that is crucial to an appropriate interpretation of the episode. Some unknown person, an agent, throws the brick. That is, the agent acts upon an instrument (the brick), which results in a whole new state of affairs which can be characterized in a proposition or indeed in a whole series of them. The brick hurtles toward the window. After a brief lapse of time, the window becomes a grammatical direct object, whose structure is radically altered by the impact of the brick. The momentum of the brick can be construed as a predication associated with it by the act of the thrower. In order to understand and react to the situation appropriately, it is first necessary to appreciate the fact that the trajectory of the brick would pass through the space

---

1. However, there is some evidence that the *distribution* of brain functions may be determined in part by certain cultural variables in experience (see Sibatani 1980).

now occupied by the head of the worker, if said worker did not negate that propositional possibility by ducking his head. Otherwise, we infer correctly, undesirable consequences would result. To understand this is to take account of a good deal of knowledge about bricks and heads. Setting aside the motoric response of the person who ducks, even for an independent observer to understand this action requires an appropriate interpretation of the textual elements of the event sequence. All of which goes to confirm the textuality of ordinary experience.

THE EXPECTANCY HYPOTHESIS

Another hypothesis which relates in fact to both sides of the schematic given in Figure 2 is the expectancy hypothesis. It says that *the activation of correct expectancies will enhance the processing of textual structures.* This hypothesis logically applies both to event-structures in experience and to the sequences of verbal elements that constitute discourse.

The importance of the effects of expectancies is perhaps best illustrated through errors or through texts that deviate from the expected form and thus cause us to do a mental double take at one or many points while processing them. For example, consider the sentence, "The pen was lost by the pier." The structure is such that we expect an agent (e.g., "by the newswoman") instead of a location "by the pier." What we seem to do in such a case is like putting on our mental brakes, cramming the gear lever into reverse, and driving by again hoping not to miss the turn. (Expectancies of this sort can conveniently be represented in the sort of grammatical system characterized by Woods 1970, 1978, as an augmented transition network. For a variety of similar examples, see de Beaugrande 1980, pp. 47–48.)

Expectancies of the most complicated sorts enter into even mundane motoric routines. For instance, one of my favorite examples came from a certain professor I knew in graduate school. It seems he had just purchased a new cigarette lighter and was driving down the highway at the speed limit. It was a warm summer day and he had the window down. Absently he lit up, shook out the flame, and tossed the lighter out the window. He had developed an expectancy for using matches to light up and continued on automatic pilot to behave as if he had just lighted his cigarette with a match instead of a brand-new lighter. His error is one of anticipatory mind-set, a sort of cognitive momentum that is set up by a false assumption. Although this example illustrates a problem in the event-structure side of Figure 2, it is not unlike common lexical confusions that occur on the verbal side of intelligence.

For an example of the latter sort, consider the tragically prophetic error of Sadat some years ago. He was asked what he would do if the peace talks with Israel did not bear fruit. He answered that he would turn in his "assassination."

He corrected himself immediately and said "resignation," but the fearful motivation for his slip of the tongue had already revealed an anticipatory mind-set—which as it turned out was not unwarranted. Of such errors was Freudian psychology made.

Interestingly, slips of the mind and tongue may also be accompanied by slips of the whole body at times. For instance, I remember an incident where a certain lawyer was preparing to take leave of a tired group of conferees. The long discussions of the day had concluded and people were beginning to look forward to a more pleasant evening. It was the sort of occasion where people are brightening up and congratulating one another on their congeniality. At just such a moment, the lawyer said he would meet the rest of us in the lobby shortly. Then, he turned briskly and ran into the door jamb. Speaking to the wall he said, "Oh, excuse me," and at the same moment gave it a couple of pats as if to say "I hope you're not injured." Then, casting a glance over his shoulder in our direction he hurried into the corridor and out of sight.

The lawyer's speech act shows that he had formed certain expectancies based on the crowded surroundings and his previous successes at getting through doorways. He apparently was more prepared to run into a person than a door jamb. His error reveals the synchronization required in order for understanding, intention, and action to be properly coordinated.

One final example will serve to illustrate that this coordination involves a delicate synchronization at more than one level of meaning and intention. Not long ago, I was checking out at a grocery store. It was late in the day and the store was crowded and noisy. The clerk said something to me as I was picking up the bag of groceries to leave. I didn't understand and asked for a repetition. She repeated herself. I still missed it, and asked for another shot. She obliged, a bit louder. I still couldn't quite make out what she had said. On the fourth try, her words were loud enough and mean enough to have stopped the front line of the Pittsburgh Steelers. She shouted, "I said T-H-A-N-K Y-O-U!!!" You might have thought that E. F. Hutton had begun to speak. Every head in the store turned.

On what Watzlawick, Beavin, and Jackson (1967) term the "content level" she was apparently intending to say that she was glad I stopped by and that she hoped I would come again. However, owing to the difficulty of putting this message (perhaps an insincere one) through the channel, on what Watzlawick et al. term the "relationship level," she ended up saying something like, "You idiot, if I never see you again, it'll be too soon."

What this example shows is that plans to communicate must be coordinated in terms of content and relationship information, and also that, as John Dewey observed long ago, the things that one says may often surprise oneself as much as anyone else.

Now we turn to a consideration of the hypothesis that provides a basis for linking the input, textuality, and expectancy hypotheses together.

THE EPISODE HYPOTHESIS

The episode hypothesis says that *text (i.e., discourse in any form) will be easier to produce, understand, and recall to the extent that it is motivated and structured episodically.* A corollary to this hypothesis is that the acquisition of a second language will be facilitated to the extent that the texts used in the instructional process are episodically organized. There are two aspects to "episodic organization"—motivation (or affect) and logical structure. Generally, it may be said that selling authors respect both of these (Braine 1974, Peck 1980, and D. V. Swain 1980).

Before we go on to consider both the motivation and structure of episodically organized texts, it is necessary to show that the episode hypothesis and its corollary relate to second language teaching. It seems to me that *these ideas lead to the supposition that perhaps second language teaching would be more successful if it incorporated principles of good story writing along with the benefits of sound linguistic analysis.* This supposition underlies all of the preceding discussion. We will return to it shortly to consider some of the ways in which it may help to bolster practical approaches to language teaching, but now it is time to illustrate more explicitly what episodic organization is.

As with the expectancy hypothesis, episodic organization may be clarified by examining cases where it is violated. There are two principal ways in which episodic organization can be made light of. The first common violation is to generate unmotivated (or poorly motivated) text. The result, as Peck observes, is "dull, dull dull," and most writers who do it, unless they happen to write for ESL or FL publishers, generally remain unpublished. Speakers who do it are rarely invited back for a second engagement. The person who persists in it is regarded as a bore.

A second common violation is to generate illogical (or jerky) text. The latter may prove interesting in the short term (provided it is motivated), but usually it loses its audience much as a devilish bronc unseats many a would-be rider. The result of the two types of violation together is almost always fatal to the text. The first violation usually quenches the spirit of any potential interpreter, and the second skins the shins and twists the nose of the would-be understander until he gives up and goes home.

Let's take the problem of textual logic first. My favorite example of an apparent narrative which jerks and twists and turns with tortured logic comes from the 19th century humorist, Samuel Foote. It is a useful piece of text because though it violates the principle of episodic *structure,* it has a surprising episodic *motivation,* which we will come to in a moment. But first a look at the text:

So she went into the garden to cut a cabbage leaf to make an apple pie: and at the same time a great she-bear coming up the street pops its head in the shop. "What! No soap!" So he died, and she very imprudently married the barber: and there were present the Picninnies, the Joblillies, and the

Garcelies, and the great Panjandrum himself, with the little round button at the top, and they all fell to playing the game of catch-as-catch can, till the gunpowder ran out the heels of their boots (S. Foote, ca. 1854, as cited by Cooke 1902, pp. 221f).

My father used to quote this passage as part of a general sales pitch on the importance of "meaningful sequence" (alias "episodic structure") in materials to be used for teaching a foreign language. His point was that the logic of Foote's text is not terribly unlike that found in many exercises written for the consumption of foreign language students. Except for its vague resemblance to narrative and its syntactic heterogeneity Foote's prose could well pass for many an ESL or FL pattern drill from a now, we may be grateful, fading era.

The trouble with Foote's prose is not so much its violation of what might be construed as a purely western style of episodic organization of discourse; rather, it is a problem of how to make an apple pie, and of the habits and haunts of she-bears. It is a matter of shaving soap, mortality, and barber shops, of weddings and the kind of folk who celebrate them. Of gunpowder and boot heels.

However, if we look back at the time and place where Foote's text was created, we discover that in fact his prose was not "unmotivated" in the sense in which we used this term above. That is, Foote himself had a pragmatic purpose in mind. His text made a point. It was a practical experiment proving one aspect of the episode hypothesis. To see this, we must look back at the context of his creation.

It seems that Foote had been attending a series of lectures in which a certain Professor Macklin was holding forth on the art of oratory. On the evening in question, Macklin boasted that using the techniques of memorization which he had ardently recommended throughout, and which he himself had mastered, he could repeat from rote any passage of prose up to a hundred words in length after having read it aloud only once. Foote casually wrote the text about the she-bear and the barber shop on the back of a scrap of paper, handed it to Macklin, and challenged him to read it once and repeat it from memory.

To the great delight of Mr. Foote, Macklin read the text but, alas, after only one pass through it, was unable to repeat it from memory. With a single stroke of humorous fantasy, Foote reduced Macklin's boast about his memory to a scrambled mess of apple pie and cabbage leaves. The trouble was that Macklin *could* memorize up to a hundred words in a single pass, provided the words fell into the sort of meaningful sequence characteristic of the logic of ordinary prose.

In retrospect, we look back and say that Foote's prose was pragmatically *motivated* by Macklin's boast, but the text itself violated many of the constraints that govern ordinary narrative. His prose lacked the internal episodic structure of ordinary discourse.

Of course, there are lots of examples of texts that are poorly motivated and/or poorly structured as well. In fact, lack of motivation especially may be singled out as one of the most common faults in texts that are written for the consumption of second language learners. For instance, consider the following conversation that supposedly took place on an airplane while Mr. and Mrs. Miller were en route to Hong Kong. They had run into Miss Yamada, again, a stewardess they had met on an earlier flight. Miss Yamada had begun to show them pictures of family and friends, and then the following dialogue is supposed to have ensued:

> Miss Yamada: This is my best friend. Her name is Fumiko.
> Mrs. Miller: She's very pretty. Is she older or younger than you?
> Miss Yamada: She's one year younger.
> Mrs. Miller: Aren't you thinner than she is?
> Miss Yamada: Yes, I am. Fumiko loves to eat.
> Mr. Miller: So do I. I hope it will be time for lunch soon.
>
> (National Council of Teachers of English 1973, p. 73.)

This text is odd because it lacks motivation. For instance, we might ask why the dialogue takes place. Does it have anything to do with getting to Hong Kong? Actually, in a tangential way it does, but it does not seem to contribute toward that end in any *significant* way. (It is not the sort of thing that one would be apt to write home about.) More particularly, we might ask why Mrs. Miller is curious about the relative ages of the stewardess and her friend. Or why Miss Yamada happens to take out the picture album in the first place. However, once the pictures are out, why is Mrs. Miller so curious about the relative sizes of Fumiko and Miss Yamada? Is the picture so bad or the stewardess's uniform so ill-fitting that the question is not superfluous—not to mention impertinent?

It isn't so much that the text lacks structure. On the contrary, Mrs. Miller seems to have an abiding concern for "structure"—especially comparatives. (She is probably an ESL teacher of the old school.) There is even a kind of temporal development in the conversation as, for instance, the mention of eating causes Mr. Miller to remark upon the fact that it is lunch time. What is missing is a motivation for Miss Yamada to take out the pictures in the first place, or for Mrs. Miller to ask about relative ages and weights or alternatively to quiz Miss Yamada on her ability to use English comparatives. Also, there is the general question as to why this conversation is reported in the course of a trip to Hong Kong.

What exactly is missing from the Miller text, and from many similar ones in ESL and FL texts? Or, putting the question differently, how come the episode does not seem to make any essential contribution to the Millers' experience or even to their trip to Hong Kong? Wouldn't it make more sense to delete the dialogue and just report, "The Millers went to Hong Kong by plane"? Apparently, the hidden agenda is to give the ESL students practice in the use of comparatives. This is probably the true motivation not only for the dialogue but for the chance meeting on the plane, and perhaps even the trip to Hong Kong in the first place. However, any such motive is simply insufficient if we take the pragmatic basis of trips to Hong Kong and the like seriously. Yes, giving practice in the use of comparative structures is a *kind* of pragmatic motive (to an ESL textbook writer), but it is too esoteric as a motive to contribute to an interesting story. The interpreter (listener-reader-hearer-learner) remains unmotivated. The outcome, in the words of Peck, is "dull, dull, dull."

What is missing?

A little more than seven decades ago, John Dewey (1910) noted that reflective thinking is always occasioned by trouble. A difficulty arises in experience and provides the incentive for reflection. Without any trouble there just isn't anything much worth bothering your head about. Not only is there nothing to write home about, there isn't even anything to converse about. Dialogue that contains no implicit conflicts, that wrestles with no troubles or difficulties, is a lot like reflective thinking without any motive. It is, in short, unmotivated.

Interestingly, Dewey's analysis of thinking presupposes that human behavior is goal-directed. There can be no trouble except in relation to thwarted purposes or desires. The very definition of the term "trouble" implies a cognitive superstructure with goals and plans to achieve them. (For analyses attempting to characterize such structures more explicitly, see Schank and Abelson 1977, Schank 1980, and Rumelhart 1975. However, we may note in passing that Rumelhart's story schema does not say anything significant about the beginnings and ends of stories precisely because he does not concern himself to explain where conflict enters and exits.)

Perhaps the single most common goal-orientation of human beings (something that can be taken for granted in *almost* all contexts of ordinary life) is the struggle to preserve life against the threat of death. This is a very practical version of the classic conflict of good and evil which appears in most novels in one form or another. Just such a classical structure motivates man's religious activities. The universal problem would seem to be the achievement of enlightenment and immortality.

Even scientific endeavors, in a very general sense, can be construed as attempts to differentiate false propositions from true ones, correct theories from nonsense. Presumably the fact that false ideas and superstitions in the end promote disease, poverty, and injustice is the primary motivation for the pursuit of scientific thinking and research.

Or, putting the whole perspective of episodic organization in a nutshell, we may refer to Robert Newton Peck's observation that "a plot is two dogs and one bone." Conflict in the pursuit of desired ends provides the motive for conversation, for writing home, and for telling stories as well as listening to them. A meaningful episode, one worth generating text about, is one that involves an experiencer pursuing a desirable goal in the face of opposition—the more severe the opposition, the more desired is the goal, and the more motivated will be the telling, comprehending, recalling, and retelling of the story. Or, casting the whole matter in Piagetian terms (see especially Piaget 1981), it may be argued that conflict is the principal source of the affective fuel that powers the cognitive engine. Dwight Swain (1980) and other teachers of writers have also often commented on the importance of feeling as a reaction to conflict and as a motivation for story telling.

The episode hypothesis thus asserts that to the degree a text is episodically organized (motivated and structured episodically), it will be easier to produce, understand, recall, and otherwise to benefit from for any practical purpose. To illustrate this, consider the fact that there are answers to many questions in reference to episodically organized texts which elicit only a blank stare when asked in reference to less organized texts. For instance:

> Why did the she-bear amble up the street?
> Who died in the barber shop?
> What killed him, the lack of soap or the bear?
> How did the gunpowder end up inside the boots of those at the wedding?
> What is the game of catch-as-catch can?

For these questions there are no determinate answers because the text in question lacks the requisite level of episodic structure (i.e., meaningful sequence).

The same is true, though less dramatically so, of the Miller text:

> Why did Miss Yamada take out her picture album?
> Why does Mrs. Miller ask about the relative ages of Fumiko and Miss Yamada?
> How does the conversation with Miss Yamada relate to the Millers' trip to Hong Kong?

Compare the absence of any determinate answers for the foregoing questions with the following:

> Why did the Embassy worker duck his head?
> What would have happened if he hadn't ducked?
> What caused the brick to come crashing through the window?

Or, consider the determinacy of the answers concerning the Foote text if we focus on the broader episodic context which motivated Foote's creation:

> Why did Foote write such an extraordinary text?
> Why couldn't Professor Macklin repeat it?
> What does Foote's demonstration prove about memory?
> Who had the better understanding of memory, Macklin or Foote?

And, obviously, many other questions could be adduced.

However, the point is by now established: *to the extent that a given text is episodically motivated and structured, it will give a richer yield of information.* Quite simply, it contains a larger quantity of accessible information than a less structured text.

SOME IMPLICATIONS

So where does all this lead us? What can we conclude from the input, textuality, expectancy, and episode hypotheses? It seems to me that several significant implications can be drawn for second language instruction, and for education in a more general sense as well. These can perhaps best be summed up as caveats which, as I indicated above, have their roots in successful story writing techniques. I am thinking here primarily in terms of second language instruction, but no doubt some of the implications which I will try to make explicit seem to have applications to other instructional objectives in other areas of school curricula.

First, I think that unmotivated texts should be avoided. We should treat them just as we would polecats with their tails in the air. Since, as we saw above, motivation seems to hinge on meaningful conflict, a text that lacks conflict relevant to the pursuit of a desired goal should not be used. This will *help* to relieve a lot of classroom boredom.

Second, the story line should be carried primarily by stageable action. This piece of advice comes from the most successful fictionalist of all time, Erle Stanley Gardner, and has been echoed many times by other successful writers. By 1979, Gardner had sold 310 million copies of his novels—mainly the mystery novels featuring Perry Mason and company. According to a 1981 publisher's release (Ballantine Books in New York), Gardner still outsells Agatha Christie, Harold Robbins, Barbara Cartland, and Louis L'Amour combined. Therefore, it seems that the advice he wrote in a letter to an aspiring writer is worthy of our attention:

Don't say that the villain is a mean man with a wicked wallop. Show him sliding down from his horse in a rage because the animal jerks away from him. Show him swing a terrific fist and crash the horse on the nose. That gives the reader the idea of the wickedness of his wallop. Then when the villain advances toward the hero with doubled fist the reader gets some suspense because he's seen what happened to the horse. But if you tell the reader the villain is bad and has a mean wallop, it's history, and the less history you get into a yarn the better (as cited by Fugate and Fugate 1980, p. 79).

Or, in the words of Robert Newton Peck, "Don't tell 'em: show 'em."

If this advice were heeded in the preparation of materials to be used in teaching languages, texts would be easier to dramatize and easier to understand, and much effort presently wasted trying to make sense out of nonsense could be better used.

Third, if the action of the story line is to be stageable, it must respect the logic of experience. (And to a surprising degree this is even true of fantasy!) That is to say, the sort of pattern drill nonsense that goes through every imaginable permutation of a given surface form without respect to meaning should never be used. In other words, we should not ask language students to practice saying drills like the following:

> John is a pilot.
> John is not a pilot.
> Is John a pilot?
> If John were a pilot, he could fly an airplane.
> John is not a pilot so John cannot fly.
> John is a pilot so John can fly.

> If John were not a pilot, he could not fly.
> Be a pilot, John, so you can fly.
> Fly to the John, pilot.
> Ask the pilot where the John is, John.
> The John is not a pilot.
> The pilot is not a John.

For the nonnative speaker there is little possibility of comprehending drills which permute structures without regard for meaning, and even less motivation to do so. In fact, meaningfulness is contrary to the intent of meaningless drills in the first place. However, meaningless drills are not logically necessary. Pattern drills, where they are used, may be anchored in pragmatically motivated text. For instance, in the Spanish program discussed in greater detail in Chapter 2, the author wrote:

Even the structure drills . . . are either based upon the known facts of the story or are cued by means of cartoons so as to render comprehension automatic . . . (Oller 1963, p. x).

Fourth, from the earliest stages of second language acquisition it makes sense to present the experience side of the pragmatic mapping first, and then to go on to analyze in greater detail the discourse side. In other words, the teacher should first make sure the students know what happens in the story, who is there, where it all takes place, what difference the events make to the characters, and what goals are being sought and thwarted. Then the student will be in a position to begin to work out an understanding of the subtleties of the target language used in that text in much the same manner, presumably, that the first language acquirer develops the usual sort of native-speaker "intuitions."

Fifth, if the text is long, it may be broken down into manageably smaller chunks. Understanding a long text is like eating an elephant in this respect: both must be consumed one bite at a time. This principle lays to rest many a complaint that texts in general are "too complicated for learners at stage X" (where X may be any point between ground zero and native speaker competence).

Sixth, it will be possible with episodically organized material to work through each episode in multiple cycles where the depth of understanding and the range of comprehension increase on each pass. On the first pass through a text or segment only the bare outlines may be understood. On the second and subsequent passes progress is made from the principal facts of who, what, and where, to the meatier details of when, why, and how, and eventually to presuppositions, associations, and implications at whatever depth suits the purpose of the instructor.

In the final analysis, the process of pragmatically linking input in the target language with the facts of experience depends, as Krashen, Burt and Dulay, and others have argued, on comprehension. This process can be facilitated by capitalizing on the textuality of ordinary experience, respecting its logic, harnessing the cognitive momentum that this logic creates, and in general by employing good story telling techniques in preparing, packaging, and presenting language teaching materials.

DISCUSSION QUESTIONS

1. In just what sense is everyday language both "situational" and "sequential," and how do these concepts relate to the process that Oller calls "pragmatic mapping"?

2. Select both a good example and a bad example of "text" (in the broad sense intended in this chapter) and examine each in terms of its episodic organization. Consider which elements of the text could be readily pragmatically mapped into a potential learner's experience and which elements would be difficult to incorporate. What factors help to determine the "comprehensibility" of a text in this sense?

3. Why is mere "exposure" not enough to bring about language acquisition?

4. Why are there answers to many more questions in the case of episodically organized material than in the case of unmotivated or poorly structured materials?

Chapter 2

An Integrated Pragmatic Curriculum: A Spanish Program

John W. Oller[1] and John W. Oller, Jr.
University of New Mexico

EDITORS' INTRODUCTION

When it began to take shape back in the late 1950s and early 1960s, the pragmatic program described here did not fit any of the theories of language teaching that were popular at the time. On the contrary, it ran in the face of many accepted dogmas. The wave of structural linguistics with its emphasis on contrastive analysis and syntactically motivated drills was just cresting. Consequently, when the first level of *El español por el mundo* appeared, it met with stiff resistance. Objections included the fact that the program in question paid virtually no attention to a contrastive analysis of the target language (Spanish) and the native language of most learners (English). Newmark's answer to this criticism (see Chapter 4) had yet to be written. Another objection was that structural sequencing had been made light of. For example, irregular verbs were used from the very beginning, as well as imperatives with attached pronominals, and subjunctive forms appeared during the first semester. Krashen's "net hypothesis" and his concept of "stage $i + 1$" would have countered the objection concerning structural sequencing, but it would be nearly two decades before Krashen's arguments were widely disseminated. Others insisted that *El español por el mundo* merely added a visual dimension to the audio-lingual approach which was standard fare at the time. However, critics failed to see that the intent of *El español por el mundo* was to immerse students in the world of the target language. But what the critics overlooked, some of the students and teachers who used the program were nonetheless able to see. There was a plan behind the program which resulted in the acquisition of Spanish, even in a formal classroom setting. This chapter discusses that plan. It also shows how a pragmatic conception differs from the now popular British approach of the "notional/functional" syllabus.

EL ESPAÑOL POR EL MUNDO: THE PRAGMATIC BASIS

The first level of *El español por el mundo—La familia Fernández*—was published in 1963 by Encyclopaedia Britannica Films. The second level,

---

1. My father, John Oller, Sr., died in September 1980. Therefore, this chapter is put together from introductory remarks which he had written years earlier for the two levels of *El español por el mundo* and from the experience I have had in using *El español por el mundo* at midschool, high school, and university levels. I would like to think that what is said here is entirely consistent with the theory and practice behind the program, but for any discrepancies I must take full responsibility. Thanks are expressed to the publisher (Encyclopaedia Britannica Films, now Encyclopaedia Educational Corporation) and to Dr. Ángel González, the coauthor of level II, *Emilio en España*.

Emilio en España, appeared in 1965 (coauthored with Ángel González). Both levels were dedicated to the belief that

language on the useful everyday level is situational and sequential and that the moment a student can react automatically . . . to a given situation identified with his own experience, he "knows" the foreign language used in *that* situation. The proper procedure then is to immerse the student in the world in which this language is used, a world inhabited by people about whom he knows and cares (Oller 1963, p. ix).

However, *El español por el mundo* did not merely bathe students in a flood of target language utterances (as in an unstructured "direct method"). Nor did it merely expose them to a series of situations or a list of examples of communicative functions in the target language (as in some applications of the "notional/functional syllabus"). Rather, *El español por el mundo* put the students into the *world* of the target language beginning with brief and simple episodes of experience and progressing to more complex ones. The objective was "immersion" not into a sea of utterances but into full-fledged contexts of living where utterances have values and meanings by virtue of their integration into the purposes, the conflicts, and the relationships of people. *El español por el mundo* was committed to the thesis that utterances do not arise in vacuo, but in the course of ordinary experience in a rich and varied world of people and events, with purposes, goals, conflicts, and relationships. Thus, it was argued in the Teacher's Manual for *La familia Fernández* that the

sharing of everyday experiences with people of a foreign tongue creates the climate of sympathy necessary and establishes the *sine qua non* for the teaching of the language, the *desire* of the students *to learn* to communicate with the people of that language . . . (Oller 1963, p. ix).

Parallels and Contrasts with the "Notional/Functional Syllabus"

About 10 years later, British theorists, notably Wilkins, Widdowson, and their disciples would offer a theoretical distinction between "synthetic" teaching and "analytic" teaching. Still more recently, Johnson capsulized this distinction as follows:

In a synthetic approach the teacher isolates and orders the forms of the linguistic system, systematically presents them to the student one by one. . . . In analytic teaching it is the student who does the analysis from data presented to him in the form of "natural chunks." Wilkins associates the synthetic approach with structural syllabuses, and the analytic approach with notional specifications (1979, p. 195).

"Notional specifications" were characterizations of language use based on semantic or pragmatic analyses. More specifically, the term "notional" came from the traditional "notional" definitions of grammatical categories (e.g., "a 'noun' is the name of a person, place or thing").

Wilkins' distinction between "synthetic" and "analytic" approaches paralleled the dichotomies of "discrete-point" versus "integrative" teaching as well as Krashen's distinction between "learning" and "acquisition" (1981, 1982). While "discrete-point" teaching tries to get students to synthesize a whole language system out of thousands of isolated bits and pieces presented one at a time, "integrative" teaching presents holistic communicative events and allows students to resolve them analytically into usable elements.

Therefore, in some respects, the British recommendations for a "notional/ functional syllabus" would parallel the pragmatic approach. However, Johnson, who is himself a proponent of the "notional/functional approach" (1979), notes that the contrast between such an approach and a "structural" (i.e., "discrete-point" or "synthetic") approach is not entirely clear. He claims that "certainly many of the materials which have been produced following notional syllabuses indicate that this type of specification *can* lead to synthetic teaching" (1979, p. 196).

The problem is that in listing "notions and functions" one merely arrives at another set of isolated bits and pieces of language cut loose from their moorings in experience. In the words of Widdowson, the goal of the applied linguist should be to "specify the nature of different communicative acts, the way they are realized, the way they combine in different varieties of language use" (1979, p. 59), or in another place, he urges that the key is "the understanding of what conditions must obtain for an utterance to count as a particular communicative act" (p. 57). The aim is to become "able to describe a type of discourse in terms of the kind of communicative acts it represents, and the manner in which they are given linguistic expression" (p. 57). He apparently sees the goal as teaching "the rules of use" instead of "the rules of grammar" (p. 50). Similarly Wilkins advocates a syllabus which will "cover all kinds of language functions" (1976, p. 19).

As a result, teaching such lists (e.g., teaching a variety of ways to apologize, or to accept an invitation, or to disagree politely with a superior) puts the student in much the same position as the old school structural approach. Students must synthesize the contexts which would motivate each notional/functional segment (i.e., type of communicative act), and they are right back in the same old boat as with the earlier discrete-point approaches with the exception that the segments, the points to be manipulated, are now longer.

A Pragmatic Approach Begins with the World of Experience

A pragmatic approach goes considerably farther than a "notional/functional syllabus." Instead of merely analyzing "concepts and functions" (Wilkins 1976, p. 19) and then attempting to plan a syllabus around the "semantic demands of the learner" (p. 19), a pragmatic approach goes directly to the *world* of experience. However, this is not the same as going to isolated and unrelated "situations" which taken as separate incidents may be as unmotivated as isolated utterances or grammatical elements. Nor is it the same as characterizations of different communicative acts or notional/functional uses of language.

A pragmatic approach assumes that the world is a spatio/temporal reality with the properties of wholeness and continuity. This is not only taken for granted by language users but is relied upon in order to make sense of experience. A pragmatic approach begins by placing the student in such a world.

A distinctive and necessary characteristic, therefore, of *El español por el mundo* was the sequentiality of its episodes—the continuity of the life experiences which it depicted, and of which it consisted. In this respect, the program anticipated, agreed with, and responded to Widdowson's observation that "language teachers have paid little attention to the way sentences are used in combination to form stretches of connected discourse" (1979, p. 49).

LEVEL I: *LA FAMILIA FERNÁNDEZ*

In *La familia Fernández,* and in fact throughout both levels of *El español por el mundo,* the events of lesson 1 led into those of lesson 2, which led into lesson 3, and so forth. The idea behind this sequentiality was an appreciation of the importance of episodic organization in both its motivational and structural aspects (see Chapter 1). The idea was for students to go *with* speakers of the target language *through* ordinary experiences and thus to learn the language of those experiences:

> In *La familia Fernández* . . . we follow through film the daily multi-situational lives of a typical family of Mexico City. Their experiences are common to those of all civilized families, and the language, carefully checked for authenticity by many Spanish language experts, both lay and professional, is that used by the middle class people of Mexico. . . (Oller 1963, p. ix).

In fact, *La familia Fernández,* consisted of

1. 54 filmed lessons
2. Each lesson accompanied by a filmstrip
3. Recorded exercises and drills
4. Recorded tests (two per lesson)
5. One student book containing over 1600 still photographs and cartoons
6. A teacher's manual, with a word index—indicating initial usage of lexical items plus the first three reentries. Initial entry of vocabulary in the exercises is in boldface type (Oller 1963, p. ix).

From the outset, the pragmatic approach in question assumed that the input in the target language would have to be made comprehensible. This assumption would later be clarified by Krashen (1980, 1981, 1982). However, it was also supposed that comprehensibility alone would not be sufficient. More than that, the language of common experiences would have to be actively operated on by the students so that the experiences of the characters in *La familia Fernández* would become personalized and appropriated by the students themselves:

> Simple "exposure" is not enough to teach a language to large groups of students. . . . Until a language becomes an integral part of the student's experience, until he can react to and activate automatically language which has been made part of his experience, he cannot communicate effectively in that language (Oller 1963, p. ix).

The object of *El español por el mundo,* therefore, was to facilitate the student's own entrance into the world of experience of the target language—to get the student to "be there." This, it will be appreciated, is substantially more than mere exposure to discourse. Even more obviously it is more than mere practice with lists of sentences illustrating syntactic patterns, or lists of communicative acts illustrating notional/functional categories.

Even in the "structure drills" of *La familia Fernández* the goal of comprehension and incorporation of the language into one's own personal world of experience remained intact:

> Believing that all language experience should be psychologically motivated and should revolve around known facts within high frequency situations, we have structured all exercises to this end. Even the structure drills . . . are either based upon the known facts of the story or are cued by means of cartoons so as to render comprehension automatic without translation (Oller 1963, p. x).

Multiple Cycles and the Communication Net

Another critical element was a systematic plan for developing facility in the language of each episode of experience. To accomplish this, the principle of multiple cycles was used (see the sixth recommendation in Chapter 1). The initial exposure to each new episode in the target language was achieved through a sound-motion film and followed by a film strip of still pictures capsulizing the events of the film and the meaning of each utterance at its point of occurrence. On the first exposure to each new lesson, the objective was comprehension. On each subsequent exposure, the objective remained the same, but the ante was upped. The progression from cycle to cycle was always intended to move the student from i to $i + 1$, $i + 2$, and so forth in manageable steps. From the beginning, the intent was to throw the communication "net" (Krashen 1980) so as to cover the student's present capacity (the "ith stage") and a little beyond (the "$i + 1$ stage").

The whole plan could be understood as a series of cycles spiraling outward to a greater expanse and a higher level of comprehension on each pass. In this series of broadening steps, the first step in each new lesson (from the beginning onward) was to show the film introducing the new material:

> It is recommended that the teacher show the film at least three times and then by means of the "stills" go through the language with the students. During this activity overall general comprehension is obtained. It is not necessary, however, to achieve at this stage absolute and complete comprehension of each lexical item. Understanding grows from exercise to exercise (Oller 1963, p. x).

Within each lesson the syllabus was designed so that many passes would be made through the target language utterances and expansions of them. The first objective, in keeping with the "input hypothesis" (Krashen 1980; also see Burt and Dulay in Chapter 3) was to establish comprehension of the facts of the story line. This was achieved largely through the film.

Anchoring Utterances in Facts of Experience

For instance, in the first episode (lesson 1 of *La familia Fernández*), the scene opens on a bright summer day with a little terrier disappearing around the corner of the house. The front door opens and out walks 5-year-old Pepito Fernández. He's looking around and wondering out loud, "¿Dónde está Imán?" He calls, "¡Imán! ¡Imán!" As Pepito comes down the front steps into the enclosed courtyard, Imán (the same little white dog we saw running off moments earlier) comes running back in response to Pepito's call. The boy sees him coming, and announces, "Aquí viene Imán." He bends down and pets the dog. About that time, the gardener walks by with a hoe. He says, "Buenos días, Pepito." Pepito looks up and answers, "Buenos días, Señor." Then, Enrique, a teenager, arrives, entering the courtyard from the street. Pepito announces to the gardener, "Aquí viene Enrique." The gardener goes on about his business and Enrique approaches and greets Pepito. Then, Enrique asks, "¿Dónde está Emilio?" Pepito hears the door opening behind him and looks around over his shoulder. Gesturing toward the door, he answers, "Aquí viene Emilio." Then Enrique and Emilio exchange greetings. Enrique asks Emilio, "¿Estás listo?" Emilio answers, "Sí. Estoy listo." Enrique gestures toward the gate and says, "Vámonos." Emilio answers, "Sí. Vámonos." As the two older boys head for the gate leading to the street, Pepito takes up pursuit. At this point, lesson 1 ends.

After the first showing of the film (while the film was being rewound for a second pass) the teacher would ask questions to begin to establish the facts of the story in the minds of the students. This is an important step in comprehending the target language utterances that occur in the film. For instance, on the first showing the teacher might ask in English (the native language of the students) such questions as the following:

> What is the little boy looking for when he comes out of the house?
> What's the dog's name?
> Who does the dog belong to?
> What are the names of the two older boys?
> What do you think is the relationship between Pepito and Emilio?
> Where do you think the older boys are going?
> What does Pepito do at the end of the film?

If any of the questions were not answered correctly after the first showing, they could be asked again after the second. For instance, it would be easy for a novice *not* to catch names like "Emilio" and "Enrique" on the first showing. So the students would be advised to see if they could catch the names of the older boys on the second viewing. Also, they might not have understood that Emilio and Enrique were going swimming on the first pass through the film, but both of these facts would probably be picked up on the second showing and certainly on the third. By then the "wh-" questions would have been answered. For example, "Who is Emilio?" The older brother of Pepito. "Who is Imán?" Pepito's dog. "Who is Enrique?" Emilio's friend. "Who is the man?" The gardener who takes care of the Fernández's yard. "What is Pepito doing when he comes out of the house?" Looking for his dog. "What does the gardener say to Pepito?" He says, "Buenos días." "Why does Enrique stop by?" He and Emilio are going swimming. "Why does Pepito run after them?" He probably wants to go with them.

The next step is to begin to establish familiarity with each utterance and its meaning. This probably could have been achieved in a variety of ways, and perhaps without plunging immediately into the production of utterances in Spanish, but firsthand experience with this program shows that students are quite capable of handling the challenge at this point. Moreover, launching production at this stage is critical to advancing the student's *i* and progressing to deeper levels of comprehension.

Incorporating the Utterances Themselves

In the Teacher's Manual for *La familia Fernández* backward buildup imitation drills were recommended—e.g., the student would hear, "¿Dónde está Imán?" on tape, or live from the teacher. Then the utterance would be broken down into manageable (i.e., repeatable) units. On the tape the student would hear "Imán" (student repeats, "Imán"). Again, "Imán" ("Imán"). Then "está" (students: "está"), "está Imán" (students: "está Imán"), "Dónde" (students: "Dónde"), "¿Dónde está Imán?"

By this method, each line of the dialogue was presented and then repeated by the student in small segments until the whole line could be uttered with some fluency. Throughout this phase students were reminded of meaning through the use of still pictures portraying the relevant events of the story. Granted, some lines of dialogue were more easily pictured than others, but throughout *La familia Fernández* virtually every line was such that its comprehension could be visually aided. From the opening imitation phase of lesson 1 and onward, it was possible (and recommended) for all the talk in the classroom to take place in the target language.

In a single 50-minute class period at the middle school or high school level it would be possible to progress through three showings of the film, and through the imitation drill for the first lesson. In the second class meeting a quick review of the film would help to refresh the students' memories.

Questions and Answers

Then, during the second meeting the teacher would progress to the question-answer cycle. By this point the students have already begun to produce the utterances of the basic dialogue with some fluency and with accurate pronunciation, and they also have a good solid understanding of the meaning of each utterance. The meaning has been developed and enriched from the first showing of the film until now. At this point the students have been through the facts of the story until they are familiar. Now the central focus shifts back to the facts again as viewed through the utterances of the dialogue.

The questions at this stage are asked in the target language and concern the familiar facts of the story. For instance, students are shown a picture of Pepito coming out of the house and they are asked, "¿Qué pregunta Pepito?" (What is Pepito asking?) By now they know that at this point in the story (the opening of lesson 1), Pepito is looking for Imán, and he is wondering aloud, "¿Dónde está Imán?" In the next picture Pepito is shown calling, "Imán. Imán." The question is "¿Qué grita Pepito?" Since new words are introduced in the questions (e.g., "pregunta" and "grita" in these cases), it takes some inferencing on the part of students to determine what is being asked. This element of uncertainty prevents the possibility of "parroting in repetition without comprehension" (Oller 1963, p. x) and ensures that *some* genuine communication must take place during the execution of this exercise. Also, each response required of students is consistently linked "to a visual representation of its meaning" (Oller 1963, p. x).

Linking of Form to Meaning and Vice Versa: Pragmatic Mapping

The emphasis on establishing the connection between meaning and form is one that is shared by proponents of the notional/functional or communicative approach. As Johnson (1979) points out, "There is a crucial difference between practice involving the linking of expression to actual meaning—and practice in which the student's attention is focused on achieving correctness of expression" (p. 200). He goes on to point out that this difference is essential to Krashen's distinction between "acquisition" and "learning." Also, he notes Savignon's caveat that students need "practice in linking expression to actual meaning" (1972; also see Savignon's Chapter 19).

From beginning to end it is always the linking of form and meaning that motivates the activities of teacher and students in working through the material of *La familia Fernández*. First, the facts are established; then the students are familiarized further with the meaning and form of each utterance; then the utterances are used to express the facts in significant but manageable ways through questions and answers. Subsequently, by graduating from talk about the facts in the film to talk (in the target language) about the talk of the film, a higher level of abstraction is achieved and a deeper level of comprehension is ensured. For instance, as the question-answer exercises proceed, it is possible for the instructor to help students understand specific grammatical elements (i.e., to establish the pragmatic mapping of utterance to meaningful context more precisely) by focusing attention on them through questions in the target language. To illustrate, consider the statement, "Pepito pregunta, '¿Dónde está Imán?' " as a response to the question, "¿Qué pregunta Pepito?" By producing the former utterance the student demonstrates at least some comprehension of the question. To push the comprehension still deeper, the teacher may ask, "¿Quién pregunta, '¿Dónde está Imán?' " ("Who asks, 'Where is Imán?' ") to which the answer is, "Pepito." Then the teacher may ask, "¿Qué hace Pepito?" ("What does Pepito do?") to which the correct response is "Pregunta, '¿Dónde está Imán?' " Probing still further, the teacher may ask, "¿Por quién pregunta Pepito?" to which the answer is "Pregunta por Imán" ("He asks about Imán"), and so forth throughout the elements of the entire episode.

Structure Drills as Paradigms of Demonstrable Meaning Changes

At about this same level of development, say, during the second or third class meeting, a simple high-frequency syntactic paradigm is developed and illustrated through the facts and meanings already established in the story and the communication that has already taken place in previous exercises concerning the story. A structure drill is introduced where each change in form has demonstrable consequences in terms of demonstrable meanings. For instance, students see a picture of Emilio pointing toward himself, saying, "Aquí estoy." Next, in the structure drill for lesson 1, is a picture of Enrique pointing toward Emilio. Enrique is saying, "Aquí está Emilio." In the following frame, Emilio and Enrique are shown together and a third voice says, "Aquí están Emilio y Enrique." Finally in the fourth frame, Emilio and Enrique are shown together and Emilio is saying, "Aquí estámos Enrique y yo."

The objective of each structure drill is to expand some element already introduced in the story line and to show how changes in meaning result in changes in its form and vice versa. The result of these drills and expansions of them along the lines of the other exercises throughout the program is a progressive internalization of the grammar of Spanish ánd development of the sorts of intuitions concerning meaning and form that native speakers of Spanish possess.

So, the students have events of experience accompanied by dialogue. Then, they have questions about the events. Next, the focus shifts to the dialogue and its meaning. Students learn to reproduce the utterances of the dialogue. Then they talk about the dialogue and there are structure drills that expand on elements that arise in the dialogue, and questions about the utterances of those structure drills. (e.g., "Oye Emilio, ¿dónde estás?"—"Hey Emilio. Where are you?"—to which a student impersonating Emilio responds, "Aquí estoy." Or the student's own name may be used.) Then we have questions about the talk about the dialogue (e.g., Pepito is shown coming out of the house looking for Imán and the teacher asks, "Por quién pregunta Pepito?" to which the student must respond, "Por Imán").

Communication Taking Place Throughout

At each phase, comprehension is necessary. Even though the exercises are repetitive and cyclic, it is generally impossible to give a correct answer at any point without understanding. Correct performance cannot be had by mere memorization of responses. Thus, the critical element of choice, something stressed by our British colleagues, is ensured. As Johnson puts it quoting Colin Cherry, "information can be received only when there is doubt; and doubt implies the existence of alternatives—where choice, selection, or discrimination is called for" (1979, p. 202). Or in another place, Johnson says, "language teaching may be seen as the provision to students of sets of options from which selection can be made. It must also provide practice in the process of selecting from these options in real time" (p. 202).

Narrative: Same Facts and Story, More Complex Language

Beyond the level of talk about talk there is narrative. Each lesson consists first of the dialogue itself, presented through the film; then talk about the dialogue in imitation drill, question-answer exercises, structure expansion exercises, and question-answer expansions of those exercises. In addition to all these methods of cycling through the material, there is full-fledged narrative. For instance, instead of saying, "Pepito pregunta, '¿Dónde está Imán?' " we may say, "Pepito pregunta por su perro. Dice, '¿Dónde está Imán?' " ("Pepito asks about his dog. He says, 'Where is Imán?' ").

Obviously it is easier to say, "¿Dónde está Imán?" than it is to say, "Pepito pregunta por su perro. Dice, '¿Dónde está Imán?' " However, by the time students are able to do the more advanced question-answer exercises of lesson 1, they will be ready to progress to the dialogue of lesson 2, and by the time they can do the question-answer drills of lesson 3 they will be able to handle lesson 1 in narrative form. Thus in the Teacher's Manual for *La familia Fernández* it was recommended that teachers work on a minimum of three lessons at a time. This gives a greater sense of progress, provides a built-in review, enhances the sense of continuity, and reduces boredom. (And by the way, can anyone truthfully claim that language acquisition by any method will not have its moments of tedium? But for some relief, see Part VI of this book.)

Reading and Writing Activities

Also, by the time students have reached the dialogue of lesson 3, provided the material has been adequately covered, they will have begun to stabilize an authentic pronunciation of all the material covered and will therefore be ready to encounter it in written form. Hence, from about the third week onward students will be doing reading and writing exercises over the material covered previously. Normally, at the beginning, reading and writing activities would lag about three lessons behind the current new material introduced first through the listening/viewing exercises of the film. In other words, the sequence was planned so that by the time the articulatory/productive exercises of imitation, question-answer, indirect restatement, and finally narrative were reached for lesson 1, the student would be about halfway through the same exercises for lesson 2, and would be working on listening comprehension of the film for lesson 3.

In the meantime, reading and writing activities would be introduced for lesson 1. It was assumed that there would be a good deal of positive transfer across modalities and that, therefore, all four of the traditionally recognized skills should be carried forward more or less simultaneously, with listening comprehension leading the way, followed by imitative production, then question-answer production, and so forth up to fuller productive use, followed by reading and writing activities in that order. However, as the students' facilities in the language progressed it was assumed that the time lag between listening, speaking, reading, and writing could eventually be reduced and finally done away with between the intermediate and advanced level.

Meaningful Sequence Prevails Throughout

The critical factor which makes possible an integrated development of all four skills and which maximizes the positive benefits of transfer across modalities is the sequentiality of the lessons. That is, the facts of the story line in lesson 1 continue into lesson 2 and throughout. This is not to say that the characters are always doing the same things from one lesson to the next. On the contrary, they are never doing exactly the same thing from one lesson to the next, but the normal continuity of the world of experience is respected.

For instance, in lesson 1 Enrique comes over to meet Emilio to go swimming. When it ends, Pepito takes up pursuit. At the beginning of lesson 2 Pepito catches up with them. He demands to know where they are going. "¿A dónde van ustedes?" With a look of exasperation, Emilio tells him, "¡No te importa!" ("It's none of your business.") Pepito starts yelling for mother. Emilio begs him to be quiet. ("Cállate, Pepito. Cállate.") Emilio concedes that he and Enrique are going swimming. Enrique agrees, "Sí. Vamos a nadar." Pepito's eyebrows rise and he asks, "Puedo ir con ustedes?" ("Can I go with you?") Emilio frowns, "No. No puedes." Pepito starts yelling for mother again. Again Emilio urges him to be quiet. "Bueno. Bueno. Vamos." ("All right, all right, come on.") Pepito has won, but now that the victory is his, he loses interest. He says, "No. No quiero ir. Voy a jugar con Imán." ("No. I don't want to go. I'm gonna play with Imán.")

And so on it goes. One episode leads into the next. As students follow the characters through the various episodes, they also learn the language of those episodes. At the beginning, things seem to go along slowly and each utterance requires considerable effort. By lesson 3 students are beginning to achieve some fluency, and by lesson 54 (the end of *La familia Fernández*) students will have achieved a considerable facility in the language and some breadth. At the midschool level it takes approximately 3 years to complete *La familia Fernández*. At the high school level the same material can be completed in 2 years, and at the college level in two semesters.

By the time lesson 54 is completed the student will have mastered many elements of standard Mexican Spanish (a vocabulary of over 3000 words, and all the basic syntax and morphology of the language). The student will have learned to read and write all the material of all the lessons and will be able to use the language creatively well beyond the confines of the particular elements practiced in exercise contexts.

LEVEL II: *EMILIO EN ESPAÑA*

In the second level of the program, *Emilio en España* (intended for use in the third and fourth semesters of college Spanish or the third and fourth years of high school Spanish), the students go with Emilio to Spain where he travels to visit his grandparents. As in the case of level I, level II continues to use the principle of multiple exposures to episodes of experience through multiple modalities of processing:

> We reiterate that all the necessary skills for effective communication should be taught at all levels of study.... Comprehension, speaking, reading, and writing should not be approached as separate and conflicting objectives but as logical, systematic and harmonious components of learning (Oller and González 1965, p. 7).

Acquisition Stressed Rather than Learning

Level II also continues to stress the inductive approach to the teaching of grammatical rules. The objective is to get students to internalize (in Krashen's terms, to "acquire" rather than "learn") grammatical rules (and a great deal more than mere grammatical rules) through use. However, in level II an appendix of explicitly stated grammatical rules is provided. Concerning it the authors point out:

> The specific rules which are printed in the appendix ... and cross-referenced to *Generalizaciones, Lecturas Gramaticales,* and *Prácticas Sistemáticas,* provide opportunity for students who may profit from the concise definition of grammatical phenomena.... [However,] the authors wish to caution teachers and students alike [that] this appendix is not designed for use in initial presentations. Study and discussions of grammatical principles per se are profitable in our opinion only when such study and discussion provide within themselves linguistic experience (Oller and González 1965, pp. 7–8).

That is to say, explicit grammatical rules ("Generalizaciones") were believed to be useful only when discussion of them could take place in the target language. In that way it would be possible for students to profit not only from the rule per se but also from the comprehensible input provided through discussion of the rule in the target language. Although *Emilio en España* was published in 1965, a thoroughgoing rationale for this approach would have to wait for Krashen's *Principles* ... not to be published until 17 years later in 1982.

Concerning the expansion of vocabulary and structural patterns the authors wrote:

> Presentation of new vocabulary and of structural patterns in a manner designed to secure comprehension by context, a technique used in Level I, assumes an increasingly important role in Level II. It is our belief that the student who has been immersed in the language, to the extent that his automatic reaction to new words and phrases is to search for meanings through mental image and situational context, is prepared to experience an explosion in comprehension (Oller and González 1965, p. 8).

Although a glossary was provided at the end of the textbook both for *La familia Fernández* and for *Emilio en España* indicating the initial entry and two subsequent entries of each new vocabulary item or grammatical form, the authors recommended, at level II, that students be encouraged to use one of several Spanish-to-Spanish dictionaries for checking meanings and usages of unfamiliar words.

Greater Creativity Allowed at Level II

There were also some significant contrasts between level I, *La familia Fernández,* and level II, *Emilio en España,* in terms of approach. Whereas in level I in the early stages emphasis had to be placed on deciphering of utterances and gaining productive control of a whole new phonology, lexicon, and grammatical system, at level II because of the development that had already taken place through level I, it was possible to move much more rapidly and to allow the student greater creativity from the beginning.

Still, the principle of multiple cycles through discourse anchored in experience was used throughout. As in level I, lesson 1 of level II (and all subsequent lessons) began with a filmed episode.

In the first lesson of *Emilio en España* an elderly man, whom we will later discover is Santiago Fernández, grandfather to Emilio, and his plump wife, Rosario, are seated in the patio of their home in Sevilla. He's reading a magazine and she's knitting. The maid enters with their customary hot chocolate. She asks, "¿Quieren ustedes su chocolate ahora?"

The old man answers, "¡Ah! Gracias."

At just that moment the doorbell rings. The old man speaks to the maid, "Ve a ver quién es, Rocío."

The maid leaves and the old man, returning to his reading with the cup in his hand, takes a sip of the hot chocolate. With a mild look of surprise he almost drops the cup, sucking air over his burned lips and tongue. He says, "Cuidado, Rosario, que está muy caliente."

His wife tests her hot chocolate carefully and answers, "Sí que lo está. Dame el azúcar por favor."

He passes the sugar.

The maid returns, and the old man asks, "¡Ah! ¿Quién era?"

She says, "Es un telegrama, señor," as she hands it to him.

"¿De quién será?" he mumbles as he opens it and begins to read. His eyes widen. "¡Por fin! Va a llegar Emilio." (At last, Emilio is going to arrive.)

"¿Mi nieto?" asks Rosario with a look of incredulity.

"¿Qué otro va a ser?" (Who else would it be?) the old man retorts.

"¿Y vendrá aquí?" she persists undaunted.

"Primero va a Madrid," he answers patiently. "El telegrama es de tu hijo Adolfo.[2] Emilio is arriving on Tuesday."

---

2. English is used here to ensure comprehension, but, of course, in the actual lessons only Spanish was used.

"¡Qué alegría!" exclaims Rosario; then she asks as an afterthought, "Pero, ¿por qué no vendrá aquí primero?" The old man answers that she knows there is no flight from Mexico City direct to Sevilla. "You're right," she answers, "we'll have to call Ignacio and tell him the good news." (See note 2.)

"Buena idea," Santiago answers, "¿Qué numero de área tiene Salamanca?"

She doesn't remember and sends him frowning to the telephone directory a few steps away from the table. He finds the number finally and dials, "dos—uno—cinco—siete . . . ¡Hola! ¿Ignacio? . . . Sí, soy yo . . . Tenemos telegrama de Adolfo . . . Que llega Emilio dentro de una semana . . . ¿A Sevilla? No; a Madrid . . . voy a ir a recibirle con Rosario . . . ¿Vas tú también? Bueno; nos vemos en Madrid . . . Saludos a todos. Adiós."

He hangs up the phone and comes back to the table.

"¿Entonces Ignacio va a estar a recibirle también?" Rosario asks.

"Yes," Santiago answers, "he's going to be in Madrid for a few days on business."

"¿Y Esperanza?" she asks.

"No," he says, "Esperanza is not coming, but Paco will arrive in the capital a couple of days later."

"¡Qué bien!" she says. "I need to buy some things in Madrid."

"Shall we fly?" he asks.

"I wouldn't think of it!" she answers with a look of horror. "For me it will have to be by train. Get on the telephone and make reservations immediately."

"Right now?" he sighs.

"Of course," she says matter-of-factly, "there are only five days till Emilio arrives."

Thus ends the opening episode.

Establishing the Facts

As in level I the first step is to establish the facts of the film. What happens? Who is there? Who is coming to visit? Where will he arrive? etc. However, unlike the opening lesson of *La familia Fernández,* at level II it is possible to carry out all of the talk (with very rare exceptions) in Spanish.[3]

Since the language of the dialogue is now considerably more challenging than was possible in level I, the first step is to summarize the events of the story at the outset. For example, "Los abuelos están en el patio. Van a tomar chocolate caliente. Suena el timbre y la doncella va a ver quién es. . . ." (Oller and González 1965, p. 36). Also, to make the transition from level I to II smoother for students who may have considerably varied backgrounds, all the tenses of the indicative are reviewed in the first few lessons.

3. It should be noted that all the dialogue and material in the films and written exercises throughout level II is in Spanish. The material is graded so as to become progressively more complex, and vocabulary entry is still controlled carefully as it was in *La familia Fernández,* but the rapidity of introduction of new vocabulary and a diversity of forms of expression is accelerated.

As before, the next exercise poses questions relevant to what happened in the film. Here the vocabulary is expanded and additional information may be filled in. For example, as this exercise progresses the students learn that Esperanza is the wife of Ignacio. Of course, this should be inferred from the telephone conversation between Santiago and his son Ignacio, but in the first question-answer exercise it is made explicit. The teacher, of course, is encouraged to expand upon this question-answer format ad libitum within the facts of the story. For instance, the teacher might ask who Paco is, to which there are a variety of correct responses. A student might answer correctly: "Es el hijo de Ignacio." Or "Es el primo de Emilio." Or the teacher might ask, "¿Quién es Ignacio?" to which a student might answer, "Es el hermano del padre de Emilio," or "El padre de Paco, el esposo de Esperanza, el hijo de Santiago y Rosario Fernández, y el tío de Emilio," and so forth.

After the question-answer exercises (accounting for a minimum of three passes per lesson through the facts of the story), there follows an expanded narrative recounting the facts of the film plus interpolations that expand upon the explicit happenings of the film. For instance, in the initial narrative (Primera Lectura) for lesson 1 we learn that in addition to Adolfo, Emilio's father, and Ignacio, Paco's father, Santiago and Rosario have another son named Rodrigo who lives in Barcelona, Spain. This is information introduced for the first time. However, there are also new bits of information that were implied in the film and in previous exercises which are now made explicit. For instance, "A la abuela no le gustan las aviones." (Emilio's grandmother doesn't like airplanes.)

Grammar

Following *La Primera Lectura,* for each lesson, are several (as many as 12) structure review exercises which refer to facts in the film and certain logical expansions of the facts. For instance, in these exercises both regular and irregular verbs are reviewed, as well as many aspects of Spanish grammar. The technique at first is inductive acquisition of rules and patterns which are made more explicit in the grammatical *Generalizaciones* which follow. For example, in the opening lesson the authors discuss,

Los usos principales del presente en español. . . a. Presente real. El verbo se refiere a una acción que está en progreso en el momento en que hablamos. Este es el presente verdadero. La acción del verbo se realiza ahora: "¿Qué haces? Tomo chocolate. . ." (Oller and González 1965, p. 43).

In addition to the explicit statement of grammatical rules and principles, there are brief narratives called *Lecturas Gramaticales* which illustrate certain subtleties of Spanish grammar in action. These readings are topically relevant to what has taken place or is about to take place in the main story line, but they are not limited to that story line. Also, they follow grammatical themes that arise in the main dialogue and related narrative versions. For instance, in lesson 1 there are readings that illustrate inductively certain facts about uses of the present indicative, also articles, and there is the following grammatical narrative

(Lectura Gramatical, c) illustrating nearly all the idiosyncratic masculine and feminine nouns ending in -*ma:*

El telegrama plantea *el problema* de cambiar *el programa.* Los abuelos discuten *el tema* de la visita y deciden usar *el sistema* ferroviario y llegar a Madrid a recibirle. No habrá dificultad en eso, a pesar de *la fama* que tiene *el sistema* de Europa. *La suma* que tendrán que pagar es pequeña. De noche *la cama* les será muy cómoda e igual el asiento de día. *La goma* que usan para cubrir *las camas* y los asientos se llama goma espuma, y resulta muy bien para el caballero or para *la dama.* Podrán contemplar *el panorama,* o entretenerse escuchando y hablando en *el idioma* del país con los pasajeros. *El esquema* que tienen parece muy bueno, ¿verdad? (Oller and González 1965, p. 44).

Following the grammatical narratives in each lesson are writing exercises which provide an opening in Spanish which is to be completed by the students according to instructions of the teacher. Also, the dialogue from the film is given in its entirety.

Handling Cultural Information

Then follows another narrative version of the filmed story. This one is called *Expansión del Tema.* Whereas the *Primera Lectura* stayed closely within the facts and experiences of characters in the film, the *Expansión* deliberately ranges beyond to incorporate relevant geographical, historical, and cultural information. For instance, in the *Expansión del Tema* for lesson 1 some details are offered concerning the city of Sevilla where the grandparents live. In addition, forecasting concerning future lessons is given:

Sevilla es la ciudad más representativa de Andalucía. Es la capital de la provincia de Sevilla, que es una de las ocho provincias de Andalucía. Más tarde vamos a visitar toda esta región con Emilio y sus parientes... (Oller and González 1965, p. 45).

Cultural similarities and contrasts are discussed in Spanish:

Los abuelos no son muy diferentes de los abuelos de cualquiera de nosotros. Los vemos por la tarde tomando chocolate. En España las horas de comer son distintas de las de los Estados Unidos. Los españoles, por lo general, no desayunan fuerte al levantarse por la mañana. Toman café, chocolate, o, especialmente los niños, leche caliente. A veces también comen panecillos o bollos. Más tarde, a eso de las diez y media de la mañana, toman el *bocadillo* con una bebida. El bocadillo consiste en un sandwich o un panecillo o cosas por el estilo.... Almuerzan entre la una y las tres de la tarde... (Oller and González 1965, p. 45).

Finally, following the *Expansión del Tema* for each lesson there are summary questions, which again may be supplemented by the teacher. As in *La familia Fernández,* the second lesson follows the experiential content of the first, and so forth throughout.

Varieties of Spanish

Because of the diversity of dialects of Spanish, the taped exercises for lessons 1 to 27 of *Emilio en España* include speakers representing a wide variety of regional variants. The authors observed:

Contrasts between cultures (foreign and native) tend to command a disproportionate share of classtime. This danger is minimized if discussions are conducted completely in the target language and thereby afford true linguistic experience [i.e., in Krashen's 1980 term "comprehensible input"] (Oller and González 1965, p. 9).

Concerning the development of cultural understanding the authors wrote:

The direct objective of foreign language study in high school and lower division college classes should always be the attainment of communication skills. Where the setting is entirely different within the culture of the target language, as is the case, with... *El español por el mundo,* the indirect benefit of cultural appreciation is a natural outcome (Oller and González 1965, p. 9).

CONCLUSION

When *El español por el mundo* first came on the market two decades ago, one of the common complaints was that it was too expensive for many small school districts to obtain it. Even back in those days of single-digit inflation it cost something over $3000 to place *La familia Fernández* in a classroom. Although many critics were willing to concede that the program did achieve its aim of bringing the world of the foreign language into the classroom and of making communicative competence in the language accessible to students (and even to teachers alike), they contended that the price tag was too high. In spite of this objection, many school districts and a couple of state boards opted to buy it anyway.

Now, however, we live in a whole new era of technology. The cost effectiveness of video recording and playback equipment has made pragmatic language teaching with a sound-motion-picture component more accessible than at any point in previous history. For this reason it may be hoped that some of the concepts embodied in the foreign language program discussed in this chapter will continue to contribute in a small way to more effective classroom language teaching.

DISCUSSION QUESTIONS

1. What is the difference between immersing the student in the "foreign language" versus immersing the student in "the world of experience" in which that language is used? How does this distinction relate to the difference between "synthetic" and "analytic" teaching, or between "discrete-point" and "integrative" teaching, or between "learning" and "acquisition"? Also, how does immersion in a world of experience facilitate the pragmatic mapping of target language utterances?

2. Traditional foreign language teaching has been criticized because it presses students to attend too exclusively to the surface form of target language utterances (e.g., their phonology, morphology, and syntax). However, in a

so-called pragmatic approach, students must still master the surface forms of target language utterances; so what's the difference?

3. What are some of the ways that the students' "$i + 1$" is systematically advanced as they progress through the episodes and exercises of *El español por el mundo*?

4. Do the structure drills of this Spanish program differ from those in other audio-lingual programs? Examine similarities and differences closely.

5. How are grammatical rules taught at the beginning of the program and how does the philosophy of explicit rule presentation change as the student progresses to level II? What argument does Krashen offer in favor of discussing target language grammar in the target language?

Chapter 3

Optimal Language Learning Environments

Marina K. Burt and Heidi C. Dulay
Bloomsbury West, San Francisco

EDITORS' INTRODUCTION

In this chapter the authors stress that *both* the context of learning *and* what the learner brings to it are important. Based on careful examination of relevant research findings, four conclusions are offered: (1) to acquire a nonprimary language, the learner's attention must be directed toward message content; (2) input which is roughly tuned to the student's level of readiness will be maximally beneficial; (3) the input must be comprehensible; (4) students will be inclined to acquire the language of peers, i.e., persons with whom they identify. Burt and Dulay also point out the basic distinction between *foreign* language teaching and *second* language teaching. In the former case, as seen in Chapter 2, the burden to provide access to the world of experience through the target language weighs more heavily upon the teacher, while in second language teaching, typically there are many sources of meaningful communicative experience outside the classroom. Among the approaches highlighted by Burt and Dulay are natural exposure methods (see Chapters 17 to 20), the Canadian and American bilingual immersion approaches (see Chapter 31), and Asher's "total physical response" method (see especially Chapters 5, 26, and 27). Also recommended are classroom activities where talk focuses on things and events in the here and now—e.g., doing a science project (for additional ideas see Chapters 21 to 25 in Part VI, Fun and Games, and Chapters 13 to 15 of Part IV) or taking a field trip (especially see Chapter 16). The point of such activities is to motivate and facilitate the pragmatic mapping of target language utterances onto meaningful contexts of experience.

Language learning is a two-way street. Learners, and all the mental and physical machinery they come with, comprise one dimension. The environment, including the teacher, the classroom, and the surrounding community, is the other. During the last 10 years of second language research, the focus was mostly on the learner: on learning strategies and styles, on attitudes and motivation, on cognitive and neurological mechanisms. In the last few years, the research pendulum has begun to swing in the other direction; researchers are paying attention to the environment surrounding the learner. Describing the kind of speech learners hear—"motherese," "teacher talk," and "foreigner talk," for example—is a favorite topic.

We have put the learner and the environment together in this effort to present facts about language learning that will be maximally applicable to teaching. We begin with the assumption that learners do not pay equal attention to, nor do they try to process, everything they hear or read. In other words, not everything available in the environment—even language directed at the learner—will trigger learning. Crucial to a description of language learning, therefore, are answers to the question: *What features of the environment enhance second language acquisition?* This chapter summarizes the results of our efforts to answer that question.

We have scoured the research literature and have accumulated a cache of relevant studies, enough to draw four major conclusions. In this paper we present these conclusions together with supporting data, and we offer suggestions for their application. Finally, we locate the environment within the broader context of the entire language acquisition process.

MAJOR FINDINGS

A Natural Language Environment Is Necessary for Optimal Language Acquisition

A natural language environment exists whenever the focus of the speakers is on the content of the communication rather than on language itself. An ordinary conversation between two people is natural, and so are natural verbal exchanges at a store, a bank, or a party. The participants in these exchanges care about giving and receiving information or opinions, and although they use language structures, they do so with virtually no conscious awareness of the structures used. Likewise, reading for information or entertainment, or film or television viewing are also natural uses of language. All these activities provide the participants with *natural exposure* to the language.

Observed effects of natural exposure

John Carroll's (1967b) much publicized survey of nearly 3000 college foreign language majors was one of the first to demonstrate the beneficial effects of natural language exposure for second language acquisition. Carroll found that most of the French, German, Russian, and Spanish majors in American colleges and universities did not demonstrate very good foreign language skills. Their average scores on the Modern Language Association Foreign Language Proficiency Test corresponded to a Foreign Service Institute rating of two-plus (out of five): between "limited working proficiency" and "minimum professional proficiency."

Naturally, some students did better than others, and this is where Carroll demonstrates the benefits of natural exposure. He found that students who reported a year's study abroad performed best; those who reported a summer or a tour abroad performed next best; and both of these groups outperformed those who had never studied in a host country but only in a formal foreign language learning environment (such as learning French in the United States).

The host language environment (such as French in France or English in the United States) is one which permits learners to talk with native target language speaking peers about issues relating to their lives in the new environment. It provides maximum opportunities for natural language exposure.

With careful planning, natural language exposure can also be made available within a foreign language environment. When it is, language learning results improve noticeably. For example, one group of researchers (Scott, Saegert, and Tucker 1974) studying students learning English in Egypt and Lebanon found that all students studying English did not automatically improve over time. Only some did. Students who had experienced learning academic subjects in English improved steadily over time, while those who studied English only in a formal language classroom situation did not improve as steadily.

Using a content subject such as biology to expose students to a new language is a way of providing natural exposure to the language. The focus of the participants is on the content—biology—and this is the necessary ingredient for a natural language environment.

The much discussed "immersion programs," such as those in Canada (Lambert and Tucker 1972), also show the value of natural language environments for language acquisition. Immersion programs were designed for students who speak a majority language (such as English in the United States or Canada) as their first language and who wish to learn the minority language (such as Spanish in the United States) as a second language. In these programs, the language the students are learning is used as the medium of subject matter instruction.

French immersion programs have existed for English-speaking children in Canada for over a decade [see Swain Chapter 31], and a Spanish immersion program for English-speaking children has been operating for several years in Culver City, California. In evaluating the programs, it has been demonstrated that the children developed a level of language competence in their second language "that even the most optimistic second language teacher would not set for a student following the traditional FLES (Foreign Language in the Elementary School) program" (Bruck, Lambert, and Tucker 1974, p. 203).

In immersion programs, the language is used as a vehicle to focus on subject matter content. Since content is the focus of the participants, immersion programs provide a natural language environment.

Communicative Interactions Must Match the Learner's Level of Language Development

When learning a new language, learners appear to pass through at least three kinds of communication phases: *one-way, partial two-way,* and *full two-way.*

In *one-way communication,* the learner listens to or reads the target language but does not communicate back. The communication is one-way, toward the learner, not from the learner. Listening to speeches and radio programs, watching films and most television programs, and reading books and magazines are examples of one-way communication.

In *partial two-way communication,* the learner may respond orally to someone, but the communication is not in the target language. The response may be in the learner's first language or may be nonverbal, such as a nod or other physical response.

In *full two-way communication* the learner speaks the target language, acting as both recipient and sender of verbal messages in the target language.

Learners appear to tend toward these types of communication at different times during the learning process.

Observations of natural language learning

When left to their own devices, learners have been shown to rely on one-way and partial two-way communication during the early stages of language learning, waiting until much later to participate in full two-way communication. This tendency is exemplified by the Vaupes River Indians in South America (Sorenson 1967) who may well be the world's leading experts in practical language learning. Almost two dozen mutually unintelligible languages are spoken in a small area populated by a group of about 10,000 people. It is the custom in this Indian culture to marry outside one's language group—people must find mates who do not speak their language! As a consequence, children must learn at least three languages from the start: their mother's, their father's, and the lingua franca of the area (Tukano). More languages are typically acquired as the individual grows up, and this extraordinary language learning continues throughout adolescence, adulthood, and even into the later years.

What do these extraordinary people do to help them learn a new language? Sorenson writes that "the Indians do not practice speaking a language they do not know well yet. Instead, they passively learn lists of words, forms, and phrases in it and familiarize themselves with the sound of its pronunciation. . . . They make an occasional attempt to speak a new language in an appropriate situation, but, *if it does not come easily, they will not force it"* (Sorenson 1967, p. 680, emphasis ours).

Sorenson's description documents learners' reliance on one-way and partial two-way communication in the early learning stages. Not until learners feel ready to speak the new language do they even attempt to do so.

Children learning their *first* language have almost always been observed to understand language before being able to produce it. Researchers and observant parents have all noticed that children begin by listening to language from 1 to 3 years before beginning to speak it (Brown 1973, Bloom 1970). All the while, of course, they are developing comprehension skills, demonstrating their understanding by doing the things asked of them, such as drinking their milk (partial two-way communication).

Researchers studying children learning a *second* language have also observed the gradual transition from one-way to two-way communication. Unless adults (teachers or others) force children to speak in the new language, they typically exhibit a *silent period* from 1 to 5 months. During this period, the young second language learners concentrate on comprehension and opt for one-way or partial two-way communication.

For example, one otherwise outgoing immigrant boy learning English at a school in southern California said nothing at all for the first 2 weeks and spoke only a few words during the next 2 weeks, mostly memorized phrases to communicate essential needs (Huang and Hatch 1978). English-speaking children aged 4 to 9, enrolled in Swiss schools where French was the language of instruction, did not volunteer anything in the new language for a prolonged period; some said nothing for several months (Ervin-Tripp 1974). Similarly, Hakuta (1974) reports that he could not begin his study until some 5 months after his subject had been exposed to English because she produced almost no speech before that time. Instead, the little girl demonstrated only comprehension of the language.

It appears that second language learners naturally begin by listening; then they respond nonverbally or in their own language, and finally they start producing the new language.

Classroom research on the effects of a silent period

Two studies on the effects of a *silent period* for the first 1 to 3 months of language instruction provide support for incorporating the natural tendencies of language learners into a curriculum. Postovsky (1974, 1977) experimented with American adult students studying Russian in an intensive 6-hour-per-day course at the Defense Language Institute in Monterey, California. Students were instructed not to respond orally but to write their answers to classroom exercises (partial two-way communication). Students who experienced the silent period during the first month of the intensive course outperformed those who were made to speak from the beginning in both pronunciation and control of grammar (Postovsky 1977, p. 18).

Fifty English-speaking children learning Spanish in a southern California school were studied during the first 5 months of instruction (Gary 1975). Half of the children received a regular Spanish course in which oral responses in Spanish were required (full two-way communication). The other students experienced a silent period first. They did not practice any oral Spanish for the first 14 weeks of the course (they indicated comprehension nonverbally) and responded orally only for the first half of the lesson during the remaining 8 weeks. At the end of the 22 weeks, both groups of children were tested for production and comprehension skills in Spanish. In listening comprehension, the partial two-way group outperformed the full two-way group, as might be expected. The partial two-way group, however, also did as well on the *speaking* tests as the group which had been practicing speaking since the first day.

Apparently, matching the type of communicative interaction with the learners' level of language development maximizes the students' likelihood for success.

Target Language Input Must Be Comprehensible to the Learner

Students' ability to organize the new language system depends largely on how well they can understand what they hear or read. When students are at the early stages of learning how to speak a new language, they know few words in the language and therefore need to *see* the meaning of much of what they hear. *Concrete referents* for verbal input comprise, therefore, an important ingredient of a learner's early language environment.

Concrete referents refer to extralinguistic items that can help the learner grasp the meaning of the sounds of the new language. They include things and activities that can be seen, heard, or felt while the language is being used. Experienced teachers usually provide concrete referents in the form of visual aids, motor activities, and other "here-and-now" kinds of extralinguistic support.

Examples of the here-and-now principle abound in the literature on children's learning of a first language. Parents or others describe what children are doing, or what they have just done: *That's a nice sandcastle! Oh, you spilled your milk!* Or they tell children what to do: *Drink your juice! Stop that!* Or they ask questions about the children's ongoing activities: *Is that a doggie? Where is your sock?*

These native speakers do not generally talk to children about activities displaced in time and space, such as what will happen next week, what is going on down the block, not to mention next year or events in another country.

Language environments for young second language learners are also often concrete. Questions such as *Is this your ball? What color is your car?* follow the here-and-now principle and give the learner the extralinguistic support necessary to understand the new language (Wagner-Gough 1975). Native speaking peers who play with the newcomers in school appear to realize the importance of concrete referents for comprehension. Fillmore (1976) notes that when an English-speaking child she studied wanted to tell a fairly new immigrant child about an upcoming television program, the first child asked a bilingual adult to tell the second one about it in Spanish, because "he won't know what I'm saying." The English-speaking child realized he could not provide any concrete referents for a future television program; so he asked a bilingual to say it in his playmate's native language.

While concrete referents are often provided in second language classrooms for younger children, they are often forgotten for older learners, who need them just as much. For example, one researcher documented the following questions being asked of a newly arrived immigrant who was 13 years old: *What are you gonna do tonight? What do you do at home? What do we mean by 'question mark'?* (Wagner-Gough 1975). Although these questions may not seem difficult to a native English speaker, the absence of a single concrete referent makes it impossible for the learner to figure out what the meaning is without knowing the meaning of the words already.

Older learners, like younger ones, benefit from adherence to the here-and-now principle, especially in the early stages of instruction. Rather than talking about doggie or toys with older students, one would select more appropriate objects and activities, such as money or food. But whatever the choice, the objects and activities chosen should have concrete referents so that learners can figure out the meaning of the language used.

Language Learners Attend to, and Acquire, the Language and Dialect Spoken by People with Whom They Identify

The source of the language the learner hears is the fourth significant environmental factor that researchers have found influences a language learner's performance. Several speaker models may be available (anyone who speaks the target language is a potential model), but learners do not draw on them equally. To date, evidence has been presented which demonstrates speaker model preferences of three sorts: peers over teachers, peers over parents, and one's own ethnic group members over nonmembers.

When both a teacher and peers speak the target language, learners have been observed to prefer their peers as models. For example, a 7-year-old Japanese-speaking child who had immigrated to Hawaii acquired the Hawaiian Creole English of his age mates, rather than the Standard English of his teachers during his first school year. When the boy moved to a middle-class neighborhood the following year, he quickly picked up the Standard English that his new friends spoke (Milon 1975).

In immersion programs where the teacher is typically the only native speaker of the target language to whom the children are exposed during the school day, children show unexpected gaps in their control of the target language, even after 4 to 7 years in the program (see Bruck, Lambert, and Tucker 1975 for the St. Lambert French immersion program; Plann 1977 for the Culver City Spanish immersion program).

The development of such "immersion varieties" of target languages does not appear to be attributable to any learning problems of the children nor to the quality of the target language spoken by the teachers during the school day. Instead, the outcome seems to be directly attributable to the preference these children have for their peers as speech models. In the immersion programs, it happens that all the preferred models are themselves struggling with the new language.

Peers are also preferred over parents as language models, whether they speak standard or nonstandard varieties of the target language. In first language learning, it has been found that when the speech characteristics of peers and parents differ, the children will tend to acquire the speech characteristics of their peers (Stewart 1964, Labov 1972).

Finally, some children have been observed to tend toward the dialect or language spoken by members of their own ethnic group. For example, Benton (1964, cited in Richards 1974) reports that Maori children learn the English dialect of their own ethnic group rather than the standard New Zealand English spoken by other children.

These examples indicate that language learners attend *selectively* to different target language speakers. They learn from some but not from others.

INSTRUCTIONAL APPLICATIONS

The environments we have discussed here that make a difference in language learning seem to be those that enhance the students' "creative construction" of the new language. They provide learners with rich exposure to natural language used by people with whom the learner identifies, at a level of comprehension and learner participation that is attuned to the learner's stage of second language development.[1]

Optimal language learning environments can be (and have been) created by teachers in classrooms. One just has to be willing to subordinate linguistic form to subject content for a major part of the curriculum. One also has to be willing to explore materials that may not have been designed for language teaching purposes but can be adapted to meet those needs. Conversely, adapting existing language teaching materials so that they more readily conform to the requisite characteristics is often necessary.

Among the activities that are most frequently suggested as effective second language lessons are science experiments. They usually involve doing things and giving and receiving instructions that have concrete referents. Although science experiments may illustrate an abstract physical law, the experiment itself involves activities firmly rooted in the here-and-now. Science in general is a good choice for the content of a second language course. Science lessons lend themselves to natural, concrete communicative interactions which may be one-way, partial two-way, or full two-way, depending on the learner's readiness to use the new language. The nature of the interactions can be planned in advance by the teacher in response to the students' states of readiness to use the language. Science projects also provide opportunities to pair or group together students of various proficiency levels, so that the less proficient have peer language models while the more proficient have opportunities to use the new language without feeling linguistically inferior.

---

1. See Dulay, Burt, and Krashen (1982) for a more detailed presentation of optimal learning environments than is possible in this short chapter.

Not all language teachers take readily to science, however. Arts and crafts, some business and finance topics, cooking, or health, nutrition, and safety provide equally effective topics for language lessons. Since the ultimate objective of a language class is to teach language, a teacher need not feel obligated to teach any particular content, unless, of course, the program is one designed for special purposes (such as scientific German or business English). Otherwise, areas in which the teacher is most at ease and the students most interested will probably be the best choice.

Other effective activities that traditionally have been part of second language classes are nonlinguistic games (such as indoor baseball), communication games, and role play. For these and the other activities described above to be successful, the focus of both teacher and students should be on the activity rather than on the language forms they are using. Correction of student errors should therefore be kept at a minimum, while communication should be maximized. Teachers should accept students' use of their native languages in the second language classroom while they themselves use only the target language.

During the silent period at the beginning of language learning, the teacher has to work extra hard, since she or he does most if not all of the talking. Films, film strips, cassettes, and records, however, may provide some respite to the teacher, while getting students used to the sounds and rhythms of the new language. Reading activities are also useful, as long as students are not asked to read aloud. The "total physical response" method developed by Asher (1965, 1969; and Asher, Kusudo, and de la Torre, Chapter 5) has been integrated into a text which provides many ideas and lessons for the silent phase of an English curriculum (Romijn and Seely 1979).

In a *host* language environment, where the target language is that used by the community at large, teachers may draw on the rich language resources outside the classroom. Taking students on field trips or arranging events in which native speakers of the target language who are peers of the second language students participate are a few such out-of-classroom activities which provide good language learning opportunities, if organized well. In a host language environment, a language teacher who can incorporate outside resources into the curriculum will be helping students make optimum use of a rich natural second language environment.

Foreign language teaching is more difficult. The teacher has virtually no outside help, since the target language is not spoken outside the classroom. Thus the teacher, along with films, film strips, records, and tapes, becomes the sole source of a learner's target language environment. In such situations, it is probably realistic *not* to expect great accomplishments from students but to be satisfied if a student reaches what Virginia French Allen calls "entry level" skill in the new language. Encouraging students to visit the countries in which the target language is spoken, and giving them cultural information to ease their initial adjustment, comprise, therefore, an important part of a foreign language course. Further, if subject matter classes in the foreign language are offered at the same institution (e.g., biology in English taught at the American University in Beirut, or physics in English taught at the University of Puerto Rico), students of English should be encouraged to attend, if only to acquire better English (rather than learn a lot of physics or biology).

Finally, in applying research findings on language learning, it is best to use Mary Finocchiaro's framework for program development as a checklist to ensure comprehensive and cohesive application. Finocchiaro suggests the acronym COMET to remember all the program components into which instructional changes should be incorporated (Finocchiaro and Ekstrand 1977, p. 217):

C-urriculum
O-bjectives
M-ethods and materials
E-valuation
T-eachers (preparation and skills)

INTERNAL CONTEXT FOR ENVIRONMENTAL INPUT

Lest we have given the impression that all that matters in language learning is the environment, we conclude with a picture of the entire language acquisition process, of which environmental input is a part (Figure 1). Elsewhere we have described in detail each aspect of the process (Dulay, Burt, and Krashen 1982; Dulay and Burt 1977). Suffice it here to say that the environment provides the raw language material which the learner filters, organizes, and monitors according to principles applicable to most human beings. These principles are

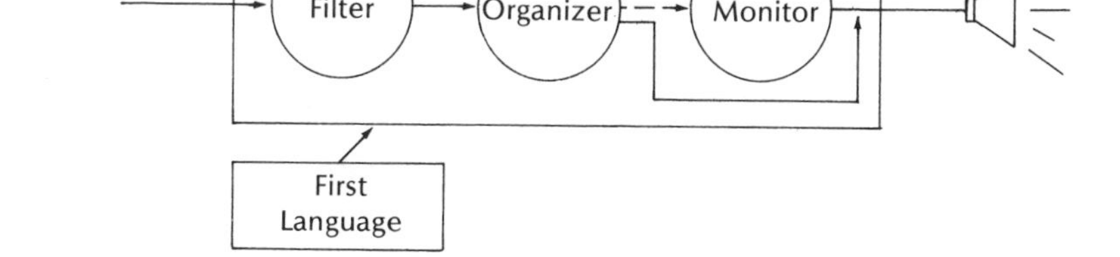

Figure 1 Working model for creative construction in L2 acquisition, an updated version of the model presented in Dulay and Burt 1977.

responsible for similarities in errors, acquisition orders, and transitional rules that have been observed in the performance of second language learners the world over. Differences in environment, age, personality, and first language background of learners also affect language processing and result in variations in verbal performance. These variations, however, do not obscure the regularities which attest to the universal internal mechanisms at work in language learning.

Teaching a second language means creating for students a part or all of their target language environment. It means working with their natural language learning capacities and tendencies in a process which is a two-way street.

DISCUSSION QUESTIONS

1. What do the authors mean by the statement that "language learning is a two-way street"? More specifically, how do the elements in Figure 1 reveal the bidirectionality of the language learning street?

2. What would you consider to be the primary characteristics of "natural exposure"? How would the concepts of "episodic organization" (see Chapter 1), especially "motivation" and "structure," figure among these characteristics?

3. In Carroll's study published in 1967, foreign language majors who traveled to the country where the target language was spoken tended to outperform students who merely studied the language in a classroom context and stayed at home. What are some of the factors that would help to account for this difference? Also, consider the results of Scott, Saegert, and Tucker (1974). Why would students studying academic content in English improve more steadily in English skills than students studying English as a foreign language?

4. In addition to the complexity of the target language per se, what else contributes to the difficulty of a communicative exchange in the target language? What relation do you see between the principle of multiple passes through a text (as discussed and illustrated in Chapters 1 and 2) and the Burt-Dulay distinctions between *one-way, partial two-way,* and *full two-way* communicative interactions?

Chapter **4**

How Not to Interfere with Language Learning[1]

Leonard Newmark

University of California, San Diego

EDITORS' INTRODUCTION

When this chapter was first published back in the mid-1960s, it struck a resonant chord with many foreign language teachers who were laboring under the heavy load placed on their backs by the dogma of contrastive analysis. The teachers of that era had been steeped in the doctrine that acquiring a postprimary language was chiefly a process of fighting off the troublesome habits of the primary language. However, in this chapter, Newmark not only combated and defeated the foolishness of the contrastive approach to curriculum design, but he also demolished any possible defense of "discrete-point" language teaching. Unfortunately, many stalwarts continued to promote that approach in one form or another for at least 18 years after any theoretical basis for it had been exploded by Newmark. The discrete-point philosophy even today persists in a variety of forms purporting to teach a language by disposing of, one at a time, an inventory of items (phonemes, morphemes, words, phrase structures, transformations, functions, notions, situations, or whatever). Newmark asserts that "acquisition cannot be simply additive; complex bits of language are learned a whole chunk at a time." He understood the principle of pragmatic mapping, the fact that chunks of language are linked to contexts of experience in systematic ways: "the language exponentiates as the number of chunks increases additively, since every complex chunk makes available a further analysis of old chunks into new elements, each still attached to the original context upon which its appropriateness depends" (p. 51). Newmark also understood the importance of episodic organization and the fundamental difference between "connected situational dialogue" and "disconnected structural exercise" (p. 51). He recommended the very sort of natural language teaching that is illustrated throughout this book (see especially Chapter 2 and Parts IV and V).

In the applied linguistics of the past 20 years much had been made of the notion of first-language interference with second-language learning. Our dominant conception of languages as structures and our growing sophistication in the complex analysis of these structures have made it increasingly attractive to linguists to consider the task of learning a new language as if it were essentially a task of fighting off an old set of structures in order to clear the way for a new set. The focal emphasis of language teaching by applied linguists has more and more been placed on structural drills based on the linguist's contrastive analysis of the structures of the learner's language and his target language: the weight given to

---

1. Published in *International Journal of American Linguistics*, 32, I, II, 1966.

teaching various things is determined not by their importance to the user of the language but by their degree of difference from what the analyst takes to be corresponding features of the native language.

A different analysis of verbal behavior has been motivated in psychology by reinforcement theory; the application of this analysis has led, of course, to programmed instruction, step-by-step instruction based in practice on the identification of what are taken to be the components of the terminal verbal behavior. What could be more natural than the marriage of linguistics and psychology in the programmed instruction of foreign languages, with linguistics providing the "systematic specification of terminal behaviors" and psychology providing "the techniques of the laboratory analysis and control" of those behaviors (Lane 1964).

If the task of learning to speak English were additive and linear, as present linguistic and psychological discussions suggest it is, it is difficult to see how anyone could learn English. If each phonological and syntactic rule, each complex of lexical features, each semantic value and stylistic nuance—in short, if each item which the linguist's analysis leads him to identify had to be acquired one at a time, proceeding from simplest to most complex, and then each had to be connected to specified stimuli or stimulus sets, the child learner would be old before he could say a single appropriate thing and the adult learner would be dead. If each frame of a self-instructional program could teach only one item (or even two or three) at a time, programmed language instruction would never enable the students to use the language significantly. The item-by-item contrastive drills proposed by most modern applied linguists and the requirement by programmers that the behaviors to be taught must be specified seem to rest on this essentially hopeless notion of the language learning process.

When linguists and programmers talk about planning their textbooks, they approach the problem as if they had to decide what structural features each lesson should be trying to teach. The whole program will teach the sum of its parts: the student will know this structure and that one and another and another. . . . If the question is put to him directly, the linguist will undoubtedly admit that the sum of the structures he can describe is not equal to the capability a person needs in order to use the language, but the question is rarely put to him directly. If it is, he may evade the uncomfortable answer by appealing to the intelligence of the user to apply the structures he knows to an endless variety of situations. But the evasion fails, I think, against the inescapable fact that a person, even an intelligent one, who knows perfectly the structures that the linguist teaches, cannot know that the way to get his cigarette lit by a stranger when he has no matches is to walk up to him and say one of the utterances. "Do you have a light?" or "Got a match?" (Not one of the equally well-formed questions, "Do you have fire?" or "Do you have illumination?" or "Are you a match's owner?")

In natural foreign language learning—the kind used, for example, by children to become native speakers in a foreign country within a length of time that amazes their parents—acquisition cannot be simply additive; complex bits of language are learned a whole chunk at a time. Perhaps by some process of stimulus sampling[2] the parts of the chunks are compared and become available for use in new chunks. The possible number of "things known" in the language exponentiates as the number of chunks increases additively, since every complex chunk makes available a further analysis of old chunks into new elements, each still attached to the original context upon which its appropriateness depends.

It is not that linguists and psychologists are unaware of the possibility of learning language in complex chunks or of the importance of learning items in contexts. Indeed it would be difficult to find a serious discussion of new language teaching methods that did not claim to reform old language teaching methods in part through the use of "natural" contexts. It is rather that consideration of the details supplied by linguistic and psychological analysis has taken attention away from the exponential power available in learning in natural chunks. In present psychologically oriented programs the requirement that one specify the individual behaviors to be reinforced leads (apparently inevitably) to an artificial isolation of parts from wholes; in structurally oriented textbooks and courses, contrastive analysis leads to structural drills designed to teach a set of specific "habits" for the well-formation of utterances, abstracted from normal social context.

Our very knowledge of the fine structure of language constitutes a threat to our ability to maintain perspective in teaching languages. Inspection of language textbooks designed by linguists reveals an increasing emphasis in recent years on structural drills in which pieces of language are isolated from the linguistic and social contexts which make them meaningful and useful to the learner. The more we know about a language, the more such drills we have been tempted to make. If one compares, say, the Spoken Language textbooks devised by linguists during the Second World War with some of the recent textbooks devised by linguists,[3] he is struck by the shift in emphasis from connected situational dialogue to disconnected structural exercise.

The argument of this chapter is that such isolation and abstraction of the learner from the contexts in which that language is used constitutes serious interference with the language learning process. Because it requires the learner to attach new responses to old stimuli, this kind of interference may in fact increase the interference that applied linguists like to talk about—the kind in which a learner's previous language structures are said to exert deleterious force on the structures being acquired.

Consider the problem of teaching someone to say something. What is it we are most concerned that he learn? Certainly not the mere mouthing of the utterance, the mere ability to pronounce the words. Certainly not the mere demonstration of ability to understand the utterance by, say, translation into the

2. I take the term and notion from Estes (1962).
3. For example, see Bolinger et al. (1960), Swift et al. (1962), Gumperz and Rumery (1962).

learner's own language. Even the combination of the two goals is not what we are after: it is not saying *and* understanding that we want but saying *with* understanding. That is, we want the learner to be able to use the language we teach him, and we want him to be able to extend his ability to new cases, to create new utterances that are appropriate to his needs as a language user.

Recent linguistic theory has offered a detailed abstract characterization of language competence; learning a finite set of rules and a finite lexicon enables the learner to produce and interpret an infinite number of new well-formed sentences. Plausible detailed accounts also abound in the psychological and philosophical literature to explain how formal repertoires might be linked referentially to the real world. But the kinds of linguistic rules that have been characterized so far (syntactic, phonological, and semantic) bear on the question of well-formedness of sentences, not on the question of appropriateness of utterances. And the stimulus-response or associational- or operant-conditioning accounts that help explain how *milk* comes to mean "milk" are of little help in explaining my ability to make up a particular something appropriate to say about milk—such as *I prefer milk*—in a discussion of what one likes in his coffee, and even less my ability to ignore the mention of milk when it is staring me in the face. An important test of our success as language teachers, it seems reasonable to assert, is the ability of our students to choose to say what they want. It has been difficult for linguists and psychologists to attach any significance to the expression "saying what you want to say"; our inability to be precise about the matter may well have been an important reason for our neglect of it in language teaching. But importance of a matter is not measured by our ability at a given moment to give a precise description of it: we can be precise about the allophones of voiceless stops in English after initial /s/, but it seems absurd to claim that it is basically as important—some textbooks imply *more* important—to teach students to make these allophones properly as it is to teach them, for example, how to get someone to repeat something he has just said.

The odd thing is that despite our ignorance as experts, as human beings we have always known how to teach other human beings to use a language: use it ourselves and let them imitate us as best they can at the time. Of course, this method has had more obvious success with children than with adult learners, but we have no compelling reason to believe with either children or adults that the method is not both necessary and sufficient to teach a language.

If we adopt the position I have been maintaining—that language is learned a whole act at a time rather than learned as an assemblage of constituent skills— what would a program for teaching students to speak a foreign language look like?[4]

---

4. I shall restrict myself here to the question of teaching a spoken foreign language. How one teaches people to read and write a foreign language depends on their literacy in another language and on their mastery of the spoken language in which they are learning to be literate. The problems involved would take me too far afield of the subject I am discussing here.

For the classroom, the simple formulation that the students learn by imitating someone else using the language needs careful development. Since the actual classroom is only one small piece of the world in which we expect the learner to use the language, artificial means must be used to transform it into a variety of other pieces: the obvious means for performing this transformation is drama—imaginative play has always been a powerful educational device for both children and adults. By creating a dramatic situation in a classroom—in part simply by acting out dialogues, but also in part by relabeling objects and people in the room (supplemented by realia if desired) to prepare for imaginative role-playing—the teacher can expand the classroom indefinitely and provide imaginatively natural contexts for the language being used.

The idea of using models as teachers is hardly new in applied linguistics, and nothing could be more commonplace than the admonition that the model be encouraged to dramatize and the student to imitate the dramatization of the situation appropriate to the particular bit of language being taught. The sad fact is, however, that the drill material the model has been given to model has intrinsic features that draw the attention of the student away from the situation and focus it on the form of the utterance. Instead of devising techniques that induce the model to act out roles for the student to imitate, the applied linguist has devised techniques of structural drill that put barriers in the way of dramatic behavior and a premium on the personality-less manipulation of a formal repertoire of verbal behavior.

If what the learner observes is such that he cannot absorb it completely within his short-term memory, he will make up for his deficiency if he is called on to perform before he has learned the new behavior by padding with material from what he already knows, that is, his own language. This padding—supplying what is known to make up for what is not known—is the major source of "interference," the major reason for "foreign accents." Seen in this light, the cure for interference is simply the cure for ignorance: learning. There is no particular need to combat the intrusion of the learner's native language—the explicit or implicit justification for the constrastive analysis that applied linguists have been claiming to be necessary for planning language-teaching courses. But there is need for controlling the size of the chunks displayed for imitation. In general if you want the learner's imitation to be more accurate, make the chunks smaller; increase the size of the chunks as the learner progresses in his skill in imitation. We do not need to impose arbitrary, artificial criteria for successful behavior on the part of the learner. If we limit our demand for immediate high quality of production, we may well find that his behavior is adequately shaped by the same *ad hoc* forces that lead a child from being a clumsy performer capable of using his language only with a terribly inaccurate accent, and in a limited number of social situations, to becoming a skillful native speaker capable of playing a wide variety of social roles with the appropriate language for each.

To satisfy our requirement that the student learn to extend to new cases the ability he gains in acting out one role, a limited kind of structural drill can be used: keeping in mind that the learning must be embedded in a meaningful context, the drill may be constructed by introducing small variations into the situation being acted out (e.g., ordering orange juice instead of tomato juice, being a dissatisfied customer rather than a satisfied one, changing the time at which the action takes place) which call for partial innovation in the previously learned role. In each case the situation should be restaged, reenacted, played as meaning something to the student.

The student's craving for explicit formalization of generalizations can usually be met better by textbooks and grammars that he reads outside the class than by discussion in class. If discussion of grammar is made into a kind of dramatic event, however, such discussion might be used as the situation being learned—with the students learning to play the role of students in a class on grammar. The important point is that the study of grammar as such is neither necessary nor sufficient for learning to use a language.

So far, I have been talking about the use of live models in language classrooms. How can such techniques be adapted for self-instruction? The cheapness and simplicity of operation of the new videotape recorders already make possible a large portion of the acquisition of a language without the presence of a model; it has been shown convincingly that under the proper conditions it is possible for human students to learn—in the sense of acquiring competence—certain very complex behaviors by mere observation of that behavior in use.[5] Acquiring the willingness to perform—learning in a second sense—seems to depend to a greater extent on reinforcement of the student's own behavior and is thus not quite so amenable to instruction without human feedback at the present time. However, extension of techniques (originally developed to establish phonological competence in step-by-step programmed instruction)[6] for self-monitoring to cover whole utterances with their appropriate kinetic accompaniment may suffice in the future to make the second kind of learning as independent of live teachers as the first and thus make complete self-instruction in the use of a language possible.

DISCUSSION QUESTIONS

1. Define "first language interference" and differentiate it from "padding."
2. Newmark allows the term "interference" in this chapter to serve a variety of pragmatic functions. Enumerate and discuss them.
3. What is the difference in "saying *and* understanding" and "saying *with* understanding" (p. 52)? How does this differentiation relate to the notion

5. For an excellent discussion of the roles of imitation and reinforcement in the acquisition and performance of complex behavior, see Bandura and Walters (1963).
6. For example, the techniques used in Sapon (1961).

that mere "exposure" is insufficient—that the target language must be incorporated into the experience of the student (Chapter 2)?

4. What does Newmark mean by "the mere mouthing" of an utterance? Further, how have discrete-point (surface-oriented) methods tended to promote and perpetuate "mere mouthings"? What is missing from such approaches?

5. In what ways do traditional structure drills tend to focus attention "on the form of the utterance"? Moreover, what does Newmark mean when he says that "the applied linguist has devised techniques of structural drill that put barriers in the way of dramatic behavior" (p. 53)?

Part II
Teacher/Individual Orientations

Although none of the orientations discussed here is uncontroversial, all have some claims to success. Each in its own way offers a practical base for making clear to language students the connection between utterances in the target language and meaningful contexts of experience. Asher's method of the total physical response (Chapter 5) accomplishes the pragmatic mapping of utterance to context through commands. These are made comprehensible through actions of the instructor, and the proof that they have been comprehended is demonstrated in the responses of the students who do on command what they have seen the instructor do. Gattegno's silent way (Chapter 6) achieves the pragmatic mapping of utterances to contexts with the help of a few little sticks of different lengths and colors. His method also incorporates commands and may have more in common with Asher's approach than has been commonly realized. Rassias's approach, discussed by Robert Wolkomir in Chapter 7, arrives at the pragmatic connection through a variety of dramatic contortions that defy the imagination and frighten the pants off most sane language teachers. Because of the highly individual nature of these three orientations (especially Rassias's), we recognize that they are not for everyone, but who can deny that they work for teachers who have the wherewithal to apply them? Finally, this section concludes with Chapter 8 by Jane Bancroft concerning Lozanov's method, more popularly known as "Suggestopedia." According to her interpretation, Lozanov's approach, like the others in this section, depends heavily on the "authority" of the teacher. For a somewhat different interpretation of Lozanov, however, see Stevick in the opening chapter of Part III.

SUGGESTED ADDITIONAL READINGS

JAMES J. ASHER.
> 1982. *Learning Another Language Through Actions: The Complete Teacher's Guidebook.* (Expanded Second Edition). Sky Oaks Productions, Inc. P.O. Box 1102, Los Gatos, California 95031.

Here Asher gives his own guided tour of the total physical response approach to language teaching. This is probably the most widely studied and the best-documented experimental method of language teaching.

CALEB GATTEGNO.
> 1972. *Teaching Foreign Languages in Schools: The Silent Way.* Second edition. New York: Educational Solutions.

Our excerpt, included as Chapter 6, comes from this volume. However, Gattegno's book itself contains a number of commentaries about applications that will be of interest to many classroom teachers who want to use his approach.

OTTO JOHNSTON.
> In press. Five years with the Rassias method in German: a follow-up report from the University of Florida. *Foreign Language Annals.*

This soon-to-appear article reports additional evidence showing that application of the Rassias madness in Florida is working. The main criterion is that enrollments are up. There are other positive indicators as well.

GEORGI LOZANOV.
> 1978. *Suggestology and Outlines of Suggestopedy.* New York: Gordon and Breach.

A work which we ourselves have yet to see but which Stevick characterizes as "indispensable." It is one of the few publications from Lozanov himself.

EARL STEVICK.
> 1980. Part II: One way of teaching: the Silent Way. In *Language Teaching: A Way and Ways.* Rowley, Massachusetts: Newbury House, pp. 37–84.

In inimitable style, Stevick reports on his own application of the Gattegno approach to teaching foreign languages. In a later section of the same book he incorporates elements of Gattegno's method with Curran's approach.

Chapter 5

Learning a Second Language through Commands: The Second Field Test

James J. Asher, Jo Anne Kusudo, and Rita de la Torre
San Jose State University

EDITORS' INTRODUCTION

Imperative drills in a target language consist of commands issued and/or modeled by an instructor and then carried out by students. The emphasis is on comprehension first as demonstrated and established in appropriate active responses, moving eventually, through a series of gentle steps at the student's own pace, into productive control of the language. Participating in such drills ensures the successful pragmatic mapping of utterances in the target language into meaningful contexts of experience. The whole person gets into the act. First, there is the auditory stimulus accompanied by a demonstrated action. The input is usually immediately comprehensible on first presentation. Then the student demonstrates comprehension by carrying out the command. The sensorimotor accompaniments of such responsive action provide a whole fabric of meaningful experience into which the utterances of the target language are woven. Unlike Gattegno's silent way (see Chapter 6), the Asher approach (also known as the total physical response, or TPR, method) insists on a listening period during which the students are not expected to produce any utterances in the target language. Asher and his collaborators contend that contrary to the claims of certain critics, the transition from TPR drills into the full scope of target language functions can be effected smoothly. They demonstrate here (and also see Chapters 26 and 27) that the TPR method is not limited to the teaching of imperatives, as some critics had contended.

Figure 1 is a still picture from a documentary film[1] produced in 1964 that showed the complexity of Japanese understood by American children after 20 minutes of training.[2] The instructional strategy was based on asking the students to be silent, listen carefully to a command in Japanese, then act immediately. The approach was called the learning strategy of the "total physical response."

1. Information on the availability of the three motion-picture films mentioned in this chapter may be obtained from James J. Asher, Psychology Department, San Jose State University, San Jose, California 95192.
2. The research here was performed under a contract with the United States Department of Health, Education, and Welfare, Office of Education, under PL85-964, Title VI, Section 602, as amended.

Since that time, the effectiveness of commands to achieve listening skill in a second language has been confirmed in a series of experimental studies in Russian, Japanese, French, Spanish, and German.[3]

The imperative drill can be traced back to 1925 when Harold E. and Dorothée Palmer (1970) observed that physically responding to verbal stimuli is "one of the simplest and most primitive forms of stimulus and reaction in the whole range of speech-activities" (p. 38). This may be the first pattern of responses by the young child to language uttered by his mother. For example, mother may say, "Look at that little cat in the garden!" and the baby turns his head and looks in the appropriate direction. Still later, mother directs the child to "fetch things or to pick things up or to put things in various places, and the baby performs all these actions so accurately and so naturally that one is almost tempted to believe that the child has an instinct for understanding his native language" (p. 39).

---

3. The references are as follows: Russian (Asher 1965, 1966, 1969a; Asher and Price 1967; Postovsky 1974, 1975, 1977), Japanese (Asher 1964; Kunihira and Asher 1965; Kanoi 1970), French (Mear 1969, Pimsleur 1972), Spanish (Kalivoda, Morain, and Elkins, Chapter 27 in this volume) and German (Asher 1972).

The Palmers then suggested in their classic book, *English through Actions*, that executing orders is a prerequisite to achieving the power of expression in a second language. Even further, they advocated that no approach to teaching foreign speech is likely to be economical or successful which does not include in the first stage an extensive period of time for classroom work involving students carrying out orders by the teacher. Twenty-five years later in 1950, Tan Gwan and Robert Gauthier introduced in Canada the Tan Gau approach, which was based in large part upon the imperative drill.

Currently, the *total physical response*, the *audio-motor approach*, and the *silent way* all have in common the imperative drill. In Tan Gau, the total physical response, and the audiomotor formats, production is delayed until listening comprehension has been developed to a considerable extent through commands by the instructor. In the silent way, there is an immediate switch from listening to production, and from the beginning an attempt is made to "fine tune" the student's pronunciation.

With few learning trials, physically responding to commands seems to produce long-term memory. This phenomenon can be generalized beyond second language learning because it has been shown that even in one's native language, responding to commands has an impact on retention. For instance, Lieberman and Altschul (1971) conducted a study in which a list of 35 simple commands (such as stand on one foot, fold your arms, and put your hands on your hips) were played on a tape recorder to groups of college students. One group ($N = 50$) was instructed to close their eyes, relax, and imagine themselves performing the commands. Another group ($N = 53$) watched a model perform, and still a third group ($N = 46$) performed when they heard the commands.

After the list of commands was played, each student had 5 minutes to write the commands he could recall. The recall of each group was significantly different. The one-way analysis of variance yielded an F of 25.6 ($p < .01$). Specifically, the mean recall for the "imagine" group was 47 percent (SD = 12 percent); for the "see" group, the mean was 53 percent (SD = 10 percent); and the group that performed the commands had a mean recall of 62 percent (SD = 8 percent).

The study by Lieberman and Altschul demonstrated short-term memory for commands. James H. Humphrey from the University of Maryland showed in 1972 that even 3 months after science concepts were learned through motor activities, the mean recall of the experimental group was 73 percent (SD = 6 percent) and the control was 50 percent (SD = 5 percent), which yielded a matched group t of 4.33 with df = 9 ($p < .01$). Humphrey published studies (1960, 1962, 1965, 1967, 1968, 1970) which indicated that a learning format based on motor activity by children enhanced the assimilation of a wide range of academic concepts and skills.[4]

---

4. Also see the work of Bryant J. Cratty (1966, 1967, 1969, 1970) and a book by George O. Cureton (1973) in which motor learning was used to teach beginning reading to inner-city students.

After viewing the motion picture of children learning a sample of Japanese, many FL teachers have commented, "Commands are fine, but what happens next? How does the student learn other linguistic features such as the verb tenses, function words and especially abstractions which are difficult to manipulate as, for instance, "honor," "justice," and "government"? How does the student make the transition from the physical and action-oriented imperative to linguistic features that seem to be nonphysical?

In an effort to answer these important questions, experimental training programs have been developed with the intention of exploring three questions:

1. Can the entire linguistic code of the target language be learned with a format in which the students physically respond to commands?
2. Can listening fluency for the target language be achieved without using the student's native language?
3. Will there be a large amount of positive transfer of learning from listening comprehension to other skills such as speaking, reading, and writing? This transfer should vary depending upon the fit between orthography and phonology. In Spanish, for instance, there should be a large amount of positive transfer because Spanish utterances are written the way they sound.

Since the independent variable was long-term training with a complex instructional program, there was not the experimental control that is possible with a laboratory problem such as eyelid conditioning. Our research strategy has been to explore the parameters of the complex instructional program in a series of field tests. By trying the program in range of situations which included different languages, different age groups, and different instructors, the expectation was that the instructional format would consistently produce significant gains in learning. The intent was to move by successive approximations in which each field test was better controlled than the previous one.

THE FIRST FIELD TEST

The first field test was reported by Asher in the March 1972 issue of *The Modern Language Journal.* Adults between the ages of 30 and 60 experienced about 32 hours of training in German with an instructor who used commands to achieve listening comprehension.

First, we found that most grammatical features of German could be nested into the imperative form. With imagination, almost any aspect of the linguistic code for the target language could be communicated using commands. For example, the *future tense* can be embedded into a command as, "When Luke walks to the window, *Marie will* write Luke's name on the blackboard!" The *past tense* can be incorporated into the command structure. For instance, say: "Abner, run to the blackboard!" After Abner has completed the action, say: "Josephine, if *Abner ran* to the blackboard, run after him and hit him with your book." As to the *present tense,* these were nested in the imperative such as, for instance, "When *Luke walks* to the window, Mary will write Luke's name on the blackboard!"

Our second finding was that basic listening fluency could be achieved in German without using the students' native language. For certain abstractions, however, the German was written on one side of a cardboard card and English on the other. Then such abstractions as "honor," "justice," and "government" were manipulated as objects. For instance, the instructor said in German, "Luke, pick up 'justice' and give it to Josephine." "Abner, throw 'government' to me."

As to the level of listening skill, the experimental group with only 32 hours of training had significantly better listening comprehension than college students completing either 75 or 150 hours of college instruction in German.

The third finding was that listening skill in German had a large amount of positive transfer to reading. Even though the experimental group had no systematic training in reading, their skill was comparable with a control group that did receive systematic instruction in reading and writing.

Concerning speaking, there was positive transfer from listening comprehension to production, as may be seen in the documentary color film, "Strategy for Second Language Learning" (see footnote 1). At the climax of 60 hours, most of which was directed to listening skill, students invented skits and acted them out. The spoken German was flowing, spontaneous, and uninhibited, but there were many errors in pronunciation and grammar. Our tolerance for production errors was similar to the tolerance adults have for production errors by children learning their first language. If the students were willing to talk and talk and talk in German without anxiety about making mistakes, eventually, when their confidence was extremely high, they could be "fine tuned" to produce the subtleties of speech that approximate the native speaker. Our goal was a spontaneous shift from listening to a level of production in which the student's vocal output was intelligible to a native speaker.

Of course we are aware that all instructional problems in teaching a second language cannot be solved with one approach. Variety is essential to maintaining the student's attention and continued interest.

It seems clear, however, that most students (about 80 percent) can rapidly internalize the linguistic code—the structure of the language and vocabulary—when language is synchronized with actual movements of the student's body. In this context, "internalization" means that the linguistic input into the student has these three properties: (1) short-term memory, (2) long-term memory, and (3) the ability to transpose linguistic elements to comprehend novelty (Asher 1965, 1966, 1969a, 1969b; and Kunihira and Asher 1965).

Theoretically, if the student can internalize listening comprehension of a second language, he can more gracefully make the transition to production, reading, and writing. If this transition is attempted too abruptly or too prematurely, before the individual student is ready, learning difficulties can be expected.

As listening comprehension is internalized, the student should eventually progress to the "naming stage" (Carroll 1964) in which the student is able to ask questions as "What's that?" "What's that called?" and "What does it mean?" The important feature of the naming stage is not that the student can ask questions but that he is able to comprehend and internalize the information he receives from the answers.

One misconception (Carroll 1970) is that when language is synchronized with movements of the body, the semantic content is limited to certain kinds of physical activity such as jumping, running, and sitting. This is a literal interpretation which does not accurately represent the parameters of instructional possibilities.

We have found that with a creative application, nonphysical vocabulary items and nonphysical structural features can be embedded in motor responses. Consider, as an illustration, these commands:

Marie, pick up the picture of the ugly old man and put it next to the picture of the government building!

Gregory, find the picture of the beautiful woman with green eyes, long black hair and wearing a sun hat that has red stripes. When you find the picture, show it to the class and describe the woman!

THE SECOND FIELD TEST

Procedure

Undergraduate college students, mostly psychology majors, enrolled in an experimental course for people without prior training in Spanish. The students ($N = 27$) received college credit for attending the class 3 hours one evening per week for two consecutive semesters.

When each experimental-course student was given the long form of the Modern Language Aptitude Test (MLAT), the mean was 114.4 with a standard deviation of 31.3. These students on the average were quite similar to the average language aptitude of college men and women reported in the MLAT test manual. After testing, the subjects were divided randomly into two separate groups that met on a different evening once each week.

Unfortunately, because of time limitations, no pretests were administered to the control groups. An ideal procedure would be to use standardized pretests with established norms for all groups so that baselines can be determined for prior language skills and aptitude.

Listening training

The students sat in a semicircle around the instructor. The students adjacent to her were asked to be silent, listen carefully to each command in Spanish, and do exactly what the instructor did. The students were encouraged to respond rapidly without hesitation and to make a distinct, robust response with their bodies. For example, if the command was "Corran!" the students were to run with gusto. A distinct response was an unambiguous signal that the student understood the command. Then the first routine was commands in Spanish as, "Stand up! Walk! Stop! Turn! Walk! Stop! Turn! Sit down!"

The instructor spoke the commands and acted together with two students on either side of her. This routine was repeated for three of four times until individual students indicated that they were ready to try it alone without the instructor as a model. Each repetition of the routine was not an exact duplication because we did not want memorization of a fixed sequence of behavior. One variation was, for instance: Stand up! Sit down! Stand up! Sit down! Stand up! Walk! Stop! Turn! Walk! Stop! Turn! Walk! Stop! Turn! Walk! Stop! Turn! Sit down!

The next step was to invite other members of the group to perform individually. Experiments have shown (Asher 1969a) that students can observe a model act, but for long-term memory, each student should then perform alone.

In the next routine, the commands were expanded to: Walk to the door! Walk to the window! Walk to the table! Then "point" and "touch" were introduced. At this juncture in training, the students had enough elements so that constituents could be recombined to move the student with unexpected novel commands as: Eugene, stand up, walk to Claudine and touch her. Claudine, walk to Norman, and touch his chair.

In manipulating the individual student, Spanish utterances were constantly recombined to present surprises and novelty which delighted the students because they realized that they usually had perfect understanding for Spanish utterances they had never heard before. As training progressed, the instructor used playful, zany, and such bizarre commands that maintained an extremely high interest level in students. Here are three samples:

When Henry runs to the blackboard and draws a funny picture of Molly, Molly will throw her purse at Henry.

Henry, would you prefer to serve a cold drink to Molly, or would you rather have Eugene kick you in the leg?

Rosemary, dance with Samuel, and stick your tongue out at Hilda. Hilda, run to Rosemary, hit her on the arm, pull her to her chair and you dance with Samuel!

Production

After about 10 hours of training in listening comprehension, the students were invited but not pressured to reverse roles with the instructor. Those students who felt ready to try speaking uttered commands in Spanish to the instructor who performed as directed by the students.

From this time on, about 20 percent of class time was role reversal in which the students spoke Spanish to move the instructor or peers, and later on there were skits created by the students and performed in Spanish, and still later in training there was problem solving in which students, presented with an unexpected difficulty while in a Latin country, had to talk their way through to a solution.[5]

Reading and writing

There was no systematic training in reading and writing. For a few minutes at the end of each class meeting, the instructor wrote on the blackboard any structure or vocabulary item requested by the students. These items in Spanish, with no English translations, were almost always utterances the students had heard during the class. As the instructor wrote on the blackboard, the students wrote in their notebooks.

Results (Midway through Training)

The midpoint in training represented about 45 hours of instruction in which class time was 70 percent listening training through commands, 20 percent was speaking, and 10 percent was reading and writing. There were no homework assignments.

There was one experimental group and three control groups. The first control was a group of high school students with one year of Spanish, the second control group consisted of college students finishing their first semester of Spanish, and the third, college students completing their second semester of Spanish.

One measure of proficiency was stories in Spanish which had the appropriate vocabulary used in the training of experimental and control subjects. None of the students had heard, during training, the exact utterances in the stories.

After listening to a story, each student answered 10 true-false statements about the story as described in the March 1972 issue of *The Modern Language Journal* (Asher 1972). The listening measure for a set of stories was followed by reading the stories in a printed booklet and answering the identical true-false questions.

Listening and reading skill for stories

First, as may be seen in Table 1, the experimental group with about 45 hours of training and no homework assignments had a keener level of listening skill for stories than high school students with about 200 hours of classroom training not including homework. (The t of 2.66 was significant beyond the .01 level for 39 df.)

---

5. Here are three sample problems: (1) You are taking a shower in your hotel bathroom, and a repairman has just come in the bathroom to fix the light. (2) You have just knocked on the door of the hotel room next door to complain about loud singing and dancing that is keeping you from sleeping. (3) You have a toothache and it is necessary to extract the tooth but you want to explain to the dentist that you are allergic to drugs used in local anesthetics.

Second, in listening skill for stories the experimental group vastly excelled college students who were completing their first semester in Spanish, which was about 75 hours of classroom instruction not including homework. (As seen in Table 2, the *t* of 6.75 was significant beyond the .001 level for 69 df.) Surprisingly, the experimental subjects also excelled in reading skills for stories. (The *t* of 3.22 was significant beyond the .001 level for 63 df.)

The third finding was rather extraordinary. The experimental group had a higher level of listening skill for stories than students finishing the second semester of Spanish, which is 150 hours of classroom instruction not including homework. (As seen in Table 3, the *t* of 3.21 was significant beyond the .001 level for 53 df.) It was surprising too that the reading skill of the second semester students did not surpass the experimental group. (The *t* of 0.60 was not significant for 47 df.)

The transitivity factor

It may be argued that an artifact of measurement accounts for the striking differences between groups. Since the stories were developed especially for this

Table 1   The Experimental Group with 45 Hours of Training Compared with Control Group 1 (High School Students Who Had 200 Hours of Training)—Listening Comprehension of Stories 1 and 2

	Mean	Standard deviation	*t*	*p*
Experimental Group (45 hours) (*N*=27)	16.63	2.15	2.66	.01
High School Group (200 hours) (*N*=14)	14.43	3.37		

Table 2   The Experimental Group with 45 Hours of Training Compared with Control Group II (College Students Who Had 75 Hours of Training)—Total Score for Four Stories

	Mean		Standard deviation			
	Experimental Group	Control II	Experimental Group	Control II	*t*	*p*
Listening	(*N*=27) 34.00	(*N*=44) 27.25	3.96	4.65	6.55	.001
Reading	(*N*=21) 34.86	(*N*=44) 33.09	1.75	2.66	3.22	.005

Table 3   The Experimental Group with 45 Hours of Training Compared with Control Group III (College Students Who Had 150 Hours of Training)—Total Score for Four Stories

	Mean		Standard deviation			
	Experimental Group	Control III	Experimental Group	Control III	*t*	*p*
Listening	(*N*=27) 34.00	(*N*=28) 29.57	3.96	6.11	3.21	.005
Reading	(*N*=21) 34.86	(*N*=28) 35.29	1.75	3.24	0.60	NS

project, there may have been an unintentional bias in favor of the experimental training.

One test of the bias hypothesis is to compare the beginning and advanced college students for transitivity. For instance, if the stories were a reasonable measure, the second semester college students should perform with higher listening and reading skill than first semester college students. Table 4 confirms transitivity since the advanced students performed significantly better in both listening and reading.

Standard proficiency tests

Midway through training, the experimental group took the Pimsleur Spanish Proficiency Tests—Form A (first level). Since the Pimsleur tests were designed for students in the typical audio-lingual program, they may underestimate the skills acquired by the experimental subjects.

As seen in Table 5, the average student performance in the experimental group was the 70th percentile rank for listening, the 85th percentile rank for reading, and the 76th percentile rank for writing. Speaking skill is assessed on the Pimsleur in three categories of "good," "fair," or "poor." The average student in the experimental group was in the "good" category.

Results (At the End of Training)

After 90 hours of training, proficiency was assessed with the Pimsleur Spanish Proficiency Tests—Form C (second level). This measurement was stringent

Table 4   The Factor of Transitivity—Total Score for Four Stories

	Mean		Standard deviation			
	Control II	Control III	Control II	Control III	t	p
Listening	27.25	29.57	4.65	6.11	1.72	.05
Reading	33.09	35.29	2.66	3.24	3.01	.005

Control II = College Students (N=44) in Control Group II with 75 hours of instruction
Control III = College Students (N=28) in Control Group III with 150 hours of instruction

Table 5   Mean and Median Percentile Rank of Experimental Subjects on the Pimsleur Spanish Proficiency Tests Form A (First Level)

	N	Mean	Median
Listening	18	70	70
Reading	17	85	85
Writing	16	76	74
Speaking	15	Good[a]	Good[b]

[a]Raw score of 70   [b]Raw score of 71

Table 6   Mean and Median Percentile Rank of
Experimental Subjects on the
Pimsleur Spanish Proficiency Tests,
Form C (Second Level)

	N	Mean	Median
Listening	16	49	55
Reading	16	69	66
Writing	17	67	60
Speaking	17	Fair[a]	Good[b]

[a]Raw score of 66   [b]Raw score of 68

because (1) it was designed exclusively for audio-lingual training, and (2) it was meant for students who had completed the second level, which is 150 hours of college instruction. Nevertheless, the experimental group performed beyond the 50th percentile rank for most skills, as may be seen in Table 6.

As with the first field test, a documentary motion picture is in preparation to show samples of student behavior during training and at the end of the second field test (see footnote 1).

Conclusions

Motivation

Most linguistic features can be nested into the imperative form, and if the approach is used creatively by the instructor, high student interest can be maintained for a long-term training program.

This experimental program started with 27 students but was reduced to 16 after the first semester. Most of those who left the program said that extrinsic reasons forced them to discontinue.

Transfer from listening to other skills

Perhaps the most important finding was the large magnitude of transfer from listening to other skills. For instance, with almost no direct instruction in reading and writing, the students were on the average beyond the 75th percentile for level I and beyond the 65th percentile for level II. The results are even more significant when one considers that the total time in training was about one-half the instructional hours usually allocated for college instruction in levels I and II.

Future plans

When language input is organized to synchronize with the student's body movement, the second language can be internalized in chunks rather than word by word. The chunking phenomenon means more rapid assimilation of a cognitive map about the linguistic code of the target language. As the code is internalized, it acts as an "advanced organizer" to facilitate the storage of information as, for instance, in the naming stage when the student begins to ask questions (i.e., "What is that called?").

The movement of the body seems to be a powerful mediator for the understanding, organization, and storage of macro-details of linguistic input. Language can be internalized in chunks, but alternate strategies must be developed for fine-tuning to micro-details.

One way to achieve this fine-tuning is to use a strategy developed by Winitz and Reeds (1973a and b), at the University of Missouri in Kansas City. In the Winitz-Reeds approach, the individual student views four pictures at a time and is directed in the target language to make a choice as, for instance, select the picture of "the men" from among these possibilities: a man, a boy, women, and men.

In a step-by-step progression through hundreds of picture sets, the student is fine-tuned for phonologic, morphologic, and syntactic features in a target language.

Future plans call for experimental training in which the student can internalize chunks of language with body movements and fine-tune in a progression of decision making with pictures.

DISCUSSION QUESTIONS

1. What evidence do Asher and his colleagues present for the claim that "almost any aspect of the linguistic code for the target language [can] be communicated using commands" (p. 62)? They have given some illustrations showing how past and future tenses, for instance, may be incorporated into commands. They also show how the TPR approach can incorporate declarative forms or questions. Is it possible to graduate eventually to full-fledged episodic structures? See p. 64, where Asher et al. answer the objection of John Carroll that TPR is largely limited to actions such as jumping.

2. What part might the extended listening period play in establishing a basis for production of target language utterances at a later point in time? How important do you feel the "silent" period is to the demonstrated successes of the TPR approach? What aspects of the pragmatic mapping process might be worked out by students during this silent time? What aspects remain to be refined at a later time or perhaps by some other method? Discuss the connection between the "silent" period and Krashen's "din in the head" (Chapter 20).

3. At one point, Asher and company seem to be suggesting that abstract nouns such as "justice" and "government" may be acquired if the teacher writes the words on cards and then issues commands referring to the words written on the cards. If this is done, what pragmatic elements of meaning which are

normally associated with such concepts are missing? Could these missing elements be incorporated?

4. Asher and his colleagues realize that the TPR method by itself will not solve "all instructional problems" and that "variety is essential to maintaining the student's attention and continued interest" (p. 63). If you were attempting to devise a complete instructional strategy or a complete curriculum, how might you integrate other approaches with TPR?

5. What do Asher et al. mean by "the ability to transpose linguistic elements to comprehend novelty" (p. 63)? How does this relate to the familiar distinction between "competence" and "performance" which linguists insist upon?

Chapter 6

The Silent Way

Caleb Gattegno
Educational Solutions, New York

EDITORS' INTRODUCTION

Gattegno uses "silence" for a purpose which is somewhat different from that of the extended listening period employed by Asher and colleagues. In Gattegno's approach the silence of the teacher is an inducement for the students to take the initiative. They must experiment with the target language internally at first and later overtly. At the outset, the teacher provides a model utterance which refers in an obvious way to a small rod selected from a set of rods which are used to provide a kind of pragmatic context. The teacher may hold up the green rod and say, "A rod" (in the target language). Then, the teacher may add, holding up the same rod, "A green rod." Then, the teacher may pick up a red one and repeat the procedure. "A rod." Pause. "A red rod." After some manageable chunk of the target language has been presented, the teacher remains silent while the pressure for some one of the students to fill the silence grows to a crescendo level. Inevitably someone speaks up, and if the utterance indicates some initial comprehension and appropriateness, the teacher reacts with nonverbal acknowledgment and encourages other students to follow suit. Or the teacher may encourage further attempts until a recognizable facsimile of the initial utterance is attained. Next a new chunk of language is introduced, and so on it goes. This method has often been criticized as "strained, artificial, intimidating," and the like, but no one who has submitted to it (and "submitted" is the right word) can deny that it generates an intense level of cognitive activity. First the students are placed under tremendous pressure to figure out what the teacher has said (comprehension) and subsequently to repeat the act of saying it with comprehension—e.g., saying "a green rod" when pointing to the green one. The silent way invites teachers and students to engage in an intense cognitive wrestling match where communicative use of the target language is both the arena and the reward.

The learning of a new language is considered to be that of a foreign language (when it is not normally in circulation in the environment). People talk of the "natural" way of learning, and of the "direct way" of teaching, referring somehow to a way similar to that of a baby learning his mother tongue. It is my contention that we shall not score much success if we continue in that way, since circumstances in the learner are on the whole incomparable with those prevailing in the first case.

If it is true that a new language will require from the learner a new adaptation, it is equally true that apprenticeships in the mother tongue and in a foreign language have little in common. In the former, a baby has no clue of what to do to reach meaning in words; in the latter, the learner has acquired a language and knows what languages are for. Consciously or unconsciously, he brings with him training in the association of sounds and situations, structures and meanings, intonation and quality of experience, sets of words and particular experience: perceptible attributes as well as words for concepts several stages removed, symbols, images, etc. He knows how to produce a verbal stream and to find in it the power of expression, the necessity of expression—mechanisms that ensure that what is said is adequate to the purpose, etc.

That all this is more unconscious than conscious is relevant in this discussion, since it can be proved that consciousness of one's own earlier activity can be brought to throw light upon the whole of the learning process.

My proposal is to replace a "natural" approach by one that is very "artificial" and, for some purposes, strictly controlled, and to use all that there is to be tapped in every mind in every school.

As a teacher, I know that no proposal of mine can be successful unless it really meets the requirements of classroom situations. It will be really successful (1) if I have taken into account the problems teachers of language meet in their own minds and in their training; (2) if I have made allowance for the capabilities of students, their habits and expectations, the demands of circumstances, etc.; (3) if I have not followed my own bent when suggesting a course, but have made my materials as flexible as will be required by the variety of conditions in the schools where languages are taught.

As I developed my techniques while subordinating my teaching to the learning, I found that I could very early transfer the responsibility for the use of the language to my students, so that I became able to teach using fewer and fewer words. It is this aspect of my techniques of teaching that prompted me to call the approach *The Silent Way of Teaching Foreign Languages.* If there is one feature I value in my approach, it is well described by the word "silent," since it will convey at once that there are means of letting the learners learn while the teacher stops interfering or sidetracking. Scores of teachers who are using the silent way recognize silence to be one of the powerful tools in their teaching.

Much Language and Little Vocabulary

Let us imagine that we are looking at a class of interested students of any age (6 or 11 or 14 or adults), and that the teacher enters the room for the first time. The class knows that it will study a foreign language, and the teacher is determined not to use one single word of the vernacular, which he may know, or which may even be his mother tongue.

The approach is, as I have insisted, most artificial. The box of colored rods that the teacher places on his desk is all he carries. He opens it and draws out of it one rod and shows it to the class while saying in the foreign language the word for rod, with the indefinite article if it exists in that language. He puts it down in silence and picks up another of a different color and says the same (one or two) words again, and so on, going through seven or eight rods and never asking for anything. The intrigued students have attentively noted the events and heard some noises which to them will seem the same while their eyes see only different objects and a repetition of the same action. Without any fuss the teacher then lifts a rod and asks in mime for the sounds he uttered. Bewildered, the class would not respond, in general, but the teacher says "a rod" and asks again in mime for another effort from the class. Invariably someone guesses (perhaps from the habits ingrained in traditional teaching) that the teacher wants back what he gave. When in his own way the pupil says something approximating what the teacher said, the teacher may smile or nod, showing how content he is at being understood. At the next trial almost the whole class repeats the sounds for a rod (very approximately in most cases). The teacher does not inquire whether some students are thinking of a piece of wood, others of lifting something, or something different. Contact has been established without the vernacular, and that is all that was wanted so far.

The teacher then introduces the names for four or five of the colors, giving the sounds for "a blue rod," "a black rod," "a red rod," "a yellow rod," "a green rod" or any other combination of the ten colors available. Because the names of the colors are now added, the pupils can no longer imagine that different expressions mean the same action and are forced to conclude that the teacher is giving the phrases that summarily describe these objects. The exercise is now shifted to practice in uttering the foreign sounds for the six or seven objects, so that as soon as one rod replaces another, one utterance replaces another, which would be the case in the vernacular.

This may be the end of the first lesson. Usually it is not, and the teacher motions two pupils to come and stand near him. He turns to one and says in the foreign language: "take a blue rod." (He has previously made sure that the set of rods on which this action is to be performed has more than one rod of each color.) Naturally, no response is to be expected, except perhaps the utterance of the words for "a blue rod." So the teacher says the words again while putting the pupil's hand over the set and making his fingers take a blue rod from the pile. Then he says: "take a brown rod" or "take a yellow rod," etc., and can expect a correct action as a response. He does this a number of times, for it is natural that while the pupil is concentrating on choosing the correct rod he does not produce the substitute in his own mind for the word "take." The teacher then turns to the other student and does what he did before but fewer times. Then dramatically he changes places with one of the students and indicates that the student should now utter the words first. Someone in the class usually gets the idea. If not, the teacher goes back to the previous situation and does what he did before once or twice again. The exchange of places this time yields the required results: the equivalent of "take a blue (or red . . .) rod" is uttered by one or the other of the students. When the teacher complies with this, he is conveying an agreement that the rules of the game are being observed.

The next lesson usually shows that the time separating the two sessions has served the students well. The quick revision of the sounds for the names of the colored rods proves that the class pronounces them on the whole much better than the previous time.

Calling two other students, the teacher says: "take . . . ," and the action is performed at once, usually correctly. But this time the teacher adds: "give it to me," and indicates with his hand that he wants it. As he does it with different rods and alternately with each of the two students, the set of noises for "give it to me" is put into circulation. Then, after saying "take a . . . ," the teacher says: "give it to him" (or "her," according to the sex of the student and the demands of a particular language) and indicates that this time it is to be given to the other student (the teacher may have to use his hands to convey the meaning).

The class has heard phrases and sentences being used from the start by a number of students, or even all of them, more or less adequately, but at least approximately recognizably. The language covered is: a rod, a yellow, red, blue . . . rod, take a . . . rod, give it to him, her, me.

What is significant is that the set of rods has helped:

- To avoid the vernacular.
- To create simple linguistic situations that are under the complete control of the teacher.
- To pass on to the learners the responsibility for the utterance of the descriptions of the objects shown or the actions performed.
- To let the teacher concentrate on what the students say and how they are saying it, drawing their attention to the differences in pronunciation and the flow of words.
- To generate a serious gamelike situation in which the rules are implicitly agreed upon by giving meaning to the gestures of the teacher and his mime.
- To permit almost from the start a switch from the lone voice of the teacher using the foreign language to a number of voices using it. This introduces components of pitch, timbre, intensity that will constantly reduce the impact of one voice and hence reduce imitation and encourage personal production of one's own brand of the sounds.
- To provide the support of perception and action to the intellectual guess of what the noises may mean, thus bringing in the arsenal of the usual criteria of experience already developed and automatic in one's use of the mother tongue.
- To provide durations of spontaneous speech upon which the teacher and the students can work to obtain a similarity of melody to the one heard, thus providing melodic integrative schemata from the start.

In the first few lessons this will be deliberate, but it will soon become a framework of conventional handling of this teaching. The students will be astonished to find that their teacher stands through much of the lessons, that he keeps them concentrating all the time, that he says less and less and they more and more, that he neither approves nor disapproves but throws them back upon their own tools of judgment, indicating that they must listen better, use their mouths differently, stress here or there, shorten one sound and prolong another. Very soon, the more or less arbitrary conventions he introduces become accepted between himself and his class.

In four or five lessons the vocabulary will have increased very little. The *plurals* of "rod," of the *adjectives* (if they exist) and of the *pronouns* are introduced, plus the *conjunction* "and"; some *possessive adjectives*, and perhaps one or two demonstrative ones. The *numerals* "one," "two," and perhaps "three" are added—generally there may be about thirty words in circulation.

These are: one noun: *rod*; color adjectives: *red, green, yellow, black, brown, blue*; numeral adjectives: *one, two, three*; articles: *a* and *the* (of one gender or neutral only, in languages that require them); verbs in the imperative: *take, give* and, perhaps, *put*; personal pronouns: *me, him, her, it, them*; possessive adjectives: *his, her, my*; the adverbs: *here, there*; the preposition: *to*; the conjunction: *and*—or 27 words.

But with them we have heard and understood, and uttered and understood:

> take a _____ rod (six or seven colors)
> give it to _____ (him, her, me)

and their conjunctions:

> take a _____ and give it to _____
> *or:* take _____ rods and give them to _____ .

These produce a large number of sentences. Obviously, there are hundreds of different utterances possible, though the general impression is that the number is much smaller because the changes between one phrase and the next may be of only one word. More utterances are easily found if we use the conjunctions as well:

take a _____ rod and a _____ rod and give them to _____ . . . , and even longer ones.

The importance of this exercise is that it allows us to work on the formation of a natural way of using the melody of the foreign language. This allows the learners to gain from the start something of the spirit of the language that is usually left for much later in linguistic studies.

It is my contention that we are giving our students something of great value by restricting the vocabulary but extending as much as we can the length of the statements uttered with ease, and in the way one uses one's own language.

Since the way we breathe has a cultural component, and since uttering statements is connected with breathing, we can see why we will be gaining more and more of the spirit of the language as we learn to alter our breathing to suit its melody.

For the teacher, the technique is a conscious way of affecting his students' unconscious relation to this new speech. As a result of it, the students will gain what cannot be passed on by explanation but can be reached by intuition and the surrender to the traditions absorbed in the spirit of a particular language.

To reinforce this awareness, the use of the disks or tapes can be invaluable. The question put implicitly to the class is: "Which of the speeches you hear is the language we have been studying?" There is no question of the students' understanding the meaning of the words used on the record, but if they can distinguish the one they are meeting in class from others as well as from their mother tongue, we must agree that their ear has been sensitized to the recognition of something that is part of each language but outside the vocabulary: this, I repeat, is part of the spirit of a language.

To further reinforce this awareness, we use a new tool and a new technique. This tool is our set of wallcharts, on which are printed in colors the words we have learned so far. Whether or not the script of the foreign language is familiar to the learner will make a slight difference. We will proceed in our argument without considering that point here, but we will do so briefly later in this discussion.

We will use only Wallchart No. 1 first. [See Figure 1.] On it are printed at random all the 27 words which have been learned plus a few more according to the demands of the language studied, one exception being that the first words are "a rod" (or "rod"). Using a long pointer, the teacher points at words, one by one, asking the class to say them (this no longer requires his saying the words, since the previous games have established the convention). When in doubt about the ability of some of the students to do it, he asks individuals to say the words on their own. In this way, the teacher can find out whether the learners recognize the printed equivalents of the oral words they have met in factual situations with the rods.

Once he is sure of this, the teacher links words, using the pointer, with the convention that if it points at one word followed by a pause (at which time the pointer is no longer pointing at a word), that word is uttered alone; if it points at two or more words in succession, all these words must be uttered and in that order. This convention is established in no time. Clearly, the teacher is silent during all the movements of the pointer and afterward, when turning to the students and waiting for a volunteer or volunteers to utter the phrase or sentence. When the class can sufficiently well utter these words in succession, the speed of pointing can be varied so that the convention of the speed of flow of words is brought in again. We call this exercise *visual dictation*.

This new technique is extremely powerful in that now the learner's mind is still more in contact with his own self. Moreover, visual imagery is brought in

une réglette -s moi a
jaune j'ai bleue noire
verte avons ici brune
aussi elle rouge vous
donnez deux la prenez
avez ils elles ont à
lui il et les oui nous
notre leur mettez sa
là ma votre est non

French
Wallchart number 1

a rod -s -s blue
green yellow black
brown take red give
as to it and not
back here her is the
them two him an me
orange the are one he
another these white
put end too his

English as a second language
Wallchart number 1

Figure 1

without any fuss or lengthy preparation, and it sustains the words heard in the foreign language as it already does in the mother tongue. Because visual images are swift and have extension and depth, they will give the learners new powers not contained in temporal sequences. In heard and uttered sentences, the temporal sequence is linear, that is, it is not reversible without real alteration of the sequence. With the chart in front of the pupils the words are all *seen* simultaneously, and contain a large number of possible choices of subsets that can be objectified by the convention of moving the pointer to create links between words. Until now, actions and perception have commanded the utterances, which were thus linked with the language and integrated as a result of the active lessons; but from now on, since it is known that words pointed at suggest noises to be made, any sequence of noises can be generated—nonsense statements as well as rational ones, including the ones that have been mastered. Here, therefore, is a new way of producing statements by simply selecting some of the words on the charts, thus giving rise to exercises that can serve new ends and test mastery of certain parts of the language.

If the teacher shows, for example, "Give me a blue rod," the pupils can obviously say it, but it is not at all certain that they will understand the meaning, since so far they have only been told in certain definite circumstances which no longer obtain: "Give it to me." Nevertheless, if someone came to the table, took a blue rod, and gave it to the teacher, no one would doubt that he had made sense of the new sequence of words. If no one can do it, all that has been gained so far is an ability to use the chart to produce sequences of sounds with a certain intonation, at a certain speed—which indicates some acquaintance with the melody of the language. This is not negligible.

As this silent exercise goes on, the teacher can increase the number of words pointed at; he can show them with quicker and quicker movements of the pointer and at the end get the whole statement from some pupils. Is it a small thing to have students of 7 or 11 who do not know much of the language breathe out, with a command of diction that is quite acceptable, a sentence of the following length?—"Take a blue rod and a green rod and give her the blue one and give him the green one."

If we have succeeded in establishing the rule that the sequence selected will be shown only once, the success of this exercise is a clear indication that the learners are now capable of behaving somehow as native speakers with respect to their breathing and their association of sound and sign. Students who can achieve such feats after so few lessons are teaching us that they can easily be taken much further than we have ever believed possible.

Visual dictation is a twofold technique in which the teacher points at words and the students say what was shown, or the students find the words on the charts after the teacher has uttered a whole sentence. This second exercise will easily be changed into oral dictation, in which a full sentence is said and the learners write it down. If all the vocabulary contained in the sentence is covered by the charts, there are two stages in this oral dictation. In one, the learners can look up at the charts to find any word they cannot write: in the other, it is agreed not to look at the charts, or these are removed.

Before pursuing this matter, let us consider the case of a foreign language whose script is entirely alien to the learners, which uses different shapes and different conventions for their formation and their alignment on paper. There are many such cases among the languages of the world: some people write from left to right, others from right to left, some above, others below the line, others vertically instead of horizontally; some use characters that are difficult to disentangle (as are the Chinese or Japanese ideograms), others use signs for whole syllables, or additional conventions that represent tone, etc. The writer's experiments have been only with some of these, and his conclusions may not be universally valid. Still, for what they are, it is a fact that there has never been need to introduce the writing conventions as such, but simply to make the writing follow the oral exercises and to associate noises already met with signs now introduced. No difference has been noted between peoples using the same script to represent different sounds (as, for example, for English and Spanish) and peoples using very different conventions (as in the case of Israelis who meet English for the first time, after being accustomed to a different script, when they write from right to left and do not write their vowels; or Amharas learning French, while their own characters are different, number 251, and are syllables and not letters). The learners could even recognize in the written speech conventions that were not pointed out to them, and used the clues to decipher written words that they had never yet heard. For example, while teaching Hindi to users of the Latin alphabet who had never seen Sanskrit letters, I wrote a sentence meaning "Take a yellow rod and give it to me." Then I showed the class which word was "give." This clue was sufficient for a Champollionesque deciphering of the whole sentence, and the formation of a list of signs whose associated sounds were ascertained by cross reference and by my silent acceptance of the solution. A number of words were then added and read correctly, though no sound was uttered for them by me.

This indicates that students have all the necessary equipment to meet the challenges presented, and that it is unnecessary to give special lessons to introduce the letters or characters of the foreign language as long as a sufficient number of clues is provided. In this approach, the clues are that part of the spoken language that has already been mastered and used. It is preferable when a new script is presented not to show a chart but to write first on the board, step by step, the words that will become the content of the first chart. No colored chalks are necessary in my experience, but if they are available they can be used with better results.

Let us stress that the introduction of the written word can be postponed until the teacher feels that it will make the greatest contribution. It has not yet been clearly established whether the fifth or tenth or thirtieth lesson is the most appropriate time for it. Each teacher will learn by trial and error, mainly by error.

It is to be understood that an approach like this one, based as it is on awareness and on personal responsibility for learning, cannot be conceived as rigid. In order to help as much as I could in the direction of flexibility, I have included in the first few charts words of the functional vocabulary that could form groups of lessons in some degree independent of each other. The teachers can work around one or the other group according to taste, circumstances, and personal philosophy.

Of special interest is the numerals chart [not pictured here]. It contains the words for the numerals 1, 2, 3, 4, and so on, that one needs in order to be able to read and say any number of any length. The various languages we publish require a different set of words, since the various cultures have developed their own description of number. The number 83 is *eighty-three* in English, *drei und achtzig* in German, *quatre-vingt-trois* in French, *ochenta y tres* in Spanish, etc. But with about 30 words, we can form as many number names as we wish. The pointer and this chart can, in a lesson or little more, provide experience in naming all numbers. Let us describe its use for the English language.

The words, arranged at random and printed in the color-code are: *one, two, three . . . ten, eleven, twelve, thirteen, fifteen, –teen, twenty, thirty, forty, fifty, –ty, eighty, hundred, thousand, million, a, and:* 26 words or signs.

The teacher has already used the rods to teach the first few numerals, and the students know how to count in their own language, but the younger students may not necessarily know how to read long strings of figures. Using the pointer, the teacher gets the class to say, in chorus, each word on the chart following the sequence 1, 2, 3. . . . When he reaches sixteen, he forms it by sliding the pointer to join *six* and *–teen;* when he reaches *twenty-one,* he joins *twenty* and *one,* thus showing that the pointer is used here to produce the name of one entity: a numeral. The analysis of its component parts is imposed upon the learner as it is on the native speakers. He must accept it as a convention if he wants to play this game. As we advance in the sequence of numerals, the numeration rules are made evident, so that we acquire the power to form millions of sounds in different combinations for millions of distinct entities. Long names of numerals provide not only exercises in elocution, breathing, and melody in the foreign language, but also an intellectual exercise. For it is permissible to use the pointer to join a number of the words on the chart and ask the learners to write the corresponding figures; we can ask the class to read it and have one of the students point out on the chart the corresponding component words. When he is mistaken, he is corrected by others. It is clear that it is not necessary to know how to read numerals in one's own language in order to carry out this exercise correctly in the new one. This exercise can, in a short time, provide the mastery of reading numerals in a new language even if it is not yet available in the mother tongue. More than a new capacity is acquired here. The new language has gained the positive emotional value of having served to increase one's insight into one's own language. This contribution is made so early in the study of the new language that it is worth mentioning here. Usually one expects such results only from much wider knowledge and from a prolonged acquaintance with a foreign language.

The use of the numerals chart is a good example of how with little vocabulary we can generate much language, since we have now potentially produced an infinite set of words in the foreign language to describe an infinite set of objects that exist, like all other objects, outside of languages. Students do feel that when this chart and its various uses have been mastered they have made a big step forward. This feeling is a positive ally that will assist progress and increase the speed of learning, the depth of awareness and familiarity with the language. It is easy to imagine that, if two or three weeks after starting the study of a foreign language children or adults can say the name of a number as long as 3,644,572,893,608, they legitimately feel that their mind and body are at par with those of native speakers. In fact, in this field, they have no reason to envy the ordinary users of that language. They have achieved the maximum; it is within themselves, and they can have recourse to it if they wish to feel the language, its melody, and its requirements upon their breathing. Since numerals form a "closed experience" on the linguistic plane, it seems sensible to introduce them early and gain all that their study can contribute: it is much more than one would ever be able to do with an equal number of words of any other category (names or colors, for example) that cannot produce meaning by being strung together. The numerals chart is a veritable mine for our purposes in this approach.

Each one of the charts will extend the powers of the learners, for they will find in it a set of words that will permit them to talk and write about relationships that occur constantly in life.

Some of the charts are linked with experiences other than the ones considered so far but which can still be described with the rods. Spatial relations such as being between, above, next to, perpendicular to, parallel to, across, on top, in front, etc., can be studied with their reciprocity of dissymmetry. *Larger than* does not reverse except to *smaller than,* while *parallel to* is a reciprocal relationship. *Between* A and B is equivalent to *between* B and A, but B *bigger than* A and *smaller than* C becomes A *smaller than* B and C. These variations on the theme are an obvious source of much language but are based upon perception and describing with very few words all that can be said within one situation.

The comparative and the superlative of adjectives are, in the case of some obvious attributes, well practiced with the rods and easily transferred to the charts and visual dictation.

Temporal relationships can be exemplified by actions in which the rods only play the role of objects that can be introduced in situations, but they could have been replaced by different ones. *After, before, successively, slowly, quickly, alternately, first, second, then, with, at the same time as, intermittently, simultaneously, while,* etc., are easily illustrated by situations produced especially for that purpose. Tenses too can be brought in by the same means, first orally, in situations, then by forming sentences with the pointer and words on the charts.

We must include in the functional vocabulary the forms of irregular verbs as well as the conjugation of most usual verbs. It is well known that irregularity in languages comes from use: the more words are used, the more they wear out, and this is shown in their irregularities. So the most often used words will require special study, but they will appear often enough in statements not to demand a special effort of memory.

On the charts are included the various forms of the irregular verbs that are most common in the description of spatio-temporal situations. A number of exercises with the pointer will provide the oral practice necessary to establish sounds in the minds of the learners. Whenever possible, situations will be generated to illustrate some of these forms. The remainder of the forms can be learned on the charts, since otherwise it would mean that true transfer of knowledge from words to general experience has not taken place and that work on previous situations is still required.

We see in the list of words on the charts that the words for box, for the lid of the box, color, length, top, end, and side are included. These are obviously not "functional," but because of their small number they will not create a problem. On the contrary, they are essential for meaningful use of the whole functional vocabulary: they will, for example, give experience of noun genders if these exist in the language.

Excluded from our charts are proper nouns or names, though they may have been used extensively in the class. This justifies the use of the personal pronouns in the first charts.

It is obvious that very soon the use of both the rods and the charts with the pointer will become second nature, and that the learners will have understood what is the meaning of a controlled linguistic situation and what one can get from it. They will soon find that as soon as some words are put into circulation their area of application is definable and it often coincides with the same area in their mother tongue. They will meet the foreign language as a language, meant to be used for communication, with the possibilities and limitations of one's own. This is one of the additional virtues everyone would want to find in any language learning approach. Words can form sentences, but contradictory statements cannot be acceptable, even though they can be uttered. This is true for any language because the statements made in each are about reality, and it is this that commands acceptance or rejection. Even imagination has its logic, and fantasy does not mean nonsense. It is not difficult to say "a black white rod," but it seems impossible to figure what it is if no alteration is brought to the statement, for example by inserting "and" between "black" and "white," or some similar change. If the learner has any understanding of the words he has met, he will know, because of his general experience, that such strings of words are no more acceptable in the foreign language than in his own.

While it is hard to think of an actual situation that is contradictory, it is very easy to produce any number of contradictory statements by pointing to the words on the charts, or with pen on paper. These can serve as tests of whether understanding of the meaning of words used in various situations exists to a sufficient degree. A statement may be grammatically correct but logically unacceptable: for example, "the largest of these rods are the smallest among them."

It now becomes clear that the work we do with our reduced number of words casts a net that would enclose almost as vast an area of experience as would the whole of the language, except for the details of special situations, which can be thought of as the spaces in the net.

The more we advance in the study of the charts, the less need will there be for detailed practice, since intelligence has a place in study and provides the generalizations, the transfers, the sense of exceptions, etc., that reduce the burdens upon memory. The way in which the charts are constructed will indicate that we have made use of the cumulative effect of learning. While in the beginning we give material that is to be used as units in their own right, later we present parts of words which can be involved in a number of words, perhaps with radically different meanings and certainly with varying meanings when connected with prefixes or suffixes. This enhancement of the challenges offered is a tribute to the increase of power in the learner, who now can tackle much harder tasks than in the earlier stages of his apprenticeship.

We have made sure from the outset that students listen to their own voices and watch all their utterances, both with respect to pronunciation and with respect to content. If this is properly carried out, the immediate formation of the inner criteria will be obvious. First, the students will have a really good diction in the new language, with a clear pronunciation of each word (as close as possible to that of natives) and an easy flow in sentence making, observing the melodic line of that language. Second, the students will feel and think in the new language, as will be evident from the correctness of their speech.

They will easily accept that their teacher never uses the vernacular and is inaccessible through it.

Because the teacher has never demanded immediate perfection, the relationship between him and his class will be conducive to constant reexamination of what can be done and what is being done. Improvement is visible suddenly and all the time: all the time through the awareness of what one is doing, and suddenly when a deeper understanding of the possibilities or of the requirements has taken place.

Teachers who refrain from pushing students who do not seem to respond or attempt to participate will be rewarded one day when these students join in as if they had never been out. Indeed, we cannot point to the particular needs of each mind to overcome the real or imaginary obstacles it is meeting. We can help more frequently and more effectively if we stop interfering.

It has been my repeated experience that whenever I am in doubt about a student's reasons for not joining in and I suspend action on, or reaction to him, the outcome is success at a later date. But whenever I enter too forcefully or too quickly into a situation of which I have inadequate understanding, my students entrench themselves in an uncooperative mood that does not serve anyone.

The pattern of progress in the gaining of skills is now well known. At first there is random or almost random feeling of the area of activity in question until one finds one or more cornerstones to build on. Then starts a systematic analysis, first by trial and error, later by directed experiment with practice of the acquired subareas until mastery follows. Emotionally, this mastery brings an inner peace which shows that one is not anxious about the results any longer. Intellectually, it shows that another level of awareness has been reached from which one can survey all activities of the past related to this area of experience. It is then that one suddenly appears to be a different person, both to oneself and to the observers. The learner's actions in this new area of experience reveal maturity and self-confidence. This provides constant confirmation of his control over his learning and gives a sense of power which is accompanied by efficiency.

Because the learner is now in control and operates with increased power, he can tackle larger tasks and more challenging developments. He can repeat the cycle of contact, analysis, mastery, not only for a different content, but also at a different tempo. This I call the cumulative effect of learning, and it is one of the results I expect through the silent approach.

If, therefore, after one term we have mastered the large integrative schemata that will facilitate the conquest of lexical items, we can expect that little memorization will be required, while much retention of related words will be experienced. Indeed, memory is a function of concentration in most of us (I exclude the pathological cases mentioned in the literature on memory). We can see this at work in very young children, who are more concentrated than the older ones and retain much more and much faster than the older ones do. We can expect that less and less repetition will be needed to reach greater retention of vocabulary and enrichment of one's analytic knowledge of a language for more specialized uses. Perhaps if the technique mentioned in various places—that the learner alone is to decide when repetition is needed—is tried out, it will be found that its yield in remembered expressions is incomparably greater than that of repetition. In fact, repetition consumes time and encourages the scattered mind to remain scattered, whereas the teacher's strict avoidance of repetition forces alertness and concentration on the part of the learners. In my experience, this increases yield and efficiency, and saves time for further learning.

For those who measure achievement through examinations, I will now estimate what can be expected after one year of study of a language through this approach.

In an oral examination, most direct questions about oneself, one's education, one's family, travel, etc., should obtain answers that are correct, expressed with ease and a good accent. Any mistakes will be simply minor slips or else due to a misunderstanding of what was communicated.

If a picture is provided, whether in a written or an oral examination, the student will be able to describe in the foreign language most of what he sees, including the existing relationships that concern space, time, and numbers. As writing has been catered for with the charts, with the color code and various texts, spelling should be more than reasonably good, and in the case of nonphonetic languages, it should show a definite insight into why alternatives are reduced. As structure has been practiced in a variety of ways (through the ear, visual dictation, use of word cards, reading, writing, and talking), grammar should be adequate, which will be implicit in the correct usage, even if all the candidates are not able to formulate it explicitly. Idiosyncrasies of each language have been met as natural features and accepted as given, without comparison and memorization. So candidates would know what to do even if they did not yet know why.

Translations are possible, for in this approach, rather than understanding the text through words checked against words, the learners have passed from text to reality (sensed or imagined). As they can talk directly of such reality (if it is suitably selected) either in their mother tongue or in the other language, translations are direct expressions in either language of what was communicated by the original text. Naturally, we expect that the essence of a situation, as expressed by the functional vocabulary which is present in a given text, will not be missed, and that only the luxury components could be overlooked or wrongly grasped, hence mistranslated. Translation is an art for the specialist, not for the novice.

We can expect questions on a selected text to be handled adequately, as on the whole (provided they are not too sophisticated) they come naturally to the mind of a reader who has been asked from the start, and all the time, to consider texts as linguistic situations.

General questions about the culture of the peoples who use the languages studied should be satisfactorily answered. As we have taken care of extending the vocabulary with texts belonging to that culture, through documentary films that are full of information for the learner, and as we have considerably assisted the learners in reaching the spirit of the language through its sociological and historical components, it is clear that students who have learned in that way will be incomparably better equipped than students taken through traditional approaches or direct methods that are purely linguistic. The benefits gained from the alertness fostered by this approach can be seen again in the amount of incidental learning that takes place, with the materials designed to give cultural awareness implicitly even if no lessons are devoted to it; and also explicitly if one cares to do so and can find the time for it.

The interest in reading, and the availability of the whole of literature in the language studied may extend to all students a situation known to exist in the case of some: they like to read the original works and do read a great deal for their own enjoyment and cultivation. If literary questions are to be included in a certain examination, they should be answered satisfactorily by these students. The novelty will be that many more candidates may be interested in answering them and will be able to do so quite well.

To sum up what I believe to be reasonable to expect from an approach like this—and I am willing to be assessed on the results of colleagues giving it a fair trial—I would list the following:

- An accent as close as possible to that of the natives who are among really cultured members of the country whose language is being studied.
- From the start, an ease in conversation related to the vocabularies presented and studied.
- An ease at dictation with speeds related to the amount of visual dictation practiced and the difficulties of the text.
- An ease in composition about all topics whose vocabularies have been met.
- An ease at narrating events, describing pictures, at shopping in various shops, ordering in hotels and restaurants, and asking for directions, etc.
- An ability to render appropriate texts of either language into the other.

Additional questions will require first that one should know whether the learners have actually passed the level of study of the language as a vehicle and reached the level where the literature can be studied as a depository of the language and of its spirit.

A word in conclusion. In this piece of work, written for a public wider than that of foreign language specialists, I have attempted to add new challenges to what learners and their teachers usually meet; but I believe I have also added many more helpful techniques and materials.

Often we hear that language studies are essential today because of the shrinking world and for the sake of international understanding. I have considered that question elsewhere, at the time when I directed the International Training Institute and ran international seminars for human education, in which people of various countries and languages participated. Linguistic studies, like all others, may be a specialization, and they carry with them a narrow opening of one's sensitivity and perhaps serve very little toward the broad end in mind.

If we now develop language teaching in such a way as to consolidate the human dimensions of being, which include variety and individuality as essential factors for an acceptance of others as contributors to one's own life, I believe that we will be moving toward better and more lasting solutions of present-day conflicts. These, to my mind, are the outcome of our living on top of each other, our sensitivities turned inward, restricting ourselves, when we need to be absorbing others as they *are* in an enhanced and more open sensitivity.

To that end this silent way of teaching is devoted.

DISCUSSION QUESTIONS

1. Discuss the similarities and differences between the Asher TPR approach and Gattegno's silent way. Are they mutually compatible? Interchangeable? For instance, is there a "listening" period in the silent way? How does it compare with Asher's "silent" period? In what ways (perhaps different ways) do the two approaches assure the pragmatic linkage of utterances to contexts of experience? Is Gattegno's approach any more authoritarian or artificial than Asher's? Is there *any* approach which absolves the teacher or some other model from serving as "an authority" on the target language? Also, consider Gattegno's remarks on p. 83 about "imaginary obstacles" and not "interfering" and still later about the "narrow opening of one's sensitivity" engendered by "linguistic studies" (p. 86). What is he getting at?

2. Gattegno is at pains to illustrate certain fundamental differences between his approach and the manner in which children acquire their primary language. However, his writing, it must be remembered, comes from a period during which the parallels between successful nonprimary language acquisition and first language acquisition were perhaps being *over*emphasized—hence his caution. In fact, there *are* some fundamentally natural aspects to Gattegno's method. Discuss what they are and also consider their relation to the "natural" approaches presented especially in Part V below. In what critical ways, therefore, is Gattegno's method *not* artificial? For instance, consider the teacher's inaccessibility through the "vernacular" of the students or the special recommendations of the silent way when it comes to error correction. Whatever happened to contrastive analysis (see Chapter 4)?

3. Does Gattegno's introduction of the famed "wallcharts" increase or decrease the artificiality of his method? What purposes are served by these charts? Can you conceive of other options that would serve as well? Are there any cognitive advantages to having visual representations of words in the target language in addition to spoken utterances of them?

4. In what ways do the practice of "visual" and "oral dictation," as recommended by Gattegno, help to provide additional information on meaning and form? Do you agree that ability to carry out commands, e.g., "Give me the blue rod from the table over there," is an adequate check on comprehension? What if the student can correctly transform a command as in an appropriate response to "Tell Judy to give me the blue rod"—e.g., "Hey, Judy. Give him the blue rod"? Or suppose the student can write down the correct form of the response.

5. What does Gattegno mean when he says "statements . . . are about reality, and it is this that demands acceptance or rejection. Even imagination has its

logic, and fantasy does not mean nonsense" (p. 82)? Also see Chapter 1 on episodic organization.

6. Is Gattegno's use of the "net" analogy on p. 83 similar to Krashen's conception of "the net hypothesis"? What does either of these concepts have to do with what Gattegno later calls "the cumulative effect of learning" (p. 84)? How do these ideas relate to Gattegno's frequent reference to the "spirit of the language"?

Chapter 7

A Manic Professor Tries
to Close Up the Language Gap

Robert Wolkomir[1]

Free-Lance Writer, Montpelier, Vermont

EDITORS' INTRODUCTION

This chapter differs from the others in this book in several ways. For one, it is authored by a professional free-lance writer rather than a professional language teacher. For another, it relies on pictures to tell the story at least as much as on words. For another, it did not appear originally in one of the usual "war" journals (e.g., *Language Learning,* or the *TESOL Quarterly, English Language Teaching,* the *Modern Language Journal,* or *Foreign Language Annals,* etc.), but in the *Smithsonian.* And for still another difference, the author reports on a professor who has the reputation with his own students of being a beloved maniac. Can language teachers at large learn anything from this nut? We think so, and so do some of our students who have worked with John Rassias in the flesh, and have gone on to apply some of his outlandish techniques. Someone has said, "All teachers are hams," and John Rassias fills the bill—completely. His whole approach to language teaching may be capsulized in the phrase "hamming it up." Personally, we are fascinated with his approach. It is, to be sure, a hodgepodge of gimmicks and foolishness tacked onto a wizard's understanding of how to motivate communicative events, but it is the sort of craziness that makes language teaching seem almost sane—even possible. We hope you'll enjoy this selection in our smorgasbord as much as we do. Also, if reading this chapter makes you curious, sample the reflections of a professional German teacher and administrator, Otto Johnston in Chapter 28, or get it from the horse's mouth (Rassias himself) in Chapter 29.

In a Dartmouth College classroom, six New York City transit policemen recite in unison: *"¡Ay Dios mío!"* Their instructor, a specially trained fellow officer, raises his arms like a choir director and the chorus repeats: *"¡Ay Dios mío!"*

Feinting, the instructor looks to the left, then abruptly snaps his fingers at a man sitting to his right. The man repeats, solo: *"¡Ay Dios mío!"*

Why are big-city policemen at an Ivy League college in New Hampshire chorusing "Oh my God!" in Spanish? They have come to learn—quickly and

---

1. The author gets by with English and halting French. Photographs by Bill Ray.

effectively—how to communicate with New York's 2.6 million Spanish-speaking citizens. And, in the process, they are demonstrating the potency of a high-voltage method of teaching foreign languages that could help to improve international relations.

Behind it all is John Rassias, a burly 54-year-old Dartmouth language professor with a bass voice, curly black hair, a lopsided grin, a boxer's nose, and a wild teaching style: he hurls chairs against walls, breaks eggs over students' heads, rips his shirt to symbolize freeing of the self, and harangues his classes in French while dressed as an 18th-century philosopher. His classroom style is unique. But his method is now used in the teaching of all languages at Dartmouth and at more than 38 other schools.

While enrollments in language classes nationwide have dropped steadily over the past 10 years, Dartmouth's language enrollments have grown substantially. And tests at Dartmouth and at other schools using this method show that it yields results far superior to those of traditional teaching methods.

Teachers from high schools and colleges elsewhere, propelled by the country's alarming language gap, are going to Dartmouth to observe the technique.

Just before World War I, 36 percent of all U.S. students at the preuniversity level studied a modern foreign language. Today, only 15 percent take a foreign language, and fewer than 5 percent ever reach the third year. One-fifth of all U.S. public high schools now offer no foreign language courses at all. Among other lamentable results:

Frenchmen had a good chuckle a few years ago on reading claims that Pepsi-Cola threw cold water on friendship. Chagrined company officials—who had intended the message to be "Pepsi is the refreshment of friendship"—promptly yanked the ads.

Cars with interiors marked "Body by Fisher" were advertised in Belgium with this unintentionally ghoulish translation: "Corpse by Fisher."

Some 10,000 English-speaking Japanese businessmen now operate in New York City alone, but of some 900 American business people in Japan, only a handful speak even rudimentary Japanese.

Government foreign-affairs agencies are worried that declining foreign-language enrollments in our schools will lower the quality of new recruits for their services and increase their language training costs ($100 million in 1978). Only 8 percent of U.S. colleges and universities now require a foreign language for admission, down from 34 percent in 1966.

In 1978, the President established the Commission on Foreign Language and International Studies to analyze the problem. In November 1979, the commission members (including Dartmouth's John Rassias) reported that our neglect of foreign language and civilization studies hobbles the country in diplomacy and international trade. "Americans' incompetence in foreign languages is nothing short of scandalous, and it is becoming worse," they charged.

The commission suggested steps that range from reinstating college language requirements to creating high schools that specialize in languages and foreign studies. But the report emphasized: "The decline in foreign language enrollments is in large measure a response to poor instruction."

Now an increasing number of language teachers see innovative approaches to teaching as a way to add vitality to their classrooms. In fact, says John Rassias, his method actually is a reaction to the dismal language teaching he encountered as a student.

The son of immigrants, he learned to speak Greek first, English second. From his earliest days, he associated languages with "the sights, the sounds, the smells, the warmth" of the Greek community in Manchester, New Hampshire, where he grew up. Then he was burned in an accident that left him bandaged like a mummy. For 9 months he couldn't see. "I knew people by their voices," he says. "From their tones I could discern happiness, I could discern sorrow—so language early became almost mystical for me."

In high school, his romance with languages ended. For one thing, his French textbook was populated by cardboard Parisians who chattered endlessly about the weather and misplaced pens. There were other drawbacks. One day, to force him to pronounce the letter "r" as the French do, the teacher used a pencil as a tongue depressor. "I couldn't help myself," he says. "I bit her." Today he keeps the same brand of pencil on his desk at all times. It reminds him of what to shun in teaching languages.

Languages must be spoken, he believes. But in a traditional class each student can speak no more than four times during the period. "That's like learning mathematics without examples," says Rassias. He also insists that reliance on vapid textbooks actually hinders a student's progress. Furthermore, the atmosphere in too many language classes is soporific—"Valium Valley," he calls it.

By the time he was graduated from high school, he was "completely turned off by languages." As a Marine stationed in postwar Japan, he found that—unable to speak Japanese—he wandered the country like a phantom, cut off from the people, baffled by their culture. Suddenly his fascination with languages rekindled.

A civilian again, he earned a degree in French at the University of Bridgeport in Connecticut, then studied in France for 2 years on Fulbright scholarships. At last he was a teacher himself, ready to fire others with his own zest for language. The results were depressing: "In the classroom I felt that I really wasn't doing much, that I wasn't making much of a difference in people's lives."

Dejected, he turned to a second love, the theater, and went back to France, this time to study drama. He earned a doctorate, and began to act professionally in Paris. But teaching was on his mind.

"One day I had this interesting thought—why only teaching? Why only acting?" he says. "Using acting techniques, couldn't a teacher improve his ability to communicate?"

He returned to the University of Bridgeport as an instructor, determined to create a new teaching system. When the Peace Corps asked him to help improve its language courses, he had his chance. The result, much refined, is today's "Dartmouth intensive language model." In action, it looks like a Gene Kelly dance number speeded up.

BEHIND THE MADNESS IS ARTFUL CALCULATION

The scene: a Dartmouth classroom. A group of undergraduates are watching their instructor, Marty Peterson, a senior from Lake Forest, Illinois. She is an "apprentice teacher," trained to conduct drills.

For a moment she studies a script in her left hand, a professor's outline of what he wants her to teach that day. Then she erupts into action, leading the class in choral renditions of sentences to be learned, zigzagging among the desks.

Looking one way, she points at someone across the room, snapping her fingers for a recitation. If the student answers correctly, she blows a kiss. If incorrectly, she stabs the offender with an imaginary stiletto, snaps at another student for the answer, then snaps again at the student who got it wrong.

Her finger-snapping gives the class a jivey beat as she paces the room, now standing, now stooping to eye level with the students. When a girl has trouble squeezing out an answer, Marty drops to her knees, smiling encouragement, trying to pull out the answer with her hands. The girl gets it right? She earns a *très bon!* and a hug. Marty jumps up and, finger-snapping and whirling, leads the class on to new material.

"You could mistake the atmosphere of this teaching method for fun," she later tells a visitor.

Actually, John Rassias has carefully choreographed every move and gesture in the apprentice teachers' repertoires. And behind his own madman antics are hours of painstaking rehearsal at home. His madness conceals artful calculation.

His strategy is to maximize the number of times each student speaks aloud in the new language. Thus, language classes at Dartmouth are limited to 22 students per section. Every day, for 50 minutes, each section meets with a master teacher, a Dartmouth professor who explains the day's lesson. Using the method's fast pace and dramatic techniques, the professors pronounce new material for the class, explain grammatical points, and clarify the lesson.

Next, the section breaks in half, each half spending 50 minutes with an apprentice teacher, an undergraduate trained in the Rassias method. Finally, the students go to a language laboratory for further practice, monitored by another trained undergraduate.

"But do you know how much homework they have? Virtually zilch!" says Rassias. "Instead of doing homework, they spend extra time in class, speaking." And one of the keys is the intense drill sessions with apprentice teachers.

At the beginning of each term, Rassias holds a 3-day workshop for students interested in apprentice jobs. A recent workshop was typical—250 candidates turned out for the approximately 30 slots open. Balancing precariously on chair arms and prowling bearlike among the candidates packing the auditorium, Rassias said, "From now on we're going to be in a fishbowl!" Observing them that night were teachers from high schools in Rhode Island and Massachusetts. "All *right*—let's go!" he exclaimed. And he outlined for the audience the

rudiments of the method. First, in all language classes, the only language spoken is the language being taught. To introduce new words, the master teachers act them out, rather than speaking in English, he said. Second, to make sure that each student speaks 65 times per 50-minute session, apprentice teachers must hustle the class along, snapping their fingers to maintain the rhythm.

After the workshop, Rassias tells the visiting high school teachers how they can adapt the method. For instance, given a 45-minute period, they can spend the first 25 minutes presenting the basic lesson. The remaining 20 minutes are for drill, perhaps led by an advanced high school student.

It's also important, he says, how teachers stress the five facets of learning a language: grammar, comprehension, vocabulary, fluency, accent. Commercial schools usually stress vocabulary, while many academic teachers stress accent. Rassias gives the most weight to grammar and the least to accent.

"I don't mean that we allow students to use an English pronunciation," he says. "But if you spend too much time harping on accent you cut people off at the pass, make them afraid to speak. If, without humiliating you, I can get you to speak even the most extraordinarily wrong thing, in the beginning I'll reward you with as much enthusiasm as if you were receiving the *Légion d'Honneur*. I tell my students, 'Have the courage to be bad, to make mistakes—but speak!' "

To encourage speaking, Rassias has devised an arsenal of techniques, such as make-believe press conferences and other skits. The New York City transit policemen learning Spanish at Dartmouth found themselves in an imaginary subway station. A heart attack victim lay on the platform; two men were picking his pockets; a crowd watched in silence. The policemen were taught how to deal—in Spanish—with the situation.

Dartmouth drill classes write their own skits in the language they are studying. They wear costumes and lug in props. Rassias, who has (to say the least) an affinity for the spotlight, once vivified a skit about the fall of Troy with anachronistic special effects: the recorded whine of falling bombs, flashing lights as they exploded, puffs of smoke.

To master counting, students may call off the numbers on rapidly rolled dice. Or they may play a game called "dots": as students call off the numerals, the teacher connects a series of numbered dots on the blackboard to spell out a word.

In a vocabulary drill, the instructor gives students a cue sentence, such as "I haven't eaten; therefore I am hungry." Then the instructor may say, "I haven't drunk," and point to a student to complete the sequence: "Therefore I am thirsty."

Into all classes, teachers inject culture. One technique is the "micrologue," a minute-long monologue on anything from French crêpes to Romanian agriculture, depending on the language under study. The teacher repeats the micrologue three times, while students write it down. Then students must repeat it for their classmates and answer questions.

After 10 weeks studying a language, Dartmouth students can opt for the "language study abroad" program. Better than half do. Students spend several months in a country where the language is spoken, living with a local family.

"One of our favorite tricks is to drive these kids out on a Friday and sort of parachute them into obscure villages lost in the countryside, which no one ever heard of," says Rassias. "They have no money and they have to get by for three days by making friends and earning their keep. Then they have to come back with a complete oral and written report on the village's history, economy and social pecking order."

Most students are positive about having fellow undergraduates as drill instructors. Michael Cooper, a freshman from New York City, says: "Students tend to be intimidated by older people, by professors, and so when you have an instructor who's much closer to your age I think you open up more."

Teachers in other schools increasingly are adapting the Dartmouth model to their own classrooms. The Exxon Education Foundation—calling the method "an educational innovation of demonstrated merit"—from 1976 to 1978 disseminated information about Rassias' method and provided funding for some colleges and universities to adopt it.

Meanwhile, jolted by the report of the President's Commission, the nation's education system may be poised for a renaissance in language studies. Already straws are in the wind, and here are a few:

In three towns along the Vermont-Quebec border, with federal funding, an English-French bilingual educational program is offered to all children, beginning with 4-year-olds. In Burlington, Vermont, the high school's 7-year-old "total immersion" program has students spend most of one semester off-campus, taking all subjects—from history and art to science—in French, then spend a month in France or Quebec.

VAPORIZING THE LANGUAGE BARRIERS

In Philadelphia, 14,000 pupils in grades 4 to 6, in 85 city schools, are taking Latin; Los Angeles has a similar program. A high school in Jamaica, New York, now offers nine languages, including Hebrew, Chinese, Russian, and Greek.

Bilingual programs are springing up in schools nationwide, in response to the influx of students who speak Spanish, Vietnamese, and other languages.

Meanwhile, at Dartmouth, Rassias continues to astonish his students, appearing one day as Denis Diderot, another as an ornately robed Chinese emperor, cold cream splotching his face to simulate leprosy.

"What we're doing is extremely simple," he says. "We're giving people the desire to communicate with others, to understand others, to be sensitive—we want to aim some big educational ray guns at these stupid language barriers and vaporize them, poof!"

DISCUSSION QUESTIONS

1. "Valium Valleys"? Haven't you been there? We have. In fact, we're sure you have too. What elements of traditional classroom approaches to language teaching tend to produce a soporific stupor?

2. Rassias insists that all communication in the classroom must take place in the target language. To realize this difficult objective, he uses dramatization. In what ways does his approach differ from that of Terrell (see Chapter 18)? In addition, compare his ideas with those recommended in Part IV.

3. The drills that Rassias uses are obviously drawn from the audio-lingual era. What, if anything, is different about the use that he and his "apprentices" make of them?

4. Wolkomir claims that the Rassias method has resulted in an upturn in foreign language enrollments at the several institutions where it has been employed. This claim is reinforced by Johnston in Chapter 28. What do you suppose is the primary reason for the attractiveness of the "Rassias madness" to students? Incidentally, in a recent version of the prime-time TV program, "60 Minutes," one student commented that "having an egg broken over your head by Rassias is an intense loving experience." One of our own students who has worked with Rassias personally confirms this reaction. How can these responses to such madness be accounted for?

Chapter 8

The Lozanov Method and Its American Adaptations

W. Jane Bancroft

University of Toronto

EDITORS' INTRODUCTION

It was difficult for us to know where to place this chapter. On the one hand it seemed to fit here in Part II since it stressed the "authoritative" position of the teacher in the language classroom. Also, it seemed to fit in this section because of its focus on individual students and their capabilities. However, there is a therapeutic side to the Lozanov method which comes through more clearly in the chapter by Stevick. We finally compromised and placed Lozanov according to Bancroft (this chapter) in Part II while we placed Lozanov according to Stevick (Chapter 9) in Part III.

Whereas the Rassias madness (as seen in Chapters 7, 28, and 29) depends on an actor who knows he is acting, the Lozanov method, here and in other publications cited by Bancroft, depends on a conception of "authority" (or Oller would say "an authoritarian conception") which is taken quite seriously by its devotees. It purports to release the deep resources of the human mind. In spite of (or perhaps because of) its assorted philosophical trappings, according to Bancroft from Yoga, Zen, and Marxism-Leninism, not to mention Baroque music, it may seem surprising that theorists such as Stevick (Chapter 9) and Krashen (1982) seem to take it seriously. Both contend that the Lozanov approach may indeed "lower the affective filter" and thus facilitate nonprimary language acquisition. To this extent Lozanov's method seems to be "therapeutic" in nature—hence Stevick's contribution in Part III.

When this article was written, back in the late 1970s, Bancroft was at pains to explain why Lozanov's method had not yet been fully understood by Americans. However, as the reader may confirm in Chapter 9 by Stevick, uncertainty about Suggestopedia has persisted into the 1980s. According to Bancroft, Lozanov's method is a collage of mimicry, memorization, role play and dramatization, grammar translation, contrastive linguistics, and parapsychology.

According to books on Soviet psychology, Western scientists often experienced difficulties interpreting and replicating Soviet (or East-European) research. "It is not an uncommon experience," says Jeffrey Gray, "for someone to read an English translation of the work of an eminent Soviet psychologist and feel almost as baffled as if he were reading an unknown tongue" (1966, p. 1). Sometimes, of course, the problem is one of language: the translation may be poor and the Western researcher is unable to read the work in the original language. The main difficulty is often philosophical: the Soviet approach to psychology derives from Marxism-Leninism and the Russian tradition of physiology. (The only acceptable explanation of the unconscious in the Soviet Union is the Georgian theory of the "set," based on the work of D. N. Uznadze.) In addition to what may be termed an ideological intrusion into scientific research, Soviet publications show, in many instances, a seeming lack of concern for methodology or statistical treatment of data. According to P. E. Jarvis (who attempted to replicate part of Luria's findings on the directive function of speech), Soviet ideas are often "novel and stimulating," but these tend to be presented "with something of a vagueness about the details of the evidence supporting them."[1]

This vagueness in Soviet research applies more to the written theoretical presentation than to the practical application of a given idea. The Soviets consider, for example, that apprenticeship is essential to learning the techniques of psychotherapy,[2] and much in Soviet psychology that is expressed orally does not find its way into print. The foreign reader of the theoretical paper is left to fill in any number of components; the visitor to the appropriate Soviet (or East European) experimental center, however, is likely to see a very structured experimental environment and will see (or hear) for himself what precise techniques or variables are involved in the appropriate research. These can then be tested in a Western setting.

In this report, it is my intention to show first, how a Soviet (or East European) idea must be investigated on the spot and second, how it can be adapted to the North American scene. The "novel and stimulating" idea is that of the Lozanov method of language learning (called Suggestopedia) which was developed, first in Bulgaria and then in the Soviet Union, East Germany, and Hungary under the direction of Dr. Georgi Lozanov, a Bulgarian physician and psychotherapist. The American adaptations are those of Dr. Allyn Prichard and Jean Taylor in Atlanta, Georgia, Dr. Owen Caskey, Director of Instructional Research at Texas Tech University, and the Society for Suggestive-Accelerative Learning and Teaching, a nonprofit organization under the direction of Dr. Donald Schuster, Professor of Psychology at Iowa State University, together with Ray Bordon and Charles Gritton of Des Moines, Iowa.

It was in 1970 that the Lozanov method was first given general attention in the West, thanks to *Psychic Discoveries behind the Iron Curtain,* a book by Ostrander and Schroeder (1970), that has become an international best seller. Based on such disciplines as yoga, classical music, parapsychology, and autogenic therapy, the Lozanov method supposedly speeded up learning 5 to 50 times.[3] Students were enabled, partly through training in special techniques of yoga relaxation and concentration, to develop "supermemories" and to learn,

---

1. Quoted in Slobin 1966, p. 133.
2. Kirman 1966, p. 59.
3. See pp. 291–296.

without conscious effort or physical fatigue, large amounts of language material in a very short time.

Ostrander and Schroeder traveled extensively in the Soviet Union and Eastern Europe in 1968, prior to writing *Psychic Discoveries*. While researching the Lozanov method, they visited the Institute of Suggestology in Sofia, Bulgaria, and conducted lengthy interviews with Dr. Lozanov and the members of the institute's staff; they saw a number of scientific laboratories in the institute but were unable to view any language classes. Their account of the method in *Psychic Discoveries* is based on interviews and on the original articles about Suggestopedia that appeared in the 1960s in Soviet and Bulgarian publications. (Some of these articles appear, in translation, in the Ostrander-Schroeder *ESP Papers*.[4]) Although the essentials of the Lozanov method are outlined in *Psychic Discoveries,* the Ostrander-Schroeder book, almost by definition, does not provide a detailed description of the suggestopedic language class.

Through Sheila Ostrander, I first became aware of the existence of the Lozanov method in the late 1960s, but the initial materials that came to my attention seemed vague and baffling. As a result, however, of a brief visit in 1970 to the Moscow Foreign Languages Pedagogical Institute (where the method was being researched), conversations with Dr. Lozanov during his visit to Scarborough College, University of Toronto in March 1971, and the subsequent reading of an unofficial English translation of the Lozanov thesis, *Sugestologiia,*[5] concerning the theory of the system, I decided the Lozanov method merited further investigation. An invitation to attend the First International Symposium on the Problems of Suggestology[6] in Varna and Sofia in June 1971 provided me with the opportunity of seeing what Ostrander and Schroeder had been unable to see: language classes in operation.

As a result of interviews conducted and classes observed in Bulgaria in May–June 1971 and subsequently; as a result of travels from 1972 to 1974 to such East-European countries as Hungary where the method was being used, I was able to piece together the original Lozanov method and to write a number of articles on the subject.[7] Knowledgeable researchers with a background in such disciplines as yoga, music, Gestalt, and parapsychology or who could read the appropriate materials in the original Bulgarian, began research in the early 1970s, shortly after the publication of *Psychic Discoveries and Sugestologiia.*[8] However, it is my article, "The Lozanov Language Class," published in 1975

---

4. Bantam, 1976.

5. *Sugestologiia* was published in Sofia by Nauka i Izkustvo in 1971. Copies of an unofficial English translation of the Lozanov thesis have been circulating in North American academic circles since Lozanov's 1971 visit to the United States and Canada. It is expected that the official English translation, to be published by Gordon and Breach, will appear in the very near future. [Editors' Note: The book was published in 1978. See References.] For an account of the theoretical bases of the Lozanov language class, see Bancroft 1977.

6. See the proceedings of the symposium, Problems of Suggestology, 1973.

7. My early articles on the Lozanov method include Bancroft 1972a, 1972b, 1972c.

8. See, for example, Robinett 1975. In their manual, Schuster, Bordon, and Gritton (1976) list a number of preliminary or pilot studies, including their own, in the bibliography, pp. 121ff.

and which gives detailed information on the original Lozanov method,[9] that has served as the basis for recent experiments in foreign languages (in addition to such subjects as science, psychology, and remedial reading) in a number of American schools and universities.[10]

Learning has not been speeded up 50 times in American experiments utilizing the Lozanov method or elements of the Lozanov method. Successful Iowa teachers in foreign languages have, however, been completing the normal language course in one-third the time using suggestopedic techniques in conventional 1-hour periods. In their investigation of the influence of a suggestive atmosphere, synchronized music and breathing on the learning and retention of Spanish words, Bordon and Schuster (1976) found that, "at a practical level, these variables when present resulted in learning 2.5 times better than when these same variables were absent" (p. 27). In the 1975–1976 remedial reading experiments conducted by Taylor and Prichard in Atlanta, 75 to 80 percent of the pupils gained a year or more on the Spache oral and silent reading subtests after 14 weeks in the program, only 12 of which were devoted to the actual teaching of reading.

THE LOZANOV METHOD

Suggestopedia has been and is indeed currently being used in a number of Bulgarian schools for the teaching of a variety of subjects. However, the principal area of concern of the Institute of Suggestology has been the teaching of Western foreign languages within the framework of a month-long intensive course. In accordance with the importance attached to the environment in Soviet psychology, room decorations are pleasant and cheerful; lighting is soft and unobtrusive. Language teachers are specially trained in such disciplines as acting and psychology in order to be able to suggest the meaning of new foreign words through gesture and intonation and in order to inspire the students to learn within the context of the group. Intensive classes normally last 4 hours a day and meet 6 days a week; 12 students (ideally: 6 males and 6 females) are the maximum number per class. In each classroom there are specially constructed chairs arranged in an open circle for the students; the instructor's chair stands at the head of the class.

The 4-hour class in the original Lozanov method comprises three distinct parts which the institute's staff calls the "suggestopedic cycle":

1. Review of the previous day's material, following the general outline of the Mauger or direct method, mainly through conversations, games, sketches, and plays. Members of the institute's staff are opposed to language laboratories,

---

9. ERIC Documents on Foreign Language Teaching and Linguistics, 1975, 53 pp. ED 108 475.

10. See especially the following: Bordon and Schuster 1976, Gritton and Bordon 1976, Prichard and Taylor 1976a, 1976b.

rigid structural exercises, and mechanistic repetition of language patterns. Although exercises are used and errors are corrected, the student is encouraged by a positive yet authoritarian teacher to react spontaneously to a given situation in the foreign language. At the start of the course, to help overcome inhibitions, each member of the class is given a new name and a new (i.e., foreign) role to play. Each "biography" contains repetitions of one or more phonemes that Bulgarians find difficult to pronounce (nasal sounds in French, for example). In the case of the sound *on,* a student is given the name Léon Dupont, told he lives at 11 (onze), rue Napoléon, that he works as a maçon, and so on. In the retelling of someone else's story, students practice phonetics, but in a humanistic setting.

2. Although as much as possible of the foreign language class is conducted in the foreign language, in the second part of the Lozanov class, new material is presented in a somewhat traditional way, with the necessary grammar and translation. This new material consists largely of dialogues and situations based on real life, i.e., dialogues and situations with which the Bulgarian students are familiar. The Institute of Suggestology believes that a student should learn a foreign language by describing, at least initially, what he sees around him. The material presented in the dialogues must be emotionally relevant and interesting to the students so that they will be encouraged to remember it and will be motivated to use it in conversational exchange. The dialogues presented in class must also be of practical value, as the students taking language courses at the institute usually plan to use their language skills in their professional work. In the first course, Bulgarian history and culture are outlined in the foreign language; the second and third courses deal with the appropriate foreign country. Special language manuals have been developed by members of the institute's staff for Bulgarians, although borrowings were made from a number of Western and East-European textbooks.

In the 10 dialogues of the first course (and in the dialogues of the more advanced courses as well), emphasis is placed on vocabulary and content. New vocabulary items are underlined in the manuals, and phonetic transcriptions are given for each new word. Emphasis in the dialogues is placed on group activities (hence the importance of verbs; all basic verb tenses are introduced to the students as soon as possible). In the dialogues as a whole and within each individual dialogue, attention is paid to a certain continuity of plot or anecdote. According to Lozanov and his staff, just as vocabulary items are more easily memorized in the context of a given dialogue (or real-life situation), so too, events or activities are better remembered than static tableaux. In addition, a series of events is easier to act out and communicate orally.

3. The third part of the Lozanov language class is the only truly original feature. Called the *séance* (or session), it provides for reinforcement (or rather, memorization) of the new material at an unconscious level. Based on the two forms of yoga concentration: outer/inner, the séance is divided into two parts: active and passive (or "concert"), with active or outward concentration on the material preceding the rest and relaxation of passive meditation on the text.

During the séance, which lasts about 1 hour, the students relax the vital areas of the body and sit in their reclining chairs in the alternate Savasana posture. They breathe deeply and rhythmically as a group—following the precepts of correct yoga breathing and according to a precise count of eight (2 seconds' inhalation; 4 seconds' breath retention; 2 seconds' exhalation). This rhythm accords with the teacher's reading of the language material, on the one hand and, during the passive or "concert" part of the séance, both with the reading of the language materials and with the slow-moving (MM 60) beat of the baroque music in the background.

Throughout the active part of the session, the students watch the language program while the instructor gives it a special reading. On the printed page, the material-for-memorization is visually arranged in threes, and each element of this trinity is presented orally with a different intonation or voice level. A simple example from the French manual follows:

> Quoi de neuf, M. Legrand? (normal tone of voice)
> J'ai un nouvel appartement, Madame. (whisper)
> Il est grand? (loud voice)

The tone of voice used for each phrase bears no necessary connection to the meaning of the word group as such. The loudness or softness of the voice and the quality of the suggestion (declarative, subtle, authoritative) are used for variety and contrast and probably also to prevent the rhythmically breathing students from falling asleep in class.

In the initial lessons, the Bulgarian translation of each word group is given first. The Bulgarian translation is for quick student reference and is considered necessary for older students who initially experience difficulties learning a foreign language by the direct method because they do not properly understand the meaning of what they are saying or hearing without some kind of clue in the native tongue. The Bulgarian equivalent of each foreign language phrase is, however, read very quickly and in a monotone. Undue attention should not be drawn to it.

In accordance with the students' breathing, the teacher reads the language materials in the following order and with the following timing: Bulgarian translation (2 seconds); foreign language phrase (4 seconds); pause (2 seconds). While the foreign language phrase is being read, the students retain their breath for 4 seconds, look at the appropriate part of the text, and mentally repeat to themselves the given phrase or word group in the foreign language. Concentration is greatly promoted by the retention or suspension of breath.[11] Inner speech is considered to be of considerable importance in Soviet linguistics (Sokolov 1972), and Lozanov and his staff have found that inner repetition is especially helpful in the memorization of difficult foreign words (for example, those which bear no resemblance to their Bulgarian equivalents). Corresponding to the continuous yogic breathing of the students, the reading of the material during the

---

11. Eliade 1969, p. 68.

active session proceeds without a break in the rhythm of 2:4:2 for a period of some 20 to 25 minutes.

The active part of the séance is immediately followed by its passive or concert counterpart. The concert session is divided into three parts: (1) a 2-minute introduction—the opening Sarabande from Bach's Goldberg Variations, for example; (2) a series of excerpts from baroque music lasting some 20 to 25 minutes over which the teacher acts out the lesson dialogue with an emotional or artistic intonation and during which the students, with eyes closed, meditate on the text; (3) a fast, cheerful flute excerpt from baroque music, lasting some 2 minutes, which brings the students out of their deeply relaxed state. During the artistic rendering of the text, the Bulgarian students are emotionally involved with the pleasant, psychologically true material and mentally reenact the scene while concentrating on the music (in other words, their attention to the language material is passive). By imagining the situation described by the text as if they were at a concert listening to program music, the students realize the process called "interiorization of language" which furthers their ability to speak and communicate, as well as memorize.

For the second part of the concert, musical excerpts are selected from 18th century baroque *concerti grossi*. Slow movements are chosen which have a rhythm of 60 beats to the minute (preferably in 2/4 or 4/4 time) and which feature a sustained melody in the violin or string section over a *basso continuo* or steady bass accompaniment. The slow movements for use in the concert are usually excerpted from the *concerti grossi* of Corelli, Handel, Vivaldi, Bach, and Telemann, representative baroque composers who favored the use of a melodic line over a ground bass. The succession of baroque slow movements contributes to the state of relaxation and meditation (the "alpha state") that is necessary for unconscious absorption of the language materials.

The teacher is expected to maintain the correct rhythm of the language dialogues over the musical background of calm, pleasant, soft, and slow-moving music while, at the same time, giving each phrase of the appropriate dialogue an inspiring or emotional tone—one that accords with the meaning of the phrase being read. Assuming that the slow movement is in 4/4 time, there would be four quarter notes, or equivalent, to the bar. Since, with a metronome speed of 60, each quarter note has the value of 1 second, each bar in 4/4 time would make up 4 seconds—just enough time for the reading of the foreign language phrase on the one hand, or a pause and a Bulgarian translation on the other.

While listening to the slow movements, the students continue to breathe in the same 2:4:2 rhythm as before, thus coordinating their breathing (as mentioned above) not only with the rhythm of the language dialogues but also with that of the music. Breath (or breathing), intelligence (or concentration), and the rhythm of the music are all united in the passive part of the séance as they are in Indian music and meditation (Daniélou 1969, p. 22). The lyrical and rhythmic music, the artistic and rhythmic rendering of the text by the teacher, the rhythmic, deep breathing, and meditative state of the students contribute to a marked decrease in fatigue and tension on the one hand, and a marked increase in memorization of the language materials on the other.

AMERICAN ADAPTATIONS

To date, research in the United States has centered on the elements of the Lozanov method, rather than on the Lozanov method as a whole, and on the variables involved in the seance. Three elements of the Lozanov method are considered essential for the system to work effectively: (1) an attractive classroom (with soft lighting) and a pleasant classroom atmosphere; (2) a teacher with a dynamic personality who is able to act out the material and motivate the students to learn;[12] (3) a state of relaxed alertness in the students (achieved by, among other things, physical exercises to relieve bodily tension; mind-calming exercises; deep, rhythmic breathing to improve concentration; rhythmic presentation of the material over a background of baroque music).

It would, of course, not be possible to use the entire "suggestopedic cycle" in a normal school situation in which 1-hour periods, rather than intensive courses of 4 hours, are the rule. The sequencing of the Lozanov class must often be changed, depending on the students and the subject taught. In the United States, the concert séance has not been reproduced exactly in its three parts (introduction, baroque slow movements, flute finale). Rather, excerpts from baroque music have been used, together with a shortened form of the active séance, in the presentation of the appropriate material-for-memorization. Or, as in the Prichard-Taylor remedial reading experiments, the varying intonations of the active session have been combined with the slow-moving music of the passive session. In some Texas classes, music has been abandoned, to be replaced by its essential element: rhythm. It is apparent, from the Lozanov thesis, that EEG recordings were taken to determine the increase in alpha waves in the students; checks for the presence of the "alpha state" have not been routinely carried out in American experiments to date.

In order to adapt suggestopedia to the American academic scene, other modifications or changes have been made. By definition, language programs suitable for Bulgarians could not be used for American students. Games, sketches, and classroom activities in general depend on preexisting American programs and on the innovative talents of the American teacher or researcher. The "ideal" number of 12 students is virtually impossible to achieve in a normal school or university situation (not to mention the selection of six students of each sex), and American researchers have been obliged to abandon, in general, the elements of number symbolism contained in the original Lozanov method. Although a circle of chairs can be formed in any classroom, most American

---

12. For the importance of the teacher's role in students' intellectual development, see, for example, Rosenthal and Jacobson 1968. [Editors' Note: We do not recommend this source.]

classrooms do not contain special chaises longues (with a pillow or headrest) for yogic relaxation; normal straight-backed chairs (with the accompanying correct posture they encourage) are being used in the United States, following the autogenic therapy of Dr. J. H. Schultz, for relaxation of various parts of the body and deep, rhythmic breathing (Schultz and Luthe 1969).

It is apparent, from the Lozanov thesis, that the Bulgarian students underwent, at least in the late 1960s and early 1970s, a period of special training in yogic breathing. Very often in American experiments, deep breathing (which may be practiced to the beat of a metronome) has been simplified: 4 seconds' inhalation, 4 seconds' exhalation. (Prichard found, for example, that very young children had difficulty breathing rhythmically.) Clicks on the appropriate tape of baroque slow movements have been used to underscore the first beat of a given bar, signaling to the students that they are to commence a new deep breath (Prichard and Taylor 1976a, p. 108). To relieve fatigue and tension, the Bulgarian students at the Institute of Suggestology had (or have) their séance or relaxation session at the conclusion of an intensive class. In the United States (as in France),[13] relaxation exercises, both mental and physical, have been used, together with positive suggestions for pleasant learning, during the 10 or 15 minutes at the beginning of a class to calm the students,[14] to improve their powers of concentration, and to motivate them to learn. In the Prichard-Taylor programs in remedial reading, the first 2 weeks of the 14-week program were devoted entirely to basic relaxation training.

The principal American contribution to research on the Lozanov method thus far has been the transformation of a Bulgarian system designed for teaching intensive language courses into one suitable for the teaching of various subjects in a normal American school situation. More especially, American researchers (in contrast to their Bulgarian or East-European counterparts) have provided a precise outline of relaxation procedures for use in the classroom.[15] Through word and gesture, the American teacher initially establishes a suggestive, positive atmosphere in which the students understand that effective learning will constitute a pleasant experience. Students in Iowa classes, for example, then perform a series of exercises derived from Hatha Yoga, exercises which leave them physically relaxed. A state of physical relaxation makes it possible for students to calm their minds with an exercise such as Zen breathing. Suggestion, in turn, is more effective when a student is mentally relaxed. Following the physical relaxation exercises and a mind-calming exercise, an early pleasant learning exercise is performed. In a state of relaxed alertness, the students are then ready to begin the work for the appropriate class.

---

13. For an account of the successful use of yoga in the French classroom (more specifically in the lycée Condorcet in Paris), see Flak 1976.

14. Physical and mental relaxation exercises were especially effective in calming hyperactive pupils in the Prichard and Taylor remedial reading experiments (1976, p. 30).

15. See, for example, Caskey and Flake (1976, pp. 20–23) and Schuster et al. (1976, pp. 19ff.).

As outlined in the SALT (Suggestive-Accelerative Learning and Teaching) manual of procedures based on the Lozanov method and in such articles as "Americanizing Suggestopedia," by Gritton and Bordon (1976, pp. 92–94), exercises include the following:[16]

1. Physical relaxation exercises (3 to 5 minutes). These exercises are performed three times by the students while standing beside their chairs.

a. Reach and stretch: While standing, raise and stretch one arm as much as possible and hold this position for 2 to 3 seconds, return the arm to the side, then reach and stretch with the other arm. (Students may also be requested to stand up, bend over, and try to touch their toes.)

b. Tension waves: Divide the body into six sections, tense one section at a time and hold, progress from the feet, to the calves, to the thighs, to the lower abdominal muscles, to the upper abdominal area, to the chest. Hold, then relax the body parts in reverse order. It is possible to do the contractions in a wavelike motion after a little practice.

c. Three turtle exercises: (i) tense one side of the neck, then the other side and the front; (ii) let head flop forward and touch the chest, then lift shoulders behind the head, then pull the head up with the neck, tighten the back of the neck, let head flop forward again; (iii) lift shoulder and rotate head, with neck tensed, three times in one direction, then three times in the opposite direction; turn neck once or twice without tension.

d. Side bends: Standing straight with hands to the side, slide hand down the side of the leg below the knee while bending the body sideways as much as possible. Repeat other side.

e. Yogic breathing: Empty the lungs by breathing out through the nose. Exhale very deeply so that the lungs are emptied of stale air. Pull in the abdomen as far as possible to help with the exhalation. Begin a slow inhalation through the nose (thus commencing to fill the lungs), continue breathing in through the nose and raise or distend the abdomen while slowly beginning to fill the lower lung. Continue the slow inhalation and distend the abdomen as far as possible and then the chest as far as possible, making this one single, wavelike movement from the abdomen upward. Continue the inhalation, drop abdomen, keep chest extended, and raise shoulders. Slowly and steadily fill in this manner the lower lung, middle lung, and finally the upper lung with air. At the top of the inhalation, after the lungs have been filled to their capacity, pause and hold breath for several seconds and then start to exhale slowly through the nose. At the same time, drop shoulders, pull in abdomen, allow the body to relax. Empty upper, middle, and lower lungs in the same slow and continuous manner in which they were originally filled. Pull abdomen well in toward the backbone at the

---

16. With the exception of the exercise on yogic breathing, which is an adaptation of ones found in texts on yoga, all the exercises described or referred to in succeeding paragraphs are taken from the Gritton-Bordon article and the SALT *Manual of Classroom Procedures Based on the Lozanov Method* (Schuster et al. 1976), pp. 19–29. The "climbing a mountain" exercise is described in the manual, pp. 26–27.

completion of the exhalation process so as to squeeze out all the stale air. Take another breath immediately; do not pause between breaths. Deep, rhythmic breathing concludes the physical exercise section and leads naturally to the mind-calming exercise(s).

2. Mind-calming exercises (3 to 5 minutes). There are several types of exercises that can be used to calm the students' minds after they have relaxed physically. These include: watching one's breathing (Zen breathing), the little white cloud exercise, or climbing a mountain.

The little white cloud exercise has the following pattern:

Imagine that you are lying on your back on the grass on a warm summer day and that you are watching the clear blue sky without a single cloud in it (pause). You are lying very comfortably; you are very relaxed and happy (pause). You are simply enjoying the experience of watching the clear, beautiful, blue sky (pause). As you are lying there, completely relaxed, enjoying yourself (pause), far off on the horizon you notice a tiny white cloud (pause). You are fascinated by the simple beauty of the small white cloud against the clear blue sky (pause). The little white cloud starts to move slowly toward you (pause). You are lying there, completely relaxed, very much at peace with yourself, watching the little white cloud drift slowly toward you (pause). The little white cloud drifts slowly toward you (pause). You are enjoying the beauty of the clear blue sky and the little white cloud (pause). Finally the little white cloud comes to a stop overhead (pause). Completely relaxed, you are enjoying this beautiful scene (pause). You are very relaxed, very much at peace with yourself, and simply enjoying the beauty of the little white cloud in the blue sky (pause). Now become the little white cloud. Project yourself into it (pause). You are the little white cloud, completely diffused, puffy, relaxed, very much at peace with yourself (pause). Now you are completely relaxed, your mind is completely calm (pause), you are pleasantly relaxed, ready to proceed with the lesson (pause).

3. Early pleasant learning recall (3 to 5 minutes). The purpose of this exercise is to stimulate or bring to the fore the sensations, feelings, and abilities which students had much earlier in their lives, for example, during a period when bedtime stories were being read to them. Typical instructions follow a Gestalt pattern in which the nonverbal components of the previous situation provoke a recall of the appropriate verbal and cognitive aspects.

Return to an experience which made you eager to learn. Get the details of this early pleasant learning experience in your mind as vividly as possible. Use your imagination to fill in the following information, if you need to, in order to put yourself in the situation once again. Where were you? (pause) Were you in a room? (pause) Were there people around you? (pause) Who were they? (pause) How did you feel about what you were reading or learning? (pause) Take a look at yourself in this learning situation. How did your hands feel then? (pause) How did your throat and head feel that day? (pause) Recall how your whole body felt (pause). Recall how naturally motivated you were (pause). Recall the thoughts you were thinking (pause). Bring your thoughts and feelings with you to the here and now and try to learn and enjoy learning the same way today.

In the adaptation of the Lozanov method to the American scene, much still remains to be done in such areas as teacher training and program development. Further experiments need to be conducted in order to confirm to what extent the Lozanov method speeds up learning and aids retention. Nonetheless, while publications on the subject are limited in number, American attempts to replicate an East-European learning system have, thus far, yielded encouraging results. As Prichard and Taylor (1976a, p. 115) point out, researchers are optimistic over the prospects of adapting the Lozanov method to the American public school setting. "As more data are generated by researchers ... improvements in applying [Lozanov's] approach will likely occur."

DISCUSSION QUESTIONS

1. In addition to the inducement of drowsiness (an effect that Bancroft comments on), what other effects might be expected from the tension-reducing exercises of the Lozanov method? In what ways might these exercises be expected to contribute to more rapid language acquisition?

2. What is the theoretical basis for the suggestion that words "which bear no resemblance to their Bulgarian equivalents" will be "difficult foreign words" (p. 106)? Are cognates (words of different modern languages that have a common root in an earlier parent language) usually easier to learn than noncognates? What about so-called "false" cognates? Are they less common than "true" cognates?

3. Acting out and dramatization play an important part in the Lozanov approach. Bancroft also argues that "events or activities are better remembered than static tableaux. In addition, a series of events is easier to act out and communicate orally" (p. 105). Why is this so? Do you see any connection between this observation and the "episode hypothesis" discussed in Chapter 1? Also see Part IV, Roles and Drama.

4. If you were given the task of modifying the Lozanov philosophy of teaching, what would you add or delete? How might the Lozanov approach be integrated with other teaching methods? Chapters 9 and 32 contain some suggestions.

Part III
Social/Therapeutic Orientations

While the orientations of both Parts I and II have been mainly concerned with the teaching and acquisition of nonprimary languages as intellectual pursuits, in Part III the emphasis shifts. It is not that previous chapters are unconcerned with personality and affect, or that their authors are disinterested in social context, but they are *primarily* concerned with the internalization of a nonprimary language as a cognitive enterprise. In Part III the emphasis moves more to the affective and social aspects of nonprimary language acquisition. In fact, here these factors become the central elements of concern. The various contributors in this section seem to view language acquisition as a basis for the establishment of self-worth or personal "wholeness." To Oller this emphasis seems somewhat misplaced, perhaps even misguided. However, we have agreed to include these chapters in the smorgasbord because there is some evidence (for Richard-Amato, some of it firsthand) that the philosophies and attendant methods recounted in this section do in fact result in success in language acquisition. At the very least, the methods discussed here provide many avenues for communicative interaction in language classrooms. Also at some points they are not incompatible with approaches discussed in previous chapters.

SUGGESTED ADDITIONAL READINGS

CHARLES CURRAN.
    1976b. *Counseling-Learning in Second Languages.* Dubuque, Illinois: Counseling-Learning Publications.

    We have excerpted and reproduced in this volume Chapters 2 and 3 from Curran's original work (see our Chapter 10). However, for teachers who want to try to apply Curran's methods, we recommend the original work in its entirety.

STEPHEN D. KRASHEN.
1982. *Principles and Practice in Second Language Acquisition.* Oxford: Pergamon.

In this seminal treatise, Krashen brings together his own thinking over more than a decade of research and practice. Especially pertinent to the discussions in Part III of this book are his observations about the "affective filter hypothesis"—the idea that when the affect is not right, input will be filtered.

EARL STEVICK.
1980. Part III: A Second Way: Counseling-Learning. In *Language Teaching: A Way and Ways.* Rowley, Massachusetts: Newbury House.

Stevick devotes no less than 11 chapters to Curran's theorizing. His insightful interpretations of the counseling-learning approach and community language learning is bound to rank high on the list of publications on this topic.

S. SIMON, L. HOWE, AND H. KIRSCHENBAUM.
1972. *Values Clarification.* New York: Hart Publishing Company.

For anyone desiring a deeper look into the principles behind this intriguing educational paradigm, this book is priority reading. Myriad activities are suggested to aid students in clarifying their values. Since the focus is on meaning rather than form, these activities are suggestive of applications in language teaching.

NINA WALLERSTEIN.
1983. *Language and Culture in Conflict: Problem Posing in the ESL Classroom.* Reading, Massachusetts: Addison-Wesley.

In Chapter 12 we include a portion of this innovative book by Wallerstein. She interprets and applies to the ESL classroom the socialist philosophy of Paulo Freire.

Chapter 9

Interpreting and Adapting Lozanov's Philosophy

Earl Stevick
Foreign Service Institute, Arlington, Virginia

EDITORS' INTRODUCTION

The material in this chapter originally appeared in Stevick's classic, *A Way and Ways* (published by Newbury House in 1980). It is presented here with only minor editorial changes. In its original form it consisted of two distinct chapters (Chapters 18 and 19 of *A Way and Ways*), which we have condensed here into one chapter with two parts. The first part gives one teacher's understanding of what Lozanov's Suggestopedia is all about. The second part offers some reflections on Stevick's own classroom applications of the Lozanov method. It will be noted that Stevick differs considerably from Bancroft in his interpretation of Lozanov. Since Stevick is one of America's most respected language teachers, in addition to being a formidable theorist on the subject, we thought that our readers would profit from his insightful thoughts on suggestopedia and its connections to other approaches, especially that of Curran, which follows in Chapter 10. Stevick's remarks in the latter part of this chapter concerning his Swahili monologues also suggest some connections with the working ideas offered in Chapter 1 above, especially the episode hypothesis. Additional ideas for applying Lozanov's philosophy are offered in Chapter 32.

It has been five years now since I first heard of Suggestopedia, and I have yet to view a significant amount of learning by this method.[1] The results which it achieves are reported to be outstanding, yet the way in which the results are reported has sometimes left them less than clear. In 1976, I wrote all that I knew about the procedures of Suggestopedia. Since that time, I have talked with three people who have had firsthand experience with the method, including one who went through the 2-month training period which Lozanov recommends for foreign teachers who want to use his system. I have also just read Fanny Saféris'

---

1. On his visit to Washington in April–May, 1979, Dr. Lozanov very kindly read the penultimate draft of Chapters 18 and 19, and also permitted me to observe a full three-hour session near the end of an Italian course which was being conducted under his direction. I have made some changes as a result of talking with Dr. Lozanov and watching Suggestopedia in operation. I would still emphasize, however, that Suggestopedia is not a fixed system, but an area of Dr. Lozanov's ongoing research; and that these chapters of mine are accounts of my own thinking, and not definitive descriptions of his method.

account of Suggestopedia and her own experiences with it. Jane Bancroft has provided some details in a recent article in the *Modern Language Journal* (reprinted in this volume as Chapter 8) and the *Journal of the Society for Suggestive-Accelerative Learning and Teaching* is largely concerned with this approach to education. Lozanov's own recent book *Suggestology and the Principles of Suggestopedy* will be indispensable, of course. Yet I am still unable to give an authoritative account of what is done and what makes it succeed. Why then am I writing about Suggestopedia again here?

For three reasons. (1) The ideas behind Suggestopedia seem to fit in with the ideas I have talked about in earlier chapters, even though they are in some ways quite different from them. (2) Reading about Suggestopedia has set me to doing some things that I'm glad I did even though they themselves could never be called examples of Suggestopedia. (3) Reading about Suggestopedia has helped me to make sense of some of the things that have happened to me as student, teacher, or supervisor of teachers in language classrooms.

Anyone who wants a readable, lively, and stimulating description of Suggestopedia at work should read Saféris' book. The course consists of 10 units of study, each of which takes exactly 6 hours of class time and (by some accounts) a little student time just before bedtime and just after getting up in the morning. The day's study consists of four 45-minute periods. Each unit consists of a long dialogue, a bit of explanation, and many activities that draw on ("elaborate") what was in the dialogue. The dialogue itself is introduced during the third period of one day. During the fourth period of that day, the teacher reads the dialogue aloud twice to the students as they sit back and listen to music (the "concert" session). The whole of the next day and the first half of the third day are devoted to activities of many other kinds.

I have not tried here to give a complete description of how Suggestopedia is used for teaching languages. I have even avoided trying to give a description that could be used as directions for organizing a course, because to do so would almost certainly be misleading and therefore destructive. Although this chapter is based on some of Lozanov's writings, and particularly on a speech he made in 1976, it will not really be a discussion of Suggestopedia either. It will be only an account of my own thoughts, and some of my actions, that have come out of my contacts with Lozanov's work.

In a bird's-eye view of what I have to say, 12 points stand out. I will number them so that we can refer to them later.

To begin with, I see Suggestopedia as being based on three *assumptions:* (1) that learning involves the unconscious functions of the learner, as well as the conscious functions; and (2) that people can learn much faster than they usually do, but (3) that learning is held back by (a) the norms and limitations which society has taught us, and by (b) lack of a harmonious, relaxed working together of all parts of the learner, and by (c) consequent failure to make use of powers which lie idle in most people most of the time.

The *strategy* of Suggestopedia, therefore, is to (4) remove these norms and (5) these tensions, and to (6) avoid introducing other limiting norms or inhibiting tensions in their place.

For these purposes, the teacher has *tools* of three kinds: (7) psychological, (8) artistic, and (9) pedagogical.

The guidelines for using these tools, and the *criteria* by which success is judged, are (10) the principle of "joy and easiness," (11) the principle of the unity of the conscious and the unconscious, and (12) the principle of "suggestive interaction." Lozanov has emphasized again and again that teaching which does not meet *all three* of these criteria will not achieve the results of Suggestopedia and should not be called Suggestopedia.

Let me then set forth my own thoughts and my own experiences in relation to these 12 points.

1. *Learning involves the unconscious functions of the learner, as well as the conscious functions.* One part of the meaning of this sentence has to do with what it is that a learner remembers. When one "studies" a particular word, for example, one may think consciously only about its translation equivalent in one's own language, or about a picture that the teacher has pointed to in presenting the word. At the same time, however, and without thinking consciously about them, one may be aware of many other things that are connected with the word: other ideas, other words, other objects or actions that are frequently associated with that word in real life; emotional impacts that the word has had on oneself or on groups that one has been in; the way the teacher acts and what the teacher seems to assume is going to happen; all these things and many more. The same range of unconscious associations exists for individual sounds, and also for larger units of language such as sentences, games, conversations, and stories.

Lozanov's point, as I understand it at least, is this: that whenever a student is consciously dealing with the overt content of a lesson—the part that he and the teacher are focusing their attention on—he is at the same time dealing unconsciously with other things which lie just outside, or far outside, the center of his awareness; and that what happens on the unconscious level affects what can happen on the conscious level. This much of what Lozanov is saying is receiving much more attention nowadays than the bare lip service that it was given at some times in the past. The "humanistic" methods place particularly strong emphasis here. This observation—that the best learning takes place when what is happening on each of these two levels supports what is happening on the other—is approximately what the word "double planeness" refers to in English translations of Lozanov's writings.

But Lozanov goes a step further. In Suggestopedia it is not merely a matter of having things generally pleasant on the unconscious level so that things will be sure to go smoothly on the conscious, cognitive level. That is to say, it is not just a matter of the one level serving as a foundation or support for the other, as lath supports the plaster of a wall. It would be more accurate to say that the two are constantly being woven or knitted into each other. To take only one example, this interplay of the two levels shows itself in the names and identities which the students take on when they enter the classroom, and which they keep until the end of the course. The name, occupation, and home of each character provide multiple examples of some one sound that the students need to learn. Thus in the English course "Robert Fox" is "a doctor from Oxford," and "Shirley Burton" is "a journalist from Birmingham." This by itself is merely a cute device on the cognitive level. But the assonance, rhythm, and (in some cases) rhyme of these identifying formulas give to them a primitive but very real aesthetic quality to which students will respond even if they never think about them—echoes and drumbeats which speak to the student's body more than to his mind. The fact that these aesthetic qualities show up dependably in all the characters implies further that the people behind the course know what they are doing. If the student draws this conclusion *unconsciously and for himself,* it will be vastly more effective than if the same idea were stated in so many words on the first page of the textbook.

Each of the occupations is also prestigious or interesting in some way, and may even be glamorous. Since the student's "real" identity is entirely excluded from the classroom, he receives from this new surrogate identity—largely on the unconscious plane—a number of positive, pleasant associations that go with that occupation. He will thus feel good about this fictitious Self, and in that *Self* will be more ready to enter into whatever is happening on the conscious level. In this character, he may take roles in dialogues which involve a whole new set of temporary characters which are being played not by his real Self, but by his surrogate Self.

If Lozanov is right about the importance of "double planeness," then a Suggestopedic teacher needs to know what is going on on both planes at the same time. But in most kinds of teaching, the teacher is not much more aware of this detailed interaction between the two planes than the student is. The training of a Suggestopedic teacher therefore involves learning to be conscious of, and to control, some of the things that the teacher does which affect the learner mostly on the unconscious plane.

2. *People can learn much faster than they usually do.* This is the side of Suggestopedia that catches the attention of the public: the claim that experimental subjects have in some sense learned the meanings of 1000 foreign words in one day, and that even in the classroom students absorb 2000 words in 60 hours of instruction. The term for this phenomenon is "hypermnesia"—"supermemory." Yet I think that Lozanov would insist that "hypermnesia" differs from what students are usually capable of not only in the amount of the material that they hold onto. The basic difference is not quantitative, but qualitative. Hypermnesia depends on activating different *kinds* of powers within the student—powers which ordinary teaching leaves untouched or even

blocks off. I regret that I cannot tell the reader exactly what these "reserve powers" are, much less give instructions on how to bring them to life. But I am fairly sure that Eric Berne, in writing about the wonderfully flexible and creative potential of the Child ego state, had seen something of what these powers can do.

3a. *Learning is often held back by absence of psychic relaxation.* I am sure that I do not understand all that Lozanov means by this point. Quite posssibly it refers to what happens biochemically inside the brain, and even in parts of the body outside of the brain. But it may also be saying that when the student is unconsciously resisting something that comes along with the new word, sentence, or whatever, he cannot at the same time welcome the word or sentence into his total system of memories. Imagine a guest at a party, a person of some charm and even of some importance, but who insists on bringing with him his pet boa constrictor. He is less likely to be kept on the list of prospective guests for future parties than is a person of comparable charm and importance who does not bring a boa constrictor with him.

In a language class, then, many of the student's resources, and much of his energy and attention, will be used up—or tied up—in defending himself from whatever is causing the "psychic tension." From this tension and from the student's efforts to deal with it, there may come not only inferior learning, but also psychosomatic disorders: drowsiness, headaches, digestive discomfort, and the like. One of the hallmarks of genuine Suggestopedia is that the students have fewer such difficulties.

Here, I suspect, is a large part of the reason why the schedule of a Suggestopedic course is so rigid, and why the teachers take charge so briskly, and why the students are not invited to contribute to decisions about what to do next. It may also account for the fact that students have absolutely no social contacts with the teacher outside of class, even during breaks. What is wanted is an image which is clear, self-consistent, and self-assured. This must be an image which will not provoke conflicts either within the student or between students— one which will not even raise in the student's mind any alternatives that are not necessary to the progress of the course.

3b. *Learning is often held back by norms which the student learned as a part of his upbringing in society.* The destructive effects of "psychic tension" have at least been mentioned by other writers. The emphasis which Lozanov places on this second limiting factor, however, is one of the distinctive features of the Suggestopedic point of view. We have been told over and over from an early age, directly and by implication, that learning a language is hard work, or that only a few people can do it as adults, or that we ourselves at least are not cut out for it, or that twenty new words a day is about all that anyone can hope to hold onto. As Lozanov tells us, the earlier an idea comes to us and the less conscious we are of its coming, the more power it will wield in shaping our thoughts and in controlling our actions. So most of us are more or less "born losers" (or at least born underachievers) even before we first set foot in a language classroom.

In this context, the large number of words per day in Suggestopedia is not only an *outcome* of the method. It is also an important *tool* of the method. The very size of the demand blasts the student out of the small orbit that was determined by what society had persuaded him were his limitations. It forces him to grasp for, and find, and use, and rely on powers—modes of learning—which he did not know were in him. The demand also implies—"suggests"—confidence in the learner and in his powers. Needless to say, an apparently unrealistic demand does not by itself lead to success. It must be one part of a total system in which the student finds out fairly soon that the demand is not impossible after all, and that he himself is able to meet it. Otherwise, it is worthless and even disastrous.

Those of us who teach non-Suggestopedic courses also have, on a smaller scale, our own opportunities to "suggest" and "desuggest" limitations on the powers of our students. One area in which this is true is in our explanations of grammar. I think we have much to learn from Lozanov here even if we are not using his method.

An example of what I mean cropped up in my own work just last week. A student who was having to leave for Turkey halfway through the Turkish course was sounding distressed because she had not yet come to the passive forms of verbs. I doubt that such situations ever arise in Lozanov's courses, and I do not know what he would do if they did. Nevertheless, the thought struck me that this student's ignorance about the passive voice was really a small matter. What was of great urgency (and here I think that Lozanov was whispering in my ear) was her idea that the passive was some mysterious forest, or some treacherous bed of quicksand, through which she could pass safely only with the help of a licensed guide and an officially published chart. To have answered her question as I used to answer such questions would have been a service to her in the short run. In the long run, however, it would have been a disservice, because I would have implied—"suggested"—to her once again that her own powers were very weak.

Instead, I said to her in Turkish, "Oh, it's not all that difficult." Then, turning to a Turk who was with us, I said, as if I were uncertain, "*Vermek . . . verilmek?*" ("to give" . . . "to be given"?). After another example or two of this kind, all without English translation, the student saw for herself what we were doing, and began to contribute examples of her own, complete with correct vowel harmonies in the suffixes. I had been right in guessing that she would be able to do this. If I had not been right, I would have had to change my technique quickly, and without her noticing that I had changed it. Otherwise, I could have ended up having conveyed the ideas that (1) she was as limited in her ability to deal with these things as she had thought she was, and that (2) she was in the hands of an incompetent teacher.

Once I saw that the student was playing happily with the kind of passive that I had introduced her to, I gave her the other essential fact about Turkish passives: "It's not all *that* simple." Then, as we had done earlier, we gave her a few examples of another passive-like suffix and let her play with it. Finally I said in English, "So you do have to know which verbs form the passive in which way. But from what we've done here, you can recognize passives when you run into them from now on, and you also know that no one way of forming passives is hard."

In earlier days, I would have responded to the student's question quite differently. First, I am sure, I would have picked up the nearest piece of chalk and made for the blackboard. Once arrived there, I would have outlined what I knew on the topic, as simply and clearly as I was able. My central purpose would have been to prepare the student for understanding and producing correct passive forms in her future encounters with the language. If I did the kind of job I was trying to do, I would leave her feeling that she now understood Turkish passive verbs, and feeling relieved from her earlier anxiety on the subject, and grateful to me for having relieved her from her anxiety by putting this new knowledge into her hands. As I gave the explanation, I would have been aiming for exactly this kind of result, and so my facial expression, my tone of voice, and all the rest would have automatically begun to convey earnest messages like, "Now always remember . . . !" and "Are you *sure* you understand . . . ?" And when, as is almost inevitable, she someday failed to apply her new knowledge correctly, she would say to herself (or she would hear me saying), "You've forgotten . . . !" We would be back to the chain, as old as the Garden of Eden, in which knowledge leads to responsibility, and responsibility leads to guilt, and guilt means that one can get no good thing except by the sweat of one's brow.

Let me say again, I do not offer this as an example of what a Suggestopedic teacher would do. It is merely one instance of conveying—"suggesting"—to the student, in an atmosphere of "joy and easiness," that her powers were greater than she had thought. This contrasts with suggesting to her what she already believed: that she was in fact dependent on me, in an atmosphere of earnestness and responsibility.

4. *The strategy of Suggestopedia includes removing the psychic tensions that would interfere with learning.* There are two obvious channels through which to reduce tension. One is the design of the materials and the other is the behavior of the teacher. Suggestopedia is concerned with both, sometimes in ways that would surprise the rest of us, or which violate some of our dearly held principles.

The best-known rule of the direct method, for example, is to speak to the students only in the target language. This allows, or forces, the students to figure out the meanings from the context. This can be exhilarating and deeply satisfying for some students, but seriously frustrating for some others. Almost any student under these conditions will feel at least a little tension. Suggestopedia avoids this tension both by allowing the students to follow the printed text in parallel NL and TL versions, and by allowing the teacher to give *sotto voce* translations when needed. (In the current version of Suggestopedia, the translations are given on separate strips of paper which can be inserted into the book when needed, and then removed later on.)

A quite different source of tension is the contents of the dialogues themselves. So, on the smallest possible scale, a student of Portuguese who expects to go to Portugal may be annoyed when one of the speakers in the dialogue calls a railway train a *trem* (the Brazilian term) instead of *comboio* (the word used in Portugal). On a larger scale, a person headed for Ouagadougou may wonder whether his precious time is being well spent in a course that is set in the shops and restaurants of Paris, and an electronic technician will not feel at home using materials that concentrate on history, politics, and the fine arts. The language professional may remonstrate with the student that the pronunciation and basic grammatical structure are the same, and that the specialized vocabulary for any particular purpose is small and easily learned. The fact remains, however, that students do become uneasy about these matters, and this kind of uneasiness can spoil the Suggestopedic environment, just as it can reduce the effectiveness of methods which are less highly coordinated than Suggestopedia.

Another source of anxiety is the very fact of being a student who is ignorant, powerless, and under evaluation every time he opens his mouth. An additional source of conflict, which we have generally taken for inevitable, lies in the custom of having each student take each part in each dialogue. Related to this is the fact that the cast of characters changes entirely, or at least partially, from one lesson to the next. Under these circumstances, no student identifies himself or herself very strongly with any of the fictional characters in the book. Speaking their lines for them becomes at worst a sterile mouthing of words, and at best an enjoyable moment of amateur theatrics.

I am beginning to see how the design of a Suggestopedic course reduces all these tensions. Most conspicuous is the *surrogate identity* which the student receives upon entering the course. This goes far beyond the ancient practice of assigning a foreign name. This identity has depth and continuity, and emotional content relative to the identities of the other students. The "world" of the classroom can therefore take on a complexity and a (provisional) credibility which are lacking in most other classes. This complexity and this credibility allow for (provisionally) real communication which for language-learning purposes is as effective as communication among students in their permanent and public identities. Communication among the surrogate identities has the further great advantage that it does not bring in any of the problems and anxieties which the students have outside the classroom. The same is true for the plays-within-the-play—the characters in the long, interesting dialogues on which the 10 lessons are based. In assuming this identity and in playing these roles, the student is less likely to fret about whether the vocabulary of the course is exactly right for his own specialized needs.

At the same time that the student uses the person of "Dr. Robert Fox" as a vehicle for entering the new language, he can also use it as a mask to hide behind. Suggestopedic teachers do not say "No," and never say "That was a mistake." So the student is safer from feeling evaluated than he would be in most courses.

Nevertheless, if he notices that he has said something that the teacher would evidently not have said, it was Dr. Fox who "made the mistake," and not he. Suggestopedia thus effectively (deliberately?) blurs the boundary between fact and fiction, so that the student can drift back and forth between them.

Unlike the reality of the student's life outside the classroom, this "fictitious reality" brings with it no embarrassments, no conflicts, no anxieties. On the contrary, it brings a series of enjoyable experiences.

Suggestopedia thus agrees with some other systems of teaching which avoid the danger of setting up an evaluative atmosphere in which people have their mistakes pointed out to them as "mistakes." It also avoids praising people because they have succeeded in doing something "difficult." To describe something, or to treat something as "difficult," is in itself "negative suggestion," which curdles the atmosphere and makes Suggestopedia almost impossible.

Suggestopedia also concurs with many other methods in the belief that it is good for the teacher to be lively, cheerful, and efficient. A difference, however, is that most other methods seem to regard the liveliness, cheerfulness, and efficiency of the teacher merely as a plus factor—important and desirable, but something that the teacher brings *to* or adds *to* the method. For Suggestopedia, these qualities in the teacher are integral parts *of* the method.

5. *The strategy of Suggestopedia includes removing the limitations which society has suggested to the student.* The trick is to lead the student to forget about or to ignore the limitations. But before he can allow himself to do so, he needs an excuse, a justification for venturing outside of the old fence even after the gate has been opened. A doctor sometimes sees that a patient's body could cure itself, except that the patient is convinced that his illness requires help from a professional. So the doctor gives the patient a prescription which costs money, and which has a scientific-sounding name, but which is made of nothing but sugar or cornstarch. The patient gets well after taking these pills, not because of any chemical action, but because the person has now used his own powers— powers which he did not know he had—to cure himself. A medicine of this kind is called a "placebo."

Lozanov makes much use of placebos in Suggestopedia in order to "desuggest" the undesirable social norm, and to leave the student open to other, positive suggestions. Virtually every element in a Suggestopedic course has, in addition to its overt effect, also a "placebo" effect.

According to Lozanov, every healthy person has three barriers to suggestion from outside. We resist suggestions that don't make sense to us in terms of what we already know. ("It's obviously impossible for me to learn 100 words a day; in the past I've had trouble holding on to even ten!") We resist suggestions that undermine our feelings of confidence and security. ("Why should I sit back and close my eyes while the teacher reads the dialogue along with the music?") We resist suggestions that we do something which we think is morally or ethically wrong. ("We shouldn't be playing all these games in class—

we should be working!'') Lozanov recognizes that without these three barriers to protect it, any personality would very quickly be torn apart by all the disorganized and conflicting suggestions that constantly strike it from outside. So he does not set out to destroy these barriers, or even to attack them directly, for that would lead to more trouble, not less. He seeks only to circumvent them, to sneak around them, or to pass through them by blending with them.

The process of desuggestion and resuggestion requires the teacher to make deliberate and skillful use of the general atmosphere—the background against which the student will see and interpret whatever else the teacher does. Even the color of the classroom walls and the style of the furnishings may be taken into account in designing a Suggestopedic classroom. But what about those of us who are not pretending to use this method in any authentic way, and who in any case are not in a position to redecorate or refinish our rooms? None of my friends would accuse me of being compulsively neat in the way I keep my own office. Yet when I walk into a classroom and see students seated around a table that is loaded down with clutter—clutter that is permanent, and unrelated to what they are doing at the moment, I wonder what kind of "suggestion" this clutter is broadcasting to the students as they try to learn.

The most important background element, though, is not paint, or armchairs, or a clear table. It is what Lozanov calls the "authority" of the teacher. By "authority," Lozanov means much more than the ability to issue instructions that will be carried out. The central element in "authority" is the teacher's apparent competence—her competence in the eyes of her students—and her reputation for being able to produce amazing results. People will not trust themselves even to a strong bridge if it looks flimsy, and if they do not set foot on it, they will never arrive at the place to which it leads. As in the case of liveliness, cheerfulness, and efficiency, Suggestopedia differs from other methods in that it considers the authority of the teacher (and of the school, and of Suggestopedia in general) to be an integral part of the method, and not just a desirable characteristic of the teacher.

We have seen this same principle at work in the history of language teaching outside of Suggestopedia. At least a portion of the early successes which swept audiolingualism to a dominant position in some parts of the world in the 1950s must have come from the well-publicized exploits of the linguistic scientists in teaching seldom-taught languages during World War II. And at least some part of the success of programmed instruction must rest on what people have read about those pigeons who were taught to appear to play ping-pong. This is not to belittle either of these methods or the sources of their success. But the same kind of "authority" which these methods have profited from generally and in haphazard fashion is in Suggestopedia developed consciously and pains-takingly, and used with great efficiency.

The desuggestion-resuggestion process also requires the teacher to make deliberate and skillful use of the conscious and unconscious elements in whatever she does against that general background of authority, pleasant decor, and all. This brings us back to the subject of "placebos." Specific combinations of objects, actions, and words used over and over again can become rituals, and Lozanov sees "ritual placebos" as among the most powerful tools of the Suggestopedic teacher. My own use of Gattegno's silence, and of an unchanging set of words that introduced the silence seemed to have something of this effect in a non-Suggestopedic course. The difference, once again, is that what is used as an isolated technique in other methods is used systematically in Suggestopedia, and woven into the very fabric of the course. The trick is to choose elements, and to combine them, in ways that will fit with—and will therefore help to join together—both the expectations of the students and the pedagogical aspects of the course.

6. *Once the tensions and the negative suggestions have been removed, it is necessary to be sure that they do not creep back in.* They sometimes sneak back in subtle ways. For example, one of my own frequent goals both as a writer of materials and as a teacher has been to break into small pieces whatever I was trying to teach, and to give it to the student in very gentle gradations so as to maintain his self-confidence and leave him with a feeling of success. Lozanov points out that this may leave the student with the impression (i.e., it may "suggest" to the student) that the language, relative to his own powers, must be very hard. In other words, his own powers relative to the task of learning the language must be weak. It is true that by our careful sequencing and grading we have left the student with a feeling of confidence. But it is confidence in power which is much narrower than what lies hidden in him. And the success which he has achieved in this way only persuades him further that the ceiling which society has placed on his rate of learning is a realistic one.

Once the student has concluded that he should not expect to learn rapidly and easily, the natural result is that he will not learn rapidly or easily. Even with the best of Suggestopedic materials, details of the teacher's tone of voice or body language may convey the impression of difficulty, unsatisfactory progress, danger of mistakes, and failure. Materials and procedures must therefore be carefully designed, and teachers specially trained, in order to maintain the conditions under which Suggestopedia will be possible.

7. *Some of the necessary tools used in Suggestopedia are psychological.* This includes the means by which the teacher makes use of emotional stimuli, and not just cognitive ones, including those that come in around the edges of awareness. We have already seen what some of these are: liveliness, cheerfulness, efficiency, the teacher's evident self-confidence and joy in what she is doing; the making of demands that imply that the student has great powers which he has never before used; the happy, successful lives of the people in the dialogues, and so on. The reader should turn for further detail to the books by Lozanov and others. But I suspect that full understanding of this point will require firsthand training which I have not had.

8. *Some of the necessary tools are artistic.* They make use of what Lozanov calls "certain harmonious art forms" which certainly include music. Some

reports also speak of special, stylized, almost "balletesque" body movement on the part of at least some teachers. It is after all in the nature of art (as contrasted with mere illustration or decoration) that it speaks to us on two levels—or on many levels—at once. This may be what Lozanov has in mind when he speaks of the "liberating and stimulating character" of the arts in Suggestopedia. The most conspicuous artistic medium, and the one which has received the most publicity, is the music which forms a part of the "concert sessions." After a new dialogue has been presented and before going home at the end of that day, the students have two of these sessions, one "active" and the other "passive," in which the teacher gives a highly skilled and somewhat dramatic reading of the new dialogue against the background of recorded music. The actual musical selections are chosen largely for the deep messages that they convey—certainty and deep but controlled emotion in the "active" sessions; order, stability, and completion of the task (of memorization) in the "passive" sessions. It is not necessary that the student be an enthusiast for music of the classical and baroque periods; the important thing is that he receive the underlying messages which they carry. Or so some of my sources report. Once again Suggestopedia differs from other methods in that the art forms are integrated into it, rather than being used as supplements for the purpose of illustrating the course or brightening it up.

9. *Some of the necessary tools are pedagogical:* materials, techniques, and so on. I am afraid that I have no very exact information concerning the pedagogical tools beyond what I wrote in 1976. Having seen videotapes of Suggestopedic classes in the Soviet Union, Canada, and the United States, and having watched a very few classes taught by people trained in Sofia, and having seen copies of a few of the dialogues, I still have not seen anything that was greatly different from what I have seen good language teachers do in non-Suggestopedic classes. This is not to say that Suggestopedia is not greatly different from other systems. It is only to say that the difference lies, not in any one element, but in the extraordinary care with which the elements are integrated into one another. The goal is to produce consistently the effects that in most methods come only at "peak moments."

One very important "pedagogical tool" is the "global" nature of the dialogues themselves. Compared with other dialogues I have seen, they are long, rambling, and variegated—Victorian mansions compared with the neat, manageable tract houses that we so often construct for our students. The purpose is that the whole will be full of life, and that each person will remember what his or her own background, interests, etc., cause to stick. No two people will hold onto exactly the same things. Yet little or nothing will be lost, because in the "elaboration" sessions the teacher is working with the collective memory of the whole group, rather than testing the memory of individuals.

In this connection, Lozanov emphasizes the importance of maintaining in the students' minds the vividness of the meaning-bearing whole, shifting away from it to analysis of details only briefly, and then coming back to the synthesis of form, meaning, and feeling.

The three principles that guide this integration are covered in points 10 to 12:

10. The first is sometimes translated from Bulgarian as "*the principle of joy and easiness*": the students should enjoy what they are doing and not see it as something hard. This implies an absence of any destructive or inhibiting tension. But psychic relaxation does not mean inattention or laziness. There are two kinds of "concentration." One is the care-full kind, the kind that teachers so often demand of their students and that the students soon come to expect of themselves. This is the "concentration" in which the student is apprehensive lest he miss something, or in which he thinks (or mutters) a new item over and over rapidly as soon as it is introduced. This kind of concentration, says Lozanov, does indeed lead to education, but to a "false education." The other kind of concentration is relaxed and care-free, yet without being care-less, and so allows learning to go on in a way that is not tiring. The principal source of tension in the former kind of concentration is the student's lack of confidence that he can do what he is asked to do. This lack of confidence is therefore a chief target of the Suggestopedic teacher's use of materials, pedagogical techniques, and artistic media. The principal source of joy in the carefree concentration that Lozanov is talking about lies in easy assimilation and easy use of the language.

A few other methods place emphasis on relaxed concentration, and some of the best teachers by almost any method help their students to reach that kind of concentration at least part of the time. But Lozanov emphasizes that a teacher whose students are working in this way is not necessarily "doing Suggestopedia," or even "doing 1/3 of Suggestopedia." This criterion must be met *along with* the two that follow.

11. The second principle that guides the integration of the various means to Suggestopedia is that *the conscious and the unconscious reactions of the student are inseparable from one another.* This is a partial restatement of point 1, above. Here, it becomes a criterion which demands that the teacher use overt means of which the student is conscious in order to pursue goals of which the student may not be fully conscious, as well as to pursue those goals that do occupy the center of the student's attention: confidence, physical enjoyment, etc., as well as accuracy, fluency, and vocabulary.

12. The last principle is what Lozanov calls "*suggestive interaction.*" He says that the level of such interaction can be measured by how fully the "reserve powers" of the learner have been mobilized. These powers are qualitatively different from those used in ordinary learning, and can lead to a new, less tiring, and more permanent type of learning. (One cannot help wondering about the relationship between this "qualitative difference" and the qualitative difference(s) between what Krashen calls "acquisition" and "learning.")

For genuine Suggestopedia, then, not one and not two but all three of these criteria (points 10 to 12) must be met simultaneously and continuously. When they are, the students become more and more able to teach and help themselves as the course goes on. But this freeing process must not be limited to the cognitive level alone, says Lozanov; freedom in the process of instruction must go hand in hand with freedom from the inner fear of one's own limited powers of assimilating new information.

SUGGESTOPEDIA AND "CONTROL"

Suggestopedia, with its carefully prepared materials and its emphasis on the authority of the teacher, is anything but a power vacuum. Yet it also requires the teacher to be warm and supportive, and to refrain from talking about "mistakes." In this way, it avoids the "evaluative paradigm." While it does try to give the student full-time security as far as the teacher's competence is concerned, it certainly does not intend to protect him from making errors. What it does produce, according to all reports, is people who enjoy using the language.

In its look inside the learner, Suggestopedia sees a person whose physical, emotional, and intellectual sides are closely intertwined. The learner-anxiety with which it deals most directly is that which arises from uncertainty about ability to handle the course and the language. Other anxieties are apparently expected to wither away naturally in the wholesome light of "joy and easiness" and "desuggestion-suggestion."

Teacher "control" is firm throughout the 6-hour cycle. To judge from what I have seen, the teacher also exercises much of the "initiative" in the beginning but allows the students a great deal of "initiative" later on. Many of the later activities involve considerable cooperation among the students, as in preparing skits. But even in the earlier and more tightly structured activities, the teacher may address her questions to the class as a whole, rather than putting one individual on the spot at a time. By doing so she appears to assume (i.e., she "suggests") that the class is a functioning *cooperative* unit, and so the students act as one. In a group of 10 to 12, moreover, there is almost certain to be someone who can come up with the answer. As a result, the "principle of joy and easiness" is maintained, and at the same time an extraordinarily strong feeling of *community* arises.

"Good vibes" are of course at the very heart of Suggestopedia, in the unnoticed positive messages which the teacher sends out at all times.

I am not sure what to say about "mask changing" by the Suggestopedic teacher. I do know that—presumably to protect the teacher's aura of authority—teachers do not fraternize with students outside of class. On the other hand, my best firsthand source reports concerning his training in Sofia, "My guide rewarded me when I relaxed into playfulness and chided me only when I undertook any exercise that smacked of drilling. I must admit I did notice a change of expression on the students' faces at such times. The sunny looks became clouded for a moment and the wary expression appeared that is seen so often in conventional classes." Perhaps the meaning of "double planeness" is precisely this: that at all times the teacher wears both masks—the mask of the director of learning, and over it the warm, engaged mask of one human being in a happy relationship with another.

This guess is consistent with my brief observation of the Italian class. During the "concert" session, as she read the new dialogue against a background of classical music, the teacher looked for all the world like the soprano soloist in an oratorio: confident and in charge of her audience, but performing in a way that gave to them what they had come to the concert for. Also as in an oratorio, her voicing of the language was highly stylized. During the "elaboration" session, there was constant give and take of one kind or another between teacher and class. In this activity, I felt that I was watching people play with a frisbee. For example, when the teacher threw out a question, she did so like a person who is sharing in a game. When the answer came back, she received it with the same gusto, very much as if she were snagging a well-placed toss of a frisbee. She very clearly did *not* do what we so often do: when the response came back, she did *not* step from in front of a target and then announce how close the student's shot had come to the bullseye.

My guess is that the Suggestopedic teacher would be a good model for the student's "Self 1" to pattern itself after.

Apparently the Suggestopedic teacher does not invite students to express their reactions to the course, at least not while it is in progress. To do so would at the very least take something away from the teacher's status as someone who has no doubts about what she is doing. And if the students expressed any serious discomforts or doubts, the schedule would be thrown off. The whole Suggestopedic basis for success might even crumble.

SOME SUGGESTOPEDIC IDEAS IN NON-SUGGESTOPEDIC METHODS

I said earlier that nothing I have ever done could properly be labeled "Suggestopedia." I have never even attempted such a thing. One reason why I have not done so is that I take Lozanov seriously when he says that Suggestopedia requires the teacher to have kinds of training that I have not had. Nevertheless, certain of my experiences may cast light on the description in the first part of this chapter, just as the theory has helped me to understand the experiences better. I will relate them in chronological order.

The Swahili Monologues

From time to time, as a methodological experience in counseling-learning for language teachers, I have taught 10 to 20 hours of beginning Swahili. *A Way and Ways* contains accounts of three such experiences, in Chapters 12 to 14. The third time I conducted a short course of this kind (not one of the experiences described in Chapters 12 to 14), one of the students said, after about four hours,

"These conversations among *us* are all very nice, but I'd like to hear how the language sounds when it's really spoken." I decided to provide a sample of fluent Swahili after the next break.

My reason for doing so was not simply to comply with the student's request. It was that I felt that we were all of us ready for a change of pace before going on with what we had been doing—an interlude which would provide relief from routine without departing altogether from what we had been trying to do.

Since this was an experience in counseling-learning, I was particularly concerned that what I did should not diminish the students' sense of security. I therefore began by saying, "I'm going to let you hear a sample of Swahili as it might be spoken rapidly outside the classroom. All you need to do is listen. I won't ask you any questions about it when I have finished." Then I talked to them for about five minutes. When I began talking, I had no clear idea of what I was going to say. I talked *to* the students, not just in front of them, and I spoke with considerable animation. I used gestures, and some of the words that they had been exposed to, as well as two or three proper names. But whenever I needed words that the students had not met, I went ahead and used them. In using them, I was not apologetic, but continued to act as though I thought my meaning was getting across. I was garrulous and somewhat repetitious, but the repetitions were of the kind that might come up in normal discourse between speakers of a language. They were not the kind of thing that a teacher uses in order to "be helpful."

When I finished, I left a few seconds of silence, as though I were catching my breath before going back to the scheduled activity. Before I spoke again, one of the students said, "Do you mind if we tell you what we understood?" I was a bit surprised, but of course invited them to go ahead. As it turned out, both they and I were amazed at how much they were able to recount in English what they had heard in Swahili. Among them, they brought back virtually everything I had said. And so a new procedure was born.

Since that incident, I have used this procedure with numerous other classes. The results have always been at least as good as the first time, and sometimes better. Here are some comments that students volunteered after one such session:

It was just about the most exciting thing that has happened in the class so far. . . . It did not seem contrived. . . . I was amazed that I could follow the story after a scant six or seven hours of study.

I didn't understand much, but the sounds were beautiful, and the gestures and facial expressions were fascinating. It was good communication. It was a beautiful drama.

I was not paying attention because I had something else on my mind, yet the story was told in a highly animated way, and was addressed to us as if we had been speaking Swahili all our lives, so that I became caught up in the story. [This comment was from a student who had reproduced in English almost everything that I had said in Swahili.]

I just let my brain go limp and let it take the story in without too much backtracking. . . . It was exciting to realize how much the human brain can piece together with very little information.

If we look carefully at these four quotations, I believe we will recognize some bits of the ore which, if refined, purified, and crystallized, might become the stuff of which Suggestopedia is made. Pleasant, relaxed emotions are evident in all of them. The unspoken attitude that I conveyed by talking to the class "as if we had been speaking Swahili all our lives" indicates that the peripheral ("suggestive") communication was consistent with my purposes, and this fact also fits Suggestopedia. All quotations but the second display success far beyond the student's expectations or previous experience. The last two show evidence of the kind of "pseudopassive" attention that Lozanov talks about. The last sentence sounds much like a reference to "the normally unused reserve powers of the mind." It is as though the very impossibility of coping with the rapid flood of language in the usual way had forced the minds of these people into a new and (to them) surprising mode of operation.

Most of the forty-some students in this class had the feeling of having followed "more than half" of what I had said. Nevertheless, there were some who felt that they had understood very little, and one reported that he felt uncomfortable because most of the others seemed to understand so much more than he had. These facts alone would be enough to keep this episode from being called an example of "Suggestopedia." In addition, the material that I used lacked careful integration of the "three tools" to the degree that Lozanov seems to call for. Even so, my contacts with Lozanov's thinking have helped me to recognize these good things when they happen; recognizing them, in turn, makes it easier for me to do them again in other classes, on other days.

It may be worthwhile to distinguish two sides of this episode. One was the relaxed way in which many of the students were able to catch and use, amid the flood of language, those bits of Swahili that they had been exposed to. No more need be said here about that side. The second side was the way in which I was apparently able to "desuggest" the limitations which could have kept the students from even trying to do such an "impossible" thing. In ordinary classroom use, these two move along together, and may seem to be parts of the same thing. But as we try to understand them so that we can learn to achieve these effects in our own teaching, it would be helpful if we could see one of them separated from the other. The following episode seems to show just that.

In September of 1976, I found myself facing an audience of about 50 people in a two-hour time slot directly after lunch. I had had two other sessions with the same audience on the mornings of preceding days, so that we were to some extent comfortable with each other. But the hour, plus the fatigue which the audience had accumulated during a week-long training program, made it clear that I could not get away with just another lecture. So I began by writing on the board two vertical columns of English words:

hairs	toiling
annulled	udder
furry	warts
starry	warts

First, I had the audience read the list aloud one word at a time. Then I recited it myself, with the intonation of someone who is telling a story: "Hairs annulled furry starry, toiling udder warts, warts welcher alter girdle deferent former wants inner regional virgin." The listeners, who were native speakers of English, found themselves *hearing* this meaningless series of *words,* but at the same time *understanding the message:* "Here's an old fairy story, told in other words—words which are altogether different from the ones in the original version." I then went on to tell them the entire story of "Ladle Rat Rotten Hut" (Little Red Riding Hood) in this way. The entertainment value of this stunt is greatest when the story is told at just the right speed, allowing the listeners to be equally aware of the actual words and of the message, and to enjoy the discrepancy.

On this occasion, however, my purpose was to do more than just keep the audience awake after lunch. At the end of the story, with almost no comment, I went into a monologue in Turkish. This monologue was conducted in the same manner as the Swahili monologues that I have already described, but this audience had never before been exposed to any Turkish at all. As a minor placebo, I drew a very rough map of Turkey on the chalkboard and made occasional references to it. At the end of the monologue, many members of the audience felt that they had understood much of what I had said. For those people, it was apparently an experience like the one that Alice had when she read *Jabberwocky:* "It fills my head with ideas, but I'm not quite sure what they are." One interpretation of their reaction is that I had "desuggested their limitations," but without going on from there and actually teaching them something, I had unlocked a door that opened on a blank wall. The experience seemed to have been a pleasantly exciting one for this audience.

The major placebo which made this possible was of course not the map. It was the story of Ladle Rat Rotten Hut. With it, the hearers had suspended their normal way of listening, and had found themselves "understanding the unintelligible." I suspect, therefore, that this was an example of the third aspect of Suggestopedia—the aspect to which language teachers least often give their attention. This episode took place in a training seminar. What we hope for in a real class is that the students will combine this feeling and this openness with some actual resources in the target language. When they do so, their progress should be many times greater than what we are accustomed to.

In connection with a counseling-learning episode (see Chapter 13 of *A Way and Ways*), I have described a technique for reading aloud to students the same sentences that they have already studied cognitively, using three different styles of speaking. As I said there, this technique was quite frankly based on my attempt to understand what Lozanov meant by the three "intonations" in his description of the "concert pseudopassive" sessions of Suggestopedia. The aspect of that technique that I wish to comment on here, however, is not the reading itself, but the way in which I introduce it. My formula goes something like this: "Now I'm going to read you the sentences in a way that will help you to absorb them. I'll read each sentence three times." I then give a brief description of the "intonations" and continue by saying, "If you have a favorite way of throwing your mind into neutral and not trying too hard, you may want to use it. I will also ask you not to look at the written words. You may want to close your eyes as I read." In reciting this formula, I use a quiet but firm voice, which is intended to convey the impression that I have used this technique in dozens of classes and that it has always worked. I leave about 15 seconds of silence before the first sentence and after the last one.

My most recent information indicates that my understanding of the "intonations" was mistaken, at least in terms of present-day practice. Nevertheless, the technique does work well. I think that its success may depend on several factors, all of which are related to Suggestopedic theory: (1) The peripherally conveyed confidence. (2) The use of an unchanging formula—almost an incantation—which becomes one part of a "ritual placebo." (3) The readiness of young adults these days to accept the value of mind-quieting exercises such as yoga and meditation. (4) The possibility that some students actually draw on their own earlier experiences in those areas. Negatively, (5) I did not use music in these sessions because I was fairly sure that my choice of selections would be more or less inappropriate, and that my handling of the tapes would be more or less clumsy, so that the overall effect would be amateurish. I am sure that music done well would have enhanced the effect still further, but done poorly it would have damaged my aura of confidence and competence (my "authority"), and so would have spoiled the overall effect. (6) For similar reasons, I did not engage in a formal, overt procedure aimed at inducing physical or psychic relaxation.

I believe that Suggestopedic factors also play a role in the success of many other methods and techniques which in themselves have nothing to do with Suggestopedia: my choice of clothing to be worn to class; the reputed miracles wrought by linguistic science in language training during World War II, as a factor in the success of the audio-lingual method.

Setting aside for the moment, the place of "miracle" in our profession, I would like to comment briefly on two kinds of activity. One is rapid-fire choral and individual "mimicry" drill which is so characteristic of orthodox audiolingual teaching. The other is the explanation of grammar, which we find somewhere or other in most methods though not in all.

The basic technique for the beginning stage of one kind of audiolingual instruction is massed choral and individual repetition after the teacher. Details vary, but in a typical procedure the teacher would say the last part of the first sentence and have the whole class say it after her. She would do the same thing again, and then go on to add another part of the sentence. She would continue in this way with larger and larger parts of the sentence, giving each part twice and having the class repeat it after her until finally they had reached the whole sentence. Then she would treat each successive sentence in the same way. At the end of the choral repetition, she would switch to repetition by individual students, correcting their pronunciation whenever she thought it was appropriate to do so. After a heavy dose of this kind of thing, students went on to try to produce the sentences by themselves, and eventually to memorize the dialogue which was made up of these selfsame sentences. What I have given in this paragraph has been a simplified description of a relatively primitive and unsophisticated version of "mimicry-memorization." My purpose here, however, is not to write a manual on the use of that technique. It is, rather, to point out one potential strength in it—a strength which I have come to see more clearly after reading about Lozanov's work.

When I first used vigorous and protracted repetition, I thought that it worked because it helped to "burn the sentence (or the grammatical pattern) into the brain." Then I noticed that this kind of activity didn't work for everyone, although it certainly worked for many. So I had to change my theory. I guessed that the technique worked best for people whose minds took the noises and the muscular feelings that were there fresh in their immediate memory, and worked with these noises and feelings, looking at them from one point of view after another, even while the words remained the same, repetition after repetition. In this way, a sentence would enter the student's memory with a richer set of associations. For this reason, the student would find that the sentence came back to him more readily when he needed it.

I still think that both of these theories may be partly right. But while I was conducting some intensive "mim-mem" drill recently, a third explanation came to mind.

An ordinary, old-fashioned radio signal uses what is called "amplitude modulation" (AM). The sound of a voice or of a musical instrument comes to us as vibrations of the air. These vibrations are at relatively low frequencies—some hundreds or a few thousands of vibrations per second. The designers of early radios wanted to take these vibrations out of the air and change them into electromagnetic vibrations so as to send them over long distances without wires. Unfortunately, however, electromagnetic waves which are of the same shape and frequency as sound waves do not travel very well. Then the engineers hit on the idea of using electromagnetic waves that vibrated at some unchanging frequency of at least half a million cycles per second. These radio waves travel very well, but they are at frequencies far above what anybody can hear. The trick was to make this "carrier frequency" stronger or weaker (in technical terminology, to "modulate" it), *and to do so at a rate* which corresponded to the shape of the sound waves:

SOUND WAVE:

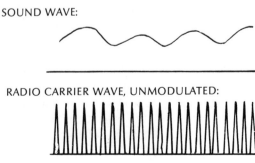

RADIO CARRIER WAVE, UNMODULATED:

RADIO CARRIER, MODULATED BY SOUND WAVE:

This was the job of the transmitter. The receiver's job was just the opposite: to filter out the radio carrier frequency but hold onto its shape, and to convert this *shape* back into sound waves by means of some sort of headset or loudspeaker.

This has been a long explanation of a matter which is not directly a part of language teaching. I apologize to those readers who understand radio principles better than I do. But I need the concepts of "carrier" and "modulation" in order to explain my third theory of how "mim-mem" can work.

If a dialogue is well chosen, and if the teacher breaks the sentences into pieces of the right size, then the rhythm of modeling by the teacher and repetition by the students becomes both rapid and quite regular. Such a rapid, regular rhythm can be soothing to the students and (in the everyday sense, not in the technical sense) almost hypnotic. This is like the radio carrier frequency, which can go places that lower, less regular frequencies cannot go. It makes its way around and past the anxieties that the student would feel if he focused on each sentence as a separate problem or set of problems. It carries with it the unspoken ideas (i.e., it "suggests") that the teacher is competent; that the teacher is in charge; that the students are "in good hands"; and that since things are going so smoothly the students themselves are also competent. Keeping up with this kind of drill can thus give to the student a general sense of personal adequacy, even elation. The bodily participation in the physical rhythm must also be a part of the total effect. (This is close to the experience that students and teacher share in Carolyn Graham's "jazz chants." [See Chapater 21 of this volume.]) The overall result, then, may be to "desuggest" many of the limitations that the students thought they had.

At the same time, the teacher may superimpose other ideas on this stable and rapid rhythm, just as a radio transmitter modulates its carrier frequency to carry the shapes of sound waves. Slight changes in technique or in facial expression or body language or tone of voice may carry such messages as, "We're making a little game of this," or "I'm enjoying myself," or "Aha! Since you did that so easily, let's move on to this new variation!" Yet if the teacher tries to transmit messages like these directly, in words like the ones I have quoted here, they will not come through as effectively. They may run afoul of the "antisuggestive barriers." If they arouse suspicion or misgivings, their net effect may even be the opposite of what the teacher intended: "Is she trying to *en*courage us because she thinks our performance must be *dis*couraging to us?" and so on.

Of course, the "modulation" which the teacher applies to the rhythmic "carrier" may be undesirable to begin with: messages like "I'm the slavedriver and you are the slaves," or "Why can't you get it right?" or "Don't let me down in front of our visitor(s)!" Any and all of these messages can come in along with the words, are stored in the student's memory along with the words, and color the student's feelings toward the language and its speakers.

Before leaving the topic of "mimicry-memorization," I should remind readers that this technique is *not* a part of Suggestopedia, for Lozanov seems to avoid mechanical drilling of any kind. I have discussed it here because I think Lozanov has helped us to see why one and the same technique can be either heavy and deadly, or light and lively.

Let us turn now to look at ways in which a teacher may "explain grammar." My own basic insights on this topic come out of counseling-learning. [See Chapter 10.] Those insights are also consistent with my understanding of Suggestopedia, while at the same time Suggestopedia makes some things explicit which are only implied in counseling-learning.

The explaining of grammar fills more than one of the student's needs. Most obviously, it helps him to see how the words, the endings, the phrases, the sentences on the mechanical side of the language all fit together. It casts light on the unfamiliar pathways and the arbitrary obstacles through which he must eventually be able to run back and forth with his eyes shut. It can thus save him a certain amount of time, energy, and barked shins. It is for this reason, of course, that the teacher needs to know these same pathways and obstacles—not only to run back and forth in them for herself, but also to see them as they look to a newcomer. On top of this are the skills of knowing when to turn on the spotlight of explanation and when to turn it off, and knowing just how to aim it so that it will help the student instead of blinding him. Everything that I have said in this paragraph is, as I said at the beginning, obvious to any experienced teacher.

But I think that the student has a second need which he hopes that grammatical explanations will meet. This is the need for power—symbolic power, almost mystical power—to protect him amid the chaos of an alien and inhospitable (language-) universe. My guess is that this second need of the student comes into being somewhat as follows:

1. Some people, by accident of nature or training, recognize and work with tastes (or spatial relations, or musical tones) better than other people do. In the same way, some people recognize and work with grammatical distinctions more readily than others do. We may call these people "Group G."

2. Group G people do relatively well at most tasks that language teachers set for them—the same tasks that non-G people find most mysterious and therefore most difficult. These tasks include the memorizing of verb paradigms and the like. They also include becoming accustomed to the fact that in one language (English) "I have _____ " is literally "there is to me," in another "I am with_____ ," and in a third "there is my_____ ." This part of their success

comes from the fact that they perceive directly the abstractions with which they must work in order to perform these tasks.

3. Group G people also do relatively well at understanding grammatical explanations; because they understand them, they also do relatively well at remembering them; and by remembering they make more effective use of them. This again helps these people to be relatively successful in language courses. But these two kinds of success are different from each other: the first (point 2, above) is like the ability of a person with mechanical aptitude to know instinctively how the parts of a disassembled bicycle must fit together; the second is the ability to make sense out of the printed instructions.

4. Group G's ordinary classmates (Group O) notice both kinds of success, but without distinguishing between them. They see Group G doing well, and they hear Group G talking about rules. They conclude that the former follows as a result of the latter, but this conclusion is valid only in a limited sense. They do not see that to a large extent both kinds of success grow out of the same basic ability to deal with a particular type of data. It is as though I, with some but very modest musical ability, were to conclude that if I were to read the same books on musical theory that professional musicians read, my own performance would improve greatly. That conclusion might not be entirely false, but it could be bad for me if it aroused false hopes or led me to misdirect my efforts to play better. We are dealing here with something akin to gnosticism, an early Christian heresy which held that salvation was to be gained through a certain body of secret mysterious knowledge.

The first need for grammatical explanations was a straightforward and relatively unemotional need. This second need, by contrast, can be highly charged with feelings, both positive and negative. It is for this reason that I have brought this topic in after discussions of both counseling-learning and Suggestopedia. Here is a scenario that plays itself out all too often:

a. A student in Group O has difficulty with something.

b. He concludes that the solution to his difficulty is greater knowledge.

c. He assumes that the best way to knowledge is to get someone to give him an explanation.

d. Someone gives him an explanation.

e. He understands the explanation to some extent, at least for the moment.

f. He feels (i) grateful to the person who provided the explanation, (ii) confirmed in his assumption (c, above), and (iii) responsible for holding onto the explanation and using it to improve his performance.

g. When performance time comes, he still makes mistakes, either because he has forgotten the explanation, or because he never had understood it fully, or because the explanation itself had been less than adequate. (Many errors in language use are in matters which are simply too complex or too subtle for ordinary explanations.)

h. The disappointing performance leads to (i) feelings of resentment toward the teacher or the book that provided the explanation, or (ii) feelings of guilt and/or personal inadequacy, or (iii) demand for additional review of the explanations or others like them. Steps d through h of this scenario can repeat themselves indefinitely. Too often, each repetition intensifies the negative feelings.

I have written the scenario from the point of view of an ordinary student (Group O). The students in Group G generally make the same assumptions as Group O concerning what happens and what needs to happen and why. Since they succeed, however, they are spared the negative feelings (h in the scenario). This reinforces their own belief, and the belief of their Group O classmates, about the scenario and the assumptions which lie behind it. As for the teacher, she is almost certainly an alumna of Group G. She understands the grammar, but she does not understand the fallacy which lies behind the scenario. If she has a personal need to "shine," or if she has a personal need to feel that she is responding to needs that the students express, or if she has a need to "give" the students information that she will later be able to grade them on in tests—*if, that is, she has her eye on anything except the students* and how her words are affecting them as she speaks—then she is likely to launch into an inappropriate kind of explanation, or an excessive amount of it. In this way, she uses her spotlight to blind the students, as we said above, or to burden them, rather than to help them.

(The gathering, studying, forgetting, and reviewing of vocabulary lists may follow a similar scenario, except that the absence of "rules" removes some of the tendency to depend on explanations.)

From the point of view of counseling-learning, the grammatical system of a language is like a picture or a series of pictures. To the teacher who knows and loves the grammar of her language, it is a wonderful, fascinating, and inexhaustible museum. The students are visitors to the museum and she is its curator. She takes a visitor by the elbow and leads him to one of the paintings on the wall. As he gazes at it and attempts to make sense of its unfamiliar style, she points out an important feature of it. Then she steers him across the room to another, somewhat different painting. There, she points out a related feature in the second painting and asks the visitor whether he sees what she has pointed out to him. Either out of politeness, or because he does see it at least halfway, he says, "Yes, of course!" The tour continues in this way, with the visitor half-comprehending each point as it is made, perhaps making careful entries into his notebook on "Art Appreciation," and ending the tour full of gratitude to the curator and admiration for her erudition. In the terminology of counseling-learning the curator has been attempting to "pull the visitor into her world." Unless the visitor has unusual ability or previous training in looking at paintings, however, he is likely to feel bewilderment, discouragement, and intellectual fatigue along with his gratitude and admiration.

In teaching English, for example, the teacher may start out to explain the tense of the verb in the sentence:

I'm going to do it tomorrow.

This could lead to the morass of trying to explain just when to use each of two similar tenses:

I'm going to do it tomorrow.
I will do it tomorrow.

and from there to the difference between *shall* and *will.* Other wilderness paths may beckon:

I'm going to do it tomorrow.	or:	I'm going to do it tomorrow.
I'm willing to do it tomorrow.		I'm to do it tomorrow.

Even if the teacher sticks to one point—or if the curator explains only one painting—it may not be one that the student/visitor was ready for. The teacher/curator has still pulled the guest into her own world.

From the new learner's point of view, the grammar of the new language is not like a museum at all. It is an alien and perplexing object which has been set before him in the midst of his own world—more like a jigsaw puzzle than it is like a meaningful collection of paintings. Counseling-learning would urge the teacher to try to enter into this world of the student's, and to look over his shoulder, and to see which gap he is trying to fill at the moment. Then the teacher, who knows what the completed puzzle will have to look like, may pick out that one piece. She will not set it into the puzzle herself, but will leave that work (and that pleasure) to the student. Or, instead of pointing out the missing piece, she may only provide the smallest hint that will help the student to locate it for himself. Exactly what she does will depend on her sensitive awareness of the student's world and where he is in it.

The place where Suggestopedia illuminates the explaining of grammar (and where I believe it can further illuminate counseling-learning in general) is in its careful attention to the unspoken, unrecognized, and therefore powerful messages that ride along with the words of an explanation. Some of them that I have "heard" from time to time (and I suppose that, as a teacher, I have also transmitted the same messages) are:

"My museum is so rich and subtle that you will never be able to see and appreciate everything in it." (The full grammatical structure of any normal language is this complex—so complex, in fact, that none has ever been completely described even by scholars. The trouble with this unspoken message is that it emphasizes the hopelessness of getting the whole, rather than the easiness of getting any one part. I think of the solicitous visitor in the hospital, who sympathetically exclaims to a patient, "Oh, you poor dear! You look terrible! You look just like Uncle Henry did just before he passed away!")

"This particular point is very hard!" (Any *one* point of grammar is easy. What pass for "difficult" points are actually clusters of related points which the teacher, operating in her own world and not in the world of the student, has never bothered to pick apart from one another. For example, "formation of the plural of English nouns" consists of a number of relationships: *key-keys, dot-dots, face-faces, house-houses, ox-oxen, woman-women,* and so on. A wise colleague of mine used to tell his students that French has 70-some classes of regular verbs—and no irregular ones! To dismiss his statement as mere playing with terminology would be to overlook the difference between his unspoken message and the message that most of us send out when we are lecturing our students on such matters.)

"Don't ask questions. I want to move ahead with the rest of my explanation." (The words that often accompany this unspoken message are "Okay?" or "Right?" or "Do you have any questions?" But something about the speaker's nonverbal or supraverbal communication says, "I'm on a fixed track, and I'm moving. If you actually ask any questions now, you may derail me. One or both of us may be slightly bruised as a result.")

"Now that I've explained this to you, remember it!" (This is a "laying on of expectations." A student who continues to make errors in the matter that has been explained is thus invited to feel either guilty or inadequate. Some manage to feel both ways at the same time!)

"See how much I know, and how expertly I have set it out for you!" (The implication is: "You could never have done this for yourself. In understanding things like this, you depend on me.")

I suppose that most teachers would agree that all of the above "messages," as I have stated them, are undesirable. Many of us, however—students as well as teachers—assume that they are unavoidable. As I try to transmit these messages less and less, I find certain tricks useful:

Find out first from the students what they already know about the point. This is quite different from asking them what their questions are, and then setting out to answer those questions. In the former, the students show us the pieces of the puzzle that they already have before them. We can then see exactly where the empty space is.

This is also different from starting out with examples taken from material to which the students have already been exposed. They may even have memorized parts of the material, but that does not guarantee that they have it alive in their minds at the time we begin our explanation.

Paraphrase many of the questions before answering them. This "counseling response" is useful in three ways: The teacher's tone of voice can imply that the question was not a stupid one, and that the mental activity which produced it is welcome. It makes the teacher less likely to answer some question which is a little different from the one that the student had in mind. It increases the likelihood that the other students will know clearly what question it is that is being answered.

Say as little as possible. Students remember what they have phrased for themselves, no matter how clumsily, better than they remember our most elegant summaries. I try to say just enough so that the "spark" can jump across the gap. Saying just enough without saying too much is a skill at which nobody can be successful all of the time. This is another example of constantly "learning the students" even while one is helping them to learn the language.

Hold each answer by the teacher to no more than 5 or 10 seconds as measured by a clock. Each time a student does something with an answer, or asks a further question, the clock starts again. This is just one more device to keep me from dragging visitors through more of my museum than they were ready for.

No matter what the length of the explanation, omit all information that is not demanded by the student's question. For example, in giving the past tense of the English verb *shine* in a sentence about shoes, I would simply say "shined." I would restrain myself from loading onto the students the additional fact that we say, "The sun *shone* all day," not "shined," but that we do not say, "I shone my shoes." This fact is quite interesting to me, and it might even be interesting to some of my students. If my purpose is to entertain or amuse or impress my students, rather than to provide the missing piece that the student needs, I may even give them this extra information. But if I mix purposes carelessly, I confuse and discourage my student. So as a teacher I need to see my purposes for what they are. I also need to discipline myself in choosing among them.

If something needs to be written on the board, get a student to do it on behalf of the class. Once we get the chalk into our own hands, it is all too easy for us to leave most of the students behind, even if we do toss a few questions like "Okay?" and "Right?" over our shoulder as we fill the board with examples. Then we are dragging the students through our own museum, rather than helping them to fill holes in their puzzle.

Invite the students to try out their knowledge, to see whether it works as they hope it will. This calls for the students to make up their own examples. It is quite different, however, from saying, "Now everybody make a sentence using this tense, or this construction." In the former, emphasis is on activity by the student, directed at a goal which has importance for him. In the latter, it is on producing a linguistic artifact with minimal depth of meaning: another instance of "Now try to do this so I can tell you whether you did it right." In the former, the teacher is a source of needed information; in the latter, she is a judge.

Leave time and opportunity for students to answer one another's questions. Often this means nothing more than just hesitating a second or two before giving one's own response to a question. It does not mean staring expectantly at the students and saying, "Figure it out for yourselves!" The latter asks the students to act like linguists doing field work. It may be very appropriate at some times in some classes, but it is not the kind of exploration that I have been describing here.

Appear interested, but nonchalant. This is the students' quest for information, and not my quest for success in explaining.

By following these rules of thumb, I hope to convey unspoken messages that are different from the ones that I listed earlier. Some of the conclusions that I want the student to draw for himself out of this kind of "explanation" are:

"My mind is O.K. at handling this kind of thing!"
"This new thing turns out to be a special case of what I already knew!"
"My classmates and I can depend on one another for much of what we need in sorting these matters out."

Several months ago, a colleague came to talk with me about a class she was teaching. The class consisted of four adults, nonbeginners, all of whom spoke the same native language. None was a highly experienced student of foreign languages, and their "aptitude" for this particular type of academic undertaking was not high. Their progress in the course had been slow, and seemed to be slowing down even more as the days went by.

What my colleague and I came up with was a set of materials which we described as "long, narrow dialogues." As of this writing, those materials have been used for 80 class hours. So far, the results have been all that we could have hoped for: fluency and accuracy have increased sharply, and so have morale and creativity. I will describe these materials briefly in the next few paragraphs, but in so doing I do not mean that I think I have found the (or a, or another) final solution to my own teaching problems or anyone else's. My purpose in describing it is only to illustrate how the three "ways" [the silent way, counseling-learning, and Suggestopedia] may intersect in, or may interpret, a method that does not completely belong to any of them.

We call the dialogues "long" because each one contains at least 75 sentences. Moreover, each dialogue leads into the next, so that they form a connected series of episodes. We call them "narrow" because few sentences have more than five words and most have fewer. The dialogues contain one role for each student, with the teacher taking bit parts such as waiter or taxi driver. Each student stays in his/her own role, rather than exchanging roles as is done in most courses that use dialogues. All of the characters in the dialogue are natives of the target culture, and all are happy, well-adjusted, and successful. Their occupations were chosen to be relevant to the student's own, though not identical with them. The events find the characters resolving uncertainties, making choices, and overcoming difficulties, but the choices are pleasant ones, and the difficulties are both minor and short-lived. The native-language translation is readily at hand in a parallel column. In all these respects, the "long, narrow dialogues" are patterned after Suggestopedia, and particularly after the sample dialogue in Saféris' book.

The techniques which my colleague is using with these materials are partially like those which have been described for Suggestopedia, but only partially. As in Suggestopedia, the students start out with activities which allow them to listen and understand without the need to produce anything at first. They are then asked to read through the dialogue once before retiring, and once on arising. As in Suggestopedia also, any drill-like activity is made into games, or at least is carried out in a manner that is gamelike. The style of dealing with mistakes is nonevaluative. And like Suggestopedic lessons, these lessons end with the students putting together their own skits.

But these lessons are quite clearly not Suggestopedia. Most conspicuously, there is no music, no "concert session," no drama or contrasting intonations in the teacher's reading of the dialogues. And, significantly, the lessons take about 20 hours apiece, much longer than the 6 hours in which Suggestopedia covers a comparable amount of material. We might have tried to use the dramatic and musical components, but neither of us had had that kind of training. We also lack the equipment for playing the music.

As I have watched some of these classes, and particularly as I have talked with the students on several occasions, certain points have stood out very clearly:

1. The students are happy. This method provides an extraordinarily high degree of security for the student, from at least three sources: (a) The fictitious character that a student has assumed, and not the student himself, is felt to be responsible for any errors. (b) The teacher's nonevaluative style minimizes the student's need to defend himself by avoiding things that he is not sure of. (c) The materials themselves prevent the anxiety that can arise from having to originate one's own conversations (as in community language learning) or from feeling that what one is studying is ephermeal, nebulous, and possibly unsuited for actual use in the target culture. On the positive side, these materials contribute to security by being easy and by consisting of happy adventures involving people who have no serious anxieties or internal conflicts. The student is thus able to leave aside many of his own anxieties about language study, about living in the target culture, etc. (I suspect that this format would be an excellent one for doing cross-cultural training, since the students are open and receptive, and the presentation is (quasi-) experiential.)

2. The continuity and the length of the dialogues effectively provide the student with a fictitious world which is large enough and vivid enough so that he can improvise within it. This is the "self-investment" which counseling-learning and other research (Stevick 1976) have seen to be so important for whole-person learning. The "self" that is "invested" here is a fictitious one, to be sure, but the investing is still *done* by the *real* self—the same self that has to do the learning. Meantime, the irrelevant conflicts and anxieties that the student brought with him are left with no *persona* through which to speak. They therefore are unable to arouse each other, to call each other forth, to build upon each other.

3. As in most methods, there is considerable reiteration and reworking of the new material. As in community language learning, this new material in some sense represents "self-investment" of the students with whom I have talked. But because the material was made up ahead of time, the teacher is not in the position of having to take fresh, unpredictable conversations and shape them on the spot into a sufficient quantity of games, drills, or whatever. She must still respond moment by moment to what she sees the students are ready for, of course. But by working from existing materials, she can prepare more fully. This contributes to her own feelings of stability and security. This stability *and* the teacher's feelings become unspoken messages which the student receives, and so they contribute in turn to the security of the student—to his confidence in the teacher and in himself.

4. These students have shown a clear increase in their ability to handle the phonological and grammatical differentiations which they need for correct production of the target language. Of particular interest was a technique for introducing some verb forms which past students have generally found to be

more or less mystifying or esoteric or threatening. The teacher simply talked with the students about material in the dialogues from earlier lessons, except that she worked many examples of the new verb form into what she said. This proved to be painless and highly effective. It appears that the context, though fictitious, had come to life, and that it was rich enough to allow these new grammatical seeds to take root in it.

This "long, narrow dialogue method" appears, then, to have been a successful way of meeting the difficulties that had been troubling my colleague's class. Let me repeat what I said above, however: I do not think that in this little fragment of method I have found the (or a, or another) final solution to my own teaching needs or anyone else's. Nevertheless, it does appear to have taken account of the many sources of anxiety and alienation about which I have written earlier and to have provided security against them; and to have drawn the students out of their shells and into self-asserting activity; and to have reused the material systematically, allowing the students' minds to work on it in enough ways so that they could hold onto it; and to have produced a growing degree of accuracy alongside a gratifying increase in fluency. It seems to have followed the formula and achieved the goals (SARD) or community language learning but without the features of the latter method which cause such strong anxiety in some students.

I have gone on at length about "mim-mem" drills and the giving of grammatical explanations, both of which lie outside of Suggestopedia proper. Few of us will be able to be trained for two months by Lozanov. If we try to "do Suggestopedia" without such training, we are doing a disservice to our students, to ourselves, and to the reputation of the method. Yet this does not mean that we must throw up our hands in despair: though we cannot "do Suggestopedia" we can at least try, as with the "long, narrow dialogues," to see "Suggesto-pedically" the methods that we do use. This may, in the long run, prove to be Lozanov's greatest gift to the worldwide profession of language teaching.

DISCUSSION QUESTIONS

1. Traditionally researchers dealing with anxiety and other forms of tension have tended to distinguish between kinds which are associated with a particular person (e.g., "trait anxiety") and kinds which are associated rather with certain performances (e.g., "task anxiety"). While the former is usually a negative factor in acquiring skills or in performances in general, the latter is not always negative in its effects. For example, it is not unknown for an athlete, musician, or speaker to comment that they do better when under pressure. Discuss these facts in relation to what Stevick says about "tension."

2.   What is meant by the term "double-planeness"? How does this relate to the concept of the "surrogate self" in Lozanov's approach?

3.   Whereas in the Rassias madness and other types of dramatic encounters the "boundary between fact and fiction," as Stevick calls it, remains clear, in Suggestopedia it is deliberately "blurred." Why this contrast? Stevick asserts, "this 'fictitious reality' brings with it no embarrassments, no conflicts, no anxieties." What is a "fictitious reality"? Is it true that it has "no conflicts," etc.? Consider the conflict issue (Chapter 1) in light of John Dewey's claim that all reflective thought is occasioned by trouble.

4.   Discuss the role of "authority" as presented in Stevick's interpretation of Lozanov. Is there any way to escape the "authority" figure? Would it be desirable in any case to do so?

5.   Stevick comments on a certain "suggestopedic" quality of mimicry and memorization drills. Discuss his reflections and your own reactions to such drills based on personal experience you may have had. Also, see Graham (Chapter 21) and Richard-Amato (Chapter 32).

Chapter 10

Counseling-Learning

Charles Curran

EDITORS' INTRODUCTION

Counseling-learning is a nondirective therapeutic approach designed to ease the learner into independence and confidence in the target language(s). Curran claims that the nonthreatening counseling relationship provides the optimal environment for learning. He borrows some of his terminology and at least one pithy aphorism from "theological" writings. For instance, among Curran's terms are "incarnation," "redemption," "rebirth," and "resurrection." More than once he repeats the statement of John the Baptist in reference to the Messiah, "He must increase, but I must decrease," as applicable to the proper relationship between counselor and client (i.e., teacher and student). He explains that the student passes through a series of cathartic phases from not knowing the language to a point of "value," "self-worth," and "wholeness" (i.e., knowing the language). Curran sees his approach as contrasting with the "exaggeratedly intellectualized" and overly "competitive" models of "Cartesian intellectualism." The teacher in Curran's view begins as an "expert knower," a kind of nonincarnate, abstract deity who imparts knowledge to the "learner." The learner starts out as a creature whose incarnated existence is a poignant form of suffering which requires "redemption." This is achieved, even to the point of "resurrection," through the knower's "incarnation" (i.e., becoming vulnerable to the community of learners, and possibly becoming one of them) and the progressive "redemption" of the "learner," who gradually becomes a knower. Hence the teacher must say, "He must increase, and I must decrease." Although Curran insists that his theological terminology is merely a manner of speaking, one of us (Oller) feels that this insistence merely conceals Curran's own godlike role in the whole discussion. Moreover, Oller is moved to ask if it is not expecting a bit much of French, Navajo, Chinese, or what-have-you, to suppose that its acquisition is a solid foundation upon which to build a sense of self-worth. Still, we agree that Curran's approach does afford a basis for interaction and communication, and that there is persuasive evidence that it may result in substantial language acquisition.

PART 1: THE MODEL

Basic to the relationship of community language learning and counseling-learning is the nature of the educative process itself. The educational process extends along a continuum from the impersonal to the highly personal. In this process, one searches for and so seeks to find adequate life meanings. He then

146

tries to make them operationally sound personal values. This discussion will consider some learning experiences from this point of view of personal involvement.

Any discussion of the educative process has really to start with the relation of conflict, hostility, anger, and anxiety to learning. This has been overlooked in many of our present educational methods because we are apparently still victimized to a considerable degree by concepts that are both exaggeratedly intellectual and competitive. The "good" student is presumed to be able to learn best in an intellectualized and individual way, with little or no consideration given to his emotional somatic involvement or his need for a community learning experience shared with other students.

Learning Model

During the last 15 years, we have been doing research in the learning of foreign languages through a counseling-therapy type of relationship.[1] The research has made increasingly clear the interweaving of the whole personality process in learning. We wish here to draw on some of these learning experiences to illustrate and clarify this, and at the same time to show how any kind of teaching or guidance encounters many of the same personality subtleties.

The learning relationship—in this case, foreign language learning—can, in fact, be viewed as a model of the process by which many other groups and individuals learn. While this discussion is directly related to the learning of foreign languages in a counseling-psychotherapeutic way, it has implications beyond this in that it can readily be adapted to the learning of other subjects, especially those that become charged with fear and anxiety.

---

1. This research has been supported since 1959 by a yearly grant from the Society for Human Relations Research. It has been carried on with groups at Loyola University, Mendel High School, Chicago, and Woodstock Central High School, Woodstock, Illinois.

Demonstrations and theoretical discussions have been presented at a variety of meetings, among them The Kansas State Language Teachers' Association, April 1960; The Spanish Language Teachers' Association, February 1963, Chicago Teachers' College; The Midwest Psychological Association, May 1963; and two National Defense Education Act Teacher Training Institutes at Rosary College, June 1962, and Mundelein College, July 1963; at a Fordham University Forum, May 1965, at Barry College, February 1968, and at the University of Windsor from June 1968 to the present.

Two Community Language Learning Institutes have been conducted by Charles A. Curran and Associates, with the endorsement of H. Douglas Brown, Ph.D., Director of the English Language Institute of the University of Michigan, May 1975, and June 1976, at the University of Michigan.

The following are books and articles related to the specific application of counseling awarenesses and skills to the learning process: Curran (1972, 1961, 1968b, 1965a–e, 1966a–b, 1968a, 1970), Begin (1971), LaForge (1975), Stevick (1973, 1974), and Tranel (1968).

Broad Implications

But the implications also extend to the areas of personality adjustment and personal value commitment, to legal and moral codes, to religious values, and to all those situations where a person must adapt himself to the demands of others, no matter what his internal preferences may be. In such situations, he cannot be guided simply by what is comfortable and secure for him. Rather he must undergo even pain and anxiety, if necessary, in order to fit himself to the boundaries and rights of others.

The struggle to learn to speak a foreign language aptly demonstrates many of the issues in this kind of conflict. To speak German, for example, one must give up one's security and comfort in English sounds and adapt to the demands not simply of the German person but of the whole grammar-pronunciation structure of what is considered proper German. This kind of language encounter contains in embryo most of the psychological experiences that any severe social adaptation entails. We can study this process psychologically and at the same time measure the effectiveness of the group process by both the psychological changes in the persons themselves and the degree to which they have learned to speak one or more foreign languages with foreign natives.

This project reveals, in a psychological research spotlight, some of the knottiest questions that arise in studying extremes like social rebels or isolated individuals who resist socialization. At the same time, we can observe more ordinary conflicts which act as barriers to personal communication, like those, for example, between husband and wife, or similar blockings in relating to others.

Resistance to Limits

We have, too, in the resistances to grammar and pronunciation, reactions that are similar to resistances to ethical, legal, and religious standards of conduct. Many times, deep personal reasons come forward—going back often to early childhood—which reveal the person's resistance is not limited to the language experience but extends to a wide area of what he sees as the outside imposition of any authority. Yet, paradoxically, he may see, too, that if he wishes to learn a foreign language, be an employee, a law-abiding citizen, etc., he must take himself in hand and submit to these demands. They do not come, as he may at first *feel*, from another person's domination of him and superiority over him (the language native in the group to whom he may at first direct his resistance) but from the whole fabric of a social structure of which, by his very presence in the class, he desires to become a part, and according to whose norms he wishes finally to change himself and learn to operate effectively.

Meaning Becoming Value

Stated another way, one could say that the absorbing of meanings so that they become values resembles and imitates the process by which I first approach and ultimately integrate and speak what was originally a foreign language. In this sense, the popular expression, "He speaks my language," or "I don't speak his language," catches something of the broader self-involving aspects of any value-learning. It comes down finally to learning to communicate comfortably and securely with oneself and others in this new value system.

As we will see, too, the learning process itself initiated here has much in it that is similar to the psychological incarnate-redemptive process by which a person in counseling and psychotherapy acquired a renewed sense of worth and value of his total self. As for the remote and almost godlike figure of the native language experts, as first viewed by the learners, we see them gradually come to share, in the learners' eyes, the common human condition. In the shared humanity of weakness and confusion, as they learn a common unknown foreign language together, there is renewed motivation for the student to identify with the expert in his language. By such deep feelings of personal belonging, the learner is then positively urged to grow more and more in this new and different manner of self-reference and communication. He thus begins to grow a new self in the foreign language, a self that sometimes, in some ways, he may prefer to his native-language self.

Constructive-Destructive

The complicated and subtle part conflict, hostility, anger, and anxiety play in learning recurred repeatedly in almost all aspects of this foreign language learning research. To a certain point, we can call these *positive* factors, for they engage one in the learning experience; they are forms of commitment and involvement. Beyond that point, however, they seem to become destructive forces; they block the student, make him want to escape the whole experience, or arouse him to a defensive kind of learning. Such a defensive learner often tends to disregard what he has learned as soon as it has served its defensive purpose, apparently because the whole experience has been so painful. Many students, for example, spoke of the deep hostility they had toward foreign languages as a result of previous classroom experiences. In their negative anxiety and conflict, most had defended themselves against this threatening situation by getting a passing grade—some even a high one. But afterward it was difficult and painful for them even to try to speak this particular language in our research group.

Learning Project

For our research project on the learning of foreign languages, at the college and graduate level, we chose four languages: French, German, Spanish, and Italian.

We thought that accepting volunteers would produce graduate students and college students, and later, groups of high school students and any interested adults, with various levels of knowledge of some of the languages, but few with a knowledge of all four. This way each one could begin fresh in at least one language, with neither advantages over others nor previous negative experiences to impede them.

But we also used this approach with individual high school language classes—in Latin and Spanish. Our project also included very small children (2 to 3 years), and elderly people in a home for the retired. Groups of "head-start" and slow learners were also taught English, as part of this research project.[2]

Initial Anxiety Conflict

To illustrate the anxiety-hostility-conflict involvement in learning, let us reconstruct an experience which we conducted a number of times in different languages. This kind of experience was not the focus of our research, but it may help clarify some initial conflicts that seem to be present at the beginning of a foreign language learning encounter. The following was in French but could be paralleled in other languages.

To begin with, we chose four people from our group who, as we knew from their scholastic records, had only a year or so of high school or college French. We put them in a room and asked them to speak as much French as they could, using English for words they did not know in French. No one of the four people knew how much French the other three knew.

The first reaction of the four was far from being simply an intellectual one. The four people confronting each other anxiously wondered how much the others knew. They experienced needs for both reassurance and group equilibrium. Each hoped that the others knew no more French than he, and so would be on his same level. In primitive and probably regressive defense of himself, each person was already prepared to resist anyone who had learned more than he. It was therefore necessary for him to begin to explore the situation causing his anxiety with something like: "je ... uh ... uh ... never really had much français." He was admitting his ignorance, defending his ego, and to some degree pleading with the others not to be any better in French than he. Another student, obviously relieved to find that there was at least one other person identified with him, would say something like: "Oh, I'm glad there is somebody here who doesn't know any French either." Two of the people were already pleased with their ignorance, and finding a degree of comfort in it, were now

2. The following people were involved as leaders or learning counselors: Latin in high school, Daniel D. Tranel; Spanish in high school, Rosina Mena Gallagher; English with slow learners, Jenny Rardin; French (in Quebec) with American college students, Yves Begin; French with the aged, Roland Janisse; English, Spanish, and French with small children, Rosina Mena Gallagher and Jenny Rardin.

fearful of the other two, lest they knew more. Soon the third person came forward and joined the group of the ignorant. Finally, when it became evident that the last person also knew no more than the others, the group settled to a security equilibrium—no one's knowledge threatening anyone.

If, however, we chose one person who knew more, he seldom felt really secure in his superior knowledge. Rather he usually tried to minimize his knowledge, and even apologize for it, since he recognized his threat to the group's security and his own isolated position in regard to the other three.

Urge to Teach

To add to the experience, in a few instances we had a native person, in one case a French girl who had been in this country only 6 months, sit outside the door and listen to these four people struggling painfully with her language. It is not hard to envisage her feelings as she sits there. During her 6-month stay in America, she had already been daily humiliated and submissive while people corrected her English. Her position in English was, in other words, much like that of a child. Now by contrast, her adult self was strongly involved. Afterward she said she was intensely identified with the four students and their obvious need of French. She wanted very much to help these Americans in return for the help she had received in English. She also wanted to be related in her French self with Americans. It would make her feel like the adult she really was, instead of the child she had been feeling. She wanted to help these people who, as she logically saw, needed her. She had, in other words, many of the qualifications and urges of an expert teacher.

Threat of Knowing

We then asked her to go into the room and sit at a slight distance from the group. The four people in the room had by this time become comfortable and at ease in their shared ignorance, and were having rather a good time exchanging whatever words they knew and using English for what they did not know. They knew this girl by sight, knew that she was French.

In a few minutes they became silent. Like a sudden draft of cold air, her entrance had frozen them. The French student was thus completely frustrated in the greatest potential fulfillment she had had so far in America. She, in turn, soon found herself disturbed, hostile, and embarrassed. In place of needing her, she realized that the people were not accepting her, had asked her no questions, did not seem to want her help. Soon after they stopped talking, she felt they were throwing angry glances in her direction. Perhaps in reality, the glances were more anxious than angry, but anxious glances were often interpreted as angry ones by the person to whom they were directed. Sometimes they were anxious and aggressive at the same time.

If one continued this process, rather than ending it here, one solution the group commonly arrived at was to become exaggeratedly dependent on the French expert, asking her reassurance and help with every word and phrase, even those they knew and may have used before. This apparently was a passively aggressive way of handling their resistance and resentment. In such a resolution, the expert gains no real relationship to the group except that of an adult to helpless children.

This reconstructed experience, while simple, serves to show some of the negative dynamics created against an expert by people who, having become secure in their comfort state, seem defensively to band together against the "enemy" who knows too much. They are resentful toward the person who tilts their security equilibrium.

Common Learning Conflict

We see here an example of the psychological conflict that is often if not always initially involved between the person who is informed, who can and is eager to give his knowledge, and the people who are blocked from accepting that help by hostility arising from their anxiety and ignorance. This is clearly a counseling therapeutic situation as well as a learning one. Yet this kind of conflict seems intrinsic to at least the first stages of learning. What often goes on in a classroom, for example, is the end effect of the attempts of both groups—the teacher and those who are to be taught—to resolve this kind of complicated psychological involvement with one another. They seldom resolve it in a counseling way, but rather almost by chance, depending on the immediate circumstances. For some students this may have serious negative aftereffects.

Inverse Ratio Paradox

By way of contrast, we found it interesting to see what happened when we chose a different group of four, all of whom knew a good deal of French, although, when the group first came together, no group member knew how much the others knew. Again, anxiety was evident at the beginning. The first speaker usually said something like: "Well, I have had some French, but . . ." Each one tended to play down his ability until it became clear that they all spoke fairly fluently. If we brought the native French person into the room after the four students had assured themselves of their security, the threat was minimal. They were usually able to make use of the French expert's help when needed, with anxiety but without serious conflict. There is, then, apparently an inverse ratio here: the greater the need, the greater the resistance to expert help; the less the need, the more willingness to accept such help. Apparently, this is, in another guise, the age-old truism—"to him who has, will be given," and the issue of "saving the saved."

Affect-Cognition Model

This brings us then to a consideration of some more complicated arrangements and procedures. As we have said, the main aim of our research was to establish a learning experience through a relationship which imitated counseling therapy and which was as deeply involving of the whole person of each student. We wanted some kind of *total experience*, not simply an "intellectual" one.

In our attempt to accomplish this, we took as our model *the affect-cognitive intercommunication* that seems to constitute a basic aspect of the counseling relationship.[3] One of the functions of the counseling response is to relate affect, emotional, instinctive, or somatic, to cognition. Understanding the language of affect, or "feelings," the counselor responds in the language of cognition. From our point of view, this is one of the chief dynamics occurring in the counseling therapy process. The person has affects for which he cannot supply adequate cognition, but which he tries to communicate in words to the counselor. He gets back from the counselor, in a sensitive and understanding relationship, a cognition of his affect that he can hear, absorb, and then compare with his affect. He often expresses successful cognition with such phrases as, "I am beginning to see." Before, he had only confusion and conflict as he tried to recognize his own feelings. It was apparently his attempt to put these confused and conflicting feelings into words, and the counselor's understanding and return communication, that slowly gave him this increase in cognition about himself.

We can say then that the counselor tries to speak the language of cognition, but also understands the language of affect, and that the client tends to speak the language of affect, but hears back, and therefore is able to absorb, compare, and understand the counselor's language of cognition. In this way, he slowly learns to speak a more cognitive language to himself. As a result, in place of confused feelings, he begins to "understand himself better," as he will often say. Seen in this way, we have a sort of two-language communication taking place.

Language-Counselor Group Communication

This awareness of a two-language model in the counseling-therapeutic process led us to choose the learning of foreign languages as the area for our attempt to interrelate counseling and learning in a unified experience. We adapted this conception to foreign language learning in the following manner. As has been said, we chose four languages: French, German, Spanish, and Italian. In this way, if a person was well trained in one language—French, for example—he could, when he desired, attempt to speak German, Spanish, or Italian. It rarely happened that a person was secure in all four languages; hence people could switch around and so experience various levels of linguistic difficulty, anxiety, and conflict in communication, in proportion to their competence.

---

3. For a more complete discussion of this affect-cognitive intercommunication model, see Curran (1976a).

To help him communicate in the foreign language, each person had a language counselor who was usually a native speaker of that language. This person came to be considered as a kind of "linguistic parent-substitute," or a language "other-self." Sometimes he was thought of as a sort of linguistic "iron lung."

The four, five, or six people sitting in a circle did not communicate with one another directly at first, but through these "other language selves." If, for example, the first person to speak wanted to say to the group in French: "It is a beautiful day today," and he knew little or no French, he turned to the French person slightly behind him, and said this in English. The others in the group overheard the English and therefore knew what the person wanted to say in French. This was called the English "overhear." We notice this was not a direct communication but more as though one might eavesdrop or monitor an exchange between counselor and client.

The French person then gave back, in the manner of a counselor's response, the French words: "C'est un beau jour aujourd'hui." The student turned to the group and repeated the French words as they were given to him. This was his first real communication to the group. He was helped by his French counselor to speak each word correctly. This same procedure was followed in the other three languages.

Speaking the Foreign Language

This process resembled the way a swimmer turns his head to breathe in the air, then turns back to the water to breathe out. It enabled the person, from the very beginning, to speak to the group in a foreign language, with the expert's help. The language counselor expert—like a psychological counselor—was warm, secure, and reassuring. The language counselor's tone and manner strived to convey the same deep understanding of the client's anxious, insecure state as he might experience in a good counseling relationship.

Handicapped Regression

This language counseling arrangement allowed us to see a number of psychological processes begin to operate. Since the foreign language counselor was a kind of parent figure, an infantile emotional regression relationship soon emerged between him or her and the client. The group in turn became both children and handicapped people. All had parent figures, and like handicapped adults, all were breathing through linguistic iron lungs as they communicated and related to one another.

In a comparatively short time the group became adapted to this handicapped way of speaking in four languages. Much like paraplegics learning to play basketball, they gradually became more natural and efficient. They soon could carry on what became increasingly an ordinary conversation, except for the much more intensive psychosomatic engagement that such a "handicapped" conversation involved.

Each one could advance independently in speaking a language according to his ability, getting help only when he needed it or made mistakes. Later, as he advanced, more minute corrections were made and special idiomatic expressions were supplied by the expert language counselors. This progress was divided into five stages, each marking a difference in his relationship to the counselor and the group as he grew more secure and independent in one or more languages.

Stages of Growth

The following outlined plan was given to each one:

Stage I

The client is completely dependent on the language counselor.
1. First, he expresses *only* to the counselor and *in English,* what he wishes to say to the group. Each group member overhears this English exchange, but is not involved in it.
2. The counselor then reflects these ideas back to the client *in the foreign language* in a warm, accepting tone, in simple language especially of cognates, in phrases of five or six words.
3. The client turns to the group and presents his ideas *in the foreign language.* He has the counselor's aid if he mispronounces or hesitates on a word or phrase.

This is the client's *maximum security stage.*

Stage II

1. Same as above.
2. The client turns and begins to speak the *foreign language* directly to the group.
3. The counselor aids only as the client hesitates or turns for help. These small independent steps are signs of positive confidence and hope.

Stage III

1. The client speaks directly to the group *in the foreign language.* This presumes that the group has now acquired the ability to understand his simple phrases.
2. Same as 3 above.
   This presumes the client's greater confidence, independence, and proportionate insight into the relationship of phrases, grammar, and ideas. Translation given only when a group member desires it.

Stage IV

1. The client is now speaking freely and complexly *in the foreign language.* Presumes group's understanding.
2. The counselor directly intervenes in grammatical error, mispronunciation, or where aid in complex expression is needed.
   The client is sufficiently secure to take correction.

Stage V

1. Same as IV.
2. Counselor intervenes not only to offer correction but to add idioms and more elegant constructions.
3. At this stage, the client can become counselor to group in stages I, II, and III.

ARRANGEMENT 1

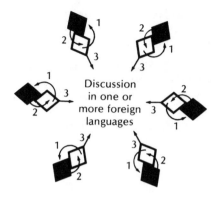

Possible foreign languages: German, French, Spanish, Italian

1 = idea in English
2 = idea in foreign language
3 = idea in foreign language to group

(White: Language clients, Black: Language counselors)

ARRANGEMENT 2

Counseling—foreign language research design of the different positions in language-counseling discussions.

As ease in conversation developed through this language-counseling arrangement, psychological complexities began to appear. Some were repeated in each successive group so that they seemed predictable. Intense relationships with the counselors emerged as well as jealousies and rivalries with other group members. Hostility to oneself and others was very strong in some. Gradually open anger was able to be expressed, especially as the members of the group grew to trust one another. There was evident regression in the group in proportion as one knew little or nothing about the language he was attempting to

ARRANGEMENT 3

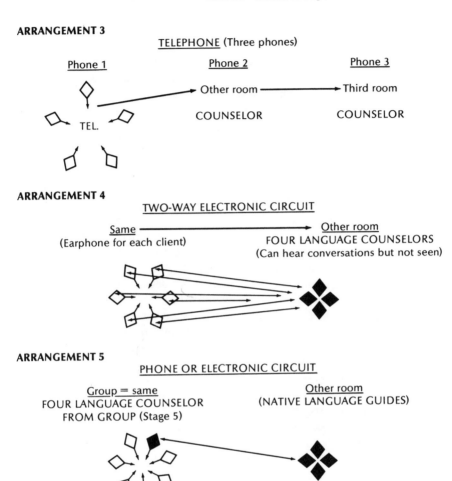

TELEPHONE (Three phones)

Phone 1   Phone 2   Phone 3

Other room ─────────────→ Third room

TEL.   COUNSELOR   COUNSELOR

ARRANGEMENT 4

TWO-WAY ELECTRONIC CIRCUIT

Same ───────────────────────→ Other room
(Earphone for each client)   FOUR LANGUAGE COUNSELORS
                                  (Can hear conversations but not seen)

ARRANGEMENT 5

PHONE OR ELECTRONIC CIRCUIT

Group = same   Other room
FOUR LANGUAGE COUNSELOR   (NATIVE LANGUAGE GUIDES)
FROM GROUP (Stage 5)

speak. Many expressed feelings, emotions, and fixed reactions similar to those they remembered from early childhood. "We are all children around a sandpile," was a commonly accepted concept for those in stages I and II.

At the other end of the scale, as people began to speak freely and independently in stages IV and V, intense resistances to the counselors sometimes emerged in a manner that appeared to be similar to that of an adolescent struggling to become an independent and self-responsible adult.

Dominant-Submissive Attitudes

In other ways, too, the relationship between the group and the counselors proved revealing. There were, among other things, implications about the hidden attitudes and needs of a person in an expert or teacher role and how this affects the group relationship. One aspect of this was the degree to which people who stayed only in their most capable languages, and so protected themselves by being superior, at the same time often felt alienated from many group members. This was especially true of the native experts.

Since people who were native expert language counselors in one language were much less expert in at least one other language, an interesting relationship usually developed between these people and the other group members. When they were expert language counselors, for a comparatively long time they were never considered part of the group by the other group members nor did they themselves really feel part of the group. This was true even though members could be deeply attached to them in their language-counselor identification.

Urges in both the group and the language expert seemed to combine to bring this about. The group, as we have seen, tended to be hostile to anyone who knew too much. This produced various reactions. One common reaction, as in controlled hostility, was to alienate the expert. One of the ways to accomplish this seemed to be to make him appear a kind of god, and so remove him from any human conditions, to put him in what we have called a "nonincarnate" state. Creatures can be seen as totally dependent on this "nonincarnate god." There is almost no communication except that of helpless, dependent people toward a god figure, who determines what is right, how things are to be done. Here we can go a step beyond the infant-parent-figure dependency to a mode of creature-creator dependency.

Alienation of Knower

This godlike position, however, while giving the native counselor great prestige, had the painful adverse effect of removing him from any sense of sharing or belonging to the group. He was simply the one who knew every word and every construction, and so seemed to have a kind of absolute, unquestioned power and supremacy.

One example will illustrate this reaction between such an individual and the group. A student in the group was an Italian who came to the United States at the age of fifteen and was now a graduate student. At the time he joined the group we were not insisting that people try any of the other languages besides the one they knew well. He was therefore in the god role in Italian and spoke fluent, correct English as well. He was also fairly competent in French. He was, however, hopelessly incompetent in German. It slowly came to him that he was almost completely alienated from the group. In other words, he was too perfect to be considered as having any share in their blundering anxiety and confusion. He felt excluded as if, he said, he did not "belong to the human race."

This is similar to the nonincarnate hostility and removal from themselves that people often express at the beginning of counseling. He was, of course, at the same time, very aware of his feeling of powerful superiority. He also felt a vengeful satisfaction at their inadequacy, which he enjoyed because of his earlier humiliations in high school when he had painfully to learn English.

In a counseling interview about this, he decided that at the next meeting of the group he would struggle to speak German for the first time. He saw that this decision meant giving up his superior position and showing himself to the group in a helpless human state. He carried out his resolution and for the first time he no longer felt alienated. He described experiencing a deep sense of his own weakness and of having his weakness understood. The group now accepted him, too. In place of his dominating power, he had gained a sense of worth through a sort of Sullivanian "consensual validation," apparently. One might describe this also as a kind of human redemption following upon the acceptance of incarnation. He felt he belonged at last, because he was now in reality an ignoramus like everyone else. He had become "engagé" in the human condition by submitting to the humiliation of his ignorance in German. In giving up his pseudo-divine power position, he had gained human community and belonging.

Will to Aid Communication

Another significant aspect was the manner in which the experts as language counselors had slowly to give up their "will to power" over their clients, and see them grow to be increasingly independent of them. One is reminded here of how the expert had to accept the ancient proposition: "He must increase, I must decrease," in regard to his client. One might suggest, too, that this resembles some of the issues between adolescents and parents, as the adolescent struggles to find his own unique and independent meaning as an adult. This began to be evident when the learner reached stage III in a particular language. Here he started to use words and phrases he had learned. With this came a surge of independence, a desire to be free of the counselor, in marked contrast to the warm, almost womblike dependency in stages I and II. Now the learners began to struggle painfully and sometimes angrily with themselves to "say it themselves." The counselor had to be very sensitive here to discern when he was really needed or when, on the contrary, persons wanted time to find, on their own, the required word or phrase.

In the third stage, as we said, the client, having gained greater confidence, independence, and proportionate insights into the relationship of phrases, grammar, and ideas, spoke immediately to the group in the foreign language, without any English communication of his ideas to the counselor. Only when he clearly needed help did he turn to the counselor with the English expression of what he wanted to say in the foreign language. Here the counselor with a surprising intuition sometimes already knew the word or phrase the client was struggling to use and could often supply it to him, without any English communication between them. The very intensity of the concentration of their communication together, and the deep relationship and security which both had, seemed to produce this joint understanding.

The following excerpt from one of the language counselors—a student from Germany—describes a subjective reaction to the client relationship at this stage:

I had to relax completely and to exclude my own will to produce something myself. I had to exclude any function of forming or formulating something within me, not try to *do* something but instead letting enter into me without any restriction, what the person says, and being completely open to everything he might say, foreseeing with calm, not hoping or wishing that or this word might come forward; not concentrated on what the person might say, i.e., on the contents of the speech, but on the person himself, completely accepting him and at the same time trying to understand what *he* wants to say, not *what* he wants to say.

Together with the other person (client), I concentrate on his process of trying to find this word or that expression joining into this process with sympathy and understanding. I do not allow myself to feel embarrassed about his hesitation, momentary silence, or stuttering, in order not to bring up any tension, which would make him self-conscious, but I sort of try to find the word myself, and as I do not know what word is wanted—I am just joining in the process of thinking with the other person. Thus, so to say, both of us are thinking in combined effort. It is important that there be in me no willing or wishing, but a relaxed state of almost passiveness, which is, however, creative as it provides additional creative force to the other person. I try to be relaxed, without any personal anxiety that he do well. I would not be disturbed in the least, if there would come forward a completely wrong sentence or word or bad pronunciation, since I do not wish to hear something particular that I have in mind myself. Thus, this situation differs widely from teaching. I am almost indifferent to what is said, or better, to how the other person puts it, as there is a deeper level of communication, which need not cling so much to words, which are but the outward appearance of what is communicated. I feel like I am walking along a path with the other person toward a common goal.

What we see here is a delicate sense of "will to community" taking the place of "will to power." The focus on teaching gave way to the joy of sharing in a person's independent learning growth.

From another language counselor:

Being a counselor to two people who want to have a conversation in my native language: Their conversation is flowing through me. I am participating in one continuous flow of thoughts, that goes through me in two directions. I have a humble role: people refer to me only when they need help. The rest of the time they are having a conversation among themselves. Nevertheless, I am not excluded from the conversation. I am participating in a passive role, giving myself to what they want to say, not producing something myself. Giving myself to the others, helping them so smoothly that they forget to realize that there is somebody without whom they would not be able to perform all this, somebody who gives them their security.

The reward here for the expert seems to be the sense of consensual validation that his presence—even in its silence—brought to the learners. To be accepted, to belong in the language of the native, to feel the warm secure approval of silence or limited correction, was a powerful motivation for the learner to speak with even greater clarity and accuracy. Almost as for a little child learning to walk or talk, the secure acceptance and approval of one's independent achievement was always there, and never more so than in silent reassurance.

Sense of Growth

The following learner comment gives both the surprise at this growing language security and the awareness of how the counselor played a part in this:

I was very much surprised at the fact that I would get anything out of the language research in German. I was more surprised by my ability to understand German, as the different speakers spoke it in our conversations. I found it much simpler than I had expected because I began to see its relationship to English and to understand it in terms of its relationship to the English words. I noticed that I did not so much discover a facility of detecting words as I discovered a facility in detecting general ideas. I found an ability to understand the general ideas and consequently to laugh at jokes in German, rather than listening for the English words. I also was very much surprised at the fluency with which the words were pronounced. I could discover that the words were flowing through me and that there wasn't a hard stereotyped pronunciation but rather the words were an extension of my English vocabulary.

Part of this I attributed to the facility of the counselor, who enabled me to feel very much at ease in the language; and consequently allowed the words to flow from herself through me into the group.

The following comment is from a person who had previously studied French but was blocked in speaking:

With regard to French, I noticed several things, one of which was definitely more of a facility in speaking French; I made more attempts to speak French. Before I would be blocked in speaking with anyone from France. I found myself now wishing to converse in French and not being so much impeded by my lack of knowledge. I found too, in French, the language flowing through me from the counselor, rather than a previous setting up the sentences in English and translating into French in my mind and then trying to speak in French. I noticed no difficulty with pronunciation whatsoever, and this was, I believe, due to the encouragement of the counselors. I found that the French was far simpler for me too, because I could again see its relationship to English and I noticed that from speaking French through the Counselor I tended to listen for the more Norman-sounding words and I tended to choose those words which were more Norman when I was speaking French.

I was also very much amazed that, when I addressed the group in conversation, there was in me no notice of the fact that I was speaking French, but rather, simply an extension of myself into the group; I was not so much concerned with how I pronounced the words, and to my amazement, I was pronouncing them with relative accuracy. I was not conscious of what word I was using or choosing, but in one span of time I found myself becoming more aware of the words which occurred more frequently and also found myself more anxious to speak on my own, without the counselor's aid.

Turning Point

Some years ago Brachfeld (1936) pointed out the turning point evident in language learning:

Many years of experience in learning languages has given me the conviction that there is a "Turning Point" in language study. This "Turning Point" has very little to do with intelligence, talent and so forth. Psychologically, it is rather akin to courage. In three foreign languages, I can clearly remember my "Turning Point." In a fourth one, I believe that I have not yet arrived at, but I am already very close to, the "Turning Point."

This "turning point" or what we call the "language threshold," was very evident in our research. Some students even recalled the precise day when this sense of belonging, this passing over the threshold, occurred in one or the other of the foreign languages. It was closely related to a deep sense of psychological belonging and sharing with the language counselor.

In fact, one of the main results of this counseling-learning relationship was that it seemed to enable students rather rapidly to pass over this threshold of confidence and away from fear, uncertainty, and strangeness. In one semester, even, many seemed to acquire a positive identification with the four foreign languages and a confidence and security that they could learn to speak and understand them. In other words, they felt strongly that they belonged to these languages. These languages were no longer strange and threatening for them.

A second result, interrelated with the first, was the overcoming of strong personal blocks against a particular language itself or the people it represented. These blocks existed in at least one language for over half the students. These resistances were caused either by unfortunate earlier experiences in trying to learn the blocked language or by national or cultural hostilities to a particular people.

This "turning point" process we might also consider the movement from meaning to value. At these stages, the language had become a value—the person had begun to invest himself in it, aided by the warm and secure personal acceptance and understanding of the expert counselor.

Deepening Commitment

Similar types of group engagement and individual change emerged in the process of these linguistic experiences. People who were just curious about the research or only vaguely interested in learning a foreign language became increasingly more deeply committed to the language experts and counselors and to one another. At first, for example, conversations would begin with the usual banal topics like "the weather" and "what did you do over the week-end?" These topics were similar to those in any group whose members do not know or feel secure with one another.

Gradually, however, relationships deepened. At this stage, one member would usually introduce the first "breakthrough" by beginning to speak of his or her feelings, especially of anxiety. Sometimes deeper communication began with freedom to express hostility toward one or more other group members or to the counselors. Thus, negative emotions emerged and the group grew able to express them with increasing security. Slowly, positive attitudes came forward, too, with the whole group sharing in the excitement of each one's language progress or new personal insights or achievements.

Community Learning

We came to call this mutual support and strengthening process "community learning," in contrast to the "laissez-faire rugged individual" learning that most classroom experiences seem to have afforded these people. There was often an atmosphere of enthusiasm and shared achievements similar to that of amputees beginning to walk on artificial limbs. Negations were still freely expressed but with little or none of the self-consciousness about, say, anger, that had marked earlier releases.

Obviously, not all students remained in the research groups long enough to attain a stage IV or V in all four languages. But a significant number did, so that easy conversation in all four languages could occur and they could then become "counselors" to new groups. More common was significant speaking proficiency in one or two languages, and less adequate comprehension of the other two or three. Some remained only two semesters. Even here, however, they often then entered regular classes in a particular language, more motivated to learn and more positive toward the language as a result of the language-counseling experience. A number of the more advanced arrranged to go to Europe, some for a year, some for a summer. As a result of the security and enthusiasm they had acquired, they now desired an even more complete linguistic and cultural experience.

As the more advanced group members became "counselors" to new groups, the native speakers of the languages became "experts" who backed up the counselors, checked recordings for mistakes, etc. Experts guided the counselors, who in turn had full responsibility for the clients. At this stage the clients, we found, could often relate more easily to these intermediate people. The counselors did not seem so distant, since they were sometimes being corrected, too.

Group Sharing and Motivation

In one study an American university group, in French-Canada to learn French, met together for 6 weeks, using this counseling-learning relationship. In their evaluation, all but one reported positive reactions and achievement, especially in motivation, to continue to study on their own:

I think eventually I will study much more on my own. If I had been forced to study, I would have learned more, but I would have never got to that point. We had to pass through that period, whether we liked it or not (Begin 1971, p. 108).

Some typical evaluative comments were:

I don't think we experienced freedom until a week and a half ago. We really expected and we still expect the person running the course to tell us what to do and what not to do. . . . At the beginning of the course, we were still thinking in the traditional methods. We are so engrained in having somebody running the course. That hindered us more than anything else.

We are just beginning to realize that it is up to us . . . up to the group to decide how you want to learn. . . . It comes from the group, and the group decides to do it: this to me was the biggest thing! (Begin, p. 105)

A strong sense of group belonging was reported by everyone but one (Edward), who insisted:

The group as such is really nonexistent. It is individuals within a group that act, and then you get accord or discord (Begin, p. 106).

His general behavior outside the language experience corresponded to this "loner" alienation.

The report commented:

Edward's behavior during the summer was perfectly consistent with those words: groups don't exist (Begin, p. 107).

This suggests that strongly isolated value patterns will persist in such a learning group, and so resist the group's efforts at acceptance and affiliation.

By contrast, the others all felt a strong group tie and its aid in motivating them:

I noticed that, when the expert started to divide the groups, no one ever said: I don't want to be in that group. I don't want to go with that bunch, because of the group feeling that was there from the start. We all wanted to help one another to learn French (Begin, p. 107).

Another comment pointed out how the student had "to learn you people" before he began to really learn French:

I think this is one of the most painless ways to learn that I have ever got into. It was left to my own motivation to study. Not only did I learn French, but I've got to know a lot of tremendous people in the meantime. This experience of living with you, guys, ya, it has been great. First of all, I had to learn you people, before we could get down to business. During the first two weeks, we were like people going to Mass without knowing each other. But after that, we could relate with everyone, even with people whom you might think you could never possibly work with (Begin, pp. 108–109).

Positive Self-Concept

We are now gathering data[4] to see if we can further determine the relationship between personality change and the learning process. Some evidence seems to indicate the possibility that significant change in positive self-regard may be related to gain in foreign language speaking competence. This seems to have been so for particular individuals. Some have commented on the notable positive changes they have seen in themselves, which also have been reported by others who know them well. These have usually corresponded to their gain in speaking ability in one or more of the four languages. Through the use of attitude scales, Q-Sort methods, personality evaluation, and similar material, we hope to gain greater understanding of the factors which bring about these positive changes as well as greater foreign language communication competence.

One study made of this research group contrasted the learners' changing views of themselves from negative to positive self-attitude toward the four foreign languages, as the group experience proceeded. As they became more

---

4. The following are doctoral dissertations related to the specific application of counseling awareness and skills to the learning process. They are listed in chronological order: LaFarga (1966), Tranel (1970), Rardin (1971), Gallagher (1973), Brady (1975).

realistic in their self-concept about what they could learn, they began, at the same time, to gain in their ability to speak and understand.

As discrepancy between self-perception and ambition is reduced, proficiency in language tends to increase (LaFarga 1966, p. 105).

There also seemed to be a more realistic self-attitude toward how much they could achieve linguistically instead of exaggerated learning goals far beyond them, or negative defeatist attitudes.

The experimental members, as a group, not only grew in self-acceptance but also in greater consistency between their self-perceptions and their aspirations (LaFarga 1966, p. 105).

Some preliminary findings seem also to suggest the rather surprising possibility that some people in this type of community language learning may be able to learn comparably in four languages what classes in one language learn in approximately the same time. This has been apparent with particular individuals who made high gains in individual languages as tested by standard language achievement tests and by an aural test especially standardized for our research. Whether this can be found to be generally evident is not yet clear. It may be that some persons are more strongly motivated by this kind of learning experience and that this accounts for their gains in foreign language competence. Differences in the experts and the counselors might also help explain some of these variations in what individuals learned. No outside assignment or study was suggested or encouraged, but this could also have made some differences.

Confidence in Learning Potential

In general, however, the main result for many seemed to be the awareness of being much less anxious in their approach to the learning of foreign languages and of having acquired confidence that they themselves could really learn to speak, as well as read and write, these languages. Such an experience might therefore better prepare them for further ordinary classroom learning in these languages. In the light of the fears that many had in the beginning, this in itself seemed a significant advance for them.

One implication here seems to be the necessity of methods that incorporate counseling more immediately into the complications of any learning experience. For this, we have to rethink the whole educative process in a non-Cartesian way, seeing it not simply as an intellectual but as a unified personality encounter. An intellectualized model gives us only a partial view, and so forces us to leave out of consideration many other significant factors. New ways of relating are necessary if we are to bring into full play the complete and genuine involvement of teachers and learners together, and with one another.

Learning is Persons

In this kind of community learning where the conflict, hostility, anger, and anxiety intrinsic to learning are shared, intellectual development would be an important and central but not an exclusive aim. Counseling and procedures patterned from it would then have a basic and effective function. This would especially open the way for making values as well as meaning, a main aim of the educative process.

One can see here a model for learning that could at the same time be personally therapeutic. The student's growth in self-worth as well as his total person are engaged. In the focus simply on intellectual knowledge, education gives, at best, meanings, not values. People often are not moved to make any real self-investment. If this is to come about, we might see the deep sense of commitment expressed by the language expert and the reciprocal sense of identity, belonging, and engagement expressed by the learners, as a model of the kind of learning experience that could be both therapeutic and constructive, as it furthered genuine and independent maturity.

What is involved here then is that "learning is persons." That is, real learning demands investment in self and others, and authentic relationship and engagement together. Knowledge of meanings can be acquired from books, lectures, and various teaching devices. But to make what one has learned a value demands "the courage to be as a part and the courage to be oneself" (Tillich 1952, p. 187). It involves, in other words, the process of maturity itself, and so engages each learner in a constructive and creative growth in greater possession of self and commitment to others, as well as in a therapeutic process.

PART 2: LEARNING AS TOTAL SELF-INVESTED PERSONS IN COMMUNITY

We are talking about learning, then, not by students in isolation and competition or with the teacher removed but as a total community with knowers and learners all engaged together, as persons, in a designated learning area. In this concept, knowers and learners deeply need and are fulfilled in one another. No one is so alienated, isolated, and alone as a knower who deeply treasures what he or she knows but from whom no one really cares to learn what they know. On the other side, no one is more lost and confused than learners who intensely desire to know something but who can find no one capable of teaching them. In this sense, we can see that knowers and learners bring personal worth, meaning, and fulfillment to one another. They need one another, one might even say desperately, when we view them not simply in a narrow way, say from the point of view of conditioning or a remote intellectualism but as unified composites, with thoughts, options, feelings, primitive instincts, and physical urges all working together at every moment in the learning process.

An Incarnate-Redemptive Regard

To catch, therefore, the complicated human engagement of all aspects of a person—what we have come to call psychosomatic engagement—we are using the word "incarnate." We mean it, as we have said earlier, not in its familiar theological sense but in its more exact literal meaning. The selves of the persons of teacher-knower and student-learners are not viewed abstractly, intellectually, or simply as reactors to stimuli but as living, mysterious, unique, "incarnate" persons. In this sense, the learning process may be viewed not in separate parts—as the six blind men viewed the elephant—but as engaging total, unified persons.

To express the degree to which teacher-knowers and student-learners mutually need, fulfill, and give a sense of value and worth to one another, we have used the phrase "redemptive relationship." Here again, the meaning is not theological but rather is intended to indicate how we gain our main awareness of our own sense of worth and value by the attitudes others show us, reflected in the way they treat us and consider us. A "redemptive relationship" in learning, therefore, would have teacher-knowers feeling themselves precious agents and most valuable, essential implements in the learning process. Student-learners, recognizing at every point the great value and gift of the knower's open, other-centered concern, and its preciousness and delicacy, would show by their intense and sensitive engagement, their skilled understanding and appreciation. In this kind of redemptive atmosphere, what is very best in the knower, and most efficacious for learning, would emerge. In Plato's sense, the learners would be midwives to the knower's redemptive-creative process.

On the other side, the student-learners, secure in the personal understanding, appreciation, and skilled sensitivity of the counselor-knower, would feel both free and secure to make a total-person, incarnate commitment to the learning relationship. Like clients who totally trust the counselor-therapists, learners could plunge without restraint, hesitation, or fear of learning trauma into the complicated maelstrom of the learning pool. Their security in the first stages would be that their anxieties would be understood by the knower and other learners, and not misused. Able to give themselves without defenses, then, at every level of their personality, they would feel, after each effort—painful, humiliating, or otherwise difficult as it might appear—that what they did had worth and significance in everyone's eyes. Reflected in this way, no matter how foolish or inadequate they might first have felt, or thought they appeared to others, their final reaction would be one of self-assurance, confidence, and courage.

The teacher-knower as the central figure would be the most redeeming agent, here contributing to the learner's self-worth. But, of almost equal importance would be the same positive redemptive attitude on the part of the other learners. All these factors joined together, and others to be subsequently considered, would be what we mean by "an incarnate-redemptive" learning relationship.

Values as Self-Investments

Here, we might treat some further aspects of what we mean by the word "values." Obviously we do not mean a kind of dogmatism or the imposition of one person's point of view onto another, as is sometimes implied; this would be something of a Kantian notion, and therefore more characteristic of the passing age. Rather, by "values" we mean something of the delicate and refined awareness of the worth and dignity of each person that modern counseling has given us. We refer also to the genuine relationship that is possible between two people that respects the rights, the integrity, the thought process, and the uniqueness of each. Such a relationship allows each person deeply and openly to understand the other, with no prejudicial notions, and allows each to be mutually convalidated. By values, in this sense, then, we mean a mutual self-investment.

Such mutual self-investment is possible in a truly understanding relationship which does not involve either approval or disapproval, either agreement or disagreement. There is simply an "unconditional positive regard" for each other, or what we would call an "incarnate-redemptive regard." Each person can be whole and incarnate. Each can invest in the other in a deep sense of understanding and being understood. Each person is "redeemed" through having his personal sense of worth and value enhanced. This is perhaps the greatest achievement that the modern conceptions of counseling and psychotherapy have produced in our awareness.

This understanding of values, while in a way new, is also quite ancient. Through it we discover, first of all what a person is genuinely invested in and what he now chooses consciously because of his investments. Through the aid of the understanding skill of another person, he can now opt to continue his previous value system or he can choose a different operational system. In the process of being understood as a whole person in this way, he comes to value his personal uniqueness and thereby discovers what he is really invested in. The very nature of one's feelings, instincts, and somatic reactions is a clue to what one has invested in. When these feelings, instincts, and somatic reactions are accepted in an understanding relationship, one can consciously choose to accept them in himself. In so doing he arrives at a more positive view of himself, of his situation, of what he wishes to do and to become.

An incarnate-redemptive model of the educative process, therefore, would stand out in sharp contrast to our present highly intellectualized, socially isolated, and teacher-centered educational methods. Its aim, as we have said, would be to incorporate teachers and learners together in a deep relationship of human belonging, worth, and sharing.

Redemption through Incarnation

In such a learning situation, the atmosphere is quite different from what one would find in a learning situation based on a purely intellectual and abstract model. In any learning situation, the anxieties of the learner are often related to other people. In the situation that we have described, these anxieties gradually work themselves out so that the person is free to learn spontaneously and openly the way he did as a child.

One phase of our research over a period of years involved the use of four foreign languages (German, French, Spanish, and Italian) simultaneously. One reason for using four languages, as we have said, was that it was comparatively rare to find a person who would know all four. If, however, a person knew one of the four, say German, he could act as a counselor to the learners of German. But his very knowledge of German gives him power over those who do not know German: in other words, he is a kind of god figure in German. But, since he knows no Spanish, if he wishes to learn it from the Spanish counselor, he must first become "incarnate"; that is, he must submit himself to the insecurity and anxiety of not knowing. In doing so, however, he is then redeemed through the sensitive understanding of the counselor.

From a state of complete security in German, for example, where he is superior to others and all are dependent on him finally, and therefore, from a kind of godlike stance, he, or she, suddenly find themselves, in the switch to Spanish, not only becoming human but placed in a dependent and even humiliating position. Incarnation in Spanish, therefore, is a terrible come-down from a divinized position in German. Such a loss of power and status, might be, therefore, almost unbearable, except for the warm understanding, openness, and security which the Spanish counselor brings. Such persons can therefore feel their own worth and value in Spanish through the positive manner in which they are reflected by the Spanish counselor. Reversely, when they return to German, they can appreciate at a deeply personal level how much a similar knower-understanding, warmth, and acceptance is necessary to the sense of worth of the people learning German.

This is one example of how the interrelating of different languages in the same learning group profoundly reflects the members' relationship with one another. Knowers and learners in this type of structure are therefore inter-changeable, with everyone open to experiencing all the intense and subtle psychological tones and attitudes that come with such interchange.

Teacher Eminence

Learning, then, as we can see in this switch from knower superiority in German to submissive inferiority in Spanish, involves the learner in a temporary psychological return to the state of a small child with its concomitant sense of weakness, anxiety, inadequacy, and dependency. With this there is both the exaggerated sense of the teacher's power to humiliate by knowledge, and a resentment, often suppressed, on the learner's part of this inferiority to the one who knows. This can, and usually does, unless it is carefully controlled, enhance, on the other side, the teacher-knower's will-to-power needs and satisfactions. The retaining of this superiority position is thereby encouraged, because it is or can be, in this way, personally rewarding. Such teacher superiority can even be rationalized as essential to learning and therefore to be maintained.

Incarnate Engagement

Present research in counseling and in the use of learning apparatus is beginning to reveal, however, that this godlike teacher stance—while of very ancient lineage—is not necessary not only to second language learning but to other forms of learning as well. It may in fact impede learning. On the contrary, what often seems to further learning is rather an incarnate engagement in an open and warm relationship between knower and learner which activates in the student a steady growth in the sense of self-worth and security. This seems to draw the student out of his anxiety that, unredeemed or worthless as he is, he cannot learn this task or language and assures him of his incarnate-redeemed learning worth and ability. In this the model of the mother and the small child seems not only to represent our earliest learning experience but also to be one from which we derive much of our later learning potential. It is the mother's loving security conveyed to the child that gives him worth and the initial courage to learn. He may, of course, learn without this, but this is a basic aid.

We are emphasizing here that consideration of an incarnate-redemptive learning experience patterned after the counseling relationship, and of the place of counseling itself in the educative process, must then start with the effects on learning of conflict, hostility, anxiety, defense, and other basic emotional and instinctive psychosomatic reactions. It must also recognize the learning experience as a community experience oriented to the fulfillment of the need to belong, to work together, and to grow in mature giving of self to others. Such learning experiences would not only be task-oriented and intellectual; they would include relations to others and involve the whole person of each learner.

Present Cartesian Tradition

In many of our present educational methods we are still victimized to a considerable degree by concepts that are fundamentally Cartesian. This Cartesian attitude, combined with models drawn apparently from economic "laissez-faire rugged individualism," has perhaps made most classroom learning both exaggeratedly intellectual and competitive. The "good" student is still presumed to be able to learn best in an intellectualized and individual way, with little or no consideration given to his emotional somatic involvement or his need for a community learning experience shared with other students.

In the Cartesian dichotomy, the psyche was conceived of as highly intellectual and removed from somatic and emotional tones. Although we have in large measure discarded this dichotomy, we still find, in our culture, structures of thought that make it difficult for us to free ourselves from its persistent influence. This dichotomy has affected the development of counseling, for example, in the way that it is so often considered only as remedial and corrective rather than as an integral part of the educative process. If, however, we look at the educative process as something experienced by a total personality, instead of viewing it with the distortions of a Cartesian intellectualism, counseling therapy skills, relationships, and models may have major roles and not simply auxiliary ones.

Persons in Community

Here we wish to consider the manner in which this whole person breaks with an overintellectualized or "angelic" idea of education—after a Cartesian-Kantian model—and incorporates the learning experience into an incarnate relationship with the "teacher" and the other learners. This incorporated sense of belonging and sharing brings with it a sense of communication, communion, and community in place of isolated competition that can be both alienating and rejecting.

As a consequence, a redemptive process emerges by which each one feels his growing worth in the achievement of learning. By this he is further encouraged to confidence and trust in his own learning capacity and self-worth as well as faith in and commitment to the other learners and the informed person, the teacher. Such faith and hope engender love and security in place of fear, anxiety, and self-mistrust and attack. The student is therefore learning in an atmosphere of respectful love of self and others and the genuine regard this produces. Personal enthusiasm, self-affirmation, and even competition are not stifled by this but encouraged. These self-assertions do not, however, break the bonds of closeness and caring which each one shares with others. They rather engage each one in a process which is the reasonable pursuit of his own excellence without encroaching on others or manipulating them for his own needs and purposes.

A wide variety of relationships were devised, some involving various learning apparatus. But whatever the method or apparatus used, it was basically intended to further the sense of belonging and sharing between the one who knew and the group, and between group members themselves. The idea was to diminish the distance, isolation, anxious state, and sense of inadequacy into which a person is placed by not knowing something. In this way, a gradual sense of incarnation between the knower—who tended initially to be seen in a nonincarnate divinized role—and the one who did not know was furthered and intensified. At the same time, the feelings of distance, strangeness, isolation, fear of failure, and humiliation which competition might bring between the members of the group were also diminished by the increase in their own capacity to give worth and confidence to one another. In this fashion they could redeem or rescue one another from the initial anxiety-bound state.

Counseling Therapy Model

The core model for this incarnate-redemptive educative process was the closeness, engagement, and sense of loving first which counseling therapy represented. Consequently the knower—for example, the native Spanish person in a group learning Spanish—strove in every way to imitate the counselor in commitment, belonging, and sensitive caring. He did not take advantage of the power and exhibitionist superiority which his expert knowing of Spanish gave him over Americans struggling to learn Spanish; rather, his whole manner conveyed openness, worth, and security. They could then begin to trust him, and through him gradually grow secure in Spanish. Conversations were initiated at the same personal level of group counseling and were carried on in that atmosphere. There was this additional element, however: they were carried out in Spanish with the Spanish expert's constant reassuring presence, support, and skilled linguistic counseling aid.

Incarnation-Redemption in the Five Stages

As we have seen, we divided the growth process of this counseling-learning into five stages, extending from total dependency, in stage I, to total independence as the theoretical goal at the end of stage V. The diagram (p. 173) illustrates this.

The various phases of the design are intended to show how the person, beginning in embryonic dependency on the learning counselor, slowly emerges to his own independent ability to communicate, so that at the end of stage V he no longer needs the language counselor's help. This, as we see, is a steady process. In proportion, for example, as he can carry on a conversation with few mistakes, and so needing corrections only in idioms and grammatical subtleties, he would have arrived at stage IV.

Individual and Group Aggression

Interestingly, the learner seems to go through a gradual process of security until stage III. Then he often experiences renewed discomfort and difficulty, especially in stage IV. This seems to be so because he is now far more aware of his mistakes even though he can be easily understood. He is therefore much more demanding of himself and more self-critical.

In addition there is, at this stage, a much greater resurgence of open aggression and self-affirmation. This seems to go with more direct responsibility for learning and a stronger determination to overcome barriers in the way of learning achievement. Sometimes this shows itself in direct hostility to other group members, especially if their behavior or manner seems to impede the person's progress in learning.

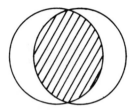

I
Total dependence on language counselor. Idea said in English, then said to group in foreign language, as counselor slowly and sensitively gives each word to the client.

II
Beginning courage to make some attempts to speak in the foreign language as words and phrases are picked up and retained.

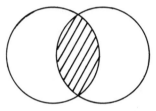

III
Growing independence with mistakes that are immediately corrected by counselor.

IV
Needing counselor now only for idioms and more subtle expressions and grammar.

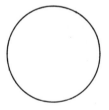

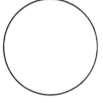

V
Independent and free communication in the foreign language. Counselor's *silent* presence reinforces correctness of grammar and pronunciation.

Stages in language counselor-client relationship from dependency to independence

This can sometimes initiate intense periods of group confrontation and exchange. Since, however, the focus is still on the learning task, the tones and attitudes seem seldom to be carried over to outside relationships. Until people are used to this, they often express surprise at the relaxed tone of coffee breaks after such sessions. For some, it was a significant experience to be able to express this kind of constructive, task-oriented anger without any feeling of guilt or of a need to apologize afterward. It was a great relief to be free to be angry and yet feel truly accepted by the group at the same time.

Adolescent-Adult

In some ways, these kinds of aggressive·struggles in the group seemed to correspond to the adolescent's need for independent self-assertion. As the group grew more secure in language achievement and moved toward the end of stage IV, much of this group aggression ceased. It became concentrated on the task itself rather than on group members. As the experiences in the group produced the rewards of successful language achievement and communication, the need for hostility and resistance among group members toward one another gradually decreased.

In these changes, one could observe a growing sense of maturity and security in the new language self. This seemed to be similar to the kind of secure self-affirmation that a young adult begins to exhibit as he arrives at a clearer delineation of himself. Stage V therefore, while concentrated in its effort for the most exact linguistic expression, was usually less tense and more relaxed. Easy personal exchanges could occur; anger could be expressed and quickly evaporate. Group members in stage V were much more at ease with themselves and one another. They had, in other words, the ease of established adult relationships that were firm and secure.

Interrelated Dynamics

These five stages, already discussed as a description of a learning process and a person's growing competence and independent knowledge in a foreign language, are also descriptive of other interrelated dynamics. They can be seen, for example, as defining the growth of a child from embryo to independent adulthood, passing through childhood and adolescence, which might be considered stages III and IV.

These five steps can also, in a special way, illustrate the process of counseling therapy. A person is anxious and insecure at the beginning of the interviews because he is in confusion and conflict about at least one area of his life. Gradually he is helped to reflect upon and see himself and his situation more clearly and so make more adequate independent judgments.

Stage I can also represent the dependent, inadequate person, unsure of himself and huddling in a group or behind others in defensiveness and fear. We can see him grow in successive stages to trust himself and allow himself to emerge in his own self-worth, as he begins to see himself as having value to himself and others. By stages IV and V he has grown to where he can take security, satisfaction, and confidence in being and becoming himself. Illustrated here then would be the emergence of Tillich's "courage to be."

But this process demonstrates at the same time a growth in self-unity in contrast to a self-rejecting dichotomy of loving to hate oneself. A person at the end would therefore be more accepting of his whole self—soma, instincts, and emotions as well as knowing and choice functions. These would all form a part of his new sense of incarnate self-worth. These five stages, then, would also show the process of growth in self-incarnate redemption. This is first achieved through the concerned understanding and knowledge of someone who consciously loved first and on whom the person can depend. This convalidates the person's own self-worth and enables him freely to grow in his own redemptive sense; that is, in his own independent convalidation of himself in the learning process.

Teacher-Knower Commitment

What is needed in an educative process, then, is the same kind of willingness on the part of the knower, the "teacher," to give up his eminence and dominance in knowing. In this he needs to abandon himself to the meaning and value of the student. The words "I must decrease, he must increase" describe the commitment that enables another person to learn from me. Starting in the ignorant dependency of not-knowing, he is free to develop into the independence of knowing. But to be needed can be self-aggrandizing for the "teacher," and to show off knowledge has an exhibitionist reward that can be very satisfying. For these reasons such a commitment is in fact most difficult.

In this commitment, the knower's convalidation of the learner enables the learner to grow in the redeemed worth of knowing. By feeling himself loved and approved not only when he is in need or depends on the teacher but also when he seeks to be free of the teacher, a student is best aided to grow in this way.

Learning As New Life

This would be *living learning*. By contrast we often have a dead structure which demands simply that the learner reflect the knower in order to please him and so protect himself from a poor grade or a classroom group humiliation. Anyone associated with, and observant of, a small child learning something new cannot help being caught up in the excitement, enthusiasm, and coming-alive feeling which the child reveals in each new learning experience. One of the frequent consequences of our present socially isolated and information-centered educational methods is to deaden learning and to take away from it all the excitement and fresh bloom of coming to new life.

But the aim of counseling therapy, as we have seen, is to encourage and aid the independent coming to life or "resurrection" of the client. He often experiences this as a movement from a dead "old" self to an exciting "new" self-birth. In the counseling therapy process, it is not uncommon for a person to describe this "new life" feeling as he struggles, with the skilled counselor's help, for a new and more integrated understanding of himself and his situation. The following excerpt indicates this:

Co: It's a new way of evaluating yourself, and therefore it needs a great deal more delineation.
Cl: Uh-huh. This is the first time I've felt free to do this.

Co: It's your first real acceptance of a positive worthwhile self in a, shall we say, a fundamentally realistic sense.
Cl: Uh-huh. (*Pause.*)
Co: Quite pleased at all that, aren't you?
Cl: Yes, and it's deep. I think I'm going to cry again. I mean, it's like a, a new baby. You're afraid its skin or something is fragile. (*Sobbing softly. Pause.*)
Co: It's a very delicate bringing something into being in yourself that you sort of see you have produced? (*The counselor, in turn, speaks very slowly and quietly.*)
Cl: And forcing it to come out this way is the only way to do it.
Co: It's one of the final stages of getting born.
Cl: Yes.

Similarly, the dead learning methods—isolated and exaggeratedly impersonal—must be brought to life through a warm, personal, and engaged living experience between expert knower and learner. The deadness of learning must be resurrected and restored to the natural joy and enthusiasm it once had for the learner when the learning experience was young and fresh.

This feeling of "new life" emerges psychologically to be a genuine and confident self-regard when, having been achieved in and through another, it finally reaches a state of independent meaning and value. At its best, this is the goal of the educative process. It should be the conscious realization of the learner that he now knows, and knows that he knows, and so can give his knowledge freely and without restraint to others.

Internalized Knowledge

We shall now consider a traditional analogy of the law as a child's schoolmaster, and how this may be applied to the expert counselor in a foreign language. He is someone who is needed in the dependency stages of growing to learn a foreign language. But a child or an adolescent, or an adult in the earlier stages, is both dependent on and yet struggling for independence of the counselor-expert. The ideal goal of such independence is when one has internalized all the linguistic knowledge of the expert and so oneself speaks the language expertly. One has in this sense cast off the teacher, as in a similar way one casts off the law. The mature person, having internalized all that the law means, has liberty not in contradiction to the law but above and beyond the law. In a linguistic sense, the laws of grammar are still basic to good speech, but when one has internalized this structure and uses the language easily, one is free because he need no longer be obsessionally concentrated on the law.

Something of this is implied by Ricoeur (1967, p. 149) in his concept of the progression from scrupulosity, as an obsession with the law and its minutiae, to freedom. Persons who are learning a foreign language tend to be obsessed with the minutiae of the grammatical construction. They may, in fact, learn the laws of grammar and be able to analyze a sentence and yet never really arrive at the freedom to speak. But representation has come into being when, in a certain sense, the law is cast off by being internalized into a living reality. Representation and being have come together in an integrity of internal meaning and value. In language learning, the person speaks correctly but without any consciousness of rules.

This progression will then work against the tendency in the one who knows, who is a teacher, to hold the eminence of "pedagogue," that is, to be a teacher of "dependent" children only. Instead, the knower must regard each person, child or adult, as having his own unique and personal learning potential. This is known only to the learner himself, and only he can unfold and activate it. In this process the "pedagogue" must decrease. He becomes rather Plato's "midwife," so that the new independent self—let us say it is a "French" self if the learner is studying French—can be born and grow in his own mysterious uniqueness.

Montaigne catches the mature relationship necessary to genuine total-person learning when he says, "To do well, learning must not be merely installed in the house but married" (Lowenthal 1956, p. 18). He goes on to say of the teacher's relationship with the learner:

At the very outset he should put the pupil on his own mettle. Let him taste things for himself, and choose and determine between them. . . . This is one of the hardest things I know of. Only the most disciplined and finely tempered souls know how to slacken and stoop to the gait of children. I walk firmer and surer uphill than down. . . . (Lowenthal, p. 23).

Mimesis

In the mimetic quality necessary to any learning situation, however, we have a clear distinction from counseling therapy. In this mimetic sense, the learning relationship would be determined by what the knower stands for or *re-presents*. It is the learner's awareness of this which brought him in the first place. In turn, it is the teacher's knowledge in a particular area which validates his position and determines the nature of his mimesis. In this the learning relationship between teacher and student clearly differs from the relationship of counseling or therapy. There the client is studying himself. He projects this study of himself in and through the counselor-therapist. In the mimetic relationship, the student is studying what the teacher knows, stands for, and re-presents. Consequently, his study and learning through the teacher extend to a field or block of knowledge beyond both himself and the teacher. Here the symbolic, more universal quality of learning appears. For in its more universalizing symbolization, as Eliade pointed out, education frees both teacher and learner to go beyond their immediate selves to the broad vistas of the whole field of knowledge (Eliade 1965, pp. 201, 207). In second language learning, it adds the whole new dimension of the growth of another self: a French-self, a Japanese-self, an English-self, etc., depending on the language learned. With this new self, there is possible a whole new self-significance, richer feelings and appreciations; in a word: a new self-potential.

Education

Knowledge is therefore given in such a clean, uncontaminated way as to stimulate real and unique experiences in each learner. Here especially, the combination of mimetic and counseling relationships is most significant since, par excellence, such learning elicits total self-investment. Knowledge alone is not enough. Feelings and values enter here as well. Significance and meaning must most surely give way to genuinely invested experience and commitment if education is to have any final effectiveness and validation. Here too, especially, the knower must truly "represent" and, having presented, decrease steadily, so that the learner may move from a diet of milk to the strong meat of adults. Only in this way can he experience the mature growth and genuine investment of an incarnate-redemptive educative process.

DISCUSSION QUESTIONS

1. What does Curran mean by the terms "language threshold" or the "turning point"? How about the phrase "Cartesian intellectualism" and "laissez-faire rugged individualism"? Do these concepts help in differentiating "counseling learning" from other approaches?

2. One of Curran's students remarked, "We are just beginning to realize that it's up to us . . . up to the group to decide how you want to learn." What was the student getting at? How would you feel about handing over the responsibility for curriculum planning to your students? What are some of the factors that influence your feelings about this possibility? Is it a practical option in your view?

3. Curran acknowledges that his method does not work equally well with all types of personalities. Discuss his example of a student who found the method unacceptable as well as Curran's criteria for students with whom the method should yield optimal results.

4. What limitations do you see in the application of Curran's method to the broad spectrum of classroom needs? Is the method, for instance, equally applicable to teaching ESL and foreign languages? What about his claim that it is possible for a student to progress as rapidly in four languages by his method as they might be expected to in only one language by some more traditional approach? What implications does this claim have for classroom settings with which you are familiar?

Chapter 11

Values Clarification Theory in ESL and Bilingual Education

Kathleen Green
Henry Sibley High School, West St. Paul, Minnesota

EDITORS' INTRODUCTION

The term "values clarification" comes from Louis Rath (Simon, Howe, and Kirschenbaum 1972). As proposed in this chapter, it is an approach to teaching which seeks to bring values under conscious scrutiny and to examine them in a nonjudgmental light. ESL teachers will agree that a classroom environment which fosters appreciation of differences is necessary. Without mutual appreciation and a willingness to tolerate and accept differences as normal and desirable, prejudice and even outright hostility can hinder language acquisition or even make it impossible. As a technique, "values clarification" seeks to enable students to understand better both themselves and others. For some practical applications see Chapter 32 by Richard-Amato. As an approach to teaching language skills, "values clarification" will elicit talk at a fairly high level of abstraction. Therefore, it may be most applicable in classes for intermediate to advanced students. It also has a certain commonality of purpose with Curran's "nondirective" counseling (Chapter 10) and Lozanov's "tension-reducing" techniques (Chapters 8 and 9).

Few linguists or language teachers would disagree that there is a relationship between language and culture. Whether language determines culture or culture determines language has been a subject of much discussion. Grammarians, like Fillmore who is searching for deep structure linguistic similarities (Fillmore 1968, pp. 1–88), and psychologists, like Lambert who believes that psychological similarities between cultures are more evident than differences (Lambert 1963, 1974), admit that cultural differences do exist (Lambert 1963, 1974) and that language is the vehicle whereby a person acquires his knowledge of those differences. He learns these differences either indirectly by having someone tell him the differences or directly through his own attempts to communicate with people who speak different languages or dialects than he does. There is absolutely nothing like the failure to communicate ideas or needs to another person to make us aware of our own differences, our own existential alienation and isolation from our audience. Conversely, success in communication, whether it be a baby's crying to be fed or changed or an adult's communication of his innermost feelings, creates a feeling of intimacy and unity with the audience. Thus, a person's failures and successes in communication determine his feelings of "we" and "they," "us" and "them." It follows (though I have no statistical proof of this) that the more people with whom a person feels he communicates successfully, the more people he will consider to be "we's," persons like himself. Thus he widens his cultural boundaries. If his ability to communicate crosses certain linguistic, geographical, and socioeconomic boundaries, he is considered to have become bilingual and bicultural.

VALUES CLARIFICATION THEORY

How does values clarification theory fit into the communication process?

First, let us look at what values clarification theory is. Values clarification is based on the principle that what we do is determined by our values and beliefs. Unfortunately, most of us are unclear about what our basic values are; so when we are faced with making a decision between two alternative courses of action, we often find it difficult. Values clarification, as first proposed by Louis Rath, looks at values not from the stative point of view of content but from the dynamic point of view of the *process of valuing* (Simon et al. 1972, p. 3). It advocates strategies which can be employed to examine the processes people use to establish their values. Often these strategies are also a means whereby a person can discover what values lie beneath those values he consciously affirms.

Values clarification strategies are not ends in themselves. They are meant to be used with other subject matter, for our beliefs as to the "value" of the subject matter determine what subject matter we learn.[1]

Use of values clarification in the classroom requires a teacher who (1) is willing to examine his or her own values; (2) can accept opinions different from his or her own; (3) encourages a classroom atmosphere of honesty and respect; and (4) is a good listener. As I see it, the qualities of a class in which values clarification is stressed are also the qualities that will foster enthusiasm for the subject matter and better communication among students and between the students and the teacher. Together, these criteria seem to me to be basic to motivating a student to learn a foreign language.

Let us examine how the above ideas might be used in two different kinds of language learning situations. First, we shall look at the use of values clarification in a college grammar-based composition class for foreign students; then let us look at some possibilities for its use with an elementary school class of bilingual students.

---

1. Lambert (1974) applies this concept to facility in language learning.

COLLEGE-LEVEL ESL

One of the major problems in the college-level English as a second language class is that foreign students with an ability to express the most complex ideas in their own language suddenly find themselves in the position of having to communicate in a language in which they have only a rudimentary knowledge of vocabulary and grammatical structures. The teacher must constantly find ways of convincing the student that he realizes that the student has intelligent, worthwhile thoughts, even though his ability to use the language is minimal. In a class with a values clarification orientation, this problem is partly solved as a part of the class. The teacher conveys the idea that he himself does not know "everything about everything" and welcomes his students' input into his knowledge about the world. One way that I have found to do this is by using various values clarification questions as composition topics. Simon et al. (1972) state that values clarification processes involve:

Prizing one's beliefs and behaviors
1. prizing and cherishing
2. publicly affirming, when appropriate
Choosing one's beliefs and behaviors
3. choosing from alternatives
4. choosing after consideration of consequences
5. choosing freely
Acting on one's beliefs
6. acting
7. acting with a pattern, consistency, and repetition

Composition topics based on these processes require students to make choices and to affirm those choices. Because values involve a variety of subject areas (Simon et al. 1972, p. 15, politics, religion, work, leisure time, school, love, sex, family, possessions, race, war, peace, rules, etc.) there is always something about which each student has sufficient knowledge to write a composition. Furthermore, because values clarification stresses choice making, the student is free to choose what aspect of a topic he wishes to talk about and how much he wants to say. He is not forced to accept the values of the author of a text as he would if he were writing a supposedly "free" composition like the following: "Write a paragraph beginning, 'The future of the world is perilous, but not hopeless' " (Robinson 1967, p. 114). Finally, while values clarification topics allow the student freedom of choice in thinking, they also allow the teacher freedom of choice in their use because they can be adapted to teach a variety of grammatical structures.

Here are some of the techniques I found successful with college-level students.

The first exercise was called "The Moon Problem." In this exercise, students were divided into small groups (three to four students) to discuss a sheet in which they were presented with the problem of being lost on the moon and having to decide, as an astronaut crew, which of 15 things are important for their survival trek to their space ship (NTL Institute 1970). Students rank order the items from most important to least important. While there is usually little question as to the most important item, the ranking of the other fourteen is largely a matter of personal choice with no right or wrong answers. As members of the group, students must convince the other students of what is important and be willing to listen to the expertise of fellow group members. Students in the sciences are able to use their technical knowledge, while students with other knowledge, such as English vocabulary or verbal persuasion skill, can use these talents in the discussion. The students combine their vocabularies for use in understanding the problem; they become involved in a task which requires communication with other members of the group; they practice both reading and communication skills in an atmosphere where they are involved in helping each other learn.

After the discussion of the Moon Problem, which should take at least 30 minutes of class time, students are asked to write a composition about the moon in which they condense their topic to a specific area that interests them or about which they are knowledgeable. Some areas I suggested were a scientific description of the moon, the value of going to the moon, the significance of the historical event of man's landing on the moon, and a legend about the moon from their country. The compositions I received ranged from an essay on the connection of the moon with poetry and love to a description of the moon's soil content, an essay praising the United States' technical progress, a biographical account of one student's activities at the time of the first moon landing, a review of science fiction about the moon, and a description of the in-class problem of moon survival. As can be seen, this topic offers an excellent opportunity for the teacher to discover the student's interests, rhetorical preferences (argument, description, analysis, etc.), and their basic compositional skills. It also provides the teacher with an opportunity to reinforce the idea that all of the students' ideas are worthwhile and that corrections on themes will be based on how well English is used to convey the ideas, not on whether the teacher agrees with the ideas. Students obviously found the topic broad enough, most seemed to enjoy it, and at least one remembered it as his favorite composition topic.

To teach adjectives and intensifiers in descriptions, the device of student-constructed riddles was used. First, students were arbitrarily assigned people to describe, such as their English teachers or commonly known world figures. A contest was held in which students guessed the answers to the riddles of their classmates. The student who gained the most points was the winner. (Points were given for being able to guess from other students' descriptions and for the number of people who could guess from the student's own description.) After analyzing some of the mistakes made in this first exercise and after providing more explanation of descriptive techniques, I wrote an example of description of myself. In a second riddle contest, students had to describe themselves in such a way that others, although not given the obvious details of name or country of origin, could guess who they were. Thus students had to make choices about what characteristics they felt would describe themselves and what characteristics others would see.

The use of descriptive riddles led naturally to the making of comparisons. Basic comparative forms were presented in a sample essay about the physical and behavioral changes of a pet. (At least in the United States pets are a suitable subject for such attention!) Then, students were asked to write their own essays on something that was changing, comparing its past with its present. Another way to initiate this activity using values clarification strategies would be to list "Twenty Things I Like to Do" (Simon et al. 1972, p. 30) and mark them for "things I liked to do five years ago" or "things my parents also enjoy." Students could then write a paper comparing their past preferences with their present preferences or the taste of their parents with their own tastes.

Comparisons are an excellent method of examining values, but the use of comparisons should not imply positive or negative traits in an individual culture, or subject; however, a teacher can fall into this trap. To avoid this, one class was devoted to showing how comparisons could be used in paragraphs with different purposes. The paragraphs included one that presupposed that the author's purpose was to convince his reader, another that was merely informative, and another that emphasized imaginative description (poetic metaphor). Thus, the students could see how the writer's purpose determined his choice of comparative forms and his choice of what to compare in the paragraph.

Of course, the most often employed use of comparisons, and especially superlatives, is persuasion. So, students were given an opportunity to use these forms in a composition entitled "The Best Country in the World." When assigning this composition, I stressed that students might choose any country, but that they should give reasons why it was better than other countries, and why they chose it as the best. Allowing students to choose which country they wanted gave them a choice of a wider range of values to express than if they had been asked to write on "My good experiences in the United States" or "Why I miss my country." Of course, many students chose to write about the United States or their native land, but many ventured into far-off places. (One Polish student wrote about New Zealand, and a French student titled his work "The Land of the Imagination.")

An even more personal essay, in that it requires the student to examine what he values about himself, would be one on the topic of "What I Do Better than Anyone Else" or "What I Do Best."[2] Both types of composition offer the student an opportunity to use both comparative and superlative forms. He also must decide whether he wishes to persuade his reader of his talents or merely describe them. Although the exercise is a type of forced choice (Simon et al. 1972, p. 94), in that the student must decide what his primary talent is, he does

2. Simon et al., based on "I Am Proud Whip," p. 134. A whip is a kind of rapid chain drill in which students must finish the sentence "I am proud that I can . . ." or "I am proud of . . . "

have the option of comparing himself with other people (this may be highly objectionable in some cultures) or simply comparing what he is able to do with what he is unable to do. One of the paralinguistic facts about American culture according to Paulston (1974) is that Americans can ask each other all sorts of personal questions, but the person asked is allowed to evade or lie about the answer. This assignment offers the teacher an opportunity for teaching this cultural idiosyncrasy. The teacher should stress that any qualities presented, no matter how trivial (a value decision) or humorous (one student suggested that he would title his paper "What I Do Best Is Sleep") are acceptable as long as the student develops the idea fully with reasons to support his statements.

Another way of teaching students about American culture, and especially how we settle our differences, is to use worksheets based on news events which demonstrate conflicting values in our society. For example, as a worksheet on subject-verb number concord, I wrote a description of the Wounded Knee Trial in St. Paul, Minnesota. The description emphasized how the different participants felt about choosing jury members and how the general public felt about the American Indian Movement. After discussing the worksheet in class, I asked students to write on "My First Encounter with the American Indian." The papers revealed that many students did, indeed, have stereotypes of Indians based on American westerns and James Fenimore Cooper, but they also revealed that being in this country had influenced their previously held beliefs. Although for many students this was an exercise demonstrating how the media influence values, one student wrote an essay on his actual physical encounter with American Indians and how that influenced his beliefs.

While it may seem that the primary purpose of the above exercise is to teach American culture or how our values are influenced by our experiences, it is a particularly adaptable method for teaching a variety of grammatical items. The teacher can construct the worksheet using either cloze or multiple-choice techniques to demonstrate the correct use of such diverse items as the use of articles, tense endings, passive versus active voice, concord, the use of modals, punctuation, etc. He can then concentrate on correcting the themes for those items which were practiced on the worksheet.

Another extremely valuable use of values clarification techniques is in teaching the meaning of the modals and their correct use. Since modals are used to convey the speaker's attitudes, they are a necessity in a composition where a student is asked to write about his beliefs and values. An especially good way to use value strategies in this area is to introduce the idea of wishing, of choosing preferred conditions. This is excellent for teaching the use of modals in the conditional. Two compositions were assigned with wishing as a basic theme. The first was "What Would You Be If You Could Be Anything" or "What Would You Do If You Could Do Anything" and the second was "If I Were President of the United States I Would . . .". The first two offered the student the opportunity to make use of *were, could,* and *would* in conditional sentences. This second topic, "If I Were President of the United States I Would . . ." is an unfinished sentence (Simon et al. 1972, p. 241) which elicited not only the *would* form but also the student's opinion of the American political system. Obviously, other values could be elicited by changing the statement to "If I Were Rich, I Would . . .", "If I Were a Member of the Opposite Sex, I Would . . .", "If I Were Seventy Years Old, I Would . . .", or "If I Were Going to Die Tomorrow, I Would . . .". The teacher should take care when assigning this type of composition that the values elicited are not too risky for the student to express. For instance, some foreign students might feel freer about giving their honest opinion about the President of the United States than about their own leaders, others just the opposite. The teacher must judge for himself which "I wish . . ." or "I would . . ." items would elicit a suitable volume of response.

One final word should be said about using values clarification techniques in the ESL classroom. Public affirmation is an integral part of value formation (Simon et al. 1972, p. 19). Every opportunity should be given students to share their opinions in class, but they should not be penalized for wishing to keep their opinions to themselves. One method of sharing compositions is to invite those students who have written particularly good or interesting compositions to make corrections of their compositions and make copies to share with the whole class. It should be made clear that they don't have to share their work if they don't want to do so. It should also be made clear that the copies the class sees are *corrected* copies, so that other class members do not feel that they are so inferior in English ability as compared with other students that they might as well give up. Special skills that the writers do show, such as sticking to the topic, paragraph organization, and sentence variety, can be emphasized as examples of why the work was chosen and the kinds of things all students should try to include in their writing. This sharing process accomplishes two goals: (1) it offers the student positive reinforcement of his communication act; (2) it assures students that they are able to communicate their ideas in English.

My experience with basing my classroom teaching on values clarification theory and using the above techniques was very successful. The classroom atmosphere was exciting and enjoyable. Students were able to work together, sharing their varied knowledge of English. They felt free to tell me when they were having trouble understanding what I was teaching and to ask questions about things they didn't understand about English. Although they were not always punctual about turning in out-of-class compositions, they did eventually turn them in, and they did their own work. Some of them made only average progress in improving their grammar, spelling, or punctuation, but they all demonstrated an ability to use the English language to convey not only thoughts but also feelings. I learned a lot about my students, which increased my enjoyment of my task and which I hope also increased theirs.

BILINGUAL EDUCATION

After reading the above, one might say, "Well, I'm convinced that values clarification theory works with college students learning English to further their studies in the United States, but aren't they a pretty sophisticated group? Do you really think this will work with elementary school bilingual students?"

The answer is an emphatic "Yes!" One of the fascinating things about values clarification strategies is their amazing adaptability for any age group. Furthermore, a teacher who bases his teaching on values clarification must create the kind of classroom atmosphere that is conducive to learning. Studies have shown that it is the teacher's attitudes and expectations of the child which most influence his ability to learn (Adkins 1971, p. 26). Moreover, a class of Anglos and non-Anglos examining their attitudes in an atmosphere of mutual respect seems an excellent way to create bicultural understanding of those cultural aspects Sancho refers to as "intangibles" (Sancho 1974).

As examples of how values clarification strategies could be used in a bilingual elementary school classroom of Anglos and Chicanos, I would like to take some of the techniques I used in the college classroom and show how they could be adapted for the elementary level. (Some had already been adapted from high school materials for the college level.)

In the Moon Problem, the technique of rank ordering is used. This can be adapted in several ways. First, instead of handing out sheets and having the students read the problem, the teacher might wish to tell a story using puppets or other illustrations. The story could be an imaginary tale about anthropomorphic animals, or it could be about children. The story need not be about the moon. It could be about other survival problems. For example, one teacher used this technique in a fourth-grade social studies class for a unit about the migration across the Great Plains. She asked the students which things they would carry with them if their covered wagon broke down and they had to abandon it. In a bilingual classroom, migrant children might find a situation in which they had to choose items to take on their migratory route especially relevant. Rather than personal survival, students might consider a story about societal survival in which they had to choose which workers of various occupations they would want to save in a disaster. It would be instructive to see whether they would save the traditional community helpers: the policeman, doctor, teacher, etc., or the ranch hand, waitress, grape picker, plumber, etc. Children would find understanding the vocabulary of any of these rank order situations necessary, and a variety of rank ordering tasks could be used to teach different vocabulary, such as household items or occupational names, as in the above examples. A picture of the items to be ranked could be used with the word to teach its meaning. Besides vocabulary, the rank order task would also have subject matter content such as history, geography, science, or career education. In addition, the class would have a firsthand opportunity to see cross-cultural differences and similarities. (Would a Chicano boy prefer to take a guitar, a football, or a radio with him on the migrant route? What would an Anglo boy take? Would the girls make different choices altogether?)

Riddles can also be used in the elementary classroom. The teacher might introduce them by reading some riddles in Spanish and English. If the students are beginning to read, he might put some of the simpler ones on the chalkboard or bulletin board with illustrations. Riddles could be used to teach question formation and adjective postmodification versus adjective premodification, both of which contrast in English and Spanish. If the teacher wishes to concentrate on question formation, he might try taping the name of a person or thing on a child's back and having the children ask each other questions about who or what they are. He might make the additional stipulation that if the person or thing is a Spanish word, the student must use Spanish for the questions, and if it is an English word, the student must use English. If he wished to stress adjectival use, he might have the students make up their own riddles to describe themselves or an object they would like to be.

Instead of using the "Twenty Things I Like to Do" list to teach comparisons, the teacher might want to use it to teach predicate forms. Or it might be changed to "Ten Things I Can Do" and "Ten Things I Like to Do" or "Twenty Things I Want to Do When I Grow Up." With the last two, students could examine their expectations of themselves and what they will have to do to fulfill those expectations. Thus, they would get practice not only in the *would like* plus infinitive and *want* plus infinitive forms, but also in setting goals for themselves.

Instead of using "What I Do Best" as a composition topic, students could use the "I Am Proud Whip" (Simon et al. 1972, p. 134). In this activity, the students rapidly fill in the blank, as in a drill, in the sentence,"I am proud of . . .". They can list a personal accomplishment, or they might be instructed to list someone else's accomplishments. This activity can also be developed into a song (Simon et al., p. 327). (Where possible the teacher might want to use other "values whips" for oral drills.) The whip gives the student an opportunity to reveal what he thinks is an important accomplishment. If he chooses to participate, he also chooses to affirm his personal worth or the worth of another individual. For some students, this may be a risky venture; so this kind of activity offers an opportunity for the teacher to stress acceptance of what people say and the ideas of not ridiculing others for what they believe. To illustrate this, he might want to tell or read a story beforehand about people or animals who say something that is ridiculed and show how they coped with the problem.

Elementary students, too, can examine the effect of their personal experiences on their beliefs. Instead of writing about their "First Encounter with the American Indian," they might tell or write about "The First Time I Crossed the Street by Myself," "The First Time I Got Paid for Working," "My First Day at School," "My First Friend," "My First Teacher," or "The Best/Worst Thing That Ever Happened to Me." These could be the subjects of small sharing groups or trios (Simon et al., p. 177) in which the students compare and contrast their experiences. Such trios could be used for conversation practice in either Spanish or English (or alternatively for both from one session to the next) or as opportunities to consolidate experiences for background materials for short stories or skits to present to the class later. Students could use the skits to illustrate how they solved the problem in the situation or leave the situation open-ended for other students to suggest solutions. The development of skits could be expanded to include imaginary situations in the past (history subject matter) or imaginary situations in nature (science subject matter).

The use of role playing, as above, is a good method for beginning the activity of wishing. Students might choose not only the situations but also the characters they wanted to play. They could discuss which characters, people, animals, or things they would like to be and why. This is an excellent way to examine cultural beliefs about animals and could also be used with nature films and texts to show that much of what we attribute to animals depends on our culture, not on scientific fact. Students might try playing both a character they admire and one they dislike. This affords a unique opportunity for the teachers to learn what paralinguistic features impress themselves on youngsters. It could also show what characteristics the children value in others. In these activities, students should become highly aware of cultural differences and similarities. If the activities are presented in an atmosphere of respect and tolerance, all students in the class should come to appreciate these differences and similarities and to feel that both their own values and the values of others have merit.

I have mentioned only a few techniques for using values clarification strategies in the bilingual/bicultural classroom. There are many other strategies focusing on different areas of value conflict that also could be used or adapted successfully for the elementary bilingual classroom. If a teacher uses even a few of them effectively, I think his rewards will be great. He will find himself inventing his own strategies and adapting others; he will find also that he has a class that is open to examining its previously held beliefs and thus is open to learning.

DISCUSSION QUESTIONS

1. Green says, "The teacher must constantly find ways of convincing the student that he realizes that the student has intelligent, worthwhile thoughts, even though his ability to use the language is minimal" (p. 181). How does this idea relate to the typical culture shock experienced by immigrants to a new culture? Discuss the feeling of helplessness you may have felt on trying somewhat hopelessly for the first time to express your ideas in an unfamiliar language and cultural setting.

2. What are some of the ways that you can encourage your students to share problems of deep concern in a nonthreatening environment? Discuss too the relaxing of inhibitions and suspicions that comes with open participation and sharing of fears, desires, and hopes.

3. What "cultural" values might enter into the recommended comparison of "the tastes of their parents with their own tastes" (p. 183)? Would such a comparison be equally comfortable to westerners and Asians, for example?

4. Paulston is reported to have asserted: "Americans can ask each other all sorts of personal questions, but the person asked is allowed to evade or lie about the answer" (p. 184). Is this sort of generalization a useful characterization of Americans in general? Is it true in your experience? What factors enter into determining how much you tell someone who asks personal questions? Do you feel free to lie? To evade the issue? What other strategies are available, and what factors influence your choice among them?

Chapter 12

The Teaching Approach of Paulo Freire

Nina Wallerstein
University of New Mexico

EDITORS' INTRODUCTION

The "problem-posing" approach is similar to values clarification. It is based on the socialist philosophy of Paulo Freire which forms the basis for the present chapter contributed by Wallerstein. Freire argues that a main task of "adult education" should be to "invite people to believe in themselves" and in the fact that they "have knowledge." In the same vein, Wallerstein, following Taba (1965), recommends "teaching students to think" (p. 197). Listening, dialogue, and action are the three main stages. The teacher is supposed to listen in order to discover who the students are both culturally and individually and to find out what their problems are. Dialogue then leads to action. Emotionally charged situations are presented in a codified form—a picture, a story, a written dialogue. The point is for the thinking of students to assume an activist thrust. According to Wallerstein, Freire's "central theme" is that "education should compel people to analyze and challenge those forces in society which keep them passive" (p. 191). Compulsory activism begins with getting students to challenge existing power structures by stating small demands first and bigger ones later on. They are supposed to progress from minor risks to more challenging ones. However, Wallerstein warns that "teachers must be careful not to impose their world view" (p. 198) but should encourage students to question not only societal values but also the teacher's views as well. As in the Curran approach to some extent, Wallerstein observes that "students and teachers communicate as co-learners" (p. 194). Also, as in Curran's counseling-learning, "students exercise control within the classroom by choosing which issues are crucial" (p. 194). Wallerstein concludes, however, by pointing out some perceived differences between Freire's approach and a number of others including counseling-learning, values clarification, and the notional/functional approach.

"Adult education should have as one of its main tasks to invite people to believe in themselves. It should invite people to believe that they have knowledge" (Freire, 1973a).

The problem-posing approach comes from the work of Brazilian educator Paulo Freire, author of *Pedagogy of the Oppressed*. Born in Brazil's impoverished northeast to a lower middle-class family, Freire eventually completed his college and legal degrees. He gave up his law practice in the late forties to set up literacy classes in factories. As a professor of education at the University of

Recife, the largest city in the northeast, he coordinated a church-sponsored adult education program and developed his "dialogue" approach with slum dwellers and peasants. In 1963, he became coordinator of the National Literacy Program, bringing basic education to tens of thousands throughout Brazil.

Freire encouraged people to view themselves as active creators of culture, not passive recipients of history. He believed people create and recreate their culture as they earn a living, pass on values, and interact in social groups. By encouraging students to reflect on their role as creators, Freire challenged his students to believe in themselves as agents of change. "Once (the students) perceive that their music has as much culture as the music of Beethoven, they can begin to break down their dimensions of inferiority. It is this inferiority which prevents them from participating in the true creation of their society" (Freire 1973a). This process, described in *Education for Critical Consciousness*, enabled his adult students to read and write after only 6 weeks of study, thus making them active members of society by gaining the right to vote (Freire 1973b).

Exiled from Brazil in 1964 after the military takeover, Freire went to Chile until 1968, then taught for a year as a visiting professor at Harvard. From 1970 to 1979 he worked as director of the Office of Education for the World Council of Churches in Geneva. In 1979, Freire returned to Brazil. His ideas have been the catalyst for many adult education and community development programs both in the third world and in industrialized nations.

Paulo Freire's phonetic literacy method is not directly applicable to the United States. His students were a homogeneous group; ESL students come from diverse backgrounds. Freire himself recognizes that "experiments cannot be transplanted, they must be reinvented" (Freire 1978). Yet with creative reinventions, Freire's central theme does apply to our classrooms. Education should compel people to analyze and challenge those forces in society which keep them passive. This theme is based on the premise that education is not neutral and does not take place in a vacuum outside society. It prepares people either to accept or to challenge their life situations.

The Freire concepts and methods that reinforce this philosophy are divided into three stages: *listening*, which begins before teaching; *dialogue*, which takes place in class; and *action*, which extends to consequences outside the classroom. *Dialogue* leads to *action* as teachers and students explore *education as a two-way process, critical thinking, problem posing,* and *codes.*

LISTENING

To develop a problem-posing curriculum, we need to know about our students, their cultural traditions, their strengths in starting a new life, and their daily concerns. But how do we learn about (and from) our students if we don't speak their languages? We can begin this process by listening.

Listening simply means employing our observational skills with a systematic approach similar to anthropological fieldwork. "Problem-posing" listening also assumes that everyone—students and teachers—can participate on an ongoing basis. Teachers do not have to work alone to discover their students' issues. Cross-cultural understandings actually emerge more easily out of an interaction of students and teachers. People can recognize each other's cultural biases and learn to avoid misinterpreting each other.

As teachers, we carefully listen to our students' conversations and interactions. To create a curriculum tailored to our students and their daily concerns, we need to listen systematically. Effective listening takes time, as does getting to know people. But the time is well spent, and the process can begin at any time by using our basic sense of watching, listening, and intuiting.

How Can We Listen/Observe Effectively?

Look for verbal and nonverbal clues, and for individual and environmental factors.

Observation is a valuable skill, especially when teachers don't speak the students' languages. Consider what a careful observer can discover about the learning styles of Cantonese students (ethnic Chinese from Vietnam) versus those of Laotian (including Mien) students.

Cantonese students tend to sit upright, focus on the teacher, and repeat individually or as a group after the teacher. Laotian students are strikingly different. They tend to lean toward each other, talk under their breath as they point out the lessons to their neighbors and laugh at (and with) each other's attempts to speak English. Observing the two classrooms demonstrates the importance of teachers having sensitivity to their students' cultural styles. With these sensitivities, teachers may be able to create a comfortable atmosphere congruent with their students' expectations.

In the classroom:

Watch students' interaction—how they greet each other, say goodbye, show respect, touch each other, express pleasure, dismay, or other feelings.

Observe body language in learning—whether they work together or alone, sit rigidly or lean toward each other, praise each other or compete.

Observe students' actions—what they reveal about priorities or problems. For instance, many Indochinese students frequently miss class due to illness. Health care could then be a major discussion issue in a class of refugees.

Ask students to share objects from their culture (kitchen implements, handicrafts, handmade household tools, clothes, anything they have made).

Listen for informal conversations held during the break or before and after class. These talks can often be the richest source of information.

Create curriculum about everyday activities—students' home and family life (where do family members live? where do students feel at home?), their neighborhood life (who do they know in the community? do they interact with other cultural/ethnic groups?), and their work life (what do they like and not like? how is work different in their home country?).

In the community:

Walk through students' neighborhoods, school, and work environs and *take photographs* to bring back to class. Be systematic—observe at the same time for a few days, or at the same place at different times, and record impressions.

Walk with students through their neighborhoods or around the school. Through field trips and walks, students' use of English in the community will increase. If possible, have students take photographs.

Draw maps of houses and services in the neighborhoods. This can be a class exercise: have students draw stores, parks, bus stops, or social places important in their lives.

Ask people on the street as well as community workers about issues in the community. Have *students conduct interviews*, and bring results and their own observations to class.

In students' homes:

Observe students' lives outside of class—their living conditions, their material expressions of culture, their manner of treating the teacher as an honored guest. Access to students' homes is a privilege and provides great opportunities to learn more about their lives.

What Are the Cultural Attributes to Observe?

Look for cultural differences and expressions of group identity.

Times of cultural transmission:

Observe social rites including rituals of becoming an adult, weddings, or baby showers. Invitations to these experiences are again a privilege.

Observe child-raising practices and parents' expectations for children's behavior. Students can discuss the differences between child rearing in their culture and in the United States. They can also tell childhood stories.

Times of cultural preservation:

Attend (or have schools sponsor) *celebrations* from students' culture and history. Learn about the foods, dress, rituals, and values.

Ask students about their home country—what they used to do, whether they want to return, what values they want to retain for themselves and for their children.

Times of cultural disruption:

Ask students about their immigration—how they felt when they left, why and how they came, what they expected, how they feel now about their lives.

Have students compare their lives in the two countries in different areas: health, work, family, education, etc.

How Can We Verify What We Hear?

This is ultimately the most important step. Cross-cultural understanding comes in what we as teachers observe, transform into curriculum, and then receive in feedback from our students. A Freire process entails constant listening for students' responses to ensure our own learning and the relevance of the curriculum for each class.

A dialogue about problems in obtaining immigration papers, for example, may reflect the concerns of a Latin American student but not apply to the problems of Indochinese refugees. Students' responses to the curriculum will help us as teachers adapt or improve the lessons. The responses may also add information that we did not or could not understand when first observing. A map of a neighborhood drawn by a teacher, for example, could not possibly include information on who has just moved in or *why* a neighbor built a fence.

In sum, listening helps select the key concerns of students to shape into culturally sensitive lessons.

DIALOGUE

To Freire, dialogue means much more than conversation; it is an exchange between everyone in a class, student to student and teacher to student. The term involves *action*—students initiate discussions, lessons, and activities to fulfill their educational needs.

Dialogue differs from the traditional lecture and seminar methods where the teacher determines the scope of discussion and students remain passive objects of learning. A Freire approach to dialogue assumes students equally determine classroom interaction. As adults, they bring their concerns and personal agendas to class. These concerns determine what's important to discuss.

In an ABE/ESL class, this dialogue assumes many forms. In curriculum content, students introduce their personal backgrounds, their needs for education, their cultural differences with each other and with Anglo-America, and the problems they confront daily. In classroom dynamics, students participate in discussion circles, divide into small groups or pairs for structured peer teaching, or learn directly from the teacher. In attitudes, students and teachers communicate as co-learners.

Teaching creatively with the dialogue approach makes ESL more than just learning a new language. As students exercise control within the classroom by choosing which issues are crucial, they will gain confidence to use English and to make changes in their lives outside of school.

EDUCATION AS A TWO-WAY PROCESS

The use of dialogue challenges the traditional role of a teacher. Rather than presenting ourselves as omniscient, we participate in a two-way process, learning alongside our students about each others' lives and cultures. For adult students, the tensions involved in learning ease as teachers become known as real people. Teachers can also relax their lecturing or performance role. As teachers and students get to know each other, they will be freer to exchange criticisms or appreciative remarks. Students will discuss their dissatisfactions more openly as well as give needed encouragement to others. Teachers will also be more personal as they emphasize their students' progress to lessen the normal frustrations in learning a new language.

As students talk about their lives, the classroom becomes a place of learning and excitement for teachers. Many ESL teachers have not had the opportunity to travel in students' home countries or interact with students in their cultural communities within the United States. Many teachers are not fluent in the students' language, and lack in-depth knowledge about their culture. Using dialogue and a multicultural curriculum established in partnership can stimulate learning and mutual understanding.

CRITICAL THINKING AND ACTION

The goal of the dialogue approach is to encourage critical thinking about the world. By discussing their personal experiences students can uncover the social pressures which affect them as members of an ethnic group. A critical view does *not* imply negative thinking. Critical thinking builds on the hopes that students have for a better life. Students have already experienced change in their lives by immigrating, and are searching for other changes in the United States. Analyzing U.S. society enables students to adopt a positive stance toward the change they want, in their personal lives or with their community. Communication with immigrants, ethnic groups, and Anglo-Americans can increase as people share their culture and move beyond stereotypes that separate groups in America.

Critical thinking in the classroom does not take place randomly; a teacher promotes inquiry by posing questions and providing information to lead the discussion into a larger social context. Students evaluate the forces that exert control on their lives. Layoffs, racism on the job, cultural discrimination, inflation, education, family—these forces limit their choices of how they live. Critical thinking begins when people make the connections between their individual lives and social conditions. It ends one step beyond perception—toward the *action* people take to regain control over social structures detrimental to their lives.

Action and change do not come easily. Many adult English students are unused to criticizing institutions or demanding reforms. They might be unhappy that their children's school system has no bilingual program, for example, but feel they do not have the privilege or right to demand such programs.

Action *can* begin in the classroom. The first step toward action is to have students reflect on their common experience. Sometimes their only shared experience is what happens in the classroom. Why are they studying? What do they learn in the classroom? What can they learn from their fellow students? What do they learn *outside* of the classroom? These discussions can elicit criticisms or suggestions for better teaching. If the atmosphere allows students to say what they think, they will have made a step toward control in one aspect of their lives.

Curriculum can also reflect students' common experiences outside of the classroom, their stories and life problems. As students identify shared issues, they may gain insight into actions to better their situations. To encourage these insights, the lesson materials themselves must include a language of action. Many ESL texts teach a language of survival or of expressing an opinion or purpose. Few, however, teach language that goes beyond identifying or accepting a situation—language that leads toward empowerment. A Freire approach considers language of action central to learning English. Lessons on neighborhood issues such as barking dogs, inadequate city services, or no heating, for example, could expand to include language about block organizing or tenants' rights. Learning language can initiate small steps toward change. Students need to be successful taking a small risk in order to gain confidence for larger ones.

Sometimes, the school setting will provide enough of a community for group student actions or programs. Students in closed-entry semester or year-long courses develop a sense of community where they may follow through on issues raised in the classroom. Or if the school creates a community providing services or a social center (like many Indochinese centers), students can get involved in self-help or collective programs. Some school centers have created farmers' food markets, selling cooperatives (i.e., the Hmong Pan Dau sales), women's groups, or parent-assisted child-care centers. When students are ready, other actions can take place within language-learning—writing letters to congressional representatives, or writing and circulating petitions, organizing neighborhood cleanups—whatever actions are important to the students.

PROBLEM POSING

Problem posing is the tool for developing critical thinking. It is an inductive questioning process that structures dialogue in the classroom. Teachers formulate questions to encourage students to make their own conclusions about society's values and pressures. The problem-posing method draws out students' shared experiences of society.

Problem posing begins by listening for students' issues. Based on the listening, teachers then select and present the familiar situations back to the students in a codified form: a photograph, a written dialogue, a story, or a drawing (see Codes). Each situation contains personal and social conflicts which are emotionally charged for students. Teachers ask a series of inductive questions which move the discussion of the situation from the concrete to a more analytic level. The problem-posing process directs students to name the problem, understand how it applies to them, determine the causes of the problem, generalize to others, and finally, suggest alternatives or solutions to the problem.

For example, a teacher questions students about a picture of unemployment lines, a situation familiar to many class members. After talking about the elements of the picture and naming the problem, students talk about their own experiences. The teacher then asks, "Why do you think it is difficult to find work?" After students state their opinions, the teacher directs the discussion beyond the students' individual experiences. Do they know other people out of work who can't get jobs? Finally, the teacher encourages discussion on alternatives. How can the students get more training and/or education? What collective actions can they take? Do they understand what affirmative action is?

The inductive questioning strategy of problem posing stresses that teaching people to think is important and applicable at all language levels. Learning to think is a step-by-step process that requires students to learn by doing. Teachers can't just communicate information; we must assume the role of asking questions of students and of expecting students to ask questions of us.

To develop thinking skills, we start at a simple descriptive level, asking students to describe people or places or events. At the descriptive level, students learn vocabulary and language structures and become interested in the discussion content.

We then move to a projective or analytic level, asking students to say what they think, to make inferences, to generalize or to evaluate. Taba pioneered a theoretical construct of a cognitive task hierarchy for teaching students to think (Taba 1965). Her cognitive steps in many ways parallel Freire's problem-posing process. Students are asked first for a literal description (Freire's naming the problem); second, an affective response (Freire's questions, how do people feel about the problem); third, inferences (Freire's why questions, asking for causes); fourth, generalization (Freire's social context); and finally, application and evaluation for other situations (Freire's step, what should be done). The major difference between the two thinkers is in the final step. Taba asks for summations and applications of a new perspective to other situations. Freire asks for *action* on alternatives to problems based on the new perspective.

To teach thinking skills, we must develop our own listening and questioning skills, and know how to focus and direct discussions to higher levels of thought.

For example, one classroom dialogue about neighborhood problems started on a descriptive level:

What's on your street?	There are houses on one side and there's a farm on the other side.
What do you like about your street?	I like the school and the Mexicans. I can talk to them.
What don't you like?	I don't like the smelly farm. I don't like the noise. There are too many dogs.

When the teacher asked the question "why," the students were forced to think on a higher level:

Why are there so many dogs?	Because there are a lot of robberies.
Why are there so many robberies?	People don't have money. They need money to eat, for clothes.
Why don't people have money?	There's too little work.

As we see, the question "why" is critical for teaching thinking skills. "Why" questions allow people to project out of their personal experiences into a broader understanding or debate of opinions.

Projective questions, however, can be too difficult for starting discussion in ESL classes, especially for people who are not used to freely expressing opinions or who are restricted by language. Problem posing therefore begins concretely in an English class, with teachers starting at the descriptive level to reinforce language. In the first days of class, students can learn the question words: who, what, where, why, when, and how, and exchange information from the very start. Some may need encouragement, as many normally expect the teacher to do the asking. An equal exchange between teachers and students is not possible with beginners, since students still need instruction in vocabulary and grammar. Yet the questioning strategy encourages students to draw from their own experience, curiosity, and language competence to communicate in English.

When problem posing, the role of the teacher is not only to ask questions but to provide any necessary information that will move the dialogue to a higher level of thinking. Teachers must be careful not to impose their world view but to encourage students in their own critical thinking. Likewise, teachers should be cautious about assuming leadership on solutions to local problems. People from the community become their own leaders; students from ESL classes could become these leaders or join others as they realize community issues can be tackled.

CODES

After teachers listen to the concerns of their students and select a theme or a series of problems, they draw up lessons in the form of codes to stimulate problem posing. Codes (or "codifications" in Freire's terms) are concrete physical expressions that combine all the elements of the theme into one representation. They can take many forms: photographs, drawings, collages, stories, written dialogues, movies, songs. Codes are more than visual aids for teaching. They are at the heart of the educational process because they initiate critical thinking.

No matter what the form, a code is a projective device that is emotionally laden and identifiable to students. Discussion of the problem will liberate energy that can stimulate creativity and raise motivation for using English. A good code should have these basic characteristics:

1. It must represent a daily problem situation that is immediately recognizable to students. (They already deeply know what is being talked about.)
2. That situation, chosen because it contains personal and social affect, is presented as a problem with inherent contradictions. The code (picture, story, etc.) should illustrate as many sides of the contradiction as possible, yet be simple enough for students to project their own experience.
3. The code should focus on one problem at a time, but not in a fragmentary way. It should suggest connections to other themes in people's lives.
4. The code should not provide solutions to the problem but should allow students to develop their own solutions from their experience.
5. The problem presented should not be overwhelming to students. There should be room for small actions that address the problem even if they don't solve it. Local community issues usually provide opportunities for students to have an impact with small-scale actions.

In essence, a code sums up or "codifies" into one statement a problem (or contradiction) that people recognize in their lives: need for English vs. loss of native culture, stress at work vs. need for work, disappointment vs. hope from expectations in the United States. Each problem is complex without narrowly defined good and bad sides. Students can project their own feelings and opinions in an attempt to negotiate solutions.

For example, students often have difficulty not being understood and not understanding English speakers. This problem can be codified into many situations; one possibility is a dialogue of a non-English speaker attempting to order food from a waitress who is pressured on her job. Teachers can ask students to identify the feelings of impatience and nervousness on both sides, the negative attitudes English speakers often have, and the defensiveness that causes students often to relinquish their equality. Solutions emerge when students realize the discomfort of both parties, and the necessity for them of taking risks to get respect.

After codifying the problem, teachers present the code and use the inductive questioning process to "decode" the problem in a five-step procedure.

These are the tools for dialogue.

Tools for Dialogue

1. Have students describe or name the content and feelings in the code: "*What* do you see?"
2. Ask students to define the problem concretely: "What is the problem here?" Address as many sides of the issue as possible.

3. Elicit similar problem situations in students' lives: "Do you also experience this? How is it the same? How is it different? How do you *feel* about it?" (Also ask if anyone has coped successfully with this issue before. Draw on their successes as well as their difficulties.)
4. Direct students to fit their individual experiences into a larger historical, social, or cultural perspective. Ask them to project opinions: "*Why* is there a problem? Why do you think?"
5. Encourage students to discuss alternatives and solutions: "What can you *do?*" Have students attempt small actions that will provide a new perspective on this problem or in some way ameliorate it. Again, ask for success stories.

Consider the following example of a classroom dialogue based on these questions. The teacher presented a picture of a Chinese home scene with the mother making wonton. The mother was speaking Chinese to her daughter; her daughter was answering, "No, I don't want to. I want to go play." The teacher showed this picture to explore the many aspects of the problem: why are children losing their parents' culture; what social pressures encourage them to "forget" the foreign language; how do parents feel; how do children feel; etc.

One class pursued the following discussion from this picture code as the teacher asked them questions in the five-step process.

First, the teacher asked students to describe what was happening in the picture.

TEACHER:	MANY STUDENTS:
1. *What do you see?*	
What's in the room?	It's a kitchen. A chair. A table.
What country are the objects from?	From the United States. That's from China.
What is the mother saying?	I don't know. It's Chinese.
What language is she speaking?	Chinese.
What is the daughter saying?	I don't want to. I want to go play.
What language is she speaking?	English.

The second step addressed the conflict between mother and daughter, with parents understanding that their children need English, though wanting their children to speak Chinese.

2. *What's the problem here?*	
What is the mother doing?	She's making wonton.
Does the daughter know how?	I don't know. Maybe. Maybe not.
Why not?	You can buy wonton in the store.
	—Maybe she not help her mother.
Does the daughter speak Chinese?	Maybe, a little.
Where is the daughter from?	Not China. She's American.
	—No, she's Chinese-American.
Does the mother speak English?	I don't think so.
Does the mother want her daughter to speak	Oh yes.
Chinese?	—But she needs English too.

Step 3 included questions applying the problem to students' lives and their feelings about the issue.

3. *Is this your problem?*	
Do your children speak your language?	Mine speak Spanish. They live with my father.
	—My son only speaks English.

Do their friends speak your language?

They only speak Spanish at home.
—Only one. He gets embarrassed with others.

When will your children speak your language?
At home?
How do you feel about it?

My daughter likes to teach the baby.
—Oh, Jessie loves Spanish TV.
Oh, I want him to speak Chinese.
—I like them to talk Spanish.

Do your children know about your country?
Do you want them to?
Do they know how to cook your food?

Yes, a little. Some things.
Oh yes.
I don't cook too much.
—Yes, they know. They help.

Step 4, asking "why," is primary to the decoding process. Often teachers only have to ask, "But why?" to move students' thinking to a higher level. The question "Why not?" solicits students' opinions equally well.

4. *Why is there a problem?*

How do they learn about your countries?
What about school?

At home.
Sometimes.
—I don't know. Kim never says anything.
—Sometimes, they teach about holidays.
—I don't think they teach a lot.

Why not? Why don't schools teach about your countries?

I don't know.
—They don't think it's important.
—This is the United States.
—But children can't speak Chinese at school.

Why not?
Do teachers speak their language?

Teachers want to teach English.
Maybe. The teacher of my children speaks Spanish a little.
—My son's teacher don't speak Chinese.

Why not?
When don't your children speak your language?
Are they embarrassed?

It's too hard.
With friends. At school.

I don't know. But my son don't speak Chinese.
—Jessie too. She gets mad and doesn't talk to my father.

Why are they embarrassed?

Their friends only talk English.
—Sometimes at school other kids call my daughter bad names.

What do they say?

Oh, I don't know. You Mexican! But she's American.

Finally, the teacher asked what students could do about the problem.

5. *What can you do?*

Can schools teach your language?

Yes, they teach Spanish one time a day.
—But why not more times a day?
—Why don't they teach my language?

Are there schools with bilingual programs?

I think so.
—That school is far. I want my son close to home.

What do you think about bilingual programs?

I like them.
—I want my children to speak English.
—But I want them to speak Chinese too.

Does your state have a bilingual education law? What does it say?	There are more than ten in my son's class. —Why don't we have bilingual classes? —I don't know. They learn at home. —My children get embarrassed. I want them to learn Spanish at school. —Send them to Mexico. —I can't. They need respect here.
What classes do you want schools to have?	Classes in language. —Yes, classes on different countries also.
What about your culture? Can you teach the teachers about your country? Your culture?	

In this dialogue, students perceived that the problem of maintaining culture and language extended beyond their personal experiences. With this understanding, they may stop blaming themselves for inadequate parenting, or they may gain the self-confidence to take action.

The decoding process creates an exciting classroom interaction. Every discussion inspired by a code will be different, depending on what issues are central to that group of students. Teachers can't and shouldn't know the answers to their questions. The inductive questions solicit students' opinions which lead to new ideas for teachers as well as for students.

In summary, the problem-posing approach has three major components:

1. *Listening:* Teachers start listening and observing before class begins and continue during and outside classroom interactions. Through their observations, teachers define and codify students' concerns for use in structured language learning and dialogue.
2. *Dialogue:* Using codes in the classroom, the dialogue approach employs decoding questions toward the goals of critical thinking and action. Teachers and students become co-learners. The dialogue approach mitigates language-learning conflict as students share their lives and culture with each other and the teacher.
3. *Action:* Dialogue is not a neutral process; it attempts to move learning from the level of information and skills to consequences and actions outside of the classroom. Action-oriented problem posing offers an opportunity for students to exercise control in class and in the rest of their lives.

To end this chapter, a chart compares problem posing with four other major ESL approaches. Though noninclusive, the chart graphically depicts the conceptual uniqueness of the problem-posing approach as applied to ESL teaching. The four approaches are counseling or community language learning, situational approaches (survival and competency-based ESL), values clarification or cultural relativism, and notional/functional.

Comparison of Freire's Problem-posing Approach and Other ESL Methodologies (Moriarty and Wallerstein)

Counseling-learning/community language learning (CL/CLL)
Similarities
- Extends beyond the artificial environment of the classroom
- Attempts to use language creatively, not just repetitively
- Topics for discussion determined by students
- Emphasizes group and social interaction
- Demonstrates relevance of conflict and emotions to learning

Differences
- Counselor/teacher doesn't ask questions, but simply translates; Freire teacher proceeds by questioning and dialogue
- Topics for discussion can be anything (Curran's examples—a trip to Tokyo, miniskirts); Freire content is always posed as a problem or central concern for the group
- CL/CLL teacher participates as expert translator; Freire teacher participates as a peer

Survival ESL, competency-based education (CBE) (situational approaches)

Similarities
- Attempts to deal with adult situations
- Shows relevance of learning to daily life
- Emphasizes needs assessment and feedback for evaluation
- Bases pattern of competencies on social inequities

Differences
- CBE emphasizes skills to cope and assimilate; Freire emphasizes skills to create and change problem situations
- Freire focuses on the survival skills and strengths that students already have
- Freire emphasizes teacher and students as co-learners

Values clarification, cultural relativism

Similarities
- Affirms students' expression of feelings and value statements
- Encourages participation by all
- Teacher is nonjudgmental

Differences
- Values clarification remains at individualistic level; Freire views values and cultural attitudes as a group creation

Notional/functional

Similarities
- Assumes communicative competence as starting point
- Uses language with its social context and purpose (opinions, intentions, emotions)
- Teaches language that students need
- Organizes teaching by content and integrated skills

Differences
- Life skills are taught for individual competence; Freire emphasizes collective approach
- Notional/functional organizes curriculum by purpose and need only; Freire takes problem orientation and thinking skills as major need
- Freire adds cultural context to expressions and communication

DISCUSSION QUESTIONS

1. Freire advocates challenging the "forces" that keep us "passive." What assumptions lie behind these words and their associated propositional meaning?

2. Discuss the progression from *listening* to *dialogue* to *action*. How does the "language of empowerment" enter into the picture?

3. When Wallerstein talks about "taking risks to get respect," what does she mean? Similarily what meanings undergird the phrase "the self-confidence to take action" (p. 202)? Is social action in the sense intended necessary to language acquisition? In what ways might it help the process along?

4. It is recommended that the teacher "listen," and then "select and present back the familiar situations to the students in a codified form: a photograph, a written dialogue, a story, or a drawing" (p. 197). In what ways would these activities lead to a progressively more thorough grasp of the target language? Consider the recommended movement from "the concrete to a more analytic level" and subsequently to recommended solutions.

5. Compare Freire's problem-posing approach with the other methods discussed throughout this book. What elements might you incorporate from it into your own teaching?

Part **IV**
Roles and Drama

The authors in this section offer practical insights into the "whys," "where-fores," and "how-tos" of drama and role-playing. In Chapter 13, Susan Stern presents some insightful observations about how it is that drama activates the body and emotions as well as the intellect. The influence of the thinking expressed in Part III can certainly be felt here, but there seems to be a shift in emphasis away from the therapeutic goals of the authors in that section back to more mundane language teaching in this section. Di Pietro (Chapter 14) praises the developers of the "notional/functional syllabi" and at the same time comments on the need for relevance of communicative devices to particular contexts of experience. His idea of the open-ended scenario leads smoothly into Scarcella's discussion (Chapter 15) of "sociodrama." Her conception stresses again the critical element of conflict and the motivating force it gives to the development of a scenario. The section concludes, then, with Chapter 16 by Rodriguez and White, who offer an explanation and exemplification of the transition from classroom exercises and activities to real-life experiences through field trips. Their example of a supermarket trip is just the sort of thing that we would have liked to learn about early in our own training as language teachers.

SUGGESTED ADDITIONAL READINGS

JOHN SCHUMANN.
   1975. Affective factors and the problem of age in second language acquisition. *Language Learning* 25:209–235.

   In this insightful article Schumann challenges the favored hypothesis that children are better second language acquirers than adults because of the greater plasticity of their brains. He contends that other factors may enter the picture as well—in particular, affective factors. Indeed he makes a plausible case for the idea that the biggest difference between children and adults may be the kinds of feedback and reactions of others to which they are exposed. (Also see Macnamara, Chapter 17, on this same issue.)

DAVID RUMELHART.
   1975. Notes on a schema for stories. In D. Bobrow and A. Collins (eds.). *Representation and Understanding*. New York: Academic, pp. 211–236.

This much criticized article may have initiated a whole new paradigm of research in artificial intelligence. We recommend it to language teachers because it offers a readable explanation of certain aspects of story structure which seem to be important to storage, memory, and recall of information. Unfortunately, it does not adequately deal with the importance of conflict, but see the following references for that.

ROBERT NEWTON PECK.
   1980. *Secrets of Successful Fiction*. Cincinnati, Ohio: Writer's Digest; and
DWIGHT V. SWAIN.
   1980. *Techniques of the Selling Writer*. Norman, Oklahoma: University of Oklahoma.

Why a brace of books on fiction at this juncture? We believe that a comprehension of the structure of readable, entertaining stories is crucial to language teachers who want to present a target language through a believable world of experience. Drama, role-play, and stories in general depend on the kinds of structures explicated in these highly readable books on fiction.

JOHN W. OLLER, JR.
   1983. Story writing principles and ESL teaching. *TESOL Quarterly* 17:39–53.

This paper explains some of the ways in which fiction writing techniques can be used in language teaching. It relies heavily on the just cited books by Swain and Peck.

F. SHAFTEL AND G. SHAFTEL.
   1967. *Role-Playing for Social Values*. Englewood Cliffs, New Jersey: Prentice-Hall.

This is a resource highly recommended by Scarcella (Chapter 15). It stresses the importance of the conflict situation for motivating the participants.

Chapter 13

Why Drama Works: A Psycholinguistic Perspective

Susan L. Stern
University of California, Los Angeles

EDITORS' INTRODUCTION

Stern assumes that drama works. She goes on then to try to say why. Among other things she notes that dramatizing communicative events leads to the necessary bodily and emotional involvement which results in the motivation to make meanings and intentions clear in the target language. This enterprise leads to competence in the language. Further since playacting removes some of the emotional burden of genuine acts of communication, yet retains much of the texture, the student has the opportunity to gain the necessary skills to carry the full communicative burden later in real acts of communication. Stern refers to the building of "specific self-esteem" in this connection, or "self-confidence," which is reminiscent of some of the remarks of previous chapters regarding the building of "self-worth," or Curran's "redemption." Criticisms of utterance forms in the target language may carry less personal threat because they are directed toward a portrayal of a character, someone other than the student. In this respect, Stern's explanation of why drama works has much in common with Lozanov's approach. However, Stern goes further than many other authors on this topic by carrying her ideas back to actual ESL students in the form of a questionnaire. The reactions of her subjects to the effects of drama in the language classroom are informative and encouraging. In general, the students agree with her assumption that drama works.

Drama is commonly used in ESL and foreign language classes for developing communicative competence, especially oral language skills.[1] Whether or not they use it themselves, most instructors would agree that drama, particularly role-play, is a standard classroom technique which "has long been recognized as a valuable and valid means of mastering a language" (Hines 1973, introduction).

It is not the purpose of this paper, however, to discuss dramatic techniques or argue for their usefulness. The intuitive assumption that drama in the ESL/foreign language classroom improves oral communication is taken as a given for this study, which approaches drama in L2 learning from a psycholinguistic perspective. The question to be explored is: Presuming that participation in dramatic activities helps L2 learners improve their communicative competence, how can this be explained in psycholinguistic terms; i.e.,

1. I wish to gratefully acknowledge the valuable and constructive comments and suggestions of Frances Hinofotis and John Schumann. I would also like to thank Donna Brinton and Meredith Pike for their contributions to the empirical study.

which psychological factors can explain why dramatic activities appear to improve the oral competence of L2 learners?

In answering this question, practical applications of drama in education and related fields were explored, beginning with ESL and foreign language classes. Any area that could illustrate the psychological basis of drama as a means of achieving a personal goal was investigated. Research revealed three such areas: drama in education, specifically in language classes; psychodrama, as practiced in the mental health field and in professional training programs; and role-playing in speech therapy.

The objectives for using drama are different for each of these disciplines. In ESL and foreign language classes, drama is directed toward language acqui-sition. In child development, creative dramatics encourages the maturation and growth of creative capacity, with particular reference to verbal skills. Psycho-drama helps restore a patient's mental health and trains individuals for new social roles. Speech therapy employs drama to help patients achieve or regain normal speech behavior and patterns.

Despite their differing aims, each of these disciplines appears to use drama for the same fundamental reason: It facilitates communication by bringing certain psychological factors into play which elicit the desired behavior in the individual. The common factors are motivation, empathy, sensitivity to rejection, self-esteem, and spontaneity. All but spontaneity are currently being investigated within the context of L2 acquisition (Schumann 1975). The focus of the present study is the insight these factors provide into the psychological effects of drama. The goal is to understand how and why participation in dramatic activities helps L2 learners achieve communicative competence.

The chapter begins with a discussion of the relationship between drama and each of these psychological factors within the frameworks of the three disciplines mentioned above. Implications for L2 learners are suggested throughout the discussion, leading to a statement of the hypothesis. The report of an informal exploratory study designed to find support for the claims made by the hypothesis concludes the chapter.

DRAMA IN EDUCATION:
ESL AND FOREIGN LANGUAGE CLASSES

Motivation

Motivation is the most frequently cited reason for using drama in ESL and foreign language classes. Dramatic activities inspire students to want to learn another language. They are a curative for the frustration and lagging interest which often occur during L2 learning, and they facilitate acquisition of the target language as a result (Hsu 1975, Via 1976, Moulding 1978).

The purposefulness of dramatic activity can provide a strong instrumental motivation for language learning. In an intermediate-level class in spoken

Chinese for American university students, for example, Hsu (1975) conducted an experiment in drama to develop the students' conversational ability and boost their sinking morale. She structured the entire course around presentation of a play, making it a group project that required students to communicate in Chinese throughout each aspect of preparation. Hsu found the activity to be highly motivating to her students, reactivating a high degree of interest in learning Chinese. Via (1976) also found play production as the culmination of a language course to be highly motivating to students when teaching English in Japan. Functioning as an end in itself as well as a topic for discussion and analysis, play production created a genuine communication need where students had to use natural conversational English in a meaningful context.

Play production can also be a source of integrative motivation by fostering cultural proximity. A play allows language learners to participate in the new culture, helping them develop a sensitivity as to how speakers of the target language interact with each other. It familiarizes them with the cultural appropriateness of words and expressions to specific settings and social situations. Ideally, this integrative experience should motivate learners to want to achieve a higher degree of language proficiency.

Moulding (1978) emphasized that drama provides the context for a meaningful exchange in which participants see a reason to communicate, and focuses on "how to do things" with the language rather than merely on "how to describe things." Maley and Duff (1978) explained that language teaching has tended to kill motivation by divorcing the intellectual aspects of language (vocabulary + structures) from its body and emotions, limiting instruction to the former. Dramatic techniques restore the body and emotions to language learning, thereby restoring motivation.

Self-Esteem

Self-esteem is an evaluation we make of ourselves and our abilities in terms of worthiness, and "specific self-esteem" is a self-evaluation particular to a specific life situation (Heyde 1977). Although this term rarely appears in TESL literature in reference to drama, the frequently cited concept of "self-confidence" seems to have the same meaning. Thus, for purpose of this study, "self-confidence" in L2 learning is synonymous with specific self-esteem—the learner's self-esteem as a speaker of the second language.

Heyde (1979) found that there appears to be a predictive quality to the correlation between self-esteem and the ability to orally produce a second language. Results indicate that students with high self-esteem received higher teacher oral production ratings than low self-esteem students. This implies that increased specific self-esteem should improve the language learner's oral proficiency. Advocates of drama in L2 learning support this hypothesis and believe that an effective way of raising self-esteem is via drama.

An analogy between acting and the martial arts suggested by Via (1976) explains one way in which drama helps self-confidence. Just as a yell accompanies the strike in order to build the confidence and increase the energy of the attacker, so a strong and clear voice (necessary when performing) gives the language learner confidence. Drama also raises self-esteem by demonstrating to L2 learners that they are indeed capable of expressing themselves in realistic communicative situations.

Sensitivity to Rejection

L2 learners who are afraid of what others may think of their less-than-perfect command of the language will be inhibited in using it. This is especially true of adults. Several educators have found that drama creates a nonthreatening situation which can reduce and even eliminate sensitivity to rejection (Hines 1973, Via 1976, Early 1977, Crookall 1978).

There are a number of possible explanations for the safety of the role-play situation. One is that it is only make-believe, and the learner needn't fear "the consequences of a lapse or miscalculation" (Early 1977, p. 34). The role shields learners against the less desirable consequences of their assertions, and their assertions thereby become freer (Crookall 1978, p. 2). A second explanation is that drama functions as a group effort, giving safety through numbers. A third is that critical judgment of what the participants say—and even how they say it—may be perceived by them as being directed toward the characters they are portraying rather than toward them personally. Consequently, they lose their normal inhibitions about speaking "relax, forget, *become* the characters they are portraying, and language flows" (Hines, 1973, introduction).

According to Via (1976), playacting is a natural activity of children, and their lack of inhibition allows them when unobserved to engage in award-winning performances. For the adult, to revive this innate ability is just a matter of rediscovery. S. Peck (1977) observed that children immersed in an L2 situation with native-speaking children will join them in play. Unfamiliarity with the second language does not seem to inhibit their involvement; on the contrary, they begin to use it themselves.

These observations, coupled with the generally accepted belief that children have the natural ability to acquire a second language, lead to some exciting speculations about drama as a strategy in adult L2 learning. If role-play can temporarily revive "the child" in adult L2 learners, then the child's natural ability to acquire a second language might also be revived to some extent.

Empathy

The empathic act is "a temporary suspension of ego functions in favor of an immediate precognitive experience of another's emotional state as one's own; ... a process of comprehending in which a temporary fusion of self-object boundaries ... permits an immediate emotional apprehension of the affective experience of another" (Guiora 1972, p. 142). Guiora explains that empathic capacity is dependent upon the ability to partially and temporarily suspend the functions that maintain one's separateness from others (usually called ego boundaries); i.e., to partially and temporarily give up one's separateness of identity. Flexibility, or permeability of ego boundaries, is the index of one's ability to take on a new identity.

Guiora et al. (1972) hypothesized that the ability to approximate nativelike pronunciation in a second language is related to the flexibility or permeability of one's ego boundaries. His experiment with alcohol, in which subjects' pronunciation in a second language was improved after their having ingested small amounts of alcohol, seemed to uphold this hypothesis. This led Schumann (1975, p. 226) to suggest that "if artificial agents such as alcohol can foster permeability of ego boundaries and reduce inhibitions, then it would not be unreasonable to assume that given the right concatenation of natural psychological factors, permeability of ego boundaries might be possible for everyone."

Actors must achieve empathy, or ego permeability, in order to give a convincing and meaningful performance. Stanislavski believed that they must pretend to live out the lives of their characters in ways that transcend the play. They must enter their characters' consciousness by temporarily giving up their own identity to take on a new dimension. A common training procedure for actors is to identify with their characters or wish they were there, and then imagine what they would do (Beutler 1976). Supporting the notion that drama fosters empathy in the participants, educators such as Shaftel and Shaftel (1952) have found that role play is a successful approach for forming positive intergroup relations because it permits the individual to understand and relate to the feelings of others.

It is therefore hypothesized that dramatic activities are an effective way of creating within the classroom setting that "concatenation of natural factors" which could make permeability of ego boundaries possible for everyone. If "the natural factors which induce ego flexibility and lower inhibitions are those conditions which make the learner less anxious, make him feel accepted and make him form positive identification with speakers of the target language" (Schumann 1975, p. 227); and if drama is one of those natural factors that induce flexibility and lower inhibitions, then one more explanation as to why drama is an effective technique in L2 learning will have been found.

DRAMA IN EDUCATION: ENGLISH FOR NATIVE SPEAKERS

A dramatic approach to the teaching of English has been practiced for a number of years in the British educational system. Instructors do not use drama to teach *about* language or the structure of the subject, or to teach *about* literature. Influenced by psychologists such as Piaget and Vygotsky, the theory of communication guiding the English curriculum focuses on personal and emotional experiences, imagination, intuition, and sensibility rather than subject matter. The question is not "how drama helps English nor how English helps drama, but how drama, English, movement and the other arts help the child" (Hoetker 1969, p. 12). Drama has also found its way into the English curricula of American schools, especially at the elementary levels as *creative dramatics*. This includes a wide range of activities, from mimic play to improvisations and from dramatizations of stories to the eventual enactment of formal plays among older children (Hoetker 1969).

The British and Americans share common assumptions about drama and employ similar techniques. It appears, however, that the goal of using drama in the British system is the total development of the child, whereas the goal of using drama among American educators more directly and specifically focuses on development of the language skills. As a strong advocate of dramatics in the American English curriculum, Moffett (1967, p. vii) sees drama as the matrix of all language activities, subsuming speech and engendering the varieties of writing and reading. Rogosheske (1972) cites a number of dedicated supporters of creative dramatics who claim it to be the most effective approach to instruction in the language skills.

Motivation

Drama can be especially effective with speakers whose skills are considered lower than average. Lazier (1969), for example, tried an experimental 12-week program in drama with a junior high school adjustment class composed of "disruptive" 13- to 15-year-olds classified as functional illiterates. Under his guidance, the students developed and staged an updated version of *West Side Story*. They rewrote the script by improvising the dialogue and recording their improvisations on paper. They then edited and refined to achieve clear and interesting communication. Although this task was extremely difficult for them, their motivation usually overcame lack of writing skill, and these students essentially formed a team of scriptwriters.

PSYCHODRAMA

Psychodrama is a general term referring to a group action technique used in psychotherapy and education, in which individuals act out roles involving social or psychological problems. Psychodrama typically begins with a warm-up period and discussion in which a theme (role, situation, problem) is agreed upon. The group members take roles and improvise a drama based upon the selected theme, then react to and analyze the performance. A scene might be dramatized a second or third time with different actors in the role, or the same actors reversing roles, followed by further reaction and analysis. There are several kinds of psychodrama, their primary difference being a matter of focus.

Sociodrama is an educational technique to train people for specific social roles, e.g., nursing, teaching. Its primary aim is the clarification of group themes, and it focuses on social problems. It involves acting out imaginary situations for purposes of self-understanding, improvement of skills, analyses of behavior, or to demonstrate how the participant operates or should operate (Corsini 1966). Sociodrama has been used effectively in ESL classes to develop vocabulary, grammar, discourse strategies, and strategies for social interaction; to promote cultural understanding; and to elicit oral production (Scarcella, Chapter 15).

Role playing is often used interchangeably with the term sociodrama. Blatner (1973) suggests, however, that most professionals would consider it to be more superficial and problem-oriented. The expression of deep feelings is not usually part of role playing. Rather, the goal tends to be the working out of alternative and more effective approaches to a general problem.

Psychodrama in the specific sense refers to the techniques employed in psychotherapy. A psychodrama is an enactment involving emotional problem solving in terms of one person's conflict. It is protagonist-centered, and moves toward relatively deep emotional issues. (*Note:* Unless specified as "psychodrama in psychotherapy," the term "psychodrama" will refer to the more general meaning.)

Empathy

Psychodramatic techniques reinforce empathic perceptions by developing interpersonal skills and sensitivity to others. For example, in a postgraduate development program for nursery school teachers conducted in a psychiatric clinic, the teachers were exploring grief due to death and bereavement when one of them asked how to deal with a child's question about death. This caused another teacher to enact the loss of a spouse, which catalyzed a dramatic and emotion-filled catharsis among the rest of the group in which they shared their own experiences of mourning. Thus, they touched their own deep feelings, and related to the hypothetical child and to each other with greater authenticity (Blatner 1973).

Role playing helps the individual become more flexible, i.e., develop a sense of mastery in many different role situations. "In turn, the components of each role can be applied more easily, in new situations, when syntheses must be developed" (Blatner 1973, p. 126). This suggests that through role play, L2 learners can experience many kinds of situations in which they will use the language; and as they develop a sense of mastery in them, they should be able to apply the language more easily to new situations.

Sensitivity to Rejection/Self-Esteem

The idea that role playing is safe is frequently expressed in psychodramatic literature. Corsini (1966) explained that in real life, patients may not attempt

214 METHODS THAT WORK

new ways of doing things; if they fail the results can be harmful. In therapeutic role playing, however, the very fact that they have the courage to demonstrate their functioning, no matter how inadequately, is a success. Consequently, patients are not embarrassed by a poor performance.

The same holds true for L2 learners. If they fail to communicate outside of class, the results can be embarrassing or even harmful. But in role play, having the courage to demonstrate the ability to use the second language is in itself a success, and they should therefore not be embarrassed by a poor performance. It follows that they should be less inhibited using the language in role play than in real life, and therefore function better than they thought they could. This in turn should raise their self-esteem.

Spontaneity

Analyses of people who have been through intensive psychodramas suggest a number of recurrent patterns which collectively might be described as "the spontaneity state" (Mann 1970). It is proposed that this state, or spontaneity, be added to the list of psychological factors currently being investigated in L2 acquisition.

Mann explains that persons in the spontaneity state completely forget about the existence of the audience or cease to be concerned about its reactions. Their temporal sense alters and they come to view time as an "eternal now," where past, present, and future are all enfolded in a dreamlike experience. Of most significance to L2 learning is that "the usual gap between thought and expression ceases to exist. Expression becomes an integrated whole" (Mann 1970, pp. 7–8). Also of relevance is the free-flowing creativity that is unleashed. "In varying degrees the person in such a state acts as though inspired. He draws on resources which neither he nor his friends may have thought he had at his disposal" (Mann 1970, pp. 7–8).

If this state can be induced in L2 learners via drama, the usual gap between thought and expression which ceases to exist in the native language might cease to exist in the second language as well. Equally relevant to L2 learning is the "free-flowing creativity" and the ability of the person to draw upon heretofore untapped resources. This might explain the following observation of an ESL student engaged in role play: "The transformation in his manner was unbelievable. He really 'hammed it up' during the phone conversation and everyone in the audience noticed" (Hinofotis and Bailey 1978, p. 15).

Corsini defined spontaneity as "natural, rapid, enforced self-generated behavior to new situations." He explained that people are frequently placed in new situations in which they have to improvise, to do something, to react. To the degree that the response is good, it is satisfying, helps one adjust, and tends to become part of one's repertoire. It is hypothesized that L2 learners undergo the same psychological process when they confront new linguistic situations in role play. To the degree that they succeed in communicating, the experience is satisfying. It helps them adjust to becoming a speaker of the second language and tends to become part of their linguistic repertoire.

DRAMATICS IN SPEECH THERAPY

Psychodramatic methods and role playing, when adapted to a particular setting, can be remarkably effective for children with relatively poor cognitive and verbal skills (Blatner 1973). Creative dramatics techniques are used as psychotherapy, as diagnostic observation, and as auditory training. Although children with speech handicaps must be individually examined and evaluated, they benefit from the group interaction central to creative dramatics.

The value of creative dramatics as an adjunct to speech therapy was demonstrated in a cooperative program offered by the creative dramatics classes and speech clinic of the University of Pittsburgh (McIntyre and McWilliams 1959). Several children with articulation and stuttering disorders were enrolled in creative dramatics classes along with children whose speech was considered normal. The program was initiated to bridge the gap between therapy at the clinic and everyday speech. The successful results of this program served to illustrate the correlation of creative dynamics to speech correction. Similarly positive results using creative dramatics to improve articulation were reported by Ludwig (1955), McIntyre (1958), McIntyre and McWilliams (1959), and Van Riper (1963). Role-playing techniques have also been adapted for adult aphasics to help them recover normal speech (Schlanger and Schlanger 1971).

Psychological Factors

The psychological factors contributing to the effectiveness of creative dramatics in speech therapy appear to be the same as those in operation in education and psychodrama. *Motivation* is a key factor. Schlanger and Schlanger (1971) claimed that the great psychological advantage of using role play with aphasics was that it helped them get closer to communicative intercourse so that they no longer felt that they were restricted to speaking in isolated and often seemingly meaningless words in a rote manner. McIntyre and McWilliams (1959) commented on the enjoyment of the role-play experience and the happy and relaxed atmosphere that it created.

Loss of *sensitivity to rejection* and heightened *self-esteem*, which also appear to be significant factors in speech improvement, are fostered by dramatics. Schlanger and Schlanger (1971) report that role playing is used to reduce aphasic patients' anxieties about communicating. In the role of another person, they can act the way they want rather than the way they are expected to act. Moreover, their attempts to communicate are reinforced by reactions of fellow aphasics, approbation of participating clinicians, and the self-satisfaction engendered by successful spontaneous communication (which brings in the factor of *spontaneity*).

Over the several years that they worked with role play, Schlanger and Schlanger noticed the following changes in their patients: (1) some relief of frustration and anxiety concerning deficient communication, (2) loss of inhibition, (3) a strong sense of accomplishment, and (4) insight into the problems of self and the feelings and actions of others. The first three changes are indicative of lowered sensitivity to rejection and heightened self-esteem. The fourth suggests that increased empathy was in operation.

THE HYPOTHESIS

This brief investigation into the use of drama in language education, psychology, and speech therapy reveals that despite their differing aims, each employs drama because it facilitates communication. For language learning and speech therapy, communication is the desired end in itself. For psychotherapy and child development, communicative ability is a prerequisite behavior that must be acquired before other behaviors, such as social adjustment and overall development of the child, can occur. But it appears to be the common assumption that drama can develop and/or elicit communicative competence in the individual.

The application of this assumption to L2 learning is the basis for the hypothesis of this study: Drama facilitates communication in L2 learners by encouraging the following psychological factors to operate: heightened self-esteem, motivation, and spontaneity; increased capacity for empathy; lowered sensitivity to rejection.

AN EXPLORATORY STUDY OF THE PSYCHOLOGICAL BASIS FOR USING DRAMA IN LANGUAGE TEACHING

Although formal empirical investigation of the hypothesis will be reserved for future research, a questionnaire was designed to explore the issue informally. The questionnaire had both a student and a teacher component. It was administered to three ESL instructors at the University of California, Los Angeles, who had recently used dramatic activities in their classes, and to the 24 advanced-level students who had participated in them. Class A was the regular university section of a course in oral communication. Class B was the university extension section of the same course. Class C was a course in phonetics also offered by university extension. The dramatic activities in which the students participated were *scenes from plays* and *improvisations*.

Dramatizing scenes from plays involved performing short scenes (about 8 to 10 minutes each) which involved two or three characters. The students were not asked to memorize lines but were told to look up and say them to the other character(s) with meaning and feeling. Both the scenes and the improvisations were videotaped, and the students viewed and discussed their performances afterward.

For classes A and C, improvisations consisted of interviews of the characters and improvisations based upon the scenes. The interview took place directly after the scene. The students had to imagine that they were still the characters they had just portrayed, and respond accordingly to questions posed by the instructor and the other students. The improvisation followed immediately afterward. The instructor described a situation to the students, similar to the scene they had just enacted, but with a significant twist in character or plot (Stern 1977). They were given 5 minutes to consult with one another, and then performed. Class B participated in the same kind of interview, but for them improvisations were a separate activity based upon a role-play game. The students were assigned character roles in pairs and were presented with a dramatic situation to improvise in front of the class.

The Student Questionnaire

There were 24 respondents to the student component of the questionnaire: the 13 students enrolled in class A, 6 of the 10 students enrolled in class B, and all 5 students enrolled in class C. The questionnaire was designed to elicit their subjective responses to the psychological aspects of drama being investigated. In order to avoid making this purpose known to the students, it was presented to them as part of the final course evaluation, and distractor items were included which focused on concrete objectives for using drama, e.g., improving pronunciation and expression. (*Note:* See the appendix for the student component of the questionnaire. Each item is labeled with the psychological factor it was designed to test, and the distractor items are identified.)

Part I asked the students to evaluate the usefulness of participating in (1) scenes from plays and (2) improvisations. Table 1 summarizes the results by collapsing the data from these two sections according to the areas of usefulness being evaluated. The items were evaluated on a five-point Likert scale. The mean scores for each class were calculated separately in order to capture any differences that might appear between the oral communication classes and the pronunciation class, and between the university and extension classes. The "Overall $\overline{X}$" indicates the response of all 24 students as one group rather than the average of the three classes in order to give a truer reading due to the differences in class size.

Part II consisted of questions relating to the students' feelings about themselves during and after performance. The results may be found in Table 2. As in Table 1, the mean scores for classes A, B, and C were first calculated separately, and the Overall $\overline{X}$ represents the average of all 24 students as one group. Three different five-point Likert scales were used, corresponding to question 1, questions 2 through 6, and question 7.

Table 1   Usefulness of Drama as Perceived by Students[a]

Item on questionnaire Part I	Potential area of usefulness	Class A mean ($n=13$)	Class B mean ($n=6$)	Class C mean ($n=5$)	Overall mean ($N=24$)
	Improving pronunciation				
1a	Scenes from plays	3.5[b]	3.2	3.6	3.4
2a	Improvisations	2.7	3.2	3.4	2.95
	Improving intonation and expression				
1b	Scenes from plays	4.6	3.2	4.2	4.1
2b	Improvisations	3.6	4.0	3.6	3.7
	Gaining self-confidence				
1c	Scenes from plays	3.9	4.2	4.0	4.0
2c	Improvisations	4.3	4.2	4.2	4.25
	Becoming less inhibited or less embarrassed when speaking in front of a group				
1d	Scenes from plays	4.3	4.0	3.6	4.1
2d	Improvisations	4.4	4.7	4.2	4.33
	Increasing/enriching vocabulary				
1e	Scenes from plays	3.0	3.4	3.4	3.0
	Learning more about American culture				
1f	Scenes from plays	3.0	3.0	4.2	3.2

[a]The data in Table 1 correspond to the items on Part I of the questionnaire.
[b]The figures are based on the following Likert scale responses: 1 = not useful; 2 = a little useful; 3 = somewhat useful; 4 = quite useful; 5 = very useful.

Part III asked the students whether or not they would like to participate in more dramatic activities and solicited their comments as to why or why not. Their responses to the yes/no question are summarized in Table 3. The students' open-ended comments are incorporated into the discussion that follows, which synthesizes and summarizes the results reported in the three tables in terms of the psychological factors under study.

Motivation

Motivation was measured in terms of the degree of enjoyment students experienced while participating in dramatic activities, and by their desire to participate in more. Responses to items 6a and 6b (Table 2) indicate that students enjoyed both activities "quite a bit." (Scenes = 4.0; improvisations = 4.1.) Seventy-nine percent expressed the desire to participate in more

Table 2   Student Reactions to Drama[a]

Item on questionnaire Part II	Topic	Class A mean (n=13)	Class B mean (n=6)	Class C mean (n=5)	Overall mean (N=24)
1	Ability to express self in English during performance	3.2[b]	3.2	4.0	3.3
2	Difficulty in understanding character	1.5[c]	1.7	2.2	1.7
3	Nervousness when participating in dramatic activities	2.5	3.2	2.0	2.6
4	Difficulty in identifying with or stepping into role of character	2.4	2.8	1.8	2.4
5	Embarrassment when acting	2.45	3.3	2.2	2.6
6a	Enjoyment when acting scenes from plays	4.1	3.8	4.0	4.0
6b	Enjoyment when acting improvisations	4.2	4.2	4.0	4.1
7	Evaluation of own performance	3.6[d]	3.2	4.0	3.8

[a]The data in Table 2 correspond to the items on Part II of the questionnaire.
[b]The figures in the first section are based on the following Likert scale:

1	2	3	4	5
Overall I was displeased with my ability. I felt very frustrated.				Overall I was pleased with my ability. I felt I was able to express myself with ease.

[c]The figures in the second section are based on the following Likert scale:

1	2	3	4	5
not at all	a little	somewhat	quite	very much

[d]The figures in the third section are based on the following Likert scale:

1	2	3	4	5
I didn't like it. It was worse than I thought it would be.		about average		I liked it very much. It was better than I thought it would be.

Table 3   Desire to Participate in More Dramatic Activities[a]

Item on questionnaire Part III	Dramatic activity	Class A % (n=13) Yes	No	Class B % (n=6) Yes	No	Class C % (n=5) Yes	No	Overall % (N=24) Yes	No
1a	Scenes from plays (with script)	92	8	50	50	80	20	79	21
1b	Improvisations (without script)	92	8	83	17	100	0	92	8

[a]The data in Table 3 correspond to the items on Part III of the questionnaire.

scenes and 92 percent indicated that they would like to do more improvisations (Table 3).

In explaining why they would or would not like to participate in more dramatic activities (Part III), students commented on the following: the enjoyment or "fun" of drama; ways in which drama had helped them achieve the objectives of the course they were taking, e.g., improved pronunciation and intonation; learning more about American culture and becoming acquainted with works of American writers. Some students commented on psychological issues, such as drama helped them "loosen up," and improvisations helped them express themselves and their feelings. A number commented on how drama helped them feel more confident when speaking in front of a group. There were four negative comments, three of which referred to the scripted scenes from plays. Only one student was negative about drama in general, explaining, "I just don't like to act."

Self-esteem

As Table 2 indicates (items 1 and 7), the students' postevaluation of their performance (3.8) was higher than their recollection of how they felt they had expressed themselves in English at the time (3.3). This suggests that while their feelings about their ability at the time of performance had been mildly positive, the postviewing raised their self-esteem. It might explain why overall the students felt that scenes (4.0) and especially improvisations (4.25) had been quite useful in helping them gain self-confidence in speaking English (Table 1, items 1c and 2c).

Empathy

Empathy was evaluated in terms of the degree of difficulty students experienced in understanding and identifying with the characters they portrayed. As Table 2 reveals (items 2 and 4), they experienced very little difficulty in understanding their characters (1.7), and only slightly more difficulty in identifying with them (2.4).

Sensitivity to rejection

Feelings of nervousness and embarrassment were the criteria used for determining sensitivity to rejection. The overall responses reported in Table 2 (items 3 and 5) indicate that the students had been slightly less than "somewhat" nervous (2.6) and embarrassed (2.6). In spite of this moderate degree of uneasiness, their overall responses to how useful scenes and improvisations had been in helping them become less inhibited or less embarrassed when speaking in front of a group (Table 1, items 1d and 2d) were 4.1 and 4.33, respectively.

Spontaneity

None of the items specifically evaluated spontaneity. However, in response to the open-ended questions which asked if participating in scenes from plays and improvisations had helped students communicate more effectively in any other way (Part I, 1g and 2e), five students commented either that drama had helped them respond "off the top of their heads" or that it had helped them respond more quickly to unexpected questions and/or situations.

Summary of student responses

Although no generalizations may be derived from the results of this informal survey, several impressionistic observations can be made. The students did feel that dramatic activities had helped them gain self-confidence in speaking English and become less embarrassed when speaking in front of a group. Along with improving intonation and expression (the instructors' primary objective for using drama), these two areas were perceived by the students as being the greatest benefits of participating in drama. They also felt that drama had helped them develop spontaneity in English. The students had felt positive about their ability to express themselves in English during the improvisations, and even more positive after seeing themselves on videotape. They had enjoyed participating in these activities and were motivated to participate in more. No comments can be made about a causal relationship between drama and empathy, but it can at least be said that the students did not appear to have any problems understanding, identifying with, or stepping into the roles of the characters.

The Teacher Questionnaire

The teacher questionnaire was open-ended, with no reference whatsoever to the psychological factors under study. This was to guarantee that any comments about the psychological effects of drama would be completely spontaneous. The questions were:

1. What were your specific objectives for using dramatic activities in your class? What did you hope to accomplish?
2. Why did you choose drama to meet these objectives, or what was it particularly about drama/role playing that lent itself to meeting these objectives?
3. Which, if any, of these objectives were met? Please comment on why you think they were successful.

The following discussion is a synthesis of the teachers' observations. The instructors are referred to as T-A, teacher of class A, the university course in oral communication; T-B, teacher of class B, the university extension course in oral communication; and T-C, teacher of class C, the university extension course in pronunciation. (*Note:* The author was the instructor of class A and felt

222 METHODS THAT WORK

it inappropriate to respond to her own questionnaire. Therefore, the instructor who had taught the university section of the same course the previous quarter, and used the same dramatic activities with her students, responded instead. The author's comments are included separately at the end of the discussion.)

T-B and T-C found that drama relaxed their students. T-A commented, "I do think the use of drama early in the term helped to lessen the nervousness the students felt about speaking in English in front of a group." She also discovered that drama appeared to create a safe classroom environment. "The students benefited from the activities almost as they would if they were interacting with Americans, but they were not under pressure to be themselves." T-B commented that drama enhanced the class atmosphere and relaxed the students' anxiety about speaking in front of each other and making oral presentations. She added that "the scenes from plays provided structure where students could 'loosen up' [their words]. We progressed from this to role-play."

T-C found drama to be a really welcome relief from the normal classroom activity, and to be highly motivating: "Affectively the implementation of drama in the classroom was very positive, in that not only the more outgoing students participated, but also (and surprisingly very willingly) the normally very passive ones." She also noted that dramatic activities helped her students lose their normal inhibitions and enabled them to assume personalities very much in contrast to their own. Another reference to empathy was made by T-B, who explained that drama facilitates adoption of a different identity.

The author's own experience with class A strongly supports the observations of these students and teachers. The students seemed to undergo a transformation when they "stepped out" of the classroom into an imaginary setting and situation, especially the shy students who normally spoke only when called upon—and then in a quiet and hesitant voice. They became more extroverted, initiating as well as responding to dialogue. Role playing seemed to stimulate them to activate their passive competence of the language. The more verbal and extroverted students were also transformed. Their speech became more fluent, and their intonation and inflection more nativelike, particularly during improvisations.

CONCLUSION

This paper has taken a speculative and theoretical approach to drama in L2 learning, with the intent of laying the groundwork and providing the inspiration for further investigation into the area. Its purpose was to present the hypothesis that drama positively affects L2 learning by encouraging the operation of certain psychological factors which facilitate oral communication, i.e., heightened self-esteem, motivation, and spontaneity; increased capacity for empathy; lowered sensitivity to rejection. This hypothesis was based upon logic, analogy, experience, and intuition. It was founded upon a literature review and was informally tested via the student/teacher questionnaire.

If the responses to the questionnaire can be taken as valid indicators, there may be some justification for the hypothesis, and drama in L2 learning is a promising area for further research. This study suggests several research possibilities. One would be a formal test of the hypothesis, i.e., to examine the psychological factors individually to determine if they are positively correlated with drama and if drama acts as a causal variable in fostering them in the participant. Related research would include further investigation into the relationship between each of the psychological factors and L2 acquisition. Another project would be to test the assumption behind the hypothesis: that dramatic activities in the ESL/foreign language classroom improve oral communication skills. Along these lines, Wesche (1977) has already found that role play correlates highly with a number of learning variables.

It is hoped that these suggestions will stimulate further research and that this theoretical study will lead to additional investigations of drama in second language learning from a psycholinguistic perspective.

APPENDIX

Student Questionnaire—Evaluation of Dramatic Activites

Your reactions to the dramatic activities that you participated in this quarter would be very much appreciated. Please answer as thoughtfully and accurately as possible.

PART I: Circle the number that most closely reflects your opinion.

1. SCENES FROM PLAYS (using script)
   How useful was acting out a scene from a play for you in each of the following areas?

			Not useful	A little useful	Somewhat useful	Quite useful	Very useful
D[a]	a)	Improving pronunciation	1	2	3	4	5
D	b)	Improving intonation and expression	1	2	3	4	5
Self-esteem	c)	Gaining self-confidence in speaking English	1	2	3	4	5
Sensitivity to rejection	d)	Becoming less inhibited, or less embarrassed when speaking in front of a group	1	2	3	4	5
D	e)	Increasing/enriching your vocabulary	1	2	3	4	5
D	f)	Learning more about American culture	1	2	3	4	5
	g)	Did acting out scenes help you communicate more effectively in any other way? Please explain.					

2. IMPROVISATIONS BASED ON SCENES FROM PLAYS (without script)
How useful was participating in an improvisation for you in each of the following areas?

			Not useful	A little useful	Somewhat useful	Quite useful	Very useful
D	a)	Improving pronunciation	1	2	3	4	5
D	b)	Improving intonation and expression	1	2	3	4	5
Self-esteem	c)	Gaining self-confidence in speaking English	1	2	3	4	5
Sensitivity to rejection	d)	Becoming less inhibited, or less embarrassed when speaking in front of a group	1	2	3	4	5
D	e)	Did it help you communicate more effectively in any other way? Please explain.					

PART II

Self-esteem

1. Think back to when you were performing the improvisations, and try to remember how you felt about your ability to express yourself in English at that time.

Overall I was displeased with my ability. I felt very frustrated.

Overall I was pleased with my ability. I felt I was able to express myself with ease.

1	2	3	4	5

Empathy

2. How difficult did you find it to understand the character you were playing?

	Not at all difficult	A little	Somewhat	Quite	Very difficult
	1	2	3	4	5

Sensitivity to rejection

3. How nervous did you feel when participating in dramatic activities?

	Not at all nervous	A little	Somewhat	Quite	Very nervous
	1	2	3	4	5

Empathy

4. How difficult did you find it to identify with, or step into the role of the character you were playing?

	Not at all difficult	A little	Somewhat	Quite	Very difficult
	1	2	3	4	5

Sensitivity to rejection

5. How embarrassed did you feel when acting in front of the class?

	Not at all	A little	Somewhat	Quite	Very
	1	2	3	4	5

Motivation

6. How much did you enjoy participating in the following activities?

		Not at all	A little	Somewhat	Quite a bit	Very much
a.	scenes from plays (with script)	1	2	3	4	5
b.	improvisation (without script)	1	2	3	4	5

Self-esteem

7. How would you evaluate your own performance?

I didn't like it. It was worse than I thought it would be.

About average

I liked it very much. It was better than I thought it would be.

1	2	3	4	5

PART III

1. Would you like to participate in more dramatic activities?
a. scenes from plays (with script)   YES   NO
b. improvisations (without script)   YES   NO
2. Why or Why Not? (Please use back of sheet to explain your answer, and to add any other comments you may have about the dramatic activities you participated in this quarter.)

[a]D = Distractor items [Editors' Note: I.e. noncriterial items, or padding.]

DISCUSSION QUESTIONS

1. How does Guiora's concept of "ego permeability" enter into the supposed effects of dramatizations? What does it have to do with "empathy"? With the acquisition of a nonprimary language?

2. Stern comments that actors must in a sense already possess the skills that language students are trying to acquire. In your view, does this element impede or enhance the effectiveness of drama as a device in the language classroom?

3. Stern cites Moffett (1967), who "sees drama as the matrix of all language activities" (p. 212). Do you agree with this assessment? If so, what in fact is the "role" of ordinary experience?

4. Do you feel that the difference between students' willingness to participate in additional contrived scenes (79 percent said they wanted to) as compared with their willingness to do more improvisations (92 percent said they wanted to) is significant? If so, why? What in your view is the proper balance between the use of contrived scenes and improvisations in the classroom? What factors might enter into the dynamics of such a balance?

5. Are you surprised that student confidence increased as a result of viewing their own improvisations on videotape? Why is this outcome unexpected (or possibly expected)? Would you expect a different outcome with less advanced students?

Chapter 14

Scenarios, Discourse, and Real-Life Roles

Robert J. Di Pietro

University of Delaware

EDITORS' INTRODUCTION

Di Pietro urges that functional/notional syllabi need to be related to ordinary experience so that they will become more than mere "shopping lists of communicational devices" (p. 233). One way of ensuring this sort of relevance is to engage students in scenarios which require that they act out roles appropriate to the demands and tensions of those contexts. Di Pietro offers a number of practical suggestions which follow up nicely the suggestions of Stern (Chapter 13) and which in fact can be carried directly into language teaching classrooms. His conception of an "open-ended scenario" where students must not only act out roles but improvise utterances based on their own decisions at various turns is a promising device for getting intermediate and advanced students fully into meaningful acts of communication. The scenario approach (whether open-ended or not) also offers many ideas for expanding upon principles and techniques suggested in earlier chapters. Also, Di Pietro's theoretical reasoning complements the following chapters by Scarcella (Chapter 15) and by Rodriguez and White (Chapter 16).

One of the most serious proposals for ESL curriculum reform to emerge within recent years is the *functional-notional syllabus* (see, for example, Wilkins 1976). An independent codevelopment is an innovative classroom technique based on group dynamics (see Curran 1976 and also Chapter 10 above). As promising as these two innovations are, neither provides the background for understanding how language and culture are associated with the many roles which learners must play in real-life interactions. This article therefore proposes a taxonomy for role types. Roles function in either long-term or short-term interactions and are thus either [−episodic] or [+episodic]. Three types of roles are established and illustrated via dialogues: social, emotive, and maturational. Through a multidimensional model of discourse, interactional exercises can be developed to lead ESL/EFL students to play roles in simulated natural settings while acquiring knowledge of the grammatical structure of English.

Suggestions have been made (Di Pietro 1978) as to how the ESL/EFL teacher can provide diverse learner personalities with strategically oriented material. These suggestions came in answer to the need for learners to generalize from the conventions of language form and use presented within the constraints of the classroom to the free options and innovations needed by them in real-life communication. We must also credit such scholars as Wilkins (1976) for first drawing our attention to the basic functions and notions of communication likely to be needed by learners of foreign languages.

As we work with functional/notional syllabi, however, we cannot avoid several problems. For example, such syllabi fail to distinguish adequately between language uses which are ritualized and those which are psychologically and culturally diverse. In order to adapt the functional-notional syllabus to a structured classroom experience, essential information must be provided on the cultural and psychological relevance of individual speech functions. That is, refutation or disagreement might be important functions to learn in the target language, but cultural constraints might exist in some instances which make the use of such functions counterproductive. Arguing with a policeman about to issue a ticket, for example, may not be appropriate if the language is Spanish and the setting is Mexico City. Even in situations where the culture might provide options for argumentation, such a style might not suit the individual involved.

Another important but usually ignored aspect of language use is *scripting*. Interaction among humans is not without an organization in which intent and purpose link one episode of interaction to another. Yet scripts in real-life are as individualistic as the people who create them. Unlike theatrical scripts fashioned by an unseen playwright and endowed with internal consistency, real-life scripts often clash. The interpretation by one person of another's intent can lead to illusion and ambiguity.

Beyond the formal structure of discourse are two other dimensions: a *transactional dimension*, in which dialogues display an exchange of strategies between the parties, and an *interactional dimension*, in which the parties assume social, maturational, and emotive roles. It is the interactional dimension which concerns us here.

TOWARD AN UNDERSTANDING OF ROLES IN HUMAN INTERACTION

What is a *role*? According to one definition, a role is "a set of norms and expectations applied to the incumbent of a particular position" (Munby 1978, p. 68). But much more must be said about this term if its application to the teaching situation is to be productive. First of all, roles do not exist in a communicational vacuum. Rather they are oppositional. To play the role of an adviser one needs someone willing to be advised. A physician requires patients to doctor just as a general needs an army to command. Even a recluse needs a society from which to be estranged. We can capture this essential aspect of roles with the expression *role reciprocation*. The following are some roles which are tied together in reciprocal pairs: host/guest, parent/child, vendor/customer, employer/employee, and teacher/student (see Di Pietro 1979 for more on role reciprocation).

The strategic function of language exchanged between persons playing reciprocal roles is for the interactants to move toward a shared goal, as illustrated in the following sample dialogue:

Grocer: May I help you, Ma'am?
Customer: Yes. I'd like a pound of coffee.
Grocer: How would you like it ground?
Customer: For a percolator, please.
Grocer: Here you are. Anything else?
Customer: No thank you. How much is it?
Grocer: $5.00.
Customer: Here. I'd like the change in ones.
Grocer: (takes money and gives her the change as requested) Have a good day.
Customer: The same to you (leaves store).

In such interactions the purpose of completing a sale is understood perfectly by both parties. The questions and answers comprising the bulk of the verbal exchange center on the specifics of the sale, i.e., item to be purchased (coffee), how it is to be prepared (for a percolator), how much it costs ($5.00), and so on. The dialogue starts with an expected opener (May I help you, Ma'am?) and comes to a close with an exchange of protocols which also might be expected (Have a good day/The same to you). While the particular verbal content of the questions and answers posed in the body of the dialogue might vary, there is no indeterminacy as to the intentions of the interactants. Their roles are so clearly reciprocating that the actual verbiage may be reduced considerably without causing any ambiguities, e.g.:

Grocer: Yes?
Customer: Pound of coffee, please.
Grocer: Percolator-grind?
Customer: Yes, thank you.
Grocer: Anything else?
Customer: No. How much is that? (etc.)

The nature of human interaction is such, however, that the roles we play are not always reciprocal. We do not always share the intentions of those whom we come in contact, even in the context of commercial transactions. Under some circumstances we may not wish to play buyer roles. Perhaps our intention is only to window shop and to do so we must fight the pressure placed on us by insistent salesclerks who want to play vendor roles. A tactic we use to counter the would-be vendor's "Can I help you" is: "Just looking, thank you." Every adult learner of English would be well advised to remember such a useful countertactic. While the vendor/window-shopper roles constitute a recurrent pair, they are not reciprocal and the language used by the players is not complementary, e.g.:

Salesclerk: Can I help you?
Window-shopper: Just looking, thank you.
Salesclerk: Call me if you need me.
            By the way, we're having a sale on gloves.

Window-shopper: I'm not interested in gloves.
    Salesclerk: Have you seen our new sweaters?
Window-shopper: I'm really just browsing.
    Salesclerk: They're marked down 35 percent.
Window-shopper: I'll call you if I need you.

This dialogue between a salesclerk and a window-shopper can be just as likely to occur as the one between a grocer and a willing customer. The verbal give-and-take bumps along until one of two events takes place: either the salesclerk converts the window-shopper into a customer (where the roles are now reciprocal) or the interaction is concluded. We teachers should provide our students with enough English (1) to recognize the role intentions of others, and (2) either to complement those roles or to counter them with personally desired ones.

A good basis for formulating the verbal strategies which fulfill both types of roles is the functional-notional syllabus. However, functions and notions must be made situationally and personally relevant. Further on, some sample scenarios are presented which are adaptable to the classroom and which allow students to play a number of different roles, complementary or not, which are coached by the teacher. But first more needs to be said about the nature of roles.

In addition to the feature [±reciprocating], interactional roles may also be [±episodic]. The effect on actual usage can be considerable, depending on the duration of the interaction. Long-standing role relationships, i.e., [−episodic], call for verbal strategies reflecting the players' familiarity with each other, whereas in short-term interactions, i.e., [±episodic], the players are not very much involved emotionally or psychologically. Compare the following dialogues, which are based on a similar theme but differ in terms of the familiarity with one or another of the interactants:

Dialogue 1: [+episodic]
Flight Attendant: Sorry sir, no smoking in this section.
    Passenger: I didn't notice. Sorry.
Flight Attendant: If you like, I'll change your seat.
    Passenger: Oh, that's OK. I smoke too much anyway.

Dialogue 2: [−episodic]
    Wife: John, you promised you wouldn't smoke!
    Husband: Oh-oh, you caught me lighting up.
    Wife: If you give me your cigarets, I'll put them where you can't find them.
    Husband: That's a good idea, dear. Here.

Politeness protocols are much more characteristic of episodic interactions than they are of nonepisodic ones. To illustrate this point, the second dialogue above would sound as inappropriate in the mouths of the flight attendant and the passenger as would the first in the mouths of the wife and husband.

To complicate matters, people often play more than one role at the same time. Business transactions on the same theme can be executed quite differently depending on the ways in which the players may be involved psychologically with each other. The dialogue that would transpire in the setting in which a man is buying a used car from his brother-in-law would be quite different from one in which the buyer and seller are strangers to each other. In fact, a recurrent ploy of used-car salesmen is to act as if there were a long-standing role relationship between him and the customer ("Call me by my first name"). It is not surprising that even we who are native speakers enter into interactions with others without always knowing whether the role being played opposite us is reciprocating or not. We also find ourselves being forced into a long-standing role relationship where we might only wish to limit the interaction to one episode. Table 1 represents an attempt to clarify which role pairs are episodic and which by nature are nonepisodic. There is evidence that some role pairs can be both.

Table 1   Outline for a Taxonomy of Role Pairs

Role pairs	[+episodic]	[−episodic]
Social pairs: Buyer/seller, Adviser/advisee, Donor/bene-factor, etc.	X	
Emotive pairs: Competitors, Rivals, Friends, etc.	X	X
Maturational pairs: Parent/child, Adult/adult, Child/child, etc.		X

Whereas social role pairs are strongly conditioned by the time limitations of the interaction and maturational roles require time to develop, emotive roles are not so constrained. They may either affect language use over several episodes or be rendered inactive after only one. For example, two businessmen might be driven to be competitors (social) in some instances but might not remain rivals (emotive) over an extended period of time. What they might say to each other as competitors is undoubtedly influenced by their long-standing relationship as nonrivals.

TEACHER/STUDENT AND KNOWER/LEARNER ROLES IN THE CLASSROOM

Against the background of group dynamics we should be able to distinguish between episodic and nonepisodic roles in the classroom. The constraints of a formal course of instruction in English as a second or foreign language inevitably lead to the creation of a long-standing, nonepisodic teacher/student role pairing. Despite this long-standing role pairing, a number of different short-term role pairs may be developed in the course of instruction. In the knower/learner pair, which is episodic by nature, students may play the part of knowers to other students (see Curran 1976 for discussion of knower/learner role playing). Even in traditional classroom settings the teacher may in some exercises enlist the aid of those students who have learned a particular point before the others have.

Going beyond the knower/learner pairing, teachers may also cast themselves episodically as coaches, thereby helping the students to achieve a communicational function without dominating the learning activity. Interactional games may be played in which students work toward a personal solution of a clear-cut social problem. In such games, the teacher sets the scenario and then asks the students to decide what kind of solution would be most appropriate in their opinion and to create a dialogue in which the solution is realized via the English language. Teams of students can be composed to work together on the various roles. As a variation the teacher can assign the roles individually to be worked on as homework. A certain part of the instructional period is then set aside for the teacher to coach the players before they enact the dialogue in class. The teacher's coaching includes not only grammatical corrections but also the use of proper intonation and gestures. Since the teacher's coaching is off-stage, so to speak, student anxiety is lessened as to the committing of errors. Only on-stage errors are significant. The following is an example of an interactional game which could be used:

The Dinner Date

Scenario (part 1): A young man has invited you (a young woman) to dinner. This occasion is your first date with him. The menu lists three groups of meals: expensive, middle-priced, and inexpensive. You must make a selection.

Questions: What price-range will you choose if you are (1) interested in getting more serious about your date, (2) uncertain as to your feelings, or (3) not very interested in going out with him again? How do you think his reaction to your choice of meals will give away his feelings about you?

Exercise: Write a dialogue between you and the young man, centering on your choice of meals and his reaction.

Scenario (part 2): It is now the second dinner date between you and the young man (that is, if you have decided to let the relationship continue). Write a sequel to the dialogue which occurred on the first date.

Another student (male) may be asked to prepare his own set of verbal strategies to use in the three choices possible made by the dinner guest. The other students in the class can serve as a panel of judges, to pass on the effectiveness of the resulting interaction.

As a cultural note, a Chinese woman on her first dinner date with a Chinese man is likely to select a very expensive dish if she is interested in continuing the relationship. The reaction of the man (and his willingness to take her out again) will let her know his feelings. If there is a second date, the woman will display a concern for the man's hard-earned money and select an inexpensive meal.

Other interactional games can be composed to take into account the various maturational levels of the role pairs. Table 2 provides some sample scenarios which are maturationally applicable.

The following are two dialogues to contrast maturational role pairings:

Dialogue 3 (Parent/Child)
Mother: Johnny, don't eat that!
Johnny: Aw, Mom, I like chocolate.
Mother: You've had enough for today.
Johnny: Can I save it for later?
Mother: Only if you eat all your vegetables.

Dialogue 4 (Two Adult Friends)
Susan: You shouldn't eat so much chocolate.
  Bill: Well, I guess I'm addicted to it.
Susan: Even so, don't you think you've had enough for today?
  Bill: Maybe you're right. I'll save it for another time.
Susan: You can't beat a balanced diet.

Table 2   Scenario Themes Grouped Maturationally

  I. Preadolescent and adolescent/parent or other authority figure.
      1. Explain a bad report to your parents.
      2. Explain to Mommy how her best vase got broken.
      3. Tell Mommy/Daddy something to avoid going to bed.
      4. Get Daddy to buy something you want.
      5. Get the teacher to excuse you from an assignment.
 II. Teenager/other teenager or parent.
      1. Get out of a date.
      2. Apologize for not showing up for a date.
      3. Make up after an argument with your boy/girl friend.
      4. Explain to your parents how you overspent your checking account.
III. Adult/adult.
      1. (man or woman) Explain to your spouse how you had an accident with the new car.
      2. (man or woman) Get your spouse to agree to a vacation in a place that he or she detests but you like.
      3. (man or woman) Explain to your spouse how you happened to rip an expensive silk screen he or she put behind your chair.

REAL LIFE AND THE CLASSROOM

Real life provides much raw material for classroom scenarios. For example, in a recent undercover action by the FBI, a member of Congress was videotaped accepting a bribe. This politician claimed subsequently that he was conducting his own undercover investigation in order to determine how far the bribers would go. He said that eventually he was going to deposit the money with government authorities. A classroom scenario based on this story might cast one student in the part of the politician who constructs convincing strategies to explain his actions. A panel of judges consisting of other students could be called upon to judge him innocent or guilty.

EFL teachers who are working in parts of the world which are remote from English language news services can utilize the news reports which are current in the area to set up similar scenarios. Of course, a certain amount of discretion is advised to avoid matters which are politically sensitive. Good and harmless sources of material for interactional games are the gossip sheets of the world of celebrities.

In any event, ESL and EFL teachers must be in touch with what is happening in the society around them. Otherwise, students will lose sight of the real functions of the language they are being taught. Functional-notional syllabi

are ineffectual if they remain nothing more than shopping lists of communicational devices.

OPEN-ENDED SCENARIOS

Teachers continue to seek ways to impart conversational skills which extend
beyond the limits of short, circumscribed dialogues. Role playing, to be sure, is
one such way, but it too has its limitations. The open-ended scenario was
developed to expand the role-playing technique by introducing new information
into a predetermined situation so as to force decisions and alter the direction of
the action. In this way, students learn to make communicational choices and to
develop verbal strategies consistent with their own interactional styles.

The language used in conversations is marked by a number of features
pertaining to role interaction. One of these features has to do with the time
constraint imposed on the interaction. I suggested [+episodic] as a way to label
those interactions which are more or less limited to one event. The opposing
feature [−episodic] would apply to those which may continue over several
occasions. The roles involved in simple acts of buying and selling in a market or
store would be [+episodic] since the action is limited to the purchasing event.
Two business rivals, on the other hand, might generate interactions which are
long-standing and therefore [−episodic].

The open-ended scenario represents an effort to capture the [−episodic]
aspect of interaction for use in the ESL/EFL classroom. This particular
pedagogical device shares obvious characteristics with traditional role plays.
Both grow from a set of circumstances dictated by the teacher. Both have some
element of dramatic tension or urgency to be resolved. However, the usual kind
of role play is one in which open-endedness is not really developed. According
to Clark (1980, p. 55), for example, the intention of role plays is to put the
students into a realistic communication situation in order to "sharpen their
listening comprehension skills, bring them into contact with new language, and
discover areas where they need additional practice." A sample role play goes as
follows: You have just moved into your new apartment and your neighbor
knocks on your door to introduce him/herself. The kind of dialogue to be
generated from the precondition might be:

> A: Hello, I'm your next-door neighbor. Nice to meet you.
> B: Nice to meet you, too.

and so on.

The sample role plays suggested by Paulston (1975) are more liable to
develop into open-ended scenarios, since they are based on events which could
be linked together in a chain. For example, there is a car accident; the driver is a
young man who has been drinking; the owner of the car is the father of another
young man who is a passenger; the police arrive and begin to gather information
for their report. The students are asked to develop a conversation based on this

description. They are also helped by being supplied with some natural-sounding expressions. While such role plays are superior to those of Clark, neither type offers any guidelines or gives any indication as to how the resultant scenario might develop. That matter is left entirely up to the students, guided by their instructor.

In open-ended scenarios, new developments and/or new information are meted out in phases rather than given all at once. The intention is to emulate those occasions which often occur in real life wherein people are called upon to redirect their communication in response to newly introduced facts and events. Nonepisodic conversations develop as the students must relate subsequent interactions to those which preceded. In preparing for this kind of exercise, the teacher should plan out the phases ahead of time in such a way that redirections or new decisions are inevitable. If desired, a data base of some sort might be employed, such as in scenario 1, given below. If a data base is used, it must lead to an interpretation which somehow refers back to the roles being played. Other themes for scenarios can be obtained from situations commonly portrayed on television. The following scenarios are offered as three illustrations of what can be done in the classroom.

Scenario 1

Phase 1. The teacher selects either two male students or two female students. They are told that they are good friends and have been placed on a diet by their physician. Each has been instructed to lose 10 pounds. They meet at the doctor's office to compare their weights, which are recorded weekly. The figures for the first three weeks are as follows:

Males	1st week	2nd week	3rd week
Friend 1	188	187	188
Friend 2	185	180	177
Females			
Friend 1	140	139	140
Friend 2	135	130	126

Each friend is to prepare his/her part of the conversation which occurs between the two on the occasion of the third weighing. The conversation is then performed in class.

Phase 2. After the first conversation is performed, the following statistics are introduced for the weights recorded on the fourth, fifth, and sixth weeks:

Males	4th week	5th week	6th week
Friend 1	184	182	179
Friend 2	177	178	178
Females			
Friend 1	138	137	134
Friend 2	127	128	129

The same students who were selected for the first conversation are now directed to prepare a second one based on the new weighings.

Scenario 2

Phase 1. Teacher selects one male and one female student. The male must invite the female to dinner at a restaurant. The female may either accept the invitation or reject it. The interactants are to develop a conversation in either case.

Phase 2. If the female accepts, the two go to the restaurant, where they encounter another male who appears to be the boy friend of the female. Develop a conversation among the three individuals. If the female rejects the offer to go to dinner, the male asks another female, who accepts. Then they go to the restaurant, where they encounter the first female seated at a table having dinner with another male. Develop a conversation with the four persons.

Scenario 3

Phase 1. The teacher selects two female students. One plays the part of an adolescent who wants to start earning money as a babysitter. Her mother (played by the other student) is of the opinion that she is too young to take on such a responsibility. Construct a conversation between the two. There are several possible outcomes to this conversation: (1) The mother does not grant permission to the daughter to babysit but does agree to change her mind when the daughter reaches her next birthday. (2) The mother grants permission but attaches several conditions; e.g., the daughter must not take on a job that will keep her up past midnight, the home where the daughter will babysit must not be at a great distance, and the daughter must show that she can handle problems which might come up. If this last condition is not met, the daughter will not be able to babysit for another full year.

Phase 2. The teacher selects another female student who plays the part of the wife of a young corporate executive being considered for a promotion in his firm. This young executive has been invited, together with his wife, to an important reception where he will be "looked over" by other top executives in the company. It is very important that both husband and wife make a good impression. However, the girl who is their regular babysitter is not available for the time of the reception. The couple becomes frantic. They must attend the reception. They decide to ask the mother (part played in phase 1, above) if her daughter will babysit for them. Develop a conversation between the wife of the young executive and the mother of the adolescent girl.

Phase 3. If the mother agrees to allow her daughter to babysit, she reminds her daughter of the last condition mentioned above, namely, that if anything goes wrong, she will not be able to babysit again for a year.

Phase 4. The babysitter is given instructions by the mother of the child. These instructions include calling the place where the reception is being held if there is any emergency. At the same time, the babysitter is told how important the reception is for the couple. She must not call for any but the most serious reasons. That evening, the child begins to cough and perspire. The babysitter must decide what to do and whom to call. Develop a conversation between the babysitter and whomever she decides to call.

As indicated above, some class time is set aside for preparations and rehearsal. Students should be led to understand that during this time they are free to ask any questions they wish about the plot of the scenario and the forms of the utterances they wish to construct. Errors made at this stage are not recorded and the instructor's pedagogical role changes to that of a consultant and/or coach, providing whatever help students may request. In this way, the instructor does not force the students to follow a predetermined path in developing the conversation but does give them help with the mechanical and/or structural aspects of what they want to say. A main purpose of the rehearsal stage is to relieve student anxieties about how to verbalize their intentions. The class should be broken down into discussion groups, with no more than nine to twelve students in each group. The dynamics of small-group interaction allows for a more equitable distribution of participation among the students and leads to the development of various interactional modes (e.g., assertive leadership, contemplative observation, cooperation, and support). It is strongly recommended that each group be assigned only one role to develop, rather than write out a full conversation. In this way, the task becomes one of allowing for a number of possible positions in the interaction while anticipating the verbal countermoves of the other interlocutors. Each group then elects one of its members to represent the combined expertise of the group in performing the scenario. Diverse rehearsal stages can be sandwiched in between phases of the scenario, thereby allowing for the new events to be turned into speech. Since each conversation develops along distinct lines, students are given the chance to experience firsthand the ways in which extended discourse affects conversational language (for a handy survey of the formal aspects of conversational language, see Richards 1980).

Each student or group of students must find some resolution to the questions suggested by the theme of each scenario. What are the desired outcomes of each communication problem? What strategies should be enacted in order to work toward those outcomes? The choice of strategies will depend on each student's personal preferences and disposition: Should I be aggressive? Is there any expectation that the other party in the conversation will acquiesce? Perhaps an apologetic stance would be preferable. And so on.

The next matter to be settled concerns the choice of speech functions for each strategy. In the case of an apology, for example, several functional expressions might be appropriate:

> I guess you're right, after all.
> You're right, you know.
> There's no question that you are right.
> You are absolutely correct and I am wrong.
> etc.

Students will also have to decide how many ways there are to make a refusal:

> I'm sorry I can't go with you. I have to study.
> I really have too much to do tonight.
> My boy friend doesn't like me to go out with other men.
> etc.

Note the subtle yet very real difference between the following:

> I really can't go out with you.
> I really shouldn't go out with you.

The second can be used to express a wavering rather than a firm decision to refuse the invitation. The author's personal experience in the classroom suggests that matters of grammatical form are best explained in strategic contexts such as those outlined above. For example, making an explanation of tense and aspect as part of an answer to a learner-motivated need renders the task a much easier one.

Dialogues in real life are not disjointed speech acts. They stand as links in chains of events which stretch over extended periods of time. In order to communicate in any language, it is necessary to acquire not only the protocols dictated by the immediacy of conversation but also a repertoire of verbal strategies to use over time. The preconditions spelled out for open-ended scenarios mirror those of many actual discourses, leading students to respond to changes in speaker intentions, just as they might do in real-life situations.

In addition to the protocols and strategies which a student must acquire in a new language, there are the features which are tied to dialogue structure. These features include openers, connectors, preclosers, and closers. There are also devices to correct false starts (called self-repair mechanisms), to mark turn taking, and to hold the right to speak while searching for just the right word (Richards 1980). At this point in our pedagogical development, we have no special techniques to impart these skills to our students other than by illustrating them. The open-ended scenario provides an opportunity for learners to become acquainted with those conversational features, such as overlap and change of topic, which mark extended discourses.

Finally, a word about composition. As more is understood about the relationships between spoken and written discourse, it becomes evident that techniques can be developed in the classroom which center on how conversations generate written narratives. One such technique is to use the learner-generated dialogues as the raw material for compositions. In this way, opportunities are provided for showing the many relationships that exist between direct and indirect discourse. Reading selections which contain reported conversations can also be employed as demonstrations of the two modalities of communicating.

The open-ended scenario presented in phases through the steps outlined in this chapter holds much promise as a means to make instructional use of the considerable knowledge we are gaining about discourse and conversation.

DISCUSSION QUESTIONS

1. What does Di Pietro mean by the term "scripting"? How does his use of that term relate to the conception of Schank as discussed in Chapters 1 and 30?

2. In what sense are roles "oppositional" in character? Are some of the tensions of communicative exchanges necessary to the mutuality or the reciprocal nature of the enterprise? Explain. Discuss the concept of "dramatic tension" in relation to the definition of a story plot offered by Robert Newton Peck—"two dogs and one bone."

3. Di Pietro suggests that "functions and notions must be made situationally and personally relevant" (p. 229). What is he getting at? What connections do you see between this remark and the idea of Chapter 2 that the student must be immersed not in the target language or in any analysis of it but in "the world of experience" in which that language exists?

4. Does Di Pietro use the term "episodic" in the same sense as in Chapter 1? Explain.

5. Consider the "dinner date" example. In what ways might the assignment be varied to accommodate different levels of student abilities? Is it possible to use the suggestions of Chapter 3 for adjusting texts to fit the students' "$i + 1$"? Be explicit in saying how adjustments could be made. How, incidentally, could your observations be extended to the "open-ended scenario," which clearly requires "improvisation" by students?

Chapter 15

Sociodrama for Social Interaction

Robin C. Scarcella
University of California, Santa Barbara

EDITORS' INTRODUCTION

The focal element of "sociodrama," as recommended by Scarcella, is a significant conflict. As suggested in Chapter 1, trouble is the universal motivator of discourse and of reflective applications of intelligence. The mind in all of its abstract independence seems to get into gear when the body in a concrete-temporal context is up against the wall. It is the conflict situation of a matrix story which provides the basis for the development of the sociodrama. The drama begins at just the point where the conflict is made clear. The students are left to their own devices to work out the scenario from the point of the dilemma forward. The sociodrama is a type of open-ended scenario (Di Pietro, Chapter 14). Because of its focus on a specific conflict, one that is relevant to the experience of the students, it may be construed as a kind of "supercharged" open-ended scenario.

It is often recognized that greater emphasis should be placed on developing communication skills.[1] Sociodrama can be used effectively to attain this goal. First, by participating in several enactments, students produce new sentences based on their own behavior or the spontaneous constructions produced by other students. Second, as in real-life communication, sociodrama obliges students to restructure their language use according to the social context. Third, sociodrama promotes social interaction, a prerequisite for communication.

Sociodrama has high student appeal. Its game structure allows students to try out new behaviors without fear of social penalty. It also encourages students to repair communication lapses occurring in both their own and others' speech. This in turn enables the teacher to diagnose communication breakdowns for future lessons. Sociodrama creates a comfortable atmosphere which promotes cross-cultural understanding.

For many years, ESL educators have been aware of the need to develop students' conversation skills. At the same time, they have experienced the

---

1. This chapter was presented at the 1977 TESOL convention, Miami Beach, Florida. The author wishes to thank Kearney Rietmann of the American Language Institute, University of Southern California, for her help in transcribing sociodrama sessions.

difficulty of creating class activities leading to the attainment of this goal. One activity which has been found to be a successful catalyst for social interaction and hence communication is sociodrama.

Sociodrama is a type of role play involving a series of student enactments of solutions to a social problem. The problem takes the form of an open-ended story containing one clear, easily identifiable conflict which is of relevance to the students. (For a complete description refer to Shaftel and Shaftel 1967, and Chesler and Fox 1966.)

Another type of role play which is frequently used in the ESL class is situation role play. However, sociodrama differs from situation role play in several important ways. First, the technique for using sociodrama is unique because it involves a series of specific steps. (See below.) Second, sociodrama is student- rather than teacher-oriented. Students frequently define their own roles and always determine their own course of action in the enactments. Only those students who seem to relate to the roles are selected to enact them. Also, sociodrama involves several enactments and therefore lasts much longer than situation role play.

TECHNIQUE[2]

Steps in sociodrama may include:

1. *Warm-up*. The teacher introduces the sociodrama topic and stimulates student interest. During this time the teacher tries to create a relaxed atmosphere.

2. *Presentation of new vocabulary*. A minimal number of new vocabulary words and expressions are presented.

3. *Presentation of dilemma*. Good sociodrama stories are written with specific teaching objectives in mind. The story must be relevant to the students and contain a clearly identifiable problem and climax. The story stops at the dilemma point. The students are asked to focus their attention on the conflict in the sociodrama story as it is related to them by their teacher. (See Appendix for sample sociodrama story.)

4. *Discussion of the situation and selection of roles*. In this stage the problem and roles are discussed. The teacher selects students who relate to the roles and who have offered solutions to the problem to come to the front of the class to participate in the enactment.

5. *Audience preparation*. Students in the class who are not selected to participate in the enactment become the audience. Members of the audience are given specific tasks. For example, they may be asked to determine why the conflict is or is not being resolved.

6. *Enactment*. The role players enact the solutions which they have suggested. To help the students initiate the enactment, the teacher may repeat the last few lines of the sociodrama, give students a minute to gather their thoughts, as well as ask the students to reformulate their description of the roles and their intended course of action.

7. *Discussion of the situation and selection of new role players*. Alternative ways of solving the problem are explored. New role players are chosen.

8. *Reenactment*. Students replay the problem situation and attempt to solve the sociodrama dilemma by using new strategies.

---

2. Adapted from Shaftel and Shaftel 1967.

At this point steps 5, 6, and 7 may be repeated until many different possible solutions have been presented and discussed in terms of their consequences.

9. *Summary.* The teacher guides the students to summarize what was presented in the enactments and asks, when appropriate, if there are any final comments or generalizations about the problems and proposed solutions.

10. *Follow-up.* Follow-up activities may include a writing exercise, extended discussion, an aural comprehension exercise, or a related reading exercise. Some teachers like to give a mini-lesson on a communication breakdown occurring in the session.

USES

Sociodrama may be used effectively to develop vocabulary, grammar, discourse strategies, strategies for social interaction, to promote cultural understanding, and to elicit oral production from all students.

Claims made here about the uses of sociodrama and the effectiveness of sociodrama as a technique are based on transcriptions of sociodrama sessions video-taped at the American Language Institute at the University of Southern California. Participants in the sessions included intermediate and advanced students of English as a second language and native English speakers.

One use of sociodrama is in the development of vocabulary. Sociodrama supplies contextual clues from which the students can induce the meanings of words. In addition to allowing the L2 acquirer to observe the vocabulary which is needed in various situations in order to carry on a conversation, sociodrama provides students with opportunities to try out the vocabulary. Participants in the sociodrama help each other communicate by supplying vocabulary items and expressions as the following examples demonstrate. R and J are advanced ESL students.

1.	R:	We plan to have dinner at 7:00 but uh uh =
	J:	= But we have a surprise for you.
	R:	Yeah. A surprise.
2.	Native speaker:	Why don't you want to eat? Are you on a diet?
	J:	On a diet. Yeah. I'm on a diet.

Furthermore, because the enactments are often very similar, the input is frequently repeated. Repetition of this kind leads to better comprehension.

Grammar can be developed through sociodrama. It has been proposed that language acquisition evolves out of learning how to participate in conversation (Hatch 1976), that the L2 student first learns communication strategies which facilitate conversation and then learns how to interact verbally. From this interaction arises the student's increasing ability to produce grammatical sentences. In sociodrama students can produce spontaneous constructions based on their own behavior or on the spontaneous constructions produced by other students, as illustrated by the following example.

3. J: Where ya gonna take me?
    K: Lovely restaurant. I'm gonna take you to a lovely restaurant.

In this case, K, an intermediate student, appears to be copying the progressive verb form used by J, an advanced student.

Another use of sociodrama is in the development of discourse strategies. Strategies for attention getting, topic initiation, and topic change may be developed through sociodrama. During the early enactments of sociodrama the students have difficulty initiating conversation and the teacher must help the students by setting the scene. However, as the sociodrama progresses the students become better at initiating conversation and no longer rely on the teacher. Students learn to initiate conversation by use of attention getters such as "Excuse me," "Hello," "What's new," and "How are you". These expressions occurred frequently in the sociodrama transcriptions and were modeled after expressions used by the native English speakers as well as by fellow students. Also, as the sociodrama advances, the students spend less time groping for the appropriate words to initiate the topic. For example, in one sociodrama session, students hesitated 3 seconds before beginning the first topic, 2.4 seconds before beginning the second topic, and did not hesitate at all before beginning the third and fourth topics. Finally, sociodrama gives students practice in changing the topic. "By the way," "I've been thinking," and "You know what else?" were some of the expressions which students in the transcribed sociodrama sessions used to change the topic. In order to encourage the development of these strategies, the teacher may choose to focus on them before introducing the sociodrama story.

Strategies for social interaction may also be developed through sociodrama. These strategies are essential for communication and language development. In fact, social interaction is often considered the first stage of L2 acquisition. Students must develop strategies for making and maintaining relationships in order to receive the necessary input. Sociodrama promotes the development of the social strategies suggested by L. Fillmore (1976). These include initiating interaction with others, establishing and maintaining relationships, providing others with encouragement, and counting on others for help.

Sociodrama can also be used to heighten awareness of cultural differences. Rivers (1972) has suggested that cultural patterns, values, attitudes, relationships, and taboos can be acquired through discourse. Since language is a part of culture, successful communication can arise only when the speaker can predict how the hearer will react and the hearer can predict the speaker's intentions. By participating in sociodrama, students become aware of discourse in relation to social expectations, formulas of politeness, social attitudes, and appropriateness of response to a cultural situation. For example, in a sociodrama story involving university professors, students get practice using politeness formulas. Any inappropriate behavior can be resolved during the discussions. Also, the sociodrama sessions which are most successful in promoting cultural understanding are those in which native speakers participate and serve as models.

Teachers may use sociodrama to elicit communication from all students, since sociodrama creates a relaxed atmosphere, one in which even shy students feel free to participate. The teacher endeavors to foster a comfortable environment by (1) calling on native speakers or the most verbal and socially accepted students to participate in early enactments; (2) not criticizing students; (3) not forcing students to participate against their will; (4) giving shy students passive roles at first to get them used to being in front of the class; (5) clearly dissociating the role players from the parts which they enact. As a consequence of these procedures, students are given practice and security in performing before others.

RATIONALE

Many reasons explain the success of sociodrama in teaching ESL. Of primary significance is the fact that sociodrama serves to increase the students' "intake." Corder (1967) describes the small part of language which *is* processed as "intake." Wagner-Gough (1975) reports that an important ingredient for "intake" is attention. It follows then that good activities capture the students' attention.

Sociodrama is an activity which obliges students to attend to the verbal environment. First, it is relevant to the students' interests, utilizing both extrinsic motivation, which refers to the students' daily interests and cares, and intrinsic motivation, which refers to the students' internal feelings and attitudes (Stevick 1971). Second, students pay attention because they expect to participate; even the audience is given an active role. Third, the participants are often friends. The importance of peers in language development is frequently noted. Furthermore, sociodrama is a problem-solving activity which simulates real-life situations and requires active student involvement.

Teaching experience tells us that different students acquire language in different ways. Some students make heavy use of learned rules while others rely more upon the language acquisition process (Krashen 1976). A further advantage of sociodrama is that it combines both formal and informal learning environments and allows the students to benefit from both so that the rule-oriented student is free to search for rules, while the less rule-oriented student can use the intake provided by acquisition alone. In the vocabulary stage the teacher isolates vocabulary, and perhaps some grammatical structures and discourse strategies in a formal way and appeals to the students' conscious learning processes. However, in the enactment stage there is no overt teaching. Thus, the students are free to accept or reject language from the enactment discourse much as speakers do in everyday language situations (Rietmann 1977).

Sociodrama cannot possibly be used to accomplish all the goals of an ESL class. Its effectiveness as a technique has yet to be experimentally validated.

Yet, on the basis of the transcriptions of video-taped sociodrama sessions, as well as my own and others' experience, sociodrama can be said to be a valuable supplementary activity. It can be used effectively to teach ESL, a subject in which social interaction is important.

APPENDIX

The following is an example of a sociodrama story used in a university ESL class to teach Advanced Spoken English.

Mrs. Watson was very upset when Robert, her youngest son, decided to marry Kathy. Mrs. Watson did not think that any girl was good enough to marry her son. "Look, Robert," she said, "you're not old enough to get married and support a wife. You're only twenty-eight. Kathy won't make you happy. She can't cook like I can. Please don't get married and leave me alone. I'm a widow. I'll be so lonely without my only son."

Nevertheless, Kathy and Robert got married. When they returned from their honeymoon, Kathy received a phone call from Mrs. Watson. "How I've missed you!" Mrs. Watson said. "Why haven't you called me? This Friday is my birthday and I've been wondering if you plan to invite me to visit you. I hate to feel lonely on my birthday."

Kathy replied, "Of course I want you to come here this Friday. We don't want you to be alone on your birthday. I'd love to have you for dessert."

That Friday Kathy was very busy. She wanted to make sure that everything was perfect for her mother-in-law. Kathy spent the entire day cleaning the house. At first, everything went very well. Mrs. Watson arrived promptly at seven o'clock. Kathy served Mrs. Watson a drink and then left her to talk with Robert while she returned to the kitchen.

When Kathy went to take the cake she was baking out of the oven, she was shocked. The cake was completely burned! Kathy quickly shut the oven door so that the smoke would not escape. Then she brought Mrs. Watson another drink. "Here, Mom," Kathy said, "Would you like another drink?"

Mrs. Watson replied, "No thanks. I don't care for another drink right now. You invited me for dessert. When are we going to eat it?"

Kathy replied, ". . . ."

DISCUSSION QUESTIONS

1. What is the significance of the "one clear, easily identifiable conflict which is of relevance to students" (p. 240)? Why is such a conflict a critical element of any successful sociodrama? What would happen if no relevant conflict were present?

2. Do you see any parallel between the several recommended steps of sociodrama as recommended by Scarcella and the phases of Suggestopedia as discussed by Bancroft (Chapter 8) and Stevick (Chapter 9)? What about the recommended phases of Freire's approach as interpreted by Wallerstein (Chapter 12)?

3. In the account of sociodrama by Scarcella, and in the open-ended scenario as recommended by Di Pietro in the preceding chapter, we see applications

of the principle of multiple passes as discussed in Chapters 1 and 2. In what ways does Scarcella recommend multiple passes through a given socio-drama? What effects does she anticipate from this procedure? Or, how are pragmatic mappings of utterance to contexts progressively refined as the students progress through the various steps of enacting the sociodrama?

4. What part, according to Scarcella, does attention play in the process of converting input into "intake" (Corder's term, 1967)?

Chapter 16

From Role Play to the Real World

Raymond J. Rodriguez
New Mexico State University, Las Cruces

Robert H. White
University of New Mexico

EDITORS' INTRODUCTION

This chapter provides a bridge from the vicarious experience of students through film, drama, and role play to interactive experiences outside of the classroom. Of course, it is tempting to assume that the classroom is not part of the real world, and yet in fact it is a very *real* context in its own right. Moreover, the dialogues and dramas practiced there in the safety of what some punster termed the "class-womb" may provide the very basis necessary for communicative interactions in what the same clumsy wordsmith called "the 'real' real world." Again, as in previous chapters in this section, the principle of multiple passes through a given text is apparent. The initial phase involves a simple dialogue which is eventually committed to memory. Subsequent role playing and dramatizations will lead to still deeper penetration of the "text" (recall the "textuality hypothesis" of Chapter 1), followed by more open-ended activities with improvisation, eventually culminating in a field-trip type of experience where the student encounters the ultimate challenge of facing off with one or more untutored natives in the "real" world. Subsequently still deeper penetration may be made into the "text" by debriefing exercises back home in the classroom with expanded narratives and additional enactments and/or embellishments of the field-trip experience.

It has become evident to many teachers of ESL students that most of the available texts and materials are based on artificial sequencing of grammatical structures and stilted, often irrelevant, dialogues and topics. Only recently, with the stimulation of current research in second language learning and teaching, have new materials appeared based on the communicative needs of students. These new research insights and materials have finally accepted a principle often discovered in the past by classroom teachers: that effective ESL teaching must be based on helping students learn the language they need to function successfully in everyday situations and in future settings where they will be using English.

Another principle derived from current research concerns the comparison of first and second language learning in children *and* older learners and the possibility of patterning second language learning experiences on the model of natural first language learning. Just as children, in learning the first language, are exposed to a variety of experiences and accompanying language in a supportive environment to which they creatively respond, the second language learner may also be capable of responding to natural open language experiences based on communication needs.

In a plan based on those principles, students would be placed in a variety of experiences with accompanying language such as a trip to the zoo, lunch at a cafeteria, learning to play soccer, going to the supermarket. In experiences such as these, the learner is exposed to language in meaningful contexts. As beginners, their task is simply to attend to the sights and sounds of the experience, listen to the language which is part of the experience, and attempt to understand what they see and hear. Language presented in this situation can become meaningful to the student because of the many audiovisual clues which accompany it. The student can then begin to comprehend some of the language appropriate to the objects and actions in the setting. Since frequent field experiences may not be possible in school settings, simulated or vicarious experiences may be provided in the regular classroom. Appropriate films, videotapes, sound filmstrips, and dramatic presentations may be used to stimulate student attention and provide the meaningful contexts in which the language is best learned.

Although it may be possible for ESL students to learn English naturally through a curriculum made up of a long series of open language experiences, it is obvious that such a program would require years of student involvement. In practice, ESL classes for children, teenagers, and adults are limited to a fraction of the school day, or the students are in mixed classes and regular teachers are asked to provide some special ESL activities for students who need it. With the limited time available it is necessary to follow open language experiences with more intensive structured situations, dialogues, and role-playing activities.

In the structured situation phase of this model, students are presented with simple but natural narratives or long dialogues of no more than 100 words based on the language of segments of the open language experience. These are accompanied by visual clues through use of pictures, objects, silent films, or filmstrips taken from the larger experience and used again to provide a meaningful context for the language presentation. Material of about 100 words in length has been found to be too long for quick memorization by students; thus the emphasis in this phase is for the student to concentrate on the meaning of the material. In addition, at least ten guide questions are presented to the student following the narration. These are constructed from the material in the narration and are designed to be answered by students with some of the language they have heard. What is encouraged here is the beginning of full responses using language understood from meaningful presentations.

In beginning classes a large difference in the ability of students to respond to the guide questions will exist. Many students will be too timid or unable to attempt responses in English although their listening comprehension may be good. For most students, therefore, an additional phase involving the learning of short dialogues will be helpful and will give beginning students the confidence of actually using the language. The dialogues should be taken from the language of the structured situations, presented in no more than eight lines but using the natural yet simple language appropriate to the experience. Dialogues can be presented orally by the teacher or other students with repetition and guided memorizing, again with visual clues. Reading and writing can also begin in the dialogue phase with the teacher use of charts containing the dialogue sentences and students learning to print their own word cards from the dialogues and arranging them in sentences as they memorize. These word cards can then be used for reviewing dialogues, constructing new sentences with the same and new words, and phonics activities based on these sight words, which will help the student make the transition to reading other relevant text materials and stories. Two or three students may be assigned to practice the dialogue until they feel confident enough to present it orally to the class.

Building of confidence through these memorized presentations will lead to students' participation in role playing and dramatic activities. After being involved in several structured situations and mastering related dialogues, students will have internalized enough of the basic language associated with the open language experience that they will be able to respond to role-playing situations planned by the teacher. These should be directly related to segments of the original open language experience. Students will be given short descriptions of a situation and asked to act out the roles of the people in these settings without looking at the printed dialogue material previously memorized. The role-playing activities should be similar to the narratives and dialogues, but sufficiently different to encourage freer use of the language.

Throughout the structured situation, dialogue, and role-playing phases, the teachers become diagnosticians, noting errors as the students attempt to respond, present dialogues, or act out role-playing situations. The teacher can categorize the errors, noting phonological (pronunciation), grammatical, and semantic errors made by a large number of class members, a small group, or an individual student. It is from these errors that the teacher plans appropriate practice activities. Recent second language learning research has indicated that making errors is a positive illustration of the students' attempts to internalize language forms by developing hypotheses based on the language material they hear. For example, students may have hypothesized from many examples and contexts that the *ed* ending indicates past tense. As a result, they may overextend this hypothesis and apply it inappropriately to an irregular verb and make an error such as eat*ed* instead of *ate*. Errors such as this may disappear after the student has been exposed to the language for a longer period of time, but the teacher must eventually judge that a persistent error continues to interfere with meaning and provide practice activities for correction or prevention of this error. A valuable use of published ESL text material is to provide the teacher with ready-made practice activities for most predictable errors. These texts are usually organized with tables of contents and indexes that make it possible for the teacher to select quickly the practices needed for phonological, grammatical, and semantic errors. In this phase, the teacher and other students may work with individuals or small groups, guiding them through the appropriate practice activities. After ESL students have learned to read and write at basic levels, they may work at these materials individually or in pairs.

The evaluation phase of this model is based on a reality principle: the effectiveness of language instruction is best tested by assessing the student's use of the language in the actual experience. Thus, the students completing the phases of the unit are asked to repeat the open language experience to which they were first exposed and during which they may have only been able to listen. For example, in an experience involving shopping at a supermarket, students are given a shopping list and a sum of money and asked to bring back a report on their activity and evidence of a successful shopping trip. If the actual field experience cannot be undertaken, a simulation of the experience may be arranged in a classroom.

Students who are unsuccessful in their performance would then be assigned repeated dialogues, role playing, and error-based activities followed by repetitions of the open-language experience. This recycling of some students need not prevent the introduction of another open language experience unit for the whole class.

Although some publishers are attempting to produce textbooks based on the communicative needs of ESL students with related phonological, grammatical, and vocabulary activities, they are unable to predict completely the needs of thousands of ESL students representing all ages and backgrounds. Only teachers struggling to meet the needs of their students can use interview techniques and interaction with students to determine and predict student communication needs and build practice activities related to the actual language errors of students.

The following outline for an open language experience unit plan and sample unit is offered as a possible model for teachers to use in their efforts to create more meaningful materials for their ESL students.

MODEL OPEN LANGUAGE EXPERIENCE UNIT OUTLINE

I. Determining needs and interests
   A. List the communication needs and interests of the target group.
   B. In what settings *will* they be using English?
   C. In what settings are they *currently* needing English?
II. Planning open language experience activities
   A. Select one of these needs or interests and develop an open language experience activity in which the students can use their natural language learning abilities.
   B. The meaning and language in this experience will be acquired by the student's *listening* and *observing* in the context.
   C. Examples:
      1. Plan a field trip to a supermarket.
      2. Show a relevant sound film.
      3. Plan to bring in a group of native speakers of English to act out a situation, e.g., eating lunch at an American restaurant.
   D. Write your plan for the open language experience activity in enough detail so that another ESL teacher can follow it.

III. Structured situations
    A. Select three parts of the open language experience. Example: checking out at the supermarket
    B. Write three narratives of about 100 words each to be presented by the teacher or another student that describe or discuss three parts of the open language experience activity.
       1. Keep the language natural and appropriate to the situation.
       2. Keep vocabulary as simple as possible.
       3. Keep sentences as short as possible.
    C. Prepare visual cues to meaning to accompany the structured situation. Examples: pictures, objects, silent film, or filmstrip
    D. Prepare at least 10 guide questions for each structured situation that can be answered by the students directly from the structured situation presentation.
    E. Have students role play what they remember.
    F. Note student errors as they attempt to answer the questions.
IV. Short dialogues
    A. Write at least six short dialogues (about eight lines each) based on the structured situations.
    B. Present each dialogue orally to the group.
    C. Have students practice each dialogue in pairs (or threes) and in front of the class.
    D. Note student errors as they present dialogues.
 V. Drama and role playing in activities
    A. Plan additional activities based on the structured situation and dialogues.
    B. Note student errors.
VI. Error analysis
    A. Analyze student phonological (pronunciation), grammatical, and semantic errors from the structured situations, dialogues, and other activities.
    B. Categorize the errors:
       1. Common class
       2. Small group
       3. Individual
VII. Planned practice—plan practice activities for the class, small groups, and individuals that focus on their particular errors and their developmental needs.
VIII. Repeated open language experience—ask students to repeat the open language experience and report the results.
 IX. Recycling—have students who were unsuccessful in the open language experience repeat dialogues and practice activities.
 X. Plan and present a new open language experience unit.

SAMPLE PLAN FOR AN OPEN LANGUAGE EXPERIENCE: SHOPPING AT THE SUPERMARKET

This is a report on the open language experience and materials used with an ESL class of Vietnamese refugees living in Albuquerque, New Mexico.

Needs Assessment

A translator was present at the first session, and through him the students were asked questions about the nature of their English needs. For instance, each student was asked how long he or she had been in the United States and whether or not he or she had had any formal schooling in his or her native country. Students were also asked what kinds of places—bank, post office, grocery store, airport, bakery—they had been to in the United States, and what they felt to be their most essential English language needs.

Planning the Open Language Experience Activity

Everyone had been to a grocery store in the United States, and each student expressed a need to learn the American system of money; hence, a grocery store setting was chosen for the open language experience, the need and current use of English in this setting having been established.

After the translator explained the purpose of the activity, the class was taken on a field trip to a small neighborhood grocery store. We took a grocery list with us and empty pop bottles to return. At the store the class was videotaped observing and listening to the teacher. The teacher asked prices of the grocer, compared prices of items and made choices of what items to buy, went through the checkout stand, got change, said goodbye to the grocer, went home, and put the groceries into the refrigerator and cupboards. The videotape of this experience, as well as the actual objects purchased, were used as vehicles or props for later lessons on various phases of grocery shopping.

The videotape was also used as a basis for discussion in class, for error analysis and correction, and for the amusement and motivation of the students. In the final stage of the open language experience, testing, when the students went to a large supermarket with a grocery list and purchased groceries "on their own," another videotape was made and used in class for error analysis and for assessment of teaching success.

The three phases of grocery shopping dealt with in this report include making a grocery list, choosing groceries, and going through the checkout stand.

Structured Situations

Narrative A

I want to make a grocery list. I get a pencil and a piece of paper to write down what I need. Let's see. What do I need? I open my refrigerator. I need milk. I need eggs. I need butter. I write down: milk, eggs, butter. Also, I need orange juice. I have plenty of vegetables—onions, carrots, celery, and tomatoes. So I don't need to buy any vegetables. Do I have any fruit? I have oranges. But I don't have any apples. I need apples. So here is my grocery list: milk, eggs, butter, orange juice, apples.

Guide Questions
1. What is a grocery list?
2. How do I make a grocery list?
3. What do I open to see what I need?

4. Which vegetables do I have?
5. What vegetables do I need to buy?
6. What fruit do I have?
7. What fruit do I need to buy?
8. Which three dairy products do I need to buy?
9. What kind of fruit juice do I need to buy?
10. What items are on my grocery list?

Narrative B

At the grocery store I get a grocery cart. I look at my grocery list. It says: milk, eggs, butter, orange juice, apples. I find the *dairy* aisle. I put a quart of skim milk and a dozen eggs in my cart. I see that a pound (lb.) of butter costs $1.99. I see that a pound (lb.) of margarine costs $0.97. I put the margarine, not the butter, in my cart. I go to the produce aisle. I see red apples and green apples. I choose six green apples. I find the canned orange juice. I put one can of pure, unsweetened orange juice into my cart.

Guide Questions

1. What is a grocery cart?
2. What is on my grocery list?
3. How much milk do I choose?
4. How many eggs do I buy? How many eggs are there in a dozen?
5. Why do I choose margarine instead of butter?
6. In what aisle do I find apples?
7. What kinds of apples do I see?
8. Which apples do I choose?
9. How many apples do I buy?
10. What kind of orange juice do I put into my cart?

Narrative C

At the checkout register I put my groceries on the counter. The quart of milk costs $0.59, the pound of margarine costs $0.97, the dozen eggs cost $0.68. The clerk says, "The apples are $0.59 a pound; that will be $0.74." The can of juice costs $0.79. The total is $3.77 plus tax. Tax is $0.15. The total bill is $3.92. I give the clerk a five dollar bill. He gives me a penny, "$3.93," another penny, "$3.94," another penny, "$3.95," a nickel, "$4.00," a dollar bill, "$5.00." He puts my groceries in a bag and says, "Thank you." I say, "Thank you and goodbye."

Guide Questions

1. At the checkout stand where do I put my groceries?
2. How much does the milk cost?
3. How much does the margarine cost?

4. How much are the apples?
5. How much money do I give the clerk?
6. How many pennies does the clerk give me in change?
7. How many nickels does the clerk give me in change?
8. How many dollar bills does the clerk give me in change?
9. Where does the clerk put my groceries?
10. What is the last thing I say to the clerk?

Dialogues

Making a grocery list

A: What do you need at the grocery store?
B: I don't know. Let me see.
A: Do you need any vegetables?
B: No, I have plenty.
A: Do you need some fruit?
B: Well, I have oranges, but I don't have apples.
A: Then you need some apples.
B: Yes, I need some apples.
A: I'm going to make out my grocery list.
B: Here's a pencil and paper. Let me write it for you.
A: Okay. Write down milk, eggs, and butter.
B: Okay. Milk, eggs, and butter. What else?
A: Write down apples.
B: Okay. Apples.
A: Write down orange juice. That's all.
B: Okay. I've got milk, eggs, butter, apples, and orange juice.

Choosing groceries

A: Where do I find the dairy products?
B: Over there. You'll see the milk, butter, and eggs.
A: How much does the butter cost?
B: It's $1.99 a pound. The margarine is cheaper.
A: Where do I find the apples?
B: Over there in the produce section.
A: Excuse me. Where can I find the orange juice?
B: Over there. It says "Canned Juice."
A: Excuse me. Where is the dairy aisle?
B: Over there.
A: Thank you.
B: You're welcome.
A: Excuse me. Where is the produce?
B: There. See the carrots and lettuce?
A: Oh, yes. Thank you.
B: You're welcome.

Going through the checkout line

A: Hello.
B: Hello.
A: How much were the eggs?
B: A dozen cost $0.79.
A: Fine.
B: That will be $3.92.
A: Here's a five dollar bill.
B: Thank you. Here's your change. Have a nice day.
A: Thank you. Goodbye.
A: Hello. How are you?
B: Hello. I'm fine, thank you.
A: That will be $3.92.
B: How much was the tax on that?
A: $0.15.
B: Thanks. Here's a five dollar bill.
A: Your change is $1.08. Thank you. Have a nice day.
B: Thank you. Goodbye.

Role-Playing Activities

Between the open language field experience of the trip to a small neighborhood grocery store and the test situation of having students purchase groceries at a large supermarket, we had several lessons that focused on role playing. We used an actual grocery cart and props of vegetables, milk cartons, margarine and butter cartons, and various other grocery items.

Role playing seemed to be the most successful phase of the open language experience. Students enjoyed and joked and created language to fit the situation. Given the dialogues, which they hadn't completely memorized but which they had understood, the students played with the possibilities of language. Given "Excuse me," to mean let me pass with my grocery cart, one student elaborated, "I want to go by you." Given "Where is the produce?" another student elaborated, "I want to find the celery." Given the format, "I want to buy a gallon of milk," a student, seeing a knife on the kitchen counter, expanded the form to say, "Excuse me. I want to buy a knife."

ERROR ANALYSIS

With this particular group of Vietnamese the consensus of native speakers dealing with the students seemed to be that pronunciation was a serious problem. Vietnamese native speakers have difficulty with the pronunciation of English to such an extent that it is not advisable to ignore it.

In particular, this group of students tended to omit the final consonants of all English words. The word for book [buk] became [bu]; the word for cap [$kæp$] became [$kæ$]. First person, singular, present tense verbs invariably were pronounced without the final *s*. The final *s* in plurals was rarely pronounced. Hence a question such as "What does she eat?" elicited the response, "She eat apple and cookie." Since this response is easily understood by a native speaker, in a "real" conversation between a native speaker and a native Vietnamese speaker using English, there was no great effort to correct pronunciation; however, when we were doing drills and patterns, we felt it was very appropriate to concentrate on the pronunciation of the final consonants of words, especially the final *s* with the plurals, and the final consonant on common words such as book and ship. We focused attention on this problem through a translator, explaining that in English the final consonants and especially the pronunciation of *s*'s was important. This explanation seemed to help; certainly it facilitated our corrections and their being understood by the students.

DISCUSSION QUESTIONS

1. How does the "open language experience" facilitate the pragmatic linkage of utterances to meanings? Is the principle of multiple passes applied? Explain how.

2. What is your feeling about the teacher serving as "diagnostician" during role-play activities? How would this role differ from that of a "counselor" in Curran's approach (Chapter 10 above)? Similarly, what is your reaction to the idea of drilling problem points? Are there any cautions to be borne in mind for the selection and/or construction and use of such drills? Refer to the caveat followed in the structure drills of the Spanish program discussed in Chapter 2 above.

3. The authors say, "The effectiveness of language instruction is best tested by assessing the student's use of the language in the actual experience" (p. 249). If this working premise is followed, do you think there will be any need for additional performance testing? Why or why not?

4. What parallels and differences do you see between the Rodriguez-White approach and the one discussed by Wallerstein in Chapter 12? Consider their unit outline with its needs assessment, planning of an experience, and so forth.

5. Is the diagnostic attention to surface forms, e.g., pronunciations, in the supermarket trip consistent with the total intent of the chapter? Explain.

Part V
Natural Orientations

It is not a new idea that people in natural settings often succeed in acquiring languages while similar persons in classrooms typically fail to make any notable progress. A common byword dating back into the distant past has been the remark, "If you want to learn the language, go to the country where it is spoken and live with the people there." Or, "Marry someone who speaks it." Or, "Develop a prolonged relationship with someone who speaks it." And so forth.

The article by John Macnamara included here as Chapter 17 contrasts and tries to explain the nearly universal success of natural language acquisition and the almost equally widespread failure of many classroom approaches to language teaching. When Macnamara's article first appeared, many teachers were impressed with its fundamental correctness and yet felt compelled to continue with the familiar failing methods for lack of any clear replacement options. Not only were nearly all the published language teaching materials prepared in the "formal" (linguistic analysis) orientation, but the methods books only gave lip service, for the most part, to "natural" alternatives.

Even some of the materials published since the mid 1970s, though they may have profusely acknowledged the need for communicative activity, often failed to provide any solid basis for it. Therefore, when Terrell first published his reflections on the "natural approach," it met with an enthusiastic response from many of the teachers. They soaked up all he had to say and cried for more. Chapter 18, reprinted from the *Modern Language Journal*, 1982, strengthens and expands his previous writing on the subject. Chapter 19 adds some observations about the "natural" approach from the vantage point of the Savignon family who, in response to the proverbial wisdom it would seem, actually did "go to the country." Then, Chapter 20 by Stephen Krashen offers some fascinating observations about the possible importance of the "din in the head"—a phenomenon that seems to accompany extensive "natural" exposure to comprehensible input.

SUGGESTED ADDITIONAL READINGS

SUSAN ERVIN-TRIPP.
  1978. Is second language learning like the first? In E. Hatch (ed.). *Second Language Acquisition: A Book of Readings*. Rowley, Massachusetts: Newbury House.

Both similarities and contrasts are considered in this classic contribution by one of the pioneers in this important area. The reader may want to compare the remarks and findings of Ervin-Tripp with those of Macnamara (Chapter 17).

STEPHEN KRASHEN AND TRACY TERRELL.
  1983. *The Natural Approach*. San Francisco: Alemany.

An in-depth treatment of the approach discussed briefly in Chapter 18 by Terrell. Combines and incorporates many of the features of methods discussed by Asher, Gattegno, Stevick, Curran, and others.

SANDRA SAVIGNON.
  1972. *Communicative Competence: An Experiment in Foreign Language Teaching.* Philadelphia: the Center for Curriculum Development.

Although it is now somewhat dated, this little book still stands as a milestone in the whole movement of language teachers toward more communicative techniques of language learning. It also contains some practical ideas about communicative teaching and testing.

GORDON WELLS.
  1981. *Learning through Interaction: the Study of Language Development.* Cambridge: Cambridge University.

Though this book deals with first language acquisition, some of its insights are no doubt applicable to the problem of the second language.

Chapter 17

Nurseries, Streets, and Classrooms: Some Comparisons and Deductions

John Macnamara
McGill University

EDITORS' INTRODUCTION

Macnamara started something with this paper. It was first published a decade ago. It appeared actually in two versions: one came out in the *Modern Language Journal* (which is the version we reprint here) and the other in *Focus on the Learner* (Oller and Richards 1973). In fact, before either of the published versions appeared, the article was circulated among a group of graduate students at UCLA, among whom was Stephen D. Krashen. No doubt Macnamara's distinction between "formal" and "informal" learning influenced Krashen's subsequent distinction between "learning" and "acquisition." Also intriguing is the fact the Macnamara reached much the same conclusion about the nearly nonexistent effects of formal instruction as contrasted with the nearly universal efficacy of natural acquisition. Macnamara's comments about the artificiality of formulas for grammatical processes which are only dimly understood (if at all) also anticipated the concept of "freak" grammars discussed in a number of subsequent publications. Concerning the relationship between child and adult capacities for language acquisition the evidence continues to support the position that Macnamara took in this paper. Adults are better than children except when it comes to certain aspects of surface form, especially phonology. Concerning the variability in acquired skills among first language acquirers, however, the jury is still out. New evidence seems to suggest that there is a great deal of variability in language abilities among natives. On one point, though, there is increasing agreement. Human beings apparently have certain genetic endowments which are universal to our own species and yet are not shared by any other species. It is this ineffable and distinctly human *faculté de langage* which provides a solid foundation for the remaining chapters of this section (Terrell, Chapter 18; Savignon, Chapter 19; and Krashen, Chapter 20).

Some things children seem to learn naturally; others they have to be taught. Unaided, they seem to learn to walk and to perceive the world visually; on the other hand nearly all children have to be taught arithmetic. Language is a peculiar embarrassment to the teacher because outside school children seem to learn a language without any difficulty whereas in school with the aid of teachers their progress is halting and unsatisfactory. It is common experience that when translated to a town where their native language is not spoken children will become reasonably proficient in the new language in 6 months. It is equally common experience that after 6 years of schooling in the second language, whatever the teaching method, most children emerge with a very poor command of the language. The first set of experiences shows that children are possessed of a very powerful device for learning languages; the second shows that the school harnesses the device only in a most inadequate manner. This chapter is my attempt to arrive at an explanation of the school's relative failure and to derive therefrom guidelines for teaching. I am encouraged to do so because of the overwhelming evidence from common experience that the child has vastly more language learning potential than he shows in the classroom. Indeed, language is the sole school subject of which we have this information, and consequently is the subject where the prospects of improving learning are the brightest and most substantial.

THE CAPACITY TO LEARN A LANGUAGE

The function of the human language learning capacity is defined with reference to a genuine language, such as French or German. If we could specify exactly the code which we call French we would have taken the first and most important step in the direction of specifying the nature of the language learning capacity. The second step would be to specify the actual learning process whereby a person grapples with the code and masters it. The troubles with this approach, however, are massive: we are very far indeed from being able to specify a code like French, and *we are even farther from being able to specify the language learning process.*

I have argued elsewhere (Macnamara 1972) that infants learn their mother tongue by first determining, independent of language, the meaning which a speaker intends to convey to them and then working out the relationship between the meaning and the expression they heard. In other words, the infant uses meaning as a clue to language, rather than language as a clue to meaning. The argument rests upon the nature of language and its relation to thought, and also upon the findings of empirical investigations into the language learning of infants. The theory is not meant to belittle the child's ability to grapple with intricate features of the linguistic code. These must be grasped even if the clue is usually—though by no means always—to be found in meaning. The theory claims that the main thrust in language learning comes from the child's need to understand and to express himself.

Contrast now, the child in the street with the child in the classroom. In the street he will not be allowed to join in the other children's play, not be allowed to use their toys, not even be treated by them as a human being, unless he can make out what they say to him and make clear to them what he has to say. The reward for success and the punishment for failure is enormous. No civilized teacher can compete. But more to the point, the teacher seldom has anything to say to his pupils so important that they will eagerly guess his meaning. And pupils seldom have anything so urgent to say to the teacher that they will improvise with whatever communicative skills they possess to get their meaning across. If my analysis of infant language learning is correct, as I believe it to be, it can surely explain the difference between the street and the classroom without placing any serious strain on the analogy between first and second language learning.

I want to carry this analysis further and apply it to the school, but before I do I want to clear up one theoretical matter. Many people imagine that babies learn languages in a special manner which is different from the way older persons learn them. They miss the obvious point that for an adult to know a language is in all essentials the same as for a baby to know it. Since the product is the same, the simplest hypothesis is that the learning process is the same. Suits of clothes which look identical are probably cut from the same pattern. There is then just as much magic in an adult's learning a language as in a baby's doing so. And in the absence of all evidence to the contrary, *we can safely hypothesize that it is the same magic.*

SOME GUIDELINES FOR THE TEACHER

Though of late some writers (e.g., Asher 1972) have proposed that language teaching in classrooms should be modeled on the communication between mothers and babies, no one, so far as I am aware, has gone ahead to make practical deductions from what we know of recent studies of language learning among babies. Yet such deductions are neither impractical nor counterintuitive to what we know of the schoolchild. Let us, then, assume that the schoolchild's mind is so fashioned that he approaches language learning largely as an infant does, and see what follows.

Our first conclusion must be *that teacher and children wallow in almost total misunderstanding.* The teacher believes that language is to be respected and caressed for its own sake, that one needs to do penance and prepare oneself to capture the fine points of pronunciation and grammar as Sir Galahad prepared himself to seek the Holy Grail. Children are simply stunned by this attitude. They believe that language is for communicating; they see it as a modest tool, but communication for them is the essence of the business. I believe the children are right and the teachers wrong. I also believe that the only way to make the linguistic magic work is to become vitally engaged in communicating something.

From this central confusion on the part of teachers follow several corollaries. Babies begin with one-word sentences and manage to communicate very well in them. Schoolchildren are usually required to speak in full sentences in an unnatural manner: "that is not a hen; that is a lawnmower." The teacher sees virtue in full sentences and the schoolchild is at a loss to know why.

Parents are proud of any effort which a small child makes to express himself in words. They welcome his phonological innovations; they accept his bits of words; and they understand his telegraphese. As a matter of fact, parents seldom correct a small child's pronunciation or grammar; they correct his bad manners and his mistakes on points of fact (see Gleason 1967). Somehow, when a child is vitally concerned with communicating, he gradually gets over his difficulties and eradicates errors, at least to the point where society accepts his speech. His parents' attention is on his meaning, not on his language, and so probably is his own. And curiously he and his parents break one of psychology's basic learning rules. Psychology would advise that he should be rewarded only for linguistically correct utterances, whereas parents reward him for almost any utterance. But then the folk wisdom of the Italians, older than experimental psychology, has created a proverb which gives the lie to psychology and agrees with parent and child—*sbagliando s'impara* (by making mistakes we learn). By contrast the conscientious teacher pounces on all departures from phonological and syntactic perfection; she does not care what the student says as long as he says it correctly. The schoolchild, unused to such treatment in learning his first language, is unnerved and finds himself at a disadvantage. He does not, of course, analyze the situation; he merely becomes bored or concludes that he lacks talent for languages.

Finally, a mother does not have another verbal language in which to talk to the baby if he fails to understand her. She has to make do with gestures, facial expressions, and exaggerated tones of voice. Because they are both involved in communicating they usually manage somehow. How different it is in the classroom! Teacher and child usually have another common language, and could communicate better if they really needed to. Indeed they often do have recourse to other language. Teachers, unlike mothers, do not exploit to the full the basic natural language of gestures, intonation, facial expressions, and events in the environment to provide the child with clues to the meaning. As a result, classroom conversations seem remote, unreal, and often lifeless compared with the conversations of a mother and child. Basically it is the same disease that we have encountered before: The teacher sees language mainly as something to be learned; the child sees it mainly as a means of communication. He is seldom interested in language, but rather in the information it conveys.

SOME COUNTERARGUMENTS

Partly in opposition to the position I am taking there is a common belief that one's language learning device atrophies rather early in life. The evidence for this is that babies pick up their mother tongue with what seems like great ease, and young children in suitable environments pick up a second language with little trouble, whereas adults seem to struggle ineffectively with a new language and to impose the phonology and syntax of their mother tongue on the new language. The argument has been supported with some evidence from neurophysiology (Penfield and Roberts 1959), but the value of this evidence is dubious, to say the least.

I suspect that the evidence which most supporters of the theory draw upon confounds two phenomena, the child in the street and the child in the school. Small children don't go to school. Older ones usually learn languages in school rather than in the street. We have already seen that these two phenomena must be distinguished. But besides all this many families have the experience of moving to a new linguistic environment in which the children rapidly learn the language and the adults do not. This happened frequently to English families which moved to one of the colonies, such as India. In such cases, the linguistic experience might well be attributed to unfavorable attitudes toward the new language which the parents but not the children adopted. However, Italian families which migrated to the United States often met with a similar linguistic fate—the children learned English, and the parents, despite favorable attitudes, did not. Is this conclusive evidence that language learning ability atrophies?

No! Let us take clear examples; let us compare a man of forty with an infant. We could not prove that the man was less skilled in language learning unless we gave the man an opportunity equal to that of the child to learn a language. We would need to remove the man from the preoccupations of his work and supply him with a woman who devoted a large part of her time and energy to helping him learn the language. Further, the woman would have to behave just like the mother of a small baby, which among other things would include treating anything the man said in his mother tongue as she would treat a child's babbling. Naturally such an experiment has never been carried out, and for that reason there are almost no grounds for the general fatalism about adults' ability to learn languages. On the contrary, what experimental evidence we have suggests that adults are actually better than children. Smith and Braine (unpublished manuscript) found adults superior in the acquisition of a miniature artificial language, while Asher and Price (1967) found adults superior at deciphering and remembering instructions given in what to them was a foreign language. Thus there are grounds for optimism in this area.

However, there is evidence that adults and even teenagers generally have difficulty in mastering the pronunciation and intonational patterns of a new language, or even a new dialect. Labov (1966) found that persons who moved to Manhattan after the age of twelve seldom came to sound exactly like persons who grew up there. Similarly, persons who learn a language after adolescence usually sound a little bit foreign. But this does not mean that they do not communicate effectively and even quite normally. It is unwise to overemphasize their phonological difficulties. *Apart from this there is no evidence that after adolescence one cannot learn a language as rapidly and as well as a small child.*

A second strategy employed to explain why infants and children in streets are better language learners than children in classrooms is to argue that the latter learn formally whereas the infant and the child in the street learn informally.

But since it is impossible to specify the elements and rules of a language, it follows that the term formal learning can be applied to language in only the loosest sense. If we cannot reduce language to formula, we cannot learn it by formula. The extent to which we cannot formulate a language is the extent to which our learning of it cannot be formal, and this is to a very great extent. On the other hand there are useful rules or formulas which capture some of the regularities of a language. It is the case that these are often explicitly taught to adults, and they are never taught to infants. May we not speak of the adults' learning as being to this extent formal, and that of the infant informal? And if so, is this an important difference? The answer is most unlikely to be an affirmative. The main reason is that the normal grammatical rules given to students are merely hints which so depend upon linguistic intuition that they constitute very little evidence indeed for anything which can justly be termed formal learning; neither do they suggest a large difference in learning style and strategy between babies and adults.

Among the most commonly canvassed explanations for the relative lack of success in language work in the classrooms is an unfavorable attitude among the students to the language or its speakers. I am sure that this is not without foundation, but I also feel that it is greatly exaggerated. The argument ought at least to deal with the fact that historically language shifts have generally been accompanied by unfavorable attitudes to a conquering people and its language. There has always been antipathy between the Irish and the English; yet English replaced Irish. The Highland Scots behaved just like the Irish, and while the Welsh proved tougher than either, they too seem to be in the process of changing to English. They are, of course, following in ancient footsteps, because centuries ago the Celtic languages of Europe succumbed to Latin. Despite determined efforts to prevent it, the people of Provence have accepted French in place of Provencal, and the Catalonians have learned Castilian in addition to Catalan. But there is no need to multiply examples.

A child suddenly transported from Toronto to Berlin will rapidly learn German no matter what he thinks of the Germans. Indeed when he makes his first appearance on the street and meets German children he is likely to be appalled by the experience. They will not understand a word he says; they will not make sense when they speak; and they are likely to punish him severely by keeping him incommunicado. I have argued elsewhere (Macnamara 1972) that he will learn German because he must understand what is being said to him precisely when it is said, and he must communicate precisely when the need arises. His need to communicate has very little to do with what is commonly understood as an attitude to a people or its language.

CONCLUSION

To return to the main line of argument, which is to take the infant or the child in the street as the model, it is clear that the teacher's job is to set up the language class so that communication in the new language is essential to the students. This can probably be best done by turning it into an activity period. If the students are cooking, or engaged in handicraft, needs to communicate rapidly arise. The teacher, then, could explain in the foreign language what needed to be done and allow the student to demand further information and clarification. What a change that would be! The teacher should be so serious about this that she would allow what is being cooked or made to be spoiled if the student failed to understand. She should never fuss about language, but rather be delighted with all attempts to talk. Perhaps, there would be a lot to be said for mixing students of various levels of proficiency in the same activities in order to increase the linguistic resources. This would be more like the family, and it has the support of the excellent experience of such cooperation in small country schools. If the teacher tells a story, she should not break off every line to note unusual usages or to ask whether the students know some word. The story should be the thing, and the students should be obliged to ask for explanations when they need them. But this is not the place to give a detailed scheme. I will have to leave that to another time, or better still, to other people.

One final point. Babies do not differ much in ability to learn a language. Leave aside the deaf ones, those who are severely retarded mentally, and a few who have pathological linguistic troubles, and the rest seem to learn with little difficulty. One may be a little more talkative than another; one may progress a little more quickly than another and learn a larger vocabulary. But we must look closely if we are to notice linguistic differences and disentangle them from other variables such as general intelligence and vitality. In foreign language classrooms the linguistic variation is enormous, and this I take as a sign of failure to engage the children's *faculté de langage*. I am not surprised to find enormous differences among people in solving mathematical problems, but I would be if I were to find them among people in walking. Walking, I take it, is "natural" whereas solving mathematical problems is somehow "artificial." It would seem that homes and streets produce "natural" language, whereas schools produce "artificial" language, and that the variation among students is an indication of the artificiality. Our task is to make the school more like the home and the street. My belief is that when we really learn this lesson, individual differences in linguistic attainment will cease to be striking. I also forecast a lean time for those whose business, as guidance counselors, is predicting such differences.

DISCUSSION QUESTIONS

1. Do you agree with the suggestion that "children seem to learn" such things as walking and visual perception? Consider the notion of "learning to see" as opposed to the biological maturation of, say, the heart or the brain. Surely one does not "learn" to have binocular vision any more than one "learns" to have a brain or any other organ. This is the beginning of an argument for the biological basis for the language faculty as advanced in recent years by

Noam Chomsky, especially in his debate with Jean Piaget (see Piatelli-Palmarini 1980). Does Chomsky's argument for the genetic basis of language strengthen or weaken the position that Macnamara is taking throughout this chapter? Explain.

2. What is Macnamara getting at when he says, "we are very far from being able to specify a code like French, and *we are even farther from being able to specify the language learning process*" (p. 260; his italics)? How does this remark relate to the claim that "the extent to which we cannot formulate a language is the extent to which our learning of it cannot be formal" (p. 264)? What additional differences between the process of language acquisition and the process of grammatical description might also enter the picture here?

3. Discuss the claim that apart from "phonological difficulties" there is "*no evidence that after adolescence one cannot learn a language as rapidly and as well as a small child*" (p. 263; his italics). In what ways is it to be expected that the rewards and punishments would enter the picture for teenagers and adults as contrasted with children before puberty? For instance, Macnamara claims that "no civilized teacher can compete" with the peer pressures placed on young children.

4. It would seem that the child's energy in acquiring a language in a natural setting is ordinarily focused on determining the relationship (the pragmatic mapping) of utterances to meaningful contexts of experience. In what ways have traditional classroom approaches tended to ignore and even to stifle this natural purpose? (For ideas about how to bring that focus back to the classroom see the preceding and subsequent chapters of this volume.)

Chapter 18

The Natural Approach to Language Teaching: An Update

Tracy D. Terrell
University of California, Irvine

EDITORS' INTRODUCTION

Terrell relies heavily on Krashen's "monitor theory" of second language learning, and more particularly on his "input hypothesis" (see Chapter 1 and Krashen's own Chapter 20). Terrell asserts that the chief aim of the natural approach is to focus on the meaning of genuine communications (rather than on the form of utterances, as in the traditional approaches criticized by Macnamara and others) and to bring anxiety down to a minimum. Terrell acknowledges the kinship of his approach to other communication-oriented methods such as Asher's total physical response approach, Lozanov's Suggestopedia, Curran's counseling-learning, and Gattegno's silent way. In Terrell's classes comprehension precedes production and during acquisition activities direct feedback on errors is not provided by the teacher. Correction, where it occurs, is quite indirect, through expansion, reiteration, and the like. The reason for this is straightforward: "Activity that promotes acquisition must allow for comprehensible input in which the focus is on the communication of messages in a low-anxiety environment" (p. 274). Direct correction of errors increases anxieties and inhibits participation in communicative exchanges. Terrell sees communicative activity progressing through three stages—"comprehension," "early speech production," and finally, full-fledged "speech activities." Just as Macnamara contended in the immediately preceding chapter, Terrell argues that first and second language learners alike are able to figure out the syntax of the target language by a prior understanding of meaning. Or, as proposed above in Chapters 1 and 2, the pragmatic mapping of utterances into contexts of experience in the initial phases of language acquisition depends on a prior understanding of the facts—persons, goals, plans, relations, and events—that are talked about. We agree with Terrell, Krashen, and others that, at least in the early stages of acquisition, the lexicon is more important to comprehension than are the surface niceties of syntax. For additional applications of Terrell's ideas see Chapter 32.

In 1977, I outlined a proposal for a "new" philosophy of language teaching which I called the "natural approach" (NA).[1] My suggestions at that time were

---

1. See Terrell (1977). Kelly (1976) and Titone (1968) make it apparent that there are no new approaches to language teaching: only rearrangements of ideas which have gone in and out of style since man began speculating on language teaching and learning. Higgs (1979, pp. 335-341) implies that I "rediscovered" the natural approach. This implication is, in a sense, true; during the audiolingual period, when I studied language-teaching methodology, we paid very little attention to methods other than grammar-translation, which we had set out to replace, and audiolingualism, its replacement. Leonard Newmark (Chapter 4 in this volume) made suggestions very similar to mine in 1966.

the outgrowth of experience with Dutch and Spanish classes in which the target languages were taught to beginners whose native language was English. Since then the NA has been used in primary, secondary, and adult ESL classes, as well as in secondary, university, and adult Spanish, French, and German classes. During these 5 years of experimentation we have concentrated on the development of teaching techniques to implement the original proposals.

This chapter has two purposes: (1) to discuss the underlying assumptions of the 1977 paper in light of recent research in second language acquisition and learning, as well as from personal experience in the classroom; and (2) to suggest specific techniques for implementing the NA in second or foreign language classrooms.

GENERAL CONSIDERATIONS

The natural approach is not the only means of language teaching that results in students who can communicate with native speakers of a given target language. Any approach in which real communication is the basis of class activities will produce students who, within a very short time, can function in communicative situations with native speakers of that language.[2] The professional literature has positive reports on numerous communicative approaches to foreign language teaching.[3]

For most students, approaches that do not normally result in the ability to communicate are grammar-translation, audiolingual, and the various eclectic cognitive-based methods. They produce skills that match exactly what is taught.

---

2. I am fully aware of the difficulties in defining these two terms. I defined communicative competence in my 1977 article and it is relatively clear despite the criticism in Higgs (note 1 above), p. 335. A "very short time" must remain vague because of the many factors which determine rate of acquisition. In any case, I see no reason to accept the radical view that the ability to communicate messages cannot be achieved in a classroom or even that many, many years of language study are necessary. The massive failure of classroom teaching to produce anything resembling communicative ability in one or two years of language study is unfortunately hidden by the almost universal practice of testing *only* grammatical competency. Students often do well with complicated grammar manipulations on written tests, and one assumes (although probably not really believes) that if the proper situation arose, they could use this knowledge for communication. Since such situations rarely arise in the classroom (because the instructor is busy teaching the next grammar point), the student's ability to transmit messages is never put to the test and the failure of the course is hidden. For a similar point of view see Diller (1971, pp. 1-2).

3. Language teachers should be familiar with at least the following "new" approaches to language instruction: Lozanov's *Suggestopedia*, see Stevick (1980, pp. 229–259 [this volume, Chapter 9]), Grabe (1979); Curran's *community language learning;* Stevick (1973), Grabe (1979); Asher's *total physical response*, see Asher (1977 [this volume, Chapter 5]); Gattegno's *silent way*, see Gattegno (1972; rpt. New York: Education Solutions, 1974 [this volume, Chapter 6]); Stevick, (1980, pp. 37-82); Grabe (1979); Magnan's *Focus approach*, see Magnan (1979); Galyean's *confluent learning*, see Galyean (1979). See also Benseler and Schulz (1980) for a brief summary of these approaches.

In the case of grammar-translation, students can translate from the target language to L1 and usually have a good knowledge of the grammar of the target language—especially if asked to perform on grammar tests. They normally neither speak nor understand the spoken language, nor should they be expected to do so. Students in an audiolingual approach usually have excellent pronunciation, can repeat dialogues and use memorized prefabricated patterns in conversation. They can do pattern drills, making substitutions and changing morphemes using various sorts of agreement rules. What they very often cannot do is participate in a normal conversation with a native speaker. Students using the various cognitive approaches now in vogue can usually do well on grammar exams and can often even produce new sentences, although slowly and laboriously. This result undoubtedly stems from the fact that they have concentrated on a cognitive understanding of the rules and must therefore apply them consciously when speaking.[4]

Although I make no claims for the NA which another communicative approach could not match, one can demonstrate informally that communicative-based approaches generally produce results superior to any cognitive or habit-drill based approach.[5] In the original NA proposal I suggested three principles on which to base language teaching: (1) the classroom should be devoted primarily to activities which foster acquisition (activities which promote learning might be assigned as homework); (2) the instructor should not correct student speech errors directly; and (3) the students should be allowed to respond in either the target language, their native language, or a mixture of the two.[6] Experience has shown that, by far, the most important principle is that acquisition activities be provided in the class. Such activities allow the development of communicative abilities through natural acquisition processes in addition to fostering the kind of knowledge that results from conscious cognitive learning exercises. The other two suggestions are only particular

---

4. See Krashen (1978, pp. 175–183). Krashen has called this strategy the "L1 plus Monitor mode" of speaking. It consists primarily of using native language word order, target language lexical items, and as much "patchwork" as possible using target language rules that have been explained and practiced. Although this production strategy works for certain individuals (those who have a "knack" for grammar) in restricted circumstances, it is an extremely inefficient mode of speech and must at some point be replaced by normal modes of speech production.

5. Given the large number of variables difficult to control in any experiment of comparative methodology, it is unlikely that any hard evidence for this claim will be produced in the near future. There are some minor sorts of evidence similar to that reported by Asher (1965 [and see Chapters 26 and 27, this volume]), Hauptman (1971), Villani (1977), Savignon (1972). See also Stevick (1980) for impressive personal accounts of successes with various communicative approaches.

6. I use the now accepted "research" definitions of *acquisition* as an unconscious process of constructing grammar rules, also referred to as "creative construction" or commonly as "picking up" a language, and *learning* as a conscious attempt to internalize grammar rules; the latter usually includes focused study and practice with various sorts of exercises.

examples of possible techniques which encourage an acquisition-rich environment. In order, then, to understand how the NA functions in the language classroom, we must examine in some detail the acquisition process and its implementation.

ACQUISITION

Available research in second language study strongly supports the hypothesis that the processes Krashen and others have called acquisition (the unconscious formulation of grammatical principles) and learning (the conscious cognitive-based study of grammar) represent two systems for internalizing knowledge about language.[7] My original proposal was that both are important ways to gain linguistic proficiency. However, since in most cases of foreign language (and often even in second language) study, the student has little chance for acquisition outside the classroom, the instructor must provide this kind of experience. Learning, on the other hand, being of secondary importance in the development of communicative competence, should be more restricted, perhaps to outside-the-class activities. The important point is that activities promoting acquisition are indispensable for all students. Learning activities are more limited in their usefulness to beginners.

On the other hand, some observers evidently believe that the acquisition process is not relevant in a language classroom. Strevens (1978) states, for example, that "first language acquisition and LL/LT (language learning and language teaching) belong in different universes of discourse which overlap in only limited ways. To see language teaching as applied psycholinguistics is to misunderstand the relationships between a predominately intellectual activity and a predominately practical one" (p. 180). In my opinion teaching languages as an *intellectual* activity is, to a great extent, responsible for the failure of the educational establishment to impart even the most fundamental communication skills to normal students in foreign language classrooms.

Overwhelming research evidence and informal reports point out that students who wish to communicate must acquire this ability in much the same way that speakers, adults or children, acquire it in natural situations. Krashen provides strong evidence that learned, rather than acquired, rules are of limited use to the student; for some, they serve as a "monitor," i.e., primarily an "editor" to make minor changes or corrections in utterances which for the most part are initiated by acquired knowledge. Research supports Krashen's hypothesis that this "monitor" can be activated only under restricted circumstances. The speakers must: (1) know the rule; (2) be focused on the form of what they are saying; and (3) have time to apply the rule.[8]

---

7. See Krashen (1977); Taylor (1978); for similar views see Bialystok (1978, 1979a, 1979c, 1981) who uses the terms "implicit and explicit knowledge."

8. For research support for this claim see Krashen (1979b, 1979c, 1980b), Larsen-Freeman (1975); Krashen, Butler, Birnbaum, and Robertson (1978); Bialystok (note 7 above and 1979b).

Most speakers meet conditions for monitoring regularly and systematically only on cognitive grammar tests. Most of us are not able to monitor to an appreciable degree in normal communicative situations. Thus, even if rules are learned by the students through explanation, drill, and practice, and even if they demonstrate that they can produce correct forms and syntax on grammar exams, such (cognitively based) knowledge is usually not very helpful in normal communicative situations, particularly in beginning stages.[9] Krashen's monitor theory thus explains that oral proficiency in communication is not necessarily related to the ability to achieve high scores on standard grammar tests, a fact usually overlooked by language teachers who claim to have communicative competence as a goal but continue to evaluate progress only in the learning of grammar rules.[10]

Krashen claims that the monitor theory also accounts for the tremendous variation in grammatical accuracy among adults. There are "underusers," those who rarely use their learned competence or perhaps those whose learned competence is low. ("Underusers" might still achieve very high levels of communicative accuracy entirely through acquisition.) "Overusers" spend so much time and effort on correctness that it often seriously interferes with communication. "Optimal users" are those who are able to monitor their speech and improve their level of grammatical accuracy, but not to such an extent that it interferes with smooth communication. A fourth category was suggested by Carlos Yorio at the 1978 TESOL convention in Mexico City: "superusers," those who are consciously able to apply learned rules quickly and efficiently so that a listener would not notice the monitoring at all. Many language instructors fall into this category, and although most have acquired the relevant rules through subsequent experience and no longer need to monitor their speech consciously, they often feel that this mode of production (supermonitoring) is the most efficient way to learn another language. Unfortunately, many, perhaps most, students are not capable of performing with the mental gymnastics of their supermonitor instructors.

Some assert that learned rules are acquired through practice. This assumption seems to underlie most cognitive approaches in which a three-part technique is used: explanation, practice, and application. Advocates of cognitive approaches, Chastain notes, believe that comprehension of the rule *must* precede its use. The learning of a grammatical principle *can* precede its acquisition. Whether it facilitates acquisition probably depends on the learning style of the acquirer (Chastain 1976, p. 135).

---

9. Bialystok (note 7 above) presents strong evidence that general exposure to the language in communicative situations is relevant to performance requiring attention to either meaning or form, but that additional formal practice after a particular point no longer facilitates performance. Rivers' comment from her diary account of learning Spanish is revealing. "You cease to think in the language when the exercises make you say things which are contradictory or do not apply to you" (1979, pp. 67–82). Both formal and informal evidence thus points to the centrality of conveying meaning in messages, not of formal practice.

10. See Mullen (1978, p. 303); Terrell, Perrone, and Baycroft (forthcoming).

Fortunately, a conscious understanding of grammar rules is not prerequisite to their acquisition. Most adults are not very good at learning grammar, but they acquire rules readily, although usually imperfectly, given the chance to interact in communicative situations with native speakers of the target language.

If the monitor theory of second language competence and performance is correct, activities that foster acquisition must assume a central role in any approach having communicative abilities as its goal. Research indicates that acquisition takes place under certain conditions. In a communication situation: (1) the focus of the interchange is on the message; (2) the acquirer must understand the message; and (3) the acquirer must be in a low-anxiety situation.

The claim that the focus must be on the message in a communicative situation is a strong one and has immediate implications for the classroom.[11] If this claim is correct, and so far we have no contradictory evidence, it means that, for the most part, acquisition will not take place during traditional grammar exercises or drills since they provide no opportunity for meaningful communication.[12] For this reason the syllabus of a NA course consists of communication goals.[13] For example, a possible goal might be to talk about what the students did over a weekend. In the activities which are used to achieve a particular goal, the necessary tools (vocabulary and structure) are supplied. However, the focus of the student during the activity must be maintained on the semantic content (in this case, the weekend activities), not the grammatical form (here, the past tense).

The second condition is that the student understand the message. Acquisition does not take place by listening to speech that is not understood by the student. Therefore, the input supplied by the speech of the instructor must be made comprehensible. That does not mean, however, that speech need be simplified to the extreme of using only lexical items, grammatical forms, and structures already studied by the student, a practice common to the audiolingual approach.

---

11. The importance of focus on content for children has long been recognized, but holds equally for adults. See Dulay and Burt (1973, 1977).

12. I do not claim that no acquisition can take place in learning activities. For example, in any exchange in which the attention is focused on verb tenses, other structures (word order, noun-adjective agreement, gender, etc.) may be acquired if the other conditions posited are met. Unfortunately, most cognitive grammar-based exercises are boring to all but the most dedicated of students. I would omit them entirely, but am convinced they are helpful to at least a few students. On the other hand, their failure as a basis for a language course is painfully obvious.

13. Notional-functional syllabuses, in use in Europe now for some time, are based on a similar philosophy of language teaching. See, for example, Wilkins (1973), Johnson (1977), B. Kennedy (1978). The difference is that when I use the term communication goals, I refer principally to the sorts of personal messages a beginner would need to communicate (information about himself, his family, his friends, daily activities, hobbies, likes, dislikes, and so forth). The notional-functional syllabus focuses also on messages, but from the point of view of what the speaker wishes to do: greeting, inviting, giving directions, expressing agreement, etc.

Language acquirers in natural situations regularly receive comprehensible input. In first language acquisition we call it "caretaker speech," in second language acquisition "foreigner talk."[14] The characteristics of this sort of simplified speech have been studied in some detail and are of interest to teachers because they seem to be useful to the learner. Hatch summarizes the most important characteristics of simplified input: *slower rate* (clear articulation, diminished contractions, long pauses, extra volume, and exaggerated intonation); *understandable vocabulary* (high-frequency vocabulary, less slang, few idioms, high use of names of referents instead of proforms); *marked definitions* (explaining a term that the speaker doubts the learner will know, repetitions, gestures, pictures); *simplification of syntax vis-à-vis the meaning* (simple propositions, focus on topics, repetition and restatement, less proverb modification, helping the learner complete utterances); *discourse techniques* (giving a possible answer within the question, yes-no question, tag questions) (see Hatch 1979).

The remarkable thing about simplified input is that the techniques to produce it are easily acquired. Native speakers do not necessarily give immediate input at the correct level for all acquirers in all situations; but, for most adults some experience talking with acquirers will result in the ability to make the above sorts of changes automatically and unconsciously.

The third condition is that the students receive comprehensible input in a low-anxiety environment.[15] I have previously (1977) asserted that affective factors are the most important in language acquisition (but not necessarily in language learning). I am even more convinced that the lowering of affective barriers must be the overriding concern in classroom activities if acquisition is to be achieved. "Student attitudes," Stevick (1976, p. 62) says, "take chronological priority [over course content]. . . . The linguistic material presented during the first week . . . is only a vehicle for getting acquainted and for finding and reducing anxieties" (see also Gardner and Lambert 1972).

A low-anxiety situation can be created by involving the students *personally* in class activities. Specific techniques for lowering affective barriers will by necessity vary from group to group because of the different personalities, interests, and aims of students and instructors. The goal is that the members of the group become genuinely interested in each other's opinions, feelings, and interests, and feel comfortable expressing themselves on the topics of discussion

---

14. An excellent collection of papers on speech to children and its significance for the acquisition process is available in Snow and Ferguson (1977).

15. I use the term "low anxiety" to mean "affectively positive." A certain level of "tension" may be good for learning, but probably not very helpful for acquisition. Schumann (1975) classifies factors in second language acquisition in some detail using a nine-way classification: (1) social; (2) affective; (3) personality; (4) cognitive; (5) biological; (6) aptitude; (7) personal; (8) input; (9) instruction. My use of affective covers his categories 1, 2, 3, and 7—i.e., factors such as motivation, attitude, self-esteem, and anxiety.

in class. From these observations it follows that no text can supply more than suggestions for the activities which actually involve students.[16]

In summary, then, affective acquisition activities rather than cognitive learning exercises form the core of the NA.[17] An activity that promotes acquisition must allow for comprehensible input in which the focus is on the communication of messages in a low-anxiety environment.

Let us now turn to the sorts of activities we use in the NA classroom. I will describe the activities which correspond to three stages of language instruction for beginners: (1) comprehension (preproduction); (2) early speech production; (3) speech emergence.

COMPREHENSION (PREPRODUCTION)

Since the ability to comprehend novel sentences in the target language is a necessary condition for acquisition to take place, we have tried to develop a series of techniques which provides listening comprehension experiences in initial stages of language acquisition. These activities do not require the students to speak in the target language. The use of a preproduction period is not an innovation of the NA, but with the exception of Asher's total physical response, it is one of the few approaches which uses it extensively.[18] Children acquiring their first language learn to comprehend before speaking (Frazer, Bellugi, and Brown 1966). Indeed, for all speakers, competence in comprehension outpaces competence in production. Winitz and Reeds (1973) estimate that in first language acquisition "comprehension antedates sentence generating by about a year. This sequence of development—comprehension first, production second—is a functional property of the human brain which should not be violated in language instruction." Strong research evidence suggests that a prespeaking phase is beneficial to students in the classroom.[19]

Comprehension in a new language, whether of spoken or written materials, is achieved in early stages primarily by learning how to make intelligent guesses. The major components are: (1) a context; (2) gestures and other body language

---

16. Particularly good suggestions are found in Christensen (1975, 1977), from whom I take the term affective [acquisition] activities. See also Galyean (1976); Moskowitz (1979, 1981); Papalia (1976).

17. Compare this position with the opposite one of a cognitive approach such as that proposed by Nahir (somewhat misleadingly called a "practical approach"), who states that "our first premise, then, is that second-language learning must, at least in the early stages, be based on basic structures and rules, introduced following careful programming and followed first by thorough exposition, discussion, and association of the grammatical units and lexical items, and then by well-planned drills, exercises, and other types of practice." See Nahir (1979, p. 595).

18. See note 3 above for references to TPR; see also Davies (1976).

19. Asher (note 4 above); see also Asher, Kusudo, and de la Torre (this volume, Chapter 5); Ruder, Hernamm, and Schefelbusch (1977); Postovsky (1979).

cues; (3) a message to be comprehended; and (4) a knowledge of the meaning of the key lexical items in the utterance.

Grammatical signals are not usually crucial to the comprehension task of beginning students. Snow notes that "children figure out rules underlying syntactic structure by using the cues provided by the meaning of the adult's utterance" and that this implies that "children must be able to determine what an utterance means on the basis of nonsyntactic information since the syntax is precisely what is to be learned." Following Macnamara, Snow describes the process for children exactly as I have suggested for adults: "Knowledge of the meaning of important lexical items plus knowledge of what is likely to be said about those entities or actions given the situation must enable the child to guess correctly what the utterance means. This implies of course that the child must be a good guesser, but also that the adult must say the kinds of things the child expects to hear" (Snow 1979, p. 369).

In his famous guide, *Teaching and Learning English as a Foreign Language* (one of the most important theoretical precursors of audiolingualism), Fries takes the opposite view: "in learning a new language, then, the chief problem is not at first that of learning vocabulary items. It is, first, the mastery of the features of arrangement that constitute the structure of the language."[20] Neither informal observations of second language acquisition nor formal studies of the same have supported this view of the priority of phonology and grammar over the lexicon. As Bolinger (1970) so clearly put it, "the lexicon is central, . . . grammar is not something into which words are plugged but is rather a mechanism by which words are served. . . . The quantity of information in the lexicon far outweighs that in any other part of the language, and if there is anything to the notion of redundancy it should be easier to reconstruct a message containing just the words than one containing just the syntactic relations."

Brown's (1977, p. 15) comments on caretaker/children interaction constitute excellent advice for the classroom teacher in teaching listening comprehension. He notes: "I do think parents are exclusively concerned with communication. I do think they continuously monitor the child for signs of distraction or incomprehension, and when they see them, promptly act . . . to correct the situation."

In the following paragraphs, I will mention only a few of the techniques we have used to develop listening comprehension; imaginative instructors can easily develop others. The important point for beginners is that they not be

---

20. Unfortunately, too many in the profession have accepted this extreme position and, even worse, Fries' definition of what constitutes learning a foreign language: "A person has 'learned' a foreign language when he has thus first, *within a limited vocabulary* mastered the sound system . . . and has, second, made the structural devices matters of automatic habit" (p. 3). Such a view of language competence is both restricted, i.e., the learner will not be able to participate in many normal communicative contexts, and unrealistic, i.e., many second and foreign language learners never learn to control the phonology and grammar as a matter of automatic habit. See Fries (1945, p. 3).

required to produce utterances in the target language until they feel comfortable with comprehension.

Asher's total physical response (TPR) techniques have proved to be very useful in the NA. In these activities the instructor asks the students to perform certain actions or act out events. Simple commands *(Sit down! Raise your hand! Close your book!)* are a part of many methodologies. TPR can be used in many other ways, however. Parts of the body and clothing lend themselves easily to TPR *(Put your hand on your right leg. Point to a blue sweater.)*. Classroom objects (or any object easily portable) work well with TPR. *(All those with pencils, point to something red. Walk to the blackboard and write your name on it.)*. These commands may become quite complex and after appropriate practice in an affectively positive situation, individualized: *Kevin, please pick up the large glass sitting in front of the woman wearing a red sweater and put it on the desk in back of the student with the beard.*

Another technique, which is useful in the first few days of class, makes use of the students' names and descriptions. The following is an example of "teacher talk," that is, comprehensible input: *What is your name? (Barbara.) Everyone look at Barbara. Barbara has long, blond hair* (using context and gestures to make meaning of *hair, long, blond). What is the name of the student with long, blond hair?* (Class responds with name only.) *What is your name* (selecting another student)*? (Mark.) Look at Mark. Does Mark have long hair?* (Use gestures to contrast long-short.) (Class responds, *no.) Is his hair blond? (No.) Is it brown* (use context and gestures)*? (Yes.) Mark is the student with short, brown hair. What is the name of the student with long, blond hair? (Barbara.) And the student with short, brown hair? (Mark.)*

This activity can be continued using physical characteristics (*positive* attributes only) and clothing, including colors and some simple descriptions. This activity not only serves as comprehensible input (key words are easily interpreted from context), but also serves as a means for the instructor and students to learn each other's names.

Another technique we use extensively from the first contact hour makes use of pictures and focuses on the learning of names. The instructor introduces pictures by describing what is in the pictures, emphasizing only key lexical items in each one. *In this picture there are two women. One is standing and the other sitting. The woman who is standing has a cup of coffee.* Each student is given a different picture. The questions addressed to the class consist of information about the picture which can be answered with the name of the student who is holding the picture. *Who has the picture with the two women? Who has the picture with a woman holding a cup of coffee in her hand?* Naturally such questions will be taken from a variety of pictures: *Who has the picture with the woman talking on the telephone? What is the name of the woman with the picture of the two men washing the dog?*

An additional technique uses learning personal details about each student in the class. For example, the purpose of the lesson might be to learn which classes other students are taking and the teacher supplies for the entire class the target language equivalent. The idea is that the target language word for a particular course is associated with a particular student in the course. As the activity proceeds the instructor asks questions like: *Who is studying psychology? Which two students are enrolled in both English literature and music appreciation?* Other possibilities for early topics which lend themselves easily to association are sports, games, birthplaces, birthdates, work experiences, etc.

The prespeaking stage should last as long as the students need it to last. In 1977, I insisted that the individual students must decide when to begin speaking. Experience has proved this suggestion to be feasible. In my experience with NA classes, elementary age students need comprehensible input for several months to begin the acquisition process. Secondary students usually begin to speak comfortably after a month or so. University-level students are normally all speaking voluntarily after 4 or 5 class hours.

EARLY SPEECH PRODUCTION

The transition to early speech production is simple if students have developed a reasonably extensive passive vocabulary. I recommend a recognition level of 500 words before extensive early production is attempted. In early production we want to encourage the use of acquired knowledge and to avoid as much as possible the use of "L1 plus monitor" mode. Early opportunities for speech should therefore consist of questions which require only single word answers. *Either-or* questions are especially valuable and evolve easily from the listening comprehension activities described in the previous section: (looking at a picture) *Is this woman standing or sitting? Is this car red or green?*

NA students go through production stages similar to those of an acquirer in a natural environment (these are not completely discrete steps): yes and no answers (*Is he eating a salad? Yes.*); one-word answers from either-or questions (*What color is this blouse? Blue.*); lists (*What do you see in this picture? woman, hat, yellow, etc.*); two words strung together (*big hat, at home, no have, me go, see nothing, etc.*); three words and/or short phrases; longer phrases; complete sentences; connected discourse and dialogue. As with children learning their first or second language, the stages overlap. Some sentences may be complex, while other ideas are still being expressed with single words.

Several activities other than question-answer encourage early speech production via the acquisition mode. Most are traditional techniques which I have simply given labels. The frame itself is unimportant, but the possibility for interesting follow-up with spontaneous conversation is crucial.[21]

---

21. Many of the examples are adapted from Christensen (note 16 above).

The *open sentence* model provides a sentence frame with a single word missing: *My mother is* _____ . *The class I like best is* _____ . The *open dialogue frame* consists of short interchanges with key elements missing: *Hi, where are you going? I'm going to the* _____ . *Would you like to* _____ *with me tonight?* The *open interview* is good for early production, especially if the frames are given for responses: *What is your name? My name is* _____ . *His/Her name is* _____ . *Where do you live? I live at* _____ . *He/She lives at* _____ . I have described another early production model, the *association model* elsewhere in some detail (Terrell 1980).

Early speech production of all students will contain errors. This reality is inevitable since grammar rules are acquired over long periods of time and proficiency with any particular grammar rule will occur only after considerable experience with real communication. For this reason, in the original NA paper I proposed that direct correction of speech errors be avoided. This point deserves some extended comment before proceeding with the third stage of the NA.

ERROR CORRECTION

My earlier proposal to avoid correction of student speech errors was seen as quite "radical" and has proved to be a "bone of contention" for many who are interested in the NA. I suggested then that "there is no evidence which shows that the correction of speech errors is necessary or even helpful in language acquisition.[22] This statement is still valid. Five years of experience in classes in which speech errors are not corrected have convinced me that the practice of correcting speech errors directly is not just merely useless, but actually harmful to progress in language acquisition.[23]

I believe that the problem language teachers have accepting ungrammatical speech from students stems from two misunderstandings. First, I claim that direct correction of speech errors is not helpful for acquisition. I have never

---

22. Terrell (note 1 above), p. 330; Lalande (1981).

23. Hendrickson (1978, p. 389) devotes a great deal of space to the "when, which, how, and who" of error correction. However, his discussion of the central question, "should learner errors be corrected?" is predictably short. In fact, his evidence in support of an affirmative answer is weak. He argues that "students unable to recognize their own errors need assistance of someone more proficient in the language than they are." This assertion is true, but correct input can be supplied in many ways without direct correction of speech errors. I believe the other arguments advanced to be so weak that they are not worth extended comment. When Hendrickson paraphrases Krashen and Seliger (1975), "Error correction is especially helpful to adult second language *learners* because it helps them to learn the exact environment in which to apply rules and discover the precise semantic range of lexical items" (my emphasis), this assertion cannot be used as evidence for the use of error correction in the *acquisition* of language rules and structure but only in *learning* easy rules for monitoring.

claimed that the correction of errors is unnecessary for the conscious, cognitive-based learning of grammar rules and structures. I proposed that no student errors be corrected during acquisition activities in which the focus by definition must remain on the message of the communication. Correction of errors would focus the students on form, thereby making acquisition more, not less, difficult. Correction of speech errors may lead to *learning,* but not to *acquisition.* Since the NA classroom consists almost completely of acquisition activities, it follows that student speech errors are not normally corrected directly. On the other hand, traditional classrooms where cognitive exercises and/or audiolingual drills form the central component of the course, not to correct speech errors would be counterproductive. It would certainly be a waste of time to perform an item-substitution drill which focused on subject-verb agreement, for example, if the student were allowed to ignore agreement. Or, if the instructor wished to check the answer to a cognitive grammar exercise in which the student had filled in the blank with correct verb forms, it would be equally ludicrous to accept an erroneous answer without correction. The noncorrection of errors in the NA stems directly from the hypothesis that acquisition is the central component in language competence and performance and that the correction of speech errors, in general, does not play a role in the acquisition of language by children or adults.

Second, misunderstanding results from the fact that teachers (and parents!) feel intuitively that the correction of errors is responsible for the students' improvement toward the form of an adult grammar; that only through the use of language and constant feedback with error correction do the students advance in their ability to express themselves in the target language. Five years of experience with several thousand students who have successfully completed language courses using the NA without overt correction of speech errors and who continue to progress and improve throughout the course is strong evidence, albeit informal, that error correction is not a prerequisite for improvement in competence and performance.[24]

If error correction of student speech is not the source of improvement and progress, then what is? Monitor theory predicts that given continued exposure to comprehensible input in the target language used in affectively positive situations, the student continues to improve in both fluency and accuracy. According to monitor theory, this improvement is the result of the nature of comprehensible input. When students hear a communication and understand the message, they do not necessarily understand all of the lexical items, grammatical structures, or forms used by the speaker. At a given level of lexical and structural complexity, students can understand speech containing lexical items, structure, and forms which is slightly more advanced than the acquirers'

24. Students who have studied a second language using the NA do make errors when engaging in normal communication in the target language; however, my claim is that they do not make *more* speech errors than students using other methodologies.

current competence, but not so far advanced as to interfere crucially with comprehension. As the acquirer advances and improves, so does the level of the input. This difference between comprehensible input and the current production abilities of students accounts for improvement.[25]

On the other hand, speech errors in the NA are not passed over without any sort of response. We use the same conversational techniques with our students that caretakers use with children and that native speakers use with foreigners in real communication. If the students' speech is extremely garbled, the instructor tries to reconstruct a possible sequence. *What are you going to do after class today? I no go do eat cafeteria, no have money.* The instructor would respond, *Oh, you aren't going to eat in the cafeteria because you don't have any money. Why don't you have money? Did you forget it? Is it at home?*

If the speech contains only minor errors, they are normally corrected indirectly by simple expansion: *What's the baby doing? Baby playing. Yes, the baby's playing. What's he playing with?* Almost any response can be commented on and expanded into more conversation.

One should not think that these expansions have immediate effects for all students. The usefulness depends on the readiness of each particular student. Hatch (1979, p. 66), discussing the conversation of a Spanish-speaking adolescent learning English, makes this point clearly: "It seems unlikely that this particular learner attends to the corrections included in the replies of the native speaker. More likely, he 'hears' them only as signals that his listener understands what he is trying to tell him. Perhaps at some later stage he will hear them and match them to his own performance.

I believe that three solid reasons exist for avoiding direct correction of speech errors: (1) correction of speech errors plays no important role in the progress toward an adult's model of grammar in any natural language acquisition situation; (2) correction of speech errors will create affective barriers; and (3) correction of speech errors tends to focus the speaker on *form*, promoting learning at the expense of acquisition.

SPEECH EMERGENCE

Classroom activities in the third stage will depend to a great extent on the goals of the course, both in terms of the situations and functions for which the language will be used, and in terms of the particular language skills desired, oral skills, reading and writing skills. I will orient the remainder of this discussion to a description of activities which foster oral skills by means of acquisition. However, it should not be thought that the NA excludes in any way reading and writing skills. Four sorts of activities promote acquisition by virtue of the fact that their focus will always be on the content of communication rather than on its form.

---

25. See Krashen as listed above in notes 7 and 8.

1. *Games and recreation activities.* Games have always been used by language instructors, but mostly as a relaxation activity rather than as a core component of the language course. Games, by their very nature, focus the student on what it is they are doing and use the language as a tool for reaching the goal (participating in the game) rather than as a goal itself. No instruction hour, even with adults, should be without an activity in which the target language is used for some sort of fun.

2. *Content.* The target language may be used to explore some content area. In language classrooms this area has been traditionally dedicated to cultural similarities and differences or to some aspect of the history of the language or peoples who speak the language. Immersion programs such as those in Canada make use of content to teach academic subject matter (Swain 1978a). The important point is that content activities, if they are interesting to the students, qualify as an acquisition activity since they use language as a tool for learning something else. Focus is necessarily on the information being transmitted rather than the means (the target language). Popular activities in this category include slide presentations, movies, reports, show and tell sessions, panels, photographs, guest speakers, and so forth.

3. *Humanistic-affective activities.* These include activities which appeal to the student on a personal level. Affective-humanistic activities explore the students' values, ideas, opinions, goals, and feelings as well as their experiences. They qualify as an acquisition activity because the focus is on the message being conveyed rather than the form of the language used to convey the messages. Christensen, Galyean, and Moskowitz have developed this sort of activity, and we use them extensively in the NA in the third stage.[26]

4. *Information and problem-solving activities.* The student must determine a solution or an answer to a specific question or problem. These activities are especially useful in preparing students to function in the country in which the language is spoken. For example, working with clothing advertisements from the newspaper, the instructor asks questions like: *How much does a suit cost? What is the price reduction on underwear this week? What time does the store close? If you had only $50 to spend in this store, what would you buy?* Or the student could be given an advertisement from a grocery store and asked to plan a meal. Charts of information are useful, and many newer English as a Second Language texts use this technique extensively.[27] A chart of daily chores for the Green family might include indications on what is done, by whom, and when. Questions center around information. *Who does the dishes in the Green family? What are the duties of the youngest child? Does the father ever wash the car?*

There are, of course, activities in which more than one of the categories is relevant. One can construct with the class, for example, a chart of daily activities of the students themselves. This activity is both problem-solving and affective.

---

26. All are listed in note 16 above.
27. See, for example, Yorkey et al. (1977).

Or, a problem-solving activity can be used as a game. The important point is that each activity provides the students a chance to use language for what it was intended: a tool in communication. Focus in all acquisition activities is on the messages being exchanged, not the form.

CONCLUSIONS: BASIC PRINCIPLES

Although the basic principles of the NA have not changed, its focus has expanded considerably. If the goal of the course is the ability to communicate using the target language, grammar rules must be acquired, since rules which have been learned are available only for monitoring. Comprehension is the basic skill which promotes acquisition and therefore should precede speech production. Production (speech and writing) is not taught directly, but rather emerges in stages from response by gestures to complete discourse. Both comprehension and production experiences are provided by a series of affective acquisition activities, the main purpose of which is to promote acquisition by (1) providing comprehensible input, (2) lowering anxieties, (3) creating opportunities to convey messages. The NA posits three stages of language acquisition with various techniques used in each stage.

1. Comprehension (preproduction)
   a. TPR
   b. Answer with names—objects, students, pictures
2. Early speech production
   a. Yes-no questions
   b. Either-or questions
   c. Single/two word answers
   d. Open-ended sentences
   e. Open dialogues
   f. Interviews
3. Speech emerges
   a. Games and recreational activities
   b. Content activities
   c. Humanistic-affective activities
   d. Information–problem-solving activities

Roger Brown (1977) attempted to answer the question "How can a concerned mother facilitate her child's learning of language?" Despite the numerous differences between first and second language acquisition, his answer is just as applicable to the classroom situation with adults as with children: "Believe that your child can understand more than he or she can say, and seek, above all to communicate. To understand and be understood. To keep your minds fixed on the same target. In doing that, you will, without thinking about it, make 100 or 1000 alterations in your speech and action. Do not practice them as such. There is no set of rules of how to talk to a child that can even approach what you unconsciously know. If you concentrate on communication, everything else will follow." Teachers of a second or foreign language can be given no better advice.

DISCUSSION QUESTIONS

1. Terrell discusses some situations in which the student's attention should be focused on form. Discuss these and consider their place in a natural approach. Can attention to form contribute to "acquisition" rather than "learning"? Under what circumstances, if any, would you expect this to occur? In this connection examine some of the suggestions in Chapter 2 above.

2. Stevick is quoted as saying that anxiety reduction should chronologically precede the teaching of the language. Consider the arguments here and in Part III above in favor of this sequence. Can you think of any settings of ordinary experience where anxiety, or perhaps excitement, may be high but have a positive impact on comprehension, recall, communicative effectiveness, and the like? For instance, how about a job interview, or a speech contest, or debate?

3. Discuss the claim that direct correction of errors tends to have negative effects. Are these negative effects successfully sidestepped by indirect corrections through expansion or restatement? What about deliberate misunderstanding (e.g., taking what the learner says at face value rather than reading between the lines, so to speak)? Reflect on the effect of error correction (both direct and indirect) in your own experience as a language student.

4. Terrell asserts that "no instruction hour, even with adults, should be without an activity in which the target language is used for some fun" (p. 281). Discuss this claim and, in this connection, examine the activities in Part VI, Fun and Games.

Chapter 19

Three Americans in Paris: A Look at "Natural" Language Acquisition

Sandra J. Savignon

University of Illinois, Urbana-Champaign

EDITORS' INTRODUCTION

In this chapter, Savignon contributes some insights about differences between the "street" and the "classroom" (see Chapter 17 by Macnamara). Among other things she writes about how language teachers can learn to understand and to capitalize on opportunities for communication as well as attitudes conducive to language acquisition in a "natural" setting. However, she cautions that in spite of our best efforts to bring the "street" setting into the "classroom," the fact will remain that in an immersion context the demands and opportunities for target language use are vastly more numerous than they could be in the best of classrooms. She sees the deemphasis of "linguistic competence" per se and the promotion of comprehension as a positive, perhaps even a necessary step. Her example from the writings of Margaret Mead is highly persuasive. It suggests that mutual understanding between the acquirer and people of the target culture far outranks the significance of a perfect accent, or flawless morphology and syntax (along this line also see Terrell's comments on "error correction" in the preceding chapter). Savignon suggests that perhaps a primary function of language teaching in classroom settings should be to equip students to succeed as language acquirers in the "street." Her comment concerning her own children acquiring French is refreshing: "My primary concern was that my children enjoy their French experience, make friends, have fun" (p. 286). Don't the best language teachers have similar hopes for their students?

A persistent concern of second language researchers has been the documentation of L2 acquisition in natural environments, the study of "street learning" as it has been called to distinguish it from classroom learning. Documentation of L2 development, much of it on the model, if not the scope, of Roger Brown's (1973) landmark study of L1 development, has been concerned primarily with the sequence of acquisition in terms of particular grammatical features. In tracing, so to speak, the interlanguage of the learner, L2 acquisition studies look for patterns of grammatical development. Is there a universal sequence? Does it resemble patterns of L2 acquisition? What is the relationship of rate of acquisition for different learners to learner error? What are the sources of errors—L1 interference, simplification or overgeneralization of L2 rules? Some of these studies have been longitudinal, on the Brown model, following one or several learners over a period of time. Far more have been cross-sectional, contrasting data from different groups of learners at a particular point.[1]

As promising and as useful as these studies are, they do not afford a full view of the L2 acquisition process. Language *teachers* are perhaps the first to recognize that learner attitudes play the preeminent role in the development of competence in a second or foreign language. Important as it is to trace the acquisition of structure, attention must also be focused on the opportunities for interaction in the second language and the use made of these opportunities by the learner. An analysis of the *occasions* for L2 use and the *attitudes* of the learner is of particular interest where the emphasis is on providing as "natural" a language learning environment as possible. In an environment where learners are expected to interact meaningfully in the language they are learning, it is important to look at the *way* in which the learner interacts.

The present study takes such an ethnographic approach to an analysis of the acquisition of French by three American children spending a year in Paris. In a sense, it is an update of a 1974 report on a conversation with my 7-year-old son Daniel, who at the time was just beginning to use French. The purpose of the earlier report was to contrast the skills Daniel had acquired in what could be called a "natural" L2 learning environment with the kind of skills typically emphasized in beginning language courses (Savignon 1972, 1974).

Since 1974, almost all new textbooks talk about communication goals, communicative competence, "real" language use. Language teachers have begun to expand the curriculum to include the opportunity for meaningful, spontaneous expression at beginning levels. And there seems to be a concern for creating the kind of a "natural" language learning environment described above.[2] From his modest beginnings, Daniel is now a fluent speaker of French and, perhaps more important to his father and me, is as proud of his French heritage as he is of his American background.

Daniel's *pattern* of L2 use, along with that of his two sisters, serves as a useful perspective from which to understand classroom models in L2 programs. The "natural" setting of three L2 learners in Paris is of interest inasmuch as it represents what I think most of us language teachers concerned with communicative competence view as an ideal language learning situation. In an immersion model such as this one there is a maximum amount of context—the learner is surrounded by the second language and uses it to convey meaning—and a minimum amount of grammar explanation. In sum, it is a 24-hour communicative competence classroom.[3] An understanding of that environment can only

---

1. For a good summary of recent research see Chun (1980).

2. For a discussion of the various theoretical underpinnings of these trends see Canale and Swain (1980), and Krashen (1978).

3. See Savignon (1978). For some methodologies, the situation I describe here would be more appropriately defined as *submersion*, the term *immersion* having come to mean the use of the L2 as a medium of instruction in an otherwise L1 environment. I am nonetheless uncomfortable talking about *submersion* in this instance as the expression lacks, for me, the suggestion of support and sustenance for the learner.

lead to an evaluation of what the classroom can and should provide. A comparison with the classroom seems compelling in light of the dilemma we currently face in setting goals for classroom foreign language programs. Considering all that we have yet to learn about the development of communicative competence—in school *or* in the street—an understanding of what happens in an immersion situation should be of help in evaluating classroom methods or materials that purport to be "communicative" or "natural" and in setting realistic goals for learner achievement.

In looking at the acquisition of French by my three children, for several reasons I decided early in the year not to attempt to trace the development of grammatical features. First, I was well aware that the process of data collection is tedious and the variables so numerous—age, native language, contact with the L2, to name just a few—as to make interpretation of findings at best speculative. Second, I was frankly afraid of interfering in the acquisition process. My primary concern was that my children enjoy their French experience, make friends, have fun. It was important that I do nothing that might be interpreted as a preoccupation with language development. I was specifically concerned that the weekly or so recording sessions required for such documentation would not only show how concerned I was with language, thus making the process a self-conscious one, but that they might even lead to competitiveness between the children. Third, and at the same time, however, I was aware of something very important happening. The result is the present report.

The Paris experience came about as a result of my husband's decision to direct the Illinois Study Abroad Program. We set out not without apprehension. Could we get used to big city apartment living? How would the children fare in school? We were particularly concerned about Daniel, who was to be a high school freshman. The school where he had been accepted made clear that he would have to take all classes at his grade level without provision for regrouping in special subjects, such as French, where he would have more difficulty. We had made our decision, however, to seek regular French classroom environments for all three children, not taking advantage of either the many private bilingual schools in Paris or the public schools with special classes for recent immigrants. In addition to Daniel, age 14, there was Catherine, age 9, and Julie, age 8. Their formal learning in French at the time of our departure consisted of a summer of private tutoring in grammar and reading twice a week for the girls and the equivalent of two semesters of beginning college French for Daniel. He completed the second semester with a grade of B the summer before we left.

As I look back at our adaptation I am struck by how well it fits the classical sociological model of cultural adaptation as described in a recent article by H. Douglas Brown (1980a [also see Brown 1980b]). Following an initial period of euphoria—isn't it great to be in France, great food, great scenery, lots of new things to explore—came the sudden realization that we were not at home and we, not the French, were the ones who were going to have to adapt. A couple of anecdotes will serve, I think, to illustrate the impact of this realization.

The first day of school Daniel met in the school courtyard with the one hundred or so other students at his grade level. The school director called out names, and students stood and indicated their class. All went smoothly until "Savignon" was called. Daniel stood up, announced his class, and was immediately and smartly reprimanded for daring to address the director with his hands in his pants pockets! We learned of the incident later in the day when Daniel came home and announced that that had done it! He was not setting foot back in school! Meanwhile, in another school courtyard, his sister Catherine whose name had inadvertently been omitted from the class roster was standing in tears, unable to explain to a concerned teacher why she had not gone with her class.

I cite these incidents to show that all did not go smoothly and that there was plenty of opportunity for anomie, or a feeling of cultural alienation, to arise as the children pursued their acquisition of French. According to Lambert's theory of motivation in L2 acquisition, the success of the experience is determined precisely at the moment of greatest alienation. Either the learner retreats back into the native culture and, consequently, fails to acquire the L2, or resolves the feelings of anomie and goes on to become bilingual (Lambert 1963).

Children and parents alike faced many sources of frustration, anxiety, and anger. At times we were given preferential treatment as Americans. Our response was to band together as a family and to provide at home an emotional security that would help us to cope with the newness of the world around us. While we were eager that our children learn French, my husband and I made no demands or even suggestions that they use French with us at home. To do so, we sensed, would have created a barrier between us and rendered impossible the very closeness we needed to maintain. On the other hand, once in a francophone environment my husband and I began using French more and more between ourselves. These patterns were to change, however, as the year progressed.

The patterns of French language use that ultimately emerged during the year can be described as four distinct stages (see Figure 1).

In stage 1 (August–December) the parents speak a combination of French and English to each other, English to the children. The children speak English to each other. English is maintained by the parents at home to provide security at the time of immersion in the francophone environment.

Stage 2 (December–April) was brought about by a further immersion, this time to a family vacation camp in Senegal with a number of other families, all French-speaking. As we began eating meals and mingling on a daily basis with many other French speakers, the family nucleus broke up. When we came together again at the end of the 2-week period French had become a natural channel of communication between parents and children. By this time, also, the communicative strategies of the children were sufficiently developed to allow this communication.

Stage 3 (April–August) emerged somewhat more gradually, beginning in certain limited contexts and spreading until by mid-April the children were

English — — — — — — — — —
French ─────────────

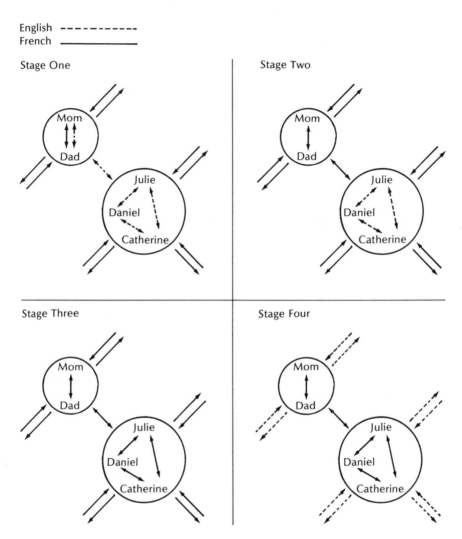

Figure 1

using French exclusively with each other. Their use of French among themselves began in dinner table and other family discussions and came to include
not only their private conversations but their games and all the taunts and
squabbles typical of a *famille nombreuse*. This third stage lasted until August of
1979 when we left France.

Stage 4 (August 1979–present) represents the continuation of stage 3
channels of communication in an anglophone environment. While the children
now speak English in the outside world, their most intimate transactions take
place in French.

The following summary statements can be made about L2 input and output for the children during the year. *Exposure to natural language:* (1) input is not all "meaningful." The children are surrounded with language sounds, only some of which are immediately interpretable. There are, however, many nonverbal clues to meaning; (2) the arrows show a gradual increase in output. From minimal output at the beginning, there is eventual total elimination of the L1 as a means of communication; (3) maximum use of coping strategies is made to survive in the outside world (Catherine's response, for example, when she was asked who she was and why she had not gone to class, was: *"je ne sais pas, je ne sais pas, je ne sais pas. . ."*). *Language learning activities:* (1) reading and writing tasks are everyday class activities (it would be wrong to say there is no formal language instruction in a "natural" environment of this kind); (2) there is no systematic speaking or listening practice (the L2 is simply the medium of interactions of all kinds); (3) there are no contrastive studies such as translation or grammar explanations that take into account the L1. The most noteworthy feature in these patterns is, of course, the gradual adoption of French until it becomes the language of the most intimate interpersonal relations with parents and siblings.

As language teachers the question we now have to ask is: how successful the experience was. The fact of now daily *use of French for communication* stands out as the most obvious mark of success. The children have very positive feelings about French and France. They write letters to French friends. They seek out other French speakers in the community.

A second criterion of success is *functional language skills.* What can the children do in French? The best measure here is their academic success. All completed the year's work and were promoted to the next level. They also made friends in French and demonstrated an ability to function in a variety of social settings. They could answer the telephone, run errands, make polite conversation. The above measures are both valid indicators of communicative competence and ones we should set for L2 programs of all kinds.

The third criterion is the *linguistic competence* of the children. How is their syntax, spelling, pronunciation, vocabulary? Is it distinguishable from a native speaker? The conversation transcribed below lets the children speak for themselves (see the Appendix).

The salient features of the conversation are the comprehension, the fluency, the ease and the nativelike pronunciation.[4] The children's positive feelings come through. All are happy to use French and use it with varying degrees of skill. If we wanted to look for grammar errors, we could find many. **Commencement*

---

4. The accent is, of course, an important concern and cannot be evaluated from a transcription of this kind. The reaction of French linguist Albert Valdman on hearing the tape recording is therefore pertinent. He characterized Julie's accent as "decidedly Parisian" while Daniel's was French but with no particular regional quality (ACTFL annual meeting, Boston, 1980).

des âges classiques, *la plus vielle (=l'aîné), *une genre, *et puis personne ne comprenne, *dès qu'on leur dise, *en Canada, *je sens bizzare, are among the more obvious. Daniel is aware that his accent and grammar are perhaps not as good as those of Catherine, in particular, who is a bookworm and a keen grammarian. Each of the girls has her own distinguishable style of speech.[5] Without going into an analysis of the children's written communicative competence, the following note provides just one example of the kinds of messages I find on my kitchen table when I return from work: *"Chère Maman, Je suis chez Cynthia, J'ai bien travalliee et je pense que sa vas aller. (sa aller très dois j'ai regardè dans ton mirroir!) Je t'aime.* Julie S."

Out of context, the message may not be clear. It has to do with violin practicing and efforts to keep a straight bow. What is important to me is that Julie takes advantage of one of the few opportunities she has to write in French. She takes risks, never sticks to what is sure. For the time being, I am just collecting her notes, and perhaps next summer, when we both have more time, we can do some spelling exercises together.

How can we summarize from this brief report of the experience of three Americans in Paris? The lesson for those of us who would like to prepare students to communicate in a second language appears to me to be threefold. First, we have to recognize the differences in environment. We cannot duplicate the L2 community in our classroom. In the "street" the opportunity for language experience is infinite, unlimited by the text, the knowledge of the teacher, or the time of day. We have to face this fact in reaching a decision as to how best to spend the time and the expertise we *do* have available to us. More important, perhaps, we need to view the L2 acquisition process as one that takes students from the classroom to street and back again to classroom. Levels of competence wax and wane with changes in exposure and emphasis. We need to analyze the occasions for L2 use in the learners' environment and help them to integrate them successfully into their language program. The role of the teacher and of the classroom depends on this analysis.

Second, we must acknowledge that the classroom has, by tradition, focused on linguistic competence. It may even be true, as Valdman and Moody (1979) have suggested, that native speakers expect classroom learners to speak with linguistic precision. Yet intelligent and successful L2 users give other accounts of how they learned to communicate. I am grateful to the late Ruth Crymes for sharing this verbatim report of a famous L2 learner, Margaret Mead:

I am not a good mimic and I have worked now in many different cultures. I am a very poor speaker of any language, but I always know whose pig is dead, and when I work in a native society, I know what people are talking about and I treat it seriously and I respect them and this in itself establishes a great deal more rapport, very often, than the correct accent. I have worked with other field workers

---

5. Julie was characterized by her violin teacher in Paris as affecting the elitist sophisticated style associated with the "Madeleine" quarter of Paris, whereas Catherine had the forthright down-to-earth manner of the popular district around the Gare de Lyon.

who were far, far better linguists than I, and the natives kept on saying they couldn't speak the language, although they said I could! Now, if you had a recording it would be proof positive I couldn't, but nobody knew it! You see, we don't need to teach people to speak like natives, you need to make the other people believe they can, so they can talk to them, and then they learn (Crymes 1980).

I find it interesting to note the number of times that both French and Americans have commented on how nice it is that our children are "bilingual." The phrase *parfaitement bilingue* has been used several times, perhaps to underscore what "bilingual" continues to mean in the minds of laymen: a parallel or identical competence in two languages. And yet the brief oral and written samples I have given are ample evidence of linguistic imperfections. The dilemma we face in the evaluation of student performance is clearly far from resolved.

Third, we do not know enough about L2 development at this point to advocate either a "communicative syllabus" or a "natural method." Any deliberate reduction of materials, i.e., language input, or stylization of the teacher's role—particularly if that role is unnatural—may not be in the best interest of the learner. Perhaps our best strategy is to prepare learners for and encourage street learning. We can do this best by not getting in the way of acquisition, by not deliberately limiting learner contact with the L2, while at the same time providing a systematic presentation of the linguistic structure of the language. More important than the analysis of linguistic structure, however, is the presence of role models, people who use the language to communicate. Members of a teaching staff who routinely use the L2 in exchanges among themselves is ideal. Native speaker visitors, exchange students, short wave, or even local radio stations all provide further access to language. They serve not only to show the range of the L2 in actual use; they provide the learner with the abundant opportunity to listen.

Finally, we should encourage the development of both linguistic and communicative competence, recognize the difference between the two, and be flexible enough in our evaluations to provide for a variety of learner strategies. The biggest factor in determining the eventual success of a program is attitude. Some measure of communicative competence is attainable by all those who seek it. It is up to us to encourage them along the way.[6]

APPENDIX

Maman: Bonsoir, Daniel.
Daniel: Bonsoir, Maman.
Maman: Je crois que la dernière fois que j'ai eu une conversation enregistrée avec toi tu avais sept ans.
Daniel: Ah oui, cela est vrai.
Maman: Est-ce que tu te rappelles de ça?

---

6. I should like to thank my colleague, Muriel Saville-Troike, for her encouraging and helpful commentary to an earlier version of this paper.

Daniel: Oui.

Maman: Nous étions à Viriville cet été là et tu venais à peine d'apprendre le français et commençais à parler un petit peu. Tu as bien accepté de parler avec moi.

Daniel: Oui, je parlais très peu mais je parlais quandmême.

Maman: Oui. Est-ce que tu peux nous dire un peu ce que tu fais. Enfin je sais que nous venons de fêter tes seize ans.

Daniel: Oui.

Maman: Est-ce que tu peux nous dire ce que tu fais cette année comme programme d'études et . . . comment va ta vie?

Daniel: Ah, ben, je fais beaucop de science et de math et j'étudie pas mal la grammaire anglaise aussi et l'histoire du monde vers le commencement, uh . . . des âges classiques et . . . ma vie va très bien à vrai dire.

Maman: Tu peux parler un peu de tes soeurs?

Daniel: Ben, j'ai deux soeurs, la plus vielle qui s'appelle Catherine qui a douze ans et la deuxième qui s'appelle Julie qui a onze ans et . . . elles sont très gentilles.

Maman: Est-ce qu'elles parlent français aussi?

Daniel: Oh oui très bien. D'ailleurs, uh . . . elles parlent mieux que moi.

Maman: Tu crois qu'elles parlent mieux que toi?

Daniel: Ah oui, je pense.

Maman: Pourquoi cela? Qu'est-ce qui te fait dire cela?

Daniel: Ben, elles ont eu peut-être plus de pratique pendant l'année qu'on a passée en France . . . et je pense que dans le cas de Catherine elle a beaucoup lu . . .

Maman: Oui.

Daniel: . . . plus que moi aussi . . .

Maman: Oui.

Daniel: . . . alors je crois qu'au moins Catherine s'est entraînée un peu plus dans la langue française que moi et puis leur accent est mieux aussi.

Maman: Tu crois?

Daniel: Je pense oui.

Maman: Est-ce que ça te gêne?

Daniel: Non, pas du tout. Je m'accepte comme je suis.

Maman: Est-ce que tu aimes parler français?

Daniel: Oui, beaucoup. C'est un plaisir de parler ce soir d'ailleurs, comme ça.

Maman: Et est-ce que tu peux m'expliquer comment tu te sens maintenant que tu parles français avec tes deux soeurs parce que avant de partir en France nous parlions à la maison toujours anglais et maintenant que nous sommes de retour vous continuez à parler non seulement français avec vos parents mais aussi avec . . . entre vous les enfants?

Daniel: Oui, ça est devenu un rite disons uh . . . je sens bizarre si je parle anglais à Catherine ou à Julie . . . ça s'est développé comme ça. Puis il y a une genre de fierté dedans aussi . . . une puissance qui vient avec . . . que je peux parler avec Catherine ou Julie dans la rue et puis personne ne comprenne quoi c'est . . . ça donne un peu de super, quoi . . . on sent bien quoi.

Maman: Tu te sens un peu supérieur?

Daniel: C'est ça. Plus spécial quoi. On sent bien.

Maman: Oui. Est-ce que tu crois que . . . quelle est la réaction de tes camarades de classe quand ils savent que tu parles français ou qu'ils t'entendent parler français.

Daniel: Ben je crois que ça les impressionne . . . dès qu'on leur dise que je sais bien parler français couramment ils veulent toujours que je leur dise quelque chose en français . . . Comment est-ce qu'on dit cela . . . ou just simplement "Dis quelque chose en français!" Alors là c'est toujours dur. On ne sait pas quoi dire quoi. C'est . . . c'est un peu gênant.

Maman: Oui. Tu penses faire quelque chose avec le français dans ta vie?

Daniel: Ben, j'aimerais peut-être m'installer quelque part en Europe oui. Si ça aiderait ou non je ne sais pas ... peut-être en Canada aussi, je ne sais pas. On ne sait jamais ... oui je pense que ça aurait un effet.

Maman: Uh ... ta petite sœur Julie est là avec nous ce soir. Je ne sais pas si elle aimerait peut-être parler un peu au micro.

Julie: Oui.

Maman: Tu aimerais dire quelque chose, Julie?

Julie: Ah oui ... je voulais dire que moi aussi je suis un peu fière de parler français dans la rue quand personne ne te comprenne mais alors comme ici on habite à l'Université où il y a beaucoup de gens qui parlent français il y a des fois qu'on parle français avec toi ... uh ma mère ... ou bien Daniel ... um il y a quelqu'un à côté de nous qui comprend le français ... ben ... ben ça gêne un peu qu'il comprend.

Maman: C'est vrai? Tu t'es trouvée gênée des fois parce que tu m'as dit des choses que tu voulais que personne n'entende et puis tu t'es rendue que quelqu'un t'avait comprise?

Julie: Oui.

Maman: Tu peux nous dire un peu ce que tu fais?

Julie: Ben ... à l'école?

Maman: Oui ... ou ... à l'extérieur ... avec des amis, ce qui t'intéresse dans la vie.

Julie: Ben ... à l'école j'aime beaucoup les math ... je travaille surtout là-dessus et ... uh ... ben ... à la maison quand je rentre je travaille mon violon ... je fais plutôt ... c'est surtout ça que je fais, mon violon.

Maman: Tu aimes ton violon?

Julie: Oui.

Maman: Tu travailles beaucoup ton violon?

Julie: Oui.

Maman: Combien est-ce que tu travailles?

Julie: Ben ... j'essaie de faire deux heures, des fois même trois heures, ça dépend.

Maman: C'est beau. C'est beaucoup.

Julie: Oui, je sais.

Maman: Oui. Et qu'est-ce que tu penses faire quand tu seras grande, dans la vie?

Julie: Uh ... je ne sais pas ... je veux peut-être être violoniste ... peut-être uh ... docteur, je ne sais pas.

Maman: Eh bien, tu as le temps de décider en tout cas.

Julie: Oui.

Maman: Est-ce que tu aimerais poser des questions à Daniel?

Julie: Ah ... je ne sais pas quoi lui poser.

Maman: Est-ce que tu es contente de parler français avec lui ou est-ce que tu trouves ça peu bizarre maintenant que tu habites aux Etats Unis et ...

Julie: Non, moi j'aime bien. J'aime bien habiter ici mais toujours parler français, parce que ... ça fait comme si on était en France mais ... mais comme on est toujours en Amérique.

Maman: Oui.

Julie: On fait des choses ici ... comme Papa est français on fait des choses ici un peu au ... à la français quoi.

Maman: Tu aimes ça?

Julie: Oui.

Maman: Bon. Alors on n'a pas eu une discussion avec Catherine parce qu'elle n'est pas là ce soir. Où est-ce qu'elle est?

Julie: A la bibliothèque, je pense.

Maman: Bon alors, merci beaucoup de cette entrevue. Vous êstes très gentils. Je crois que c'est l'heure d'aller vous coucher bientôt maintenant, n'est-ce pas?

Julie: Ben oui.

Maman: Quelle heure est-il?

Daniel: Ben il est neuf heures cinq.
Maman: Oui ben alors effectivement il est l'heure d'aller se coucher. Allez. Bonne nuit tout le
        monde. Au revoir.
Daniel: Bonne nuit.
  Julie: Bonne nuit.

DISCUSSION QUESTIONS

1. Savignon says that "it would be wrong to say there is no formal language
    instruction in a 'natural' environment of this kind" (p. 289). What is she
    getting at?

2. Discuss the observed stages of development through which the Savignon
    family progressed in their use of French. What critical factors seemed to
    contribute to the children's switch to French addressed to Mom and Dad?
    Addressed to each other?

3. Savignon distinguishes "functional language skills" from "linguistic
    competence." List and discuss the parallel distinctions encountered in
    earlier chapters.

4. Concerning application of her findings to the language classroom, Savignon
    asserts, "More important than the analysis of linguistic structure . . . is the
    presence of role models, people who use the language to communicate"
    (p. 291). She also stresses the role of listening. Why do these two
    observations necessarily go together?

Chapter **20**

The Din in the Head, Input, and the Language Acquisition Device

Stephen D. Krashen
University of Southern California

EDITORS' INTRODUCTION

Krashen recounts several paragraphs from the personal experience of Elizabeth Barber in acquiring and using Russian and some experience of his own in using German. He attempts to explain what appears at first to be a side effect of intimate and extended contact with a nonprimary language—a phenomenon he calls (inspired by Barber), "the din in the head." Is it possible that this fascinating mental phenomenon, something that all successful language acquirers have experienced from time to time, is somehow crucial to language acquisition much as dreaming may be to mental health? In addition to offering some interesting reading on this possibility, Krashen also gives a thumbnail sketch of his own theoretical framework—a viewpoint that has been ground out of years of thinking, teaching, and research. It stresses the fundamental difference between *formal* "learning" and *natural* "acquisition." It advocates "the input hypothesis" and the notion that acquisition will progress optimally when comprehensible input is provided just a little beyond the student's present stage of development (at "$i + 1$"). Further, it suggests that the "affective filter" must be down (i.e., turned off, or very low) in order for acquisition to proceed at an optimum rate. Is it possible that the "din phenomenon" may in fact help to link natural acquisition to classroom practices as Krashen suggests?

Elizabeth Barber of Occidental College has recently described a phenomenon in her personal second language acquisition experience that is extremely interesting. It is an experience many of us have had in attempting to acquire a second language in natural circumstances and sometimes in formal circumstances. I will suggest here that this experience, the "din in the head," may be of importance both theoretically and practically. It may be a result of the operation of the LAD, the "language acquisition device" itself, and may be utilized for some very practical ends. It may well be able to tell us, for example, how long language lessons should be, and when they are effective.

The early sections of this chapter describe the "din in the head." I repeat here Barber's insightful and lucid description of her experience, then add one of my own. The next section briefly reviews some recent work in second language acquisition theory that is relevant to the final section, some hypotheses about the din phenomenon, and some suggestions as to its utility in language teaching and acquisition. The hypotheses are based entirely of what can be termed "anecdotal" and self-reported data. They may be, however, testable using more rigid experimental procedures and are consistent with both the reports and what is currently known about second language acquisition.

DESCRIPTIONS OF THE DIN

We first turn to Barber's description, taken from a very interesting paper on language acquisition and applied linguistics (Barber 1980). Barber is both a linguist and an archeologist, and this excerpt describes her language acquisition and language use experiences on a recent trip to Europe:

I spent last fall traveling in a dozen countries, mostly in Eastern Europe. Since I was working rather than touring, I had to communicate in any language I could. I had studied Russian ten years ago and had read it some since, but I had never spoken it much; I had learned Greek by traveling one summer in the backwoods of Greece, with some help from my classical Greek, but I had never read it and had not used it at all in the intervening seventeen years. French, which I had learned in a French schoolyard at age twelve and had studied in high school, and German, which I had studied one summer by correspondence, were more immediately serviceable: I had read and spoken both from time to time.

It turned out that the curators I was working with at the Hermitage in Leningrad spoke nothing but Russian. The first day I was tongue-tied, but by the third, I was getting along well enough. That is, we were managing to get the information back and forth and to enjoy one another's acquaintance, even though I was acutely aware that I was making grammatical errors everywhere. But it was either that or hopelessly stall the conversation and the work. Any self-respecting adjective in Russian gives you on the order of forty possible categories of forms to choose from, according to case, number, gender, and animacy, not to mention long and short forms and declension classes. If you have to dive into this labyrinth to select a form consciously, you find when you surface proudly with your hard-won morpheme that the conversation is ten miles down the road. Either that, or your interlocutor is sound asleep. Social pacing turns out to be more important than grammatical correctness, even in a scientific conversation.

By the third day also, the linguist in me was noticing a rising din of Russian in my head: words, sounds, intonations, phrases, all swimming about in the voices of the people I talked with. This din blocked out all my other languages to a degree inversely proportional to how well I knew them. Many times on the trip, after a few days of a given language, my social signals always came out in that language, regardless of what I was trying to talk at the moment—except English, of course. And interestingly, French. I had learned my basic French as a child, by child's methods, and I have always retained the ability to switch in and out of it cleanly at a moment's notice. And whereas German was difficult to switch to, Spanish, my most recent language, was hopeless . . .

The sounds in my head became so intense after five days that I found myself mindlessly chewing on them, like so much linguistic cud, to the rhythm of my own footsteps as I walked the streets and museums. Whenever I noticed this din, the linguist in me would demand to know what I was saying. Half the time I had to look up what I was saying, or somehow reconstruct what it meant from the context in which I had heard it hours or days earlier. The constant rehearsal of these phrases of course was making it easier and easier to speak quickly; things popped out as prefabricated chunks. But I had no control over what my subconscious fed into my "chewer" each day. It fed me what it considered to be memorable—usually from a surprising or stressful or isolated incident—not what I considered maximally useful. Nonetheless, my overall command of Russian improved more in a single week than it would have in a month or two of intensive reading (Barber 1980, pp. 29–30).

I add now my own experiences, not because they are unique, but because they are not. Last year (1980) the Goethe Institute in New York kindly invited me to participate in a workshop/symposium on second language acquisition, along with several other North American and European scholars. The working languages of the symposium were English and German, the usual practice being that scholars would present their work and make their comments in their own language, assuming that all others would be able to understand.

I came to the conference with some linguistic hesitation. I had not used German to any extent since 1962, when I had spent 10 months in Vienna. On the first day of the symposium, all the presentations were in English with only part of the discussion in German. When German was used, it made me somewhat uncomfortable—I felt "German-shy," not sure I would understand, and in the casual talk that evening, not at all eager to use German. The next day was different. A major presentation was made in German, lasting well over an hour. It was on a topic that not only interested me but concerned me personally. My work was even cited several times! After a while I was so engrossed that I "forgot" that the presentation was being made in German. I followed it easily, thanks to a large extent to a very familiar extralinguistic context.

Barber's din began soon after. From New York, I flew directly to San Francisco to another Goethe Institute, where I conducted a weekend workshop on language teaching. On the plane, walking to the hotel, I felt the din rattling in my brain, exactly as Barber described it. When I got to the workshop I was, for the first time in years, not only willing but eager to communicate in German, and I chatted in German with the participants during the breaks and at get-togethers in the evening. I noticed that I was confident and fairly fluent, but not perfect. I was not overly concerned about my errors and unashamedly asked for repetition and clarification when someone said something I did not understand.

The din lasted only for a little while after the San Francisco weekend. After a few days back home in Los Angeles, with no contact with German, it began to wear off. Soon I was German-shy again.

These two anecdotes should give readers some idea of the din phenomenon, enough to relate to their own experience. I present more such data later. We turn now to a very brief review of some concepts in current second language acquisition theory that will be useful in stating hypotheses about the din later on.

SECOND LANGUAGE ACQUISITION THEORY

What follows is a brief sketch of the main points of my own work. For supporting evidence and more detail, see Krashen (1981, 1982).

Second language acquisition theory distinguishes subconscious language *acquisition* from second language *learning*. Acquisition is hypothesized to be subconscious in the sense that while it is happening we are not usually aware of it; our focus is elsewhere, on the message that is being communicated. The results of acquisition are also subconscious—we cannot always describe our acquired knowledge but rather have a "feel" for correctness in a language we have acquired. Conscious learning is "knowing the rules," or explicit knowledge. In everyday speech, it is "grammar." In my view, research suggests that acquisition is far more important than learning. Acquisition is responsible for our fluency in second languages, while learning serves only as a monitor, or editor: we use our conscious knowledge of rules only to make corrections, either before or after we produce our sentence in the second language.

The theory hypothesizes that we acquire in only one way: by understanding messages in the second language that utilize structures we have not yet acquired. Put differently, if an acquirer proceeds along an order of acquisition of structures:

$$1 \ 2 \ 3 \ 4 \ \dots \ i$$

where i is his or her current stage of development, he or she can proceed to the next structure $i + 1$ by understanding input that contains $i + 1$.[1]

We acquire, in other words, via *comprehensible input*, by listening or reading for meaning. We do not acquire by practicing speaking. Speaking is now thought to be a result of acquisition, not a cause. Real language production happens only after the acquirer has built up competence via input. (Speaking can help indirectly in that it encourages people to talk to you!)

I have hypothesized that the best input for acquisition need not be (and should not be) "grammatically sequenced." When communication is successful, when the input is understood and supplied in quantity and variety, $i + 1$ will be provided automatically and recycled in optimum quantity for language acquisition.

Comprehensible input is necessary but not sufficient. Even with comprehensible input, some acquirers fail to make progress. This is because, we have hypothesized, the input does not reach those portions of the brain that do language acquisition, even if it is understood. This happens when acquirers are overanxious or unmotivated to acquire the language, and results in the presence of an affective filter, a mental block that keeps the input out of the LAD (language acquisition device).

A very interesting hypothesis is that we acquire best only when the pressure is completely off, when anxiety is zero, when the acquirer's focus is entirely on communication; in short, when the interchange or input is so interesting that the acquirer "forgets" that it is in a second language.

We can summarize the above by saying that second language acquisition occurs when comprehensible input is delivered in a low-anxiety situation, when real messages of real interest are transmitted and understood.

---

1. This is a vast oversimplification. See Krashen (1981, 1982) for more discussion.

THE DIN HYPOTHESIS

I present now a central hypothesis concerning the din phenomenon, a hypothesis consistent with the reports as well as the theory described above:

The din is a result of stimulation of the language acquisition device.

This hypothesis has two corollaries:

1. The din is set off by comprehensible input.
2. This input needs to contain significant quantities of the acquirer's $i + 1$, structures which the acquirer has not yet acquired but is "ready" for. (Note that $i + 1$ is probably a set of structures and not just one.)

This hypothesis is clearly consistent with Barber's report as well as my own. In both cases, there was considerable comprehensible input. In Barber's case the input came from interaction and in my case the din was triggered by a good dose of pure input.

Corollary 2 predicts that the din will not occur in very advanced performers, since they will receive less input containing $i + 1$, having acquired most of the target language. This prediction is satisfied in the two cases reported earlier as well as the following report. Tracy Terrell, a professor of Spanish and Linguistics at the University of California at Irvine, is a very advanced performer in Spanish but reports that he is only an intermediate in French. Terrell was in Toronto last year and visited some French immersion classes. He reported that he sat in on about three hours of class one morning and subsequently experienced the din. His hosts at the Ontario Institute for Studies in Education were quite surprised to hear him chatting easily in French with a department secretary upon his return from the immersion school. Terrell said that after the session, he was no longer French-shy, and like me in San Francisco, he desired some interaction in French. The case confirms corollary 2, since Terrell experienced the din in an intermediate language; he reports that he never experiences the din in Spanish (any more!). It also confirms corollary 1, since the din was set off by input only.

The din hypothesis makes several other predictions, consistent with the case histories but requiring further cases: The din will *not* occur after output practice without input. It will also not occur after pattern drills or grammar exercises.

Also, it seems to be the case that the din takes a certain amount of time to start up. The case histories suggest that it takes at least one to two hours of good input. Of course our usual procedure in language teaching is to give classes lasting an hour or less. Perhaps those teachers who prefer the two-hour class are also saying that it takes a two-hour dose of input to get the LAD moving.

The din also seems to wear off after a few days. My experience studying French in a class in the summer of 1978 supports this, as well as the previous generalization. Our class met two and a half hours, twice a week, and was conducted entirely in French. Each class produced a clear din for me, and a desire to use French. Monday's din was enough to last until Wednesday, and I usually started Wednesday's class eager for more French. The Wednesday din, however, had generally worn off by Monday, despite my efforts to keep it going over the weekend by reading, and I generally came to Monday's class just a little French-shy.

This last case raises the question of whether aural input is more effective than written input for starting up the din. It may be, but I have no study hypothesis as to why, since written input should help language acquisition as well.[2]

Barber also notes in her case that the din made it difficult to switch into other languages. Could this be because the LAD prefers to work on one language at a time? Barber noted no problem in switching into her first language, English, and into her advanced French, only having problems with those languages that she was less advanced in.

A final conjecture concerns the craving for input and language use that both Terrell and I experienced. We, of course, are professional linguists who came into linguistics partly because we enjoy language acquisition. Does the din produce this craving among "civilians"? If so, we are led to the hypothesis that language acquisition is a natural and enjoyable process for anyone, even a drive, as long as the right kind of input is provided!

THE "LANGUAGE IN THE CRIB" PROBLEM

The din hypothesis may help to solve at least one theoretical issue. When Ruth Weir's book, *Language in the Crib* appeared in 1962, her study was cited as supporting evidence for the audio-lingual technique of pattern drill. Weir tape-recorded her 28-month-old son's evening monologues, and found that some of them did, in fact, resemble rehearsal of patterns (many did *not*, being coherent stretches of discourse). This phenomenon has been interpreted as *practice* and therefore as evidence that production, and a certain kind of production (pattern practice) is helpful or even necessary for language acquisition.[3]

My interpretation of the language in the crib phenomenon is different: it is simply the din externalized. The child is much more likely to react this way to the din, actually uttering the sounds he or she hears inside. James Cummins reports that his daughter, a student in a French immersion program in Toronto, often utters what appears to be random French when playing alone after school. Could this be the same thing?

---

2. Barber discusses the possibility that some people may experience a visual din. See her footnote 6.

3. I cannot cite any published source for this assertion. It has come up a good deal in conversation over the years, however.

CONCLUSION

The din may have real practical value. If the above speculations are correct, and if we can get reliable reports from students on when the din is "on" and when it is "off," it may help to tell us when our instruction is effective, how long lessons should be, their optimal frequency, what topics should be discussed, etc. In short, it may tell us when we are providing truly interesting and comprehensible input and thus when we are causing real second language acquisition.

DISCUSSION QUESTIONS

1. Recount your own experience with the "din phenomenon." Also, consider its connection to the process of being "_____-shy" (the blank is to be filled in with the name of any nonprimary language you know fairly well).

2. Discuss how operating within the confines of a language only partially known constrains the language user. To what extent do you feel that the constraints in question are "intellectual" (cognitive) in nature, and to what extent do you feel that they are "emotional" (affective)? What do your observations imply for the importance of the "din" or the "affective filter"?

3. Krashen suggests that the *apparent* "pattern drills" of first language acquirers, e.g., Ruth Weir's child, may be nothing other than an externalization of the "din." Discuss your own observations on this point.

4. What sorts of evidence would be relevant to the suggestions in Krashen's concluding remarks? For instance, how could it be demonstrated that the "din" is somehow linked to the effectiveness of instruction? What sorts of research procedures might be employed to empirically establish this hunch? Compare your reactions to anecdotal evidence of the sort found in this chapter with some of the more traditional sorts of empirical evidence found in Part VII, Program/Experiment Reports, below. In terms of gut-level feelings, which sort of evidence seems more solid? Why?

Part VI
Fun and Games

The notion that language teaching *can be,* and perhaps even *ought to be,* fun has already been a recurrent theme in the previous parts of this volume. Terrell (Chapter 18), for instance, in the preceding section, argues that not a single classroom hour should go by without some activity which is undertaken for the sake of enjoyment. Savignon (Chapter 19) suggested that it was her hope that her children would not only learn French but also have fun doing it. Several of the contributors have also stressed the importance of in Krashen's terms "getting the affective filter down" so that students can loosen up and move wholeheartedly into communicative activities in the target language. According to the popular wisdom, "Time flies when you're havin' fun," and this is probably due to a temporary loss of self-consciousness, or just plain self-*ish*ness. We believe this is not only desirable but in some sense necessary to the language acquisition process.

Who could deny that exhausting mental work is a necessary element of language acquisition? Or for that matter who could offer a method that would remove all the social and psychological risks of language acquisition? On the other hand, the need to adjust the pace and lighten the atmosphere from time to time is also well recognized by successful teachers.

The several contributions in this section offer a variety of ways to break up the routineness of classroom work. Chapter 21, excerpted from Carolyn Graham's *Jazz Chants,* offers a form of verbal play that to some extent disengages the intellect while appealing to the senses. Chapter 22 on treasure hunts by Camy Condon also offers a means of breaking the routine but at the same time encouraging students to both seek out and render comprehensible input in the target language. Jigsaw reading as interpreted by Jonathan de Berkeley-Wykes in Chapter 23 offers another optional activity which engenders lively interaction while at the same time fostering the development of useful skills. Planned argumentation, or "the debate" as suggested by Leong in Chapter 24, is yet another option for promoting intense communicative exchanges. Finally, Rinvolucri's "action mazes" in Chapter 25 offer still another alternative.

SUGGESTED ADDITIONAL READINGS

CAROLYN GRAHAM.
    1978. *Jazz Chants*. New York: Oxford University.

This jazzy book is recommended by Stevick in Chapter 9 above. It is excerpted as Chapter 21 in this section. Also see Chapter 32 for an application of some of its recommendations by Richard-Amato.

MARIO RINVOLUCRI AND MARGE BERER.

    1981. *Action Mazes*. London: Heinemann.

Another innovative book, this one is available in the United States from Heinemann Educational Books, Inc.; 4 Front Street; Exeter, New Hampshire 03833. Also, see Chapter 25 about the technique by Rinvolucri himself.

Chapter 21

An Excerpt from *Jazz Chants*

Carolyn Graham

EDITORS' INTRODUCTION

"Jazz chants" are catchy repetitive drills that draw attention toward the rhythm and kinesthetic properties of utterances. As such there is the danger that they may become mere "meaningless" exercises. However, if they are linked to contexts of experience through imaginative dramatization (see Part IV, Roles and Drama, above, and also Chapter 2 of Part I, Pragmatic Orientations), and if they are successfully mapped into meaningful events of experience, they can be a powerful tool for enabling students to achieve a greater fluency and naturalness in uttering the forms of the target language. They may be used to help students over significant pronunciation stumbling blocks—as for instance, the little rhyme,

> Erre con erre barril.
> Erre con erre carril.
> ¡Qué rápido corren las ruedas del ferrocarril!

has helped many Spanish students over the difficult hurdle of the Spanish trilled "r." The danger of focusing attention too narrowly on surface form can be avoided by using the "jazz chant" technique sparingly and with sufficient dramatic props to make certain that whatever meaning exists in the chant is brought before the student's consciousness. Of course, they may be used for a variety of purposes, some oriented toward surface form, others toward pragmatic effect.

Jazz chants are the rhythmic expression of Standard American English as it occurs in situational contexts. . . . Just as the selection of a particular tempo and beat in jazz may convey powerful and varied emotions, the rhythm, stresses, and intonation patterns of the spoken language are essential elements for the expression of feelings and the intent of the speaker. Linking these two dynamic forms has produced an innovative and exciting new approach to language learning.

Although jazz chanting's primary purpose is the improvement of speaking and listening comprehension skills, it also works well in reinforcing specific structures used in a situational context. The natural rhythms and humor of the chants are highly motivating and may be used effectively for both classroom practice and individual home study. . . .

The student of jazz chanting learns to express feelings through stress and intonation, while building a vocabulary appropriate to the familiar rituals of daily life. . . . [See the following example.]

OUCH! THAT HURTS

Ouch!
What's the matter?
I stubbed my toe.
Oh, that hurts, that hurts.
I know that hurts.
Ouch!
What's the matter?
I bit my tongue.
Oh, that hurts, that hurts.
I know that hurts.
Ouch!
What's the matter?
I got a cramp in my foot.
Oh, that hurts, that hurts.
I know that hurts.
Ouch! Ouch!
What's the matter now?
I bumped into the table,
tripped on the stairs,
slipped on the carpet,
fell over the chairs.
Gee! You're clumsy today!

The chants are written in two-part dialogue form. . . . The dialogues include three basic forms of conversational exchange:

1. Question and response. This includes information questions, . . . yes/no questions, . . . and questions created by intonation pattern alone. . . .
2. Command and response. . . .
3. Response to a provocative statement. . . .

The material in the chants includes the most frequently occurring structures of conversational American English and is intended to provide the student with patterns and vocabulary that he can comfortably use in the world outside the classroom. . . .

In performing the chants, the students are actually learning to distinguish difficult vowel and consonant contrasts while they are actively engaged in a verbal exchange which can easily be related to their own experience.

The chants are particularly useful in developing listening comprehension skills. A comparison of the written text and the tape [which accompanies it] illustrates the striking difference between the written word and spoken American English. The students are being trained to comprehend the language of an *educated native speaker* in natural conversation. . . .

THE PRESENTATION

The essential element in presenting a jazz chant is the clear, steady beat and rhythm. By setting the dialogue to a beat, we are not *distorting* the line but simply *heightening* the student's awareness of the natural rhythmic patterns present in spoken American English. A student practicing a specific rhythm and intonation pattern within the chant form should be able to use that same pattern in normal conversation and be readily understood by a native speaker.

The chants are based on a combination of *repetition* and *learned response.* Initially, the students should repeat the lines of the chant following the model provided by the teacher and/or the tape. This choral repetition allows the students to experiment with expressing strong feelings and, in some instances, raise their voices to an angry shout, without the natural shyness that would occur when speaking alone in class.

Once the students are familiar with the material, they progress from the simple choral repetition to giving a group response in answer to a question or statement. This introduces an important new element, as the class is now engaged in a dialogue with the teacher. This dialogue may then be transformed into a three- or four-part exchange.

It is extremely important that the students have a clear understanding of the meaning of the words they are saying and the appropriate situations in which they might occur. . . .

Presenting a Jazz Chant, Step by Step

The following step-by-step plan for presenting a jazz chant is intended to suggest one of the many possible ways of using the material and to share some of the methods I use with my classes in jazz chanting at New York University. The teacher should feel free to experiment, improvise, and adapt the chants to the needs of the students. In short, if it works, use it.

1. The teacher explains the situational context of the chant. For example, in *Baby's Sleeping* we are learning the different ways in which you tell someone to be quiet. In this case we are asking for silence because the baby is sleeping. The teacher should clearly explain any vocabulary items or expressions which might present difficulties, and may wish to discuss the cultural implications of the material.

SH! SH! BABY'S SLEEPING!

I said, Sh! Sh! Baby's sleeping!
I said, Sh! Sh!, Baby's sleeping!
    What did you say?
    What did you say?
I said, Hush! Hush! Baby's sleeping!
I said, Hush! Hush! Baby's sleeping!
    What did you say?
    What did you say?
I said, Please be quiet, Baby's sleeping!
I said, Please be quiet, Baby's sleeping!
    What did you say?
    What did you say?
I said, Shut up! Shut up! Baby's sleeping!

I said, Shut up! Shut up! Baby's sleeping!
   WAAAAAAAAAAAAAAAAAAA
   Not anymore.

2. The teacher gives the first line of the chant at normal speed and intonation. The students repeat in unison. This simple choral repetition continues for each line of the chant. At this stage the teacher may stop at any point to correct pronunciation or intonation patterns. You may wish to repeat each line several times in chorus.

3. The teacher establishes a clear, strong beat by counting, clapping, using rhythm sticks, or snapping his fingers. The teacher continues to demonstrate the beat and repeats step 2.

4. The class is divided into two equal sections. There is no limit to the number of students in each section. A jazz chant can be conducted with two students or two hundred students. The teacher now establishes a clear, steady beat and gives the first line of the chant, using normal speed and intonation. The *first section* repeats the line. The teacher gives the second line of the chant. The *second section* repeats the line. This pattern is continued for each line of the chant, with the teacher's voice providing a model for the repetitions.

5. The chant is now conducted as a two-part dialogue between the teacher and the class. The teacher establishes a clear, strong beat and gives the first line of the chant. The class answers in unison with the second line of the chant. Until the students are thoroughly familiar with the material, they will probably wish to refer to their open text in class. This two-part dialogue between the teacher and the class is clearly illustrated in the accompanying tape. Notice that at this stage the class is no longer divided into two sections but is *responding* to the teacher as one choral voice, *without* the teacher's model.

DISCUSSION QUESTIONS

1. The author speaks of "situational contexts." Discuss the problem of accessibility of such contexts from the vantage point of the student. How can maximal accessibility be assured?

2. What precautions could be taken to select or create "chants" that are directly linked to meaningful contexts? (Consider the recommendation of Chapter 2 concerning the linking of pattern drill material to the episodic context of the main story line of lesson material.)

3. Take a sociodrama (or other role-play situation) and create a "jazz chant" to help students over some of the difficult surface syntax, morphology, or phonology. Be careful to create the chant so as to maximize meaningfulness and accessibility of the experiential context.

4. Discuss any constraints you foresee on the use of jazz chants with students at various levels of development. Consider the relative appropriateness of the technique to beginning, intermediate, and advanced students (roughly defined).

Chapter 22

Treasure Hunts for English Practice

Camy Condon
San Diego, California

EDITORS' INTRODUCTION

In this chapter Camy Condon describes a different kind of "treasure hunt." The difference is that instead of merely looking for old objects, as in a traditional "scavenger hunt," the game is to complete a list of tasks which often require group interaction. For instance, instead of looking for "an old left shoe," the group may be asked to find the person in their group who has "the largest shoe size." Or, instead of hunting for "an old bent spoon," students look for "something useless." Also, abstract tasks are included, such as "naming eight cities where English is spoken" or action-based tasks that require the cooperation of other students, such as "collecting the autographs of three people not in your group." Every imaginative teacher will think of many additions and expansions of the treasure hunt concept. Moreover, teachers will also readily see the pragmatic value of many of the recommendations of Condon—value for heightening interest and communicative energy and for lowering anxiety and inhibitions to talk. This activity can generate lots of comprehensible input. Tasks which require value judgments such as finding "something beautiful" are especially conducive to interaction because they require some consensus.

A cleverly planned treasure hunt can be a successful and lively educational language activity for English students of all ages. Students work in small groups competing to satisfy the various requests on the list of treasures. Treasure hunts may be used in the classroom as a 15-minute diversion from the textbook, while longer hunts, lasting an hour or more, may be played outdoors. An imaginative teacher can even invent a list of treasures to fill an entire day. (See sample list below.)

As a teenager in the United States I played this kind of game, called a scavenger hunt, at birthday parties. We raced around the neighborhood collecting old objects from neighboring families and competed to be the first to return with all the treasures.

In Japan I have adapted this hunt idea to the English classroom, eliminating the need to disturb neighbors. The items on these treasure lists can easily be found, or the activity completed, by the group members themselves.

Treasure lists are prepared in advance, one copy of the same list for each group. The items should be matched to the age and ability of the class. A 10-minute hunt might include only five items.

TREASURE-HUNT INSTRUCTIONS

1. Divide the class into groups. Any number may play. Each group should have from three to six members.
2. Give the same list of treasures to each group.
3. For younger or beginning students, the teacher should read over the items on the list with the whole class to make sure all of the vocabulary is understood.
4. A time limit may be given, e.g., 30 minutes.
5. At the signal "Go!" the groups begin to compete in finding and doing everything on the list.
6. At the end of the time limit, or when the first group returns, everyone is called together. (The first group to complete all the items is not necessarily the winner.)
7. The teacher and all the learners check each item. Points are given for each correct one. This conversation should be conducted in English. For example:

Teacher: What is number 1?
Students: Something green.
Teacher: Group A, what do you have?
Group A: We have a green leaf.
Teacher: Group B, what do you have?
Group B: We have a green pen.

Everything should be checked and shown to the whole group.

8. The teacher may give five points to each team for each completed item. Points are deducted if the request is not satisfied. The team with the most points is the winner.

EXAMPLES OF ITEMS FOR INCLUSION IN A TREASURE-HUNT LIST

Senior High-School Level

1. Find something ugly.
2. Find something made of gold.
3. List five countries the members of your group would like to visit.
4. What is the largest shoe size in your group?
5. Eight things your group would like to eat now.
6. Five mistakes high-school students often make when speaking English.
7. Find something useless.
8. Draw a picture of five animals and name them in English.
9. Make a dinner menu in English.
10. Count how many red things you can see in the room.
11. Five things you use when swimming at the beach.
12. Find something long and black.

Junior High-School Level

1. Find a photograph.
2. Find something that makes a noise.
3. How many windows are there in the classroom?
4. Name five animals you have seen in the zoo.
5. What are the three colors the teacher is wearing?

6. Add up the number of family members in your group.
7. What is the favorite food of each person in your group?
8. Name eight cities where English is spoken.
9. Find something beautiful.
10. Name five parts of the body in English.
11. Collect the autographs of three people *not* in your group.
12. Make up a short four-line conversation in English.

Crazy Hunt (Children or Adults)

1. Invent crazy English names for each member of your group.
2. Write an English word for every letter of the alphabet.
3. Find something that smells good.
4. Find something that reminds you of each of the four seasons: fall, winter, spring, summer.
5. Find something good to eat.
6. Make a crazy hat for your teacher.
7. Count from 1 to 50 backward.
8. Write a short ghost story in English. (Include sound effects: screams, wild laughter, wind, crying, etc.)

Christmas Hunt

1. Find something red.
2. Draw a picture of Santa Claus.
3. Make a Christmas card for your teacher. (Everyone in your group must sign it.)
4. Make a list of five nice Christmas presents for a mother.
5. Make a funny toy out of anything.
6. Find something to eat.
7. Make a list of five nice Christmas presents for a father.
8. What are four English-speaking countries in which snow falls in the winter?
9. Write down six ways of making people laugh.
10. Write down five things you need to make Christmas cookies.
11. What five colors can you see in Christmas-tree lights?
12. Find something green.
13. What are ten good Christmas presents for your school friends?
14. What are five foods you would like to eat at a Christmas dinner?
15. What are three ways to make your English teacher happy?
16. What does each member of your group want as a Christmas present?

DISCUSSION QUESTIONS

1. What are some arguments for varying the difficulty of the tasks in a treasure-hunt list? What guidelines could be given for calibrating the tasks so that they are not too easy for the least competent or too hard for the most competent students in a group?

2. Some tasks seem more likely to generate comprehensible input than others. Selecting tasks that require value judgments can heighten the amount of interaction. However, a task that seems to be surface-structure-oriented,

e.g., find "five mistakes high school students often make when speaking English," may result in some comprehensible talk. Or it may prove, with some students, to be impossibly difficult. Why, and what cautions would you impose to guide the selection of tasks?

3. How might the tasks selected for a treasure hunt be related to the stories, dialogues, dramatizations, and the like with which students are already familiar? Consider this question especially in light of Chapter 16 by Rodriguez and White. Is there any way that a treasure hunt could be episodically organized?

4. What criteria might you propose for sequencing the items in a particular treasure-hunt list?

Chapter 23

Jigsaw Reading

Jonathan de Berkeley-Wykes
University of New Mexico

EDITORS' INTRODUCTION

"Jigsaw reading" (JR) has been called by other names. For instance, a more colorful term which has been applied to much the same technique is "the strip tease." It is a kind of puzzle. Pieces of text are cut up and scrambled. The objective of the student, then, is to restore the pieces to their proper order—to make sense of the text. The treatment of this technique in this chapter is perhaps a bit more scholarly than other selections in this part. De Berkeley-Wykes attempts not only to introduce the method as a practical classroom activity but also to justify it in terms of previous research on reading and related psycholinguistic processes. If used as a group activity where students communicate about the decisions of how to order the various pieces of the text, JR can elicit a great deal of communicative interaction. It also finds a fairly solid basis in reading research and in theories of discourse processing. (Also see Chapter 30 by Adams on scripts and second language reading.)

Research into the reading process has led to many theories, and some models of reading, e.g., Gough (1972), LaBerge and Samuels (1976), and Rumelhart (1980). Interest in the processes underlying reading has not, however, been matched by a comparable interest in the production of classroom materials and applications of them for the teaching of reading to students of English as a second or foreign language.

Traditionally, reading series for classroom use have been produced to follow prescriptive bases such as:

1. Graded structural complexity
2. Vocabulary frequency counts
3. Reading skills and strategies development (concentrating on sound-symbol correspondences and the like)

The assumption implicit in the derived reading courses is that identification of the language components, and improvement of each of those components separately, will eventually produce a cumulative improvement in student reading. Such atomistic approaches fail to recognize that reading, like language, is an integrated functional system. To quote a trite but true phrase, "the whole is greater than the sum of the parts" (Watzlawick, Beavin, and Jackson 1967).

Atomistic approaches to reading in a nonprimary language also seem not to recognize that reading in a second language may depend on many of the same psycholinguistic processes, conceptions of discourse, and affective factors which enter into reading in the first language. However, these three aspects of reading can interact to good effect only if the materials selected naturally draw them into the process. Materials which are "episodically organized" in the sense of Chapters 1 and 2 will facilitate the necessary interaction. Jigsaw reading (JR), an interesting and highly interactive classroom activity, can help to integrate the skills of communication and reading in a more holistic manner.

INTERRELATED PSYCHOLINGUISTIC PROCESSES

As Goodman has argued,

There is no possible sequencing of skills in reading instruction since all systems must be used interdependently in the reading process even in the first attemps at learning to read (1975, p. 25).

Therefore, sorting out the elements that go into the totality of the reading process may be not only unnecessary but actually counterproductive.

To begin with, a JR is based on a full-fledged, relatively self-contained text (that is, it should not require access to other texts for its comprehension). The text is cut into segments and the task of the students is to restore it to its proper order. A JR may include a title, or in the case of new articles, headlines. The value of titles has been shown, by Bransford and Johnson (1972), to establish a link in the reader's mind with his knowledge of the subject of a text. Activation of this knowledge sets up, in the reader, certain *predictions* of what he might expect to find in the text.

A similar orienting effect can be achieved by including pictures, cartoons, drawings, maps, charts, diagrams, or tables. Brown and Murphy (1975) show how the logical sequencing of pictures will cause a learner-reader to impose a *logical sequencing* on a narrative. Also Paulson, Kintsch, Kintsch, and Premack (1979) show how a sequence of pictures can create a "story proposition" which subsequently facilitates reading.

In addition to *specific* predictions in text processing there are also *general* expectations. Readers always expect, for example, that a piece of writing will make sense (Bever 1970) and will adhere to the cooperative principle (Grice 1975) of being relevant, informative, more or less concise, and truthful. Presumably these general expectations come either from previous experience with texts in the first language or from innate cognitive universals (or both). Peck (1980) argues that failure to take account of reader expectations explains why so many aspiring writers produce so much unpublishable fiction. On the other hand, recognizing the importance of such expectancies (see "the expectancy hypothesis" of Chapter 1) serves as a theoretical basis for the kind of text operations involved in JR.

Writers cater to detailed expectations about person(s) place, time, and setting by offering this information early. The fact that readers can sometimes remember the first sentence of a paragraph verbatim while the remainder is only recalled in outline (Garrod and Trabasso 1973) suggests (among other things) that reader expectations are particularly strong at the beginnings of passages. Expectations about how texts should begin may be due to a universal need in discourse processing to pragmatically tie down the context. Weaver (1980) has suggested that effective readers use context to confirm their unfolding tentative interpretations. A clear context will assist comprehension and set up further useful predictions concerning what is to follow later in the text (McCullough 1976).

Olson (1974) has noted that a written text has to define the spatial and temporal terms of reference to enable the reader to accurately interpret it. Therefore, a useful constraint on JRs is that they should give the reader clear contextual frames of reference. Through them, the learner-reader can make tentative comprehension decisions which will be confirmed, rejected, or refined (Goodman 1975) as more pieces of JR are put together.

The JR is cut into pieces at meaning boundaries. Johnson and Friedman (1971) showed how sentences which are meaningfully segmented are more easily comprehended and remembered. Also, Cohen and Freeman (1978) have shown how good readers naturally segment a text into phraselike units. By presenting the JR in pieces, the learner-reader processes the passage in clausal units (Garrett, Bever, and Fodor 1966), since these segments act as psychological units (Carroll and Bever 1974) in comprehension. Each piece of the JR, therefore, should be a natural "*chunk*" (Clark and Clark 1977). Jarvella (1971), Caplan (1976), and Klieman (1975) have shown how comprehension processing tends to chunk material according to a semantic interpretation which is not necessarily related to surface syntax. Cutting the JR into pieces at meaning boundaries therefore encourages the student to use the normal psycholinguistic method of comprehension.

Psycholinguistic theories of the processes involved in reading are often characterized by "top-down" or "bottom-up" descriptions (see, e.g., Kamil 1978). Neurolinguistic research suggests that the two hemispheres of the brain process different types of information in different ways (Wittrock 1977), but comprehension is the joint result of those differential processing systems. JR, therefore, engages both holistic "top-down" processes as well as sequential, analytic "bottom-up" methods which jointly contribute to meaningful reading.

At any point during its assembly, JR enjoins the reader to match the piece he intends to add against the text already completed. This matching involves both holistic and *sequential considerations*. In order to fit correctly, each piece will have to be matched to a number of particular aspects of the text (Collins, Brown, and Larkin 1980).

The addition of pieces, at a grammatical level, shows the student that agreements of gender and number can reveal constituent clauses of a sentence.

Tense consistency within paragraphs can help with assignment of the pieces to the correct paragraph in longer passages. Similarly, punctuation may help. For example, pieces which end with a comma or a semicolon have to be followed by a continuation beginning with a small letter, whereas pieces ending with a full stop have to be followed by a capital letter. Using this awareness of grammar and punctuation can assist the student to arbitrate in cases of uncertainty.

Since the JR retains the natural redundant features of language, the learner-reader can use this redundancy to reduce the number of plausible contextual alternatives as the text progresses. As the student's ability to activate psycholinguistic processes improves, the number of plausible alternatives will presumably be reduced, thus enhancing comprehension (Smith 1978). As the reader draws on different aspects of language redundancy, at the same time using different processing mechanisms, his "psycholinguistic guesses" (Goodman 1976) become more accurately constrained. Thus JR engenders a self-reliant approach, to use the known to aid in understanding the unknown. Self-directed handling of language aims to prepare the student to cope better with language outside the classroom.

CONCEPTIONS OF DISCOURSE

Not only can the student utilize psycholinguistic processes to aid in reading another language, but also he has experience and knowledge of discourse. Oller (Chapter 1) proposes that language comprehension involves crossing the pragmatic bridge between individual experience and texts. Accomplishing this requires intricate and complex mental negotiations of the connections between structures of discourse and elements of experience. Rosenblatt (1978) has stressed the importance of the reader's personal store of knowledge in achieving this sort of comprehension. JRs are helpful in this respect because they encourage the reader to draw on prior knowledge and understandings of discourse in a surprisingly natural way.

Such interaction sets up an extralinguistic link between the reader and a piece of text. When the text is in a foreign language, that interactive link can assist comprehension, for experience and knowledge of discourse are not necessarily bound to any one language. JRs capitalize upon a reader's non-language-bound knowledge; therefore, JRs should relate to the interests and knowledge of the learner. With learners who are learning to read for a specific purpose, specialist texts can be used. Voss et al. (1980) have shown how subject knowledge, or specialized "expertise" (their term), is involved in compre-hension. For learners with less specifiable purposes, passages on current affairs, topics in the news, and the history or geography of their country can be used. Such subjects bring the learners themselves more actively into the process of comprehension. This process, it is claimed, relies as much on the "information in the reader's mind as on the information in the written text" (Adams 1980, p. 12).

Regardless of the kind of information contained in a piece of text, Morgan and Sellner (1980) have shown that effective readers naturally impose some kind of organizational structure (also see Coulthard 1977). Rumelhart (1975) clarifies the nature of textual expectancies in terms of his "story schema." Together with the foregoing arguments this fact supports Oller's "expectancy hypothesis"—the notion that cognitive momentum aids in the unraveling of a text. JR encourages the reader to appeal to this expectancy momentum in assembling the pieces and thus restoring the text.

Completion of the JR relies on the coherence (Halliday and Hassan 1976; or conceptual connectivity," De Beaugrande (1980) of a discourse being realized by means of the cohesion (Halliday and Hassan 1976; or "surface connectivity," De Beaugrande 1980) of the language of the text. Anaphoric expressions are examples of cohesive language devices. They are intersentential elements which maximize comprehension (Huggins and Adams 1980) by helping the reader update and refine hypotheses about the discourse (Webber 1980).

In many texts written for language classes, however, natural anaphora is deleted. This attempt at preadaptation of passages is based on the mistaken belief that it makes the passages simpler and therefore easier for the nonnative to understand. Though such a method may make passages seem simpler, it does the student two disservices: it "short-circuits" comprehension systems, since it upsets the surface connectivity of the passage by removing much of its cohesion, and it encourages the development of false expectations about texts. These freakish expectations violate universal notions of conceptual connectivity and will, it would seem, over the long run, hinder the comprehension of discourse outside the classroom.

AFFECTIVITY

A further effect of artificially preadapted reading materials is that they are less interesting than natural texts. D. V. Swain (1980) has suggested that prose momentum is essentially a linked series of units consisting of motivating stimulus and consequent reaction. These motivation-reaction units, Swain argues, are the basis for sustained involvement of the reader. Peck (1980) contends that interest is also naturally heightened as a character in a story encounters obstacles in the pursuit of a desirable goal. Similarly, linking the pieces of a JR may produce in the student sustaining interest due to the synergistic character of the text itself, and also the puzzle-solving aesthetic of assembling the pieces. As each piece fits into the developing discourse, momentum builds in the reader.

Clearly the best-designed classroom reading materials still depend to a great extent on reader interest. Piaget (1981) has argued similarly that

The technique by which a goal is attained requires coordinations, regulations, and always presupposes an energy whose origin appears to be essentially affective (p. 8).

An additional aspect of affectivity which Piaget emphasizes is "valuation." How much value does the subject place on a particular goal? According to expert writers (e.g., Swain, Peck, and others), the valuation of a goal is best judged in terms of what the character will endure to obtain the goal. However, Piaget (1981) rejects any simple cost/benefit explanation which would attribute value strictly on the basis of potential reward. [Also see Piaget 1947, 1970.] He argues that valuation of goals exceeds the limits of mere behavioristic "reinforcements." Corder (1978), following a similar line of thought, has claimed that a learner will move along the continuum toward more accurate language use only when the improvement has merit in the learner's own eyes.

Partly because of its gamelike character, in JR, the value of the completed task is constantly reaffirmed as the student works through the puzzle. In keeping with Wilkins' (1976) observation that using language as a tool is intrinsically rewarding, JR affirms the student's efforts through a satisfying solution of the puzzle. Also, in solving the puzzle, the student refines necessary skills in the target language. The intrinsic valuation of such performances helps to produce self-dependent learning and gives the students a sense of personal achievement. achievement.

In an oft-quoted remark, Huey described reading as "the most remarkable specific perfomance that civilization has learned in all its history" (1908). JR is a modest step toward making this skill more accessible to language students. It depends for its effectiveness on the three-way interaction of psycholinguistic processes, prior experience and knowledge, and interest. It conscientiously avoids the prescriptive bases of artificially contrived reading materials. What is more, it works.

A SAMPLE JIGSAW READING

The text which follows has slashes inserted at cut points. The text would be typed on cardboard, cut up into segments, and then shuffled. The object of students is to restore the segments to their original order.

Sadat's Assassination

On 6th October, 1981/ there was a military parade/ in Al-Nasr stadium./ The President of Egypt, Anwar Sadat,/ the Vice-President,/ and their guests/ were sitting in the President's box./ Some planes flew over the stadium,/ so everyone looked up at them./ While they were looking up,/ a lorry stopped in front of the box,/ and four young soldiers jumped out of it,/ and ran toward the box./ When Sadat saw them,/ he stood up,/ because he thought they were coming to greet him./ Suddenly, three of them began shooting at the President/ and the other people in the box./ Everyone got down on the floor,/ and some tried to hide/ on the floor under the chairs./ The fourth soldier ran round/ to the side of the box/ and shot at the people/ under the chairs./ When the shooting stopped,/ 11 people were dead/ and 18 were injured./ One of those was Sadat./ The Defense Minister radioed for a helicopter/ and it took Sadat to the hospital./ When he got there,/ the doctors tried to save him,/ but he died two hours later.

INSTRUCTIONS

1. The supervisor gives the student the pieces of the jigsaw and the check card.
2. The supervisor tells the student to turn the check card face down.
3. He explains to the student that the pieces will fit together exactly to form an account, in this case, of the assassination of Anwar Sadat. (If appropriate visual material is to be used, the supervisor lets the student look through it at this point.)
4. The supervisor then tells the student to lay out the pieces of card in front of him, one by one, so he can read them easily.
5. The student should be warned that some items in the passage may not be familiar to him, but that this is to be expected.
6. The supervisor tells the student to scan the pieces for a few moments.
7. The student should be told to pick out the title and place it at the top of a clear space of the surface he is using.
8. The student is told to begin to assemble the text, piece by piece, under the title, placing each strip directly under the one preceding it. (The supervisor may need to prompt, with suggestions, during its assembly.)
9. When all the pieces have been assembled, and the student has both understood the passage and physically completed the jigsaw to his satisfaction, he should then compare it with the check card.
10. Once any necessary self-correction has taken place, and the student understands any mistakes he may have made, he should read through the jigsaw once again.
11. After a short interval, the supervisor may ask the student to write out the passage from memory, as near to verbatim as he can.
12. Finally, the supervisor and the student should compare the student's written version with the check card, and discuss acceptable and unacceptable deviations from the original text.

Note: Once both student and supervisor have followed these instructions once or twice, the student should be able to use new jigsaws self-reliantly, self-critically, and self-motivatedly.

DISCUSSION QUESTIONS

1. Consider ways in which the three factors discussed in this chapter (psycholinguistic processes, knowledge and experience, and affect) might interact in solving a JR based on the Sadat example.

2. What specific and general expectations are utilized in solving the Sadat example?

3. De Berkeley-Wykes uses the terms "top-down" and "bottom-up" in reference to reading comprehension. What is he getting at?

4. Suppose the activity of the JR is done in small groups. What kinds of interactive discussion might be expected to occur? Would this activity be equally feasible to all levels? How might it be calibrated for maximal effectiveness?

Chapter 24

The Debate

Hugh Leong
Chiengmai University, Thailand

EDITORS' INTRODUCTION

Some ideas about how to stage a debate in a TEFL classroom are presented here by Leong. Presumably his framework can be extended to second language or foreign language classrooms in general. Ways of linking up the debate technique with topics or dilemmas set up through sociodrama (see Chapter 15) or through social activism (see Chapter 12) can readily be inferred. Advance preparation might also be arranged employing ideas from Chapter 16. The debate could be linked up, therefore, with an episodically organized context (Chapters 1 and 2). At any rate, debate is yet another activity which, if it is properly gauged to the level of the students as Leong cautions, will generate high levels of interaction and communication. It can also help to lower the level of self-consciousness as students abandon themselves to the heat and humor of either real or feigned argumentation.

A debate is a good way to get students talking, but it sometimes presents problems when the students are not native speakers of English. The reason is easy to understand. The foremost problem is that the students may not have the skills to work around the subject matter of a free debate. Some kind of control is usually needed for the students to feel comfortable and confident in using the debate form.

However, too much control in a debate will make for stilted and unnatural production. For example, if the students are asked to prepare an argument for or against something, they may come the next day prepared to read their arguments or to recite them from memory. This would be all right if all that was wanted was to have the students practice pronunciation or speak in front of the class, but a debate should be a "give-and-take" activity with the students spontaneously responding to what their opponents have said. Presented here is a suggestion for setting up a classroom debate that is both semicontrolled and free enough to give the students a feeling of real communication; it is an activity using "controlled spontaneity."

Before presenting a debate as an activity in your classroom you must make sure that the atmosphere in the classroom is conducive to free speech and friendly competition. This would mean that the debate should not be attempted until the students have achieved a level of cooperation at which you believe they can handle the expression of their own ideas and the refutation of someone else's. In choosing a topic for the debate we should choose something that is controversial and current. A topic being debated in the school or community is always good. Furthermore, choices the students must some day make are appropriate, such as "Is living and working in a big city preferable to living and working in the countryside?"

The following are some of the steps we can take in preparing for our semicontrolled debate:

Step 1: The day before the debate is to be scheduled the students are told there will be a debate on such and such a topic. The idea of a debate may have to be explained, but the students may already know the form from debates they have seen or taken part in in their native language. The assignment is for each student to go home and think about and list the various arguments on both sides (e.g., "Working in the city is good because there are more opportunities, but it is bad because of air pollution"). They should try to think of as many arguments, pro and con, as they can. They should come the next day prepared to argue on either side.

Step 2: On the day of the debate two teams are chosen. These should be made up of four or five members each. More than five is hard to handle and would take too long. Fewer than five would not involve enough students. After the teams have been chosen they are told what stand they will take. This works much better than it sounds, for a number of reasons. The students seem to like the fact that they can argue a point they do not really believe in. This may be because they can argue a point without being held personally responsible; they can say anything, no matter how crazy it may sound (e.g., "Working in the city is better because there are more pretty girls there than in the country"). Not telling the students beforehand also ensures that what is said will be more or less spontaneous.

Step 3: Each team is then told they will have 20 minutes to choose the order in which they will speak and prepare their arguments. The members are advised to help each other, so that they cover all the arguments they have listed and thought about. If there is another room for them to go to, they should be sent out of the classroom. If this is impossible, they should be given some space in the classroom where they can work together as groups, maybe at the back of the room. While the groups are preparing their presentations the class will have a chance for discussion. The class will be smaller by 10 students, and a conversation about some of the ideas the other students have can develop.

Step 4: The teams are recalled and sit together in the front of the room, with the teacher sitting between them as moderator. One team is designated A and the other B. Each speaker is given 2 minutes. Team A begins with its first speaker and team B answers with its first. The teams alternate until everyone has spoken. The only rule concerns how to begin. If our debate is between the city and country people, team A members must begin with "I think the city is better because . . .". This small measure of control is enough to get the students on the way to stating their positions. The team B member is to respond with "I disagree with team A . . .".

Step 5: While the teams are arguing, what are the listeners doing? This could cause a problem with a large class, as there will be many inactive students. One way to solve the problem of inactive students is to encourage them to ask questions or to make their own statements about what anyone has said. After everybody has spoken, the teacher can ask for questions from the listeners. It can be made a requirement that the students listening should be prepared to ask at least one question of each speaker. If the team member is asked a question, he will have to respond with a spontaneous answer defending his position. This part of the debate (absent from formal debates) makes it more interesting and exciting for the TEFL classroom.

Step 6: After all the students have spoken, it is time for the listeners to vote for the winner. They may do this by clapping for the team of their choice. The listeners are told they should choose the team that presented the best arguments. This can be fun, as the teacher is the sole judge as to who was clapped more, and many drawn contests can result.

What does this kind of activity accomplish? It is usually a lot of fun, but more than that it is an amusing way for the students to put their ideas into words of their own. The student who does not really agree with the stand his team had to take (e.g., he hated the city but was in team A) will have to use his imagination and some abstract thinking to come up with a reasonable response. Listening comprehension is reinforced and a fairly normal conversational situation, the argument, is set up. Spontaneity is something we may not be able to teach our students, but with a few controls a classroom situation can develop in which the students feel secure enough to create meaningful language.

DISCUSSION QUESTIONS

1. Following Leong's suggestions, how would you go about selecting a topic for debate in a classroom setting?

2. How might you prevent the "reading of prepared speeches"? Can you conceive of ways to prepare students in advance so that they might be prepared instead to engage in spontaneous argumentation? To improvise arguments on the spot?

3. Discuss the concept of "controlled spontaneity." Can there be spontaneity without controls?

4. Discuss more specifically how techniques recommended by other authors in this volume might be used to either prepare students for debate or to motivate the selection of topics, or both.

Chapter 25

Action Mazes

Mario Rinvolucri
Pilgrims (Teacher Training), Canterbury, England

EDITORS' INTRODUCTION

The "action maze," an activity genre invented by Rinvolucri, engages students in reading, listening, and speaking activities through a kind of puzzle-solving, decision-making activity. As such, the "action maze" has elements common to "jigsaw reading" (Chapter 23), "sociodrama" (Chapter 15), and even "debate" (Chapter 24). Students are presented with an initial communication problem printed on a card (e.g., your neighbor insists on blocking your driveway). They must decide on a course of action by choosing from several possible alternatives printed on the same card. After they select their preferred course, by arguing their way through the options, they proceed to the next card, which is designated by the number of the option they have selected from the previous card. The next card poses some additional communication problem which again must be solved (e.g., you decide to talk to him and he complains that there just isn't any place else to park). Several options are presented (e.g., you threaten to have his car towed, etc.). The selected option leads to another consequent problem, and so on it goes. A criticism that might have been heard some years ago is that this approach mixes the traditional skills all together in a single classroom method. Nowadays with the increasing attention to holistic communication objectives, this apparent weakness must be regarded as a strong plus for the "action maze."

MAZES AS READING ACTIVITIES

Who are the people in our society who have a right to ask other people long strings of questions? Policemen, teachers, doctors, torturers, insurance brokers, toddlers . . . the list is a long one but one thing that all the above categories of people have in common is that they have power over the person being questioned.

The continual asking of questions is one of the main verbal ways in which teachers show their status superiority to their students. Of course, many colleagues would justify their interrogations on the ground that they must find out how much the students have understood, especially after reading a passage of difficult English. Below I will suggest that there are better, simpler ways of checking.

When students have finished reading a passage their minds are at the end of the passage. They are then frequently confronted with a string of questions that ignores this fact and asks them to switch back to the start of the passage, thus ignoring their temporal reality. So another objection to the question of true/false statement methods of checking comprehension is that it takes no account of the students' standpoint in time vis-à-vis the passage just read.

When you are at lower intermediate level, say, reading any great length of text in the foreign language is a strain, and so it is vital that extensive reading should be broken up by other activities, which is exactly what happens in the action maze below.

A maze is a series of reading cards—the number of cards may vary from 15 to 40. Card 1 outlines a problem situation and offers readers four or five possible courses of action. Students tackle the maze in groups of three or four and they have to reach agreement in their groups on what action to take. (Four is a better group number than three because three often leads to a majority-minority situation, which tends to discourage real discussion, the individual in the minority feeling he or she should simply give way.)

Once a small group has agreed on a course of action, they turn to the appropriate card and read the result of their choice. The new situation opens up a new set of choices, and so on.

Here is Card 1 of the Parking Maze:[1]

PARKING Card 1

You are a reasonable sort of person but you have a very difficult neighbor. This neighbor insists on parking his car in the street across the entrance to your driveway. This means you can't get your car into your own driveway. What are you going to do about it?

11   You decide to do nothing, which means parking in the next street most of the time, as there is no room in your street.

2   You leave a note on his windshield asking him not to park across the entry to your driveway.

4   You go up to him and ask him not to park across your driveway.

10   You wait until he has driven away one morning and put large wooden boxes where his car was.

13   You let the air out of his tires.

The alternative courses of action are numbered, so that students know which card to turn to once they have picked a course of action.

Suppose a group of students opts for alternative 4 on card 1, they then have to turn to card 4 of the maze:

PARKING Card 4

You have approached your neighbor and asked him not to block your driveway. He says he's a very busy person and has nowhere else to park. He has no driveway or garage of his own. What do you do?

3   Warn him you'll have his car towed away.

21   Threaten to call in the police.

7   Ask him what he expects you to do if you can't get into your own driveway and can't park on the street?

---

1. The Parking Maze is from *Mazes I* by Rinvolucri and Berer, obtainable from Pilgrims, 8 Vernon Place, Canterbury, Kent. [Also see the address given for *Action Mazes* on p. 304, this volume.]

Most students have to read and discuss 10 to a dozen cards before they manage to get out of this maze (a 24-card maze). As they read and discuss the teacher gets called over to help with language people can't work out for themselves—in fact, a very great deal of peer teaching also goes on.

Let us return for a moment to the points made at the beginning of the article. The teacher's role in this reading exercise is not one of questioner-interrogator—he or she acts as a roving comprehension consultant called in when and where needed by the students. The students have a task to perform and decisions to make, which puts them in an unusual position of power. The teacher becomes a language technician and counselor, abandoning the boss role. The students become subjects, instead of being objects.

Comprehension difficulties are dealt with card by card during the reading process—there is no question of asking students to refocus on language problems they may have had on card 1 when they triumphantly reach the maze exit card. They have to understand the few sentences on each card before they can possibly reach any decisions. Since they have to process the information on each card, they are acutely aware that they need to have grasped it correctly. Interesting differences of opinion sometimes arise from different understandings of the text, which then have to be sorted out. There is clearly no need for the teacher to resort to linearly sequenced, heavy-booted comprehension questions.

A maze provides lower intermediate students with extensive reading but metes it out to them in assimilable bits broken up by a mixture of thinking, listening, and speaking activities. In this way the learner is not discouraged by having to face an extensive text all in one long piece.

MAZES AS WRITING ACTIVITIES

When students have done two or three mazes as reading-to-discussion work, they are ready to try writing their own as a discussion-to-composition exercise. The teacher asks them to look at the tree diagram of a maze they have read. Here is the top half of the diagram that underlies the Parking Maze:

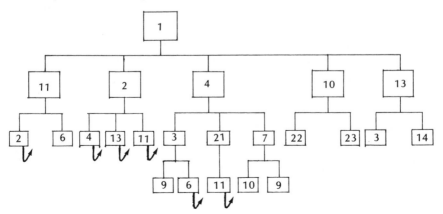

A student then comes to the chalkboard and acts as secretary to the group. Students try to think of problem situations on which they might want to base a maze.

After this brainstorming phase the students split into groups of three or four and choose one of the problem situations. They write out a card 1 which defines the situation and suggests three or four courses of action.

Card 1 should be written out in full, but the rest of the tree should be done in note-form only.

As homework, one person in each group can be asked to turn the tree diagram into a fully written-up maze on cards. The cards then have to be randomly numbered, and corrected mazes can be used by the teacher as reading material in other classes. In this way students actually produce material for each other of a sort appropriate to their age and interests, be they 14-year-olds or fifth-year electronics students in a Grande École. If students produced more of their own learning materials, we would be much closer to the sort of classroom that the late Charles Curran envisioned when he created his community language learning approach.

DISCUSSION QUESTIONS

1. The "action maze" is designated as a "reading activity." What other skills must the student possess in order to successfully participate? What advantages would this approach have in your view over more traditional sorts of reading practice?

2. How could mazes be coordinated with other episodically organized classroom activities? Could you, for example, devise an action maze for the Sadat text (see Chapter 23)? Could this technique be adapted to "texts" in general?

3. In what way would the teacher become a "counselor" as recommended by Curran in Chapter 10?

4. What are some of the social and cultural variables that a sensitive teacher would need to take into account when dividing students into groups for this sort of activity?

Part VII

Program/Experiment Reports

This section includes reports either on program experience or on practical experiments bearing on ideas and methods offered in earlier chapters. It seems likely that there is no single method about which so much experimental work has been published as J. J. Asher's total physical response (TPR). In Chapter 26, he himself reviews this compelling research. However, the TPR has not been without its critics. Among them have been a team of researchers at the University of Georgia—Kalivoda, Morain, and Elkins (Chapter 27)—who have applied an adaptation of TPR in more traditionally structured foreign language classes for the teaching of German, Spanish, and French. Perhaps their most important revision of the TPR technique is to insist on "meaningful sequence" (alias "episodic organization," see Chapter 1) in the imperative drills.

Surprisingly, the technique which has made headlines in many popular media outlets and has even been featured on prime time television is less well known to the consumers of classroom research in the language teaching business. We are speaking of the Rassias approach. Therefore, we are happy to be able to include two articles which will help to refute the common complaint that there is no "empirical evidence" that the Rassias madness works. Quite the contrary, Johnston shows in Chapter 28 that increasing enrollments and other evidences at the University of Florida where the method has been applied in foreign language classes show that the Rassias madness must have something going for it. Further, John Rassias himself (Chapter 29) generously permitted us to reprint his own paper from a little-known Peace Corps publication in 1970 showing some of the details of the approach not covered by the popular press and also some of the evidence that the philosophy is deeper than a few snapshots could possibly show.

In Chapter 30, Shirley J. Adams offers some evidence on second language reading and the importance of "scripts" or background information on texts.

Her findings tie in nicely with much of what is said in other chapters on the importance of meaningful sequence (e.g., see Kalivoda et al. in Chapter 27). Then, in Chapter 31, Merrill Swain gives an overview of the Canadian experiments in teaching French to anglophones through immersion. And, finally, Richard-Amato (Chapter 32) concludes the volume with a report on an ESL center for refugees and immigrants in the Jefferson County Schools of Colorado.

SUGGESTED ADDITIONAL READINGS

TED ROGERS.
  1978. Strategies for individualized language learning and teaching. In J. Richards (ed.). *Understanding Second and Foreign Language Learning.* Rowley, Massachusetts: Newbury House, 251–273.

  Different types of individualized language teaching are discussed including programmed learning, sequential learning kits, factlets (topical study packets), and contracts.

EARL STEVICK.
  1980. *Language Teaching: A Way and Ways.* Rowley, Massachusetts: Newbury House.

  Although we have mentioned it in reference to both Parts II and III above, we mention it again here because it is one of the few "methods" books that presents evidence from actual applications of its own recommendations. Stevick talks about applying the silent way in Honolulu. One of his students, Irene Dutra, describes an experience with Stevick in learning Swahili via an adaptation of the counseling-learning model, and Dieter Stroinigg and Betsy Bedell both write about the same model as applied in their own teaching in rather different settings. The book is packed with ideas of interest to language teachers. It is one of a kind.

MERRILL SWAIN.
  1978. Bilingual education for the English-speaking Canadian. In J. Alatis (ed.). *Georgetown University Roundtable on Languages and Linguistics,* 141–154.

  One of the successful approaches to second language teaching has been immersion, and the immersion experiments in Canada are the best-studied cases in history. In this Roundtable paper, and in Chapter 31 below, Merrill Swain talks about the relative successes of different approaches to immersion.

Chapter 26

Motivating Children and Adults to Acquire a Second Language

James J. Asher
California State University, San Jose

EDITORS' INTRODUCTION

The present entry comes from an article that appeared in the Canadian journal *SPEAQ* in 1979. It is modified only slightly to remove overlapping content which would have repeated material appearing in Chapter 5. It summarizes very briefly many of the studies that have lent support to the claim that the method of the total physical response works. In this chapter positive results from studies in the teaching of Japanese, French, German, Spanish, and even American Sign Language are offered. A variety of sources of evidence are cited along with references which may be consulted for more detailed information. Also, Asher here expands somewhat on the theoretical basis of his approach. His remarks about Krashen's distinction between "acquisition" and "learning" offer a familiar theme in a new key. Asher proposes that perhaps instruction should progress from the former to the latter.

Achieving skill in a second language can be divided into initial, intermediate, and advanced training. If the training starts with explicit learning such as audio-lingual that emphasizes (1) error-free production, (2) correct form, and (3) conscious rule learning, the risk is that most children and adults will give up before reaching even the intermediate level (Carroll 1960, Lawson 1971).

As an alternative model that motivates most children and adults to persist in the training program, it is suggested that the initial training start with implicit learning and gradually make the transition to explicit learning as students progress into the advanced stages of language acquisition.

IMPLICIT LEARNING

Krashen (1978) calls implicit learning a kind of "subconscious language acquisition" as compared with the explicit way that is "conscious language learning." The implicit approach may be how children acquire their first language. For example, in the infant's home environment, caretakers are not concerned with the form of their utterances, but with communicating messages that the child understands. There is an absence of error correction and no attempt at the explicit teaching of rules (Brown and Hanlon 1970; Brown, Cazden, and Bellugi 1973). Snow and Ferguson (1977) have observed that the caretaker's speech is modified to increase the child's understanding. Further, caretakers communicate through directions to the young child such as:

> "Let's wash your hands."
> "Pick up your teddy bear and come with me."
> "Give Daddy a kiss."

There are also many questions from caretakers that require either a nonverbal response from the infant such as a nod or a simple "yes" or "no." Examples would be:

> "Do you want more orange juice?"
> "Where is your teddy bear? Go find your teddy bear!"
> "Do you want to go for a walk?"

The order for the internalizing of structures by the child seems to be rather predictable (Brown 1973, Dulay and Burt 1975). As the infant develops, certain structures are acquired before others, but children do not seem to be conscious of the "rules" they are using and "may self-correct on the basis of a 'feel' for grammaticality" (Krashen 1979b, p. 2; Sutherland in press).

Implicit learning seems to occur during a pretalking stage when the infant is silent except for babbling, but "may be building up acquired competence via active listening" Krashen 1979b, p. 13; Cross 1977).

Understanding the target language through listening may involve "intake" rather than production (Scarcella and Krashen 1980; Newport, Gleitman, and Gleitman 1977). One important intake mode may be observed in transactions when the caretakers gently direct the infant's behavior with commands such as "Stand still while I wash your face," and simple questions that usually require a physical reaction as when the caretaker says, "Do you want some more milk?" and the child reaches for the glass or perhaps nods her head (Ervin-Tripp 1973).

It is important to note that while caretaker speech has a high proportion of imperatives and questions, teacher talk (Trager 1978) and foreign talk (Freed 1978) appear to have a larger percentage of declaratives.

Krashen (1980b) speculates that the caretaker's transactions with the infant enable the child to decode easily and directly the meaning of the target language including its semantics and gross structure. This Krashen calls an "acquisition-rich environment." In comparison, the teacher in the typical classroom uttering mostly declaratives may be providing input but not necessarily intake. That is, this is an "acquisition-impoverished" environment in which most students may have difficulty deciphering the meaning and structure of the target language except at a painfully slow pace in which there is conscious attention to rules and explanations (Wagner-Gough and Hatch 1975; and Krashen, Long, and Scarcella 1979).

It may be that before the child is ready to produce language, there must be months of intake in which caretakers utter directions to the infant who responds with nonverbal physical behavior such as looking, reaching, grasping, turning, and smiling. During this pretalk period, the infant may be expanding an unconscious map of how the language works and what it means. When the map is sufficiently intricate, speech is released (Gesell and Thompson 1929, Bühler and Hetzer 1935).

When speech appears, it will not be perfect, but gradually as the child develops, production will shape itself in the direction of the mature speaker. Production, like skill in tennis as described by Gallweys (1974), is "apparently better acquired than learned" (Krashen 1979a, p. 46).

When acquisition (implicit learning) is allowed to occur, production errors correct themselves naturally, which suggests that these errors are part of the normal developmental process (Belasco 1965, Corder 1967, Krashen 1979a).

PRACTICAL APPLICATION

Our research supports Krashen's view (1979a) that "the best approach (to second language instruction) might be one in which both learning and acquisition are fully utilized in the classroom" (p. 50). That is, the instructional model is to start with implicit learning (or acquisition) and gradually as the individual's understanding of the target language becomes more sophisticated make a transition to explicit learning. During implicit learning, intake is provided with an "acquisition-rich" classroom environment. Elsewhere (Winitz 1981 and Asher 1977), this has been called "comprehension training."

The model is a mirror of first language acquisition in which the "caretaker" in the role of the teacher utters directions to students who respond with physical actions.

Children or adults can acquire understanding of a second target language through comprehension training in a fraction of the time that was necessary for the infant acquiring its first language. One reason, we believe, is that the second language student has a network of physical response possibilities that is several hundred times larger than the infant who is restricted to responses such as crying, laughing, reaching, touching, looking, grasping, eliminating, and eating.

Another reason that acquisition is speeded up in comprehension training is that the student is willing and capable of following directions. Also, it is important to note that directions are uttered in the target language, which short circuits the interference and delay that usually occur when the person translates into the individual's first language.

COMPREHENSION TRAINING: WHAT THE RESEARCH SHOWS

It has been well established in experiments and classroom studies that when students "acquire rather than learn" (to use Krashen's terms) the target language, there are statistically significant gains in (1) short-term retention,

(2) long-term retention, and (3) the understanding of novel utterances in which already acquired constituents are recombined to produce surprise utterances. The generalization seems to hold for both children and adults acquiring a second language in English, French, German, Japanese, Russian, or Spanish. Further, the acquisition through comprehension training has shown positive transfer of learning to other skills such as speaking, reading, and writing.

The documentation to support each generalization may be found for adults acquiring *Japanese* under controlled experimental conditions (Kunihira and Asher 1965, Kanoi 1970), children and adults acquiring *Russian* under controlled experimental conditions (Asher 1965, 1969a, 1969b; Asher and Price 1967; Nord 1975; Ingram, Nord, and Dragt 1975), children and adults acquiring *French* in controlled experiments (Mear 1969; Davies 1976, 1977, 1978a, 1978b), adults acquiring *German* in classroom studies (Asher 1972; Reeds, Winitz, and García 1977; Swaffar and Woodruff 1978), adults and children acquiring *Spanish* in classroom studies (Kalivoda, Morain, and Elkins Chapter 27; Asher, Kusudo, and de la Torre Chapter 5; Asher 1977; Gary 1975) and adults and children acquiring *English as a second language* (Asher 1979, Jackson 1979, Sutherland in press). Pilot demonstrations by Paul Coulton (Murphy 1979) suggest that acquisition rather than explicit learning will significantly enhance the student's mastery of the sign language of the deaf.

Student attrition

Data on student attrition were obtained recently in a large-scale study at the University of Texas at Austin by Swaffar and Woodruff (1978). Twenty-three classes of 398 students experienced the first four weeks of comprehension training in beginning German by being silent but acting when directed by utterances in German spoken by the instructor. After two weeks of understanding spoken German through actions, students were encouraged to speak spontaneously on a voluntary basis. Except for a 5-minute question and answer period at the close of each hour, German was the exclusive language of instruction.

In the 5th week of instruction, a transition was made to reading using *Deutsch 2000*. After 17 weeks of comprehension training in which the students were acquiring skill in understanding spoken German and in reading German, individuals spontaneously expressed a readiness to memorize principal parts of verbs, the rules of German word order, and idiomatic prepositional phrases. (This is an example of the natural transition from implicit to explicit learning.)

As to results, in prior years, using the traditional explicit learning, only 55 percent of first semester students elected to continue their study into the second semester, but after a switch to implicit learning through comprehension training, 78 percent of first semester students decided to continue their study of German. Since these results have held for each year after the conclusion of the initial study, it seems reasonable to conclude that the dramatic increase in enrollments is not due to the Hawthorne effect.

Student attitudes

The reason for the dramatic increase in motivation to continue studying German may be related to the positive change in student attitudes. For example, the Harvard University study showed that when the instruction was the traditional explicit learning, one-third to one-half of the students in required foreign language courses had no intrinsic interest in the language they were taking (Jakobovits 1969) and a survey at the University of Illinois (Jakobovits 1969) found that "76 percent disapprove of the foreign language requirement and 40 percent feel that foreign language study in college has actually been detrimental to them." In comparison 76 to 84 percent of the University of Texas students acquiring German through actions said that their interest in Germany and the German language had increased. From 80 to 84 percent said that the course gave them a feeling for contrasts and similarities in German and American culture.

As to student achievement, 59 percent of the first semester students and 78 percent of the second semester students felt that they could now read German and grasp the main ideas, at least most of the time.

After the first semester 31 percent said they felt able to understand spoken German in everyday usage (a high-level expectation given the small number of instructional hours) and this proportion increased to 48 percent following the second semester.

Student achievement

After one year in the innovative, implicit learning program the students were administered the listening comprehension and reading measures of The Modern Language Association. The University of Texas students scored on the average at the 70th percentile rank in listening comprehension and the 58th percentile rank in reading German. Both scores were substantially above the expected 50th percentile rank for the national norms.

Student evaluation of the faculty

When the instructional format was explicit learning, the first semester student evaluation of the faculty was 64 percent on the average, which increased to 84 percent when the format was changed to implicit learning.

Second semester students assigned an average evaluation of 78 percent for explicit learning, which increased to 88 percent for implicit learning.

Transfer of learning

When students acquire understanding of the spoken language through implicit learning, an important finding has been a large magnitude of positive transfer to other skills such as reading, writing, and speaking.

For example, after only 45 hours in an experimental program for college students learning to understand spoken Spanish through implicit learning

(Asher, Kusudo, and de la Torre, Chapter 5), the students were given the Pimsleur Spanish Proficiency Tests—Form A (First Level), which was designed for audio-lingual students completing about 90 hours of instruction.

For listening comprehension, the average student performance was at the 70th percentile rank and there was a large amount of transfer of learning from listening competency to other skills. For example, the average student proficiency in reading was at the 85th percentile rank and for writing it was at the 76th percentile rank. Speaking skill is assessed on the Pimsleur in three categories of "good," "fair," or "poor." The average student in the experimental group was in the "good" category.

After 90 hours of experimental training, the students were administered the Pimsleur Spanish Proficiency Tests—Form C (Second Level), which was designed for audio-lingual students completing about 150 hours of college instruction. Nevertheless, the experimental group showed excellent transfer of learning from listening skills since they performed at about the 65th percentile rank, on the average, for reading and writing. Their speaking skill was classified between "fair" and "good."

Recent findings for English as a second language

A 3-year research project supported by a federal grant has just been completed by Jackson (1979) and her colleagues at the Whisman School District in Mountain View, California. Children in elementary school with deficiencies in English language skills were matched on vocabulary, language comprehension, and expressive skills. Children in the experimental group experienced comprehension training through the total physical response. There was systematic receptive training using nonverbal motoric responses such as "whole body, manipulatives, and pictures," which gradually advanced the students into complex production. The matched students in the control group experienced a traditional audio-lingual production-oriented training program.

After 3 years, the experimental group had the following gains when compared with the control group: (1) on the average, a 1.5-year advantage in vocabulary, (2) 80 percent more comprehension on the average, and (3) an average comparative increase in expressive skills of 130 percent. All gains were statistically significant using multivariate analysis of variance.

SUMMARY

Clearly, children acquiring their first language seem to offer a stress-free model for second language acquisition. An optimal approach is to maximize intake of the target language during a pretalking stage when students are silent but responding with an appropriate action when they hear a direction in the target language. An example would be "Stand up. Walk to the door. Turn, run to the chalkboard and draw a funny face . . .".

Gradually, the patterns become more and more sophisticated when grammatical features are nested in the imperative as illustrated in this direction: "When Maria begins to dance with Juan, Pilar will run to them and hit Juan with her newspaper."

Just as in the infant's development, the student's understanding of the target language expands and expands until the person is ready to talk. At this point, the student has the opportunity to reverse roles with the instructor and utter directions in the target language to peers or to the teacher. Of course, the student usually will attempt to utter commands from earlier lessons, and like the infant, pronunciation will not be perfect. But gradually, as in the normal development of children's speech, production will shape itself in the direction of the native speaker.

Future research should be designed to map, in a long-term study, exactly what can be expected in the appearance of errors and their extinction. From prior research (Asher and García 1969, Krashen 1979a), we would expect that children starting the stress-free training before puberty would have the most promising chance to attain eventually a near-native pronunciation. Students starting after puberty can expect to communicate fluently in the target language but with a noticeable accent.

APPLICATION IN THE CLASSROOM

Teachers may see demonstrations in several documentary films that show how the approach works with children and adults acquiring Japanese, French, Spanish, and German. For further information on films together with training materials, write Sky Oaks Productions, 19544 Sky Oaks Way, Los Gatos, California 95030.

DISCUSSION QUESTIONS

1. Asher writes about the significance of "caretaker" speech in first language acquisition. He does not mention the fact that "caretaker talk" is often episodically organized, yet this idea comes up in the following chapter by Kalivoda et al., where they recommend series of related commands which are sequentially connected within an activity such as sampling a stew or pinning a map on a bulletin board. (See Chapters 1 and 27.)

2. Why might student attitudes be expected to improve because of the adoption of TPR methods? What variables could be expected to contribute to the positive change observed in the teaching of German at Harvard, for example?

3. Asher claims that his model is "stress-free." Discuss.

4. Asher's views on the significance of errors are somewhat at variance with the traditional conception. What advantages and disadvantages would you expect to accrue over the long term to Asher's approach to errors?

Chapter 27

The Audio-Motor Unit: A Listening Comprehension Strategy That Works

Theodore B. Kalivoda, Genelle Morain, and Robert J. Elkins

University of Georgia   University of Georgia   University of West Virginia

EDITORS' INTRODUCTION

Kalivoda et al. apply the Asher method (see Chapters 5 and 26) with a couple of differences: they insist on "meaningful sequence" (a term familiar especially from Chapters 1 and 2), and they contend that the command approach should function only as part of a total curriculum—not as the core. Their own imperative drills are miniature dramas where the teacher functions somewhat like a director first showing and telling, then just telling, the actors what to do (also see Part IV, Roles and Dramas). They see potential for vocabulary enrichment through imperative drills and they also point out how subtleties of cultural difference can be incorporated in such a way that they become obvious to the students, e.g., how to eat steak the European way. Their recommendations have the greater force because they have demonstrated that they work in French, Spanish, and German. It is not difficult to see them working, in fact, in just about any language. Reactions of students and teachers, solicited by questionnaires, were generally very positive and confirmed Asher's claims for positive transfer from listening to speaking, reading, and writing. Some of the teachers claimed that directing the drill dramas resulted in significant gains in their own target language skills.

The classroom teacher is not indifferent to the theorist. We listen attentively to the grammarian, the audiolingualist, the cognitive-coder, and the eclecticist. But while we wait for the Revelation, we have to go on teaching the language Monday through Friday from September to June. The question we ask most fervently when two or three gather together is, "What are you doing that works?"

Teachers who are searching for a way to improve students' listening skills may want to investigate the "audio-motor" unit, a supplementary device that seems to "work." Simply, it is a daily 10-minute activity designed to develop the listening skill (*audio-*) by requiring an immediate physical response (*motor*).

James J. Asher (1969b) has pioneered research in the area of listening skill coupled with physical activity. He attributes the current failure to produce students fluent in the language to the fact that most language teaching is multiple in dimension—involving the simultaneous presentation of different skills. Asher advocates a change to "serial learning" of the four skills, with "listening fluency" the first to be acquired. His experiments with the "total physical response technique," which combines listening with enacting, showed that students who learned by this strategy were superior in retention of the foreign languages to those of control groups.

However, Asher's "total physical response technique" is conceived as the sole learning activity for an extended period. Its use in the classroom would require a radical restructuring of the first-level language program and would render obsolete many of the materials now in use across the land. In addition, those students who leave the program after one year would have little or no contact with speaking, reading, and writing skills. Furthermore, it is questionable whether a unidimensional approach could be satisfying to students for an extended period of time.

The audio-motor unit described in this paper is indebted to Asher's work but varies markedly in approach. It is designed as a supplementary, not an exclusive, learning activity, and thus is immediately applicable to any class-room. It provides one answer to Wilga M. Rivers' call in 1966 for increased use of listening comprehension materials at regular intervals in the language learning program.

THE AUDIO-MOTOR UNIT

Format

The average length of the audio-motor unit is 10 minutes. This may be shortened or extended as class needs change from day to day.

To begin the unit, the teacher walks to a tape recorder and activates the voice of a native speaker. The voice, speaking at a comfortable speed which retains natural rhythm and intonation patterns, gives a series of some 20 commands, structured around a central theme.

The teacher acts out the appropriate responses to the commands, making use of gesture, pantomime, and facial expression. Sometimes a simple prop (a billfold, an eraser, an apple) may be used to illustrate meaning. The students listen to the tape and observe the actions of the teacher.

An audio-motor unit involving activities in the kitchen might include the following fragment. (The imaginary drawer might be one which has been sketched on the black-board. The onion, knife, and spoon may also be sketched for the teacher to "pick off" the board on command.)

> Tape: Open the drawer. (Teacher pulls out imaginary drawer.)
> Tape: Take out a knife. (Teacher pantomimes.)
> Tape: Place the onion on the table. (Pantomime)
> Tape: Chop the onion. (Pantomime)
> Tape: Your eyes are watering. Wipe them. (Pantomime)
> Tape: Add the onion to the stew. (Pantomime)

Tape: Pick up the spoon. (Pantomime)
Tape: Stir the stew. (Pantomime)
Tape: Take a spoonful. Blow on it. (Pantomime)
Tape: Taste it. (Pantomime)
Tape: It's good. Smack your lips. (Pantomime)

Childish? Maybe. But how many students (and teachers for that matter) know how to say: "Your eyes are watering," "Blow on it," "Taste it," and "Smack your lips"? Teachers should not misinterpret the purpose behind such commands. It is recognized that the student may never be in a situation where he will give the direct command, "Smack your lips." He may, however, eventually encounter such forms as "Don't smack your lips," or "He smacked his lips." The value of the command, then, lies in learning the vocabulary and in the transfer to other situations.

When the taped lesson is finished (2 to 3 minutes), the teacher replays it. This time he invites the students to join him in acting out the appropriate responses. If the activity does not require extensive movement, all students participate simultaneously, standing in the aisle by their desks. If a great deal of action is called for, the teacher may designate several students to represent the class, although once the class acquires the feel of pantomime they can simulate at the side of their desk even the actions required by such commands as "Climb the ladder" and "Run to the window."

The taped sequence is repeated on ensuing days until the teacher is satisfied that most of the students can associate the proper physical response with a given command. To test this, the teacher takes over the giving of the commands and presents them in scrambled order. The entire class may respond, or individuals may be designated to demonstrate the responses. This portion of the unit offers opportunities for a competitive game situation which makes testing a positive activity.

In summary, then, the format of the audio-motor unit is simple: (1) the teacher acts out responses to taped commands; (2) students listen and observe; (3) the tape (or the teacher) repeats the commands; (4) the students respond physically.

As John B. Carroll (1965) has pointed out: "The more kinds of association that are made to an item, the better is learning and retention" (p. 280). With the audio-motor technique, the student first *sees* meaning as he *hears* sound; then he himself supplies the *muscular response* which fulfills meaning. Thus visual, auditory, and motor sense combine in this listening comprehension strategy.

Subject matter

The content of each audio-motor unit is organized around a central theme. The prosaic world of the classroom is a logical starting place, but the nature of the activity required need not be humdrum. The familiar requests to "Open your books" and "Hand in your papers" are valid, but so are "Plug in the projector" and "Don't scribble on the desk."

The activities as initially presented on tape are given in a meaningful sequence. The student may be told to take out a piece of paper, draw an outline map of France, take it to the bulletin board, pick up a thumbtack, pin the map to the board, stand back and look at it, shake his head, remove the map, crumple it up, and throw it in the wastebasket.

Once the students grasp the audio-motor technique, there is no need to limit lesson horizons to the classroom. The teacher can set the scene by holding up a single picture or making a rapid sketch on the blackboard. Students play the game with alacrity. There is no limit to the imaginative setting they seem willing to accept—as long as it lies within the normal scope of experience. A lesson on "How to Wind the Maypole" would lack the relevance which today's students demand.

Vocabulary acquisition

Audiolingualists have minimized the importance of vocabulary learning in the early stages of language study. Valid though their urgings may be, our students are left with a rather pallid lexicon. They know the equivalent of "book," "window," "door," "sweater," and "record." They can "go," "come," "take a walk," "play tennis," and "drive a car." But in a world where involvement means perception on many levels, this is not enough. It is a distortion of culture to strip the physical and emotional content from language learning.

The audio-motor unit can teach recognition of a rich supply of nouns in the affective domain: the sneer, the sigh, the giggle, the guffaw, the shrug, the wink, the frown. It can provide a powerhouse of verbs to be assimilated with vigor and humor. There is no reason to limit today's bright students to "standing up" and "sitting down." They also want to wince, twist, squat, lurch, spit, stoop, and clutch. The audio-motor unit is an exceptionally efficient way to teach kinesics. By presenting the vocabulary of movement and emotion, it can restore life to an anemic lexicon.

Reentry of materials

Careful structuring of the audio-motor units provides for reentry of materials at regular intervals. In a discussion of listening comprehension, Rivers (1966) emphasizes reentry and suggests that it is effective when presented through the use of games:

Games imaginatively devised give the students comprehension practice in a situation where interest is heightened by the competitive element . . . A few minutes of listening comprehension games at regular intervals, usually at the end of class lessons, will enable the teacher to reintroduce systematically material which is not currently being actively practiced. In this way, retention of material from earlier lessons will be constantly reinforced by active recapitulation without tedium.

The audio-motor unit provides a palatable form of reentry where physical involvement and the spirit of competition reinforce the learning experience.

Cultural concepts

Audio-motor lessons have the advantage of linking culture to language in a way which makes the cultural phenomena immediately obvious. Simply talking about an aspect of culture or looking at pictures which illustrate it cannot provide the learning impact which results from physical involvement.

An example of cultural learning may be seen in the following Spanish lesson:

You are at a restaurant.	Estás en un restaurante.
Pick up your napkin.	Coge la servilleta.
Unfold it.	Desdóblala.
Put it on your lap.	Ponla sobre las piernas.
Pick up your fork in your left hand.	Coge el tenedor con la mano izquierda.
Pick up your knife in your right hand.	Coge el cuchillo con la mano derecha.
Cut a piece of meat.	Corta un trozo de carne.
Put it in your mouth.	Ponlo en la boca.
Chew it.	Mastícalo.
Swallow it.	Trágalo.
Put down your knife and fork.	Deja en el plato el tenedor y el cuchillo.
Leave your hands on the table.	Deja las manos en la mesa.
Pour a glass of wine.	Sírvete un vaso de vino.
Take a sip.	Bebe un poco.
You want some bread. Break off a piece.	Quieres pan. Parte un trozo.
Eat it.	Cómelo.
Pick up the bill.	Coge la cuenta.
Look at it.	Mírala.
Take out your wallet.	Saca tu billetera.
Pay the bill.	Paga la cuenta.
Leave a tip.	Deja una propina.
Leave the restaurant.	Sal del restaurante.

At least four significant cultural points are illustrated in this unit, each reinforced through physical enactment:

1. Techniques of eating meat: holding knife and fork in right and left hands, respectively, cutting one piece of meat at a time, lifting the cut piece to the mouth with the fork still in the left hand.
2. Leaving both hands resting lightly on the edge of the table when not in use.
3. Using wine as the common beverage at mealtime for young people as well as adults.
4. Eating bread by tearing off small pieces from the larger individual portion, instead of biting them off.

These four Spanish eating habits differ markedly from those commonly practiced in the United States and could serve as a springboard for a discussion of cross-cultural differences at a later moment.

Such cultural differences come to light unexpectedly in the preparation of audio-motor units. The authors, working French, Spanish, and German to create a unit involving activities in the kitchen, wanted to set up the sequence:

> Go to the refrigerator.
> Open the door.

At this point the German writer suggested that a command was missing. He insisted that "Bend over" should follow immediately after "Go to the refrigerator." His French and Spanish colleagues were mystified, until the resultant discussion brought out the fact that the typical German refrigerator is a low unit which falls far short of the height of an American refrigerator. One must "bend over" if he is to open the door and look inside. Absorbing a tiny fragment of culture such as this may not seem important, but it might prevent an American student from blurting, "Oh, what a funny little refrigerator!" to a sensitive German hostess.

Variation in routine

The inclusion of the audio-motor unit within the regular classroom session has another value. It provides a salutary relief from the pattern drill and directed dialogue. With instant physical involvement, the student "comes alive" in every sense—muscular as well as intellectual.

The nature of the activity ranges from the relatively mild act of entering a phone booth, consulting the directory, and placing a call, to the really gymnastic efforts of a lesson in calisthenics, where students, participating simultaneously, are required to bend, stretch, jump rope, and do knee bends.

The chance to get up and move around the room is appealing to students. Not only does it offer rest from the sedentary pursuit of knowledge, but it also represents meaningful activity in terms of the language learning which students are seeking.

THE AUDIO-MOTOR UNIT IN PRACTICE

Small-scale pilot programs using the audio-motor unit have been conducted in high schools in Florida and Georgia. The first large-scale use of the audio-motor strategy took place at the Southeastern Language Center on the University of Georgia campus during an intensive 6 week course for high school students in the summer of 1970.

Procedure

Coordinate lessons were used in French, Spanish, and German classes. The language background of the students ranged from 1 to 6 years of language study. Six different audio-motor units, each composed of 20 commands, were presented at the rate of one unit per week. Classes with 1 and 2 years of language study participated in the audio-motor lesson daily, allocating the last 10 minutes of the hour to this activity. Advanced classes required only one or two 10 minute intervals to master the designated unit for any given week.

The teachers who conducted the audio-motor lessons received only the minimal instruction necessary to ensure similarity of presentation. There was no discussion concerning possible drawbacks to or benefits from such a program. One instructor asked to be excused from participating, explaining that he would "feel foolish" during the teacher-modeling phase of the unit. A total of eight teachers took part in the audio-motor program.

Results

At the end of the 6-week period, students were asked to fill out a questionnaire (see Appendix I) giving their attitude toward the audio-motor units at the beginning and at the end of the 6 weeks, as well as their perception of their instructors' attitude at the same intervals. Students were also asked to enumerate their positive and negative criticisms of the audio-motor strategy (see table).

A total of 180 students took part in the study. The response of 90 percent of these (162) students were positive. Neither the sex of the respondent nor the language studied proved to be significant in analyzing the questionnaire results.

Students indicated strongest approval for the following aspects of the audio-motor unit:

1. They felt it increased their language learning in terms of listening comprehension and vocabulary building.
2. They appreciated the change of pace it gave to classroom procedure.
3. They found it stimulating and entertaining.

On the other hand, negative reactions included such comments as: "too easy," "boring," "silly." Nine students expressed dissatisfaction in being unable to see the written form of the commands. Two students indicated a desire

Student Questionnaire

Items	Number of students rating items by categories					
	Very positive	Positive	Somewhat positive	Somewhat negative	Negative	Very negative
1. What was your attitude toward this activity at the beginning of the 6 weeks?	29	55	47	34	10	5
2. What was your attitude toward this activity at the end of the 6 weeks?	54	76	32	5	11	2
3. What was your instructor's attitude toward this activity at the beginning of the 6 weeks?	71	71	26	6	5	1
4. What was your instructor's attitude toward this activity at the end of the 6 weeks?	84	63	20	5	4	4

to participate orally in the lesson. It is interesting to note that a total of fifty-six students did not list a negative reaction of any kind.

Instructors who had worked with the audio-motor units filled out a different questionnaire, evaluating their own reaction to the technique, as well as their students' reaction as perceived by the professors. They were also asked to list strengths and weaknesses of the audio-motor strategy. (See Appendix II.)

Of the eight teachers involved, six responded with positive reactions. They were principally impressed with four benefits derived from the use of the units:

1. Lexical and structural items and their syntactic arrangements which were being practiced through other classroom activities were reinforced by the physical response lesson. This subjective reaction would tend to uphold Asher's assertion (1969a) that "listening skill seems to have a large positive transfer to reading and writing depending upon the fit between phonology and orthography of a specific language" (p. 4).

2. Cultural learnings illustrated by the lessons and strengthened through physical enactment caused strong interest on the part of students.

3. Although the lessons were designed to facilitate development of the listening skill, evidence of their impact on student oral expression was seen in the students' spontaneous use of the commands both in and out of the classroom. Idioms and individual words seemed to become a part of the students' system of expression. Some teachers felt that there was an accompanying improvement in pronunciation, although they added that "This is hard to verify." Asher does cite evidence that "the skill of listening comprehension has high positive transfer especially to speaking a foreign language (p. 4).

4. Nonnative speakers of the staff indicated that the lessons helped them with their own ability to say certain things in the foreign language. It is possible that teachers in secondary schools often fail to use the foreign language in the classroom because they are not sure how to say what the situation demands. Audio-motor lessons contain high-frequency situations found throughout the language hour and thus provide the teacher with useful expressions for greater communication in the foreign language.

Objections from the teachers who participated in the audio-motor lessons included two principal criticisms:

1. Some felt that the exclusion of the written word narrowed the benefits to be derived. They wanted the students to read and speak the commands as well as hear and enact them.

2. One would have preferred more explicit orientation to the procedures to be used and a chance to meet with other staff members to evaluate the program at its conclusion.

Analysis

In generalizing from the results of the questionnaires, it should be remembered that participants in this program were not "typical." Students who enroll at the Southeastern Language Center must have at least a B average in prior language study. Furthermore, students who are willing to devote 6 weeks of summer vacation to intensive language study are obviously highly motivated. It should also be kept in mind that participants at the Language Center attend class at least 5 hours per day. They might be more receptive, therefore, to a 10-minute departure from usual classroom activity than would students whose contact time with a foreign language consists of 50 minutes per day. On the other hand one might speculate that students with average or lower grades, and students with weak motivation, would be even more responsive to an audio-motor unit than their more favored peers.

It is to be regretted that no controlled attempt was made to evaluate the effect of the audio-motor strategy upon retention. However, instructors did reenter materials from past units at frequent intervals, and reported that student response was highly accurate.

At the conclusion of the 6-week period, video tapes were made of the audio-motor units in action. In an attempt to more nearly approximate the "beginning language" stage, German students were taught a French unit, French students learned Spanish, and Spanish students received instruction in German. The video tapes did capture the sense of concentration, the release that comes with physical involvement, the spontaneity and the learning satisfaction which characterize the audio-motor technique.

SUMMARY

The audio-motor unit as a device for teaching listening comprehension has met with an overwhelmingly positive response in a large-scale operation.

Using a visual and an audible stimulus initially to elicit a physical response, this strategy brings sight, hearing, and kinesic participation into interplay. Later the visible stimulus is dropped and the student relies only upon the oral command to motivate his physical response.

It is suggested that regular use of carefully prepared audio-motor units can provide listening comprehension activities which increase knowledge of lexical and structural items, add dimension to cultural understanding, and enliven the learning situation with zest and humor.

Appendix I   Student Questionnaire: Audio-Motor Units

Language studied: _____		Please circle one:	Male	Female	
Very positive	Positive	Somewhat positive	Somewhat negative	Negative	Very negative
1. What was your attitude toward this activity at the beginning of the 6 weeks?					
2. What was your attitude toward this activity at the end of the 6 weeks?					

	Very positive	Positive	Somewhat positive	Somewhat negative	Negative	Very negative
3. What was your instructor's attitude toward this activity at the beginning of the 6 weeks?						
4. What was your instructor's attitude toward this activity at the end of the 6 weeks?						

5. Which lesson did you like most? _____
6. Which lesson did you like least? _____
7. Give your positive reactions to the audio-motor units.
8. Give your negative reactions to the audio-motor units.

Appendix II   Instructor Questionnaire: Audio-Motor Units

Language taught: _____		Please circle one:	Male	Female		
	Very positive	Positive	Somewhat positive	Somewhat negative	Negative	Very negative
1. What was your attitude toward this activity at the beginning of the 6 weeks?						
2. What was your attitude toward this activity at the end of the 6 weeks?						
3. What was the attitude of your class toward this activity at the beginning of the program?						
4. What was the attitude of your class toward this activity at the end of the 6 weeks?						

5. With which group did you use the AMU, students of beginning, medium, or advanced language ability?
6. How many minutes each day did you use this activity? _____
7. How many days per week did you use it? _____
8. At what time slot during the class hour did you use this activity? Beginning? Middle? End? At varying times?
9. Why did you present the activity at this time?
10. Please evaluate the activity in terms of the following areas:
    a. Vocabulary enrichment _____
    b. Grammatical reinforcement _____
    c. Carry-over into students' pronunciation _____
    d. Cultural learnings _____
    e. Your own acquisition of knowledge (if nonnative speaker) _____
11. Please add any further comments or suggestions you would care to make.

DISCUSSION QUESTIONS

1. What advantages do you see to drills that incorporate the element of "meaningful sequence" (alias "episodic organization")?

2. One teacher asked to be excused from participating in the experimental application of the strategy recommended in this chapter because he said it would make him "feel foolish." Discuss this reaction. Is such a dramatic strategy for everyone?

3. Another teacher suggested that students should see the imperatives written down as well as hear them. Further, according to the same teacher, they should be required to say and read them. What consequences good or bad would you expect as a result of taking these suggestions?

Chapter 28

The Intensive Language Model at Florida

Otto W. Johnston
University of Florida

EDITORS' INTRODUCTION

Johnston reports on an application of the Rassias-inspired "intensive language model" in the teaching of German at the University of Florida. The "intensiveness" of the program has nothing to do with condensation of material covered. The curriculum is not collapsed into a shorter space of time; rather, the program is "intensive" because it requires students to spend more contact hours working with the target language than normally would occur in the traditional 3- to 5-hour-a-week course. In the intensive model students spend a minimum of 2 1/2 hours per day in drill or class sessions. These sessions are an interesting mix of traditional audiolingualism, minimal-pair phoneme discrimination, and dramatic Rassias madness. Students report that the highlight of their language study is the preparation and presentation of "skits" in the target language. These are videotaped and then examined in great detail in debriefing sessions. Visits by "surprise" guests who communicate with students in the target language also generate high interest levels and help to reduce absenteeism. To help smooth the transition to literacy in the target language (German in this case), Johnston also reports on an innovative dictation technique which makes a kind of communication game of the whole process. Also see Wolkomir, Chapter 7, and Rassias's own contribution in Chapter 29.

The intenstive language model developed by Dartmouth Professor John Rassias has generated widespread popular acclaim, largely because of favorable press reports in *Time Magazine* (August 1977), *Newsweek* (December 1977), *Change Magazine* (December 1977) and *The New York Times* (Jan. 8, 1978). For the most part, the news stories focus on the unusual techniques Rassias employs with advanced-level students of French literature. Disguised as Voltaire's Candide or Molière's Misanthrope, Rassias, by "dynamiting language," in his words,[1] elicits emotional responses from his listeners not previously experienced by American students. Pelting seminar participants

---

1. Rassias (1968, 1972); *Congressional Record* (1974); *Time* magazine (1976); and Bacon (1977). *Effective Language Teaching,* a film on the method available without charge through Association-Sterling Films, Department OB, 866 Third Avenue, New York, N.Y. 10022. Accompanied by a descriptive manual. (See also Chapter 29.)

with eggs, igniting firecrackers in his classroom, and telephoning students in the middle of the night are routine occurrences in his course. Thus, the French language is purported to become the medium for a wide range of feelings familiar to the native speaker, but strange to a 19- or 20-year-old American. This "emotional involvement" provides the incentive for further language learning.

Yet Rassias's exploits in transmitting French culture constitute only one aspect, and by no means the most important part, of the intensive language model. Neglected in these news bulletins is the structure of the beginning language courses, which represents a considerable improvement over the traditional approach to language learning. By developing audiolingual techniques to a high degree of efficiency and dividing his "master class" (20 to 22 students) into smaller sections (6 to 8 students) taught by undergraduate apprentice teachers, Rassias greatly accelerates the rate at which students can learn a foreign language. His adaptations are based on experiences in Africa where he trained Peace Corps volunteers.

Rassias has also perfected drill techniques which he practices with his highly skilled apprentices. Since the latter are often only a course or two ahead of their pupils, these peer tutors, trained in workshops by Rassias himself, generate an incredible amount of enthusiasm for the process of language learning. With the intensive language model, the vitality of both master and apprentice teacher becomes in itself a subject for scrutiny. The student is motivated to learn by the enthusiasm and objectified "hard work" of his instructors.

The intensive language model has been highly successful at small liberal arts colleges.[2] But of the 17 institutions in the United States currently employing the model (Luxemberg 1976), only CUNY (Baruch), Florida State University, and the University of Florida are large state-supported universities with enormous student-teacher ratios, shortages of classroom space, and marginal, if not inadequate, funding. Despite these handicaps, the Department of Germanic and Slavic Languages at the University of Florida (Gainesville) sought, with the aid of a $6000 Impact Grant from the Educational Foundation of the Exxon Corporation, to implement the intensive language model in Beginning German in the 10-week summer quarter of 1978. As a basic text, we used Helbling/Gewehr/von Schmidt, *First Year German* (New York: Holt, Rinehart, and Winston, 1975), Chapters I–VI. The experiment can be documented in terms of (1) preparation, (2) initial student reaction, (3) student input and motivation, (4) funding, and (5) teacher evaluation.

---

2. The following schools have announced their participation in the intensive language model: Claremont Men's College, Clark University, College of William and Mary, CUNY (Baruch), Earlham College, Florida State University (Tallahassee), Immaculata College, Lenoir-Rhyne College, Northern Illinois University, St. Martin's College, St. Olaf College, University of Denver, University of Detroit, University of Southern Mississippi, University of Montana, prospectively University of Florida (Gainesville).

PREPARATION

In 1974, the German Department at the University of Florida supported a large-scale computerized evaluation of its three quarter program for beginners, which primarily serves those students seeking to fill a language requirement in the College of Arts and Sciences (VonGal 1974). Questionnaires were distributed to 363 students at three levels of beginning instruction; the results were tabulated by computer. The response indicated that, despite faculty suppositions to the contrary, beginning students were generally enthusiastic about learning a language. Those recently enrolled in our program expressed a desire, beyond meeting their college requirement, to gain proficiency in German. Nevertheless, the initial interest waned after about 5 weeks, as more emphasis was placed on the fine points of syntax. Midway in second quarter German, students panicked when confronted with the complexities of German grammar. By German III, virtually all enthusiasm for the subject had disappeared; students were ill-disposed to the material, although 75 percent felt that the instructor had covered the subject satisfactorily. The disenchantment was a result of the complexity of the subject matter rather than a product of inadequate teaching. Seventy percent felt they were not getting their money's worth: despite some ability to recognize grammatical structures, the students expressed disappointment at their inability to speak. The oral component was a conspicuous omission in their early language training. On the other hand, 30 percent were happy with our program. These students felt that the emphasis on reading and comprehension had been put in the right place and voiced no desire to increase proficiency in speaking.

A similar study conducted in 1976 with a select group of 90 students produced the same general results. Again, the absence of oral proficiency was cited by 68 percent of those responding as a glaring weakness in our established program.

In 1977, the department revised its goals. The primary tasks with regard to the 350 students enrolled in Beginning German had been perceived by the faculty as (1) providing a basic knowledge of German grammar, (2) building vocabulary, (3) preparing for more difficult reading material. However, the results of our questionnaires as well as the increased interest in foreign trade shown by Florida's Bureau of Trade Development (Department of Commerce) prompted the German Department to deemphasize traditional grammar methodologies and offer in their place live speaking situations which call for specific responses. In the past we had prepared students for the study of language, literature, and culture; we thought now to move into commercial and technical language training. Our aim was to build flexibility into our program in order to meet student needs.

Classes conducted in a traditional mode had depended on readings, conversation, grammar exercises, and pattern drills. The focus was on textbook and teacher; some sections were taught by graduate student teaching assistants.

Clearly, we were training future German language teachers for high school, junior college, and the university. But now we sought accommodation with both our changing economic infrastructure and the current academic situation. We were determined not to add to an overcrowded field of linguists and literary scholars. By implementing the intensive language model, we hoped to diversify the course content. Instead of preparing all students to respond in a single mode, we sought to tailor our courses to practical student needs.

INITIAL STUDENT REACTION

The first step in implementing the model was a revision of class scheduling. Traditionally, our 5-hour German course met once a day, Monday through Friday. Therefore, the initial problem was to work the drill session with an apprentice teacher into the student's already crowded schedule. A typical study plan in our College of Arts and Sciences appears as follows:

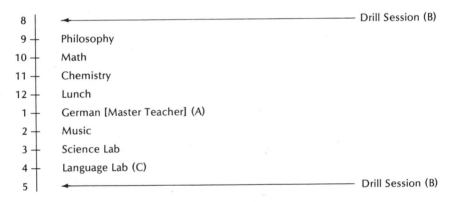

(A) The student schedules a section of Beginning German in accordance with his or her study plan.
(B) He or she is signed up for a drill session at a time prior to the beginning of the school day (8:00 a.m.), or in the afternoon regular classes (4:45 p.m.). The choice is made by the student. The reputation of the particular apprentice teacher became a decisive factor for the second group instructed in this way.
(C) The student visits the language laboratory for 20 minutes each day whenever he or she can fit it in.

The scheduling of these segments of this particular class produced the following structure:
These tables indicate an immersion in Beginning German comprising 2 1/2 contact hours per day. The faculty anticipated a furor over so much exposure in a five-credit course, especially after announcing that an absence for whatever reason from any session would result in a letter grade reduction. For example, a student who missed any one session needed a 90 to 100 percent average on examinations to obtain a B; those who were absent for two sessions were

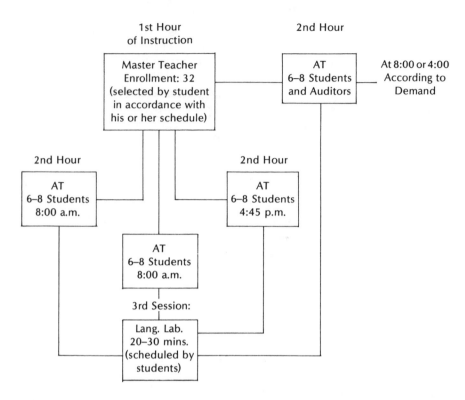

required to maintain the same average for a C. Anyone who missed more than three sessions could not pass and was counseled to drop the course.

Despite the severity of such regulations, we encountered surprisingly little opposition. Beginners were told that the drill session represented a "supervised assignment hour" which could be deducted from homework otherwise done alone. Within a week, students showed no negative reactions whatever and professed pleasure at meeting with classmates in a mutually rewarding endeavor and not having to learn by themselves. Each drill group, whether scheduled at 8:00 in the morning (three groups), or 4:45 in the afternoon (one group), developed an astonishing *esprit de corps;* in addition, the members of each session became fiercely competitive with regard to other groups. Each strove to outshine the others in oral recitation, grasping of grammatical concepts, and as we shall see in more detail later, performance in the master class.

STUDENT INPUT AND MOTIVATION

On the first day of class, students were handed a letter from the master teacher informing them of their status as participants in an experiment funded by the Exxon Corporation. They were asked to keep a diary in which they related their reactions to our innovations. Each participant was asked to comply with every regulation (as indicated above) no matter what inconvenience this might cause. They were then to record the extent of the inopportunity. In this way, we attempted to distinguish fact from fiction with regard to student excuses for missing classes.

This innovation proved remarkably effective. When students realized that class absence could not be adequately justified, they confessed to all sorts of ploys used to gain the sympathy of previous instructors. The act of journal keeping became a means of self-scrutiny; motives and reactions were constantly challenged. More importantly, students felt they could gauge their own progress as well as critically evaluate the entire process of language teaching and learning.

These journals proved to be a valuable data source for the experiment. Student attitudes toward each phase of the program could now be assessed with remarkable ease. We were able to ascertain on a weekly basis which of our scenarios excited student interest and which should be discarded. We also obtained a rare glimpse of the trials and tribulations of student life, the incredible problems neophytes encounter with a large, insensitive university bureaucracy.

The component most appreciated by our students was the element of surprise. Since grammar explanations, dialogues, and exercises were constantly interrupted by calculated interference, students were eager to attend classes. Virtually no one complained about having to come to class, because no one wanted to miss the day's bolt out of the blue. In the middle of a grammar explanation, for example, the department secretary might walk into the classroom and demand the keys to the office, explaining in German that she had been locked out. The instructor's wife might appear, bringing his lunch which he had purportedly forgotten; she would then explain in German what Herr Professor did and did not like to eat. An unexpected guest, either a colleague or a native speaker, would pose as a character from a fairy tale (*Cinderella, Sleeping Beauty*), or famous German short story (Gregor Samsa, from Kafka's *Metamorphosis*), a drama (*Faust, Wilhelm Tell*), or an epic (Siegfried, from the *Saga of the Nibelungen*). The students were required to ask this person questions in German until his or her identity was revealed. The response was enthusiastic; participants prepared (on their own) a barrage of questions to ask any extraordinary personage who might happen to "drop in." By the sixth and seventh weeks, students were proficient at asking specific questions and could figure out the identity of the ghost personality in a very short time. These interruptions generally lasted 15 minutes, whereupon the instructor picked up the grammar point again; the difference, as compared with the traditional method, was that he once again had the undivided attention of his class. More than two dozen such short breaks occurred throughout the 10-week course. In their diaries, students described in great detail the impact each visitor or interruption had made on their desire to learn German. Virtually everyone wanted to communicate with our guest.

In the third week of class, the master teacher, with the aid of the apprentice teachers, acted out a skit which they wrote themselves, based on vocabulary familiar to the students. The beginners were astonished at how much they had learned, what they had understood, and what they had been able to figure out. Each drill session leader was then encouraged to devise a similar scenario and present it to the class. By the seventh week, the individual groups were ready. Their skits ranged from "Alice in *Wunderland*," to "*Die Entführung von Patty Hearst*," from "Charlie Chan in Germany" to a parody of the hippie movement of the mid-sixties. Each scene required hours of dedication, energy, and hard work from the students, who admitted they would never have spent so much time studying for any traditional test, regardless of the consequences. The self-produced skits became the highlight of the course.

On the day of each group presentation to the class, a "special surprise" took place. Videotape equipment was utilized to record and play back to the participants the entire presentation. Each was then asked to analyze his or her own speaking role; evaluations were elicited from the class; finally, the instructor offered his critical commentary. This process, by first showing the student what he or she looked and sounded like to a German and allowing for self, peer, and teacher evaluation, had a far greater impact upon the beginners than any midterm or final. Students recorded a highly favorable response to this technique.

Early in the fourth week, we encountered the most serious problem with the method: students had major difficulties spelling German words. Although able to express verbally rather complex thoughts and to pronounce words with near native intonation, participants, when required to write sentences, confused *ihr* and *er, ist* and *es,* as well as a host of other diphthongs and consonant clusters. One reason for confusing the [i:] and [e:] sounds is, of course, the difference between the German and English vowel systems: German vowels are higher and tenser than their English counterparts, so that German [e:] is often perceived as an [i:] by an American speaker. We had solved that verbal problem by using minimal pairs which allowed the student to hear the phonemic contrast. Nevertheless, the difficulty reappeared despite such drills whenever the student was asked to write down words containing those pairs. Moreover, participants also confused the *ie* and *ei* sounds in their written work, suggesting to us that we, in our zeal to prompt verbal responses, had neglected the written component. We countered the problem by increasing not only the minimal pair drills, but also the frequency of dictations. The apprentice teacher's session had been devoted entirely to drilling verbally the material covered in the master teacher's hour. No new material was presented by the apprentice teacher; instead, students answered questions or repeated structured patterns, responding individually almost 60 times per hour. With the discovery of an unacceptable number of spelling errors, however, time was set aside for written comprehension exercises.

In both master and apprentice teacher sessions, these dictations were handled in the following unorthodox manner: one student was asked to step forward; he or she did not write but listened intently to a complete, 1-minute monologue in German (usually a coherent anecdote, occasionally a dialogue with question and answer spoken by the master teacher). A second student wrote this dictation at the back of the room on a blackboard which the other participants could not see. A third kept time, signaling the end of the monologue after 1 minute. The master teacher spoke initially at less than normal speaking tempo as the class copied what was said. In the second minute, the same monologue was repeated at a faster pace, approximating normal conversational speed. This enabled the writers to correct their first draft. Because his rate of speaking accelerated during the second minute, the master teacher, once he reached the previous stopping point, continued the monologue for one or two sentences, which the students also wrote down. In the third minute, the participant who had only listened answered questions pertaining to the material he or she had, by now, heard twice. Since the questions were phrased in such a way as to prompt the listener to repeat the more complex aspects of the monologue, those writing used this opportunity to correct their work once more. After answering the master teacher's questions, the listener was asked to relate in his or her own words, but still in German, as much as he or she could remember of the monologue. Thus, each student except the listener had written down as much as he or she could grasp during the first reading, corrected and added to the draft of the second, and amended his or her work the third time as the listener answered the master teacher's questions. A final opportunity for corrections and insertions was afforded the writers when the listener, who related as much of the monologue as he or she remembered, repeated once again most of the master teacher's words. Occasionally, prompting by the master teacher was necessary. At this point, the teacher went to the back of the room, had the students turn their chairs around, and corrected the dictation written on the board. Students, who had been asked to exchange papers with their neighbors, corrected each other's work.

Drills of this kind proved very effective in eliminating orthographical errors. Theoretically, they have the added advantage of taking up only 5 minutes of class time! In practice, of course, whenever mistakes were frequent, this drill might involve 10 to 15 minutes. Although such efficiency may seem incredible, a master teacher who has perfected the technique can easily complete such an exercise in remarkably little time. Moreover, the increased activity generated by a listener, a timekeeper, and a writer at the rear of the room maintains student interest, while the listener's recitation underscores the verbal component in an otherwise totally aural exercise. By asking each student who made a mistake in any drill during either of the sessions to go to the board and write out the sentence in which the error occurred, we were able to supplement this response to the problem of inadequate orthography and poor writing. The final examination, which was basically a composite of "traditional" tests given by the department in past semesters, indicated that spelling errors had not been eradicated completely. Nevertheless, substantial improvement over earlier tests was recorded.

FUNDING

The intensive language model relies on interpersonal contact between teacher and language learner. Whereas American foreign language educators have become increasingly more dependent upon such modern gadgetry as foreign language records, films, slides, tapes, and even the computer (PLATO), the Rassias method eliminates the need for expensive equipment. The master and apprentice teachers serve as models for the learner; they drill by means of a four-part technique, including (1) voice modulation, (2) snapping the fingers, (3) pointing at designated responders, and (4) intense eye contact. Through "surprise" and personal involvement, teachers motivate students to share in the unique experiences a foreign language can transmit. The language laboratory is the only essential aid integrated into the model. Those sums previously designated for purchasing and maintaining other hardware can be allocated as salaries for the apprentice teachers.

The $6000 grant we received from Exxon suffices merely to initiate the model. As student motivation increases and enrollments in these sections grow, the university administration will be called upon to fund more sections taught in this way. In order to ensure continued financial support, the intensive language model relies on good public relations. The news releases referred to earlier demonstrate the effectiveness of publicity in creating good will for language teaching. The success of the experiment at the University of Florida was due in no small part to good press.

Prior to implementation, the intensive language model was highlighted in a feature story in the local newspaper (Prine 1978). Press releases were issued after each "surprise." Although these did not appear in print, they aroused the interest of the campus press (an independent newspaper not affiliated directly with the university but concerned primarily with campus affairs [Morris 1978]). The editor asked for permission to send a journalist and photographer to the class. Both arrived in the seventh week as skits were presented. Appearing as a news item, rather than a feature article, the description of the experiment excited participants, interested their parents, and influenced administrators who were, at the time, in the process of making budget allocations.

The excitement of being interviewed by reporters, having pictures appear in the paper, and "making news" prompted students, who by now greatly appreciated the efforts of master and apprentice teacher, to appeal to the dean for a continuation of the experimental methodology. Through personal interview and signed petition, the students, now eager to continue their language training according to the intensive model, succeeded in obtaining the necessary allocation increments for the department. The popularity of the method became the pillar of its fiscal report.

The news coverage also got the parents involved. Mothers and fathers of the undergraduate participants wrote to the college administration, requesting a continuation of the intensive language model. University officials admitted that such appeals had, in fact, secured their support. They were willing to allot a supplemental fund to the department since parents, students, and the press had clamored for it. A sequel was prepared at once and the new offering publicized on broadsheets all over campus. Public relations had generated the needed academic dollars.

TEACHER EVALUATION

Assessing teacher strengths and weaknesses became a twofold process. The first aspect involved the training and choosing of apprentice teachers; the second concerned the student appraisal of both master and apprentice teacher. The latter were chosen in the following manner: a 3-day workshop was announced before the semester began. Prospective ATs were enlisted from all levels of German instruction with prospects of financial gain and extra credit. The session began with a 15-minute film illustrating the model as developed at Dartmouth. After an explanation of the experimental nature of this approach and the anticipated administrative problems, the four-phase drill technique was demonstrated. The master teacher trained the workshop participants in the proper coordination of voice, finger snap, point, and look. Each person was then asked to write out a simple pattern drill. Using backward buildup, each student worked with the group until everyone could recite the drill, make substitutions, and respond adequately. The next day at 8:00 a.m. practice continued. Videotape equipment was brought into the room, and each performance was recorded and played back for the performer. Self-criticism, peer evaluation, and teacher analysis followed each presentation. Both sessions lasted until after 5:00 p.m. On the morning of the third day a panel of five master teachers chose four apprentice teachers according to the following criteria:

Evaluation of Workshop Participants

Participant	Dramatization Technique	Tempo	Voice	Gestures	Stage Presence	
					Impression:	Personality and Creativity
A						
B						
C						
D						
E						
F						
G						

- Each participant wrote and presented three five-line monologues. From the story emerged a pattern drill, including progressions and substitutions.
- Each scenario (4 to 6 minutes) was videotaped for subsequent evaluation.
- Aspirants were judged by the five "master teachers" on a scale from one (poor) to five (excellent) in each category.
- AT positions were awarded to those with the most points.
- Throughout the quarter, the master teacher visited each AT drill session periodically in order to evaluate the AT and suggest improvements in the technique.

Student evaluation of the ATs and the master teacher were conducted both informally and formally. First, the daily journals alerted us to problems on a weekly basis. Second, an informal get-together was held each Friday afternoon at 4:30 p.m. Students were encouraged to talk about any aspect of the experiment at that time. Complaints regarding teacher performance on the program were noted. Third, a seven-part questionnaire was completed by each participant at the end of the quarter. The form, which had been used previously by the faculty to evaluate graduate assistants and was now employed by students to comment on the performance of both apprentice and master teacher, contained 50 rating questions, and 4 questions calling for more detailed answers. The students judged such items as (1) command of German, (2) organization of class meeting, (3) presentation of material, (4) classroom interaction, (5) effectiveness of methods and techniques, (6) self-confidence, tolerance, manners, and (7) strong and weak points. Student commentary may be summarized as follows: initial apprehension gives way rapidly as sessions become fun. Comradeship emerges as a motivating factor; however, fast learners become impatient with slower classmates. Disappointing either the AT or the MT leads to self-reproach. Because they are able to correct mistakes immediately, participants seldom repeat errors and are astonished at their own progress. The high motivation of the class generates peer pressure to continue working at maximum potential. A very positive effect was the large number of students inquiring about majoring in German.

Improvements Suggested by Students

1. More positive reinforcement of right answers through such compliments as *sehr gut, prima, ausgezeichnet.*

2. More visits of master teachers to drill sessions. This keeps everyone working at optimal efficiency.

3. More exact coordination between the lesson plans of master and apprentice teacher. The work sheets for the AT compiled by the master teacher must leave no room for insertion of additional material.

4. More written work. In order to enhance the concept of an additional contact hour, we had played down the need for individual homework. Participants pointed out, however, that such deemphasis assumed that all students learned at the same rate. Moreoever, it is not self-evident in this model, especially in the early stages, that individual students are falling behind.

Participants should be advised that language learning takes place at different rates; therefore, some would have to spend more time than others on written assignments.

5. More reading. As emphasis shifted from the traditional to a more verbal approach, students requested more reading material. Students appeared willing to read more provided the suggestion came from their own ranks, rather than from the master teacher. Participants were advised that additional reading would be forthcoming at more advanced levels.

These suggestions for improvements contained an essential recognition on the part of the students: in order to say what they now ardently wished to articulate, they must continue language study. They are spurred on by a personal desire to communicate.

Survey of Responses to Evaluative Questionnaire

This questionnaire was administered to 14 students who participated in an experimental course in the Rassias method in the summer quarter of 1978 at the University of Florida.

1. With regard to classroom atmosphere, what level of interest was maintained?
2. Did the instructor require the participation of everyone?
3. Were the students aware of what was expected of them?
4. During or after the grammar presentation and drills, did the instructor provide opportunities for the class to use German in meaningful situations?
5. Were the explanations of content clear, with sufficient examples?
6. Did the students seem to understand?
7. Was the level of questions and discussions appropriate?

The following aspects of general teaching performance were also rated on a scale of 1 (low) to 6 (high) by each participant.

A. Command of German
B. Organization of class meeting
C. Presentation of material
D. Classroom interaction
E. Teaching methods and techniques
F. Self-confidence, tolerance, manners

From the data, it is evident that students had recognized full participation as a course requirement, that we had, in fact, found the appropriate levels for questions and discussion, and that students were genuinely interested in what went on in German class. Less enthusiasm was shown for the examples we chose in explaining grammar points. Surprisingly, the participants thought less of their own proficiency than we did.

What about actual success? Could students really speak German better than their counterparts taught by more traditional, less expensive means? Admittedly, the results of our efforts to answer such questions can be regarded at this early stage as merely tentative. Establishing through empirical data the speaking proficiency actually attained by our participants presented a problem which we were unable to solve to the complete satisfaction of all faculty members. Nevertheless, four concrete indications of better speaking performance were recorded:

1. *The "Cartoon" Test.* Before implementing the intensive language model, we had begun testing each beginning student for verbal proficiency at the end of traditional German One. In the last days of the term, all regularly enrolled students were interviewed by their teachers at assigned times. A series of related cartoons, which told a pictorial story based on assigned vocabulary, was placed before each test candidate. His or her proficiency was judged on a scale from 1 (low) to 6 (high) in the areas of (a) pronunciation, (b) correctness of expression, (c) proper syntax, and (d) active vocabulary. A typical statistical breakdown for classes averaging 30 students appears as follows: (a) 2.5, (b) 3, (c) 1.5 to 2.5 (if the student attempted even a relatively uncomplicated compound or complex structure, the resulting utterance was, more often than not, unintelligible), (d) 2. Clearly, such low levels of achievement were discouraging.

When we repeated similar "cartoon tests" with each candidate on the intensive language model, the average ratings were appreciably higher: (a) 4, (b) 3, (c) 3 (a persistent problem in this connection was the student's overeagerness to "say something;" too often he or she sought to express complex thoughts, calling for grammatical structures to which he or she had not yet been exposed), (d) 3.5. The higher rating in (d) was fiercely disputed by some faculty members, who argued that traditional classes are geared more toward reading; therefore, the earlier test candidates would have had larger passive vocabularies. This is likely, primarily because the traditional students had, in fact, moved through the textbook at a faster pace and covered one more chapter of reading and grammar material than the intensive language model trainees in a similar 10-week period. Our reluctance to proceed before the latter could verbalize material presented in the master class had retarded the pace at which material was covered.

2. *Pronunciation, intonation, fluency of speech pattern, and lack of hesitancy compared favorably with more advanced students.* Prior to the experiment, the Grant recipient administered the MLA Cooperative Foreign Language Tests in German (Form M.A.) to 22 students who were about to complete German Four (equivalent to 40 weeks of German instruction). Responses to the oral section were recorded on cassette tape. At the conclusion of the summer experiment, the responses to our cartoon test, which is designed along similar lines, were recorded and compared with the tapes of the MLA test candidates.

Although the two tests involved very different material, many of the participants in our summer experiment sounded more like native speakers than did our more advanced speakers. Because of the inherent differences in the test material, testing conditions, and procedures, we do not claim that our comparison is in any way conclusive; the results were encouraging nonetheless.

3. *High ratings in the workshop.* As called for in Rassias's blueprint for the intensive language model, a workshop was held at the beginning of fall quarter in order to recruit and train new ATs for beginning German One and Two, both of which were to be conducted as intensive language models. Two of the eight available positions went to participants in our summer experiment in accordance with the rating procedure outlined earlier. Two others were appointed as alternates. This was a considerable achievement, since applicants for AT positions in the fall who had participated in our summer experiment were qualified to teach at only one level, whereas students who had completed more advanced courses in German competed for positions in both German One and Two.

On the other hand, our trainees did not compare favorably with those seeking AT jobs who had just returned from our Junior Year in Bonn (Germany); they earned the other six apprentice teacher positions. However, even the most adamant opponents of the Rassias method on our faculty were favorably impressed by the pronunciation and motivation of our intensive model applicants.

4. *The native speaker visit.* Toward the end of the quarter, we initiated a supersurprise. During a grammar presentation, four German exchange students visited our class. We prepared them beforehand in those basic areas in which the students had acquired a large enough vocabulary to hold a reasonably intelligent conversation (riding a bus, in a café, smoking and health, music, stereo equipment, etc.), and now divided the class into small groups. The native-speaker guests spoke with our students without resorting to English. The German visitors, who had been prepared equally well in the vocabulary of the three groups, found it easier to converse with our students than with German Two's or Three's. In contrast to the traditionally taught, our intensive language model participants responded eagerly and proficiently whenever the guests ventured into a familiar situation. To be sure, this test is more impressionistic than empirical. We offer the results merely as a suggestion of greater fluency, as we continue working on a more objective instrument for measuring the oral proficiency of participants in the intensive language model.

In conclusion, we feel justified in claiming positive initial results for this experiment. Students responded enthusiastically to the concrete efforts of their teachers to excite their interest. The general attitude can be summarized as "you can't help but learn." The potential for expanding the intensive language model seems inexhaustible. By adding scenarios tailored to student interests and needs, the department will be able to realize its goal of maximum flexibility. Once the entire faculty is convinced of the intrinsic value of a practical approach to language training, and each member becomes a magician who can create tricks and surprises on the spot, we will have a modernized stimulating program. In other words, language learning will cease to be a requirement; it will become, at least at the University of Florida, a self-motivating experience.

DISCUSSION QUESTIONS

1. In a subsequent paper, to appear in *Foreign Language Annals*, Johnston (in press) reports that after implementation of the Rassias model enrollments at the University of Florida dramatically increased in both German and Russian. What factors might have contributed to these results?

2. What relation do you see between the "esprit de corps" observed by Johnston in Florida German classes and the camaraderie characteristic of courses taught in the Curran style? Aren't these approaches radically different? If so, how is it that they seem to produce similar effects.

3. Journal keeping seems to be a suitable method of documenting student growth in target language skills at least on an introspective, intuitive level. What other sources of data might regularly be used to check further on the effectiveness of the German Intensive Language Model or any other institutionalized method of language instruction?

4. What about the role of error correction in the German Intensive Language Model as compared with Terrell's natural approach? Also discuss the use of explicit grammatical explanations and the reaction of students.

Chapter 29

New Dimensions in Language Training: The Dartmouth College Experiment

John A. Rassias
Dartmouth College

EDITORS' INTRODUCTION

We have saved this chapter, the one "from the horse's mouth" so to speak, until now in spite of the fact that chronologically it preceded the two earlier chapters that have dealt with the Rassias method (7 and 28). It will be seen that Rassia's whole perspective on language teaching, acquisition, and use is somewhat broader than the applications described by others. Not only does Rassias insist on thunder and lightning audio-lingualism in this paper, originally published by the Peace Corps in 1970, but he gives somewhat deeper insight into his perception of what other authors have referred to as the "spirit" of language. The "dynamism and histrionics" of Wolkomir's commentary are still apparent and yet are noticeably subservient to the grander scheme which includes all sorts of opportunities and pressures to communicate in the target language. The conceptions of the "language dormitory" and the "in-country laboratory" are articulated to the Rassias madness in an eminently sane manner. It is easy to believe that students who participated in the whole process would indeed excel. Rassias says that the 70 students who participated during the second year of the program achieved the highest scores on the CEEB "ever recorded at Dartmouth."

Not too long ago the Peace Corps sought to stampede American universities from pastures of intellectual self-contentment by challenging them to assist in the new task of training volunteers for service abroad. As with most stampedes, chaos ensued.

In the beginning universities engaged "scrub" teams to do their jobs. They found language coordinators who were not integrally involved in their programs; they whipped together teams of nonprofessionals who were hired by an agency of the university, but not by the departments of languages themselves. Host country nationals brought over from their own countries, or hired from graduate schools in this country along with other native speakers of various languages, underwent intensive language workshops and were converted to semiprofessional teachers, who often displayed more enthusiasm, admittedly, than competence. Nevertheless, through constant supervision a highly effective level of proficiency was maintained and the job of language instruction was accomplished; it was accomplished so well that language instruction was often the most outstanding component of many Peace Corps training programs.

Slowly, at first, the impact of the Peace Corps made itself felt. The agency's prestige heightened when previously accepted methods of language instruction were seriously challenged by the special demands created by training programs on campus. The new techniques that were then brought to focus on the problem made language learning quick, accurate, and enduring. Language instruction proved effective, rewarding, and real. It became so real, in fact, that the acquisition of a foreign language became for many students a useful and inspiring experience. Questionnaires distributed to Peace Corps trainees (and later to our own students when we introduced the new courses) revealed: (1) that language learning was exciting, (2) that language teachers were alive, involved, capable, and (3) that the learning process was a practical, measurable, understandable phenomenon, not a vague, unrelated investment in one's future betterment.

In 1964, Dartmouth picked up the challenge. We have since had 5 years of experience with the Peace Corps in academe, and we are thoroughly satisfied with the results, which have been tested in every conceivable manner.

The Peace Corps became meaningful to Dartmouth College in quite the same way that it has become meaningful to host countries. Its effect was not immediate or radical, but it stirred things up: people began to talk about it; it created a climate of controversy and self-evaluation. Eventually, its influence helped change our approach and our philosophy of language instruction. We experimented and learned a lot in those years, and most of what we learned was channeled into our academic program.

It is obviously not the purpose of this chapter to say why language study is necessary. Are there among us those who still need convincing? The purpose of this chapter is to demonstrate two points: (1) the impact the Peace Corps exerted at Dartmouth, and (2) a different approach to the fulfillment of a language requirement in a humanities curriculum.

THE INSTITUTIONAL DINOSAUR IN PERSPECTIVE

Historically, language held its position in the humanities curriculum principally because of its contributions to general culture. Language training was not conceived primarily as an instrument to teach conversation or communication in any mundane sense; it concentrated largely on reading skills so vital to the appreciation of literature in the original language. Literature, that refined expression of a gentleman's liberal education, was viewed as the most important facet in language instruction. There is a strong case to be made in favor of this argument; however, our disagreement is less with the traditional assignment of priorities than with the injudicious use of these priorities.

A university, one feels, should deal in elevated thought. Literature, philosophy, history, science, and the like are fitting and proper for study.

Language learning, a more mechanical process, ought not therefore to be taken seriously by a respectable institution. The ethereal zones of thought cannot tolerate struggling utterances and—logic dictates—this mechanical and mechanized instruction ought to be consigned to high schools. A most respected member of our profession told me some time ago that language study is of such unsophisticated intellectual stature as to preclude it from ever being taken seriously, and a language teacher cannot consider distinguished instruction in this area a reason for promotion. This form of reasoning is still widespread in our universities, and some language departments treat books by grammarians as inferior pedagogical garbage; further, they assign the most inexperienced staff members to the instruction of languages. What new Ph.D. does not dread such courses? And given the conditions under which most Ph.D.s are reared, it is difficult to find a cogent argument to change their attitude.

The accumulation of experience over this long span of time should have wrought radical and frequent changes in the instruction of languages. Instead, language instruction became entangled in ivy-cloistered concepts of a gentleman's education.

Dartmouth College catalogues reveal certain mutations in the concept of language instruction through the years. (Catalogue, as a term, appeared first in 1820, but courses were not described to any extent until 1895.) In 1876, the study of French began in the sophomore year with Knapp's *Grammar* and *la France littéraire*.

In 1895, French was studied in the freshman year. In 1900, the word "pronunciation" appeared in the description of the "First Year Course," and held its place in all subsequent descriptions until 1956. Apparently, little was done to make pronunciation a part of language learning through realistic conversation; it was studied in a disembodied form, and never articulated properly to the language. The 1900, description then stressed: "Elements of Grammar (Fraser and Squair's *French Reader*, Erckmann-Chatrian's *Contes fantastiques*); memorizing and simple paraphrasing in French of portions of the text read."

The substance of the French 1 courses continued approximately the same up to 1918, when "Reading, writing, and speaking of easy French prose" appeared in the description. World War I taught members of the Department that, like Monsieur Jourdain, what they were actually speaking was prose, and in 1919 a significant change was made: one was taught the "speaking [of] simple French."

No further change was made until 1946 when Professor François Denoeu offered a substitute course for French 1, labeled "French 3–4 [credit for two courses], Intensive Course for Beginners." The course met 9 hours per week and aimed at a thorough grounding in spoken French and a "considerable ability in rapid silent reading." In 1947, the optional French 3–4 continued for two credits, and three of the nine meetings were devoted "to very small conversation groups."

In 1958, Dartmouth replaced the semester system by the trimester and its French courses were patterned this way:

French 1: An introduction to French as a spoken and written language. The work includes regular practice—both in class and in the laboratory—in understanding and using the spoken language. Elementary reading materials drawn from literary and other sources serve for vocabulary building, analytical exercises, and discussion.

French 2: Extensive reading of French classics of intermediate difficulty, with intensive analysis and interpretation of passages selected from them. Continued vocabulary building and more advanced practice, both in the classroom and in the language laboratory, in the use of the spoken language.

French 3: Further development of fluency in reading, skill in literary analysis, and oral competence, through the study of representative major works, discussed as far as possible in French. Laboratory exercises designed to complete mastery of basic language patterns and active vocabulary.

The optional French 3–4 was dropped, and the new 1, 2, 3, courses remained the same until 1963, when the phrase "drawn from literary and other sources" in the French 1 description was eliminated.

In 1966, a new approach was attempted. A double course (French 1–2: Intensive Introductory French) was designed to achieve in a single term maximum proficiency in the spoken language. "Class preparation," the catalogue reads, "is largely replaced by supervised work in the classroom and in the laboratory. Special language tables and dormitories provide maximum contact with the language. Course enrollment limited to twelve students."

The results obtained were acceptable, but not spectacular—in spite of the fact that students devoted two out of their three courses to the study of French. The program was perhaps still too "academic" and needed a stronger dosage of vigor and reality. We dropped this program from the curriculum after the first term, but it was a start in the right direction.

Before the present courses were established, we reviewed the entire panorama of language learning, its role in the humanities, and what we wanted it to accomplish.

PEACE CORPS LANGUAGE MODEL IN THE CURRICULUM

In the past, then, our courses embraced the following priorities: development of the student's speaking and comprehension capacity in French 1; improvement of the student's speaking ability, along with the enrichment of his vocabulary through literature and culture in French 2; deeper concentration on literature and culture in French 3.

Our experience in regular Peace Corps language training taught us that a beginning student can comfortably attain a speaking level of S-2+[1] in 1 month under immersion pressure. We decided to concentrate on achieving a year's goal in one term (10 weeks), if possible, and in two terms at the most.

This new approach would not neglect training in reading and writing, lest the end result be the creation of orally fluent illiterates. Nor would we depart from the humanities tradition, for along with the excitement of language instruction in

---

1. A short definition of this level of proficiency, established by the Foreign Service Institute, Washington, D.C., is S-2: able to satisfy routine social demands and limited work requirements with confidence but not with facility; S-2+: exceeds S-2 primarily in fluency or either grammar or vocabulary. (See Allan Kulakow, To speak as equals. *Faculty Paper* 1, p. 6.)

a new mold, we wanted to continue broadening a student's comprehension of culture and literature. We would attempt to do the job more efficiently by making it possible, according to accomplishment on the College Board examinations, for a beginner to proceed to relatively sophisticated literary studies in his second term.

A thorough overhaul of procedures was required. We decided to block off the amount of time a student traditionally devoted to a course and immerse him in language study during that time span. A team-teaching staff was established to carry out the operation. We assigned 5 hours per week to classroom study of the language with a faculty member (master teacher), 5 hours to drill in a class with a qualified undergraduate (apprentice teacher), and 5 hours to work in the language laboratory under the close supervision of a qualified student monitor. We based our scheduling on the traditional and unwritten law which commits a student to 2 hours of preparation for every hour devoted to class. This gave us a combination of 5 hours of actual class time, together with 10 hours of controlled study time—a formula that obviously excluded unstructured homework. The student would receive one course credit for his work.

We designated our French classes for pilot experimentation, along with one class of Modern Greek. Further, we decided to make all sections intensive: no freshman had a choice in deciding whether to study these languages in the "traditional" or in this "new" way. In our second year we included Spanish and Italian in the program.

Once the schedule was decided we took a close look at our instructional needs. I have defined elsewhere the qualities we sought in our Peace Corps language teachers (Rassias 1968); we used the same criteria to staff this new program. In a word, along with indispensable professional competency in the language, we sought *vitality* in our people. Our teachers must be in total command of the language, and they must also be firebrands and actors. Dynamism and histrionics are requisite not only to convey the subject matter more effectively, but also to give students a model of the uninhibited suppleness they will need to live the language experience more thoroughly.

We were aware that some of the apprentices would seek careers in teaching. The vitality we insisted on served notice to them to abandon our ranks if they could not lose the stuffed-shirt dignity that prevented them from exuding the reality of a language. "Language," we said in our workshop for teachers, "is a living, kicking, growing, fleeting, evolving reality, and the teacher should spontaneously reflect its vibrant and protean qualities" (Rassias 1968).

Our professional staff was asked to dedicate itself to the task by accepting the many new strains this program would place on them. This degree of commitment is rarely demanded in a normal academic setting.

Next, we turned to our most qualified undergraduates—French nationals on campus, senior students (majors or nonmajors) who had spent time in France and whose spoken French was excellent—and invited them to attend a workshop one week prior to the fall term. These students knew that they would not all be selected for positions, and the atmosphere of competition was electric.

Again, using the same techniques we employ in language workshops for the Peace Corps, we conducted demonstration lessons in modern Greek for the apprentice teachers. Each demonstration covered a variety of teaching skills: backward buildup, pattern drills, dialogue learning, conversation exercises, testing the learning of materials, and means of energizing a class. Greek was used to acquaint the apprentice teacher with the problems his peers have when they approach the study of a foreign language.

The apprentice teacher was obliged to prepare and present several lessons every day during the workshop. Each session was followed by general criticism, self-criticism, and group evaluation: strengths and weaknesses were frankly evaluated in relation to the method. We worked hard to establish the ultimate model of teaching effectiveness. The commandments we use as guidelines for the Peace Corps were carefully reviewed and the relevancy of the concepts was discussed with the apprentice teachers. The basic and inescapable theme was that no other method would be tolerated in this program. Some of the "commandments" which the apprentice teacher learned to obey are:

1. Always stand, move about; your animation should be natural and should involve the class.

2. Do not be too slow or too fast. Always speak at your normal conversational pace.

3. Pronounce everything distinctly.

4. Keep students' books closed.

5. Do not name the student before asking him to recite. Make all students participate in class. Indeed, if you do not name them or give other outward indications before asking a student to recite, *all* the students will be on the alert since they know that it may fall arbitrarily upon one of them to answer. In order not to lose a single student's interest, use a "shotgun" approach, viz., look at one student but point to the one whose turn it is to recite *after* you pose the question. Like lightning, the question should strike first, and like the thunder that follows (stimulated by a loud finger snap), you should immediately designate the person to be queried.

6. Do not follow a set pattern in your interrogation. Do not ask questions in the order of student A, student B, then student C, etc., but change the pattern of interrogation each time.

7. Do not wait for a delayed answer. If the student hesitates go to the next person and then return to the one that did not answer.

8. Correct every mistake and make the student repeat the correction properly.

9. Do not abandon a subject which the students do not grasp.

10. Speak only in the target language—in and out of the class.

The need to close gaps in time, experience, and expertise was apparent here, as with Peace Corps training. To teach skills to teachers who are largely inexperienced calls for a well-conceived methodology to which all staff members must subscribe. Our problem was more difficult because we were dealing with students who had never taught before in their lives. They not only lacked experience and the resources of imagination that experience creates, but also the confidence so necessary to an effective classroom presentation.

To withhold instruction to the staff because of some sense of misdirected academic freedom, or to allow the staff to do as it pleases, might cause differences of a harmful nature to arise. Teachers may gain or lose popularity by their individual performances, but students will, in general, suffer the consequences.

It is important that all master teachers and apprentice teachers adhere to one system in order to make possible staff rotation. This allows the student to be exposed to various accents, intonations, and speaking personalities which are part of language or which in fact are language. Peace Corps taught us that one person—the teacher—is not the language. It is too great a danger to allow one model to serve as a symbol of a country. This may lead to an identification with the teacher's deficiencies, creating psychological blocks toward the whole country. One then runs the risk of developing love or hatred for the language by exposure to a single model. In addition, rapid rotation creates new pressures which keep instructors and students alert. The instructors gain more objectivity through the changes; the students lose any sense of overconfidence or other bad habits developed under one instructor (for familiarity also breeds tolerance). Thus, benefits accrue from rotation and no time is lost by forcing students to adjust to individual techniques.

After the workshop training, the apprentice teachers were ready to begin teaching. They worked in close cooperation with their master teachers and they met with me weekly to discuss problems in teaching. These weekly sessions also involved continuing shock lessons in Greek, in order to remind the apprentice teachers of the necessity to adhere to a single methodology.

To reinforce further the necessity of our methodology I visited daily as many classes as other duties would allow, and then gave each of the apprentice teachers a critique of his work.

It is important to stress that the apprentice teacher never attempted to instruct material not previously covered by the master teacher and reviewed by the students in the language laboratory.

We also decided that the apprentices may work only two of the three terms in any given year. This is a precaution we exercise so that they will in no way neglect their own studies.

In our first year of operation we employed 22 apprentices in French in the fall term, nine in French and one in modern Greek in the winter, and in the spring, one in French. In our second year (1968–1969) we employed 27 apprentices in French, 11 in Spanish, 2 in Italian in the fall, 16 in French, 6 in Spanish, 2 in Italian, 1 in modern Greek in the winter, and in the spring, 5 in French.

It has been pointed out that the amount of energy apprentice teachers channeled into their teaching generated a greater interest on their part in different levels of departmental activity. This interest was demonstrated partially by more frequent discussion with the professorial staff. More to the point, this new system encouraged the present generation of students to become directly involved in education at Dartmouth.

The student teachers were placed in demanding circumstances, and every one of them benefited from the experience. They were forced—like Peace Corps volunteers—to function at their highest level of ability. Unlike regular teachers in university work, they could not afford *not* to be at their best every day. And this experience had salubrious effects in more than a personal sense: the apprentice teachers' grades all improved in their academic subjects during their employment.

SOME MEASUREMENTS OF ACHIEVEMENT

What did this course accomplish? A very distinct rise in morale and achievement occurred. On the first day of classes we asked the students not to question the validity of our procedures at the outset. We asked them to cooperate and let time, their good will, and their assiduity prove the efficacy of our methods.

Interest in foreign languages rose sharply, along with the belief that knowledge of a foreign language makes one a better student. Not only did student morale attain levels never before encountered in language instruction at the college, but the morale of our instructors rose accordingly. One wrote to me, and I quote at length:

> There is no question in my mind that the new French 2 . . . represents a vast improvement over the old French 2. Above all the students enjoyed the work in this course, partly because the material they dealt with was stimulating, partly because they realized that after many years (some of them had already had some high school French) they were at last learning some French.
>
> The increased exposure to public oral practice and drill through the use of drill masters meant not only the student's work was under close supervision and available for immediate correction of errors, but that he had ample opportunity to overcome his fear and self-consciousness at speaking in a foreign language. The students did not evince resentment of the teaching role assumed by their peers. . . . The presence of the drill masters had a salutary effect in that it was a constant reminder to the students that French could be learned by others like themselves.
>
> They gained in this course a spontaneity in all skills which they lacked in the past. The improvement in student response and the new level of morale in French 2 more than justifies continuing this course under the present new system.

Statistically, we were able to raise the scores on the College Board examinations. We had truly outstanding results in comparison with previous years. In French 2 the *average* midterm increase of each student in CEEB scores in our first term of operation was 75 points. Although we were pleased with the results of the fall term, those of the winter term were conclusively superior. A comparison of the average grades earned by our students in both the *Reading* and *Listening* exams at the end of the fall and winter terms shows an improvement over the "old," traditional methods, and further demonstrates that students prepared in French 1 at the college (under "new" methods) do decisively better in French 2 than their classmates prepared elsewhere.

In no case do we abandon liberal arts values in this new approach. Our experimentation in language never strays from the liberal arts tradition of shaping the whole man; as efficiently as possible we want to give that man more than one voice. We value the aid language learning contributes to thought processes, but we also recognize the stark necessity of working up to that goal, rather than starting from the top with the hope that the oral phase will somehow take care of itself. For one to appreciate what language can do he should logically appreciate what it does. We considered communication our fundamental goal and got fully behind the attempt to realize that goal.

In reviewing our class structure, we decided that normal class sizes would have to be lowered to accomplish the task. Adapting Peace Corps criteria to class enrollments, we placed a ceiling of 14 students on each class with the regular faculty, and reduced our drill sessions to 7 each. Student involvement in class increased considerably and morale rose as our students found themselves talking, participating in the language. Language, as they experienced each day, could be lived and they were living it.

Students indicated in a questionnaire that their participation in the work and their steady, measurable progress in speaking, comprehending, reading, and writing were among the course's outstanding features.

Our priorities were: (1) communication, (2) cultural orientation, (3) literature.

Behind each class was a concept of dynamism that carried instructors and students through hard work. Not one minute was wasted in the business of teaching and learning. No slackness in pacing induced sleep; no distractions led students off their course. We used telephone calls to inject realism in the language, psychodrama to force students to use their vocabulary in conditions of stress, and debates and interviews to create the unpredictable nature of language usage.

THE LANGUAGE DORMITORY

Supplementary motivation was designed into this program by the addition of two distinctive features: (1) a language dormitory, and (2) the possibility for any student *after one term of language study at Dartmouth* to continue study and involvement in-country.[2]

We deem it essential to house in one dormitory language students involved in the ongoing phase of our foreign language program. The language dormitory has language booths available for use at any time.

---

2. We have been operating a foreign study program since 1958. Today we have foreign study centers in 17 cities in 10 countries. Participation in the foreign study programs requires an advanced knowledge of a language (six courses) and is open to all students regardless of major. Foreign language programs are available to any student who takes one course of beginning French, Spanish, or Italian.

It is in the language dormitory that we will benefit from the expanded education and outlook of students returning from foreign study and eager to communicate new information to their classmates, as well as to speak in the foreign language with them. This exchange of views and the additional practice in language better prepared our prospective foreign study students for their stay abroad.

The language dormitory permits immersion to occur in the language. The vocabulary involved in this area—the daily living routine—reinforces the basic elements in language learning and permits class hours to become involved in more sophisticated patterns of thought. This environment has also proved conducive to relatively sophisticated "bull sessions" in the foreign language.

The language dormitory serves as a Foreign Language Center in which students have the opportunity to meet and present papers. They also have the opportunity to read foreign language newspapers and periodicals. The Foreign Language Center houses collections of records, tapes, and books.

Ultimately, the language dormitory will serve as the home for a visiting writer in residence whose function will be to talk to our students on subjects of his personal interest. He will not teach a regular course but will, on occasion, call seminar sessions to discuss contemporary topics, or his own work.

THE IN-COUNTRY LABORATORY

In 1968, our first group of students to go abroad in the new foreign language program reported to Dartmouth on August 25. They were immersed in French. The schedule was a straightforward 8 hours per day in language classes for 4 weeks, including 1 hour of language laboratory per day. In addition to their daily classes, they shared a common dormitory and ate together in an isolated dining room on campus. All of our Peace Corps expertise was put into action by three dynamic teachers (one master teacher and two apprentice teachers). On September 25 they flew to Bourges, France, where they continued their studies in our Centre d'Enseignement Intensif du Français.

In Bourges they lived with French families (one student per family) and took on a heavy program of studies. The students devoted 4 hours each morning to intensive language study in small groups with native instructors who had been prepared in our methodology of teaching. The students took all their meals with their French families. In the afternoon they were involved in one course in culture-civilization and another in literature. All told, they devoted 44 hours weekly to study in class and to homework assignments.

Our experience with the Peace Corps in in-country training programs enabled us to establish a substantive approach to immersion in French culture, and not merely to involve our students with languages in a French setting.

We tried to structure the courses so that the students would be completely involved in what they wanted to learn, while maintaining a sound academic control on presentation of the subject matter. To introduce the subject of religion, for instance, we had the students first read topical articles involving the role of religion in contemporary France. We discussed its meaning in the cultural life of the city, and then we brought in a priest to give his own views and answer student questions. When the local press was discussed we had the students study local newspapers and we arranged for the director of the *Nouvelle République* to speak on the influence of the regional press on French political thinking. This was followed by a review of the political structure in France. The pattern was always similar, i.e., study of articles on the subject, discussion in class, confrontation with spokesmen in each area, and continued discussion of the subject in the homes. In this light the families chosen to participate in our program gave us full assurance of their willingness to become involved in all necessary efforts.

In the second year of operation (and over three terms) we sent 70 students to Bourges, France, to continue their in-country training, and 18 to San José, Costa Rica, for study of Spanish in the spring term.

Upon returning to campus these students took the CEEB examinations. Their scores were the highest we have ever recorded at Dartmouth. Their oral facility was uniformly excellent, as established by the FSI testing.

CONCLUSION

Our continuing goal is to serve the cause of the humanities in an effective way. (Students in our Foreign Language Centers will be able to apply two course credits toward fulfillment of the humanities distributive requirement, in addition to satisfying the language requirement.) More significantly, we want to place our students in the culture and give them the opportunity to realize the goals of a true education in the humanities by actually communicating with other people and by actually understanding them. Then, in the best meaning of John Stuart Mill's definition of a liberal education, they will return—as a result of this experience in language—as sensitive students to become sensitive doctors, sensitive engineers, and sensitive lawyers.

A substantial number of students who participated in these programs continue their studies of literature, carrying over into their work an entirely different set of attitudes compared with their nonparticipating classmates. They do not worry about performing in the language; they move rapidly into our most advanced courses. They have experienced a process of change and growth in another culture, and these new dimensions in a liberal education have made them more sensitive, more curious, and more concerned students.

DISCUSSION QUESTIONS

1. Rassias writes of language instructors who are "firebrands and actors" capable of "histrionics" and "dynamism" in order to give students a "model of the uninhibited suppleness they will need to live the language experience more thoroughly" (p. 367). Compare this remark and the meaning it entails with the philosophies of other authors who advocate a lowering of the "affective filter" and a consequent unshackling of the self within.

2. Discuss the merits of studying an exotic language (or at least an unknown one; at Dartmouth in the late sixties they used Greek) while in training to become a language teacher. What perspectives can be gained from putting yourself into the shoes of the students you will eventually be teaching?

3. Compare Rassias' use of "general criticism, self-criticism, and group evaluation" with the nonevaluative methods advocated by other language teachers and teacher trainers. The carefree use of the term "commandments" creates a certain authoritarian impression. Is it possible that such limits might enhance the freedom of the teacher who wholeheartedly accepted them? Or, would you perhaps prefer to amend the Rassias "commandments"? If so, how?

4. Discuss Rassias' argument for multiple models rather than a single teacher who "represents the language."

5. To what extent would you attribute the successes of the Rassias method to thunder and lightning audiolingualism, as opposed to high levels of input generated by the dormitory concept, psychodrama, debate, and the like?

Chapter 30

Scripts and Second Language Reading Skills

Shirley J. Adams
American Council of Teachers of Foreign Languages

EDITORS' INTRODUCTION

This chapter may seem a bit out of place in view of the fact that all of the others in this section deal with language acquisition as a whole rather than any particular modality of processing. However, we believe that reading skills per se merit special attention. In the last couple of decades, of the language teaching methods that have achieved some evidence of success, nearly all emphasize oral skills above literacy. To be sure literacy is not excluded in any of the methods included in our smorgasbord, but usually it isn't served up as a main dish either. Therefore, we believe that many readers will find that the present entry will help to balance off the meal, and it does fit into this section insofar as it reports on research results. Further, it complements many of the previous entries (but especially Chapters 1 and 2 of Part I, Pragmatic Orientations). Although her tone and methodology are decisively more technical than those of other authors, Adams's conclusions are highly pertinent to much of what is said elsewhere in the volume. The importance of "meaningful sequence" and of the sort of script-based knowledge which makes the negotiation of such a sequence possible is experimentally demonstrated. The critical hypothesis which is established is that script activation helps both first and second language readers. As expected, first language readers outperform second language readers, but interestingly scripts help both types of readers about equally.

Several first-language reading studies demonstrate the importance of vocabulary in the reading comprehension process. Davis (1971) conducted factor analyses of component skills in reading and found a knowledge of words to be the essential component in reading comprehension. Kruse (1979) states that vocabulary is of prime importance in reading. In a critical review of readability formulas, Chall (1958) found that a measure of vocabulary load was the major factor in almost all readability formulas. Loban (1970) points out that studies of children's language development show a high correlation between preschoolers' knowledge of word meanings and achievement in reading at higher grade levels.

Two studies in second language reading also point to the importance of vocabulary in the reading process. Yorio (1971) administered a questionnaire to native speakers of Spanish and found that students felt vocabulary constituted their main problem in reading English. In her analysis of the second-language reading process, Phillips (1974) found that vocabulary and syntactical errors often prevented correct interpretation of a sentence.

Along with vocabulary, a reader's background knowledge has been shown to be an important component of reading comprehension. The background experiences children bring to a reading selection affect how well they can understand it, according to studies by Gordon, Hansen, and Pearson (1978). Chiesi, Spilich, and Voss (1979) created a knowledge structure for the game of baseball. The researchers presented passages of baseball-related information to individuals with high or low knowledge of that game. The experiments demonstrated that high-knowledge individuals anticipated a greater percentage of high-level baseball information than did low-knowledge individuals. In addition, high-knowledge individuals recalled more event sequences than did low-knowledge individuals. Results from these and other studies in first-language reading prompted an investigation of the possible effects of relevant background knowledge upon an aspect of comprehension that is particularly important in second-language reading—guessing the meaning of unfamiliar vocabulary.[1]

Background knowledge, however, is difficult to assess when conducting an experimental study. Script theory therefore was used in this research. Schank and Abelson (1977) have developed a model of comprehension based on scripts. A script is defined by these authors as "a structure that describes appropriate sequences of events in a particular context . . . a script is a predetermined, stereotyped sequence of actions that defines a well-known situation" (p. 41). One example is a restaurant script [also see Schank 1980]. People generally know what to expect and what to do when entering a particular restaurant. They have certain expectations of the order of events that will occur in a three-star restaurant or in one specializing in fast foods. According to script theory, this order of events and information concerning types of restaurants is found in the various slots or components of the restaurant script. For example, before going to a three-star restaurant, one would call to make a reservation, arrive at the restaurant at the appointed time, have drinks, order, eat, pay the bill, leave a tip, etc. Once this script has been established, it can be applied to almost any three-star restaurant. The procedures and sequences of events at a fast-food restaurant will differ, of course, from those associated with its three-star counterpart. To emphasize the importance of scripts, consider the uneasiness that one might feel when trying to apply a fast-food restaurant script in a three-star restaurant, or in a restaurant in another country such as Japan, where procedures vary from those in an American restaurant.

Researchers have conducted studies using script (schema) theory in conjunction with reading comprehension. The different schemata (or scripts) that individuals bring into play when reading a text can be manipulated by giving them ambiguous passages to read. Schallert (1976) developed passages that could be given two distinct interpretations. The interpretations that subjects

---

1. For other studies see Pearson, Hansen, and Gordon 1979; Ribovich 1979; Spilich, Vesonder, Chiesi, and Voss 1979; Bransford and Johnson 1972.

gave to the passages were strongly related to the title. When no title or introduction was present, the script by which subjects processed ambiguous passages depended on their background experiences. Obtaining similar results, Anderson, Reynolds, Schallert, and Goetz (1976) constructed one passage that could be interpreted as an evening of playing cards or as a rehearsal of a woodwind ensemble, and another passage that could be interpreted as a convict planning his escape from prison, or as a wrestler hoping to break the hold of an opponent. The two passages were read by a group of physical education students and a group of music students. Test scores indicated that the interpretation given to passages was strongly related to the subjects' background. As the research by Schallert demonstrated, a particular script can be activated (i.e., a particular interpretation can be given) by presenting the subject with a title or introduction that tells what the passage is about.

A relationship between script theory and vocabulary recognition was established by Wittrock, Marks, and Doctorow (1975) in experiments with sixth grade children. The researchers found that stories familiar to the students facilitated the learning of unfamiliar, undefined vocabulary words as well as comprehension of the text. A situation in which stories are already familiar to the students is similar to a situation in which students possess the appropriate script for a reading passage. Both situations allow the readers to predict and anticipate events or information contained in the text.

People possess many different scripts that are "called up" or activated, often unconsciously whenever they are needed. For this study, the reading passages were based on common knowledge (scripts) about everyday tasks or activities that would be familiar to American college students. Background knowledge about a task or activity was controlled by either activating the scripts (telling the students what the passages were about) or not activating them (not telling the students what they were about to read).

PURPOSE OF THE STUDY

This study investigated the effects of statements designed to activate scripts on measures of unfamiliar vocabulary with American college students reading in French and in English. Specifically, the following directional hypotheses were tested: (1) subjects receiving script activators before reading will score higher on measures of unfamiliar vocabulary than subjects receiving no script activators; (2) subjects reading in their native language will receive higher scores on measures of unfamiliar vocabulary than subjects reading in the second language (French); (3) a greater difference will exist between the unfamiliar vocabulary mean scores of the French script/no script activator groups than between the mean scores of the English script/no script activator groups. This third hypothesis was based on the assumption that script activators would aid second-language readers more than their native-language counterparts because the former do not have the same facility with a second language as the latter have with their own. Native-language readers should be able to obtain cues from the written text and create context even when no script activator is provided, whereas second-language readers often need additional or extralinguistic cues to aid comprehension.

DESIGN

A partial hierarchical design was used for this study (J. Kennedy 1978). The first independent variable, language, had two levels—French and English. The second one, availability of script activator, also had two levels—script activator and no script activator, and was nested within levels of language. Groups or classrooms were built into the design as the third independent variable to control for individual classroom effects. The dependent variable consisted of one response measure–the total score received for the number of times the target word was correctly recognized by each subject for all six passages. Each passage consisted of five responses worth one point for each correct response for a total of thirty possible points for all six passages. An incorrect response was scored as zero. If an item was left blank, it was scored as minus one.

POPULATION AND SAMPLE

The population from which the sample of subjects for this study was drawn consisted of all students enrolled in third-quarter French and in an introductory psychology course at Ohio State University. Eight French classes and eight groups of psychology students took part in the study. The students from psychology were not enrolled simultaneously in any of the French classes and vice versa. A total of 298 subjects participated—124 French students and 174 psychology students. Most of the French and psychology students were fulfilling a course requirement, and were between 18 and 22 years of age. Participation in the study was voluntary, owing to procedures required by the Human Subjects Committee of the university.

MATERIALS AND PROCEDURES

The construction of the six reading passages used in this study was similar to those in Hoffman (1979) who used contextual buildup during reading. A target word was established that was closely associated with the activity or task described in the passage. The target word from each passage was replaced by a nonsense word that resembled real French. The nonsense words used in this study were rated by six native French speakers and eight French-speaking colleagues as to how French-looking they were. Each passage consisted of five sections with each section containing one instance of the target word.[2] Each of the six passages contained approximately 70 to 75 words. Topics included everyday tasks or activities that American college students could be assumed to have in their realm of experience. Two of the topics were adapted from a study on comprehension and recall by Bransford and Johnson.[3] Topics included playing tennis, grocery shopping, flying a kite, doing laundry, washing dishes, and a wedding. The passages were written first in French, then translated into English for use by the psychology students.

The same procedures were used for both the French classes and the psychology students. Four of the French classes and four of the psychology groups (randomly selected) were given statements (script activators) telling what the passages were about, while the remaining groups received no statements. All students received a booklet of instructions and answer sheets. Students completed an example in English before they began reading the six passages.

The passages were presented to students on transparencies by means of an overhead projector. This medium was used to control the length of reading time. Each section of each passage was masked and then revealed one at a time for 30 seconds. The amount of time was determined by the pilot study. Students were

---

2. Following are two of the reading passages used in the study:

A. Script activator (given orally in English): "This passage is about flying a kite."

1.   Favorable conditions are necessary in order to do this activity. That is, you have to have
     1
     enough *rouche.*
                    2
2.   If there is too much *rouche*, the object might break.
                                                           3
3.   But if conditions are too calm, you will have problems because the *rouche* makes the objects go up.
4.   If there are obstacles, a serious problem can result because you cannot control the
     4
     rouche.
             5
5.   Usually the *rouche* is most favorable during the spring.

B. Script activator: "This passage is about playing tennis."
                                                           1
1.   Il faut avoir certains objets pour cette activité—surtout un *rauvre.*
2.   On peut faire cette activité à l'extérieur ou dans un bâtiment, mais en tous cas, le   2
     rauvre doit avoir des dimensions spécifiques.
                    3
3.   On peut rester très prés du *rauvre* ou on peut en être assez loin.
                                                                       4
4.   Le but de cette activité est d'envoyer un des objets nécessaires au-dessus du *rauvre.*
     5
5.   Mais quelquefois le *rauvre* devient un obstacle pour un des objets nécessaires.
     3. See note 1 above.

not permitted to look back at the preceding section because it was masked after the allotted time. Those groups randomly selected to receive script activators received them orally in English before the first section of the passage was revealed.

ANALYSIS AND RESULTS

An analysis of variance appropriate for a partial hierarchical design was conducted on the data. Table 1 presents the means and standard deviations of the unfamiliar vocabulary scores for the language and script activator variables. An examination of Table 1 suggests strong main effects for both variables. Students who received script activators before reading the passages achieved higher vocabulary scores ($\overline{X} = 20.93$) than students who received no script activators ($\overline{X} = 0.75$). Students who read in English received higher vocabulary scores ($\overline{X} = 13.58$) than those reading in French ($\overline{X} = 8.10$).

Table 2 summarizes the analysis of variance. The main-effect variables (language and script activator) proved to be significant. The analysis of variance confirmed the findings suggested by Table 1. The language variable was significant beyond the .001 level ($F[1, 12] = 895.53$) as was the script activator variable ($F[1, 12] = 66.10$).

DISCUSSION AND CONCLUSIONS

A review of results confirmed two of the three hypotheses tested in this study. Significant differences were found between the means of both the language variable (French/English) and the script variable (script activator/no script activator). Students who read in English scored significantly higher than those who read in French. Likewise, students receiving script activators received significantly higher scores than those who received no script activators. The third hypothesis (the interaction of the script and language variables) was not confirmed by the study. Although the interaction was not statistically significant, the difference between the mean scores of the French script/no script activator groups was slightly higher ($\overline{X} = 20.87$) than the difference between the mean scores of the English script/no script activator groups ($\overline{X} = 19.44$). The French no script activator groups also tended to leave more blanks than their English counterparts ($\overline{X} = -2.37$ for French as opposed to $\overline{X} = 3.86$ for the English). The English no script activator groups appeared to be able to create some kind of context from the readings and to supply responses to the unfamiliar vocabulary words even though the responses were often incorrect.

One explanation for the lack of significant interaction could be found in the level of language proficiency of the students who read in French. The script activators might be more beneficial to second-language readers with low language proficiency than to readers with high language proficiency. That is, the

Table 1   Means and Standard Deviations of Vocabulary Scores by Language and Availability of Script Activator

	French			English			Overall		
	N	Mean	SD	N	Mean	SD	N	Mean	SD
Script activator	65	18.56	1.95	83	23.30	2.76	148	20.93	2.43
No script activator	59	− 2.37	3.50	91	3.86	1.47	150	.75	2.47
Overall	124	8.10	2.79	174	13.58	2.17	298	10.84	2.44

Table 2   Analysis of Variance of Vocabulary Scores by Language, Script Activator, and Group

Source	df	MS	F
A (Language)	1	26898.4870	895.53*
B (Script activator)	1	1985.5678	66.10*
AB	1	36.8077	1.23
C/AB (Group)	12	30.0365	1.20
S/C/AB	282	25.0246	
Total	297		

$*p < .001$

higher the proficiency level, the less impact the script activators would have because the students would be able to create a context from the linguistic cues in the text itself. This explanation would be consistent with Mueller's research (1979, 1980). Although his study dealt with a contextual visual, the principle involved is similar. Mueller found that a contextual visual does not seem to enhance comprehension in higher levels of language proficiency. Context is derived from the actual *Linguistic* cues rather than the visual.

In order to lend support to the above explanation further research should be conducted that incorporates levels of language proficiency along with the language and script variables used in this study. Another avenue of investigation lies in studying the same variables used in this study, but testing one student at a time rather than testing groups of students. By using this method of testing, time latencies could be recorded, and comparisons could be made with regard to the time a student required to record the first response as opposed to each succeeding response for a passage. Information from these data could be used to study characteristics of reading passages that would facilitate the decoding of unfamiliar vocabulary.

This study revealed the importance of preparing readers for what they are about to read. Teachers who create or select reading materials should keep in mind the backgrounds and present knowledge of their students. For example, reading selections for a beginning French class should include topics with which the students are already familiar rather than selections dealing exclusively with the target country or culture. Even though beginning students may not know all of the vocabulary in a reading selection, they are less likely to feel frustrated in their first attempts with a new language if the topic of the reading selection is already familiar to them.

DISCUSSION QUESTIONS

1. Discuss the components of a "restaurant script" and how they might enter into the task of reading a text that is set in a famous Parisian restaurant. Consider other scripts as well. In what ways might psychodrama, socio-drama, the audio-motor units of Kalivoda et al., and similar techniques from other authors be used to help students build or modify appropriate scripts? By the way, should scripts be "learned" or "acquired" in the second language classroom?

2. In what way does a script typically incorporate the principle of "meaningful sequence" or "episodic organization"? Discuss the exemplary texts used by Adams (in footnote 2). In what ways do they possess the normal properties of episodic organization and in what ways do they fall short?

3. Do you agree with the prediction that second language students should rely more on script activation than native speakers operating in their first language? Why or why not? How would you account for the fact that there was no significant difference in the benefits of script activation for natives and nonnatives?

4. What implications for teaching of texts and in particular for the teaching of reading skills do you see in this chapter? How do you see it linking up with the sort of task recommended by de Berkeley-Wykes in Chapter 23?

Chapter 31

Home-School Language Switching

Merrill Swain
Ontario Institute for Studies in Education

EDITORS' INTRODUCTION

In this chapter, Swain discusses one of the largest and best-documented educational experiments of this century—namely, the Canadian experience for nearly two decades with French "immersion" programs. She also discusses why it is that such programs have proved to be successful in teaching French as a second language as well as in teaching school subject matter while some corresponding "submersion" programs in the United States and elsewhere have resulted only in weak to inadequate second language acquisition and failure in school achievement. To help explain the contrast, Swain invokes Cummins's "threshold hypothesis." It suggests that in order to profit from instruction in subject matter provided through the medium of a second language it is necessary for the students first to have achieved a certain minimal level of comprehension and skill in the second language—they must be at "threshold" level. This achievement, Cummins argues, can only be accomplished comfortably if the students have first reached "threshold" in their native language. Swain goes on to discuss, then, some of the contrasts between the skills of children in French immersion programs and native speakers of French. For instance, she observes that the immersion students tend to retain certain "errors" which tend to become "fossilized" (in Selinker's term). It may be of some interest to compare Swain's observations about these "fossilized forms" with those of Savignon (Chapter 19) concerning the retention of certain nonnativisms by her children in a "natural" environment.

The term "home-school language switch" has been used to refer to contexts in which the language of communication at home is different from the language of instruction in school[1]—a situation not uncommon for students in many parts of the world. Under these circumstances, second language learning necessarily becomes an integral part of the students' lives. In this chapter, three types of programs involving a home-school language switch are described and compared in order to account for contradictory research findings which have emerged in relation not only to second language learning, but to academic achievement as well.

---

1. Although I refer to *languages* of the home and school throughout this chapter, the situations described incorporate as well those in which home and school *dialects* differ.

SECOND LANGUAGE IMMERSION

Immersion refers to a situation in which children from the same linguistic and cultural background who have had no prior contact with the school language are put together in a classroom setting in which the second language is used as the medium of instruction.

One example of an immersion program is that of French immersion in Canada. The initiative for such a program in the public school system began with a small group of parents in St. Lambert, a suburb of Montreal, whose primary concern was that the level of French attained by their children in a traditional French-as-a-second-language (FSL) program would not be sufficient to meet their needs in a community and country that was increasingly emphasizing the importance of French as a *langue de travail.* As one parent put it, "many of us had learned French in high school, but had graduated with very little proficiency in it, in addition to having a big inferiority complex about second language learning" (Parkes 1972). They did not want the same for their children—they wanted their children to be able to function in an environment in which the language of work was French. Nothing was said about attaining a nativelike command of the language. They were, however, convinced that if French was used as a medium of communication—as a means to an end rather than as an end in itself—second language learning would be enhanced.

Today, French immersion programs exist in every province and in every major city of Canada. The students in a French immersion program are for the most part English-speaking children who have had little or no exposure to French before entering school. English is the language of their home and immediate community environment.

The typical format of a French immersion program at the primary grade levels is that all instruction is given in French until grade 2 cr grade 3, when English Language Arts is introduced and taught in English for approximately an hour a day. With each successive year thereafter a larger proportion of the curriculum is taught in English until an approximately equal balance is reached between the time devoted to instruction in each language.

The term *immersion* has led to many a misconception of what actually occurs in a French immersion class. Although it *is* the case that French is the only language used by the teacher, it is *not* the case that it is the only language used by the children. During much of the first year in a primary-level French immersion program, the children continue to speak English among themselves and to their teacher, who, although a native speaker of French, is bilingual and therefore can understand the children when they use their native language. It is not until the second year of the program that the teacher begins to insist that the children attempt to express their ideas in French and, through a gradual transition, French comes to be established as the language of the classroom.

Many of the French immersion programs in Canada have been evaluated, and the results have been remarkably consistent across programs and geographical areas (see Swain 1976a for a bibliography of research on immersion education).

Generally speaking, in the evaluations of French immersion programs, four basic questions have been examined:

1. Are the children enrolled in the French immersion program more proficient in French than they would be if they took an FSL program (20 to 40 minutes a day of formal French instruction)?

2. Does prolonged exposure to a second language result in some loss of facility in the students' native language?

3. Does instruction in a second language about a specific subject (for example, mathematics) affect the students' achievement in that subject?

4. Does the learning of a second language affect the child's IQ and general cognitive development?

Answers to these questions have been sought by administering tests of French language skills, English language skills, subject-area knowledge, and IQ to the students in the French immersion program and comparing their results with those of students with similar background characteristics enrolled in a regular English program and studying FSL.

Generally speaking, the results show:

1. French immersion programs lead to the development of French skills far superior to those of students following an FSL program. How the French immersion children perform in relation to native speakers of French will be discussed below.

2. Prior to the introduction of formal training in English Language Arts, students in the primary French immersion program do not perform as well as their English-taught peers in English skills. However, they quickly catch up to their peers if they are introduced to formal instruction in English Language Arts at the grade 2, 3 or 4 level. In fact, the data suggest that in some aspects of English language skills, the immersion students outperform their English-instructed peers by grade 5 or 6.

3. Where achievement in subject areas taught in French has been tested in English, French immersion students perform as well as their English-taught peers.

4. Students who have attended several years of a primary French immersion program do not appear to be disadvantaged in terms of cognitive development. They continue to perform as well on standardized IQ tests as their English-taught peers. Additionally, there is some evidence which suggests that by the later grades, certain aspects of cognitive functioning may have been enhanced (see Cummins 1978b for a review).

Thus the overall picture which emerges from the studies related to primary-level French immersion programs is a positive one. Many educators have referred to the documented success of the French immersion programs in

Canada as evidence that it is in fact possible to learn both a second language *and* subject matter at the same time. Indeed the success of the immersion programs has led to a tenuous extension of this line of reasoning. The success of the immersion program has been used to argue against the necessity of education in the mother tongue in cases where the mother tongue is not the same as that used in the schools. In other words the French immersion program has, for some educators, legitimized home-school language switching and has provided an argument against vernacular education for minority language groups. It is therefore important to examine closely the validity of this generalization. To do so, we will examine another type of program which has often been referred to as immersion but which has been relabeled as *submersion* to draw attention to essential differences (Cohen and Swain 1976).

SECOND LANGUAGE SUBMERSION

Second language submersion refers to the situation encountered by some children wherein they must make a home-school language switch, while others can already function in the school language. Within the same classroom, then, one might find children who have knowledge of the school language, varying degrees of facility in the school language through contact with the wider community, and native speakers of the school language.

Typical of this situation are the children of migrant workers, first and second generation immigrants, as well as the children of our indigenous populations for whom low academic achievement, low target-language proficiency, low self-esteem, and first language loss have been reported in submersion programs (see, for example, Yarborough 1967; Skutnabb-Kangas and Toukomaa 1976).

The contradictory results for children experiencing a home-school language switch in an immersion program and in a submersion program indicate clearly the need to look beyond the home-school language switch as a causal variable. Some of the factors which contribute to an explanation of the differences in linguistic and academic outcomes between the two programs have been discussed by Cohen and Swain (1976), Swain and Bruck (1976), Burnaby (1976), and Paulston (1978).

First, it is the case that most of the children enrolled in the French immersion programs are from middle- to upper-middle-class homes; whereas many children involved in the submersion type of home-school language switch programs are from lower-working-class homes. It is a recognized fact that socioeconomic class correlates with school achievement. Thus, with children in the French immersion program it is not surprising to find that although working-class children do as well academically and linguistically in French immersion programs as their working-class counterparts in English programs, it is not the case that they do as well as middle-class children in similar programs (Bruck, Jakimik, and Tucker in press). (Similar conclusions hold true for children with learning disabilities and below-average intelligence; see Genesee 1976 for a review.) Similarly, there is evidence to suggest that children from middle-class homes who undergo a submersion experience can come to pass for native speakers of the target language without any noticeable loss in the first language (Macnamara, Svarc, and Horner 1976). Thus comparisons of results across programs without taking account of socioeconomic differences are obviously inadequate.

The way in which socioeconomic class affects second language learning and academic achievement is not well understood. Cummins (1976, 1978a) has suggested that the development of skills in a second language is a function of the level of the child's first language competence at the time when intensive exposure to the language begins (developmental interdependence hypothesis).[2] Cummins points out that in the case of most middle-class anglophone children in Canadian immersion programs, the first language is adequately developed and reinforced by the out-of-school environment, while this may not be the case among lower-class or "disadvantaged" minority language children. If the developmental interdependence hypothesis is correct, then children whose first language is not adequately developed should not be exposed to a language switch until it is. Developing and maintaining the first language will provide the potential for equivalently high levels to be attained in the second language.

Cummins has also proposed the "threshold" hypothesis—its import being linked intimately with the developmental interdependence hypothesis. Basically the threshold hypothesis claims that one must attain a threshold level of competence in the second language in order to be able to profit by instruction in that language. But because the level of competence in the second language is dependent on the level attained in the first language, it is important to ensure that the threshold level is also attained in the first language. It must not be forgotten, however, that not only might socioeconomic variables be related to first language development, but also so will variables such as language use patterns in the home and perceived prestige value of the home and school languages.

Concerning the perceived status of the languages in question, in the French immersion program the children are members of the dominant linguistic and cultural group. Learning the second language does not portend the gradual replacement of the first language and the loss of cultural identity associated with that language. Furthermore the second language being learned is a socially relevant, nationally and internationally recognized language, through which individual economic advantages may accrue to the learner. Lambert (1977) has referred to this situation, that is, where the first language is maintained while a

---

2. Cummins appears to use "language competence" and "cognitive competence" interchangeably, by which he means "the ability to make effective use of the cognitive functions of the language, i.e., to use language effectively as an instrument of thought and represent cognitive operations by means of language" (1978b, footnote 21).

This description is obviously not applicable to the situation where two languages are learned simultaneously from birth.

second language is being learned, as an "additive" form of bilingualism. This is in contrast to the situation faced by many immigrant groups and indigenous populations who perceive knowledge of the majority school language to be the gateway to social and economic gains, and the home language to be of no consequence except in enabling them to communicate with their friends and relatives. The overwhelming use of the dominant language in school and in the wider community often results in a "subtractive" form of bilingualism (Lambert 1977), where the learning of the second language may reflect some degree of loss of the first language and culture.

Program variables also have been considered to play an important role. As has been noted, the French immersion program involves a home-school language switch which is the same language switch for all children, and where all children begin the program with essentially the same level of competence in the school language—nil. In the submersion program, the children experiencing the language switch are mixed together with students whose native language is that of the school. In the immersion program the use of the second language by the children receives praise and reward, leading to feelings of progress and accomplishment. In the submersion program, use of the second language with competence and fluency is *expected*. Limited proficiency is often treated as a sign of limited intellectual and academic ability, resulting in feelings of inferiority and lack of self-esteem. In the immersion program, second language learning is a recognized goal, and attended to by the teachers. In the submersion program, second language learning is presumed to have occurred, and students are instructed as if they were native speakers of the school language. The teachers in the French immersion program can understand the children's home language and respond appropriately. The teachers in the submersion program typically cannot understand the home language or languages being used by their students, who are left frustrated by their inability to make their needs known and their ideas understood. Furthermore the teachers may have little understanding of the complexity of the task facing the second language learners as they grapple with new ideas presented in a form intended for native speakers. In the French immersion program the children's home language is introduced as a subject at some stage in their educational program, providing institutional recognition of the importance of that language. In the submersion program, the home language is neither taught nor used, reinforcing the attitude that it is of little import.

Participation in a French immersion program is *optional*—at the choice of the parents—thereby ensuring the interest and support of the parents. Participation in a submersion program is obligatory. No other options are available to the children. Because of the home-school language difference, parents are reluctant or unable to communicate with school personnel about their interests or concerns related to their child's development within the educational setting.

Thus, submersion and immersion programs are clearly different programs which lead to different results. Those who have recognized the failure of submersion home-school language switch programs have argued that what is needed is education in the vernacular, an argument not incompatible with Cummins's hypothesis.

TRANSITIONAL AND MAINTENANCE BILINGUAL EDUCATION PROGRAMS

Transitional and maintenance bilingual education programs both involve a home-school language switch. Both, however, involve beginning the educational process in the home language of the children, shifting at a later stage to the partial use of the language typically used in the school setting (maintenance bilingual education programs) or to the complete use of the language typically used in the school setting (transitional bilingual education programs).

Through this process, educators are hoping to accomplish several things at once: increase the level of academic achievement, strengthen self-image, and develop second language skills. Whereas in the immersion program, the main aim is to develop second language skills without a *decrease* in academic achievement or mother tongue development, in the immersion program, no one is concerned with improving the child's self-image; it is not judged to be low. The fact that different criteria of success have been applied to each program indicates that it is not valid to simply look at the success rate of the programs in order to determine whether a program of home-school language switch or of vernacular education is better.

In the case of the transitional and maintenance programs, there is evidence to suggest that in many—but by no means in all—programs, measures of first *and* second language skills, of academic achievement, and of self-concept were higher among those participating in the bilingual program than those participating in a unilingual (submersion) program (see, for example, Belkin, Graham, Paulston, and Williams 1977; Hébert 1976; Skutnabb-Kangas and Toukomaa 1976; Claydon, Knight, and Rado 1977). In the French immersion program all programs have been judged successful because a second language is learned without loss in academic achievement or mother tongue skills relative to children in the regular English program.

But what does a comparison of this sort mean? Very little indeed. A comparison of those goals which the programs have in common would be considerably more meaningful. One goal which the programs have in common is second language learning.

SECOND LANGUAGE LEARNING

In considering the studies associated with the programs, it is important to note that many of the comparisons of the second language skills of the French immersion children have been in relation to children who have learned French as a *second* language through more traditional language-teaching programs; whereas comparisons of the children in the other programs have been in relation to children who are *native* speakers of the target language.

Consider for example, the following description of the second language skills of French immersion children as summarized by Tucker and d'Anglejan (1972):

> In addition and at no cost they can also read, write, speak and understand French in a way that English pupils who follow a traditional program of French as a second language never do. These children have already acquired a mastery of the basic elements of French phonology, morphology, and syntax; and they have not developed the inhibition which so often characterizes the performance of the foreign or second language student.

More recently, comparisons with the French used by native speakers of the same age have become more frequent. Swain (1978b) concluded that:

> The results reveal consistently superior performance of the immersion students relative to students following a program of FSL instruction. Furthermore, immersion students perform better than at least 30% of native-French students who served as norming populations for the standardized tests employed. After six or seven years in an immersion program, student performance in the areas of listening and reading approaches native-like levels; whereas in the areas of speaking and writing, many differences between immersion and francophone students still remain. Second language acquisition research, as well as teacher opinion, suggest that additional language "input" through sustained interaction with francophone peers is an essential component of a program if the attainment of native-like speaking abilities is to be a program goal.

What are some of the differences between the speech of the French immersion students and students whose first language is French? To date almost no systematic analyses have been undertaken which have compared in detail the French spoken by the immersion students with that used by their francophone peers. One exception is a study (Harley and Swain 1977, 1978) which examines the productive control of the verb system in French by grade 5 immersion children in a completely English-speaking community, grade 5 French-English bilingual children, and grade 5 unilingual French children from Quebec. The data analyzed for this study were obtained through individual interviews conducted by a native French-speaking adult.

Questions were directed to in-school and out-of-school topics of relevance and intrinsic interest to children of the age group concerned. The interviewer was free to extend the conversation in any direction that seemed appropriate, and was asked to introduce a minimum set of questions in as natural an order as possible. This set of questions was designed to elicit a variety of discourse types—narrative, descriptive, and expository—which might be expected to contain differences in time, aspect, and modality, with a corresponding variety of verb forms. For example, the students were invited to tell the interviewer about personal experiences from the past, to describe some classroom activities, and to talk about their dreams for the future.

The study was carried out with a view to determining whether or not there are systematic differences in the spoken French of the immersion pupils vis-à-vis the comparison groups. The findings indicate that there are such differences.

In general, the immersion children may be said to be operating with simpler and grammatically less redundant verb systems. They tend to lack forms which are of minimal import for the conveyance of ideational meaning, or for which grammatically less complex alternative means of conveying the appropriate meaning exist. The forms and rules that they have mastered appear to be those that are the most generalized in the target verb system (for example, the first conjugation -er verb pattern). In the area of verb syntax, it appears that where French has a more complex system than English (for example, in the form and placement of object pronouns), the immersion children tend to opt for a simpler pattern that approximates the one that they are already familiar with in their mother tongue. It is significant, however, that in the area of vocabulary, of major importance in the realization of meaning, the immersion children seem, in general, to be relatively close to the comparison groups.

One interpretation of the systematic differences between the immersion children's speech and that of the comparison groups is that such differences are clearly connected with the language acquisition setting in which the immersion children find themselves. The French immersion classroom provides a setting for second language acquisition that resembles a natural language acquisition setting in some important respects. Not only do the pupils receive several hours of exposure to French each day, but they have the opportunity to use the second language for real communication about a wide variety of topics. Indeed it may be hypothesized that, as in a natural setting, it is their communicative needs that largely determine what French is acquired. Their communicative needs in the classroom are oriented most strongly toward the conveyance of cognitive meaning, and once the children have reached a point in their language development where they can make themselves understood to their teacher and classmates (as they clearly have), there is no strong social incentive to develop further toward native-speaker norms. Many of the errors noted in the speech of the grade 5 immersion students appear to be *fossilized;* that is, they appear to have been in their speech for several years (see, e.g., Swain 1976b; Selinker, Swain, and Dumas 1975) and show little sign of being eradicated.

What makes the French immersion setting different from the natural setting is that the children are for the most part exposed, in any one year, to only one native French-speaking model—the teacher. Otherwise, the spoken French language input that they receive is largely that of their nonnative French-speaking classmates in interaction with the teacher or with each other. This and the lack of interaction with native French-speaking peers suggests that there may be insufficient input, or social stimulus, for the immersion children to develop completely nativelike speech patterns. This isolation, or "social distance" from native speaking peers, experienced by the immersion students may, however, be quite similar in important ways to that experienced by some language learners in natural settings (Schumann 1976). It is interesting to note that the simplification evident in the immersion children's speech is similar in kind to that found in the speech of many "natural" second language learners, in whose speech certain forms may also become fossilized (see, for example, Schumann, 1978).

Although a similarly detailed, comparative study of the product of second language learning in the other home-school language switch settings described has not been undertaken, it is highly probable that the learners attain a more nativelike command of the second language, especially if interaction with native speakers of the target language is one of the critical variables: children in the submersion programs have contact with native-speaking children of the target language both within and out of school; children in the bilingual education programs typically have contact with native speakers out of school. Perhaps what the linguistic product of the French immersion program represents is the best that can be accomplished in terms of developing second language skills in a school setting alone.

However, the extent to which nativelike command of the second language is accomplished at the expense of the first language is the extent to which a valuable resource has been lost, both to the individual and to the society. And if the threshold and developmental interdependence hypotheses are substantiated, then the extent to which the first language is not developed must be seen as a limiting factor in second-language development. One of the important educational tasks of the future is to structure school settings so that they convert subtractive forms of bilingualism into additive ones. This structure will necessarily involve a home-school language switch at some stage in the educational process, but when and how much must be determined in relation to the linguistic and socioeconomic characteristics of the learner and of the learning environment.

DISCUSSION QUESTIONS

1. Based on the hypotheses and ideas offered in previous chapters, why is it reasonable to expect that French immersion programs should be more successful than typical programs in French as a second language? Is this a necessary outcome, or is it merely a product of weak second language instruction?

2. One of the problems noted in some immersion programs is the paucity of native models. For most classroom settings the only model for French is the teacher. In what ways might this limitation be expected to hinder students' development of fully nativelike skills in French?

3. Compare the remarks about the "fossilization" of certain typical errors in immersion classes with the errors observed by Savignon in the French of her own children who were in a more "natural" setting, surrounded by the target language.

4. What kinds of precautions would you recommend to school districts who are considering "submersion" or "immersion" programming? If you were going to attempt to determine whether or not the potential students had reached "threshold" level either in the target language or in the native language, how would you go about this?

Chapter 32

ESL in Colorado's Jefferson County Schools

Patricia A. Richard-Amato
University of New Mexico

EDITORS' INTRODUCTION

The sudden appearance of sizable numbers of students who do not speak English and who clearly fall below the Cummins's threshold in English skills (see Chapter 31 by Swain) is a problem that many American school districts have had to accommodate. This report discusses some of the ways that methods recommended in this volume were applied in a pilot ESL program for refugees and immigrants at Alameda High School in Lakewood, Colorado. It worked well enough to become a model for other ESL centers throughout the Jefferson County School District, and since then in other states. Methods and techniques that resulted in certain demonstrable successes are discussed in this chapter. Whereas other chapters have dealt with foreign or second language teaching in settings where students have the luxury of choosing to participate or not, in this chapter, the program under consideration was an emergency effort to help refugees and other newcomers adjust to the traumatic shock of a whole new world. In their case learning English was a matter of survival. They had been "submerged" so to speak and they were being held under in an unfamiliar English-speaking environment.

In recent years school districts throughout the nation have experienced a tremendous influx of students from all over the world, but predominantly from southeast Asia.[1] Generally speaking the schools were not prepared to handle these newcomers and tended to place them in regular or remedial classes designed for native speakers of English. As a result, meeting their specific needs in their new culture was either neglected altogether or relegated to a secondary or even incidental status.

In many cases these students lost valuable time without making significant progress in acquiring English because the teachers, for the most part, had to concentrate on the majority, consisting of native speakers of English. Teachers

1. I am grateful to Salman Saeed, presently a Ph.D. candidate in applied linguistics at Georgetown University, for sharing his topic ideas with me, and to my collaborator, John Oller. I must also thank my students and coworkers at Alameda High School without whom this chapter could never have been written. Nonetheless, I alone remain responsible for any errors and for the ideas expressed here.

were unable to take the time necessary to make the subject matter comprehensible to those who had limited English. A few such students were fortunate enough to have a tutor assigned by the school for as much as one period each day, but for many of them, one period a day wasn't enough.

In attempting to cope with the problem of growing numbers of these students, the Jefferson County Schools in Lakewood, Colorado, opted to provide Intensive ESL Learning Centers in selected schools. It was felt that the centers could serve three purposes: (1) to begin with, they would provide environments for immersion of the students in comprehensible English input suitably adjusted to their potential levels ("$i + 1$"—Krashen's term); (2) they could, through the help of a competent staff who understood the students' special needs, provide help in making the eventual transition into the mainstream somewhat smoother; and (3) they would also provide highly positive environments, where cultural differences were respected and valued rather than being thought of as undesirable.

Alameda High School became a pilot school for one of the first centers, and I was asked to organize and direct it. A cultural awareness program was established for the student body and staff, and an ESL Intensive Learning Center was created. It was first necessary for us to consider the students themselves. What were their backgrounds? What were their most immediate and pressing needs?

With regard to our first question, concerning the background of the students, we found that they represented eight different countries—Vietnam, Laos, Korea, Taiwan, Somalia, Romania, Colombia, and the Philippines. Altogether the students spoke nine different languages including two dialects of Chinese. Seventy-eight percent of them were refugees from Southeast Asia—namely, Vietnam and Laos. The others, from the remaining countries, were immigrants rather than refugees, but nearly all 41 of them planned to make the United States their home.

Next we began to consider their needs. Based on what we were able to learn by talking with the students and other teachers, a number of specific goals were agreed upon. We decided to try to help them learn English, but at the same time to encourage them to maintain their own languages. Rather than prepare them for an indefinitely long period in the ESL center, we decided to prepare them for the mainstream, both *academically* and *socially*, as quickly as possible. We wanted to encourage them to maintain an appreciation for their own cultures while they also learned to function effectively as members of a multicultural society here in America.

PLACEMENT

Through oral interviews and writing samples we tried to examine each student's interlanguage and to determine roughly each student's approximate $i + 1$. To begin with we asked simple questions such as "What is your name?" and we progressed to more difficult ones such as "How did you happen to come to Lakewood, Colorado?" When we felt we had reached the level at which the student could profit from instruction, the interview was terminated. While the interview was going on, responses were written down for subsequent evaluation.[2]

We also obtained samples of writing abilities by asking the students to describe pictures or relate personal experiences. Although our initial approaches could have probably been improved upon in detail, they worked fairly well in dividing the students into three traditional categories: beginning, intermediate, and advanced. We held no illusions about the boundaries between one level and another, realizing that there would be overlap. Also we were aware throughout that the categorization into the three levels would, in part, be a function of the particular communication task at hand. We knew too that the groups would be fairly heterogeneous, and we considered that an *advantage* in that through group interaction the students could learn much from one another. In fact, we often purposely created an environment in which beginning students had a chance to interact with the more advanced students.

We then tried to determine the needs of students at each level. Students at the beginning level typically would be in the center for most of the day for 1 or 2 weeks, and gradually they would add mainstream classes. We found that all the beginning students needed at least 2 to 4 hours in the center for intensive work just to help them survive the immediate problems of everyday living, e.g., finding an apartment, for themselves or their parents, or entering into content-area classes (art, physical education, music, math, etc.). In order for the transition into the content-area classes to be as smooth as possible, we had the teachers of those classes list basic words and concepts that students needed before entering. We then attempted to teach these basic concepts in ESL. The procedures we used are detailed below. The length of time before mainstreaming into content areas varied depending upon the content area involved and the individual student. Usually the student went into gym, art, physical education, or music within just a couple of weeks. Then math followed and then science and eventually social studies, which required a higher level of English skills.

Most intermediate students needed 1 to 2 hours a day in the center to develop language skills through interaction before certain interlanguage elements had a chance to fossilize. Also, the intermediate stage in the student's partial recovery from culture shock seemed optimal for acquisition and intensive work. By the time they had reached the intermediate stage, most students were into a full schedule of regular classes except for mainstream English.

Advanced students required 1 to 2 hours in the center to work in a specific skill area in which language analysis might help or to practice their interlanguage.

---

2. A less obtrusive way to record the students' responses would be to use a tape recorder after students have been familiarized with it.

By then most were ready for the gradual transition into mainstream English classes. A student who came to us with almost no English skills could expect to be placed in a mainstream English class within 1½ to 3 years. Much depended upon the student's motivation, willingness to work, and degree of inhibition.

CLASSROOM ACTIVITIES

In the following section the activities and outlines of work with each of the three levels of students are discussed in the framework of four phases: Prespeech Activities, Early Speech Production, Speech Emergence, and Toward Full Communication. The first three phases are roughly parallel to those proposed by Terrell in the natural approach (see Chapter 18).

Prespeech Activities

To create trust, decrease inhibitions, and avoid the requirement of verbal responses, the beginning students were at first involved in purely physical activities such as the following:
  1. The students joined hands in a circle. The teacher then guided them to move (with hands still joined) until the group was all tangled up and didn't look like a circle anymore. A student who had been sent out of the room came back to untangle the group. The activity was repeated until all volunteers had a chance to go out and come back to restore the circle.
  2. Mirror dancing was used. We divided the students into pairs and had the members of each pair stand opposite each other. Rock music was played. One member of the group danced while the other member mirrored every move the first member made. Then they switched roles. This activity provided a way of communicating and establishing relationships without verbalizing.

Early Speech Production

To make the transition to early speech production smoother, the principal tools were activities that relied heavily on Asher's total physical response (TPR) method as described above in Chapters 5 and 26 and the audio-motor unit as recommended by Kalivoda, Morain, and Elkins in Chapter 27. These were integrated with some of the drama techniques recommended by the authors in Part IV, Roles and Drama. An especially useful approach involved the teacher acting as director and the students often as mute actors and actresses in mini-scenarios. These activities merged and overlapped to some extent with the third phase, speech emergence.
  They often began in a story which was read and acted out by the teacher and teacher-assistants. Later the teacher acted as director and the students performed the parts. Directions would include lots of comprehensible input in the form of commands such as "Please move to the right" or "Walk around the

chair" or "Ask Joe (a character in the story) to eat dinner with you." Students sometimes practiced phrases aloud. Later, when the students were ready, they took turns being the director while the teacher and other students acted out the roles. However, in all of these activities there was a more or less established script. The students were not yet required to invent their own agenda for communication.

Perhaps the method that helped most to establish a relaxed state preceding and during early speech production was Suggestopedia (see Chapters 8 and 9 above). While soft music played in the background, students were asked to close their eyes, breathe deeply, exhale slowly but completely while tensing and relaxing specific muscle groups. Then, I would say something like, "Try to remember when you were a child. You were sitting very close to someone who was reading to you . . . maybe it was your mother or your father or an older sister or brother. That person was reading to you softly. You felt very warm and secure. You knew you could learn just about anything at that moment."

Through this suggestive technique, students were reminded of a comfortable childlike state at a time when they were presumably highly capable learners. Even though they may not have understood all the words, just the tone of voice seemed to soothe them. Again we would go through the deep breathing. Then they would open their eyes. After that, I would begin showing them pictures of objects while I read the names of the objects dramatically. The vocabulary items selected were ones suggested by the content-area teachers who would eventually have these students in their classes. First the students just listened. Later they were shown the pictures and had to supply the names of the objects. Since the procedure falls far short of real communication, and is a discrete-point approach to vocabulary, presumably it worked as well as it did partly because the students were highly instrumentally motivated to learn just those items in order to get into the relevant mainstream classes later on.

In another type of activity with characteristic features of TPR, Suggestopedia, and counseling-learning, the students learned numbers, days of the week, months of the year by simply bouncing a ball. For instance, seven students in a circle would each represent a day of the week. The "Sunday" student would bounce the ball and call out "Sunday, Saturday." The student who was "Saturday" would have to catch the ball before it bounced a second time. Conscious attention was focused on catching the ball while *the series of terms was being internalized at a more or less peripheral level of consciousness.* TPR came into the picture as students were being directed into the different roles of the game. Because of the nature of the games themselves, students were encouraged to relax and become more comfortable in their relationships with each other. The routine and repetitiveness had a kind of suggestopedic effect, and the teacher's role as facilitator was functionally like the "expert counselor" in Curran's approach.

Obviously the foregoing technique of using names for days of the week, for instance, still falls short of ordinary communication in English. The words internalized will not normally be used in a situation resembling the game.

However, this type of activity merely serves to initiate minimally difficult productions in a *highly supportive low-tension context*. It also provides a great deal of comprehensible input leading to more advanced production later on as found in the mini-scenarios mentioned earlier.

Speech Emergence

Throughout the entire process of teaching ESL, we were always trying to make progress toward *full communication*. We tried to create situations in which the students were taken through the natural process of language acquisition, from a silent period, to games, to chants, and subsequently to increasingly demanding communicative situations. In the initial phase the objective was to recapture, in the sense of Lozanov's Suggestopedia, that malleable period when first language acquisition was occurring. For instance, I personally remember, as a child acquiring my first language, when words themselves were fascinating to me. There was something about their rhythm and the kinesthetic feedback associated with the articulatory events. Verbal play did not depend on the meanings of the words which were not always clear. I can remember thinking the words "London Bridge is falling down" really said "Log and breeches falling down." It didn't make much sense but that didn't matter at the time. What mattered was the melody and the game that went along with it. Later I did begin to wonder what the words meant, and actively tried to figure them out.

With this sort of thing in mind what we hoped to accomplish in the ESL classroom was to appeal to the universal interest, curiosity, and uninhibited spirit associated with first language acquisition. One means for accomplishing this was to use jazz chants (see Chapter 21). With student input we even wrote our own jazz chants. Although such exercises are often written for beginning levels, the following one was written for a group of intermediate to advanced students as a means of teaching idiomatic expressions. I had placed a sheet of paper on the door where the students could list phrases they heard in the halls that they wanted to know the meaning of. Then, based on the problems that they had noted, I constructed the following chant:

> What do you say when your friend's sad and blue?
>> Hang in there!
>> Hang in there!
> What do you say when your love's not true?
>> I'm feeling down.
>> I'm feeling down.
> What do you say when your sister misbehaves?
>> Don't mess around!
>> Don't mess around!
> What do you say when you feel like slaves?
>> We're fed up!
>> We're fed up!

What do you do when someone is shy?
    Break the ice!
    Break the ice!
What have you done when you can't remember why?
    I've spaced it out!
    I've spaced it out!

Students would snap their fingers to the rhythm of the words as they read them aloud.

Toward Full Communication

Moving toward more challenging production, we created situations where one student had vital information that another did not have but needed. Intuitively we employed the idea of the "information gap" as described by Johnson (1979) and Allwright (1979). We had one student go to the chalkboard and another student go to the back of the room with a simple drawing in hand (geometric shapes worked best at first). The student at the back of the room gave directions to the student at the chalkboard so he or she could reproduce the drawing. This activity generated a lot of comprehensible input and TPR-type mappings of utterances to actions. Afterward there was a debriefing activity where students got feedback from the teacher and other students. This aspect of the teaching would seem to parallel some aspects of Curran's counseling-learning approach. Also, the debriefing phase resulted in acquisition of vocabulary and structures near the student's "zone of proximal development" (Vygotsky 1934) or "$i + 1$" (Krashen 1981, 1982).

But perhaps the most effective kind of communication was what took place between the teacher and the student on a one-to-one basis. The resulting interactions were not unlike those between caretaker and child (e.g., see the discussion by Burt and Dulay in Chapter 3, and by Terrell in Chapter 18 and their references). For instance, here is an example of a typical conversation:

Teacher: What are you drawing?
Student: Drawing?
Teacher: You know "drawing." (The teacher makes drawing motions in the air.)
Student: Oh, "drawing." (The student makes drawing motions in the air.)
Teacher: What are you drawing? (The teacher emphasizes "what" and points to an object on the student's paper.)
Student: House.
Teacher: A house? You are drawing a house."
Student: Yes, a house.

This kind of conversation provides individual attention and comprehensible input. However, when classes are large, as is usually the case, the teacher simply cannot provide a sufficient amount of such individualized attention. Fortunately, in a typical American school such as Alameda High, one omnipresent resource is a supply of potential peer teachers. After preliminary training, they can provide highly effective comprehensible input and involve the students in meaningful interaction. (Dykstra and Nunes 1973, and Rogers 1978).

PEER TEACHERS

English-speaking students with native or near native competence were selected from mainstream English classes on the basis of the recommendations of their teachers. These students were trained in two workshops of 4 hours each before they started teaching. The workshops included an orientation to the various cultures represented by the students and a discussion on how to interact with students to encourage, motivate and communicate effectively.

The next two workshops, which each lasted 2 hours, were held within the first couple of weeks in the semester. In the meantime the peer teachers were given a chance to observe and become acquainted with those groups or individuals with whom they would be interacting. During these sessions the peer teachers became familiar with the materials and the methods they would be using. They spent part of the time in role play using the materials and experimenting on each other with the methods. Thereafter, they attended one 2-hour workshop every month to share successes and to discuss problems.

In addition to the peer teachers, two adult lay assistants were hired from the community by the school district. They too participated in the workshops. The teacher met with each of the lay assistants and each of the peer teachers at least once a week. During these sessions we discussed student progress and planned ahead week by week. At the beginning to lower intermediate levels, each of us worked with small groups of three or four students. With the upper intermediate to advanced levels, the work was often one-to-one. For each student we had a folder in which we kept the student's work. We reacted to written work constructively, providing positive feedback and asking relevant questions. The peer teachers and lay assistants were encouraged to have students write and rewrite frequently. In addition to the individualized work, peer teachers and lay assistants were able to lead their respective groups in activities such as play writing and dramatization (see Part IV); reading and/or acting out stories (see Chapters 1 and 2); writing expository paragraphs; small group discussions; and in general any sort of activity which would result in comprehensible input and which necessitated interaction.

During their ESL experience, students were encouraged to express themselves *without fear of criticism*. Sometimes sociodramas (see Chapter 15) were used to elicit problems for discussion or composition. For intermediate to advanced students, in particular, we had a picture folder to stimulate ideas for stories and expository paragraphs and a topic box out of which students could draw ideas such as the following:

If you had to choose between love and money, which would you choose?

You are Phil Donahue. Select someone to interview and decide on the questions that you will ask.

You are making your own greeting cards to save a little money. Write a verse for one of the following: Get Well, Happy Birthday, or Wish You Were Here.

Disneyland has just come up with a new ride. People say it takes your breath away. Tell all about it.

Select a line from a popular song. Use it as the starting point for a short story.

Or, students made up topics of their own. They often chose to write about poignant memories out of their own experience. One student, for example, wrote about how the people on the boat from Vietnam gathered rain water on a plastic sheet in order to have enough to stay alive. Another wrote about being a nurse in a Thai refugee camp where at the age of 13 he delivered babies. Yet another contemplated what might be happening to a mother or a father in a Vietnamese concentration camp.

Values-clarification activities (Simon, Howe, and Kirschenbaum 1972) were also used to strengthen self-concepts and further the development of communication skills at the same time. One type of activity which proved to be popular with the students was a variation on the values-clarification theme. Five large signs were placed at strategic visible locations around the room. They read: Strongly Agree, Somewhat Agree, Neutral, Disagree Somewhat, Disagree Strongly. During this activity, I would read a statement such as "Parents should be strict with their children," and the students would go to the sign that best described their reaction to the statement. Usually there would be groups at all or most of the positions. Then each group would be asked to designate a spokesperson to verbalize the group's position on the issue. During the explanations *the teacher remained impartial.* As each student expressed his or her group's viewpoint, the others usually just listened, but sometimes someone would interrupt to offer a point of clarification. This activity encouraged complete involvement. Students soon forgot their self-consciousness and speech began to flow freely.

We also discovered other values-clarification-type activities which resulted in total involvement. For instance, in one activity, students sat on the floor in two concentric circles with equal numbers in each circle. The members in the inner circle faced outward toward corresponding members of the outer circle. The activity would begin with a question, e.g., "What has been your biggest problem since you got to the United States?" The students in the outer circle would answer the question first, and as soon as a lull in the conversation became apparent (after a minute or so), the students in the inner circle would answer the same question. Then the inner circle would remain stationary while the outer circle rotated clockwise until each student was aligned with the next person to the left. A different question would be asked. This time the inner circle would answer first. Then, after those in the outer circle had also answered, the inner circle would rotate counterclockwise to the next person. And so on it would go for perhaps as much as a full class period.

A variation on the same theme, with somewhat different interpersonal dynamics, used groups of three. This variation, of course, was preferred when the activity was to be used with relatively small numbers of students. One person in each group answered the question while the others listened. When time was called, the second member of each group answered the same question, and so on.

Another approach which had interesting results was the "mock telephone" conversation. I would pretend to hold a telephone receiver up to my ear and say, for example, "Hello, is Carlos there?" Carlos would pretend to answer and a conversation would ensue. After a weekend or a vacation, we often used this method to get in touch with one another again. When we had visitors in the classroom, we used it as a way to get to know them. This pretend procedure seemed to relieve some of the tension of classroom performance. Although the student was "on the spot," so to speak, there was still freedom to contribute without fear of being evaluated since corrections were only done indirectly (see Terrell, Chapter 19 above). In the case of visitors, it brought them into the game, forcing down any affective barriers that might be standing in the way of communicative interaction.

Mock-up talk shows were yet another way to encourage student involvement. Students would interview each other, or they would invite in friends, other teachers, administrators, or school personnel and interview them. Sometimes we would prepare questions in advance and the students would go outside the classroom to interview other students around the school. After completing several such interviews, they would return to the center and report on whatever interesting things they had learned. The questions fell mostly into two categories depending on the person or persons to be interviewed. Here are some of them:

For other ESL students
What advice would you give a foreign student who was planning to come to the United States?

What do you miss the most about your country?

What one thing would you change about your current situation if you could?

For friends, teachers, and administrators
Have you ever been to another country outside of the United States? If so, how did you feel about it?

Suppose you wanted to escape your country for some reason and had to do it by crossing a large ocean in a small boat. How would you react?

What do you think it would be like if you had to go to a different country and live in a completely different culture?

When tensions seemed particularly high, for instance, after a pep assembly, before final exams, or after an unpleasant incident, we sometimes used techniques from Lozanov to calm down. If there had been a particular incident, we would usually take time out to discuss it. We made it clear that other less important things could wait. Another approach was to have students role-play the difficult situation. For example, if someone had been shoved in the hall, or if someone had been teased, role play was effective in teaching coping strategies and alternative approaches to conflict resolution (see Stern, Chapter 13 and also Scarcella, Chapter 15).

Another activity which *reduced tensions and strengthened rapport within the classroom* was deliberate, therapeutic stroking. The students would be seated in a circle. Then, concentrating on one student at a time, each of the other students, the teacher, the peer teachers, and the lay assistants would say one thing they really liked about that person. One of the assistants or peer teachers would write down on a separate sheet of paper the comments made about each individual. At the end of the session each person went away with all these strokes in writing. This activity was especially helpful in reducing tensions before final exam week, and it also generated a good deal of comprehensible input which each student was highly motivated to comprehend. We used this activity several times during the year. Even the teacher got a boost once in a while.

Yet another tension-reducing technique was to use music. I mention it last because music seems to combine many approaches to building self-esteem as well as communicative skills. Also, music requires physical involvement through its rhythms, and where lyrics are used, the cognitive element of meaningfulness may be introduced through the words. Music not only diminishes inhibitions but it seems to heighten sensitivity to meaning and thus suggests topics which may lead into meaningful discussions. For example, following are a few lines from one of several songs that stimulated a lot of conversation at our ESL center:

Bridge Over Troubled Water
When you're weary, feeling small,
When tears are in your eyes, I will dry them all;
I'm on your side. When times get rough
And friends just can't be found,
Like a bridge over troubled water
I will lay me down

[Copyright ©1969 Paul Simon. Used by permission.]

Questions for discussion
How would you describe the person who is speaking?
What does Simon mean by "troubled water?
Who is the "bridge?"
What will that person do?

Music was one means by which the ESL student was encouraged to deal with nostalgia and with the inevitable feelings of depression and loneliness which sometimes relentlessly pursue immigrants and refugees. We realized that repression of such feelings could only be detrimental. Still, we did not pressure anyone to talk about the past, but we did try to provide an open atmosphere where they could if they wanted to. The objective was for them to feel secure in expressing whatever feelings they might choose to reveal. In some cases, we engaged the help of one of the school counselors, the school psychologist, or the psychiatric social worker depending on the difficulty of particular cases.

EVALUATION OF THE STUDENTS

Grading is a difficult and usually onerous task at best, but in most school settings a necessary one. At the ESL center, we looked at progress in oral skills and in writing. Also, as much as possible, we took account of the amount of student effort we had observed. We used speech samples and writing samples taken at 9-week intervals (similar to the diagnostic procedure described earlier). At the end of every 9-week period, we had individual conferences with each student to emphasize gains made during the previous period. The positive approach did much to build self-esteem. We sent home progress reports translated and written in the respective languages by the students themselves (see Illustrations 1 to 5).[3]

One benefit of the evaluation process at Alameda High was that each student received full credit for time spent in the center. This included the peer teachers as well as the ESL students themselves. However, the long-term goal was not merely to provide a pleasant, nonthreatening environment conducive to the acquisition of English, but to prepare the students at the center for the demands of mainstreaming with which they would eventually have to cope.

MAINSTREAMING

For the sake of the transition from the relatively protective environment of the center into the mainstream, we tried to involve as many people in the process as possible. The idea was to move the students at the center as rapidly and comfortably as possible toward full participation in the English-speaking world at the school and at large.

Teachers invited the students to share in family outings; peer teachers invited them to movies, sports events, and other activities; clubs and organizations involved them in parties and retreats. Even the members of the Alameda High student government volunteered to write personal letters to them at the center. These personal letters were especially appreciated as they were received and answered every few weeks. Some of the ESL students became close friends with their "pen pals."

THE NATIVE LANGUAGE

A principle followed implicitly throughout all of our activities was to encourage the students to maintain their own languages and to build appreciation for their own cultures as well as the cultures of other students. We felt that it might do

---

3. I wish to thank Patricia Bonilla's students at TVI in Albuquerque, New Mexico, who assisted in the preparation of these illustrations.

PROGRESS REPORT

(1) Student's name _____

(2) Teacher _____

(3) School _____

(4) Date _____

Following is an evaluation of the student's progress in _____ .

(5) (name of course)

	usually	sometimes	seldom	never
is progressing satisfactorily (6)				
maintains a positive attitude (7)				
is sensitive to needs of others (8)				
participates in activities (9)				
is strongly motivated (10)				
maintains excellent attendance (11)				
demonstrates good study habits (12)				
is cooperative (13)				

Comments: (14)

If you wish to call the teacher, please call _____ (phone). (15)

If a translator is needed, please call the TESOL office (231-2327) or call the ESL teacher in your center school.

Illustration 1   A progress report in English

REPORTE DE PROGRESO

(1) Nombre de estudiante _____

(2) Profesor _____

(3) Escuela _____

(4) Fecha _____

La siguiente es una evaluación del progreso del estudiante en _____

(5) (nombre del curso)

	usualmente	algunas veces	tara vez	nunca
esta progresando satisfactoriamente (6)				
mantiene una actitud positiva (7)				
es sensitivo con las necesidades de los demás (8)				
participa en actividades (9)				
está fuertemente motivado (10)				
mantiene una excelente asistencia (11)				
demuestra buenos hábitos de estudio (12)				
es cooperativo (13)				

Comentarios: (14)

Si Ud. desea llamar al profesor, por favor llame _____ (teléfono). (15)

Si un traductor es necesitado, por favor llame a la oficina TESOL o al profesor de ESL en su escuela.

Illustration 2   A progress report in Spanish

BẢN BÁO CÁO TIẾN BỘ

(1) Tên học sinh _____

(2) Giáo sư   _____

(3) Trường   _____

(4) Ngày   _____

Dưới đây là sự đánh giá của học
có tiến bộ trong _____
(5) (Tên người trải qua.)

	Thường	có khi	Hiếm	Không bao giờ
Sự tiến bộ và làm tròn nhiệm vụ (6)				
Duy trì rõ ràng thái độ (7)				
Có cảm giác cần đến những cái khác (8)				
Tham dự vào may mắn (9)				
Giãi bày mạnh dạn (10)				
Phục dịch giữ gìn tốt (11)				
Thói quen học hỏi (12)				
Có sự hợp tác (13)				

Lối phê bình (14)

Nếu anh chị muốn gọi giáo sư, vui lòng gọi : _____ (15)

(Điện thoại)

Nếu cần thông dịch viên, vui lòng gọi
văn phòng dạy Anh ngữ - (231 - 2327)

Illustration 3 A progress report in Vietnamese

ລາຍການກ້າວໜ້າ

(1) ຊື່ຂອງນັກຮຽນ _____

(2) ມາຍຄຣ _____

(3) ໂຮງຮຽນ _____

(4) ວັນທີ _____

ເບຶ່ງຈົ່ງໄປນີ້ ແມ່ນວງກການຂອງນັກຮຽນໄດ້ ໃນວງຈາ _____

(5) (ຊື່ຂອງ ເພີ່ນທາງ)

	ເລວຍ ໆ	ບາງເວລາ	ນວຍ/ຄ່ອຍທີ່ສຸດ . ບໍ່ ,ຄຍ.
ຮຽນໄດ້ວ່ງໄວວ່ດີ (6)			
ຕັ້ງໃຈຮຽນດີ (7)			
ຮ່ວມເຮື່ອ ຄນ ອນ ທໍ ຫຍໍ ການ (8)			
ເຮັດຫຼກສັ່ງຫຼກ ປ່ຽ ບໍ ຄດຄວ້ (9)			
ຕອງໃການ ຮຽນ ປ່ຽ ຄຄນ ແອງ (10)			
ສະ ຸຄງວ່າ ນີ ສັບການ ຮຽນ (11)			
ຮັກສາ ລະ ບຽບຫຍນດີ (12)			
ການ ຮ່ວມນີ (13)			

ອອກຄວາມ ຄດ: (14)

ຖ້າເຈາກທ່ານມີຄວາມຍະ ສົງ ຍປະ ໂທຫານມາບຄຣກຮຸນທີ່ເຮະ: _____ ນ້າຍ ຶ ເຄຣໂຟນ (15)

ຖ້າເຈາກ ຕອງ ການ ຮ່ວຍແປ ພາສາ , ກຮຸນກໂທຫາ ໄຮ ການ
(ຂວ - ຂຈຂ) TESOL

Illustration 4   A progress report in Laotian

활동 사항 보고

(1) 학생 이름 _____
(2) 담당 교사 _____
(3) 학 교 _____
(4) 날 짜 _____

다음은 _____(학과명) 학과에 대한 상기 학생의 (5)
활동사항 보고 입니다

	항상	보통	때때로	좋지않다
만족할만큼 향상 되고 있다 (6)				
적극적인 태도를 유지한다 (7)				
다른사람 에게 협동심이있다 (8)				
여러가지 학과 활동에 참여 한다 (9)				
어떤 사항에 강한 관심을 가진다 (10)				
우수한 출석율을 유지한다 (11)				
학습방법이 우수 하다 (12)				
교사 와의 관계가 협동적이다 (13)				

교사 의견 : (14)

만약 담당교사 에게 전화 문의를 원하시면
_____ 로 하십시오 . (15)
(전화 번호)
만약 통역이 필요하시면 TESOL 사무실
(231-2327)로 전화 하십시오 .

Illustration 5 A progress report in Korean

irreparable harm to discourage them from using their native languages in the class. To outlaw or even to deliberately diminish the use of the native languages would have been tantamount to saying that they weren't good enough for use in an American school. Or perhaps that English was just that much better. On the contrary, we tried to stress the advantages of being able to use more than one language and therefore to encourage our students to hang onto their native languages and cultures.

We also compared and talked about cultures a lot. One activity which was especially useful in this connection was to have each cultural group choose a national holiday to celebrate. Students planned ahead for these events weeks and months in advance. They invited people from the community, content-area teachers, administrators, counselors, and other friends to join them. During the festivities of each special event, the students shared their customs, dances, songs (in their own languages), games, and food.

SOME REFLECTIONS AND RECOMMENDATIONS

Obviously, a brief overview of a program that extended over several years cannot cover anything but the barest essentials. Therefore, it seemed reasonable to include some thoughts and conclusions drawn from the overall picture that might be of use to teachers in training or others who might one day find themselves in the position of having to set up a similar program. In that vein, here in outline form, are some elements of an ESL Intensive Learning Center (ILC) which one might want to include.

Staff

A. *A full-time ESL teacher* to (1) manage the ILC each day; (2) be responsible for curriculum planning; (3) make decisions on academic mainstreaming; (4) coordinate programming for individual students with content-area teachers and other personnel; (5) provide inservice training for lay assistants, peer teachers, and content-area teachers; and (6) order materials, supplies, and equipment for the ILC.

B. *Two part-time lay assistants* (each at 4 hours per day) and *one peer teacher* for every four to five students (one period each per day) who would be responsible for (1) participating in workshops in order to become familiar with methods and materials; (2) teaching on a one-to-one basis; (3) playing a facilitative role in small-group situations; (4) assisting in student evaluation; and (5) helping the teacher in materials preparation.

C. *Resource persons* to help out in a variety of ways that should be more or less obvious according to category—(1) a reading teacher, (2) one or more counselors, (3) a librarian, (4) a media specialist, (5) a school psychologist, and (6) one or more social workers. In addition, of course, the school administrators should be apprised of and sensitized to the special needs of non-English-speaking students.

The Room and Furnishings

To allow space for multiple simultaneous activities the room should be fairly large, about 25 by 35 feet. To accommodate the physical activities it should be well ventilated and attractively decorated, preferably with movable furniture, for example, as shown in Figure 1.

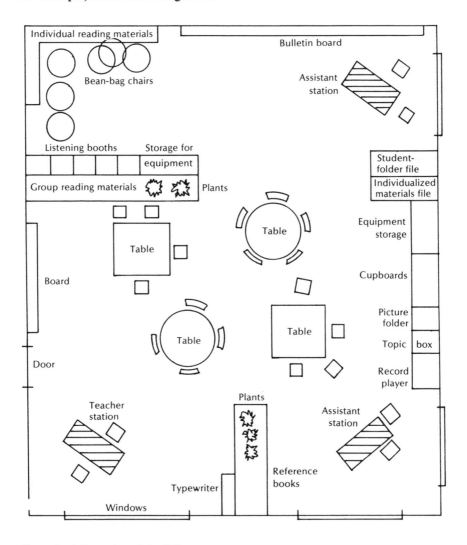

Figure 1 A floor plan of the ILC

It should include:

Furniture—tables, comfortable chairs, bookshelves (used for partitioning as well as for shelving books), listening stations, bulletin boards, chalkboards, files, and enclosed cupboards.

Equipment—tape recorders, cassette players, listening stations with headsets (for private listening), record players, and one or more typewriters.

Materials—folders for student work, a topic box with topic ideas for writing and discussion, a picture folder to stimulate ideas for writing and discussion, audio-visual aids (hand-manipulated clocks, maps, telephone dials, picture cards, etc.), records to provide music for many purposes (background music, music to promote discussion, etc.), games, magazines, and current newspapers.

Student reference books—dictionaries in various languages, traditional subject matter books from the content-area teachers, idiom dictionaries, simplified dictionaries, special-interest books (how to get a job, colleges and universities, etc.).

Some Ideas for Content-Area Teachers

Content-area teachers can be trained in a workshop type of setting to do the following:

Provide a warm environment by eliminating pressure on the ESL student. One way to do this is to set up a "buddy" system in which native English-speaking students are paired with ESL students. Another useful technique for the content areas is peer teaching, in which a native English speaker teaches one or more ESL students.

Acknowledge and incorporate the ESL student's culture whenever possible. For instance, differing number systems can be introduced in math, customs and traditions in social studies, folk medicine in science, native dances and games in physical education, songs in music, ethnic calendars in art, Haiku in language arts, etc.

Increase possibilities for success. Keep goals within the student's reach by alternating difficult activities with easier ones so that the ESL student can experience some success.

If possible use a pass/fail grade option until the ESL student is able to compete with native speakers successfully. (Teachers should be told that this may occur sooner than they expect, since many ESL students adapt very rapidly.)

Communicate individually with the ESL student as much as time permits. At first ask questions which require only "yes" or "no" for an answer. Avoid using complicated words or complex sentences. Speak slowly but with normal intonation. Don't shout or overenunciate and avoid the "Me Tarzan"—"You Jane"—"Me go sleep" approach.

Reassure the student that his or her own language is acceptable and important. (The content teacher needs to be aware that this is true even if he or she does not understand or speak the language in question.) If other students from the same language group are present, do not insist that they use only English in class.

Make all corrections indirectly by repeating what the student has said in correct form. For example, suppose the ESL student says, "My book home," the teacher can repeat, "I see. Your book is at home" or "Oh. You left your book at home." It must be remembered, however, that simplified (ungrammatical) forms are to be regarded as normal while the student is progressing toward more complete competence in English. When the student is ready to move to another level, the indirect correction will probably be picked up and internalized after it is heard a few times in a variety of situations.

Try to answer all questions that the student asks but avoid overly detailed explanation. Simple answers which get right to the point will be understood best. If possible point to objects, pictures, or demonstrate actions to help get the meaning across.

DISCUSSION QUESTIONS

1. Discuss some of the salient contrasts between teaching a foreign language and teaching a second language in a "submersion" context. What about teaching a second language in an "immersion" context (see Swain, Chapter 31).

2. What are some of the practical ways it might be possible to tell if ESL students are ready for mainstreaming or not? Is the concept of a "threshold" relevant? If so, how can you tell whether or not your students have met it?

3. Which do you feel is more important to the ESL submersion student, feelings of self-worth, or practice in the target language? Or why is this not a meaningful question?

4. In a game activity such as the ball-bouncing examples, for instance, in what ways does the TPR method become relevant? What aspects of Curran's counseling-learning can be seen? Suggestopedia? Does such a game activity have episodic organization? Is there, for instance, a relevant conflict?

References

Adams, M. J. 1980. Failures to comprehend and levels of processing in reading. In Spiro, Bruce, and Brewer, 12–32.

Adkins, P. 1971. An effective classroom climate for Mexican-American students. *Education* 92:26–27.

Alatis, J. E. (ed.). 1980. *Current Issues in Bilingual Education.* Washington, D.C.: Georgetown University.

Allwright, R. 1979. Language learning through communication practice. In Brumfit and Johnson, 167–182.

Anderson, R., R. Reynolds, D. Schallert, and E. Goetz. 1976. Frameworks for comprehending discourse. Champaign-Urbana: University of Illinois, Center for the Study of Reading. ERIC ED 134 935.

Asher, J. 1982. *Learning Another Language through Actions: The Complete Teacher's Guidebook.* (Expanded Second Edition.) Los Gatos, California: Sky Oaks Productions.

Asher, J. 1979. *Learning Another Language through Actions: The Complete Teacher's Guidebook.* Los Gatos, California: Sky Oaks Productions.

Asher, J. 1977. Children learning another language: a developmental hypothesis. *Child Development* 48:1040–1048.

Asher, J. 1972. Children's first language as a model for second language learning. *Modern Language Journal* 56:133–139.

Asher, J. 1969a. The total physical response approach to second language learning. *Modern Language Journal* 53:3–17.

Asher, J. 1969b. The total physical response technique of learning. *Journal of Special Education* 3:253–262.

Asher, J. 1966. The learning strategy of the total physical response: a review. *Modern Language Journal* 50:79–84.

Asher, J. 1965. The strategy of the total physical response: an application to learning Russian. *International Review of Applied Linguistics* 3:291–300.

Asher, J. 1964. Toward a neo-field theory of behavior. *Journal of Humanistic Psychology* 4:85–94.

Asher, J., and R. Garcia. 1969. The optimal age to learn a foreign language. *Modern Language Journal* 53:334–341.

Asher, J., and B. S. Price. 1967. The learning strategy of the total physical response: some age differences. *Child Development* 38:1219–1227.

Bacon, R. 1977. The thunder and lightning professor. *Yankee* magazine, September.

Bancroft, W. J. 1977. Suggestology and suggestopedia: the theory of the Lozanov method. ERIC ED 132 857.

Bancroft, W. J. 1975. *The Lozanov Language Class.* ERIC Documents on Foreign Language Teaching and Linguistics, 1975, 53. ED 108 475.

Bancroft, W. J. 1972a. Foreign language teaching in Bulgaria. *Canadian Modern Language Review* March:3–13.

Bancroft, W. J. 1972b. The psychology of suggestopedia or learning without stress. Toronto: *Educational Courier* February:16–19.

Bancroft, W. J. 1972c. The teaching of foreign languages through suggestion. *Michigan Foreign Language Newsletter* January:6–7.

Bandura, A., and Walters, R. H. 1963. *Social Learning and Personality Development.* New York: Holt.

Barber, E. 1980. Language acquisition and applied linguistics. *ADFL Bulletin* 12:26–32.

Begin, Y. 1971. *Evaluative and Emotional Factors in Learning a Foreign Language.* Montreal, Canada: Editions Bellarmin.

Belasco, S. 1965. Nucleation and the audio-lingual approach. *Modern Language Journal* 49:482.

Belkin, J., J. Graham, C. Paulston, and E. Williams. 1977. Appendix B: excerpts from abstracts of U.S. dissertations on bilingual education. In C. B. Paulston (ed.). *Research in Bilingual Education: Current Perspectives.* Arlington, Virginia: Center for Applied Linguistics.

Benseler, D., and R. Schulz. 1980. Methodological trends in college foreign language instruction. *Modern Language Journal* 64:88–96.

Benton, R. 1964. *Research into the English Language Difficulties of Maori School Children,* 1963–1964. Wellington, New Zealand: Maori Education Foundation.

Beutler, S. 1976. Practicing language arts skills using drama. Report prepared at Bryant Community School; Ann Arbor, Michigan. ERIC ED 136–295.

Bever, T. G. 1970. The cognitive basis for linguistic structures. In J. R. Hayes (ed.). *Cognition and the Development of Language.* New York: Wiley, 288–331.

Bialystok, E. 1981. The role of conscious strategies in second language proficiency. *Modern Language Journal* 65:24–35.

Bialystok, E. 1979a. An analytical view of second language competence: a model and some evidence. *Modern Language Journal* 63:257–262.

Bialystok, E. 1979b. Explicit and implicit judgments of L2 grammaticality. *Language Learning* 29:81–104.

Bialystok, E.1979c. The role of conscious strategies in second language proficiency. *Canadian Modern Language Review* 35:372–394.

Bialystok, E. 1978. A theoretical model of second language learning. *Language Learning* 28:69–83.

Blatner, H. 1973. *Acting-in: Practical Applications of Psychodramatic Methods.* New York: Springer.

Bloom, L. 1970. *Language Development: Form and Function in Emerging Grammars.* (Research Monograph No. 59). Cambridge, Massachusetts: MIT.

Bobrow, D., and A. Collins (eds.). 1975. *Representation and Understanding.* New York: Academic.

Bolinger, D. 1970. Getting the words in. *American Speech* 45:257–262.

Bolinger, D., et al. 1960. *Modern Spanish.* New York: Harcourt.

Bordon, R., and D. Schuster. 1976. The effects of a suggestive learning climate, synchronized breathing and music on the learning and retention of Spanish words. *Journal of Suggestive-Accelerative Learning and Teaching* Spring:27–40.

Brachfeld, O. 1936. Individual psychology in the learning of languages. *International Journal of Individual Psychology* 2:77–83.

Brady, T. 1975. A study in the application of a counseling-learning model for adults. Unpublished Ph.D. dissertation, Walden University, Florida.

Braine, J. 1974. *Writing a Novel.* New York: McGraw-Hill.

Bransford, J., and M. Johnson. 1972. Contextual prerequisites for understanding: some investigations of comprehension and recall. *Journal of Verbal Learning and Verbal Behavior* 11:717–726.

Brown, A. L., and M. D. Murphy. 1975. Reconstruction of arbitrary versus logical sequences by preschool children. *Journal of Experimental Child Psychology* 20:307–326.

Brown, H. D. 1980a. The optimal distance model of second language acquisition. *TESOL Quarterly* 14:157–164.

Brown, H. D. 1980b. *Principles of Language Learning and Teaching.* Englewood Cliffs, New Jersey: Prentice-Hall.

Brown, H. D., C. Yorio, and R. Crymes (eds.). *On TESOL '77—Teaching and Learning English as a Second Language: Trends in Research and Practice.* Washington, D.C.: TESOL.

Brown, R. 1977. Introduction. In Snow and Ferguson, 1–27.

Brown, R. 1973. *A First Language.* Cambridge, Massachusetts: Harvard University.

Brown, R., C. Cazden, and U. Bellugi. 1973. The child's grammar from I to III. In C. Ferguson and D. Slobin (eds.). *Studies of Child Language Development.* New York: Holt.

Brown, R., and C. Hanlon. 1970. Derivational complexity and order of acquisition in child speech. In J. Hayes (ed.). *Cognition and the Development of Language.* New York: Wiley.

Bruck, M., W. E. Lambert, and G. R. Tucker. 1975. Assessing functional bilingualism within a bilingual program: the St. Lambert Project at grade eight. Paper presented at the TESOL Convention, Los Angeles, California.

Bruck, M., W. E. Lambert, and G. R. Tucker. 1974. Bilingual schooling through the elementary grades: the St. Lambert Project at grade seven. *Language Learning* 24:183–204.

Bruck, M., J. Jakimik, and G. R. Tucker. In press. Are French programs suitable for working class children? In W. von Raffler-Engel (ed.). *Prospects in Child Language.* Amsterdam: Royal Vangorcum.

Brumfit, C. J., and K. Johnson (eds.). 1979. *The Communicative Approach to Language Teaching.* Oxford University.

Bühler, C., and H. Hetzer. 1935. *Testing Children's Development from Birth to School Age.* New York: Farrar and Rinehart.

Burnaby, B. 1976. Language in native education. In M. Swain (ed.). *Bilingualism in Canadian Education: Issues and Research.* Yearbook of the Canadian Society for the Study of Education, 3, Edmonton, Alberta: Western Industrial Research Center, 62–85.

Burt, M., and H. Dulay (eds.). 1975. *New Directions in Second Language Learning, Teaching, and Bilingual Education.* Washington, D.C.: TESOL.

Burt, M., H. Dulay, and M. Finocchiaro (eds.). 1977. *Viewpoints on English as a Second Language.* New York: Regents.

Canale, M., and M. Swain. 1980. Theoretical bases of communicative approaches to second language teaching and testing. *Applied Linguistics* 1:1–47.

Caplan, D. 1976. Clause boundaries and recognition latencies for words in sentences. *Perception and Psychophysics* 12:73–76.

Carroll, J. B. 1970. Interview. *Modern English Teaching* February. Kenkyusha, Tokyo.

Carroll, J. B. 1967. Foreign language proficiency levels attained by language majors near graduation from college. *Foreign Language Annals* 1:131–151.

Carroll, J. B. 1965. New directions in foreign language teaching. *Modern Language Journal* 49:273-280.

Carroll, J. B. 1964. *Language and Thought.* Englewood Cliffs, New Jersey: Prentice-Hall.

Carroll, J. B. 1960. Wanted: a research basis for educational policy on foreign language teaching. *Harvard Educational Review* 30:128–140.

Carroll, J. B., and T. G. Bever. 1974. Sentence comprehension: a case study in the relation of knowledge and perception. In E. C. Carterette and M. P. Friedman (eds.). *Handbook of Perception,* Volume 7, *Language and Speech.* New York: Academic.

Caskey, O., and M. Flake. 1976. *Adaptations of the Lozanov Method.* Society for Suggestive-Accelerative Learning and Teaching.

Chall, J. 1958. *Readability: An Appraisal of Research and Application.* Columbus: Ohio State University.

Chastain, K. D. 1976. *Developing Second-Language Skills.* Chicago: Rand McNally.

Chesler, M., and R. Fox. 1966. *Role-Playing Methods in the Classroom.* Chicago: Science Research Associates.

Chiesi, H., G. Spilich, and J. Voss. 1979. Acquisition of domain-related information in relation to high and low domain knowledge. *Journal of Verbal Learning and Verbal Behavior* 18:257–273.

Chomsky, N. 1981. *Rules and Representations.* New York: Columbia University.

Christensen, C. 1977. *Explorando: Affective Learning Activities for Intermediate Practice in Spanish.* Englewood Cliffs, New Jersey: Prentice-Hall.

Christensen, C. 1975. Affective learning activities. *Foreign Language Annals* 8:211–219.

Chun, J. 1980. A survey of research in second language acquisition. *Modern Language Journal* 64:287–296.

Clark, H. H., and E. V. Clark. 1977. *Psychology and Language.* New York: Harcourt.

Clark, R. 1980. *Language Teaching Techniques.* Brattleboro, Vermont: Prolingua Association.

Claydon, L., T. Knight, and M. Rado. 1977. *Curriculum and Culture: Schooling in a Pluralistic Society.* Sydney, Australia: George Allen and Unwin.

Cohen, A., and R. Freeman. 1978. Individual differences in reading strategies in relation to handedness cerebral asymmetry. In J. Requin (ed.). *Attention and Performance VII.* Hillsdale, New Jersey: Lawrence Erlbaum.

Cohen, A. D. and M. Swain. 1976. Bilingual education: the immersion model in the North American context. *TESOL Quarterly* 10 (1), 45–53. Reprinted in J. E. Alatis and K. Twaddell (eds). *English as a Second Language in Bilingual Education.* Washington, D.C.: TESOL, 1976, 55–63.

Collins, A., J. S. Brown, and K. M. Larkin. 1980. Inference in text understanding. In Spiro, Bruce, and Brewer, 385–410.

Congressional Record. 1974. A call for madness. March 29, volume 120, no. 44:8916–8917.

Cooke, W. 1902. *The Table Talk and Bon Mots of Samuel Foote.* London: Myers and Rogers.

Corder, S. P. 1978. Language-learner language. In Richards 1978, 71–93.

Corder, S. P. 1967. The significance of the learner's errors. *IRAL* 4:161–169.

Corsini, R. 1966. *Roleplaying in Psychotherapy—A Manual.* Chicago: Aldine.

Coulthard, M. 1977. *An Introduction to Discourse Analysis.* London: Longman.

Cratty, B. J. 1970. *Perceptual and Motor Development in Infants and Children.* New York: Macmillan.

Cratty, B. J. 1969. *Perception, Motion, and Thought.* Palo Alto, California: Peek.

Cratty, B. J. 1967. *Movement Behavior and Motor Learning.* Second edition. Philadelphia: Lea and Febiger.

Cratty, B. J. 1966. *The Perceptual-Motor Attributes of Mentally Retarded Children and Youth.* Monograph. Los Angeles, California: Mental Retardation Services Board of Los Angeles County.

Cratty, B. J., and M. M. Martin. 1969. *Perceptual-Motor Efficiency in Children.* Philadelphia: Lea and Febiger.

Crookall, D. 1978. The design and exploitation of a role-play/simulation. *Recherches et Echanges* 3:1.

Cross, T. 1977. Mothers' speech adjustments: the contribution of selected child listener variables. In Snow and Ferguson, 151–188.

Crymes, R. 1980. Current trends in ESL instruction. *TESOL Newsletter* 14:1–14, 18.

Cummins, J. 1976. The influence of bilingualism on cognitive growth: a synthesis of research findings and explanatory hypotheses. *Working Papers on Bilingualism* 9:1–43.

Cummins, J. 1978a. Educational implications of mother tongue maintenance in minority language groups. *Canadian Modern Language Review* 34:395–416.

Cummins, J. 1978b. The cognitive development of children in immersion programs. *Canadian Modern Language Review* 34:855–883.

Cureton, G. O. 1973. *Action-Reading.* Boston: Allyn and Bacon.

Curran, C. 1976a. *Counseling and Psychotherapy: The Pursuit of Values.* Dubuque, Illinois: Counseling-Learning.

Curran, C. 1976b. *Counseling-Learning in Second Languages.* Dubuque, Illinois: Counseling-Learning.

Curran, C. 1972. *Counseling-Learning: A Whole-Person Model for Education.* New York: Grune and Stratton.

Curran, C. 1970. *Chromacord Simultaneous Leader Group Communication.* Chicago: Loyola University.

Curran, C. 1968a. *Chromacord Learning Systems: The Process of Development.* Chicago: Loyola University.

Curran, C. 1968b. Total involvement: toward an education unified field theory. *Jubilee Magazine* May.

Curran, C. 1966a. *Counseling in the Educative Process: A Foreign Language Integration.* Chicago: Loyola University.

Curran, C. 1966b. *Group and Individual Dactylochrome Learning Apparatus.* Chicago: Loyola University.

Curran, C. 1965a. *A Counseling Psychotherapeutic Methodology and Associated Learning Apparatus.* Chicago: Loyola University.

Curran, C. 1965b. *Forward: Implications of a Counseling-Psychotherapeutic Approach to Learning.* Chicago: Loyola University.

Curran, C. 1965c. *Theory and Description of Language Machines.* Chicago: Loyola University.

Curran, C. 1961. Counseling skills adapted to the learning of foreign languages. *Menninger Bulletin* 25 (2).

Daniélou, A. 1969. *Northern Indian Music.* New York: Frederick A. Praeger.

Davies, N. F. 1978a. Putting receptive skills first: An experiment in sequencing. *Proceedings of the 6th AILA Congress.* Montreal.

Davies, N. F. 1978b. *Putting Receptive Skills First: An Investigation into Sequencing in Modern Language Learning.* University of Linkoping: Department of Language and Literature.

Davies, N. F. 1977. Ett Realistickt mal for skilans sprakundervisning (A realistic goal for school language teaching). *Skolvarlden* (Stockholm) 3.

Davies, N. F. 1976. Receptive versus productive skills in foreign language learning. *Modern Language Journal* 60:440-443.

Davis, F. B. 1971. Psychometric research on comprehension in reading. In F. B. Davis (ed.). *The Literature of Research in Reading with Emphasis on Models.* East Brunswick, New Jersey: Iris, 8–3 to 8–30.

De Beaugrande, R. 1980. *Text, Discourse, and Process.* Norwood, New Jersey: Ablex.

Dewey, J. 1910. *How We Think.* Boston: D. C. Heath.

Diller, K. 1971. *Generative Grammar, Structural Linguistics, and Language Teaching.* Rowley, Massachusetts: Newbury House.

Di Pietro, R. 1979. The semiotics of role interpretation. In S. Chatman, U. Eco, and J. Klinkenberg (eds.). *A Semiotic Landscape.* The Hague: Mouton, 511–515.

Di Pietro, R. 1978. Verbal strategies, script theory and conversational performances. In C. Blatchford and J. Schachter (eds.). *On TESOL '78.* Washington, D.C., 149–156.

Dulay, H., and M. Burt. 1977. Remarks on creativity in second language acquisition. In Burt, Dulay, and Finocchiaro, 95–126.

Dulay, H., and M. Burt. 1975. A new approach to discovering universal strategies in child second language acquisition. In D. Dato (ed.). *Developmental Psycholinguistics: Theory and Applications.* Washington, D.C.: Georgetown University, 209–234.

Dulay, H., and M. Burt. 1973. Should we teach children syntax? *Language Learning* 23:245–258.

Dulay, H., M. Burt, and S. Krashen. 1982. *Language Two.* New York: Oxford.

Dykstra, G. and S. Nunes. 1973. The language skills program of the English project. In Oller and Richards, 283–289.

Early, P. B. 1977, Postscript to games, simulations and role-playing. London, England: ELT Documents, British Council. ISBN 0–90029–40–3.

Eliade, M. 1969. *Immortality and Freedom* (translated by W. Trask). Princeton, New Jersey: Princeton University.

Eliade, M. 1965. *Mephistopheles and the Androgyne Studies in Religious Myth and Symbol.* New York: Sheed and Ward.

ERIC Documents on Foreign Language Teaching and Linguistics. 1975. ED 108 475.

Ervin-Tripp, S. 1974. Is second language learning like the first? *TESOL Quarterly* 8:111–127. Reprinted in E. Hatch (ed.). 1978. *Second Language Acquisition: A Book of Readings.* Rowley, Massachusetts: Newbury House, 190–206.

Ervin-Tripp, S. 1973. Some strategies for the first two years. In A. Dil (ed.). *Language Acquisition and Communicative Choice*. Stanford: Stanford University.

Estes, W. K. 1962. Learning theory. *Annual Review of Psychology* 13:110.

Fillmore, C. 1968. The case for case. In E. Bach and R. Harms (eds.). *Universals in Linguistic Theory*. New York: Holt, Rinehart, 1–88.

Fillmore, L. 1976. The second time around: cognitive and social strategies in second language acquisition. Unpublished Ph.D. dissertation, Stanford University.

Finocchiaro, M., and Ekstrand, L. 1977. Migration today: some social and educational problems. In Burt, Dulay, and Finocchiaro, 205–218.

Flak, M. 1976. Se relaxer pour mieux apprendre. *L'education* November: 23–25.

Fraser, C., U. Bellugi, and R. Brown. 1966. Control of grammar in imitation, comprehension, and production. *Journal of Verbal Learning and Verbal Behavior* 2:121–135.

Freed, B. 1978. Talking to children, talking to foreigners. Paper presented at the Los Angeles Second Language Research Forum, University of Southern California, October.

Freire, P. 1978. *Pedagogy in Process; The Letters to Guinea-Bissau*. New York: Seabury.

Freire, P. 1973a. By learning they can teach. *Convergence* 6:78–84.

Freire, P. 1973b. *Education for Critical Consciousness*. New York: Seabury.

Freire, P. 1970. *Pedagogy of the Oppressed*. New York: Seabury.

Fries, C. 1945. *Teaching and Learning English as a Foreign Language*. Ann Arbor: University of Michigan.

Fugate, F. L., and R. B. Fugate. 1980. *Secrets of the World's Best-Selling Writer: The Story Telling Techniques of Erle Stanley Gardner*. New York: Morrow.

Gallagher, R. M. 1973. Counseling-learning theory applied to foreign language learning. Unpublished Ph.D. dissertation, Loyola University, Chicago.

Gallweys, W. T. 1974. *The Inner Game of Tennis*. New York: Random House.

Galyean, B. 1979. A confluent approach to curriculum design. *Foreign Language Annals* 12:121–127.

Galyean, B. 1976. *Language from Within*. Long Beach, California: Prism.

Gardner, R. C., and W. E. Lambert. 1972. *Attitudes and Motivation in Second Language Learning*. Rowley, Massachusetts: Newbury House.

Garrett, M. F., T. G. Bever, and J. A. Fodor. 1966. The active use of grammar in speech perception. *Perception and Psychophysics* 1:30-32.

Garrod, S., and T. Trabasso. 1973. A dual memory information processing interpretation of sentence comprehension. *Journal of Verbal Learning and Verbal Behavior* 12:155–167.

Gary, J. O. 1975. Delayed oral practice in initial stages of second language learning. In Burt and Dulay, 89–95.

Gattegno, C. 1972. *Teaching Foreign Languages in Schools: The Silent Way*. New York: Education Solutions. Expanded edition, 1974.

Genesee, F. 1976. The suitability of immersion programs for all children. *Canadian Modern Language Review* 32:495–515.

Gesell, A., and H. Thompson. 1929. Learning and growth in identical twins: an experimental study by the method of co-twins control. *Genetic Psychology Monographs* 6:1–124.

Gleason, J. B. 1967. Do children imitate? Paper presented at the International Conference on Oral Education of the Deaf, Lexington School for the Deaf, New York City, June.

Goodman, K. S. 1976. Reading: a psycholinguistic guessing game. In N. A. Johnson (ed.). *Current Topics in Language*. Cambridge, Massachusetts: Winthrop, 370–383.

Goodman, K. S. 1975. *Strategies for Increasing Reading Comprehension*. Glenview, Illinois: Scott, Foresman.

Goodman, K. S. 1970. Psycholinguistic universals in the reading process. *Journal of Psycholinguistic Research* 4:103–110.

Gordon, C., J. Hansen, and P. D. Pearson. 1978. Effect of background knowledge on silent reading comprehension. Paper presented at the annual meeting of the American Educational Research Association, Toronto. ERIC ED 159 255.

Gough, P. B. 1972. One second of reading. In J. F. Kavanagh and I. A. Mattingly (eds.). *Language by Ear and by Eye.* Cambridge, Massachusetts: MIT.

Grabe, W. 1979. Three methods for language learning: community language learning, the silent way, suggestopedia. *Ohio University Working Papers in Applied Linguistics* 5.

Graham, C. 1978. *Jazz Chants.* New York: Oxford University.

Gray, J. 1966. Attention, consciousness, and voluntary control of behavior in Soviet psychology: philosophical roots and research branches. In O'Connor, 1–38.

Grice, H. P. 1975. Logic and conversation. In P. Cole and J. Morgan (eds.). *Syntax and Semantics,* Volume 3, *Speech Acts.* New York: Academic, 41–58.

Gritton, C., and R. Bordon. 1976. Americanizing suggestopedia: a preliminary trial in a U.S. classroom. *Journal of Suggestive-Accelerative Learning and Teaching* Summer:83–94.

Guiora, A. 1972. Construct validity and transpositional research: toward an empirical study of psychoanalytic concepts. *Comprehensive Psychiatry* 13:139–150.

Guiora, A., B. Hallahmi, R. Brannon, C. Dull, and T. Scovel. 1972. The effects of experimentally induced changes in ego status on pronunciation ability in a second language: an exploratory study. *Comprehensive Psychiatry* 13:421–428.

Gumperz, J., and J. Rumery. 1962. Conversational Hindi-Urdu. Unpublished manuscript.

Hakuta, K. 1974. Prefabricated patterns and the emergence of structure in second language acquisition. *Language Learning* 14:287–298.

Halliday, M. A. K., and R. Hassan. 1976. *Cohesion in English.* London: Longman.

Harley, B., and M. Swain. 1978. An analysis of the verb system used by young learners of French. *Interlanguage Studies Bulletin* 3.

Harley, B., and M. Swain. 1977. An analysis of the spoken French of five French immersion pupils. *Working Papers on Bilingualism* 14:31–46.

Hatch, E. 1979. Simplified input and second language acquisition. Paper presented at the Annual Meeting of the Linguistic Society of American, Los Angeles, January.

Hatch, E. 1976. Discourse analysis, speech acts, and second language acquisition. *UCLA Working Papers in TESL* 10:51–64.

Hauptman, P. 1971. A structural approach versus a situational approach to foreign language teaching. *Language Learning* 21:235–244.

Hébert, R. 1976. Rendement academique et langue d'enseignement chez les élèves franco-manitobains. Saint-Boniface, Manitoba: Centre de Recherches du College Universitare de Saint-Boniface.

Hendrickson, J. 1978. Error correction in foreign language teaching: recent theory, research, and practice. *Modern Language Journal* 63:389.

Henning, G. (ed.). 1977. *Proceedings of the Second Language Research Forum,* University of California, Los Angeles.

Heyde, A. 1979. The relationship between self-esteem and the oral production of a second language. Unpublished Ph.D. dissertation, University of Michigan.

Heyde, A. 1977. The relationship of self-esteem to the oral production of a second language. In Brown, Yorio, and Crymes, 1–13.

Higgs, T. 1979. Some pre-methodological considerations in foreign language teaching. *Modern Language Journal* 63:335–341.

Hines, M. 1973. *Skits in English as a Second Language.* New York: Regents.

Hinofotis, F., and K. Bailey. 1978. Course development: oral communication for advanced university ESL students. *UCLA Workpapers in TESL* 12:7–19.

Hoetker, J. 1969. *Dramatics and the Teaching of Literature.* NCTE/ERIC Studies in the Teaching of English. Champaign, Illinois: NCTE.

Hoffman, J. 1979. Studying contextual build-up during reading through cumulative cloze. Paper presented at the Pacific Reading Symposium Annual Meeting, Tucson, Arizona. ERIC ED 181 410.

Hsu, V. 1975. Play production as a medium of learning spoken Chinese. Paper presented at the Asian Studies on the Pacific Coast Conference. ERIC ED 112 667.

Huang, J., and E. Hatch. 1978. A Chinese child's acquisition of English. In E. Hatch (ed.). *Second Language Acquisition: A Book of Readings.* Rowley, Massachusetts: Newbury House, 118–131.

Huey, E. B. 1908. *The Psychology and Pedagogy of Reading.* Reissued in 1968. Cambridge, Massachusetts: MIT.

Huggins, A. W. F., and M. J. Adams. 1980. Syntactic aspects of reading comprehension. In Spiro, Bruce, and Brewer, 87–112.

Humphrey, J. H. 1972. The use of motor activity learning in the development of science concepts with slow learning fifth grade children. *Journal of Research in Science Teaching* 9:261–266.

Humphrey, J. H. 1970. Teaching slow learners science through active games. In J. H. Humphrey and D. D. Sullivan (eds.). *Teaching Slow Learners through Active Games.* Springfield, Illinois: Charles C. Thomas, 145–182.

Humphrey, J. H. 1968. Use of the physical education learning medium in the development of certain arithmetical processes with second grade children. *American Association of Health Physical Education and Recreation Abstracts.*

Humphrey, J. H. 1967. The mathematics motor activity story. *Arithmetic Teacher* 14:14–16.

Humphrey, J. H. 1965. Comparison of the use of active games and language workbook exercises as learning media in the development of language understandings with third grade children. *Perceptual and Motor Skills* 21.

Humphrey, J. H. 1962. A pilot study of the use of physical education as a learning medium in the development of language arts concepts in third grade children. *American Association of Health Physical Education and Recreation Research Quarterly,* March.

Humphrey, J. H. 1960. Physical education and science concepts. *Elementary School Science Bulletin,* March.

Ingram, F., J. Nord, and D. Dragt. 1975. A program for learning comprehension. *Slavic and East European Journal* 9:1–10.

Jackson, P. 1979. Final report on quick-start in English. Unpublished manuscript. Whisman School District; 1975 San Ramon Ave.; Mountain View, California 94043.

Jakobovits, L. 1969. Research findings and foreign language requirements in colleges and universities. *Foreign Language Annals* 4:448.

Jarvella, R. 1971. Syntactic process of connected speech. *Journal of Verbal Learning and Verbal Behavior* 10:409–416.

Jespersen, O. 1904. *How to Teach a Foreign Language.* London: Allen and Unwin.

Johnson, K. 1979. Communicative approaches and communicative processes. In Brumfit and Johnson, 192–205.

Johnson, K. 1977. The adoption of functional syllabuses for general language teaching courses. *Canadian Modern Language Review* 33:667–680.

Johnson, R. J., and H. L. Friedman. 1971. Some temporal factors in the listening behavior of second language students. In Pimsleur and Quinn, 165–170.

Johnston, O. In press. Five years with the Rassias method in German: a follow-up report from the University of Florida. *Foreign Language Annals.*

Kamil, M. L. 1978. Models of reading. In S. Pflaum-Connor (ed.). *Aspects of Reading Education.* Berkeley, California: McCutchan.

Kanoi, N. 1970. The strategy of the total physical response for foreign language learning. Unpublished manuscript. Hanover College, Hanover, Indiana.

Kelly, L. G. 1976. *25 Centuries of Language Teaching.* Rowley, Massachusetts: Newbury House.

Kennedy, B. D. 1978. Conceptual aspects of language learning. In Richards, 117–133.

Kennedy, J. 1978. *An Introduction to the Design and Analysis of Experiments in Education and Psychology.* Washington, D.C.: University of America.

Kirman, B. H. 1966. Psychotherapy in the Soviet Union. In O'Connor, 39–62.

Klieman, G. M. 1975. Speech recording in reading. *Journal of Verbal Learning and Verbal Behavior* 14:323–339.

Krashen, S. 1982. *Principles and Practices in Second Language Acquisition.* New York: Pergamon.

Krashen, S. 1981. *Second Language Acquisition and Second Language Learning.* New York: Pergamon.

Krashen, S. 1980a. The input hypothesis. In J. E. Alatis (ed.). *Current Issues in Bilingual Education.* Washington, D.C.: Georgetown University 168–180. Also in J. Oller (ed.). 1983. *Issues in Language Testing Research.* Rowley, Massachusetts: Newbury House, 357–366.

Krashen, S. 1980b. The theoretical and practical relevance of simple codes. In Scarcella and Krashen, 7–18.

Krashen, S. 1979a. Adult second language acquisition as post-critical period learning. *ITL* 43:39–52.

Krashen, S. 1979b. The monitor model for second-language acquisition and foreign language teaching. In R. Gingras (ed.). *Second Language Acquisition and Foreign Language Teaching.* Arlington, Virginia: Center for Applied Linguistics, 1–27.

Krashen, S. 1979c. A response to McLaughlin, the monitor model: some methodological considerations. *Language Learning* 29:151–168.

Krashen, S. 1978. Individual variation in the use of the monitor. In W. Ritchie (ed.). *Principles of Second Language Learning.* New York: Academic, 175–183.

Krashen, S. 1977. The monitor model of adult second language performance. In Burt, Dulay, and Finocchiaro, 152–161. Also in K. Croft (ed.). 1980. *Readings on English as a Second Language.* New York: Winthrop, 213–221.

Krashen, S. 1976. The monitor model of second language performance. Paper presented at the 6th Annual California Linguistic Association Conference.

Krashen, S., J. Butler, R. Birnbaum, and J. Robertson. 1975. Two studies in language acquisition and language learning. *International Review of Applied Linguistics*, 73–92.

Krashen, S., M. Long, and R. Scarcella. 1979. Age, rate, and eventual attainment in second language acquisition. *TESOL Quarterly* 12:573–582.

Krashen, S., and H. Seliger. 1975. The essential contribution of formal language instruction in adult second language learning. *TESOL Quarterly* 9:173–183.

Krashen, S., and T. Terrell. 1983. *The Natural Approach.* San Francisco: Alemany.

Kruse, A. 1979. Vocabulary in context. *English Language Teaching Journal* 33:207–213.

Kuhn, T. S. 1962. *The Structure of Scientific Revolutions.* Chicago: University of Chicago.

Kunihira, S., and J. Asher. 1965. The strategy of the total physical response: an application to learning Japanese. *International Review of Applied Linguistics* 3:277–289.

Labov, W. 1972. *Sociolinguistic Patterns.* Philadelphia, Pennsylvania: University of Pennsylvania.

Labov, W. 1966. *The Social Stratification of English in New York City.* Washington, D.C.: Center for Applied Linguistics.

LaBerge, D., and S. J. Samuels. 1976. Towards a theory of automatic information processing in reading. *Cognitive Psychology* 6:293–332.

LaFarga, J. 1966. Learning foreign languages in group counseling conditions. Unpublished Ph.D. dissertation, Loyola University, Chicago.

LaForge, P. 1975. *Research Profiles with Community Language Learning.* Apple River, Illinois: Counseling-Learning Institutes.

Lalande, J. 1981. An error in error-correction policies. *ADFL Bulletin* 12:45–47.

Lambert, W. E. 1977. The effects of bilingualism on the individual: cognitive and sociocultural consequences. In P. A. Hornby (ed.). *Bilingualism: Psychological, Social, and Educational Implications.* New York: Academic, 15–27.

Lambert, W. E. 1974. Culture and language as factors in language and education. Paper presented at the TESOL Convention, Denver, Colorado, March 7.

Lambert, W. E. 1972. *Attitudes and Motivation in Second Language Learning.* Rowley, Massachusetts: Newbury House.

Lambert, W. E. 1963. Psychological approaches to the study of languages: II. On second language learning and bilingualism. *Modern Language Journal* 47:114–121.

Lambert, W. E., and G. R. Tucker. 1972. *Bilingual Education of Children*. Rowley, Massachusetts: Newbury House.

Lane, H. 1964. Programmed learning of a second language. *International Review of Applied Linguistics* 2:250.

Larsen-Freeman, D. 1975. The acquisition of grammatical morphemes by adult ESL students. *TESOL Quarterly* 9:409–419.

Lashley, K. 1951. The problem of serial order in behavior. In L. A. Jeffress (ed.). Cerebral Mechanisms in Behavior. New York: Wiley, 112–136. Reprinted in S. Saporta (ed.). 1961. *Psycholinguistics: A Book of Readings*. New York: Holt, 180–197.

Lawson, J. H. 1971. Should foreign language be eliminated from the curriculum? *Foreign Language Annals* 4:427. Also in J. W. Dodge (ed.). *The Case for Foreign Language Study*. New York: Northeast Conference on the Teaching of Foreign Languages.

Lazier, G. 1969. Dramatic improvisation as English teaching methodology. *English Record* 20:46–51.

Lieberman, L. R., and S. Altschul. 1971. Memory for a list of commands: imagining, seeing, doing. *Perceptual and Motor Skills* 33:530.

Loban, W. 1970. Stages, velocity, and prediction of language development: kindergarten through grade twelve. Washington, D.C.: USOE.

Lowenthal, M. (ed.). 1956. *The Autobiography of Michel de Montaigne*. New York: Vintage.

Lozanov, G. 1978. *Suggestology and Outlines of Suggestopedy*. New York: Gordon and Breach.

Ludwig, C. 1955. The effect of creative dramatics upon the articulation skills of kindergarten children. Unpublished M.A. thesis, University of Pittsburgh.

Luxemberg, S. 1976. All the class a stage. *Change Magazine* December:30–33.

Macnamara, J. 1972. The cognitive basis of language learning in infants. *Psychological Review* 79:1–13.

Macnamara, J., J. Svarc, and S. Horner. 1976. Attending a primary school of the other language in Montreal. In A. Simoes, Jr. (ed.). *The Bilingual Child: Research and Analysis of Existing Educational Themes*. New York: Academic, 113–131.

Magnan, S. 1979. Reduction and error correction for communicative language use: the focus approach. *Modern Language Journal* 68:342–348.

Maley, A., and A. Duff. 1978. The use of dramatic techniques in foreign language learning, *Recherches et Echanges* 3.

Mann, J. 1970. The present state of psychodramatic research. Paper presented at the American Psychological Association Convention, Miami Beach , Florida. ERIC ED 043 055.

McCullough, C. M. 1976. What should the reading teacher know about language and thinking? In R. E. Hodges and E. H. Rudorf (eds.). *Language and Learning to Read: What Teachers Should Know about Language*. Boston: Houghton Mifflin, 2–7.

McIntyre, B. 1958. The effect of creative activities on the articulation skills of children. *Speech Monographs* 42–48.

McIntyre, B., and B. McWilliams. 1959. Creative dramatics in speech correction. *Journal of Speech and Hearing Disorders* 24:275–278.

Mear, A. 1969. Experimental investigation of receptive language. Paper presented at the Second International Congress of Applied Linguistics, Cambridge University, Cambridge, England. In Pimsleur and Quinn, 1971, 143–156.

Milon, J. P. 1975. Dialect in the TESOL program: if you never you better. In Burt and Dulay, 159–170.

Moffett, J. 1967. *Drama: What Is Happening*. Champaign, Illinois: National Council of Teachers of English.

Morgan, J., and Sellner, M. B. 1980. Discourse and linguistic theory. In Spiro, Bruce, and Brewer, 165–199.

Morris, L. 1978. German professor turns classroom into a stage. *Independent Florida Alligator* August:17, 27.

Moskowitz, G. 1979. *Caring and Sharing in the Foreign Language Classroom.* Rowley, Massachusetts: Newbury House.

Moskowitz, G. 1981. Effects of humanistic techniques on attitude, cohesiveness and self-concept of foreign language students. *Modern Language Journal* 65:149–157.

Moulding, S. 1978. The development of appropriacy through drama techniques. *Recherches et Echanges* 3:1.

Mueller, G. 1980. Visual contextual cues and listening comprehension: an experiment. *Modern Language Journal* 64:335–40.

Mueller, G. 1979. The effects of a contextual visual on recall measures of listening comprehension in beginning college German. Unpublished Ph.D. dissertation, Ohio State University.

Mullen, K. 1978. Direct evaluation of second language proficiency: the effect of the rater and scale in oral interview. *Language Learning* 28:303. Also in J. Oller and K. Perkins (eds.). 1980. *Research in Language Testing.* Rowley, Massachusetts: Newbury House, 91–101.

Munby, J. 1978. *Communicative Syllabus Design.* Cambridge: Cambridge University.

Murphy, H. J. 1979. Book review of J. Asher, *Learning Another Language through Actions: The Complete Teacher's Guidebook. American Annals of the Deaf* 124:346.

Nahir, M. 1979. A practical progression in the teaching of a second language. *Canadian Modern Language Review* 35:595.

National Council of Teachers of English. 1973. *English for Today, Book Two: The World We Live In.* Second edition. New York: McGraw-Hill.

Newport, E., H. Gleitman, and L. Gleitman. 1977. Mother, I'd rather do it myself: some effects and non-effects of maternal speech style. In Snow and Ferguson, 109–150.

Nord, J. R. 1975. A case for listening comprehension. *Philologia* 7:1–25.

NTL Institute for Applied Behavioral Science. 1970. Lost on the moon—problem sheet. Washington, D.C.

O'Connor, N. 1966. *Present-Day Russian Psychology.* Oxford: Pergamon.

Oller, J. W., Jr. (ed.). 1983. *Issues in Language Testing Research.* Rowley, Massachusetts: Newbury House.

Oller, J. W., Jr. 1983. Story writing principles and ESL teaching. *TESOL Quarterly* 17:39–53.

Oller, J. W., Jr. 1979. *Language Tests at School.* London: Longman.

Oller, J. W., Jr., and D. H. Obrecht. 1969. The psycholinguistic principle of informational sequence: an experiment in second language learning. *International Review of Applied Linguistics* 7:117–123.

Oller, J. W., Jr. and J. Richards (eds.) 1973. *Focus on the Learner: Pragmatic Perspectives for the Language Teacher.* Rowley, Massachusetts: Newbury House.

Oller, J. W., Sr. 1963. Teacher's Manual: *El español por el mundo/primer nivel: la familia Fernández.* Chicago: Encyclopedia Films.

Oller, J. W., Sr., and A. González. 1965. *El español por el mundo/segundo nivel: Emilio en España.* Chicago: Encyclopedia Films.

Olson, D. 1974. From utterance to text: the bias of language in speech and writing. Paper presented at the Epistemetics Meeting at Vanderbilt University in Nashville, Tennessee.

Ostrander, S., and L. Schroeder. 1976. *ESP Papers.* New York: Bantam.

Ostrander, S., and L. Schroeder. 1970. *Psychic Discoveries behind the Iron Curtain.* Englewood Cliffs, New Jersey: Prentice-Hall.

Palmer, H. E., and D. Palmer. 1970. *English through Actions.* London: Longman.

Papalia, A. 1976. From manipulative drills to language for real communication. *Canadian Modern Language Review* 32:150–155.

Parkes, M. 1972. Perspectives on the Montreal programs. In Swain, 22–27.

Paulson, D., E. Kintsch, W. Kintsch, and D. Premack. 1979. Children's comprehension and memory for stories. *Journal of Experimental Child Psychology* 28:379–403.

Paulston, C. B. 1978. Bilingual bicultural education. *Review of Research in Education* 6:186–228.

Paulston, C. B. 1975. *Developing Communicative Competence: Roleplays in English as a Second Language*. Pittsburgh: University.

Paulston, C. B. 1974. Linguistics and communicative competence. *TESOL Quarterly* 9:4.

Pearson, P. D., J. Hansen, and C. Gordon. 1979. The effect of background knowledge on young children's comprehension of explicit and implicit information. Champaign-Urbana: University of Illinois, Center for the Study of Reading. ERIC ED 169 521.

Peck, R. N. 1980. *Secrets of Successful Fiction*. Cincinnati, Ohio: Writer's Digest.

Peck, S. 1977. Language play in child second language acquisition. In Henning, 85–93.

Penfield, W., and L. Roberts. 1959. *Speech and Brain Mechanisms*. Princeton, New Jersey: Princeton University.

Phillips, J. 1974. A study of the applicability of task analysis methodology and learning hierarchies to second language reading. Unpublished Ph.D. dissertation, Ohio State University.

Piaget, J. 1981. *Intelligence and Affectivity: Their Relationship During Child Development*. Tr. and ed. T. A. Brown, C. E. Kaegi, and Mark R. Rosenweig. Palo Alto, California: Annual Reviews.

Piaget, J. 1970. *Genetic Epistemology*. Tr. E. Duckworth, New York: Norton.

Piaget, J. 1947. *The Psychology of Intelligence*. Tottowa, New Jersey: Littlefield Adams.

Piatelli-Palmarini, M. (ed.). 1980. *Language and Learning: The Debate between Jean Piaget and Noam Chomsky*. Cambridge, Massachusetts: Harvard.

Pimsleur, P. 1972. Children get pointed lesson in French. *Knickerbocker News*. Albany, New York, May 15.

Pimsleur, P., and T. Quinn (eds.). 1971. *The Psychology of Second Language Learning*. Cambridge: Cambridge University, 165–170.

Plann, S. 1977. Acquiring a second language in an immersion classroom. In Brown, Yorio, and Crymes, 213–225.

Postovsky, V. 1979. Effects of delay in oral practice at the beginning of second language learning. *Modern Language Journal* 58:229–239.

Postovsky, V. 1977. Why not start speaking later? In Burt, Dulay, and Finocchiaro, 17–26.

Postovsky, V. 1975. The priority of aural comprehension in the language acquisition process. Paper presented at the 4th AILA World Conference, August. Monterey, California: Defense Language Institute.

Postovsky, V. 1974. Effects of delay in oral practice at the beginning of second language learning. *Modern Language Journal* 58:5–6.

Prichard, A., and J. Taylor. 1976a. Adapting the Lozanov method for remedial reading instruction. *Journal of Suggestive-Accelerative Learning and Teaching* Summer:107-115.

Prichard, A., and J. Taylor. 1976b. An altered states approach to reading. *Educational Courier* February:28–30.

Prine, J. 1978. Firecrackers, eggs . . . language too. *Gainesville Sun* May 25:5D.

Problems of suggestology. 1973. *Proceedings of the Symposium*. Sofia: Nauka i Izkustvo. (As cited by Bancroft, Chapter 8.)

Rardin, J. 1971. Task-oriented counseling experiences for slow-learning third graders. Unpublished Ph.D. dissertation, Loyola University, Chicago.

Rassias, J. 1972. Why we must change. *ADFL Bulletin* March.

Rassias, J. 1968. A philosophy of language instruction. Hanover, New Hampshire: Dartmouth College.

Reeds, J., H. Winitz, and P. Garcia. 1977. A test of reading following comprehension training. *International Review of Applied Linguistics* 14:308–319.

Ribovich, J. 1979. The effect of informational background on various reading-related behaviors in adult subjects. *Reading World* March 240–246.

Richards, J. 1980. Conversation: what it is and what it isn't. *TESOL Quarterly* 14:413–432.

Richards, J. (ed.). 1978. *Understanding Second and Foreign Language Learning*. Rowley, Massachusetts: Newbury House.

Richards, J. 1974. *Error Analysis: Perspectives on Second Language Learning*. London: Longman.

Ricoeur, P. 1967. *The Symbolism of Evil*. New York: Harper and Row.

Rietmann, K. 1977. Error repair and discourse strategies in socio-drama and other formal and informal second language environments. Unpublished manuscript.

Rinvolucri, M., and M. Berer. 1981. *Action Mazes*. London: Heinemann.

Rivers, W. 1979. Learning a sixth language: an adult learner's daily diary. *Canadian Modern Language Review* 36:67–82.

Rivers, W. 1972. *Speaking in Many Tongues*. Rowley, Massachusetts: Newbury House.

Rivers, W. 1966. Listening comprehension. *Modern Language Journal* 50:196–204.

Robinett, E. 1975. The effects of suggestopedia in increasing foreign language achievement. Unpublished doctoral dissertation, Texas Tech University.

Robinson, L. 1967. *Guided Writing and Free Writing*. New York: Harper and Row.

Rogers, T. 1978. Strategies for individualized language learning and teaching. In Richards, 251–273.

Rogosheske, P. 1972. Creative dramatics—a pragmatic approach to second language learning. Unpublished M.A. thesis, University of California, Los Angeles.

Romijn, E., and C. Seely. 1979. *Live Action English for Foreign Students*. San Francisco: Alemany.

Rosenblatt, L. 1978. *The Reader, the Text, and the Poem*. Carbondale, Illinois: University of Southern Illinois.

Rosenthal, R., and L. Jacobson. 1968. *Pygmalion in the Classroom*. New York: Holt.

Ruder, K., P. Hernamm, and R. Schefelbusch. 1977. Effects of verbal imitation and comprehension training on verbal production. *Journal of Psycholinguistic Research* 6:59–72.

Rumelhart, D. 1980. Schemata: the building blocks of cognition. In Spiro, Bruce, and Brewer, 33–58.

Rumelhart, D. 1975. Notes on a schema for stories. In Bobrow and Collins, 211–236.

Saferis, F. 1978. *Une Revolution dans l'Art d'Apprendre*. Paris: Robert Laffont.

Sancho, A. 1974. Culture in the bilingual-bicultural curriculum. Paper presented at the TESOL Convention, Denver, Colorado, March.

Sapon, S. 1961. *Spanish A*. TEMAC Series, Encyclopaedia Britannica Films.

Savignon, S. 1978. Teaching for communication. In E. Joiner and P. Westphal (eds.). *Developing Communication Skills*. Rowley, Massachusetts: Newbury House, 12–20.

Savignon, S. 1974. Talking with my son: an example of communicative competence. In F. Grittner (ed.). *Careers, Communication and Culture*. Skokie, Illinois: National Textbook, 26–40.

Savignon, S. 1972. *Communicative Competence: An Experiment in Foreign Language Teaching*. Philadelphia: Center for Curriculum Development.

Scarcella, R., and S. Krashen (eds.). 1980. *Research in Second Language Acquisition*. Rowley, Massachusetts: Newbury House.

Schallert, D. L. 1976. Improving memory for prose: the relationship between depth of processing and context. *Journal of Verbal Learning and Verbal Behavior* 15:621–632.

Schank, R. 1980. Language and memory. *Cognitive Science* 4:243–282.

Schank, R., and R. Abelson. 1977. *Scripts, Plans, Goals, and Understanding*. Hillsdale, New Jersey: Lawrence Erlbaum.

Schlanger, P., and B. Schlanger. 1971. Adapting role-playing activities with aphasic patients. *Journal of Speech and Hearing Disorders* 35:229–235.

Schultz, J. H., and W. Luthe. 1969. *Autogenic Methods*. New York: Grune and Stratton.

Schumann, J. 1978. *The Pidginization Process: A Model for Second Language Learning*. Rowley, Massachusetts: Newbury House.

Schumann, J. 1976. Social distance as a factor in second language acquisition. *Language Learning* 26:135–143.

Schumann, J. 1975. Affective factors and the problem of age in second language acquisition. *Language Learning* 25:209–235.

Schuster, D., R. Bordon, and C. Gritton. 1976. *Suggestive-Accelerative Learning and Teaching: A Manual of Classroom Procedures Based on the Lozanov Method.* Des Moines, Iowa: Society for Suggestive-Accelerative Learning and Teaching.

Scott, M., J. Saegert, and G. R. Tucker. 1974. Error analysis and English Language Strategies of Arab Students. *Language Learning* 24:69–98.

Selinker, L., M. Swain, and G. Dumas. 1975. The interlanguage hypothesis extended to children. *Language Learning* 25:139–152.

Shaftel, F., and G. Shaftel. 1967. *Role-Playing for Social Values.* Englewood Cliffs, New Jersey, Prentice-Hall.

Shaftel, G., and F. Shaftel. 1952. *Role-Playing the Problem Story: An Approach to Human Relations in the Classroom.* New York: National Conference of Christians and Jews.

Sibatani, Atuhiro. 1980. The Japanese brain. *Science* December 1980:24–27.

Simon, S., L. Howe, and H. Kirschenbaum. 1972. *Values Clarification.* New York: Hart.

Skutnabb-Kangas, T., and P. Toukomaa. 1976. *Teaching Migrant Children Mother Tongue and Learning the Language of the Host Country in the Context of the Socio-Cultural Situation of the Migrant Family.* Tampere, Finland: Tutkimuksia Research Reports.

Slobin, D. 1966. Soviet psycholinguistics. *Present-Day Russian Psychology.* Oxford: Pergamon.

Smith, F. 1978. *Reading without Nonsense.* Cambridge: Cambridge University.

Smith, K., and M. Braine. Miniature language and the problem of language acquisition. Unpublished manuscript.

Snow, C. 1979. Conversations with children. In P. Fletcher and M. Garman (eds.). *Language Acquisition: Studies in First Language Development.* Cambridge: Cambridge University, 363–376.

Snow, C., and C. Ferguson (eds.). 1977. *Talking to Children.* Cambridge: Cambridge University.

Šokolov, D. N. 1972. *Inner Speech and Thought.* Tr. G. T. Onischenko. New York: Plenum.

Sorenson, A. 1967. Multilingualism in the Northwest Amazon. *American Anthropologist* 69:674–684.

Spilich, G., G. Vesonder, H. Chiesi, and J. Voss. 1979. Text processing of domain-related information for individuals with high and low domain knowledge. *Journal of Verbal Learning and Verbal Behavior* 18:275–290.

Spiro, R. J., B. C. Bruce, and W. F. Brewer (eds.). 1980. *Theoretical Issues in Reading Comprehension.* Hillsdale, New Jersey: Lawrence Erlbaum.

Stern, S. 1977. The teaching of contemporary American drama in advanced ESL. Unpublished M.A. thesis, University of California, Los Angeles.

Stevick, E. 1980. *Language Teaching: A Way and Ways.* Rowley, Massachusetts: Newbury House.

Stevick, E. 1976. *Memory, Meaning and Method.* Rowley, Massachusetts: Newbury House.

Stevick, E. 1974. Language instruction must do an about-face. *Modern Language Journal* 58:379–384.

Stevick, E. 1973. Review of Curran 1972. *Language Learning* 22:259–271.

Stevick, E. 1971. *Adapting and Writing Language Lessons.* Washington, D.C.: Foreign Service Institute.

Stewart, W. A. 1964. Nonstandard speech and the teaching methods in quasi-foreign situations. In W. A. Stewart (ed.). *Nonstandard Speech and the Teaching of English.* Washington, D.C.: Center for Applied Linguistics, 1–15.

Strevens, P. 1978. The nature of language teaching. In Richards, 179–203.

Sutherland, K. In press. Accuracy vs. fluency in the foreign language classroom. *CATESOL Occasional Papers.*

Swaffar, J., and M. Woodruff. 1978. Language for comprehension: focus on reading, a report on the University of Texas German program. *Modern Language Journal* 62:27–32.

Swain, D. V. 1980. *Techniques of the Selling Writer.* Norman, Oklahoma: University of Oklahoma.

Swain, M. 1978a. Bilingual education for the English-speaking Canadian. In J. Alatis (ed.). *Georgetown University Roundtable on Languages and Linguistics*, 141–154.

Swain, M. 1978b. French immersion, early, late, or partial? *Canadian Modern Language Review* 34:577–585.

Swain, M. 1976a. Bibliography: research on immersion education for the majority child. *Canadian Modern Language Review* 32:592–596.

Swain, M. 1976b. Changes in errors: random or systematic? In G. Nickel (ed.). *Proceedings of the Fourth International Congress of Applied Linguistics* 2. Stuttgart, Germany: Hochschulverlag, 345–358.

Swain, M. (ed.). 1972. *Bilingual Schooling: Some Experiences in Canada and the United States*. Toronto: the Ontario Institute for Studies in Education.

Swain, M., and M. Bruck (eds.). 1976. Immersion education for the majority child. *Canadian Modern Language Review* 32, all of no. 5.

Swift, L. B., et al. 1962. *Igbo: Basic Course*. Washington, D.C.: Foreign Service Institute.

Taba, H. 1965. The teaching of thinking. *Elementary English* 42, May, 534–542.

Taylor, I. 1978. Acquiring versus learning a second language. *Canadian Modern Language Review* 34:455–472.

Terrell, T. 1980. A natural approach to the teaching of verb forms and function in Spanish. *Foreign Language Annals* 13:129–136.

Terrell, T. 1977. A natural approach to the acquisition and learning of a language. *Modern Language Journal* 61:325–336.

Terrell, T., C. Perrone, and B. Baycroft. Forthcoming. Teaching the Spanish subjunctive: an error analysis. *International Review of Applied Linguistics*.

Tillich, P. 1952. *The Courage to Be*. New Haven: Yale University.

Time Magazine. 1976. Dynamiting language. August 16, volume 108:56.

Titone, R. 1968. *Teaching Foreign Languages: An Historical Sketch*. Washington, D.C.: Georgetown University.

Trager, S. 1978. The language of teaching: discourse analysis in beginning, intermediate and advanced ESL classrooms. Unpublished M.A. paper. Department of Linguistics, USC.

Tranel, D. 1970. Counseling concepts applied to the process of education. Unpublished Ph.D. dissertation, Loyola University, Chicago.

Tranel, D. 1968. Teaching Latin with the Chromacord. *Classical Journal* 63:157–160.

Tucker, G. R., and A. D'Anglejan. 1972. An approach to bilingual education: the St. Lambert experiment. In Swain, 15–21.

Valdman, A., and M. Moody. 1979. Testing communicative ability. *French Review* 52:552–561.

Van Riper, C. 1963. *Speech Correction—Principles and Methods*. Englewood Cliffs, New Jersey: Prentice-Hall.

Via, R. 1976. *English in Three Acts*. Honolulu, Hawaii: East-West Center, University of Hawaii.

Villani, S. 1977. Communication in an experimental foreign language class. *Canadian Modern Language Review* 33:372–378.

VonGal, C. 1974. A proposal for a systematic approach to the evaluation of an ongoing first-year college language program. Unpublished M.A. thesis, University of Florida.

Voss, J. F., G. T. Vesander, and G. J. Spilich. 1980. Text generation and recall by high and low knowledge individuals. *Journal of Verbal Learning and Verbal Behavior* 19:651–667.

Vygotsky, L. 1978. *Mind in Society*. Tr. and ed. M. Cole, V. John-Steiner, et al. Cambridge, Massachusetts: Harvard University.

Vygotsky, L. 1934. *Thought and Language*. Tr. E. Haufmann and G. Vakar, American edition 1962. Cambridge, Massachusetts: MIT.

Wagner-Gough, J. 1975. *Comparative Studies in Second Language Learning*. M.A. thesis, University of California at Los Angeles.

Wagner-Gough, J., and E. Hatch. 1975. The importance of input data in second language acquisition studies. *Language Learning* 25:297–308.

Wallerstein, N. 1983. *Language and Culture in Conflict: Problem Posing in the ESL Classroom.* Reading, Massachusetts: Addison-Wesley.

Watzlawick, P., J. Beavin, and K. Jackson. 1967. *Pragmatics of Human Communication.* New York: Norton.

Weaver, C. 1980. *Psycholinguistics and Reading: From Process to Practice.* Boston: Little Brown.

Webber, B. L. 1980. Syntax beyond the sentence. In Spiro, Bruce, and Brewer, 141–164.

Weir, R. 1962. *Language in the Crib.* The Hague: Mouton.

Wells, G. 1981. *Learning through Interaction: The Study of Language Development.* Cambridge: Cambridge University.

Wesche, M. 1977. Learning behaviors of successful adult students in intensive language training. In Henning, 355–370.

Widdowson, H. G. 1979. Directions in the teaching of discourse. In Brumfit and Johnson, 49–60.

Wilkins, D. A. 1976. *Notional Syllabuses.* London: Oxford University.

Wilkins, D. A. 1973. The linguistic and situational content of the common core in a unit/credit system. In *System Development in Adult Language Learning: A European Unit/Credit System for Modern Language Learning by Adults.* Strasbourg: Council of Europe, 136–137.

Winitz, H. (ed.). 1981. *The Comprehension Approach to Foreign Language Instruction.* Rowley, Massachusetts: Newbury House.

Winitz, H., and J. Reeds. 1973a. *Comprehension and Problem Solving as a Strategy for Language Training—The OHR Method.* Prepublication monograph. Kansas City, Missouri: University of Missouri.

Winitz, H., and J. Reeds. 1973b. Rapid acquisition of a foreign language by the avoidance of speaking. *International Review of Applied Linguistics* 11:295–317.

Wittrock, M. C., C. B. Marks, and M. Doctorow. 1975. Reading as a generative process. *Journal of Educational Psychology* 67:484–489.

Wittrock, M. C., et al. 1977. *The Human Brain.* Englewood Cliffs, New Jersey: Prentice-Hall.

Woods, W. A. 1978. Generalization of ATN grammars. In W. Woods and R. Brachman (eds.). *Research in Natural Language Understanding.* Cambridge: Bolt, Beranek, and Newman (*Quarterly Progress Tr.* 4:3963).

Woods, W. A. 1970. Transition network grammars for natural language analysis. *Communications of the Association for Computing Machinery* 13:591–606.

Yarborough, R. W. 1967. *Bilingual Education Hearings before the Special Subcommittee on Bilingual Education of the Committee on Labor and Public Welfare, United States Senate, Ninetieth Congress* (in two parts). Washington, D.C.: Government Printing Office.

Yorio, C. 1971. Some sources of reading problems for foreign language learners. *Language Learning* 21:108–109.

Yorkey, R., et al. 1977. *Intercom: English for International Communication.* New York: American.

Author Index

Abelson, R. 15, 376, 427
Adams, M. J. 316, 317, 415, 422
Adams, S. iv, xv, 213, 316, 327, 375–82
Adkins, P. 186, 415
Alatis, J. E. iv, 2, 415, 418, 422, 429
Allen, V. F. 46
Allwright, R. 399, 415
Altschul, S. 61, 424
Anderson, R. 377, 415
Asher, J. iv, xiii, xiv, 38, 46, 57–72, 87, 258, 261, 263, 267–69, 274, 276, 327, 329–38, 344, 396, 415, 423, 425

Bach, E. 420
Bacon, R. 348, 415
Bailey, K. 214, 422
Bancroft, W. J. v, xiii, 101–12, 115, 116, 244, 415, 427
Bandura, A. 54, 416
Barber, E. 295–97, 299, 300, 416
Baycroft, B. 271, 429
Beavin, J. 11, 213, 430
Bedell, B. 328
Begin, Y. 147, 150, 163, 416
Belasco, S. 331, 416
Belkin, J. 389, 416
Bellugi, U. 274, 330, 417, 420
Benseler, D. 268, 416
Benton, R. 45, 416
Berer, M. 304, 324, 427
Berne, E. 119
Beutler, S. 211, 416
Bever, T. G. 314, 315, 416, 420
Bialystok, E. 270, 271, 416
Birnbaum, R. 270, 423
Blatchford, C. 419
Blatner, H. 213, 215, 416
Bloom, L. 41, 416
Bobrow, D. 206, 416, 427
Bolinger, D. 51, 275, 416
Bonilla, P. 404
Bordon, R. 102–4, 416, 421, 428
Brachfeld, O. 161, 416

Brady, T. 164, 416
Braine, J. 12, 416
Braine, M. 263, 428
Brannon, R. 211, 421
Bransford, J. 314, 376, 379, 416
Brewer, W. F. 415, 418, 422, 425, 427, 428, 430
Brinton, D. 207
Brown, A. L. 314, 416
Brown, H. D. 147, 286, 416, 426
Brown, J. S. 315, 418
Brown, R. 41, 274, 275, 282, 284, 330, 417, 420
Brown, T. A. 426
Bruce, B. C. 415, 418, 422, 425, 427, 428, 430
Bruck, M. 40, 44, 386, 417, 429
Brumfit, C. J. 415, 417, 422, 430
Buhler, C. 331, 417
Burnaby, B. 386, 417
Burt, M. iv, xiii, 1–3, 18, 24, 38–48, 272, 330, 399, 417, 420, 423, 425
Butler, J. 270, 423

Canale, M. 285, 417
Caplan, D. 315, 417
Carroll, J. B. 39, 48, 64, 70, 315, 329, 339, 417
Carterette, E. C. 417
Caskey, O. 102, 109, 417
Cazden, C. 330, 417
Chall, J. 375, 417
Chastain, K. D. 271, 417
Chatmant, S. 419
Cherry, C. 28
Chesler, M. 240, 417
Chiesi, H. 376, 417, 428
Chomsky, N. 417, 426
Christensen, C. 274, 277, 281, 417, 418
Chun, J. 285, 418
Clark, E. V. 315, 418
Clark, H. H. 315, 418
Clark, R. 233, 234, 418

431

Subject Index

Acquisition *vs.* Learning 19, 21, 27, 31, 32, 36, 127, 259, 269–83, 270, 278, 279, 283, 295, 297, 298, 329, 331, 382. *See also* Formal learning *vs.* Informal learning.
  child *vs.* adult 261–65; classroom *vs.* natural settings 259–65, 270–84, 290; L1 *vs.* L2 284–85. *See also* Natural approach.
Action Mazes 323–26
Additive bilingualism *vs.* Subtractive bilingualism 388
Affective factors 273. *See also* Environment, low anxiety
Affective filter 47, 101, 114, 295, 301
Analytic teaching *vs.* Synthetic teaching 21, 36. *See also* Integrative *vs.* Discrete-point teaching.
Apprentice teachers 100, 357–58, 367–70. *See also* Peer teachers.
Audiolingual instruction 37, 100, 133, 268, 269, 272, 279, 300, 329, 334, 340, 349, 352, 374. *See also* Drills.
Audio-motor approach 61, 337–47, 396. *See also* Total physical response.
Authority (teacher eminence) 87, 101, 124, 145, 169–70, 177

Bilingual education 185–88, 291, 328
Bottom-up processing *vs.* Top-down processing 315, 318

Caretaker speech 273, 335
Cartesian intellectualism 146, 165, 170, 171, 178
CEEB (College Entrance Examination Boards) 363, 370, 373
Cognitive approaches *vs.* Natural approaches 268, 269, 271, 274
Cohesion or surface connectivity 317
Communication (full two-way, partial two-way, and one-way) 40–41, 48

Communication net. *See* Net hypothesis.
Communicative approach. *See* Notional/functional approach.
Community language learning. *See* Counseling-learning.
Competence *vs.* performance 71, 284, 289, 294
Comprehensible input 3, 5–8, 24, 36, 43–44, 273, 399. *See also* Input hypothesis.
Comprehension training 331–32. *See also* Silent period.
Concrete referents. *See* Here-and-now principle
Content area classes 395–96
  teachers 412
Contrastive analysis 49, 51, 87
Counseling-learning 114, 136, 138, 142, 144, 146–78, 190, 202, 203, 267, 268, 328, 397, 399, 413
  incarnate-redemptive process 146, 149, 158, 159, 167–70, 172, 178; language threshold 161–62
Creative construction 45, 47, 269
Cross-cultural understanding 194
Cultural values 35, 188, 242, 341, 342, 410
Culture shock 188

Dartmouth College language program 89, 363–74. *See also* Rassias Method.
Debate 320–23, 374
Dialogues 14, 16, 20–36, 247, 248, 368
Din hypothesis 70, 257, 295–301
Direct method 21, 72, 104
Discrete-point teaching *vs.* integrative teaching 21, 22, 36, 49, 55
Drama 207–58, 354, 396, 397. *See also* Psychodrama, sociodrama, role-playing, and open-ended scenario.
Drills 17–18, 26, 28, 49, 51, 53, 55, 133–36, 144, 145, 255, 301, 308, 347, 357, 368. *See also* Audiolingual instruction.
Dynamism 363, 367, 374